44 95

OSCAR MICHEAUX AND HIS CIRCLE

Oscar Micheaux (1884–1951)

African-American Filmmaking and
Race Cinema of the Silent Era

OSCAR MICHEAUX & HIS CIRCLE

Pearl Bowser, Jane Gaines, and Charles Musser

EDITORS AND CURATORS

INDIANA UNIVERSITY PRESS
BLOOMINGTON AND INDIANAPOLIS

This volume is published on the occasion of the world premiere
of the Oscar Micheaux and His Circle programme at the 20th
Giornate del Cinema Muto (Sacile-Pordenone, 13-20 ottobre 2001).

This project was made possible by grants from the Ford
Foundation and the Connecticut Council for the Humanities.
The publication of this book was facilitated by a grant from
the Hilles Publication Fund.

The curators express appreciation to the University Seminars
at Columbia University for assistance in the preparation of the
manuscript for publication. The ideas presented have materially
benefited from discussions in the University Seminar on Cinema
and Interdisciplinary Interpretation.

This book is a publication of
Indiana University Press
601 North Morton Street
Bloomington, IN 47404–3797 USA

http://iupress.indiana.edu
Telephone orders   800-842-6796
Fax orders   812-855-7931
Orders by e-mail   iuporder@indiana.edu

The paper used in this publication meets the minimum require-
ments of American National Standard for Information Sciences—
Permanence of Paper for Printed Library Materials, ANSI
Z39.48–1984.

MANUFACTURED IN THE UNITED STATES OF AMERICA

Library of Congress Cataloging-in-Publication Data

Oscar Micheaux and his circle : African-American filmmaking
    and race cinema of the silent era / edited by Pearl Bowser, Jane
    Gaines, and Charles Musser.
          p.   cm.
      Chiefly papers presented at a conference held Jan. 1995, Yale
University.
        Includes filmographies, bibliographical references and index.
        ISBN 0-253-33994-4 — ISBN 0-253-21484-X (pbk.)
        1. Micheaux, Oscar, 1884–1951—Criticism and interpretation—
Congresses.   2. African Americans in motion pictures—
Congresses.   I. Bowser, Pearl, date   II. Gaines, Jane, date
III. Musser, Charles.
PN1998.3.M494 O83   2001
791.43'0233'092—dc21
                                                                        2001001386

1 2 3 4 5 06 05 04 03 02 01

for Spike Lee

In memory of
Toni Cade Bambara

CONTENTS

III. MICHEAUX'S CONTEMPORARIES

THE TOURING PACKAGE:
Programs and Credits

PROGRAM 1

Happy Though Married. Screen Snapshots Corporation. 1920. 35mm. 10 minutes. Produced by Jack Cohn and Louis Lewyn. Includes footage of director Oscar Micheaux. Print courtesy of the British Film Institute.

Within Our Gates. Micheaux Film Corporation. 1920. 35mm. 5,935 ft. (originally 8 reels). Produced, written, and directed by Oscar Micheaux. Evelyn Preer (Sylvia Landry), William Starks (Jasper Landry), Mattie Edwards (Jasper Landry's wife), Grant Edwards (Emil Landry) E. G. Tatum (Efrem, Girdlestone's faithful servant), Jack Chenault (Larry Prichard), S. T. Jacks (Reverend Wilson Jacobs), Grant Gorman (Armand Girdlestone), Flo Clements (Alma Prichard), Jimmie Cook, Charles D. Lucas (Dr. Vivian), Ralph Johnson (Philip Girdlestone), James D. Ruffin (Conrad Drebert), Bernice Ladd (Mrs. Geraldine Stratton), Mrs. Evelyn (Mrs. Elena Warwick), William Smith (Philip Gentry, detective), LaFont Harris (Emil as a young adult). Filmed at the Capitol City Studios, Chicago, and in the Chicago area in 1919. Print courtesy of the Library of Congress.

PROGRAM 2

A Pictorial View of Idlewild. Chicago Daily News Film Service. 1927. 35mm. 2,234 ft. (3 reels). Filmed at the black summer resort of Idlewild, Michigan. Re-edited and copyrighted by Benjamin C. Wilson and Edward Reed, 1979. Print courtesy of Library of Congress.

The Symbol of the Unconquered. Micheaux Film Corporation. 1920. 35mm. 3,852 ft. (originally 8 reels). Produced, written, and directed by Oscar Micheaux. With Iris Hall (Evon Mason), Walker Thompson (Hugh Van Allen), Lawrence Chenault (Jefferson Driscoll), Edward E. King (Tom Cutschawl), Jim Burris, Mattie V. Wilkes (Driscoll's mother), E. G. Tatum, Leigh "Lee" Whipper (Tugi Boj, Indian fakir), George Catlin (Dick Mason), James Burroughs, Edward Fraction (Peter Kaden), Lena L. Loach (Christina). Filmed in the New York City area. Fall 1920. Print courtesy of the Museum of Modern Art.

PROGRAM 3

[*Zora Neale Hurston.*] 1927–1929. 16mm. 400 ft. (Selected 100–foot rolls). a) [Logging, April 1928]; b) [Children dancing and girl rocking on porch, January/February 1929]; c) Children's games and baptism, August 1929]; and d) [Kossula, last of the Takkoi slaves, February 1928]. Field footage taken by Zora Neale Hurston at the Everglades Cypress Lumber Company near Loughman, Florida. Funded by Mrs. Rufus Osgood Mason. Print courtesy of the Library of Congress.

The Flying Ace. Norman Film Manufacturing Company. 1926. 35mm. 5,005 ft. (6 reels). Produced, written, and directed by David Norman. With J. Lawrence Criner (Captain William Stokes), George Colvin (Thomas Sawtelle, stationmaster at Mayport), Kathryn Boyd (Ruth Sawtelle, his daughter), Harold Platts (Finley Tucker, local aviator), Steve Reynolds ("Peg," Stokes's mechanic), Boise DeLegge (Blair Kimball, paymaster of the MN&O Railroad), Lyons Daniels (Jed Splivens, local constable), Sam Jordan (Dr. Maynard, the local dentist), Dr. R. L. Brown (Howard Mac Andrews, general manager of the MN&O Railroad). Produced at the Norman Studios, Arlington, Fla. Print courtesy of the Library of Congress.

Program 4

Body and Soul. Micheaux Film Corporation. 1925. 35mm. 7,700 ft. (originally 9 reels). Produced, written, and directed by Oscar Micheaux. With Paul Robeson (Rgt. Rev. Isiaah T. Jenkins, Sylvester), Mercedes Gilbert (Martha Jane), Lawrence Chenault (Yellow Curly Hinds), Julia Theresa Russell (Isabelle), Marshall Rodgers (saloon owner), Chester A. Alexander (Deacon Simpkins), Walter Cornick (Brother Amos), Madame Robinson (Sister Lucy), Lillian Johnson (Sister Ca'line), and Tom Fletcher. Filmed in the New York–New Jersey area in late 1924. Print courtesy of the George Eastman House.

Program 5

Hell-Bound Train. ca. 1930. 16mm. ca. 20 minutes. Produced by James E. Gist, Jr., with commentary and additional contributions by Eloise King Patrick Gist. Print courtesy of the Library of Congress.

Ten Nights in a Barroom. Colored Players Film Corporation. 1926. 35mm. 4,559 ft. (originally 8 reels.) Written and directed by Roy Calnek; presented by David Starkman and Louis Groner. With Charles S. Gilpin (Joe Morgan), Lawrence Chenault (Simon Slade), Harry Henderson (Willie Hammond, the judge's son), Arline Mickey (Mehitable Cartwright), Myra Burwell (Jannie Morgan, Joe's wife), William A Clayton, Jr. (Harvey Green), William R. Johnson (Judge Hammond), Edward Moore (Sample Swichel), William F. Milton (Alfred Romaine), Reginald Hoffer (William Carr), Ethel Smith, Sam Sadler, and Boxana Mickelby. Based on William W. Pratt's play *Ten Nights in a Bar-Room* (1858). Produced at Colored Players Film Corporation studio, 58th Street and Woodlawn Avenue, Philadelphia, during June 1926. Print courtesy of the George Eastman House.

Program 6

The Scar of Shame. Colored Players Film Corporation. 1929. 35mm. 8,023 ft. (8 reels). Directed by Frank Perugini; story by David Starkman; cinematography by Al Liguori. With Harry Henderson (Alvin Hillyard), Lucia [Lynn] Moses (Louise Howard), Lawrence Chenault

(Ralph Hathaway), Pearl McCormack (Alice Hathaway), Norman Johnstone (Eddie Blake), William E. Pettus (Spike Howard), Ann[ie] Kennedy (Lucretia Green). Produced at the Colored Players Film Corporation studio, 58th Street and Woodlawn Avenue, Philadelphia, during February–March 1929. Print courtesy of the Library of Congress.

Program 7

Eleven P.M. ca. 1929. Maurice Film Company. 35mm. 5,103 ft. (6 reels). Written and directed under the personal supervision of Richard D. Maurice. With H. Marion Williams (Roy Stewart), Sammie Fields (Frank [Louis?] Perry), Leo Pope (Bennie Madison), Orine Johnson (June Blackwell, Hope Sundaisy), Richard D. Maurice (Sundaisy), Wanda Maurice (Little Hope Sundaisy), Eugene Williams (Harry Brown, editor of *The Search Light*), J. M. Stephens (Rev. Hacket). Filmed in Detroit. Print courtesy of the Library of Congress.

ACKNOWLEDGMENTS

The Oscar Micheaux and His Circle Project has several broad, interrelated goals: 1) to focus attention on the surviving works of African-American filmmakers and, more generally, on race cinema (films made for black audiences in the United States) of the silent era; 2) to foster the preservation, restoration, distribution, and exhibition of these race films, where possible in their original format but also to encourage their broad dissemination in video and digital formats using high-quality film masters; 3) to encourage scholarship and discussion about these films so that they will receive the respect and understanding they deserve; 4) to strengthen the vitality of our African-American cultural heritage and to change the ways we view American and world cinema (and so, more broadly, twentieth-century culture) in light of these achievements. In many respects, this has been a vital but modestly budgeted undertaking, dependent upon the cooperation and goodwill of many individuals and institutions (and will continue to depend upon their generosity as we move forward with the touring program). There are, therefore, many people and organizations to acknowledge and thank.

To begin at home: we have benefited from a happy collaboration among ourselves as curators of the show and editors of this catalog. Each individual has brought crucial skills, talents, experience, and insights to the process. This was only possible because of the support we received on many fronts. The Oscar Micheaux and His Circle Project began with a strong foundation: the work already done by a small band of pioneer historians that included Pearl Bowser, Henry T. Sampson, Donald Bogle, Sister Francesca Thompson, Charles Hobson, Dan Leab, Richard Grupenhoff, and Thomas Cripps. Most lent their active support to this present effort in more or less crucial ways. One of these figures was slated to contribute to this book (a preface or introductory essay) but could not: Toni Cade Bambara. Writer, poet, and documentary filmmaker, she was born on March 25, 1939 and died on December 9, 1995, only 56 years old. Bambara is well known for her dazzling literary output—her short stories, essays, and novels. Her first book, a collection of short stories, *Gorilla, My Love,* was published in 1972. Her first novel, *The Salt Eaters* (1980), won the National Book Award. In a *New York Times* obituary, Abby Goodnough wrote: "What critics found most striking about Ms. Bambara's fiction, though, was the structure and language she used. Rather than using traditional linear plots, she would often use flashbacks, stream of consciousness and interweavings of plot and subplot to tell a story. She would frequently weave black dialects into her prose, creating a unique, complex language that was widely admired by critics." (In short, her writing has a certain affinity to African-American filmmaking of the silent era—to the work of Micheaux and Maurice.) Bambara also worked in documentary film. With Louis Massiah she made *The Bombing of Osage Avenue* (1986), about the police assault on MOVE headquarters in Philadelphia, and *W. E. B. Du Bois: A Biography in Four Voices* (1995).

We should not forget, however, that Bambara introduced and discussed innumerable programs at various black film festivals of the 1970s and 1980s. Often she was the keynote speaker. On March 13, 1987, at the Journey Across Three Continents film festival in Detroit, she asked the rhetorical question "Why new black cinema?" And she responded:

A classical people demand a classical art.

TO BE ENTRAPPED IN OTHER PEOPLE'S FICTIONS PUTS US UNDER ARREST. To be entrapped, to be submissively so, without countering, without challenging, without raising the voice and offering alternative truths renders us available for servitude. In which case, our ways, our beliefs, our values, our style are repeatedly ransacked so that the power of our culture can be used—to sell liquor, soda, pieces of entertainment, and the real deal: to sell ideas.

The idea of inferiority.

The idea of hierarchy.

The idea of stasis: that nothing will ever change.

We had hoped that Toni Cade Bambara would be the keynote speaker at our Yale conference (discussed below), but illness and then her premature death put that much-hoped-for possibility on hold forever. The only gesture left to us, completely inadequate, we recognize, is to dedicate this book to her memory.

This project would not have been possible without the funding that came from various organizations. Foremost was the Ford Foundation, where we benefited from the support of Sheila Biddle. In this respect Jane Gaines, director of the Duke University Program in Film and Video, provided the crucial support needed to attract and administer that grant. Virtually all of the essays in this book were first presented as working papers at the Oscar Micheaux and His Circle conference at Yale University in January 1995. Charles Hobson and Thomas Cripps generously served as commentators at this event. This conference was a joint Yale-Duke event based at Yale's Whitney Humanities Center in New Haven. A grant from the Connecticut Council for the Humanities for this conference helped to make it possible in the form we had wanted. Charles Musser, co-chair of the Film Studies Program, and Hazel Carby, chair of the African and African-American Studies Program at Yale, were co-organizers of that event. Jayna Brown was its coordinator. We also benefited from the advice and assistance of Jim Vivian and the Yale–New Haven Teachers Institute, including Gerene Freeman. Many of the authors in this catalog also participated in the University Seminar on Cinema and Interdisciplinary Interpretation, where Micheaux was a favored subject for presentation over a period of many years. Indeed, it provided a meeting place for the three curators. We are doubly appreciative to the University Seminars at Columbia University since it helped to support preparation of this catalog through the late Dean Aaron Warner.

The Oscar Micheaux and His Circle Project also benefited from the activities and support of various archives in the United States and (indirectly) at least two in Europe. Two European archives, the Cinémathèque Royale in Brussels and the Filmoteca Española in Madrid rescued two of Micheaux's silent films—*Within Our Gates* (1920) in Spain and *The Symbol of the Unconquered* (1920) in Belgium, and kindly made them available to American archives for restoration. Without these efforts, this project would have been almost inconceivable, or at least would have been conceived in very different form. During the course of our undertaking, both pictures were restored with English-language subtitles. At the Library of Congress, David Francis, Head of the Motion Picture, Broadcasting, and Recorded Sound Division; Patrick Loughney, Head of the Motion Picture Section; and freelance scholar Scott

Simmons were crucially involved in the restoration of *Within Our Gates*. Here we joined Phyllis Klotman, director of the Black Film Archive at Indiana University, and Susan Dalton, film archivist for the American Film Institute, to create an environment that fostered this restoration project. Later we also intervened on behalf of the Library of Congress to make sure that *Within Our Gates* and *The Scar of Shame* (1929) were distributed in 35mm by the Museum of Modern Art—supporting an idea that had already been put forward by David Francis. Indeed, these were the first films to be distributed in 35mm by the Circulating Film Library of the Museum of Modern Art. Because it has proved a success, these efforts to show films in their original format are gaining ground. Likewise, we supplied the impetus and intertitle translation for the restoration of *Symbol of the Unconquered,* which was funded and executed by Turner Entertainment and the Museum of Modern Art. In this regard, Richard May at Turner and Stephen Higgins and Peter Williamson at the Museum of Modern Art were the key contributors. In July 1998, Turner Classic Movies (TCM) also organized an extraordinary film premiere at the Apollo Theater in Harlem, where Micheaux's films had once played. Max Roach provided dazzling musical accompaniment. Those of us lucky enough to attend that event experienced a vital and revealing response from New York's black community. We want to thank Katherine Evans, vice president of marketing, and her TCM staff for making the restoration as well as the premieres at the Apollo and on the TCM Cable Channel possible. Pearl Bowser's vision and determination ensured that this took place in the form that it did.

Curators, readers, and viewers owe a great debt to those family members and collectors who have deposited films and papers in public archives, particularly Richard E. Norman, Jr. (the Norman Collection to the Black Film Center/Archive, Indiana University), Homoiselle Patrick Harrison (the James and Eloyce Gist Collection to the Library of Congress), and Benjamin C. Wilson and Edward Reed (*A Pictorial View of Idlewild* [1927] to the Library of Congress).

We also owe much to the patience and support provided by Mary Lea Bandy, director of the Department of Film and Video, and Bill Sloan of the Circulating Film Library at the Museum of Modern Art (New York). It is through them that the seven-part touring program of films will be realized. Paolo Cherchi Usai, Senior Curator, Motion Picture Department at the George Eastman House, and his staff, particularly Ed Stratmann and Caroline Yeager, have provided critical cooperation and support. Madeline Matz, Brian Taves, and Michael Mashon at the Motion Picture Broadcasting and Recorded Sound Division have smoothed the way at many critical moments. At the Museum of Modern Art, Charles Silver, Ron Magliozzi, and John Harris at the Film Study Center as well as Larry Kardish, Josh Siegel, and Ytte Jensen in Film Exhibition provided friendly assistance. Thanks also to Larry Richards and his colleague Geraldine Duclow, head of the Theatre Collection at the Free Library of Philadelphia and to Howard Dodson, director of the Schomburg Center for Research in Black Culture. While curator of film at the George Eastman House, Jan-Christopher Horak did much to ensure the availability of *Body and Soul* (1925) and *Ten Nights in a Barroom* (1926) in 16mm at the Circulating Film Library of the Museum of Modern Art. *The Oscar Micheaux Newsletter,* edited by Charlene Regester and Jane Gaines, has been an important source of support for our efforts. Lisa Poteet, Hank Okazaki, Fred Neumann, and Vince Brown of the Film and Video Program at Duke University, along with director Michael Kerbel and Senior Administrative Assistant Jonathan Iannone of Yale's Film Study Center, handled important administrative responsibilities for this project. Thanks also to Matthew Bernstein, Rae Alexander-Minter, and Cheryl Finley.

We are particularly thankful for our authors, whose patience has been often tested as this catalog gradually moved toward completion. Many have contributed far more than simple essays. They have also played crucial roles in the curatorial and editorial process. Like us, they are very pleased that this catalog and program of films will have its premiere at the 20th Giornate del Cinema Muto in Pordenone-Sacile, Italy. We are immensely grateful to the members of the Giornate del Cinema Muto and the Cineteca del Friuli for co-publishing this catalog and the organization of their annual silent film festival. Our deepest thanks to Livio Jacob (president), David Robinson (director), Lorenzo Codelli, Paolo Cherchi Usai, and Piera Patat. We are also fortunate to have worked with Indiana University Press, our editor Michael Lundell, and copyeditor Kate Babbitt, who made possible the realization of this catalog in its present form.

After much spirited discussion, we dedicate this book to Spike Lee. Lee's work as a producer, director, and writer; his willingness to address controversial topics; and his perseverance and productivity in the face of sometimes disingenuous and ungenerous criticism has kept alive the spirit of Oscar Micheaux. Lee's films have forever changed the politics of race and kept alive the vitality of cinema in the United States. Lee's films and the New Black Cinema, which he did much to spur, have also given new relevance and meaning to our scholarly exploration of race cinema in the silent period. Micheaux, in turn, enriches our understanding of Lee's work. Indeed, since the 1980s many have remarked on the uncanny parallels between these two filmmakers. Both have been figures of controversy throughout their careers.

Spike Lee's work has been addressed by many of our authors, if not in this catalog then elsewhere. In his recent book, *The Mask of Art: Breaking the Aesthetic Contract—Film and Literature*, Clyde R. Taylor celebrates Spike Lee's cinema for "bringing the arts of the not-perfect within the citadel of commercial movies. Among his intriguing moves in this direction is the artistic heresy of being funny and entertaining in a vernacular tradition—'street'—without surrendering to the antics of minstrelsy. Lee's jazz-inspired, improvisational directing style is a departure from classical notions of cinema form." His work has also been critically engaged—within a framework of respect, support and concern—by Toni Cade Bambara in her essay on *School Daze* (1987), which appeared in *Five for Five: The Films of Spike Lee* (1991). It is in the interplay between this dedication to Spike Lee and to the memory of Toni Cade Bambara that we locate the spirit that has guided us in our work on this catalog and exhibition program from its initial stages to eventual completion.

PEARL BOWSER, JANE GAINES, AND CHARLES MUSSER

INTRODUCTION: OSCAR MICHEAUX AND RACE MOVIES OF THE SILENT PERIOD

Pearl Bowser, Jane Gaines, and Charles Musser

This catalog accompanies a seven-part program of American race films, which is premiering at the Giornate del Cinema Muto and will then be distributed by the Museum of Modern Art (New York) in a 35mm film format. The resulting *Oscar Micheaux and His Circle* package embraces virtually all of the surviving feature-length race films from the silent period as well as a selection of related shorts. These pictures were made between the end of World War I and 1930. Of the seven features, three were made by African-American filmmaker Oscar Micheaux (based in Chicago; Roanoke, Virginia; and then New York), two by the Colored Players Film Corporation located in Philadelphia, one by the Detroit-based Richard Maurice, and one by Richard Norman's film company in Arlington, Florida. The shorter films were made for a wide variety of purposes: some are 35mm shorts that might be shown before a feature. Others were shot in 16mm: for the church circuit by James and Eloyce Gist and for ethnographic purposes by Zora Neale Hurston. Oscar Micheaux, recognized in his time as the foremost African-American filmmaker of this period, emerges as the central figure of this book. Enough films by his contemporaries survive for us to gain a context for his work. While these other films are certainly of considerable importance in their own right, it is Micheaux who emerges as a major figure of the New Negro Renaissance that flourished in the wake of World War I. In truth, Micheaux also emerges as one of America's great directors, someone of absolutely world-class stature whose work is dense, rich, and complex. His films demand and reward repeated viewing and extensive critical engagement.

As Charles Hobson remarked at the recent Yale University conference on the African-American filmmaker, "If there hadn't been an Oscar Micheaux there wouldn't have been an Oscar Micheaux." This multitalented novelist, director, and screenwriter, virtually self-taught, belonged to no movement or school and appeared literally out of nowhere—from the South Dakota prairie. The odds were historically against the appearance of such a prolific African-American filmmaker at such an early date and so suddenly out of the plains. How Micheaux, born in 1884 to former slaves as one of eleven children in Metropolis, Illinois, came to homestead near Gregory, South Dakota, is another story, a story he told in his first novel, *The Conquest* (1913) and returned to in other writings, notably *The Forged Note: A Romance of the Darker Races* (1915), *The Homesteader* (1917), and finally *The Wind from Nowhere* (1943). In fact, Micheaux launched his film career with the adaptation of *The Homesteader,* which premiered in 1919. Of course, Micheaux never stopped telling his homesteading stories, which were the basis of so many of the seven novels and approximately forty feature-length films that he produced between 1918 and 1948. And he was always pioneering—as he sold stock to finance the Micheaux Book and Film Company, as he "hand-

Charles Lucas as Jean Baptiste and Evelyn Preer as Orlean in Oscar Micheaux's *The Homesteader* (1919).

carried" his films from theater to theater, and as he sold the rights to foreign distribution for his early films.

Micheaux's life and career can be divided into three phases: his years as homesteader and novelist (part I, 1910–1917); his years making silent films (part II, 1918–1930); and his years as a maker of sound films and as a novelist (part III, 1931–1948). If this simplifies a complex life, his work does have a certain symmetry. His novel-writing was concentrated during both World War I and World War II; except for his final feature film, his work as a published novelist bookended his film career. Micheaux's entrance into moviemaking coincided with the coalescing of the Hollywood system of representation, production, and distribution. He worked outside of it as well as against it. This strategy proved successful because, in the silent period in particular, Hollywood was ill-equipped to make and uninterested in making films for African-American audiences. Such disinterest opened a space for companies to make race movies—and for Micheaux to produce, direct, and write an extraordinary number of films. Inevitably, he continued to make silent films until the end of the decade—late by Hollywood standards (Warner Brothers' *The Jazz Singer* opened in 1927) and more typical of filmmakers in countries such as the Soviet Union, Italy, India, and even France. The absence of resources— film stock was rationed during World War II—perhaps encouraged his return to novel-writing in the mid-1940s. With these books enjoying only modest sales, Micheaux risked his life savings in a return to filmmaking—and lost. This last film, *The Betrayal* (1948), proved that, for Micheaux at least, there was no going back. 1948 was also the year of the Paramount decrees which broke up the studio system. The era of race cinema—and the vertically integrated Hollywood system of production, distribution, and exhibition—was quickly coming to a close.

In *Oscar Micheaux and His Circle,* we have concentrated on the middle phase of Micheaux's career (the silent film years), hoping that future work will be done on Micheaux the novelist and on the director's sound-era films. This focus has many motivations, not least the exciting new silent film discoveries that have completely transformed our ways of thinking about this fascinating filmmaker. While we have focused on Micheaux's work, we have also sought to open up the larger phenomenon of silent race movies, about which too little is known. Although Micheaux was an independent—even a loner—our aim is to restore the names as well as the surviving work of black and white producers who catered to black audiences who were such loyal fans in this period. The touring package of films highlights the work of five other African Americans—Richard Maurice, James and Eloyce Gist, and Zora Neale Hurston—but there were others whose work, sadly, has been lost. The first African-American producer to make films specifically for black audiences was William A. Foster, whose Chicago-based Foster Photoplay Company was flourishing by 1913. This was two years *before* the appearance of D.W. Griffith's *The Birth of a Nation* (1915), the film that, as it is often said, stirred black Americans to produce their own stories in motion picture form. Perhaps that picture motivated Noble and George P. Johnson, whose class act, The Lincoln Motion Picture Company, booked its films out of Omaha, Nebraska, between 1916 and 1921 and the Frederick Douglass Company in Jersey City, New Jersey, which distributed between 1916 and 1919. Thanks to the tireless work of Henry T. Sampson and Thomas Cripps, we know something about these companies, Hunter Haynes's Afro-American Film Company in New York, and the Peter P. Jones Photoplay Company in Chicago. They have also provided leads on a host of others that attempted a start before 1927: among these are the Rosebud Film Corporation, Paragon Pictures Corporation, Colored Feature Photoplay Incorporated, Monumental Pictures Corporation, Whipper Reel Negro News, the Western Picture Producing Company, the Eagle Film Company, the Royal Gardens Motion Picture Company, and the Unique Film Company. That no black-focused newsreels survive from the 1920s is a terrible loss. The inclusion of *A Pictorial View of Idlewild,* made by the Chicago Daily News Film Service in 1927, suggests some of these nonfiction materials.

Race movies may have played almost exclusively to black audiences in the United States, but as business ven-

Afro Weekly News Reel

Passed By State Board Of Censors

No. 1. A HEATED ARGUMENT AROUND A COAL TRUCK—The camera man just happened along at the corner of Madison avenue and Dolphin street as the driver of the coal truck sent the Chevrolet of the gentleman at the right swerving to the pavement. Both are explaining to Johnny Law how it happened.

No. 2. HE WAS A MEXICAN CHIEFTAIN—Taking part in two or three revolutions was apple pie for James Henry who attained the rank of Lieutenant-Colonel in the Mexican Army. He was snapped in an unconventional moment in front of the barber shop at 1100 Madison avenue where he is now using scissors instead of a bayonet.

No. 3. BUILDS MODEL AEROPLANES—In his spare moments Clarence Small, a mechanic, finds time to build various types of aircraft. The model here is an exact replica of the one in which Lindbergh crossed the Atlantic. It is complete in every detail to the controls which are operated from the pilot chamber.
Photos by Staff Photographer.

GET IN THE AFRO MOVIE GAME

You don't have to be a scenario writer to play this new game which will net you both pleasure and money. Just dig out some unusual person, place or happening worthy of publication and ring Vernon 6016. The cameraman will be there quicker than you can say Jack Robinson and if your picture is published, walk, don't run to the AFRO office identify yourself and presto! You will be one dollar richer.

Silent newsreels of African-American life have been lost. One such enterprise is documented in an article from the Baltimore *Afro-American,* January 14, 1928.

A Pictorial View of Idlewild (Chicago Daily News Film Service, 1927) shows off this summer resort for the black middle class. Among those featured is the local postmistress.

tures they often encouraged interracial collaboration. The white-controlled companies are represented in the touring package by Richard Norman's Norman Film Manufacturing Company of Florida. Although David Starkman's Colored Players Film Corporation started out as a white-owned business and operated on this basis while making *Ten Nights in a Barroom* (1926), by the time the company made *The Scar of Shame* (1929), African-American Sherman H. Dudley had become company president and was actively seeking black financing. Robert Levy's Reol Productions made ten features between 1920 and 1924; all are lost, which is particularly unfortunate because the company was so closely connected to the Lafayette Players, the leading African-American theatrical repertory company of the 1920s. The Lafayette Players supplied much of the on-camera talent for the silent race movies, not only for Reol but for Colored Players Film Corporation, Richard Norman, and Micheaux. Historical Feature Film and Ebony Film Corporation of Chicago were white-dominated companies that made black-cast comedy shorts between 1915 and 1919, primarily for distribution through the General Film Corporation. Playing with often-painful racial stereotypes that were criticized in the black press, the companies made films that were not strictly race films, for they were meant to appeal to white and black audiences. Although several examples of their work survive, we decided against including them in our touring package for these reasons.

Spread across the country—from Micheaux offices in Chicago, New York, and Roanoke, Virginia, to Lincoln production headquarters in Hollywood, the Colored Players studio in Philadelphia, and Norman's operations in Florida, these race movie pioneers were aware of each other and kept up a rivalry in the black box office throughout the twenties. They often corresponded and compared notes. Actors such as Lawrence Chenault, William A. Clayton, Jr., J. Lawrence Criner, and Shingzie Howard worked for two or more of these companies. The stars of these companies worked on a circuit that often included the Lafayette Players Dramatic Stock Company. And their films played the same circuit of race theaters and catered to the same audiences. We can thus talk of a circle—a loose federation of production companies and producers who competed with and depended on each other. They did not, so far as we know, ever sit around a table together. They were not a circle of friends. The circle—or circuit—was of a different kind. They certainly saw each others' films. They shared circumstances and aspirations. Of this group, however, only Micheaux was able to remain an active producer of race films throughout the entire period between the end of World War I and the beginning of World War II. Indeed, he was easily the most productive—the most prolific and significant, thus the title of our seven-part program and this book.

Although the production of race movies flourished in the immediate aftermath of World War I and, according to Henry Sampson, peaked around 1921, only two of the films in this package—Micheaux's *Within Our Gates* (1920) and *The Symbol of the Unconquered* (1920)—

The Lafayette Theatre in Harlem during the 1920s (photographed by Eddie Elcha). The theater was the home of the Lafayette Players Dramatic Stock Company and a venue for many race films.

were made in this period of maximum productivity. Unfortunately, films by other producers in these years have not survived. In quality, if not quantity, race cinema continued to develop and change until the decade's close. Oscar Micheaux's *Body and Soul* (1925) was one of several controversial and often-denigrated films made by the black filmmaker at mid-decade. In many respects, Colored Players Film Corporation made *Ten Nights in a Barroom* (1926), starring the renowned Charles Gilpin, as an alternative to Micheaux's goals and sensibilities—one meant to appeal to the very critics Micheaux had profoundly alienated. In this they succeeded. Norman's *The Flying Ace* (1926) avoided Micheaux's didacticism altogether, offering "simple" entertainment. His picture was in the detective genre with plenty of action and a dynamic, attractive hero. As Phyllis Klotman shows, however, even simple entertainment was not so simple in the race cinema context.

The last two feature films in our series were made at the end of the silent era. *The Scar of Shame* was made in the winter of 1929 and released in April of that year. It has luscious cinematography, a melodramatic story, and attractive stars who made it extremely popular. None of Micheaux's film from the last half of the decade survive, which is unfortunate in that dur-

Publicity still for Richard Norman's *The Flying Ace* (1926).

ing this period he seemed to regain a certain grudging admiration from many African-American commentators. Nonetheless, Richard Maurice's *Eleven P.M.* (circa 1929), with its dream structures and flashbacks, owed much to Micheaux's storytelling methods and subject matter. Maurice, however, was more experimental in his use of cinematography and location shooting. Both *The Scar of Shame* and *Eleven P.M.* were the last efforts by film producers who faced limited opportunities for financial recoupment as the film industry and movie theaters changed over to sound. At the very least, these seven films demonstrate that silent race cinema was as vital as it was low-budget and ephemeral.

Lynching and racial violence were central subjects of Micheaux's *Within Our Gates* (1920).

One of the most thrilling aspects of following silent race cinema is the chance that new company records will turn up or that a print will be discovered in a basement or an archive. The Richard Norman Collection at the Black Film Center/Archive at Indiana University is one such example, and it was used by the Archive's director Phyllis Klotman for her essay in this volume. Another invaluable resource for scholars has been the George P. Johnson Negro Film Collection, deposited in Special Collections at the Young Library,

UCLA in the 1960s. Johnson was very focused on the old "race movie" distribution network (particularly in Chicago and New York) by the time he moved to the West Coast and started the news service that forms the basis of the microfilm collection that we have today. Consulted by many of our contributors, it was invaluable in our efforts to establish a reliable filmography of Micheaux's silent film career. Despite George P. Johnson's extensive records, we know little about Richard Maurice other than the fact that he directed and starred in at least two feature films shot in Detroit, Michigan: *Nobody's Children* (1920) and *Eleven P.M.*

Some productions, like those of James and Eloyce Gist, who worked in Washington, D.C., were missed by the otherwise-thorough Johnson. The Gists' shorts were written and directed for a different exhibition circuit, the non-theatrical circuit of black churches and race organizations, and represent an entirely different genre in the touring package. The discovery of the Gist films is the result of the work of the film archivists in the Motion Picture and Sound Recording Division of the Library of Congress. Likewise, film archivists would have been aware of the 16mm black-and-white film footage of children playing games somewhere in the South, but it was not until Zora Neale Hurston became well known as a prolific author that scholars began to look more closely at the footage she shot. Her short 100–foot films, shot in Florida between 1927 and 1929, provide an ethnographic view of people living in relative isolation in a company town. We can also see these shorts as providing a framework of time and place in which we might situate Norman's imaginative *The Flying Ace.*

The chance phone call out of the blue may turn up reels of our lost African-American film heritage, as happened in the discovery of the old film cans in a warehouse in Tyler, Texas, in 1983. Enterprising Texas journalists created a story about the discovery of "lost" black films that was picked up nationally and carried into U.S. living rooms on *CBS Morning News* and *Nightline.* In retrospect, however, we know that of the 100 shorts and features discovered, only twenty-two were produced for black audiences and most of these were not "lost" films at all but merely additional prints of titles that, although not in commercial distribution, were housed in various film archives.

For *Oscar Micheaux and His Circle,* the real kudos go to hardworking local and international collectors, scholars, and archivists. One pair of highly dramatic achievements was the repatriation of two silent films from Belgium and Spain in the late 1980s and early 1990s. Here, cooperation within FIAF (the International Federation of Film Archives, or Fédération Internationale des Archives du Film), the seventy-five–member consortium of film archives, made all the difference. In the late 1980s, the Library of Congress acquired a 35mm print of Micheaux's second film, *Within Our Gates* (1920), from the Filmoteca Española in Madrid in exchange for a print of *Dracula* (1932). The film, considered lost for decades, had appeared under the title *La Negra* on a FIAF list circulated in 1965. A 35mm print of Micheaux's fourth feature film, *The Symbol of the Unconquered* (1920), was located on a list of American film titles circulated by the archive in Brussels, and the double intertitle format in both French and Flemish is evidence of its distribution in Belgium. A copy from the preservation negative was subsequently obtained by the Museum of Modern Art (New York) and screened before small groups in that format. In 1998, Turner Classic Movies (TCM) restored *Symbol of the Unconquered* using our English-language translation. The results premiered at Harlem's famed Apollo Theatre with a score and live percussion accompaniment by jazz musician Max Roach. TCM subsequently aired a video version with Roach's studio rendition as a kickoff to five weeks of black film programming on the channel. The Museum of Modern Art has since undertaken its own restoration, which is premiering with the Oscar Micheaux and His Circle series.

The discovery and restoration of these two films bring the number of Micheaux's surviving silent films to three. Over thirty years ago, the International Museum of Photography

Paul Robeson in the role of a sociopathic criminal posing as a preacher in Oscar Micheaux's *Body and Soul* (1925).

at the George Eastman House in Rochester acquired a 35mm nitrate print of Micheaux's *Body and Soul* (1925), made from the original negative. The Eastman House subsequently preserved the film by generating a new 35mm acetate negative from this material. A 35mm print as well as a 16mm negative were made from this duplicate negative. 16mm prints of this (and *Ten Nights in a Barroom*) are available for rental through a joint distribution project with the Circulating Film Library of the Museum of Modern Art. Besides being one of Micheaux's most remarkable achievements (and until recently his only silent film available with English intertitles), *Body and Soul* represents Paul Robeson's first film acting role and his only opportunity to work with an African-American director. Interest in the film was considerable; and in the late 1980s and early 1990s, several "budget" videotape distributors marketed low-quality videos made from poor-quality, "dupy" 16mm prints that were generally far from complete. Most people thus viewed the film in a version that had a highly tenuous relationship to the original production. When people discussed the film's "low production values," were they talking about Micheaux's actual film or the poor-quality videotape they were unfortunate enough to encounter? Only with the centennial of Paul Robeson's birth could we finally view a high-quality videotape of *Body and Soul,* distributed by Kino International (from 35mm material provided by private sources—the Douris Corporation). Even here, according to Paolo Cherchi Usai, the film is not as complete as the Eastman House material. We offer here some history of the surviving film materials as they find their way into commercial distribution in an effort to clarify the problems facing archivists, scholars, and unsuspecting viewers alike.

Archivists like to remind us of two facts: 1) there is always more footage somewhere that needs to be restored before it decomposes and 2) it is difficult to conceive of an early film that can be guaranteed as "complete." In fact, shortly after the Library of Congress released a videotape of *The Scar of Shame* in 1993, Pearl Bowser located a print with a missing, tinted scene (the wedding scene) from that film. This only underscores the "chicken or the egg" dilemma of archival projects such as these. It was the release of the video that brought her attention to this discrepancy. Future discoveries of this kind may be more likely in the case of Micheaux, who had to contend with aggressive censors and often had to re-edit his films as he moved from town to town (or state to state).

THE ESSAYS

The essays that follow explore, to a greater or lesser extent, the surviving examples of silent race cinema that we have assembled for this touring show. Thus it is that this book is a catalog focusing on a group of films and not simply a collection of essays on our chosen subject. The catalog sets out to clear new critical ground but also to clear up some critical misconceptions that, although associated with Micheaux, could be seen to apply to other race movie makers in this period. Perhaps the most persistent criticism, one that was heard early in the pages of the black press, was that these films were only "imitations" of white motion pictures. And this is the one question that all of the articles address as they demonstrate that race movies were totally unlike mainstream American cinema at the same time that they owed something to it. A companion criticism has centered on the technical achievement of these films, which have been accused since their inception of somehow falling short of the accepted and acceptable standard. It is this question of "production values" that Clyde Taylor addresses squarely with a concept imported from third world and post-colonial studies. Technical proficiency is purely a question of economics, he says, and race cinema is best understood as "underdeveloped" in relation to Hollywood, which might then be seen as an "overdeveloped" cinema. Underdevelopment is the "invisible hand" that "determines everything," says Taylor, from the budget constraints that dictate a single "take" on the set to the number of black theaters that, as he says, "limits the take" in another sense. The consequences of underdevelopment are dramatized in Richard Norman's assertion, as quoted in Phyllis Klotman's essay here, that whereas white films could play 15,000 theaters, race films could only count on the 105 theaters that catered to the black trade, all facilities that would have been more or less segregated in these years.

Cinematographer Arthur Jafa, whose credits include Julie Dash's *Daughters of the Dust* (1992) and Spike Lee's *Crooklyn* (1994), explores related dimensions of race cinema. He suggests that an appreciation of African-American creativity requires the audience to focus on "the space of treatment rather than the space of material. So, if you're assessing [a work of art] from a classically Western vantage point, which is primarily about the material, whole dimensions of the African American creativity are going to be rendered invisible." He goes on to argue that both Oscar Micheaux and Jean-Luc Godard "were equally impacted by the same aesthetic community, that is, Black aesthetics, and in Godard's specific instance its sub strand—modernism." As with Godard's own filmwork, "some of the most interesting aspects of Micheaux's films are their refusals, . . . how they resist certain Hollywood tropes and ways of organizing things."

Sister Francesca Thompson and Charlene Regester each examine specific historical contexts for enhancing our understanding of race cinema: African-American theater and the black press. Micheaux, Starkman, and Norman all drew heavily on the acting talent of the Lafayette Players Dramatic Stock Company—the legendary group that grew out of the Anita Bush Stock Company. Thompson gives us a portrait of the Lafayette Players in an overview of the career of her own mother, Evelyn Preer, and her father, Edward Thompson. Preer was an accomplished stage actress who was also one of Micheaux's most popular stars, appearing in *The Homesteader* (1919), *Within Our Gates* (1920), *The Brute* (1920), *The Gunsaulus Mystery* (1921), *Deceit* (1923), and other films. The fact that Micheaux used the finest acting talent available in the black community would seem to contradict any argument that he was an indifferent director or a sloppy craftsman.

Clearly any substantive reevaluation of Micheaux involves taking a closer look at the black press which, as Charlene Regester tells us, *made* race movies in so many ways but also became their harshest critic. Micheaux, the most prolific of the race filmmakers, benefited in the early years of his career when the press was extremely enthusiastic and bore the brunt of their negative appraisal toward the end of the silent era. The black press was vital to the success of race movies in many different ways. Columnists at the *Chicago Defender* and the *New York Age,* for example, both worked as booking agents for the Lincoln Motion Picture Company. However, as Regester suggests, we do not really know the extent to which their editorial and critical policies damaged Micheaux's box-office returns at any given time.

Having established a broad theoretical and historical framework, our catalog presents six essays that focus on different aspects of Oscar Micheaux's work. The first four focus on his

Evelyn Preer as Mildred, the mistreated wife in Oscar Micheaux's *The Brute* (1920).

three surviving silent films: *Within Our Gates* (1920), *The Symbol of the Unconquered* (1920), and *Body and Soul* (1925). As all four of these essays demonstrate, Micheaux engaged issues of race and representation in complex and sophisticated ways that were unrivaled by his contemporaries. This achievement, in combination with his radical stylistics, compels these in-depth explorations of his work. Michele Wallace, continuing her important challenge to the comparisons between stereotypes and "reality" as the basis for criticism, writes here about the way Micheaux transformed existing popular types. Wallace offers one answer to the complaint that Micheaux offered too many negative portrayals of blacks: "After inundation with the negative taking up so much room, there is no alternative but to repossess and redefine" existing types, whether "tom, coon, buck, mammy, or mulatto." Wallace shows how Micheaux transformed the stereotypes found in Griffith's *The Birth of a Nation* in *Within Our Gates,* a film also considered by Jane Gaines. Gaines, who argues that Micheaux had an oblique relationship to turn-of-the-century African-American

The Dunbar Theatre, a Bennett Family theater in Atlanta, Georgia (circa 1934). A black movie house. Little more than 100 theaters could be counted on to show race films, limiting the potential box-office return of producers such as Oscar Micheaux, Richard Norman, and David Starkman.

sentimental melodrama, finds that Micheaux's new-opportunity narratives displace the older fiction that had its origins in the slave narrative. Although this may raise questions about the degree of Micheaux's commitment to radical positions, *Within Our Gates* is probably his most political film. In it, Micheaux created a devastating portrait of the white racism that produced lynch mobs as well as the white lust that produced generations of mixed-race peoples.

Likewise, Pearl Bowser and Louise Spence view Micheaux's fourth feature film, *The Symbol of the Unconquered* (1920), as a black-centered melodrama depicting a world of good versus evil in which racial affirmation, self-loathing, passing, and miscegenation are crucial elements. The Ku Klux Klan is a gathering place for criminals, many of whom are concealing their own mixed bloodlines. But the film is also a western evoking the filmmaker's own biographical legend as a pioneering sodbuster in South Dakota. For Micheaux, the frontier is a "mythic space of moral drama and site of golden opportunities." The film thus brings these two genre conventions into creative play. Charles Musser explores the ways *Body and Soul* involves another set of collisions—the way the film condenses and reworks three plays about the Negro soul, all written by white playwrights: Nan Bagby Stephens's *Roseanne* and Eugene O'Neill's *The Emperor Jones* and *All God's Chillun' Got Wings*. By his radical treatment, Micheaux deformed and criticized these plays, along with their underlying racial assumptions. Micheaux's method is never straightforward, and, in this case, he worked an oblique connection through Paul Robeson, who starred in all three plays during a brief time span—the spring and summer of 1924—a few months before Micheaux shot *Body and Soul*. The filmmaker thus combined genres and played off texts in ways that underscore, as Jafa articulates it, "the space of treatment."

A widely printed newspaper advertisement for Micheaux's *The Symbol of the Unconquered* (1920).

The last two essays in the Micheaux section consider aspects of the filmmaker's relationship to literary forms. Many of Micheaux's silent films were either based on well-known novels or were said to be adaptations of novels by Micheaux himself (either unpublished or never actually written). In a study of what she calls Micheaux's "fictional autobiography," Jayna Brown reads the author-filmmaker as a complicated regionalist, divided between the urban and the rural, and perhaps looking forward as he looked backward to an agrarian ideal, an "obsolete model of black progress." And then, as Jayna Brown tells us here, Micheaux did not approve of either W. E. B. Du Bois or Richard Wright. In his novels he attacked their radicalism, styling himself instead as a follower of Booker T. Washington. Neither was his relationship to African-American novelist Charles Chesnutt a close one, even though Micheaux twice adapted the important literary figure's novel *The House Behind the Cedars* and adapted a Chesnutt short story from *The Conjure Woman*. As Corey Creekmur suggests in his article here, although the historical parallels between the two are striking, the actual relationship between them was one way: Micheaux was deeply influenced by Chesnutt, but

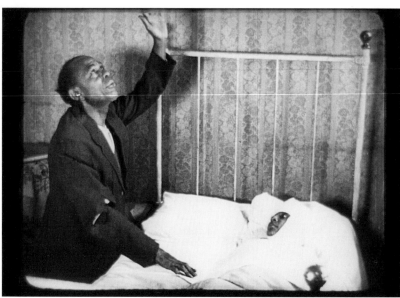

Joe Morgan, played by Charles Gilpin, swears off liquor over the body of his dying daughter in *Ten Nights in a Barroom* (Colored Players Film Corporation, 1926).

Chesnutt did not like Micheaux's versions of his work. Creekmur further elaborates the relationship between these two men's work by exploring the ways in which Micheaux reworked essential elements of Chesnutt's novel *The Marrow of Tradition* (1901) in *Within Our Gates*.

Although Harlem Renaissance artists and intellectuals, like Micheaux, shared an interest in Chesnutt, they also shared Chesnutt's dislike for the former black homesteader (as novelist and as filmmaker). The question of the controversial filmmaker's relationship to the Harlem elite is by no means settled in this collection, but the evidence thus far points to the fact that the elite literary figures were either unaware of or hostile to his films. (As Ron Green remarks in his bibliographic overview of Micheaux scholarship, James Weldon Johnson was apparently unaware that *Body and Soul* existed.) Micheaux can reasonably be described as an "outcast" in the Harlem Renaissance community. This challenges us to think where and how we should situate black independent filmmaking in the 1920s, the period coincident with the famous literary flowering in Harlem and African-American cultural activity in many parts of the United States (what is more broadly referred to as the New Negro Renaissance). Certainly there are ways Micheaux can be connected to a larger cultural and political project. As Pearl Bowser and Louise Spence remind us, like Harlem Renaissance figures Zora Neal Hurston and Langston Hughes, Micheaux "spoke as a Negro." Nonetheless, the essays in this collection mark the investigation of black cultural production that cannot be easily lumped together with the aspirations of Harlem Renaissance artists. Micheaux and other feature filmmakers belonged to the world of black *popular* culture because they spoke to the masses who patronized the all-black movie theaters, facilities that were often owned and managed by blacks.

Our decision to name this collection *Oscar Micheaux and His Circle* is meant, in fact, to signal the existence of a culture of race filmmakers who defined themselves by their audience, who had no choice but to function as businessmen and promoters adept at thinking up ways to "sell" their product. The third section of our catalog is thus devoted to

Harry Henderson as the hero Alvin Hillyard and Lucia Lynn Moses as Hillyard's wife Louise Howard in *The Scar of Shame* (Colored Players Film Corporation, 1929). She is holding a doll that will be crushed under the indifferent foot of her husband.

MICHEAUX FILM CORPORATION
Producers and Distributors of High Class
Negro Feature Photoplays
200 WEST 135TH STREET
NEW YORK CITY

August 7th, 1926.

Norman Film Manufacturing Co.
Jacksonville, Florida.

Friend Norman:

    The Franklin Theatre here, would like to play your "REGEN-ERATION". So if you will get in touch with them, the Franklin Theatre Lenox Avenue at 132nd Street, you will be able to consumate a deal with them if your rental is not too high.

    Understand that you have produced a new feature and should like to hear from you. Some Jews have produced a couple of features, the first of which appears to draw very well although mighty badly acted and poorly photographed, due to the use of some Cooper-Hewitt banks alternating current which flicker alternately through all the interiors and refuse to permite a fade-out with any degree of smoothness at all. The first is called "A PRINCE OF HIS RACE" which, while having drawn very well at the Royal in Philadelphia, and I understand at the Royal in Baltimore, if they screen the same, have serious difficulty in getting a booking with critical houses.

    All the first run houses here turned it down, and also in Washington. Nevertheless, it was a mistake and they would have made money had they played it. We could help them a great deal, but since they seem to think they know it all, and regard all of us who have endured through the years gone by as dubbs, and know nothing, I am letting them find out for themselves the things we have learned from experience. Their second picture is "TEN NIGHTS IN A BARROOM" which I am advised is not as good as the first. Since they expect to make between one hundred seventy-five and two

---

Complete selected list of MICHEAUX PRODUCTIONS With all Colored Players.
Produced and Distributed by MICHEAUX FILM CORPORATION, *800 W. 135th St., New York City*
Tel. Edgecombe 4814. OSCAR MICHEAUX, *President;* S. E. MICHEAUX, *Gen'l Mgr.;* A. F. BROOKS, *Treas.*

8 Features Starring	1 Feature Starring	2 Features Starring
EVELYN PREER	PAUL ROBESON	WM. E. FOUNTAINE
"THE HOMESTEADER"	"BODY AND SOUL"	& SHINGZIE HOWARD
"DECEIT"	2 Features Starring	"THE DUNGEON"
"WITHIN OUR GATES"	ANDREW S. BISHOP	"VIRGIN OF SEMINOLE"
Supported by	Supported by	3 ALL STAR CAST
LAWRENCE CHENAULT	LAWRENCE CHENAULT	Productions
"THE DEVIL'S DISCIPLE"	& SHINGZIE HOWARD	"THE SPIDER'S WEB"
"THE BRUTE"	"HOUSE BEHIND THE CEDARS"	Zora Neale Hurston's
"THE GUNSAULUS MYSTERY"	"A SON OF SATAN"	"VANITY"
"BIRTHRIGHT"	Starring Lawrence Chenault	Louis De Bulger's
"THE CONJURE WOMAN"	"SYMBOL THE UNCONQUERED"	"DEADLINE AT ELEVEN"

-2-

hundred thousand dollars, you can appreciate the disappointment in store for them.

    We are very comfortably located at the above address, and when you are up this way again, make our office your headquarters, and any service that we can render you, will be pleased to perform it. Wishing you a successful season with your new production, we beg to remain

             Cordially and sincerely,

             MICHEAUX FILM CORPORATION

OM:DS   *Oscar Micheaux*

Micheaux corresponded with fellow producers of race films about opportunities and rivals.

Micheaux's contemporaries. That these producers were interconnected and competitive is confirmed by Phyllis Klotman, who gives us the first complete portrait of the Richard Norman Company based on the company papers deposited at the Indiana University Black Film Archives as well as an analysis of *The Flying Ace* (1926), one of the only surviving Norman titles.* Klotman also calls our attention to one key point of overlap among race movie makers—the itinerant actors they used were often the same, particularly in the case of Micheaux and Norman, both of whom drew regularly on the talent of the Lafayette Players, the legendary group founded by Anita Bush in 1915. Charles Musser and Pearl Bowser have likewise sought to broaden our knowledge of the Colored Players Film Corporation, which is represented in this collection by two feature films, *Ten Nights in a Barroom* (1926) and *The Scar of Shame* (1929), and of Richard Maurice and the Maurice Film Company.

    By widening the circle of black filmmakers around Micheaux, we also include those makers who did not produce for commercial theaters but who, on the contrary, were interested

---

*The lengthy gestation of this catalog has meant, among other things, that Matthew Bernstein and Dana F. White have published an article, "'Scratching Around' in a 'Fit of Insanity': The Norman Film Manufacturing Company and the Race Film Business in the 1920s," in *Griffithiana* 62/63 (maggio 1998): 81–128, long after Klotman's essay was in our hands. We apologize to Klotman and the other authors for this delay and appreciate their patience.

in the possibilities of motion pictures for entirely different motives. No better example exists than anthropologist and author Zora Neale Hurston, the one genuine link to the Harlem Renaissance, whose ethnographic filmmaking activities have only recently come to light. In her article here, Gloria Gibson finds a commonality between Hurston and religious filmmaker Eloyce Gist, both of whom were deeply interested in folk culture. The answer to her question "Can these women be considered filmmakers?" must certainly be "Yes," despite the fact that only fragments of their work remains for scholars to analyze.

Finally, a catalog such as this one is only as good as its appendices. We are pleased to begin this fourth section with Ron Green's detailed report on the state of Micheaux criticism, an invaluable and comprehensive overview that begins with Thomas Cripps's 1969 essay and brings us up to the present. If Taylor urges us to think of unequal development, Green demonstrates a related uneven development in the critical field that ranges from the dismissal by some black press reviewers to *Village Voice* reviewer J. Hoberman's more recent rave evaluation: "And if Oscar Micheaux was a fully conscious artist, he was the greatest genius the cinema ever produced." The authors in this catalog offer diverse assessments of Micheaux's work that echo these long-standing debates while taking the discussion to a higher level of analysis and contextualization. At the same time, many of the leading Micheaux scholars have combined forces to produce a filmography of Micheaux's silent pictures, one that will provide an important resource for future scholars and Micheaux's many devotees. Essayists have also contributed similar information for the Norman Film Manufacturing Company and the Colored Players Film Corporation. We conclude with an updated bibliography on the topic of this project: "African-American Filmmaking and Race Cinema of the Silent Era."

I

OVERVIEWS

1.

Black Silence and the Politics of Representation

CLYDE R. TAYLOR

With conferences such as Oscar Micheaux and His Circle at Yale University and the celebration of 100 Years of Black Cinema at the National Museum of American History, Smithsonian Institution, we approach a new stage in the understanding of American cinema and its relation to Black Americans. We have come to the end of the beginning. Even in contemplating the amazing history of Black-oriented "race movies," we ought to be beyond the a-ha! stage, and should have gotten past the "gee whiz" experience.

So positioned, the agenda now should be to provoke cinema studies toward a serious examination of racism as a slice of the apple-pie history of U.S. cinema. Too often, presentations on American cinema smoothly sidestepped the issue in favor of anecdotal nostalgia. This examination demands an integration of "race movies" into the whole history of Black people in cinema. Such an agenda would also offer valuable lessons that illuminate other cultural histories.

There are many interpretive tools for this task, but few serve better than the concept of unequal development. This is one of the points where the politics of representation can use some input from political science. To make my sources plain, I am influenced here by two books, Samir Amin's *Unequal Development* and Walter Rodney's *How Europe Underdeveloped Africa.* Rodney's title contains an important warning. We cannot tolerate the trap of thinking that the sub-development of some societies is all their fault. Rodney wants us to treat *underdevelopment* as a verb. In African society, as elsewhere, somebody underdeveloped somebody else. As William Blake said, "Pity would be no more, if we did not *make* somebody poor" [my italics].

Unequal development takes place wherever there is an exploitative/dependent relationship. Unequal development means that less powerful societies must join the competition for survival and prosperity at a pace set for the convenience of more aggressive societies. Unequal development means that a more powerful society draws from the less powerful selected goods and resources without regard for what the loss of those resources will mean to the exploited.

The experiences of women vis-à-vis men in almost every social arena serve as a continuing example of unequal development.

Unequal development is a major factor in the construction and development of Black cinema. Just as Karl Marx noted that it is alienation that hires a coach and goes to the opera, unequal development, which we might call "Undie" here, for its resemblance to those garments that are seldom seen but considered fundamental to anyone's public equipment, is a constant almost-embodied companion in the filmmaking process. Undie's role is crucial in the development or mal-development of the screen, though rarely given top billing or even a credit. Undie is an executive producer, along with the executive producer; Undie directs beside the director, helps pick the cast, fires some of the crew, determines the narrative line—in fact, its fingers work to shape the whole film. Unequal development is as much an invisible hand in the making of the movie as any force of capitalism functioning silently in the marketplace. So even though Undie is less glamorous than some of the players we'd rather talk about—the stars, the aesthetic thrills, the sexy gossip abut personalities, the dial-a-dream stories—we've got to account for him (*him* advisedly) or else be chumped off as dilettantes in the wind.

Samir Amin talks about the *distortion* of some societies and their economic life under unequal development. Perhaps the most significant damage is to a society's history, which is sharply interrupted and rechanneled by outside pressures above and beyond the external pressures that impinge on any society at all times. You can know what I mean by thinking of a moment in a people's collective memory after which everything changed radically because *they* came: their boat sailed into the harbor, and a peaceful group of folks suddenly became "natives." Alongside this trauma stands the amputation of the society's decision-making process. Also implanted in this moment is the awesome wound to the group personality: if "we" are no longer making decisions for ourselves, where is the "us" in our actions, and who, then, are "we"?

In the period of Black silents, there are certain signifiers of Undie's presence. For instance, there is the relatively small number of race movies actually completed between 1910 and 1930—say 500—compared to the thousands coming out of Hollywood in the same period. This number might direct us to the legal and economic prohibitions against competition. Even though there are popular arguments against measuring "equality of results," the inequality of production on this scale tells us something. That is, if one population is making thousands of movies and another, admittedly smaller, one is making proportionately fewer, and yet another group is making none, we might look for the reasons beyond the answer that they didn't want to or didn't have the talent and guts—or to some other such jingoistic "science."

One of the explanations for the relatively small number of Black silent films is segregation laws. (Given the selective national memory, there will soon be a need to recall and verify this system, lest some youths begin to disbelieve it ever existed.) Legal segregation of people in movie theaters took different forms—from separate "White" and "Negro" theaters to different sections in theaters to different screening times ("midnight rambles" for Blacks after regular hours)—and gave race movie producers such as Noble Johnson of the Lincoln Motion Picture Company a captive audience of people who wanted the experience of watching themselves in a movie where they were not humiliated. But it also made the invisible hand of capitalism visible and forbidding when it came to reaching a larger audience or finding the most suitable venues for race films. The memoirs of George P. Johnson (Noble Johnson's brother) document the frustration of not being able to book a theater where their company was certain it could do good business with a White audience and speaks of a very profitable run in a White theater to White audiences in Long Beach, California, as proof that it could be done. Some of these theater owners were downright indignant at the thought that films that did not inferiorize Blacks were being proposed for their spaces. The limited number of movie houses where Blacks could see a race movie created an upper limit on the profit that could be made. Right away we can see the distortion of what might be thought of as artistic creativity. Oscar Micheaux soon learned that with this absolute cap on profits, another rehearsal or another take would mean dollars spent that could never be recouped.

Censorship was another signifier of Undie's presence at work. To be sure, in the era of silent movies, censorship applied to everyone. But the unequal burden of censorship for non-Whites is made evident by the number of times Micheaux was faced with censorship for a variety of possible offenses, usually connected to race in one way or another. Apparently, local censorship boards had wide or varying leverage with regard to what they deemed inappropriate for their communities. We know, to take a couple of casual examples, that Micheaux's *Body and Soul* (1925) was pressured in some communities because of its unflattering portrait of a Black preacher. The story persists that Micheaux then started showing the film with alternate

Noble M. Johnson, producer and star for the Lincoln Motion Picture Company.

endings, whichever got over in the territory he was working. And the anti-racist *Within Our Gates* (1920) faced banning in Chicago and other cities on two grounds; first, that it might inflame recently riotous neighborhoods, and second, that it again contained scurrilous depictions of ministers. Micheaux soon suppressed the historically important *Within Our Gates,* and never made another major assault on racism in his movies, nor did other filmmakers until Melvin van Peebles in *Sweet Sweetback's Baadasssss Song* in 1971.

Along with the repression of social commentary about racism, censorship worked hand in hand with Undie to inhibit race movies through the unofficial and official taboo against *miscegenation.* When the widespread prohibition was formalized in 1934 under the Breen Office, it made official what was already in place. Under the category of Sex, not Race, comes the injunction: "Miscegenation (sex relationships between the White and Black races) is forbidden." Censorship, particularly sexual censorship, obviously pressured movie expression for all filmmakers. But the ban on miscegenation was particularly burdensome for Black Americans, since it was based on the inference that the goal was to protect Whites, who would be unequally *lowered* in social symbolic status by such imaginary commingling. Such a prohibition silently reinforced the policy of denying directorial roles to Blacks in the industry.

Just as White directors made an advantage out of sexual censorship, overcoming the obstacles with cutaway shots to waterfalls or raging fireplaces, so Micheaux toyed with the boundaries of the permissible regarding race-mixing. Declaring that nothing would attract so racialized a society as an advertisement saying "SHALL RACES INTERMARRY?," he played throughout his career with the scenario in which an apparently White woman discovers in the eleventh hour that she possesses one drop of Black blood (enough in those apartheid days to finalize a Black identity) and can therefore marry her Black lover. Micheaux was even ac-

Noble M. Johnson as
Sweeney Bodin.

cused of trying to "pass" one of his films as a "White" film with actors so light and the story so general that a White audience might take it for a typical Hollywood product. Micheaux's witty outfoxing of the system provides a certain *malandro* satisfaction. But look at what this particular bit of unequal development did to the possibilities of Black cinema. Can we miss the multifarious messages that translate into a disproportionate number of light-skinned Blacks in race movies, particularly among women? And how does that disproportion, combined with a similar imbalance in Hollywood movies, affect African-American self-perception?

The destructions in the wake of unequal development are sometimes casual accidents—the grass that is trampled when elephants fight. But sometimes they arrive through a conscious, aggressive will to dominate. When the exploited population begins to pool its resources to shape alternative plans for prosperity, the counteraction from the more powerful sector may be neither casual nor accidental. There is a telling exemplum in the dilemma Universal Studios presented Noble Johnson. This handsome, athletic actor was a featured player who played all the races between White and Black in Universal movies, including Douglas Fairbanks's *Thief of Bagdad* (1924). But when he became the star of Lincoln's race movies (made by Lincoln, his own company), Universal saw it as unwanted competition and gave him an ultimatum (if I were in Amos 'n Andy, I would be forced to say "ultomato"): do one or the other, but you can't do both.

The course of race movies was significantly altered by Johnson's resignation from Lincoln Pictures, the most adventuresome and promising Black movie company of its day, which collapsed soon after his departure. This repressive action carries several features of Undie dynamics. Like Edison, Kodak, and other industry entities, Universal was exercising the power of monopoly against weaker competitors, in this case monopolizing talent the way the industry did through contractual development of superstars. By all accounts, Noble Johnson had the potential to become a very large star in race movies, a phenomenon they had never produced. So his departure was also a kind of brain drain, yet another one of Undie's skills. Thereafter, major African-American performers such as Paul Robeson and Lena Horne got involved in race movies but usually left as soon as crossover bridges were stable enough, and they never looked back, except maybe with embarrassment. Observing this pattern, we need not assess blame; the whole point, in fact, is to watch the curvature of Black cinema in the making and how it was influenced by factors *other than* commitment, race loyalty, or other personal issues.

The need of Undie is to take from a less technologically sophisticated society those things of use to the developers, whether they be educated leadership or material resources, without regard for whether the host society needs the resource or for the imbalance the removal of that resource will leave behind. The revolutionary actions of capitalism have driven populations away from subsistence agriculture, whether it be enclosures in sixteenth-century England or the colonially administered taxation that forced farmers in Africa and other places into a money economy. The force of action has been against what capital does not want. Also prominent in this transformation is the implantation of what capital does want, frequently a single cash crop such as coffee, cocoa, bananas, sugar cane, slaves, or tobacco, the kind that original farmers could not subsist from alone. What this commoditizing drive eliminates often includes the cultural identity of the people and societies in its path.

Similarly, the American culture industry has consistently taken what suits it from

African-American culture, what amuses it or strokes its illusions of superiority or infuses the deadness of its industrialized mentality with spirit. And it does so with a single-mindedness consistent with stereotyping. It makes raids on Black culture in ways that suggest single-crop economic exploitation rather than exchanges that facilitate sustained growth. The stereotypes embodied in Step 'n Fetchit comedy were a single cash crop for the U.S. image industry. In fact, Black comedy, inflected by minstrelsy, has been a perennial U.S. cultural cash crop whose economic vitality only highlights the difficulties and the importance of serious Black drama as a force to restore cultural balance. All-Black cast musicals became a single cash crop briefly during the *Cabin in the Sky* (1943) period, enough to cripple the growth of race movies, along with

A scene from *The Thief of Bagdad* (1924), directed by Raoul Walsh and starring Douglas Fairbanks. Noble Johnson is in the center, playing the role of Indian Prince. On his left is Sojin as the Mongrel Prince; on his right Mathilde Comont as the Persian Prince.

the "Negro interest films" of roughly the same period. And in the late 1980s, New Jack gang-banging movies became a single cash crop, while more nourishing forms of film representation languished.

The challenges Hollywood encountered in the face of Hays Office moral censorship can give us, through metaphor, a lesson. The prohibitions against explicit eroticism, as said before, provoked cute substitutions. The camera pans away from the steamy, groping lovers to waves crashing onto rocks on the beach. The waves can be read as an image displacement, using one image where another might have naturally, realistically been put into place. The question then becomes: Given the prohibitions against picturing Blacks as humans, which also implied the muzzling of attacks against their dehumanization through racism, how did the various framers of Black imagery "make waves"? In other words, when we look at this body of representation, particularly the self-portraits of Blacks in silent race movies, what is a direct projection of unequal development, the signature work of Undie, and what is image displacement, including the self-censorship of the oppressed? Are the stuffy, genteel manners of Black characters in race movies the "waves" that, first of all, compensate for the demeaning stereotypes and then stand in place for a more realistic portrayal that had to be rejected as possible ammunition for further denigration? Might not the same calculation enter into the quotient of brilliance smuggled into the minstrel performances of Step 'n Fetchit as "waves" winking at another reality?

The development of character types is a place where this image displacement shows up as a major determining factor in race movies. In Hollywood, a powerful change came through the rise, along with sound movies, of the common man as hero—the likes of John Wayne, Clark Gable, Henry Fonda, Spencer Tracy, and so forth—to supplant a more European gentleman type, such as John Barrymore or Ronald Coleman. The advance in the power of films to communicate effectively with large democratic audiences was retarded in race movies by the mimicry of refined snob behavior. It was not until Ralph Cooper injected an entirely new style of acting—a more demotic language of personal presentation—in *Dark Manhattan* (1937)

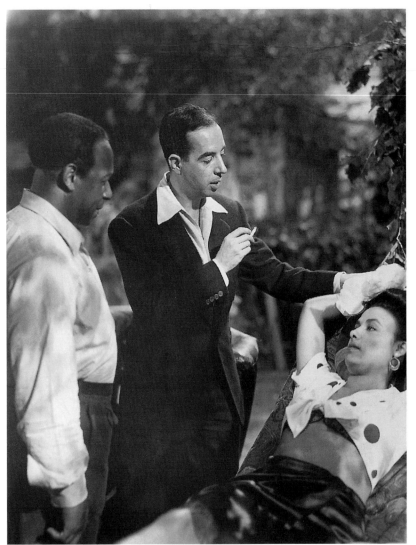

Vincente Minnelli directing Lena Horne and Eddie "Rochester" Anderson in *Cabin in the Sky* (1943).

that we can measure the loss (through stiffness) in earlier race movie performances. This overcompensation toward "proper manners" counts as one of the distortions Samir Amin attributes to unequal development. The number of such distortions in the personal fates of minority cultural producers soon become too astronomical to contemplate except in individual biographies. But to cite one more, as emblematic of the many, Cooper was arguably the most charismatic actor to come out of race movies since Noble Johnson, but his potential was squashed between Hollywood and race movies, at great loss to the American screen.

For this history, the image displacement of race is more important than any personal losses. After the debacle of *Within Our Gates*—it was banned or challenged by censors in several cities—Micheaux altered his course. He stopped trying to distribute the film, in the United States at least, and never made another film addressing racism so frontally. And other race films became, if possible, even more timorous than before. The attitude of social uplift was present throughout the race movie era, but in attenuated form, in which many issues of group improvement were addressed—any issues other than race and racism. At a time when apartheid was the law of the land and savage lynchings were too common, this was the most macabre silence of Black silent cinema.

One imaginable response to this history and its interpretation through the notion of unequal development might be "Get over it! To brood over what might have been is a wasteful luxury." This makes sense, if what has been said so far is read as a guilt trip over the horrors and injuries of bigotry. But that perhaps oversensitive reading misses the object lesson—the impact on the screen in terms of supposed "aesthetics"—of these social and political circumstances. To the practical reaction that these film directors should not have worried about racism but instead made do with what they had, I want to suggest that that is just what they did (particularly Micheaux, who attacked leaders who made an issue of racism), and then to turn our attention to what came out of their adjustments.

Looking at these films from this history, I am convinced that the concern with racism and the caste-like status of African Americans was sublimated within several themes that encoded the motif of racial/social development upon the body of the young Black woman. Just as the metaphor of children as the future is pivotal in several African and contemporary Black independent films, the perils and fate of the young Black woman is the issue around which many—I think I can say most—surviving Black silent race movies revolve.

And through this narrative motif, anxieties about "the Race" were aired, debated, and maybe purged. The figure of the endangered young Black woman was not constructed as a quintessential spirit of the people, as a Joan of Arc might be. Instead, she is presented as an iconic representation of the dilemma and situation of Black people.

Her role in this narrative redresses, with resentment, the exclusion of Black women from "the cult of true womanhood." From the nineteenth century, Black women had been counted out of the mystique cultivated around the woman of breeding who was idealized as carrier and nurturer of civilization and its higher values. Sojourner Truth was challenging this assumption when she questioned, "Ain't I a woman?" And Harriet Jacobs apologized in her ex-slave narrative for the unseemly side of her tale, which involved sexual harassment, narrow escapes from rape, and so forth, that raised spectacles common to the experience of Black women but which refined women were not expected to read about or mention. Black people generally were outraged by the public perception that Black women's honor was not something deserving of respect, from Blacks nor Whites. Just as during the campaign against slavery there had been an anxiety to demonstrate that despite the mythology, Black people cared about their families, now there was eagerness to show that they were determined to protect their young women. This was a concern particularly troublesome to the egos of Black men, exacerbated by the extreme difficulty of protecting Black women against sexual assault and harassment in reality.

With this motif in the foreground, race movies can be read as allegorical, national melodramas. The story where a young Black woman in peril is rescued by a principled Black gentleman functioned almost as a master narrative. The one surviving clip from the early race movie melodrama, *By Right of Birth* (1921), shows a young lady on horseback when the horse bucks and runs wild, until a Negro gentleman who happens to be happening by comes gallantly to her rescue. These films take pains to frame the young Black woman as treasured object and in need of protection. That this protection usually arrives, and in time, vouches for the viability of Black society and the social optimism that race movies tried to cultivate. Through this allegory, the will to struggle and survive is re-articulated as insistently as in any corpus of cultural mythology, however derivative and convoluted.

Very few silent race movies escaped this theme. In *Ten Nights in a Barroom* (1926), the evils of drink are demonstrated when, in a saloon brawl, a thrown glass strikes the daughter of a sympathetic but pathetic alcoholic, and she is killed. The very fact that this warhorse temperance drama was adapted for Black audiences hints at the intent to upgrade Black representation by serving it up through the same vehicles that were used to address White audiences. The title of Micheaux's *Symbol of the Unconquered* (1920) might very well apply to the young African-American woman who moves into strange territory to claim an inheritance and is aided by an eligible Black man against those who would defraud her. Other race movies in which the endangerment of a young Black woman is central to the story are *Body and Soul*

Armand Girdlestone (Grant Gorman) is about to rape Sylvia Landry (Evelyn Preer)—until he discovers that she is his biological daughter.

(1925), *Eleven P.M.* (ca. 1929), *The Scar of Shame* (1929), *Ten Minutes to Live* (1932), *The Girl from Chicago* (1932), *The Girl in Room 20* (1943), *Within Our Gates* (1920), and *God's Step Children* (1938).

If we see the construction of this theme as a massive, rather dominant, note in race movies, then we also see how forceful was the effect of unequal development in producing a disproportionate focus on this narrative pattern. The films deserve the hard scrutiny they will get in feminist readings. The portrayal of young Black women shows the thumbprints of what Toni Cade Bambara calls the "protection racket," the further subjection of women under the guise of protecting them—one of the disabilities of the cult of true womanhood that also befalls Black women once they are written into that narrative. The movies were, however, very popular among Black women. However that may be, in drumming the theme of the woman in peril, race movies were treating Black women to the leftovers of the mystique of true womanhood.

If this thematic pattern is inadequate for the needs of women's liberation, it is even more bizarre as image displacement for a discourse on race. But rather than ride its curiosity as an excuse to vent our ideological superiority to an earlier historical epoch, we might address the challenge of reading these films through this complicated network of recoded and miscoded significations. In race movies, we see the collision and negotiation, often under heavy pressure, of several discourses, including the self-serving narrative of (unequal) social development, the muzzled resistance to racism, and the dated discourse of "true womanhood." I maintain that much of the pleasure we take in watching race movies comes from being opened up to these complex historical dialectics, even by way of their sometimes cardboard delivery, as well as their capacity to evoke in us admiration for the determined and radical resistance that went into the making of these films, however much that political energy might have been refracted on its way to the screen. These films have a way of speaking vehemently, even through the veil of their silence. The distortion and oblique resistance in race movies under Undie's influence may also suggest interpretive angles through which we can more articulately read many films outside the sphere of overdeveloped cinema.

2.

The Notion of Treatment: Black Aesthetics and Film

AN INTERVIEW WITH ARTHUR JAFA

Editor's Introduction

Arthur Jafa is a visual artist who has worked extensively in film and video. He was born in Tupelo, Mississippi, and raised in Clarksdale, Mississippi. Later, he attended Howard University, where he studied with Haile Gerima and Ben Caldwell, going on to work as the assistant cameraman on Charles Burnett's *My Brother's Wedding* (1983). His interests span a broad range of artistic practices, all of which center around his investigations of Black aesthetics, cultural specificity and universality, psychoanalytical theory, and image processing. As director of photography he worked on numerous projects, including Julie Dash's *Daughters of the Dust* (for which he received the cinematography award at the 1991 Sundance Film Festival), John Akomfrah's *Seven Songs for Malcolm X* (1993), Spike Lee's *Crooklyn* (1994), Ada Griffin's *Audre Lorde* (1995), Manthia Diawara's *Rouch in Reverse* (1995), and Louie Massiah's *W. E. B. Du Bois: A Biography in Four Voices* (1995).

In February of 1994, Swiss graduate student Peter Hessli interviewed AJ in New York as a part of his dissertation on Black American cinema. The following is drawn from that interview, supplemented with additional discussions with Arthur in 1995. During the course of these conversations, AJ expressed his ideas as an artist and filmmaker on Black Aesthetics, linking music, art, and history to the roots of the African and Black Diaspora experience. Black music in particular appears to be at the center of his developing theories—shaping and reshaping Black artistic expression and creativity. His theories are very much in tune with contemporary discourse around the "Africanization of Western cultures."

PEARL BOWSER

AJ: Afro-American creativity has this totally reactive dimension. It's often hard for outsiders to see the full complexity of what's happening. Much of the heaviest stuff is situated in the space of treatment rather than the space of material. So, if you're assessing it from a classically Western vantage, which is primarily about the material, whole dimensions of African-American cre-

Arthur Jafa, 1994. Photographer: Carlton Jones.

ativity are going to be rendered invisible. It'd be like trying to understand the creativity of an Ikebana master in the same terms you'd bring to a sculptor. The Ikebana master doesn't make the flowers, he arranges them. African-American creativity has been shaped by the specific circumstances Black people found themselves in; we weren't generally able to dictate the materials we were given to work with. When we were brought to the Americas as slaves we were generally seen as material ourselves. You don't really have the leeway to go out and select your own materials. So a lot of our creativity coalesced around the notion of treatment, that is, transforming in some meaningful fashion, given materials. Take for example John Coltrane's repeated performance of Rogers and Hammerstein's *My Favorite Things.* What's interesting to me is how Coltrane's improvisations never seek to entirely erase the original melodic material. In fact, one can better appreciate Coltrane's permutations if you've seen Julie Andrews singing on a mountaintop in the film *The Sound of Music,* for instance, or whatever. Coltrane keeps his transformations and the original sources equally evident. That's because it's not primarily about the point of departure or the point of arrival, but the spaces between these points.

If you want to talk about the conscious development of Afro-American aesthetics in film, you've got to go to UCLA in the mid '70s when Charles Burnett, Haile Gerima, Larry Clark, Julie Dash, Alile Sharon Larkin, Barbara McCulloch, and Ben Caldwell were all there in Los Angeles. This is the first time you have a group of filmmakers who were not just making films, but consciously discussing and thinking about what a Black cinema was, what it might be, and how it could be implemented. This was a critical juncture. And it worked for a number of reasons, the foremost of which were financial support, access to equipment and a shared agenda. As soon as the filmmakers began to graduate and step outside of the academic context, they scattered, and because there was no alternate infrastructure, technical or economic, their level of productivity largely evaporated.

PH: What about the early Black film movement? Some people believe the independent film movement today operates in the same way as the African-American film movement in the early part of this century. Would you agree that the Black film movement of the 1910s and 1920s was the first independent film movement in American cinema history?

AJ: Perhaps, but a more important question is how to develop a Black film culture that is as sophisticated as the culture of Black music. I've come to realize that whatever we embrace, whatever we decide is aesthetically significant, becomes part of the tradition. Even when we build on the seemingly arbitrary, the arbitrary repeated becomes intentional, the intentional acquires meaning, and this meaning empowers the tradition. What's interesting to me about Oscar Micheaux and Eloyce Gist, Richard Maurice and Spencer Williams,[1] is that they all created cinema with a Black audience in mind, at a point when the Hollywood codes weren't hegemonic. There was a lot more space. At the point I decided I wanted to make film, I had already seen thousands of hours of films made the "right" way. "Right" according to the dominant paradigm, which didn't develop in response to, or have anything to do with, the ex-

Charles Burnett behind the camera and Arthur Jafa (assistant cameraman) filming a blues guitarist and singer for *Mississippi Triangle* (Third World Newsreel, 1984). Photographer: Pearl Bowser.

pressive desires of Black folks. So it is not possible for me to operate from a position of innocence. There is no edenic space from which my culture can operate, from which it could dictate aesthetically coherent approaches. That's why Micheaux is interesting to me, because his work is completely inscribed with what one could argue are "Africanisms." Imagine for a moment—just hypothetically—what Black people would do if our culture—the music, dance, and, most of all, our feelings—were allowed to determine the kinds of cinema we created. What would this sort of Black cinema look like? So Micheaux and others—Black filmmakers of this period—become incredibly valuable, because they offer evidence of what sort of directions our cinema might have taken in a less culturally antagonistic environment.

PH: Some have said of Micheaux's sound pictures that the music and dance sequences were tacked on for entertainment.

AJ: I hate when people make these kinds of simplistic statements about Micheaux's work—"It's just put in to entertain." People say ignorant stuff like this about Black expression all the time. That's like saying about Nkonde Nkisi, "All those nails driven into the figure, that's just to make it look scary." As if it's just arbitrary, as if the Nkonde Nkisi [West African judicial figures—Ed.] are just fetishes and not profound judicial symbols, as if each nail didn't represent a specific arbitrated and resolved conflict. And yeah, it is meant to be scary. The way Micheaux uses those music and dance sequences is both entertaining and formally radical. They're totally jagged and they completely disrupt the narrative flow. It's certainly pretty different from anything I've found in Hollywood films of the same period.

PH: I think as far as music goes he is such a pioneer and so original.

AJ: Micheaux's *Ten Minutes To Live* (1932) is one of my two or three all-time favorites. And the thing is, when you try to talk about certain aspects of film, it's fairly impossible to do so

Cabaret scene from an Oscar Micheaux film, possibly *Ten Minutes to Live* (1932).

with any kind of precision. It's like what Harold Bloom said about painting: "There's really no advanced, cognitive vocabulary to talk about visuals." And if you look at the history of criticism of painting, it's really literary criticism. Literary critics were the first to try to talk about images and they used the language they had, which was the language of literary criticism. Toward the end of his life, Clement Greenberg said, "I challenge anyone to tell me why a painting works. You can talk about what you like [about a painting], but when a painting works it just does. Beyond a certain point, you can't really describe it because images are resistant to being contained by language." By the same token, when people say they like a film, they really mean they like the narrative. But obviously there are other things as well that make up films, that determine whether they're received with pleasure or displeasure. Some of the most interesting aspects of Micheaux's films are their refusals, what they don't do—refusal as act; how they resist certain Hollywood tropes and ways of organizing things. One of the things I've often talked about is the critical importance of the work done by film theorists and historians Kristin Thompson, David Bordwell, and Noel Burch on Japanese film director Yosujiro Ozu. They profoundly affected my understanding of Micheaux. Donald Ritchie, the first western authority on Ozu, spent his entire career arguing for Ozu's mastery and formal precision, but when confronted with the "bad" spatial continuity of Ozu's later work he basically explained it by saying Ozu had gotten sloppy. That's ridiculous. The work of Thompson and Bordwell completely refuted this. They showed definitively how Ozu's spatial continuity isn't a deficient version of "Hollywood's spatial continuity but a wholly alternative system that has its own set of rules. The same can be said about Micheaux's work. There's no doubt about it. I've drawn diagrams of his camera placements and stuff—I mean his shit is not bad Hollywood, it's his own thing.

PH: I agree. I've been digitizing some of Micheaux's film on the Macintosh. I was pulling up sequences how he would edit them and it's just amazing how he would make contrasts with "colors" in his black and white films. Even the lighting is very special.

AJ: Yeah, definitely. When I look at *Ten Minutes To Live,* what really hits me is that the shape of the thing is so amazing. That film—I understand it in terms of volumes that contract and expand, but I can't get too much more precise than this. It's largely felt. It's how he juxtaposes short sequences with long drawn-out sequences, then short, then long, then it'll have a complex sequence dissolving people back and forth across a room while the camera's completely static. Then there'll be a hard cut which completely demolishes the 180-degree axis. And it's all got this rhythm and timing that's completely like Thelonius Monk. Is it accidental? Perhaps. Is it aesthetically arbitrary? I'm sorry, I don't think so. J. Hoberman points out, in a classic piece on Micheaux and Ed Woods, that if Micheaux was, as some have claimed, the baddest filmmaker of all time, then what's remarkable is that over a thirty-year career he got badder and badder.[2] This in itself refutes the logic that what Micheaux did was arbitrary.

Even the films of the worst hack will stabilize on a certain level if they continue to work. It's like Cecil Taylor said—"If you do anything long enough, order will impose itself." Even if you're just screaming as loud as you can. Do it forty times, it'll all start sounding pretty much the same; you are only going to get so much variance. If, that is, there's no artistic intelligence at work. But Micheaux's work got badder. I always insist that there is nothing arbitrary about Micheaux's work, that it displays the most lucid kind of coherency. I think he was actually in the process of developing something equal to the aesthetic coherency of jazz. His development was, of course, limited by economic constraints, amongst other things, but one can identify a fairly clear line. Micheaux was making work not just for Black people but work that was open to being shaped by the audience, meaning that he was modifying it as he was going along in response to and acting on their responses to his films.

There've been two major instances in which Black aesthetics redirects Western art practice in the past century. The first is the advent of African "Art" in Europe. Europeans are confronted with an artifact which is essentially alien. There is no real understanding of the cultural context that generated it, how the forms were arrived at and what they might mean to their makers.

Then you get a second major impact of Black aesthetics on Western art in this century; that is, the arrival of jazz. In the first instance—the arrival of African sculpture in Europe— you get artifacts without their creators. But with the arrival of jazz, the impact isn't solely the result of the music made, the artifact, but it also results from the way its creators dressed, the way they spoke and behaved, their individual styles and philosophies, and their articulations of the aesthetic priorities and processes in their work. So you get Jackson Pollack and De Kooning. There would be no Jackson Pollack and no De Kooning without jazz, the artifact, and without jazz, the aesthetic modality. I'd even argue that if large numbers of African peoples had been transported to Europe along with the African artifacts, we probably would have seen something very much like abstract expressionism in Europe.

On the second point of this, this impact. . . . If you look at modernism in terms of cinema, I would say you've got to start with Godard, in a lot of ways, because *Breathless* (1960) is the film that, in a sense, you say is modern.

PH: Maybe we've got to start with Micheaux.

AJ: Well, I think one could, but what I'm trying to get at is a little different. I mean no one is characterizing Olowe, the Yoruba master sculptor, as avant-garde, particularly in relationship to Picasso. Similarly, with Godard, many of the formal qualities that designate *Breathless* as modernist cinema can be found in excess in Micheaux's work thirty years earlier! I'm not trying to suggest that Micheaux has any direct influence on Godard. What I am saying is that in a sense, both Micheaux and Godard were equally impacted by the same aesthetic community, that is, Black aesthetics and in Godard's specific instance its substrand—Modernism. In effect Micheaux preempts Godard. The primary direct influence on Godard's *Breathless* is Jean Rouch's *Moi, Un Noir* (1958). One could even argue, as Manthia Diawara has suggested, that *Breathless* is essentially a remake of *Moi, Un Noir*. What's interesting to me is how, yet again, there is this suppressed Blackness around the concept of certain modernisms. Rouch, by his very relationship to Africa, is a line of contact between Black aesthetics and Godard.

With specific respect to *Moi, Un Noir,* and I've suggested this to Jean Rouch, the very nature of the film suggests a very different sort of relationship between the artist and his subject. One in which the artist isn't the sole, and perhaps not even the primary, author of the created artifact but is in fact a co-author with the activating subject matter. For example, I'm

Spike Lee with Tracy Camila Johns (Lola Darling) in *She's Gotta Have It* (1986).

the photographer and I take a picture of you; the art is mine—I created and dictated what it is. But what would it mean to invert this notion, the physics of this notion, that perhaps the person who is being photographed exerts as much authorship on the artifact as the photographer? The photographer's story is classically the trajectory of agency and is typically read from the gaze outward, from power downward. History is something I make which happens to you. So from this sort of vantage point, it is extremely difficult to perceive the full impact Black aesthetics has had. Say, for example, it would be difficult, from this vantage, to understand the saxophone as an African-American invention despite the fact that it was created by an Austrian, or that basketball is an African-American sport created by a white man. I believe you see something similar in the instance of *Moi, Un Noir*. I think it was largely dictated, invented, by the Africans who were photographed. The very way they penetrated space forced him to shoot them in a certain fashion. At the very least, they co-authored the film with Rouch. See, most cinema histories give the director all the credit.

AJ: I remember going to the Library of Congress in 1982 or '83 to research Micheaux's work. I got a whole lot of articles, many of which Micheaux had written himself, most of which I'd never seen in print. They were right there, in the library, for anyone who cared to look. I'm not a scholar, and I found them. Understand what I'm saying? Micheaux spells out his whole aesthetic, so I don't understand why people can't give him the benefit of the doubt. He says "Look, my films haven't always been everything I've wanted them to be, because I have to work inside of certain limitations but I've always sought to"—and he goes on to articulate, in very lucid, very eloquent terms, pretty much the kinds of things I'm saying are going on in his work.[3] Now, if we could interview Micheaux and ask him about some of the structural and formal logic of his work, would he have been able to respond in those terms? Probably not. But that's not really the point. Louis Armstrong wouldn't have been able to either. I mean, when they asked Armstrong what he thought of bebop, which was really just an extension of

16 | AN INTERVIEW WITH ARTHUR JAFA

J. T. Tagagi, Louis Massiah, and Arthur Jafa on the set of the W. E. B. Du Bois film project. Photographer: David Lee.

what he had started to do—a more pronounced conclusion, he said that it was "Chinese music." Now it's up to us to interpret what he meant. On a certain level it's clearly intended as an insult. But what he was really speaking to when he said "Chinese" is its seeming Orientalism, its "alienness." Now Armstrong's music was the apotheosis of one of the most radical artistic breakthroughs of the century, so in essence he's saying, "Look, I'm out, and this shit is too way out for me, so as far as I'm concerned, it's some Oriental, some non-Western shit." But his work epitomizes this kind of alienness, so I don't think people have to necessarily articulate their work in the same terms in which we discuss it.

I read this article about Igor Stravinsky's anxiety over his status in the Western tradition of classical music. He's basically, as someone said, "the most Russian composer there will ever be." Essentially, he took traditions of Russian folk music and fused them with the whole history of Western classical music. The problem is that the Russian classical tradition was this really marginal thing, out in left field. Russians weren't even considered Europeans for a long time. Russians were thought of as a people who existed somewhere between Europe and Asia. They were just this group of folks who had a fairly indeterminate relationship to whiteness. Now Stravinsky had a profound anxiety about this, because he felt like his status as a Russian, as a non-white, as a non-European was going to prevent him from getting his due consideration as the most significant classical composer of the century. So Stravinsky spent the next thirty years of his life lying about his background and his history, what he did and didn't study. The article quotes this book, *Europe and Humanity,* in which the author, Prince Nikolai Trubetskoy, claims that "the enlightened cosmopolitanism of the West is really a form of chauvinism." He calls it "pangermanoromanic chauvinism" and says that Russians infected by it can't help turning hostile toward Russia. This is all about the psychological dimensions of anxiety about inclusion in, or not being included in, the European tradition and how even someone as bad as Stravinsky could be infected. So Stravinsky spends the latter part of his career attempting to disassociate himself from the sources of his greatest work, *The Rites of*

Spring—which is some sho 'nuff primitive shit, primarily because it signals him as essentially a non-Western, and certainly non-European, composer. People rioted when it was first performed, because it was like jungle music. When the Ballet Russe hit Paris, that was like, for all practical purposes, an "African troupe in Paris."

Between Diaghalev, Nijinsky, Stravinsky, and the rest, they were dropping some heavy Russian shit—it was definitely alien contact time. It's fascinating to me the complexity of people's responses to even their own work and what it signifies about who they are. It's deep that he would turn his back on the most powerful work of his career because he wanted to be included. If you look at someone like Spike Lee, for example, and I don't think he's consciously doing this, but you see a very similar type of dynamic. I still find *She's Gotta Have It* (1986) Spike's most interesting film. When I first saw it, I said "Wow, this is a really interesting film. But the challenge is gonna be whether or not all those aspects of the film that may get read as accidents, or amateurishness, are gonna be developed or fixed." Looking back now, clearly he decided to fix them. It's like a person who had a top twenty hit, and what was interesting about their sound was the accent; but the more successful they got, the more they could take vocal lessons, and they started to sound more or less like everybody else. The voice still has some quirky interest, but in terms of the flow—the tone and the tenor of the work, that certain original distinctiveness is lost. Basically you see a person that is interesting as an artist in spite of themselves. But they were more interesting when they were left alone. When they have resources and are worried about whether Hollywood is going to give them an Academy Award, the work becomes less and less interesting, precisely around this anxiety over recognition. I want my films to get worse and worse the farther I go on. The work should be less and less like film, and more and more like things. It's like having somebody draw you a picture; they turn it around and it is what it is. It's not a representation. And it cannot be reduced to language. I want it to be like that. I want it to have something that I and my friends call "the alien familiar." If a work succeeds in a way or is able to conjure what a Black cinema would be or what this hypothetical manifestation of this particular tradition in the cinematic arena might be, it should be both alien because you've never seen anything quite like it, and at the same time, it should be familiar on some level to Black audiences. It's like a person, let's say, who grew up in a Black family but never heard Black music. So you've gotten everything your parents give you, on the level of how they hold you, how they rock you, all the culture they bring, but you've never heard any music. You've just heard Beethoven all your life, right? But you grew up in a Black family. Or say you grew up in a Chinese family and you never heard any Chinese music, but your parents related to you, they speak to you in Chinese, do all the things they do, but you've never heard Chinese music, you just heard Beethoven. I insist that the first time you hear Chinese music it's going to move you in a really significant kind of way. Not that you're going to like it, but it's going to move you because it is going to be the musical manifestation of all the other culturally specific modes of interaction that you're familiar with. Yet it's going to be alien, because you would have never heard it before. So it's the same thing with Black films, I think. When they're successful, they will be both alien and familiar. And the whole idea is that they should become both more alien the farther they develop and also more familiar because people will begin to see the relationship between the films and the more familiar modes of Black cultural expression.

3.

From Shadows 'n Shufflin' to Spotlights and Cinema: The Lafayette Players, 1915–1932

SISTER FRANCESCA THOMPSON

Often we hear or read that the first time African Americans had an opportunity to act in legitimate drama was when the WPA Federal Theatre Project gave them that opportunity in the 1930s. Not so! In attempting to help set the record straight, I would like to introduce you to the Lafayette Players. This distinctive group of black actors performed in legitimate dramas from 1915 to 1932 and was one of the first major professional black stock companies in this country. Making a very significant and noteworthy stride forward, this ambitious group of artists achieved success in their attempt to step, at long last, outside and above the existing roles forced upon them by white writers, producers, managers and by both white and black audiences in the early formative years of American theater. Many of these same actors went on to star in numerous silent race films made after World War I—recognized personalities and trained talent essential for the flourishing if commercially marginal production of black-cast films of the 1920s.

CREATING A NEW KIND OF BLACK THEATER

In the early days of theatrical endeavor, a destructive pattern was firmly established upon the American stage. A black performer was considered merely a source of ridicule and sport. It was a "fool's place" filled by white performers who, donning black cork, set about creating a black caricature based on a reality that had rarely, if ever, existed. This minstrel-show mentality pervaded the theatrical world and reigned supreme during the nineteenth and early twentieth centuries, doing irreparable damage to the black entertainer's image.

Not until the late 1800s and early 1900s did blacks begin to create their own images and roles that would allow them to cast aside the accepted tradition of the past. It was an exciting time of great change in many areas, and hope for a place as first-class citizens in the main-

One company of the Lafayette Players, 1924. From left to right: Andrew Bishop, Edward Thompson, unidentified actress, Charles Moore, two unidentified actors, A. B. DeComathiere, Evelyn Preer, and Susie Sutton. During their stay in Nashville, Thompson and Preer were married.

stream of American life grew stronger among black performers. A new breed appeared upon the scene, and among them was a young entertainer from New York, Anita Bush, who would later work with the Norman Film Company, as Phyllis Klotman discusses in her essay in this collection. Bush, the daughter of a tailor who worked for theatrical folk, had long been associated with the theater and had harbored an unspoken dream of producing and starring in legitimate dramatic productions. Strange and far-fetched as this dream seemed in 1915, Anita Bush was able to eventually see her dream emerge as a reality. On November 15, 1915, the Anita Bush Stock Company opened in a legitimate drama at the Lincoln Theatre in Harlem. This premiere marked an ambitious beginning. The new group with its new idea gave new hope to aspiring black actors of the period.

The young company did much more than merely provide entertainment for its black audiences. It also afforded an education for its participants. The generous applause that nightly greeted the company's efforts was proof beyond doubt that its eager public, unaccustomed as they were to this particular fare, was very appreciative of what was being offered to them. Their audiences not only found the entertainment more palatable than what had been offered in the past, they found it savory and nourishing. To those who warned Miss Bush that "the time was not right" or "the hour has not yet come," the daring neophytes defiantly cried with each successful performance, "Now *is* the time and the hour could not be more right. We have talents yet unexplored and now is the time for us to begin to prove this fact to all and any who would doubt us or our abilities."

We may say at this point—in retrospect, of course—that they were far from being accomplished, sophisticated, or polished in today's sense of these words. They were still groping in the dark in so many ways. But, while limited in many respects, they did bring to the existing material the tools they had—their own native talent combined with an innate tendency to mimic. Their own lives, so often filled with tragedy and pathos, were the training schools for these black artists who attempted what had not been attempted before. The very fact that the company was succeeding in its venture engendered a love of race and pride in accomplishment. That, in itself, was no small feat. Certainly, the understanding of and appreciation for this "new form of entertainment" did not develop overnight among all its audiences. Inclined by past experience to be satisfied with what was incorrectly and falsely considered "the Negro's limitations," both audiences and performers would need time to become reeducated. Thanks to Anita Bush and her brave company, "school time" had begun.

The New York–based group, which soon moved from Harlem's Lincoln Theatre to its nearby rival, the Lafayette, grew quickly from its original five members and, after their move to the Lafayette, they were forever known as the Lafayette Players. The original group consisted of Anita Bush, Charles S. Gilpin, Arthur "Dooley" Wilson, Carlotta Freeman, and Andrew Bishop. All of these actors went on to have significant theater careers, and all but Freeman played noteworthy roles in the cinema. Prior to the advent of the Lafayette Players, there had been no black actors performing in significant roles on Broadway. Gilpin was the first black actor to break this barrier and receive serious attention from Broadway critics and audiences when he was cast to play the title role in Eugene O'Neill's drama, *The Emperor Jones* (1920). He went on to star in *Ten Nights in a Barroom* (Colored Players Film Corporation, 1926). Andrew Bishop went on to star in a number of Micheaux films, including *A Son of Satan* (1924) and *The House Behind the Cedars* (1924/1925). Arthur "Dooley" Wilson thrived as a film actor in the late 1930s and early 1940s, most famously as Sam in *Casablanca* (1942).

From their beginnings in Harlem, the Players soon branched out and, by invitation, moved into other areas of the country. In 1922, Anita Bush was called to Chicago to help form a second company, and by 1924, there were four separate groups of Lafayette Players. One of these companies traveled across the country and was often responsible for introducing legitimate theater to black audiences in states such as Kansas, Louisiana, Arkansas, Georgia, Virginia, Alabama, Tennessee, Oklahoma, and California. In more than twenty-five cities, black audiences were given the opportunity to view black entertainers performing in a medium that differed greatly from the usual comedy or minstrel fare with which they had grown familiar. This was especially true in southern cities, where blacks were seldom permitted to attend theaters. Among the larger cities where the Players performed by "invitation" were Washington, D.C., New Orleans, Indianapolis, Memphis, and Kansas City. By the time the company disbanded in 1932, there were over 300 performers who could claim to have been a part of the Players at one time or another during its seventeen years of existence.

I believe—though I admit to some bias—that the Players had a great influence upon the history of black American theater. Even under the handicaps of exploitation and mismanagement—the prevailing style of the theater at the time—the existing sociological problems, and the lack of financial support, they persevered in their artistic determination to successfully perform in legitimate drama. Thus, they helped raise the standards of black entertainment. Questioned many years later about the ambitions of the neophyte group, Clarence Muse, one of the early members of the Lafayette Players, said that their aim had been to give vent to their

Lawrence Chenault and Charles Gilpin in *Ten Nights in a Barroom* (Colored Players Film Corporation, 1926).

talent and to prove to everyone willing to watch or to listen that they were as good at performing serious drama as anyone else had been or could be. Muse claimed that "the door opened a tiny bit to the black actor and, as always when faced with an open door, no matter how small the wedge, the black performer eased on in."[1]

Muse first joined the Players in 1916 and worked off and on with them until 1931. Muse's first starring film role was in the comedy *The Custard Nine* (1921), a stereotype-filled picture that was badly received in the black press. After this painful experience on a white-produced film, he stuck to the stage and avoided filmmaking for the remainder of the silent era. With the coming of sound, Muse again appeared in motion pictures, beginning with *Hearts in Dixie* (1929) for Fox.[2] In later years, Muse was to boast of having performed in over 200 motion pictures. He also had a prominent role in a popular TV series, *Daktari.* Showing that he was well aware of the chances the Players were taking by stepping outside of the accepted mold, Muse wrote an insightful and telling account of his position titled *The Dilemma of the Black Actor,* which he published himself in 1924. This short work states the problem very clearly and highlights the question that faced so many black entertainers during this period: "Does a black actor do what pleases him or does he play 'the coon' and please his audience?" This question persists and plagues many black performers even today.

In my research about the Lafayette Players, which turned into a detective job, I heard many wonderful and truly humorous accounts about the initiation of audiences to the legitimate work of the Players. Many involved my mother, Evelyn Preer, who was a star in Micheaux films before she joined the Players in 1920, and my dear father, Edward Thompson, who had joined the group somewhat earlier. My father's favorite story concerned a performance that he and my mother gave in Mississippi. Because the law of Jim Crow prevailed during that time, the Players were not permitted to stay in hotels in the South. Although they usually lodged in a black-operated YWCA or YMCA, the actors sometimes stayed in the homes of leading black dignitaries. Often this meant that my parents, the stars of the company, were graciously housed and fed at the home of the leading black minister. This happened to be the case when they were performing and starring in the company's production of *Branded.* A typical "heavy melodrama," *Branded* told the woeful tale of a wealthy cattle rancher and his beautiful but unfaithful wife. At the end of the play, the rancher, catching his erring wife in a compromising circumstance, determines to teach her a lesson not to be forgotten and to ensure that she will never cheat on him again. He decides to brand her on the forehead just as if she were one of his cattle. Pulling my mother roughly by her hair with one hand and forcing the sizzling brand onto her forehead with the other, my father's character then twisted his fallen wife to face the audience. As the curtain slowly descended, he declared venomously, "Now, you are mine and everyone will know. . . . You are mine! MINE!" Curtain!

My parents had earlier enjoyed a lovely dinner with the pastor and his wife and had given them complimentary tickets for the opening night performance, urging them to attend the theater and to stop by their dressing rooms backstage after the show. Their hosts did not appear, however, and my parents assumed that they had not attended the performance or for one reason or another had not had time to visit backstage. Because they had been given a key to the house, they attended a party before returning to the rectory. There, to their great surprise and consternation, they found their bags packed and waiting for them on the front porch of the parsonage. Bewildered and not certain just what to do at one o'clock in the morning, my father timidly knocked at the door, hoping for an explanation.

Clarence Muse as Nappus in *Hearts in Dixie* (Fox Film Corp., 1929). The role of Nappus was originally assigned to Charles Gilpin.

The irate minister opened the door only a crack but wide enough for him to hiss contemptuously at my puzzled and very weary parents, "How dare you impose yourselves upon my wife and me? We are God-fearing Christians and we truly love the Lord. We thought that you, too, were decent folk, and your poor wife appeared so sweet. You have deceived us greatly, sir, and you are no longer welcome here. Do you think that I would allow you to spend time under our roof after what we saw you both engage in upon that stage tonight? We have heard of degraded persons like yourselves, and we will pray for you, but you cannot stay in this house." With that stern reproach, the door closed firmly. Education often takes a long time. I don't know if my poor roofless parents were ever able to explain that they were only pretending to be so "vile," but let us say they got an A+ that particular evening for being believable.

So unaccustomed were some of these novice audiences to serious dramatic entertainment that an audience member told me that on at least one occasion, before a performance in an Atlanta theater, the white manager of the theater stood before the curtain to instruct the black audience about what to expect and how to behave during the performance. Of course, he did it as "delicately" as possible, paying what I am sure he considered a tremendous compliment to the Lafayette Players. In serious tones, he announced: "Now, we got some high-class niggers performing here for you tonight and I want you all to act right, behave yourselves and appreciate what you're going to see. It's a real treat because these niggers are first-rate!"[3] It is not only the smokers of a popular cigarette who can proudly declare, "We've come a long way, Baby!"

Edward Thompson and Evelyn Preer. Partners on and off stage. The inscription on his portrait reads "With Best Wishes to Taunia in Memory of a Pleasant Engagement. Edward Thompson 8/4/28."

Thus, the Players became in a special way educators as well as entertainers. They were certainly instrumental in guiding their audiences to accept a more sophisticated and intellectually superior form of entertainment. Especially advantageous was the fact that the black performers were patient with the occasional disruptions caused by those who came to see them. Because of their lack of previous exposure to drama, black theatergoers were not always prepared to enjoy or to appreciate properly what was being presented to them for the first time. Clarence Muse, with obvious glee, told a story of one of his performances when he was using a white makeup that he himself had created. In order to demonstrate his versatility during the early years of his association with the Players, Muse had had a German wig maker design a blond wig for him, and he invented a white makeup that he used successfully to disguise himself while portraying different characters. According to Muse, no other member of the group ever did this. He felt that if whites could use cork to create black characters, then he surely could use white makeup to create white ones.

The story Muse told was of a performance when his first line was to be said offstage. Because of his very distinctive, gravely voice, the audience knew he would enter following the line. What a surprise, then, to see this "white" actor stride across the stage. Muse walked swiftly to the side of the leading lady, who was costumed in flowing black chiffon. After clasping her ardently to his breast, Muse was supposed to utter his first onstage line, but because of the clapping, stomping, and whistles of approval which filled the theater, he was forced to wait two or three full minutes for the uproar to subside. The audience finally quieted down, but before Muse could say his next line, an appreciative fan from the balcony screamed forth his approval of Muse's changed appearance: "By God, look at that! Clarence, he don't even rub off on black!"[4] Needless to say, the loudest applause of the evening went to the spectator in the balcony rather than to the actors *on* stage. Nevertheless, over time, many skeptical cynics were taught by the Lafayette Players that legitimate drama was good entertainment and could be appreciated and enjoyed by black audiences.

Appearing in more than 250 different plays, the Lafayette Players performed in productions never before or since presented by an entirely black company of actors. Some of their more popular presentations included plays that were also being done by white actors on Broadway. Such period classics as *Anna Christie* by Eugene O'Neill, *Camille* by Alexandre Dumas, *The City* by Clyde Fitch, *The Count of Monte Cristo* by Dumas, *Dr. Jekyll and Mr. Hyde* adapted for the stage by T. R. Sullivan, *East Lynne* by Mrs. Henry Wood, *The Eternal Magdalen* by Robert McLaughlin, *Madame X* by Alexander Brisson, *On Trial* by Elmer Rice, and *Salomé* by the then-popular Oscar Wilde were all a part of the Players' large repertoire and just a few of their long list of popular and audience-pleasing attractions.

Through each of these productions the Players were instrumental in educating both whites and blacks to an awareness that black performers did possess dramatic talent and were capable of performing in serious dramatic productions that did not include singing or dancing. By acquainting black audiences with legitimate theater and by providing white audiences, directors, and producers with proof that black actors were capable of successfully performing serious drama, the Lafayette Players helped pave the way for other black dramatists, who were heartened and encouraged by their success. A few of the most important of these groups were The Negro Art Theatre, The Rose McClendon Players, the Alhambra Theatre, The Gilpin Players, and even the WPA Federal Negro Theatre Project. Each of these groups included members who had begun their careers in theater with the Lafayette Players.

The Players also served as incentive to black businessmen who began to venture into theater management and even theater ownership at this time. Prime examples are E. C. Brown, Andrew F. Stevens (who eventually purchased and owned the Lafayette Players for a short period), and Lester A. Walton, the outspoken critic of drama and film for the *New York Age.* Walton also worked as theater manager of the Lafayette Theatre for many years. Through his columns in *The Age,* he spoke out again and again on behalf of struggling black entertainers in their continuing fight for fair treatment from directors, theater managers, and owners.

Several of the Lafayette Players were to become well known in theatrical circles in later years. A few were to leave lasting marks upon their profession. In every instance where former members of the group "made good" or were recognized elsewhere, they gave credit to the Lafayette Players for having afforded them entrance into the main theatrical scene, for having given them the opportunity to perfect their craft, and also for having provided the space and place in which they could "grow and mature" as performing artists. In a 1936 article appearing in *The Afro-American,* a popular black newspaper, the Lafayette Players were lavishly praised for having given numerous black celebrities a chance to "pioneer." Over fifty names of prominent black entertainers were listed as having won much of their success and subsequent fame through their association and training with the Lafayette Players. Though the list is far from complete, there are enough names listed to substantiate the claim that the Lafayette Players served, until their closing, as a "training school" for an impressive number of accomplished black performers.[5]

Many of the early members of the Lafayette Players responded to the offers of movie producers such as Oscar Micheaux, Richard Norman, and David Starkman. Among them was Lawrence Chenault, one of Anita Bush's first leading men. In a 1969 interview, Bush said that Chenault was considered a "real heart throb" by many of his Harlem female fans.[6] In spite of his extraordinary good looks and capabilities, he and Anita were to part company with hard feelings between them in 1919. Bush felt that he often took advantage of her because she was a woman and that his "male vanity" made him believe he did not have to follow her orders since his popularity with audiences had secured him a stable and secure place as "the romantic leading man" of the time. He was mistaken, and he misjudged Bush's determination as a producer of quality theater. After he had too frequently exhibited unprofessional and unpredictable behavior with regard to his obligations to the Bush Company, she informed him that he was being terminated as a member of her troupe. Although Bush said Chenault scoffed at her "threat" and bragged that she would come "begging" for his return, as she had in the past, Bush proudly reported that she "stuck to her guns" and after firing him on Friday night, had a "more than suitable replacement" for him by the following Monday.[7] (The young, inexperienced replacement was Edward Thompson, who became a well-known "romantic lead" with the Players; in 1924, he married Evelyn Preer, becoming the leading romantic interest in their private life as well as in their professional pairing on stage.) This "split" between Bush and Chenault must have been mended at some later date because the two were to make several films together, notably the Norman Film Company's Western *The Crimson Skull* (1921). They seemed to have made a striking and attractive romantic couple on screen.

The first Chenault to appear in the movies was Jack Chenault, who played a villain in Oscar Micheaux's *Within Our Gates* (shot in 1919, released early in 1920). Lawrence Chenault followed, playing featured and starring roles in numerous Micheaux films, beginning with *The Brute* (1920), which introduced a real-life black boxer, Sam Langford, and proved very popular to its excited audiences. Lester A. Walton did not give the film his complete approval, but despite his criticism of Micheaux's use of "dives and crapshooters," he did offer an endorsement, and it was apparent to Micheaux's fans that at last the filmmaker had arrived.[8] Chenault was subsequently featured in Micheaux's *The Symbol of the Unconquered* (1920), *The Gunsaulus Mystery* (1921), *Son of Satan* (1924), and *Birthright* (1924).[9] Micheaux also cast Chenault in *The House Behind the Cedars* (1924/1925), adapted from the novel by Charles W. Chesnutt and filmed on location in Roanoke, Virginia. Although Micheaux made extensive use of local talent, familiar professional faces were also included in this film, such as Shingzie Howard and Douglass Griffin.[10] This particular film was to break all attendance records at the Roosevelt Theatre in New York City.[11]

Chenault did not lack for work during the 1920s. We find his name in cast lists for films almost every year during that decade. He worked for Robert Levy's Reol Productions, appearing in *The Burden of Race* (1921), *The Sport of the Gods* (1921), *The Call of His People* (1921), and *Spitfire* (1922). He also appeared in four films produced by the Colored Players Film Corporation, including *A Prince of His Race* (1926), *Ten Nights in a Barroom* (1926), and *The Scar of Shame* (1929).[12]

Chenault evidently got his start in theater working in the famous Pekin Theatre in Chicago, where many of the black performers of his era began their careers. He was one of those pioneer performers who dared to step outside the minstrel roles and coon caricatures which had been accorded even the most talented of our black theatrical professionals. As sound-era filmmaker George Randol noted, Chenault joined that growing band of black performers who were tired of playing small, distasteful parts in films produced by the major

The Norman Film Mfg. Co. Presents the

CRIMSON SKULL

Baffling Western Mystery Photo-Play

CO-STARRING

ANITA BUSH AND LAWRENCE CHENAULT

Supported by **BILL PICKETT**, World's Champion Wild West Performer, the one-legged Marvel, **STEVE REYNOLDS** and 30 Colored Cowboys.
Produced in the All-Colored City of Boley, Okla.
AN EPIC OF WILD LIFE AND SMOKING REVOLVERS

ALL-COLORED CAST   SIX SMASHING REELS

(Sample Window Card—Space for Dates at Top Not Shown)

After Anita Bush and Lawrence Chenault parted ways on the stage, they continued to appear together in films for the Norman Film Manufacturing Company, including *The Crimson Skull* (1921).

(white) film companies and thus began to insist vehemently upon better scripts and roles and in so doing dared to defy the convention of the time.[13] These brave front-runners joined those who decided to write and produce their own work. Micheaux must certainly be given credit and praise for allowing and aiding the talented Chenaults of the time to practice their craft more honestly and to do so with dignity and success.

Evelyn Preer was another of the Players who answered the call of film and who worked repeatedly with Micheaux. Evelyn Preer (née Jarvis) was born on July 26, 1896, in Vicksburg, Mississippi, to Blanche and Frank Jarvis. Following her father's death, she was taken by her mother to Chicago while still quite young. There she received her formal though minimal education. After graduating from high school, she was, after much cajoling, finally permitted by her devoutly religious mother to respond to the call of the theater. She accepted what her Pentecostal mother considered to be the most respectable of the multiple theatrical job offers, traveling briefly with a group of musicians and dancers, but she finally signed a contract with Oscar Micheaux. It was the beginning of a long and successful association for both parties, for Preer was to become one of Micheaux's brightest and most favored stars.

In 1918, she worked on *The Homesteader,* the first of Micheaux's many popular films.[14] The film was based on a novel by Micheaux of the same title, which is examined in depth in Jayna Brown's essay in this volume on the director's literary career. Establishing herself as an actress of worth while starring in Oscar Micheaux's *Within Our Gates* (1920), *The Brute* (1920), and *The Gunsaulus Mystery* (1921), Preer joined the Lafayette Players in 1920 while they were performing at the Lincoln Theatre in Chicago. It was there that she met and acted with the man whom she was later to marry, Edward Thompson, the son of the black composer and musician De Koven Thompson. After the Players split into separate companies, all bearing the name of Lafayette Players, Preer and Thompson became the leading stars of the traveling group. During a Lafayette Players tour of the south in 1924, one day prior to a matinee in Nashville, Tennessee, Preer and her leading man slipped away to a small town near Nashville and were quietly married.

As Preer steadily rose in the company's ranks to become one of their most popular leading ladies, she continued to appear in subsequent Micheaux films, including *Deceit* (1923), *Birthright* (1924), *The Devil's Disciple* (1925), *The Conjure Woman* (1926), and *The Spider's Web* (1926). She remained with the Players until her untimely death in 1932, which partly accounted for the demise of the group. Starring with the Lafayette Players, she appeared in countless dramas never before or since produced and acted by entirely black companies. Some of the dramas in which she won critical acclaim, from both white and black critics, include the following: *Salomé* (1923) in which she was advertised as "the most beautiful colored woman in the world,"[15] *Over the Hill to the Poorhouse* (1922–1923), *The Follies of Scapin* (1923), *The Comedy of Errors* (1923), *The Taming of the Shrew* (1923), *Paid in Full* (1926), *Rain* (1927), *Within the Law* (1928), *What Price Glory* (1928), *The Cat and the Canary* (1929), *Irene* (1929), *Dr. Jekyll and Mr. Hyde* (1929), *Branded* (1929), *The Yellow Ticket* (1929), *Under Cover* (1929), *Anna Christie* (1928), *Porgy* (1931), and *Desire Under the Elms* (1932). Theodore Dreiser wrote a glowing letter of praise after viewing the Players' production of *Salomé.* Dreiser particularly praised the performance of the leading lady, Evelyn Preer, and declared that he had seen many different productions of the play but had seen no performances to equal those of the Lafayette Players.[16]

Black actresses had never been given any serious attention, nor had they been accepted for their true worth by audiences or critics. In the *New York Age* on October 24, 1925, a critic reviewing Micheaux's *The Devil's Disciple,* the film Preer considered her best work, stated, "Very often do our people reach the heights of musical comedy stardom, but seldom do they reach the enviable position that Evelyn Preer holds in the history of dramatic art." He goes on to say that Preer is "an actress of rare ability and intelligence."[17] Leigh Whipper, the black actor who appeared in the original Broadway production of *Of Mice and Men,* said that he, Paul Robeson, and Clarence Muse all agreed that Evelyn Preer was the "most accomplished dramatic actress that our race has ever produced."[18]

Evelyn Preer, Lawrence Chenault, and Alma Sewell in *The Conjure Woman* (1926).

In Hollywood, the black performer was still equated with a comic stereotype, but this assumption was belied by the performance given by the Lafayette Players, who were highly regarded by many leading theatrical personalities of the time. The famous producer and director David Belasco used many members of the Players for his lavish Broadway production of *Lulu Belle,* which opened on Broadway on February 12, 1926.

In April 1927, Floyd J. Calvin, a reporter for *The Pittsburgh Courier,* the popular and widely distributed black newspaper, headlined the paper's theatrical page with "Evelyn Preer Ranks First as Stage and Movie Star." In this article, Calvin comments favorably:

> After a year on Broadway as an important figure in David Belasco's *Lulu Belle,* and after a long record as a star and leading lady . . . and her present popularity as a phonograph record star, Miss Evelyn Preer, who is also Mrs. Edward Thompson, takes her place in the front rank with colored theatrical celebrities. . . . Miss Preer is a pioneer in the cinema world for colored actresses.[19]

In the same article, Preer is quoted as stating that she was "crazy about films" and that she felt there was a good future for black performers in this medium. However, she declared that she was still certain that black entertainers would get their best chances from white directors who, realizing that blacks have talent, would finally be willing to employ them just as they would entertainers of any other race.

In June 1927, *The Pittsburgh Courier* carried a series of articles authored by Miss Preer, which were titled, "My Thrills in the Movies." Evidently, the Players were performing in Pittsburgh during this period and the newspaper decided to take advantage of her presence in their city. In these articles, Preer chronicled various exciting incidents that had occurred while filming Micheaux's *Birthright, The Brute, Deceit,* and *Within Our Gates.* Written very simply and honestly, the pieces are entertaining and informative for those wishing a back-of-the-lot view of early filming techniques and the practices of producer-director Micheaux. The articles also exhibit a tremendous sense of humor on the part of the glamorous young star.[20]

Having excelled on the stage and in film, Preer also used her musical talents. On June 11, 1927, Preer appeared in *Rang Tang* at the Majestic Theatre in New York. Adapted from a script by Kaj Gynt, this production was a musical comedy, with music written by the famous team of Miller and Lyles. That same year Preer recorded with Duke Ellington and also recorded a few sides and was backed occasionally by a group featuring Red Nichols and Miff Mole. For several months during 1930 and 1931, Preer performed with other well-known vocal entertainers such as Lottie Gee, Edith Spencer, and Ethel Waters at the famous Sebastian's Cotton Club in Los Angeles, California. Among the recordings still available to collectors are the following:

When The Red, Red Robin Comes Bob-Bob-Bobbin'
Breezing Along With the Breeze
No One But You Knows How to Love
What Does My Honeydew Do?
Bye-bye Blackbird
Make Me Know It
Lucky Day (The Birth of the Blues)
Sadie Green (The Vamp of New Orleans)
It Takes a Good Woman to Keep a Good Man at Home
If You Can't Hold the Man You Love
I Gotta Get Myself Somebody to Love
Magnolia
One Sweet Letter From You
Someday, Sweetheart
I Got a Papa in New Orleans, Another Papa up in Maine
After You've Gone
When Tomorrow Comes
One More Kiss
Looking for the Sunshine, Walking Around in the Rain
Black in Your Own Backyard
Nobody Know How Much I Love You
Baby, Won't You Please Come Home
Some of These Days
Slow River
Lucky Day
Do! Do! Do!
My Baby's Back[21]

Although talented as a singer, it was as an actress that Preer was to leave a lasting mark. Legitimate theater was an arena closed to black performers for the most part until the advent of Anita Bush's Lafayette Players. After Preer traveled to Los Angeles with the Lafayette Players in 1928, she appeared in a popular and much-hailed production of *Rain*. Ina Duncan, the dancer who rose to fame in *Hot Chocolates,* subsequently declared:

Prior to the appearance of the Lafayette Players in Hollywood, race actors were refused serious parts in the movies. When the Lafayette Players first came to the Pacific Coast they produced the drama, *Rain.* At the time, Gloria Swanson had just finished the drama for screen use. One night, feeling that they wanted a laugh, about 200 white stars of Hollywood came to the Lincoln, presumably with the idea of being amusingly entertained. Included in the groups were Miss Swanson, Sid Chaplin, Harold Lloyd, Sid Grauman (the big producer who has given many race actors a break), and countless others. If they came to laugh, they remained to cheer. Following the performance they went backstage to compliment Miss Preer, her husband, Eddie Thompson, and other members of the cast. This was the dawn of a new day for the Negro in Hollywood.[22]

Just as complimentary is Clarence Muse, who once said of Preer, "She was so true to her craft; so great an artist that no human critic could possibly select her great achievement. Nor could they honestly deny her ability."[23]

Preer is reported to have appeared in several films for Paramount Studio and, according to her husband Edward Thompson, in 1931 she worked under the well-known director Cecil B. DeMille, who lauded her acting and singing ability. She also worked for Christie Studios in Hollywood and starred in at least three productions for them: *The Melancholy Dame, The Framing of the Shrew,* and *Oft in the Silly Night,* which were all comic shorts written by Octavius R. Cohen, a well-respected white writer for *The Saturday Evening Post.* Today they might be considered throwbacks to the minstrel style or the "coon shows" of the nineteenth century. At various times during Preer's career, she was cast in small roles in films produced by Paramount, Fox, MGM, Columbia, and Warner Brothers Studios.[24]

In December 1931, Evelyn Preer and her husband proudly and happily announced to the press that she would soon be starring in the real-life role of mother. It was the fulfillment of a cherished dream for the versatile actress, who had been informed by numerous doctors that she could never bear a child. After announcing ecstatically to the press and numerous friends that she would not be able to work for a time, Preer happily declared that she was certain that her baby would be a girl and subsequently a famous actress.[25] In April 1932, Preer gave birth to a daughter; she and her husband Edward combined names to call the child "Edeve."

Evelyn Preer as Sadie Thompson in the Lafayette Players production of *Rain* (Los Angeles, 1928).

It was, therefore, a tremendous shock to members of her profession, her theatrical "family," and to her numerous loyal fans when just seven months later, word of Evelyn Preer's death was announced over a Los Angeles radio station. On Wednesday, November 19, 1932, Evelyn Preer succumbed to double pneumonia months after the birth of her only child.[26] During her too-brief lifetime, she had been hailed and lauded as "the Race's most famous and most versatile actress."

Oscar Micheaux, who first starred Miss Preer at the beginning of her meteoric career, said in stirring tribute upon hearing of her death:

Evelyn Preer (left) and Edward Thompson (seated) in dark makeup. A still from one of their Hollywood productions, probably a comic short for the Christie Studios.

> Beautiful and intelligent, she became immediately popular. . . . Miss Preer was a born artist and her early passing will leave her missed greatly by the profession. . . . More versatile than any girl I have ever known, Miss Preer could play any role assigned her and always did so cheerfully and without argument.[27]

At her funeral, one of the most impressive ever witnessed, even by Hollywood standards, thousands passed Miss Preer's bier to pay their respects. One reporter from a Los Angeles newspaper wrote:

> Perhaps never before has comment on the death of a Negro stage woman cut below the surface of tinsel and light as in the regretful words heard almost everywhere since the untimely ending of this brilliant star.
>
> She made the most of her gifts and in the process brought pleasure to the great American commonality, and honor to her race. Her work was always that of a conscientious artist. Her column of life as an actress was firmly set in the ground work of happiness that she brought to others. Although cut off untimely, her life was not uprooted. It stands, even in death, beloved as have but few colored members of the stage fraternity. Certainly, no colored actress ever inspired such adoration from her own people as did Evelyn Preer, and there has never been a death in this city to equal the passionate sincerity of devotion which mourning friends have shown for Evelyn Preer.[28]

In a beautiful and soul-stirring eulogy delivered at Preer's funeral, her former leading man, Clarence Muse, concluded by saying, "And so, Evelyn Preer, go on! The Lafayette Players have profited by your visit here. The world has been uplifted."[29] It was a fitting, final tribute to a rare and dedicated artist who had made her final exit and taken her last bow.

In February 1931, the *California Eagle,* the leading black newspaper of Los Angeles, carried the bold headline, "Depression Hits Stage and Screen."[30] The entire theatrical community went into a staggering recession. This was a financial slump from which the black theater was not to revive fully until years later with the opening of the WPA Federal Theatre Project in Harlem, headed by Hallie Flanagan. Not until that time was there once again an opportunity for black performers to earn money while plying their craft.

In 1932, in the midst of the depression, the Lafayette Players closed and the curtain fell upon them for the last time. It is true that at the time of their closing, black actors handicapped by race still had a long and arduous way to go and had many gains yet to win before finally achieving the long-hoped-for and much-sought-after acceptance as serious entertainers. The long, rugged road up which they would still have to climb had at least become less rocky to travel. It has always been easier and more satisfying to step forward than to be forced to crawl.

Recognition of merit was a long time coming, and we well know the difficult situation that still exists today for our black actors and performers. Bias and discrimination are, unhappily, not yet dead in many areas. However, the role played by the Lafayette Players in preparing the theatrical world to deal with the black performer on new terms and in new circumstances did help to hasten the day and hour when the black artist could become a "first-class citizen" in the world of theater and film.

Evelyn Preer at the height of her fame as a movie star, circa 1927.

What the Lafayette Players, as artists, gave to American theater history can never be taken from them. Nor can the mosaic of our great theatrical history in this country ever be complete without them. Their contribution has great value and worth beyond mere measuring. It was a positive contribution that permeated the theatrical circles of their time and paved the way for many who followed after them. This brave band of true pioneers effectively achieved what their initiator and originator had set out daringly and courageously to achieve for herself and for her group of actors: recognition as legitimate stage artists who were to be taken seriously. Anita Bush has been called "The Little Mother of Black Drama,"[31] and well she might, since she gave birth to and nourished a creative idea. That idea, because of her care, grew and blossomed and continues to bear abundant fruit. We cannot—we must not—forget. We owe remembrance and gratitude to Anita Bush and her dream which became a living reality.

4.

The African-American Press and Race Movies, 1909–1929

CHARLENE REGESTER

*T*he African-American press has been in existence since the 1800s. According to Martin Dann, it was founded to respond to white racism and to promote self-determination, and it has adhered to these principles throughout its existence.[1] This essay will examine the particular relationship between the African-American press and race movies during the years up to 1929. While the American film industry was shifting to sound in 1927, this essay extends its examination through 1929, the year that Oscar Micheaux stopped working in silent film. In three sections, it will discuss: (a) the African-American press and cinema before 1918 (the year that marked both the end of World War I and the production of Micheaux's first film); (b) the African-American press and race movies from 1918 to 1929 (Micheaux's first period of filmmaking); and (c) the African-American press and its specific relationship with one of the cinema's most prolific black filmmakers, Micheaux, during the silent period.

THE AFRICAN-AMERICAN PRESS AND EARLY CINEMA

It is widely assumed that African Americans did not respond publicly to their screen representations until *The Birth of a Nation* (1915). This assumption is simply not true. At least six years before the release of this film, the African-American press had already responded to the negative representations of African Americans on the screen. The press played a dual role in its response, both denouncing the negative screen representations and encouraging African Americans to assert themselves in the industry by becoming actors, actresses, filmmakers, producers, directors, and technicians. As early as 1909, Lester Walton, film critic for the *New York Age,* publicly aired his objections in an article entitled "The Degeneracy of the Moving Picture Theatre."[2] Expressing his dissatisfaction with the way that blacks were portrayed on the screen, Walton urged his fellow African Americans to protest such pictures:

While passing a moving picture theatre on Sixth Avenue several days ago the writer was surprised to see a sign prominently displayed in front of the place bearing the following in large print: JOHN SMITH of PARIS, TEXAS, BURNED at the STAKE. HEAR HIS MOANS and GROANS. PRICE ONE CENT! A crudely painted picture of a colored man being burned at the stake completed the makeup of the offensive as well as repulsive-appearing sign. . . . It is very likely that in Greater New York there are many other moving picture theatres featuring the scene of a colored man being burned at the stake, which means the planting of the seed of savagery in the breasts of those whites who even in this enlightened day and time are not any too far from barbarism and to whom such acts of inhumanity would appeal.

The promoters of moving picture theatres make the assertion that their pictures are of an educational nature. . . . We would like to know where do the elements of education come insofar as the picture in question is concerned? . . . The authorities will see that no offensive pictures are presented for public view if a strong protest is made by the colored citizens of New York. . . . These pictures can be suppressed if proper steps are taken to do so. However, if we do not start now to put an end to this insult to the race, expect to see more shocking pictures with the Negro as a subject in the near future.[3]

Robert S. Abbott, 1927. He was editor of the *Chicago Defender,* which covered race cinema extensively in the early 1920s.

Equally offended by the insulting representations of African Americans on the screen and responding to the general white racism that permeated motion pictures, an unidentified critic for the *New York News* in 1914 condemned white theater owners for exploiting African-American audiences to promote such pictures. This columnist charged that

too often white moving picture houses built for the patronage of colored people present pictures that are contrary to the true sentiment of our race. First of all they obtain comedy releases containing caricatures of the black race. These watermelon-[eating], chicken-stealing comedies are elaborately billed in black belts as colored moving pictures. The young of our race who see too often these pernicious libels on our character become imbued with the loss of self-respect. Therein lies the danger. And in addition to the danger is the gruesome thought that members of our own race, some living in Harlem, participate in these productions. Let us say that the pittance they earn is as vile as the pieces of silver Judas threw into the Potter's field.[4]

Indeed, African Americans were well aware of the negative representations that emerged in early motion pictures and publicly denounced such representations in the black press. Obviously, their outrage at these images was heightened when *The Birth of a Nation,* a most inflammatory picture in its demeaning portrayal of African Americans, was released in 1915. African-American author John O. Killens described D. W. Griffith's *The Birth of a Nation* as "Hollywood's first big gun in its war against the black American."[5] And this war was often fought on the pages of African-American newspapers. Most press reports document African-American efforts to prevent the film's exhibition. When the picture met with riots in Boston, New York, Philadelphia, and other northern cities, one newspaper cautioned: "Be assured, dear fellow citizens, that violence begets violence, and that we have nothing to gain by it—only possible harm. Stay away from the play, as your feelings will suffer terrible hurts and you will be tempted to express yourselves in ways that may not be tolerated."[6] One columnist ignored such warnings:

> I went last night to see *The Birth of a Nation* and the contempt I have always had for that dangerous hypocrite, the Rev. Thomas Dixon, was intensified a thousand fold. . . . However, it is not the first time the devil has worn the habit of a monk, or that brotherly hate has spoken in the accents of brotherly love. A man who seeks to degrade Lincoln to his level, and does not stop at sacrilege to the Christ, will surely meet sooner or later the universal contempt he deserves.[7]

These defaming representations of African Americans stimulated the press to promote self-determination by encouraging the race to penetrate all phases of the motion picture industry. If African Americans were to gain control of how they were presented on the screen, they would have to create their own images.

The black press promoted principles that were based on the writers' personal standards: these were generally extensions of black middle class values. Critics have often seen these middle-class views as problematic for many African Americans because, as Jane Gaines has argued, "the black bourgeois uplift philosophy was that the better society it proposed was not significantly different from the one that held all blacks down."[8] Furthermore, underlying this philosophy was the assumption that if African Americans adopted middle-class standards, they would automatically achieve middle-class status, but this strategy ignored the fact that they still had to contend with obstacles related to race alone. Nonetheless, if white racism was a universal experience for all African Americans and knew no class distinctions; members of the press, though themselves a product of the black middle class, were perhaps operating out of a sincere desire to raise the level of all constituents of the African-American community.

The black press tried to be evenhanded in its response to the complex dilemma it faced with the cinema. For example, in 1913, the Indianapolis *Freeman* commended an African-American actor who was featured in an unnamed white-produced picture while at the same time it encouraged blacks to make their own films. This report stated, "While it is a good thing for colored actors to get into the game among the whites, there is nothing like the genuine, all-colored pictures produced by the Foster company, and the quicker they become in demand, the better it will be for colored actors and picture houses. . . . It will be the duty of all the race to support the Foster movement."[9] This reviewer was referring to William Foster, credited as being the first African-American filmmaker.[10] He organized his own motion picture company, the Foster Photoplay Company, to prove that African Americans could use this medium to improve their image both in the United States and abroad. Foster contended that

> in a moving picture, the Negro can offset so many insults to the race—can tell their side of the birth of this great nation—can show what a great man Frederick Douglass was, the works of Toussaint L'Ouverture, Don Pedro, and battle of San Juan Hill, the things that will never be told except by the Negroes themselves. . . . It is the Negro businessman's only international chance to make money and put his race right with the world.[11]

A sports and entertainment columnist for the *Chicago Defender* and Indianapolis *Freeman*, Foster was fully aware of the need for African Americans to take control of their own screen images. His comments reflected the position often articulated by the press.

The African-American press became even more adamant in promoting self-determination in the aftermath of *The Birth of a Nation.* One critic charged, "Not in this whole picture, which is supposed to represent the birth and growth of the nation, is there one single Negro who is both intelligent and decent."[12] *The Birth of a Nation* spurred on the black press, which continued to urge African Americans to use film as a vehicle to promote self-determination and to encourage filmmakers to provide complimentary representations of African Americans and African-American life in their pictures.

By responding to white racism and promoting self-determination, the black press had begun to play a role in African-American film history. Between 1918 and 1929 (Micheaux's first period of filmmaking), African-American newspapers exerted a positive influence by applauding the efforts of companies that produced films appealing to black audiences. They helped to expand the market for black productions by providing reviews, advertisements, behind-the-scenes gossip, and discussion of these films. In an attempt to gain even more influence, however, the African-American press positioned itself in a sometimes unwelcome advisory capacity by commenting on what filmmakers could do to improve, promote, and distribute their films and, thereby increase their exposure and proceeds at the box office. Increasingly, this policy of encouragement was mixed with more negative comments. Writers gradually became much more critical, noting the strengths and weaknesses of race movies, and were sometimes outspokenly intolerant of productions they considered substandard. The African-American press did not hesitate to advise film companies that they needed to improve their pictures. Although they condemned those filmmakers whose pictures duplicated the un-complimentary images often witnessed in Hollywood productions, the press nonetheless remained a positive factor overall.

Even before the end of World War I, the black press was applauding the works of African-American film companies such as the Lincoln Motion Picture Company, operated by Noble and George P. Johnson, which had released its first film in 1916. (The Lincoln Motion Picture Company is further discussed by Clyde Taylor in this collection.) Complimenting this company, the *Chicago Defender* reported:

> There is only one race film company worthy of the name, that is the Lincoln Motion Picture Co. Inc., of Los Angeles, Cal. It is distinctly a Racial proposition, owned, operated and financed by our people only—not a white person even being allowed to own one share of stock. Three productions have been released, and have been booked with remarkable success; these are *The Realization of a Negro's Ambition, The Trooper of Troop K,* and *The Law of Nature. . . .* In all of them the entire casts are people of Color and the remarkable manner in which these dramas were acted was a revelation to those who had the idea that if our folks didn't cork up and pull a lot of rotten, so-called comedy, there was no chance for success.[13]

Still in its early phase of positive reinforcement, the press applauded the efforts of this African-American film company for its quality productions. Simultaneously, however, columnists denounced other film companies (whether white-owned or African-American) that specialized in race movies if they forced African-American actors to appear in blackface and play comic roles. It is interesting to note that early on the African-American press was not so subtle in its influence but outright condemned race companies that were producing films that in its opinion were undeserving of recognition. It reserved its applause for those companies that provided positive representations of African Americans, representations that were consistent with its own views.

When the Lincoln Motion Picture Company released *A Man's Duty* in 1919, the press heaped praise on both the company and the film. *A Man's Duty* "is without a doubt the greatest of all the 'All Race' productions, and is right up with the finest output of any of the large companies, regardless of color," said one report.[14] The same weekly also praised the Maurice Film Company's *Nobody's Children*, produced in 1920. One complimentary review stated, "This picture comes highly recommended and it is said to carry more actual thrill to the reel than anything ever produced by colored people. Indeed, it is doubtful if there has ever been a five-reeler made that will hold you in the manner that is claimed for this

Flora Abbott Sengstacke, mother of publisher Robert S. Abbott, at the unveiling of the *Chicago Defender's* first press in 1921.

one."[15] As this suggests, however, we should always consider that some journalists provided favorable reviews based on promotional materials and may never have actually viewed the film praised in their columns. Historians, therefore, must read some of the these reviews cautiously when analyzing the reaction of African-American journalists and critics.

During 1921, the Lincoln Motion Picture Company released *By Right of Birth,* a film that focuses on a woman reared by adoptive parents. She leaves her family in search of her biological parents. Through the assistance of a young attorney who has secretly admired her for years, the young woman's identity is ultimately revealed and she receives an inheritance that she rightly deserves as a result of a land scheme that was foiled (a plot strikingly similar to Micheaux's *Symbol of the Unconquered*). The picture was heralded by the African-American press. In the *Chicago Defender,* for instance, Tony Langston wrote:

It offers proof that Colored players can develop histrionic talent above that required for straight comedy, though it must be admitted that the comedy touches in the pictures are yet the best, as they are obviously the most spontaneous. Comic pantomime ability unquestionably is instinctive in the Afro-American. . . . Important action is played straight away without wasting time on preliminary scenes. . . . Finally, there is crude strength about the story showing that the Colored author, George P. Johnson, had his theme in mind from beginning to end. Every detail of the plot supports the theme partly expressed in the title—the right of the transplanted Race to a little pride of its own.[16]

This reviewer critiqued the film on the basis of the acting, theme, and narrative, even commenting on the implication of the film's title.

The press also commended white-owned companies such as the Norman Film Manufacturing Company, operated by Richard Norman (which is discussed extensively by Phyllis Klotman in her article in this collection). The *Chicago Defender* applauded Norman's *The Green-Eyed Monster* (1920), remarking that "this picture is one of the most spectacular productions ever shown at a local house and has created a furor everywhere it has been exhibited."[17] In a later review, the film was further commended for featuring "characters . . . from many different walks of life. The lawyer, doctor, banker and finished actor and actress portray the story, which in a subtle way suggests the advancement of our folks along educational lines and financial lines."[18] The film focused on a love triangle in which two men compete for the attentions of a woman. These men also represent rival railroad factions and compete to secure government contracts for mail distribution. Of course, the winner of these professional pursuits is equally successful in his personal pursuits. Undoubtedly, *The Green-Eyed Monster* appealed to African-American critics in part because it articulated middle-class perspectives that were shared by those writers. African Americans are shown as professionals, pursuing lofty goals that allow them to achieve some degree of economic success.

When the Reol Motion Picture Company, operated by white producer Robert Levy, released *The Call of His People* (1921), one writer stated, "It is without a doubt the finest picture

There Is Only One
GREEN EYED MONSTER
There Never Will Be Another

A 100 PER CENT PICTURE IN 5 SMASHING REELS OF THRILLS! ACTION! PUNCH!

$1,000,000 Worth of Railroad Equipment was used in the filming of this production. An $80,000.00 Train Wreck is part of the Story. The characterizations were enacted by colored people chosen from many different walks of life. The Lawyer, Doctor, Banker and Finished Actor and Actress portray this strong appeal to the highest ideals of nature and lesson of the lowness and result of jealousy, The Green Eyed Monster.

THERE IS NOT A WHITE MAN IN THE CAST, or is there depicted in the entire picture anything of the usual mimicry of the Negro. This photoplay has been indorsed by the most prominent colored people of America.

This picture wins for the theater manager the support of the public and sentiment that spells success, where they are catering to colored audiences.

WE HAVE RECEIVED HUNDREDS OF LETTERS AND TELEGRAMS INDORSING THIS PICTURE

The Green Eyed Monster is the best colored picture we have played in our houses. It made real money for us.
R. H. MURRAY,
Dunbar, Hiawatha, Foraker Theaters, Washington, D. C.

The Green Eyed Monster broke house records in our 1,200-seat Gem Theater.
W. C. KENNEDY,
Gem Theater, Knoxville, Tenn.

Very few, if any colored pictures are equal to the Green Eyed Monster. We believe that you have made the best colored picture yet produced in your Green Eyed Monster.
PAUL E. THOMPSON,
Palace Theater, Dallas, Texas.

The Green Eyed Monster is a picture that can be played every year. It is one of the few pictures that does big repeat business.
PAUL BARRACO,
Washington Theater, Houston, Texas.

I am writing you these few lines just to let you know that the showing of your photoplay, "The Green Eyed Monster" at the Douglas Theater, was a knock-out for the one-week stand and really, this is not expressing myself very much. I am glad to state that we turned them away daily through the showing. The story is good and the photography excellent. You are to be congratulated and I sincerely hope that your next one shall not have less merit.
E. SILVERMAN,
Douglas Theater, New York, N. Y.

Business on The Green Eyed Monster, second run, surpassed first runs on other colored company's features.
ALDRIDGE THEATER,
Oklahoma City, Okla.

I am glad to advise you that your picture, "The Green Eyed Monster," has proven to be a wonderful attraction. We did an excellent business at the big Royal, and also at the Keystone. Our patrons were well pleased with it.
M. WAX,
Royal and Keystone Theaters,
Philadelphia, Pa.

A PICTURE YOU CAN REPEAT AGAIN AND AGAIN

We have a fine line of advertising consisting of Ritchey Lithographs in Ones, Threes and Sixes. Heralds, Window Cards, Teasers, 11 x 14 Photos and slides.

REPEAT BUSINESS ON THIS PICTURE HAS SURPASSED FIRST RUNS ON OTHER COLORED PICTURES

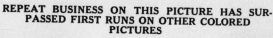

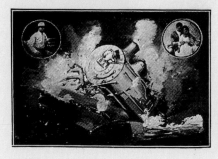

Press book for *The Green-Eyed Monster* (1920). Images and endorsements were to be run in the black press.

ever made with an all-Colored cast, the story being a gripping one, the directing being perfect and the photography the best that could possibly be made. . . . The story, as has been published, is taken from the magazine feature 'The Man Who Would Be White,' and the resultant production places the Reol Corporation in a class far in advance of any producing companies making pictures in which our people are featured."[19] The reviewer commented on the directing, photography, and plot—again delivering a much more comprehensive critique than earlier reviews of race movies.

As more and more race movies were produced, film reviewers became more thorough as well as more critical, moving into a second phase of response to race movies. *Spitfire* (1922), another Reol Motion Picture Company release, was harshly criticized. A reviewer at the Baltimore *Afro-American* asserted,

> The first fault is to be found with the story which is of the most commonplace themes and its treatment is even more commonplace still. Added to this [is a] cheap production which was made with apparently no consideration for the verisimilitude of certain parts of its locale. For instance, the audience [is] asked to believe that one of the characters of the story is a wealthy Washingtonian who keeps a butler and a maid, and yet the interior of the home of this wealthy man is that of any ordinary middle class family. Possibly, in real life, yes; but not according to acceptable movie standards.[20]

Film critic D. Ireland Thomas likewise strongly criticized *Hearts of the Woods* (1921), released by the Superior Arts Productions and directed by R. E. Carlile:

> The less comment on this production will be the better. When I tell you that the cast was composed of green amateurs and the director of no experience, you can judge the kind of production I saw. . . . We don't know the name of the writer of the story because he is not given credit on the titles. What we could make out of the story was something about the life of our people in the woods and around the saw mills. We saw a small saw mill cutting logs; we saw the men in the log pond; we saw the workmen walk through the woodland; we saw the lumber shacks. Sometimes we were unable to see anything as [the] photography was very bad. We saw the villain marry the girl in a church without pulpit or seats. . . . We saw his wife appear on the scene and denounce him and everything end happily. This [is] about all we could get out of the plot. A fair-sized audience laughed at the efforts of the heavily billed "all-star cast" and kidded them along. They had seen better Race productions than this one.[21]

During 1922 and 1923, African-American reviewers continued to be more critical of race films. Though acknowledging both the weaknesses and strengths of these pictures, they confirmed that race movies were indeed marketable and continued to promote them. For example, in a review of *His Great Chance* (1923), Leigh Whipper wrote,

> *His Great Chance* is by far the best Negro picture it has been my fortune to see, and I think I have seen all that have been shown in the vicinity of New York. . . . It was indeed a pleasure to see a picture of this kind and I am very much of the opinion that it will pave the way for a higher standard of films among us. It was entirely free from propaganda, totally devoid of any offensive features and carried a smile and a tear with grace throughout.[22]

This review, however, provoked a response from D. Ireland Thomas, who questioned Whipper's high praise in light of the quality productions released by other companies.[23] Affirming Thomas's opinion, the Baltimore *Afro-American* added that the film "misses a great chance. And that is, missed by lack of competent direction what could have made a capital comedy."[24]

To examine race movies fairly, it seems necessary to examine the socioeconomic context in which these films evolved. Race movies were made with a limited and unstable amount of capital; they were distributed in a limited market to theaters catering exclusively to African-

American audiences; and their appeal as entertainment was less than that of the more technically sophisticated Hollywood pictures. This is the phenomenon Clyde Taylor terms "underdevelopment," a concept elaborated in his essay for this volume. Producers of race movies deserved to be commended. That these films existed at all is extraordinary given the circumstances they endured. Reflecting upon the difficulty of marketing race movies, D. Ireland Thomas wrote about one occasion in which a white theater owner refused to believe that race movies would attract sizable African-American audiences to his theater. To convince the owner that race movies were a drawing card, the salesman rented an "airdrome" and showed race movies, while the white theater owner promoted his white Hollywood productions, which featured such stars as Tom Mix and William S. Hart. When only two moviegoers arrived at the white theater, while "the crowd [was] fighting to get into the airdrome across the street," the theater owner was convinced of the marketability of race movies.[25] Thomas concluded, "No picture draws like a good Race production."[26]

D. Ireland Thomas attempted to encourage African-American filmmakers by touting the marketability of race movies. "All managers are asking for good Race productions. The people are demanding them,"[27] he insisted. By 1923, however, he noted that the production of race movies had been narrowed to three filmmaking companies (the Lincoln Motion Picture Company, the Norman Film Manufacturing Company, and the Micheaux Film Corporation).[28] Thomas recognized that race movies had to be widely exhibited if they were going to succeed. He argued that the African-American press should play a more assertive role and apply pressure to theater owners to exhibit race films:

> Our newspapers will have to take the matter up and demand that the producer be given a fair chance at the Race theater. . . . Just think, until very recently the city of Philadelphia had not seen a Race picture for nearly a year, yet there are many good ones available and our people of that city are crying for every one that they can get. The same conditions exist in many other cities. What are we going to do about it? Are we going to continue to patronize the man who refuses to show our own people upon the screen in the theater that we and we only patronize? Let us get together on this and save ourselves from this threatened disgrace.[29]

Apparently Thomas's exposé of the theater owners' practices worked, because one week later he received several letters of support for his position; many of these letters were from theater owners themselves. Thomas claimed that he "received 15 letters up to this date and every one endorsed my action and remarks in regard to the theater owners not encouraging the producers of Race motion pictures. The funny part of it was, a few [were] from the theater owners. They all will do the right thing if the right people and right Race papers get after them."[30]

The African-American press tried to explain why makers of race films were encountering such difficulties. The *Chicago Defender* printed an article entitled "Are Race Pictures a Failure?" in which the reviewer stated, "In my mind, I think the failure is due to the fact that the Colored picture has to star the actor instead of the actor starring the picture; and then, too, the photography and details are left out of the colored picture."[31] He suggested that African-American filmmakers capitalize on the talent of some of the more recognized stars such as Sherman Dudley, Evelyn Preer, or Edna Morton. They would undoubtedly guarantee an audience and proceeds at the box office. The reviewer commended Oscar Micheaux for featuring Sam Langford, a champion boxer, in his picture *The Brute* (1920), offering its success as evidence that such recognized names should serve as box-office attractions.[32]

Unfortunately, strong pictures did not always guarantee box-office success. The Baltimore *Afro-American* decried the failure of several companies despite "a sincere effort . . . to contribute to the screen the much needed colored picture. Attempts in other sections have

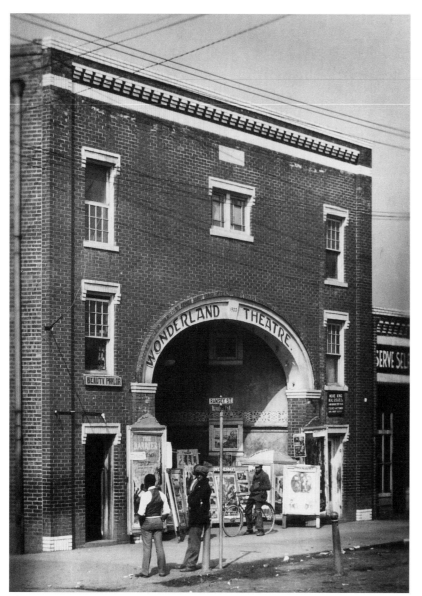

The Wonderland Theatre catered to a black clientele. Built in 1920, it was operated by the Movie King Real Estate Company.

likewise proven nominally abortive, but let's 'Carry On.'"[33] This newspaper, concerned with the lack of support for race movies among African-American audiences, declared:

The worst enemy of these race productions is the race movie fan himself. Colored Americans are governed by the standard set by white producers, and because the former have not measured up to this standard, they are scoffed at and sometimes boycotted altogether. The cinema game within the race is in its infancy and it is within the power of every race fan to crush it in its cradle. Moving pictures cannot be made without money. These pictures are shown in houses catering to colored patrons only; from them must come the means that will determine whether the industry will live. To bear with such men as Oscar Micheaux and other pioneers today means bigger and better pictures tomorrow. Make it your slogan to see these picture[s] if it hurts.[34]

In 1927, a similar sentiment was expressed by Will Smith in the same paper. Smith encouraged African Americans to support the efforts of Sherman Dudley, who was trying to launch a million-dollar production company to make race movies. Optimistic about the future of these films, Smith stated,

With the proper handling of a corporation of this caliber, we could soon develop in our race a rival to Mary Pickford, Douglass Fairbanks, Charles Chaplin, and Rudolph Valentino. When Mr. Dudley gives out his definite plans for launching his campaign, let us all as a race put our shoulder to the wheel. . . . Let us all start boosting colored pictures.[35]

W. R. Arnold echoed the position of Smith, contending that "once the public becomes interested in the colored picture the same as it is interested in white ones, the battle is over. . . . But as I said, it's going to take money and picture corporations are not created over night."[36] Indeed, Dudley's effort was, unfortunately, never realized.

In the final phase of its response to silent race movies, the African-American press became highly critical of what it perceived as substandard race movies. By the mid-1920s African-American audiences had become more sophisticated and critical of race movies. Although they craved African-American images on the screen, black moviegoers only patronized or applauded "top-quality" productions. Moreover, race movies were affected by both the advent of sound and competition from Hollywood as Hollywood captured the attentions of African-American moviegoers with productions such as *Hallelujah* (1929) and *Hearts in Dixie* (1929).

In spite of such threats, the black press continued to encourage the production of quality race films, although it did not insist on African-American film companies. For example, one critic for the *New York Amsterdam News* complimented *The Scar of Shame* (1929), produced by the Jewish theatre owner David Starkman of the Colored Players Film Corporation. He remarked, "It is difficult for me to find words to express the pleasure it gave me and the pride I felt during the unreeling of the production. In contrast to the incoherent and poorly directed stories without reasonability or plot that are released by another well-known colored picture company, *The Scar of Shame* was a refreshing achievement."[37]

Historian Thomas Cripps contends that after the Lincoln Motion Picture Company faltered, "black attention turned not to Micheaux but to white Hollywood, in part because [Noble] Johnson, Harry Levette, and others began covering the major studios in a rush to support the whites' hesitant steps toward better use of Negroes."[38] Cripps adds that not only were African-American newspapers relinquishing support of race movies in general but the *New York Amsterdam News* in particular "judged all-black movies lame and inept beside Hollywood pictures, resented them and granted them no support."[39] Although Cripps is accurate in stating that these papers began to provide a much broader perspective on African-American involvement by giving more coverage to black participation in Hollywood cinema, the press abandoned neither its support nor its coverage of race movies.

Even though some reviewers were more critical than others of race movies, none was naive enough to believe that Hollywood would provide the representations of African Americans that they desired on the screen. Ron Green's views offer a counterbalance to Cripps, asserting that "we are left wondering whether or not to agree with Cripps because he has not provided us with the criteria to resolve the historical judgment."[40] Green contends that "it is pointless to blame criticism [such as that provided by African-American film critics] for contributing to the demise of Black independent 'race' movies."[41] The press played a major role in shaping the development of race cinema in the early years by providing the coverage that the cinema needed to function as an alternative to Hollywood for black audiences. To what extent the press then undermined the same cinema that it so eagerly helped to launch remains an open question. The African-American press never completely abandoned race movies, despite its criticisms, and it would later apply these same criticisms to Hollywood productions as African Americans landed screen roles in increasingly greater numbers, often in uncomplimentary roles.

The relationship between the African-American press and race movies during the 1918–1929 period involved three phases: first, encouraging and applauding race movies in the early years; second, becoming more critical of race movies by noting both their strengths and weaknesses but still encouraging the filmmakers and their audiences; and third, becoming intolerant of most productions while demanding higher, and perhaps unattainable, standards, given the obstacles faced by black filmmakers.

OSCAR MICHEAUX AND THE AFRICAN-AMERICAN PRESS, 1918 TO 1929

Oscar Micheaux entered the ranks of African-American filmmakers in 1918 with the production of his first motion picture, *The Homesteader* (released in 1919). By 1928, Micheaux's company had filed for bankruptcy. During this eleven-year period, Micheaux produced his greatest number of films (approximately twenty, including remakes or retitled films) and his greatest number of quality films. He sought to present films that would be an answer to whites' demeaning representations of African Americans, and he also sought to present lifestyles

African Americans could emulate. However, as literary critic bell hooks asserts, Micheaux was never interested in the "simple reduction of black representation to a 'positive' image."[42] On the contrary, hooks continues, "In the spirit of oppositional creativity, he worked to produce images that would convey complexity of experience and feeling."[43] Such images emerged in his screen representations and were in part responsible for much of the criticism he received during his filmmaking career—particularly from critics who wrote for the African-American press, as he endured a sometimes turbulent relationship with these writers.

In the first few years of his career, the African-American press heaped praise on Oscar Micheaux's pictures whenever and wherever the pictures were shown. *The Homesteader* received favorable reviews despite its nearly three-hour length and the censorship difficulties in Chicago caused by three African-American ministers who objected to Micheaux's portrayals. For example, one review acclaimed, "To the credit of the producers, among other things, must be given the fact that every detail of the production has been given the most minute care; the characters for their particular parts have been chosen and conform to the description in the book so fully that it is marvelous."[44] A subsequent review pointed out, "The demands for rebooking speak well for the quality of the picture which leaves for a long transcontinental tour."[45] Although it is not clear if *The Homesteader* took this tour, Micheaux's first film clearly established him as an important black filmmaker who had wide audience appeal.

Micheaux's second release, *Within Our Gates* (1920), also encountered censorship difficulties: this time because it featured a lynching on the screen and Chicago had just witnessed one of the worst race riots in the city's history (see the essays by Michele Wallace and Jane Gaines in this volume). Once again, however, the *Chicago Defender* was complimentary. Its initial review of *Within Our Gates* declared, "The author has not minced words in presenting the facts as they really exist. . . . People interested in the welfare of the Race cannot afford to miss seeing this great production."[46] Or as an advertisement for the film would have it, the film was "the greatest preachment against race prejudice and the glaring injustices practiced upon our people—it will hold you spellbound—full of details that will make you grit your teeth in silent indignation."[47] Another advertisement in the *Houston Informer* described it as "the most spectacular screen version of the most sensational story on the race question since *Uncle Tom's Cabin*."[48] The enthusiasm for *Within Our Gates* deserves further explanation, since the picture was regarded as even more politically threatening than *The Homesteader*. Thus, it is conceivable that *Within Our Gates*, although favorably received by the press, may not have been as widely distributed as was *The Homesteader*.

As Micheaux continued his filmmaking, the press became more critical of his work, commenting on the weaknesses of his films as well as their strengths. When Micheaux produced his third picture, *The Brute* (1920), Lester Walton of the *New York Age* argued:

> So far as the story which *The Brute* unfolds, it is neither original nor any too pleasing to those of us who desire to see the better side of Negro life portrayed. . . . As I looked at the picture I was reminded of the attitude of the daily press, which magnifies our vices and minimizes our virtues. . . . As at no time in the history of motion pictures have white producers sought to represent the Negro in [a] complimentary light; it therefore is the duty of race producers to gladden our hearts and inspire us by presenting characters typifying the better element of Negroes.[49]

Although Walton pointed to those features he considered objectionable, he also commented on its favorable attributes:

> Its photography is more meritorious than any of Oscar Micheaux's pictures. At times there are lapses between important intervals which one is compelled to span by using the imagi-

nation, but these errors of omission are forgotten when Langford knocks out Cutler. As a photoplay produced by Negroes, The Brute is the best of its kind that has been offered for the amusement of the colored movie devotee.[50]

By the mid-1920s Micheaux was among the leading producers of race movies. But as the black press became more sophisticated and critical of race movies, reviewers began to qualify their compliments of Micheaux's films. This is evident with *Birthright* (1924), Micheaux's adaptation of T. S. Stribling's novel about an African-American Harvard graduate's return to his hometown and the resulting racial strife that tore it apart. In much the same manner as Walton had done with Micheaux's *The Brute,* J. A. Jackson edged his praise of *Birthright* with guarded reservations:

Within Our Gates (1920): a white mob fires on a fleeing black boy before returning to the immediate business of lynching his parents. "The facts as they really exist," noted a *Chicago Defender* columnist.

> Whatever may have been the motive that prompted the writing [of] the book, and however distasteful it may be to proud members of the race, there is no denying the faithfulness with which it brings out the condition in pictures. It is not a nice story in many of its aspects, but if the truth it reveals can be carried to the country at large, it will have served a most useful purpose. . . . Its brutal frankness hurts, and some of the titles put a sting into the evening's entertainment and just because it has been so well done; everyone of us should see it.[51]

By the time *Birthright* was shown in Philadelphia, it had been subjected to harsh criticism. Micheaux was forced to defend the film by discussing his personal aims and explaining why he had included such disturbing representations of the race in the film. In an effort to protect his work, which included pictures that often stirred the emotions of African-American audiences because of their implications with respect to race and class differences, Micheaux insisted:

> I have always tried to make my photoplays present the truth, to lay before the race a cross section of its own life, to view the colored heart from close range. My results might have been narrow at times, due perhaps to certain limited situations, which I endeavored to portray, but in those limited situations, the truth was the predominant characteristic. It is only by presenting those portions of the race portrayed in my pictures, in the light and background of their true state, that we can raise our people to greater heights. I am too much imbued with the spirit of Booker T. Washington to engraft false virtues upon ourselves, to make ourselves that which we are not. Nothing could be a greater blow to our own progress.[52]

Equally controversial was Micheaux's *Body and Soul* (1925), a film that was similarly praised and condemned by the press. One reviewer reported that when the film was shown at the Twentieth Century Theatre in Chicago "patronage slumped in the middle of the week owing to the fact that the story was void of interest. The [act] of beating a woman and common use of the deity in church meeting [not only] ridicule[d] [the race] but was all [too] commonplace in its development of lost art in elevation."[53] Another vehemently critical review associated *Body and Soul* with *The Birth of a Nation,* insinuating that Micheaux's film

Advertisement for *The Gunsaulus Mystery* (1921) in the *Chicago Defender*, 30 April 1921, 6.

was equally dangerous because of the degrading representations provided of African Americans. According to this reviewer,

> When a Negro-hating sky pilot of the other race takes up his pen to write concerning us we must expect anything. He has to make it strong to fan the flame of hate within the breast of people. But what excuse can a man of our Race make when he paints us as rapists of our own women? Must we sit and look at a production that refers to us as niggers? Now as to the merits of the picture. None exist. . . . There is no greater influence than the pulpit and screen, yet how many of our preachers and producers will plant proper seed in this fertile soil?
>
> In their great haste to gather in a few dollars they forget their Race. And even the merit of their own work.
>
> Yet, I am thankful that we have some real Race-respecting artists, preachers and producers who will continue to work for the benefit of their Race regardless of such filth as *Body and Soul.*[54]

Almost a year after the release of *Body and Soul,* another critic also targeted Micheaux for providing unflattering screen representations of African Americans, observing:

> As a constant theatergoer, I have had the pleasure of observing several of Oscar Micheaux's productions and [am] damn forced to ask with no offense to Mr. Micheaux whatever, why they are so suggestive of immoral and degraded habits of the human race? In several instances I have taken particular notice that only the wors[t] conditions of our race are shown and the worst language is used with no attempt whatever to portray the higher Negro as he really is.[55]

These reviewers were deeply concerned with the proliferation of negative representations in Micheaux's films and only wanted the positive aspects of African-American life to be unveiled on the screen. This position, however, was one that Micheaux often challenged because he viewed elevation as being consistent with exposing the social ills that all too often kept African Americans politically and economically disengaged from the lifestyles that whites enjoyed.

By the late 1920s, Micheaux had fallen into complete disfavor with the African-American press. This increasingly negative criticism can be partially attributed to Micheaux's sacrifice of production values in order to reduce costs. Lorenzo Tucker, one of Micheaux's leading actors, told film scholar Richard Grupenhoff that the limited financial circumstances under which Micheaux operated forced the filmmaker to employ a variety of cost-cutting strategies. These included refusing to allow retakes, using title cards to condense a film's narrative, and paying little attention to editing techniques. Moreover, Micheaux's financial woes were exacerbated by the negligence and financial mismanagement of Swan Micheaux (Oscar's brother, who at one time worked for his company).[56] Micheaux's efforts to survive as a filmmaker resulted in films of lesser quality, and the press, entering the third phase of its response to race movies, lost no time in attacking him. In this period of intolerance for low-budget productions, black commentators made Micheaux a prime target for their denunciations.

One reviewer, while acknowledging Micheaux's financial state of affairs, asked some pointed questions about Micheaux's *Thirty Years Later* (1928):

> One realizes that colored photoplays suffer from comparison because of limited capital available for making them and the small returns possible to be realized in a class theatre. Mr. Micheaux deserves credit for keeping at the game and paving the way for some followers who will realize more than he. But for improving future releases we might ask three questions:
>
> Why was William Edmondson not given a screen test before being cast as a supposed white man?
>
> Why does the heroine not "sport" a few more changes of clothing as almost any New York stenographer in real life would?
>
> Why have so many dreams or fainting spells during which all the "heavy" acting occurs?[57]

The *Chicago Defender* was cautiously critical of *Thirty Years Later,* declaring that while "there are some pleasing moments in the film . . . the consensus of opinion does not give it much of a break. The shots are not well put together and the story disconnects in many places. The crowds have been eager to see this picture, as the same company [has] put out some wonderful screen dramas in the past."[58] The *Pittsburgh Courier,* unsympathetic with Micheaux and growing impatient with his low-budget productions, stated, "While this man gradually improves, there is nothing in the picture to thrill with interest."[59]

Since Micheaux continually presented himself as wanting to advance self-awareness among African Americans, it is interesting to consider the perception of Micheaux held by political newspapers such as the *Negro World,* published by Marcus Garvey and his United Negro Improvement Association (UNIA). Overall, the *Negro World* provided few reports of Micheaux and his pictures. Although this minimal coverage can be partially attributed to the paper's scanty theatrical news, many of Micheaux's uncomplimentary representations of blacks were also inconsistent with the journal's political views. At the same time, however, Micheaux's promotion of black self-

Body and Soul (1925). The local saloonkeeper (Marshall Rodgers) pours another drink for one of his more insistent clients—Rev. Isiaah Jenkins—an escaped convict posing as a man of God. "Now as to the merits of the picture. None exists," remarked a reviewer in the *Chicago Defender.*

WEDNESDAY, THURSDAY, FRIDAY, SATURDAY
Oscar Micheaux's Biggest Colored Production
Son of Satan
starring
Andrew S. Bishop

and a Powerful Supporting Colored Cast
Adapted from the story
"THE GHOST OF TOLSON MANOR"
A hair-raising story of adventure in a haunted house, where rattling chains and walking ghosts are as common as parrots and puppies.

Advertisement for *A Son of Satan* (1924), in the Baltimore *Afro-American,* 19 June 1926, 4.

NEW DUNBAR

PROGRAM FOR WEEK BEGINNING MONDAY, JANUARY 31st

Monday and Tuesday 2 Days Only Don't Miss It

OSCAR MICHEAUX'S

"THE Spider's WEB"

Mighty
Melodrama
of
New York's
Harlem

WITH AN
ALL STAR
COLORED
CAST OF
WELL
KNOWN
PLAYERS

FEATURING

The Screen' Most Beautiful Colored Star

EVELYN PREER

SUPPORTED BY

Henrietta Loveless   Grace Smythe   Marshall Rogers

Lorenzo McLane   Eddie Thompson   Billy Gulfport

???—And Several Well Known Baltimore Actors—???

YOU'LL BE SURPRISED---COME AND SEE THEM

Behind prison bars she asked God to forgive those who had sinned against her I saw her stealing the money. Who ? When? After the shooting. You shall not take her, she could not have killed a man. Positively as good a crook melodrai a as you ever want to see.

Advertisement for *The Spider's Web* (1926), in the Baltimore *Afro-American*, 29 January 1927, 8. Such films showed uncomplimentary aspects of African-American life that many critics found reprehensible.

sufficiency, race consciousness, and economic independence would have solicited the approval of Garveyites and in fact may have received their praise. Micheaux's sound film *A Daughter of the Congo* (1930) did receive coverage in the *Negro World,* as it held political implications for Garvey's movement. The newspaper covered Micheaux's film primarily because the lead actor, Roland C. Irving, had toured Africa where the film had been set and because the story, at least, was in the interest of Garvey's back-to-Africa movement.[60]

By the end of the 1918–1929 period, Micheaux had fallen victim to dwindling financial resources and found himself in bankruptcy. There were many factors that contributed to his difficulties. As already mentioned, Swan Micheaux's mismanagement of the corporation's financial affairs further strained Micheaux's already limited resources. Thomas Cripps points to additional factors that may have contributed to Micheaux's difficulties: "The coming of [the] depression, costly technology, new techniques, and a . . . threatening Hollywood [that] promised only to shut down 'race' movies."[61] Micheaux faced not only these problems but also devastating financial difficulties and harsh press reviews.

In fairness, negative reviews were not just directed at Micheaux's films; however, the central disagreement between Micheaux and the African-American press, the point of contention (particularly in the later years), was not his technique but his depiction of the unsettling behavior he observed and deplored in the black community. Micheaux's representation of a corrupt African-American middle class directly contradicted the image the press wanted to see. His portrayals invited criticisms. By the late 1920s, the press expected race movies that were technically as well as thematically superior. When Micheaux, struggling with dwindling finances, lowered the production values of his filmmaking in order to continue to produce race movies, the press took offense. They also considered his featuring of African-American millionaires, professionals, and entrepreneurs excessive. However, their strongest criticism against Micheaux came when he provided uncomplimentary portrayals of an African-American middle class involved in vice and corruption. Micheaux felt such undesirable behavior needed to be exposed, lest it interfere with the progress he desired for the entire race. He must have realized that featuring hypocritical ministers who engaged in gambling, drinking, assault, and rape would be unacceptable to many, if not most, reviewers. Negative characterization of the ministry was simply not tolerated within the African-American community. Such representations were bound to result in the bruising criticism that he received from the press.

Although Micheaux made motion pictures that differed substantively from those made in Hollywood, he has sometimes been accused of emulating white, mainstream cinema. According to Jane Gaines and Ron Green, this aspect of Micheaux can best be understood by applying the term adopted by W. E. B. Du Bois, who asserted that an African American views the world in terms of a "'double-consciousness,' [that] sense of always looking at one's self through the eyes of others, of measuring one's soul by the tape of a world that looks on in amused contempt and pity."[62] Micheaux, however, was not providing this ambivalent representation of the African-American middle class without "celebrating blackness," to use bell hooks's phrase.[63] Micheaux was merely "subtly [urging] black spectators to re-evaluate the internalized racism that lead them to respect white or light skin and devalue blackness."[64]

The African-American press had a fluctuating relationship to race filmmaking. While applauding films that provided positive images of the black middle class, the press extended praise to virtually all race movies in the early years. Subsequently, these newspapers both praised and criticized race pictures and later still became highly critical of filmmakers. Intending to encourage African-American filmmakers to strive for higher-quality productions, the African-American press harshly criticized race movies at a time when African-American filmmakers were engaged in a desperate struggle for survival. Although the African-American press never really abandoned its role of attacking white racism and encouraging the promotion of racial self-determination, its harsh words for African-American filmmakers may have unwittingly harmed this dimension of the industry, at least to the extent that press reviews affected the box office.

II

OSCAR MICHEAUX

Within the closed world they create, stereotypes can be studied as
an idealized definition of the different. The closed world of language,
a system of references which creates the illusion of completeness and
wholeness, carries and is carried by the need to stereotype.
                    —Sander Gilman, *Difference and Pathology*[1]

5.

Oscar Micheaux's Within Our Gates: *The Possibilities for Alternative Visions*

The role of stereotypes is to make visible the invisible, so that there
is no danger of it creeping up on us unawares; and to make fast, firm
and separate what is in reality fluid and much closer to the norm than
the dominant value system cares to admit.
                    —Richard Dyer, *The Matter of Images*[2]

MICHELE WALLACE

*T*he most prominent conceptions of black stereotypes in cinema studies, as conceived by
Donald Bogle and Thomas Cripps, define such representations too narrowly—as harmful,
reductive, and denigrating.[3] Even recent endeavors to revise old approaches, for instance that
of Ella Shohat and Robert Stam, do not quite succeed in addressing some of the most problematic issues. Rather, their emphasis is on devaluing stereotype analysis generally as an outmoded and not sufficiently subtle "negative/positive images" criticism.[4] If we are to avoid
throwing the baby out with the bathwater, we need to follow the deconstructive work of Sander
Gilman, Eve Sedgwick, and Richard Dyer and reconceptualize stereotypes or "types" as something of greater importance, ambiguity, and theoretical sophistication.[5] Otherwise, distin-
guishing aesthetic achievement from the presumably deadening influence of stereotypes becomes all but impossible.

It is difficult, if not impossible, to explain the importance of Oscar Micheaux's project
in the silent film *Within Our Gates* (1920) without considerable reorientation with regard to
stereotypes. To the uninitiated eye, this film might first appear to be a rather inept, unshapely
attempt to imitate in blackface the entertainment values of early American film. From this
perspective, a few lame swipes at lynching and white racism might appear to be hopelessly
upstaged by a seemingly endless visual fascination with the goodness and beauty of light-
skinned, bourgeois blacks.

Of course, I have no way of seeing inside of Micheaux's mind (or the mind of any artist
living or dead), nor is it my goal to unearth Micheaux's original intentions at this late date.
Yet it is possible to retrieve some relevant characteristics of Micheaux's historical context in
order to illuminate the relationship of his work to cultural ambivalences regarding race, gender, and sexuality of that time and so bring greater clarity to the contribution of a notable
minority cultural practitioner. By so doing, I hope we will come to understand unimagined
aspects of Micheaux's oeuvre. Micheaux's *Within Our Gates* focuses on race, very possibly in

The Birth of a Nation (1915). Rehearsing the scene in which Silas Lynch (George Siegmann in blackface) tries to force Elsie Stoneman (Lillian Gish) to marry him. Actor Ralph Lewis, playing Austin Stoneman, looks on.

response to D. W. Griffith's assault on the race in the hugely successful *The Birth of a Nation* (1915). In order to understand more precisely what Micheaux had to say about race, we will progress from a redefinition of stereotypes to a particular reading of black stereotypes in Griffith's *Birth* as they impacted on Micheaux's *Within Our Gates*.

According to Donald Bogle, the best known of contemporary black film historians, black stereotypes in cinema were originally codified in the Edison film version of *Uncle Tom's Cabin* (1903). They subsequently changed very little until the blaxploitation films of the 1960s and 1970s when the "black buck" stereotype was allowed to make his first convincing appearance as the heroic, hypersexual black stud in such films as *Sweet Sweetback's Baadasssss Song* (1971), *Shaft* (1972), and *Superfly* (1972).[6] The black buck first emerged as Gus in *The Birth of a Nation* (1915), Bogle says, but was judged too threatening, even in blackface, for southern audiences.

About his short list of stereotypes, which doubles for the title of his book *Toms, Coons, Mulattoes, Mammies, and Bucks: An Interpretive History of Blacks in American Films,* Bogle says, "All were merely filmic reproductions of black stereotypes that had existed since the days of slavery and were already popularized in American life and arts."[7] Mostly uninterested in any kind of theorization or historicization of stereotypes, Bogle credits individual black actors and performers with endowing these lifeless figures with unanticipated dignity and range. Or, as he writes, "Often it seemed as if the mark of the actor was the manner in which he individualized the mythic type or towered above it."[8]

Cripps, Shohat, and Stam, as well as numerous other commentators who focus primarily on contemporary film, seem to accept Bogles's history of race representation in American film, and his breakdown and classification of stereotypes, without question. But the more I look at the films supposedly described by these categories of stereotypes, the more inadequate I find the categories to be.

To call a character a stereotype has long been a way of dismissing the character, the actor who played it, and often the entire picture. Indeed, I suspect this is why little is said in a critical mode about the so-called stereotypical black characters who occupy the background in many otherwise much-discussed films. There isn't anything to say about a stereotype, is there? It has all been said. Stereotypes are supposed to die a quick and natural death of their own superficiality and dullness.

To what conclusion should we come if we really believe, as Bogle suggests, that five character types—four of them invented by Harriet Beecher Stowe in *Uncle Tom's Cabin* and the fifth invented by Griffith in *Birth* (the brutal buck)—have continued to multiply and thrive across the spectrum of American popular culture for over 100 years? It should be clear, it seems to me, that these stereotypes must have considerable adaptive powers.

I would also argue that they and other more contemporary stereotypes and figures provide a sensitive historical template of the status of issues of gender and sexuality as well as race. To consider the ramifications of race in their construction without also taking into account gender, sexuality, class, and anything else of a historically specific nature seems to me pointless, especially since alternative constructions of gender, sexuality, and class are inextricably present in the formulation of the "difference" of "race." Indeed, even as they simplify reality, these stereotypes have also assumed the weight of myth, which mystifies and unnecessarily complicates reality. And the problem with disposing of a myth is that people are often a great deal more attached to it than they realize.

Sander Gilman proposes, correctly, I think, that stereotypes of race, sexuality, and pathology or illness (physical and/or mental) are inextricably connected. I have come to share his psychological view that racism, misogyny, and homophobia are attempts to externalize inner conflict, self-hatred, fragmentation, and incoherence—all psychological mechanisms inevitable to human existence. As Gilman writes,

> Order and control are the antithesis of "pathology." "Pathology" is disorder and the loss of control, the giving over of the self to the forces that lie beyond the self. It is because these forces actually lie within and are projected outside the self that the different is so readily defined as the pathological.[9]

Given the worst-case scenario, when such inner turmoil coincides with onerous economic exigencies (as was the case in Weimar Germany and the postbellum South), then the result is liable to be genocide and/or protracted collective sadism aimed at the externalized "Other." At such times, the object of hatred becomes a shifting, expanding and, in some ways, arbitrary one.

As Eve Sedgwick points out, difference will always be found everywhere one looks for it.[10] As long as one persists in pining for a lost homogeneity and social cohesion, the situation can only deteriorate. Also, since such relatively blunt categories as race, sexuality, gender, and class can hardly begin to accommodate the range of possible differences of personality or their conceivable historical permutations, the more one enforces social homogeneity, the more problematic and potentially explosive difference becomes.

In the late-nineteenth- and early-twentieth-century American context, propelled by constant outbursts against blacks in the form of lynchings and race riots, the flames of hatred were also directed at immigrants, Asians, Jews, and Native Americans.[11] This synergistic incubation of fear and loathing was both deliberate and conscious on the part of some hatemongers *and*, at the same time, as Shohat and Stam have pointed out, internalized and structural.

Yet, cultural expressions and symbolizations of this contempt for "difference" within the arts or popular culture signals the possibility of negotiation and intervention, precisely because symbolizations also intersect with the realm of the unconscious. I realize that this view of cultural expression as capable of positive intervention is not popular. Current practices of cultural criticism constantly incite us to see the representation and the reality as interchangeable, although they are often far from it. As Richard Dyer reminds us, "what is represented in representation is not directly reality itself but other representations," and "cultural forms do not have single determinate meanings—people make sense of them in different ways, according to the cultural (including sub-cultural) codes available to them."[12]

There is a lesson to be learned, for instance, from the saga of the way in which blackface minstrelsy, despite its portrayal of blacks as alien, non-sensical animals/children, has impacted on still-emerging forms of black representation in theatre, dance, the visual arts, and film. How white audiences progressed from the enjoyment of the Christy Minstrels in blackface to the enjoyment of "the real thing" of the Fisk Jubilee Singers, ragtime, and Bessie Smith—to the enjoyment of black musical theatre, Pigmeat Markham, Moms Mabley, and Richard Pryor—is no sugarcoated fairy tale.[13] But life has never been a picnic for an impoverished ethnic minority within the heart of an overprivileged nation flexing its muscles.

In my view, the attempt to find some other ground, far from the poisonous terrain of blackface minstrelsy, upon which to judge and evaluate the politics and aesthetics of black artists, performers, directors, and technicians is doomed from the outset. When we are inundated by visual representations generally thought to be profoundly negative, it becomes very difficult to tell negative from positive and not to succumb to viewing virtually all black images as negative. This process inclines toward regarding anything discernibly "black" and/or dark as negative. As Gilman puts it,

The "pathological" may appear as the pure, the unsullied; the sexually different as the apotheosis of beauty, the asexual or the androgynous; the racially different as highly attractive. In all of these cases the same process occurs. The loss of control is projected not onto the cause or mirror of this loss but onto the Other, who, unlike the self, can do no wrong, can never be out of control. Categories of difference are protean, but they appear as absolutes. They categorize the sense of the self, but establish an order—the illusion of order in the world.[14]

Moreover, blackface minstrelsy's cast of characters, images, and narrative expectations easily shook loose from the formal structure of the conventional three-part minstrelsy show to widely influence performance practices across the board—in vaudeville, burlesque, tent shows, musical theatre, drama, and film.

I break the most prevalent influences of minstrelsy down into three categories for purposes of this essay. The first of these involves whites playing black characters in blackface, usually but not always for comedic effect in the silent film period. This may actually be a much richer category than it first appears because U.S. films frequently employed white stars to impersonate people of color in both dramatic and comedic contexts. In the case of Asians, Latin Americans, and Native Americans, lead actors were commonly cast as white in "redface" or "yellowface." Then, visually authentic-looking Asians, Latins, and Native Americans are frequently used as background, a kind of human mise-en-scène, for crowd scenes and to establish veracity. One also finds this convention persistently employed in casting dramatic black leads as white actors in dark makeup, with real blacks providing background until the early sound period. This policy is particularly noticeable in D. W. Griffith's *The Birth of a Nation*: black characters with lines of dialogue are played by whites in blackface or brownface, whereas the violent actions of the black mobs are generally carried out by phenotypically and obviously black actors. Indeed, Cripps reports that these black players were confined to segregated camps during the filming process.[15] The presence of large numbers of apparently black actors in the frame—a sight one rarely saw in silent films—lends further weight to the film's visceral impact.

The other side of this blackface tradition became the automatic association of black characters, particularly when played in blackface and in a mundane or everyday performance context, as humorous or "low" subjects. Thus there ensued the practice of black performers (especially those who had light skin) blacking up to enhance their comedic effect (i.e., Bert Williams).[16]

The second borrowing from minstrelsy was the menu of conventional stereotypes originating in either the *Uncle Tom's Cabin* narrative or the antebellum plantation South scenario generally favored by blackface minstrelsy. These are the ones spelled out by Donald Bogle: toms, coons, mulattos, mammies, and bucks. I propose, however, that the ongoing visual reinforcement and repetition of these iconic figures reveals more about their inner dynamics than the question of when, where, and how they originated. The point is not who dreamed them up but rather that they continue to survive as a kind of self-referential sign system with its own intrinsic logic. Indeed, the incorporation of these figures (in all their superficiality and performativity) into the very core of American popular culture directly parallels that which is usually thought to be its antithesis—the incorporation of black folk culture deemed by cultural authority to be authentic. In the present day, the legacy of this process is that the two have become virtually inseparable.[17]

Although Uncle Tom was not old in Stowe's novel, under the rigors of minstrelsy he becomes elderly, some say in order to desexualize him, thus rendering him the nemesis of the "black brute" of later vintage.[18] Also, between the publication of *Uncle Tom's Cabin* and the first silent film versions, another crucial postbellum text appeared with a figure genealogically related to Uncle Tom but decisively different. Uncle Remus, the creation of southern apologist and plantation school writer Joel Chandler Harris in the 1880s, provided a narrator for several collections of African-American folktales. A seemingly deliberate parody of Uncle Tom, Uncle Remus was essentially a retired slave with little apparent work to do, a profane storyteller (whereas Uncle Tom's text was the Bible), and an elderly retainer of a formerly great plantation left under the care of the women and children (the men having died in the Civil War). Uncle Remus's companions were the little white boy (a stand-in for Chandler) to whom he told his stories and Brer Rabbit, a stand-in for the resourceful slave clever enough to trick himself out of any dangerous situations with such dullards as Brer Fox and Brer Bear. Whereas Uncle Tom dies well before his time, Uncle Remus is a cunning survivor of the increasingly Jim Crow South.[19]

Mammy, I suspect, has intercontinental African diasporic roots, which remain to be fully researched and articulated.[20] But if we confine ourselves to the United States, Harriet Beecher Stowe's version of Mammy, Aunt Chloe, seems an unlikely beginning indeed. If we refer to the charming *Slave in a Box: The Strange Career of Aunt Jemima* and Grace Hale's contribution to the subject, we will discover that Aunt Jemima, as a cousin of Mammy, goes well back into the earliest history of coon songs and blackface minstrelsy as a relic of the folk culture. Needless to say, she survives intact to this day not because she is dangerous and self-destructive but because, like Uncle Remus, she is a cunning survivor.[21]

The coons, including Topsy and, later in films, black children in general, always appear as ridiculously dressed, energetic clowns. Often, as with the conventional portrayals of Topsy or Buckwheat, the hair is made to assume an asymmetrical configuration (for current examples of this sort of things, look at styles of hairdressing among African-American males with dreds). Or there are the Zip Coons, incompletely urbanized dandies, and the soldier coons, who don't know which end is up, which led to the convention of physical demonstrations of mental confusion, fear, and duplicity (i.e., Step 'n Fetchit). All of these dissemblers, I would submit, are, in fact, trickster figures of various types, cousins of Brer Rabbit and Uncle Remus.

Participating in a logic largely mysterious to us today, the figure of the mulatto has changed the most of all the stereotypes. There really is no contemporary counterpart to this figure in our current lives, nor is she generally reinvoked as a stereotype in portrayals of mixed-race people in contemporary films. Jay in *The Crying Game* was no "tragic mulatto" in the nineteenth-century sense.

Since mulattos were viewed by some whites as being nearly indistinguishable from themselves in dress and demeanor—and certainly nothing like most freed blacks who were disfigured by poverty and abuse—the question was: Would mulattos form a separate intermediate caste between blacks and whites, as had happened before in the wake of slavery in the Caribbean and in South America? Or would the test of the "one drop of black blood," regardless of what a person looked like, be the determining one?[22]

Stowe's idealization and sentimentalization of mulattos has been linked to their whiteness.[23] Partly in reaction to this, novelist and preacher Thomas Dixon, with *The Leopard's Spot* (1903) and *The Clansman* (1905), and Griffith, with *The Birth of a Nation,* made the invisible difference of mulattos (their blackness) visible, then demonized them. Griffith's male mulatto Lynch in *Birth* is constantly grimacing, and the female mulatto Lydia is sometimes seized by fits of laughter and lust that throw her to the ground. Is it any wonder, then, that the mulatto figure, both male and female (whose real-life counterpart had, after all, played a central and pivotal role in Reconstruction politics),[24] was rendered particularly upright and dignified in subsequent "race" films, including Micheaux's, the better to disprove Dixon's and Griffith's slander? After a brief heyday in the "race" films, the male mulatto principally emerges in mainstream film as a browner model: he's not an Uncle Tom, but he's not a black brute either. Significantly, such parts don't really appear until the 1940s and 1950s, with such actors as James Edwards, Sidney Poitier, and Harry Belafonte, some of whom are light-skinned but whose skin color no longer signifies "mulatto" or mixed-race parentage.

We can trace the female type to the infrequent appearance of a black femme fatale in American films of the 1940s (with the exception of *Pinky* [1949], which harks back to the older debate about mulattos) and after—films which feature Lena Horne, Eartha Kitt, and Dorothy Dandridge—but this woman is not allowed to be light enough to be mistaken for white. As a consequence, Fredi Washington could not find work in movies after *Imitation of Life* (1934) because she was too light, and Lena Horne had to submit to "dark Egyptian" makeup to blacken her up in order to work in the few films in which she was featured before being semi-blacklisted by Walter Winchell.[25]

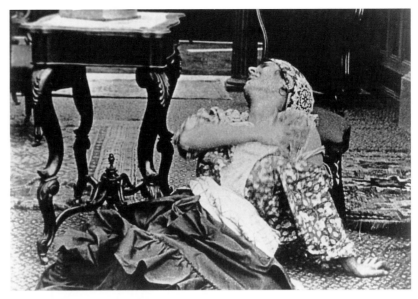

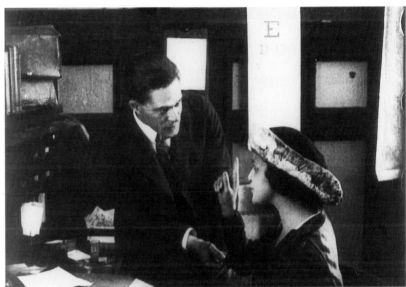

Micheaux's reorientation of stereotypes. *The Birth of a Nation* (1915) versus *Within Our Gates* (1920). Griffith has Lydia Brown (Mary Alden) in a frenzy after a flirtatious interaction with Austin Stoneman. Sylvia Landry (Evelyn Preer) has an intimate conversation with Dr. Vivian (Charles D. Lucas) in his office.

Not only can one trace these various black visual stereotypes into the present in film and theatre, but one can also observe that they have been particularly resilient and widespread in other more static kinds of visual representations, such as advertising, photography, graphic arts, cartoons, and the visual arts generally.[26]

In its treatment of race, the third borrowing from minstrelsy by film was its narrative adaptation of this menu of conventional stereotypes, originating in the antebellum plantation South scenario favored by blackface minstrelsy generally. Although both Griffith (in *Birth*) and Dixon (in *Leopard's Spot* and *The Clansman*) seemed to be engaging in aggressive re-readings of the sentimentalism of *Uncle Tom's Cabin* as well as the levity of *Uncle Remus*, they differ considerably in strategies and emphasis. Griffith's story begins before the Civil War, whereas Dixon's novels both begin at the close of the war and focus entirely on its aftermath in the South. Griffith's approach, which is only marginally concerned with establishing a linear narrative, enables him better to idealize the simplicity and contentment of the antebellum South as represented through the warm friendships between the northern Stoneman girl and boy and the Camerons, who live in South Carolina.

The slaves are shown dancing and singing, the children laughing and frolicking. And the camera lingers upon a close-up of two furry puppies at the elder Cameron's feet, as though this image of innocent nature was a direct reflection of the quality of life in the South under the "peculiar institution."

In contrast with Dixon's meretriciousness, Griffith establishes this paradigm with very few words, or intertitles, but rather with a series of shots at the beginning of the film, many of them close-ups which linger upon the photogenic good looks of the young people.[27] None of these, in and of themselves, are particularly meaningful, but in accumulation they establish the viewers' sense of connection with the characters. Their poetry and whiteness is emphasized in a manner almost as emphatic as, but ten times more effectively than, Dixon's incessant harping on the importance of preserving the purity of white bloodlines.[28]

Back in the North, Senator Stoneman and his daughter Elsie are in attendance at the theatre when Lincoln is shot. Lincoln's murder is Stoneman's license to enforce the radical terms of Reconstruction that he would prefer. This means, quite specifically, elevating the black man to equality with white men because his mind is poisoned by his perverted relationship with his mulatto housekeeper, who is also his mistress.

Historian Patricia Morton points out that "in turn of the century literature, the mulatto woman emerged as a figure as menacing as the stereotypical black male threat to white 'purity.'"[29] Stoneman sends Silas Lynch, his mulatto protégé whom he has educated and trained, to conquer South Carolina, and he follows to Piedmont with his daughter Elsie and his son. The full splendor of a raucous "black" Reconstruction is lavishly displayed: blacks frolicking and snoozing in the fields refusing to work, liquor bottles tipped to their mouths in the hall of the state legislature, flagrantly assaulting white women and marching with placards demanding "interracial marriage." While Lydia, a negligibly sustained character, disappears from the picture, Silas Lynch encourages "Gus," a mean-spirited former slave, to ask the youngest Cameron girl to marry him.

There is an interesting contrast with this idea in an earlier scene when an ordinary white Union soldier stares longingly at Elsie but doesn't dare to speak to her. The inference is that the good man of superior race holds his tongue and settles for unrequited passion whereas the man of inferior race has no control over his passions. Mammy and Uncle Tom are visible as the old couple who attend the Cameron household. Although neither forceful nor convincing (they wear slipshod blackface makeup that robs them of their appeal), they remain virtuous and loyal to their former masters during Reconstruction. Mammy may even be, in fact, a heavyset, cross-dressing male. Their deeds are completely upstaged by the dastardly carrying-on of the bad blacks and the mulattos. It would be hard to imagine either Dixon or Griffith making Uncle Tom or Mammy central characters in a film or a narrative, although this is exactly what occurs in some of Griffith's earlier films, such as *His Trust* and *His Trust Fulfilled*.

The most striking feature of Dixon's stereotype of blacks is his emphasis on the physical ugliness of blacks and the repugnant, animalistic features of their bodies—their flat feet, their yellow eyes, their large noses and mouths, their inability to stand up straight, and so forth. In *The Birth of a Nation,* Griffith seems much less interested in conveying this kind of information. One thing is for sure: in Dixon and Griffith's world, blacks are neither the harmless children of *Uncle Tom's Cabin* nor the shrewd survivors found in *Uncle Remus;* rather, they are dangerous if not kept under control. The coon stereotype is transformed into a mis-

The Birth of a Nation (1915). Gus (Walter Long in blackface) is captured by the Klan.

creant. These blacks are not allowed to appear either entertaining or amusing. The camera shows no empathy for their conviviality and celebration, as was the case in various versions of *Uncle Tom's Cabin*.

The idea of the brutal black buck, which Bogle traces back to *Birth of a Nation,* is represented by Gus, who is played by an actor who is clearly a white man in blackface. Gus goes on a rampage, during which he drives Flora (Mae Marsh) to jump off a cliff in order to escape his proposal of marriage. Needless to say, he is duly punished by the Ku Klux Klan. One might see Gus as a forebear of Richard Wright's *Native Son,* although this is stretching the comparison. But I cannot see how Gus foreshadows anything about Sweetback, Superfly, or Shaft. Indeed, either "brutal buck" is a misnomer or the figure needs to be divided into at least two or three versions which evolved over time. Sweetback, Superfly, and Shaft are all presented as cool, fearless, daring, first-rate fighters, good-looking and sexually proficient. And they never get caught. Gus has none of these qualities. Gus is not a heroic figure, nor can he be made into one, while the protagonists of blaxploitation films are obviously intended to be heroic, whatever one may actually think of their antics.

Within Our Gates (1920), Micheaux's earliest extant film, was so controversial that it was repeatedly banned by state censors. It owed its notoriety to a frank presentation of racial prejudice, discrimination, lynching, and miscegenation.[30] The film's overall plot is highly convoluted, constituting a fascinating and cogent response to the racist accusations of Griffith and Dixon, the paternalism of Harris, and the naiveté of Stowe and subsequent versions of *Uncle Tom's Cabin.* Micheaux moves his narrative to the present, the Jim Crow era, and contrasts black rural existence, which seems to represent the past, with black urban existence and the future of the race. By situating his narrative in the present of the early twentieth century, Micheaux wasn't just curbing his production budget. His emphasis is firmly placed upon what

Within Our Gates (1920). Sylvia Landry, having received an education, keeps her adoptive father's books and so challenges the power of a southern landowner.

blacks are suffering now, not why they came to suffer or even whose fault it is.

Nevertheless, Micheaux focuses on the broken promises of Reconstruction by making a number of specific references to lynching and the lack of enfranchisement, land, and education among poor blacks of the rural South. These are all gripes of Reconstruction vintage and not at all the complaints of Booker T. Washington, who was one of Micheaux's personal heroes. W. E. B. Du Bois, who had already become a prominent black leader of the Niagara Movement and the editor of the NAACP's publication *The Crisis*, expressed concerns similar to Micheaux's. Two primary targets of the NAACP's early efforts were lynching and *The Birth of a Nation*.

Micheaux makes his points through his presentation of a poor rural black family that comes to a school in the South where the protagonist, Sylvia Landry, is a teacher. In a few shots, we are presented with the tableaux of the father, who is a sharecropper, huddled with his two children in the schoolroom. Such shots are inversions of Griffith's tableaux of poor white families victimized by "black" Reconstruction in *Birth*. The intertitles have the sharecropper say, in dialect, that he has no money but will do whatever work is necessary in order to provide his children with an education. Of course, with clients like these, the school is having a lot of financial problems. So Sylvia goes to Boston to seek funding for the school and has the great good fortune to be hit by the car of a very rich white lady philanthropist. After a brief detour under the influence of a rabid racist southern lady, who insists that blacks have no use for education, the philanthropist decides to endow the school with $50,000, ten times the sum she had originally intended.

Micheaux's educated professional people are almost entirely light-skinned, and his poor people are brown-skinned. According to Williamson and other historians, this is not an unrealistic portrayal of the class structure among blacks in the early twentieth century.[31] His villains tend to be light-skinned. Another way to look at it is that many of his actors were light-skinned. Perhaps this too

Within Our Gates (1920). Sylvia, a mulatto, is nearly raped by a sexually licentious white man, who turns out to be her biological father.

was a realistic reflection of the pool of dramatic actors available to him. Later on, in his sound work, in which he almost always included some song-and-dance features and some comedy, Micheaux was able to draw on a wider range of physical types.

Moreover, it seems that Micheaux was intent upon correcting the false impression that Griffith had tried to give that mulattos were malicious and scheming by portraying them with as much dignity and humanity as possible. Also, he makes it clear that this is a serious-minded class of people who are more concerned about education, thrift, virtue, and decency than they are about trivial matters such as caste or social status within the race.

I suggest that there was a debate over how "mulattos" would be viewed and defined. Indeed, the word "mulatto" itself names an antique and obsolete concept. The concept may have died precisely under the weight of the subtle polemics of Micheaux and other artists in the theatre and in film who felt as he did but who are not so well remembered today. Remember, Micheaux himself was not a mulatto. Yet he employed the palette of African-American skin colors with skill and imagination.

In the most important, penultimate sequence of *Within Our Gates,* Micheaux constructs a flashback of Sylvia's life. Sylvia Landry is shown as the adopted daughter of a sharecropper and his wife. The education they have provided her, with great difficulty, enables her to figure out her stepfather's accounts exactly, and she determines that the white landowner owes him money. When he goes to the landowner to claim his money, they get into a fight. In the process, the white landowner is shot, not by the black sharecropper but by a disgruntled white sharecropper who has also been cheated of his money. Of course, the black sharecropper is assumed to be guilty of the murder. He and his wife are brutally beaten and lynched—by a group of poor whites who are kin to the cheated white sharecropper. Within this context, Micheaux is revealing the dynamics of a southern class structure which feeds and confirms racial hierarchies.

Sylvia Landry is nearly raped by the white landowner's brother, but he discovers just in time that she is his daughter. As a consequence, we are told, he pays for her further education although he never lets her know that he is doing so, perhaps out of a sense that the upright Sylvia might refuse help from such as he. In a scene earlier in the film, which may be a mistake due to Micheaux's hasty editing, the white benefactor is shown trying to seduce Sylvia in a parlor in the North, presumably after he has discovered that she is his daughter. Or perhaps Micheaux wanted to have another shot at the hypocrisy of white upper-class morality.

To return to the segment in the South, Micheaux expands imaginatively upon the conventional menu of black stereotypes. Sylvia's sharecropper father is not an Uncle Tom figure, as one might expect; he is young, vigorous, attractive, clean-cut rather than grizzly, honest, heroic, and falsely slain. Her mother—middle-aged, buxom, and brown-skinned—is a potential Mammy, but she is sympathetically and sensitively portrayed. A real woman who exists in the bosom of her family, she loves her spouse and children. There is a lovely shot in which the mother is lying in the camp they have made: in hiding, weeping, her hair undone, she is afraid but resigned to endure whatever happens to her and her family. Subsequent contemporary portrayals of lynchings frequently seem to double the erasure of black humanity.[32] Micheaux, on the other hand, through a few subtle compositional moves, is able to convey the humanity and the normalcy of these lynch victims.

Micheaux's reinterpretation and historicization of the coon figure is also extremely noteworthy. In an earlier scene, the preacher Old Ned openly regrets his buffoonery for the sake of whites. One minute he is grinning and performing to the delight of his white benefactors; the next, as he shuts the door between himself and them, he is scowling for the viewer's benefit

Within Our Gates (1920). Sylvia's sharecropper father, Jasper Landry (William Starks), and mother (Mattie Edwards): characters that expand imaginatively upon the Uncle Tom and Mammy stereotypes.

alone. In a medium close-up, he confides to the camera that he is a serious and wounded man who does not have the courage to reveal his real self to whites for fear that the punishment may be death. It is an extraordinary filmic moment which confronts the material basis of the racism of this period directly.

The second coon figure, Ephrem, is brilliantly foreshadowed by Old Ned. He ends up being lynched, even though he loves white folks and betrays the black sharecropper.

The flashback, which progresses over thirty minutes near the end of *Within Our Gates,* is a film within the film. This mini-film attempts to directly refute the claims of white popular culture with regard to "black" Reconstruction by demonstrating through analogy who is thrifty, God-fearing, and hardworking: working-class black people such as the Landrys as well as middle-class blacks such as the principal of the school and his sister. It also shows who is wicked, violent, and duplicitous: the poor whites who shoot the boss, pin it on the Landrys, and then hunt them down and lynch them as well as the rich whites, who exploit their workers economically, physically, and sexually.

In response to Griffith's and Dixon's assertion that blacks are ignorant and misguided, Micheaux shows them as studious, always reading and desirous of education. In response to Griffith's assertion that black men are undisciplined and have sexually unquenchable appetites for white women, Micheaux counters that most blacks—whether working-class or educated—are hardworking, disciplined, and subject to the sexual whims of an out-of-control class of southern white aristocrats. Even Micheaux's bad blacks are not animals or children; they are cunningly devious kin of Brer Rabbit who mindfully pursue deception for personal gain. Also, each criminal black is countered with a portrayal of a resourceful, ethical antidote, such as the police detective and the doctor whom Sylvia ultimately marries.

Griffith's portrayal of blacks and whites is grounded in the myth of the family romance. The offspring of the slavocracy, the long-lost children of a noble race, are restored, via the vigilantism of

Within Our Gates (1920). Behind closed doors, Uncle Ned curses his own hypocrisy.

Within Our Gates (1920). The coon character Efrem (E.G. Tatum) wants white people to love him, but for that very reason he ends up being lynched by them.

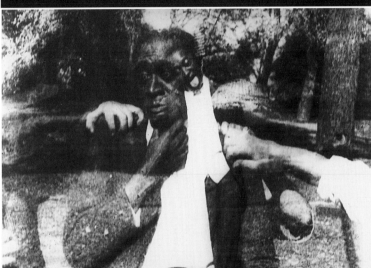

the Ku Klux Klan, to their presumably rightful position as benign leaders of an infantile, inferior, and essentially pleasure-loving race of savages. The appeal of Griffith's utopia to its audience is precisely its almost insane ahistoricism and intoxicating impracticality.

While Micheaux often succumbs formally to the generic requisites of melodrama and the family romance, his use of the genre is often inspired and effective, especially given his financial shortcomings in comparison to Griffith's lavish budgets. Even as he embraces some of the conventional notions of women's roles, his portrayal of blacks is, nevertheless, largely grounded in a realistic sense of the opposition. He was conversant with the realities of history in a way that will perhaps prove as useful and instructive in our own time as it was in his.

6.

Within Our Gates: *From Race Melodrama to Opportunity Narrative*

JANE GAINES

Audiences viewing any one of African-American filmmaker Oscar Micheaux's three surviving silent films are often surprised at how distinctly different they seem from his more well-known sound work, dating from 1931, many more examples of which have been available for exhibition in the decades since his death in 1951. It is, of course, difficult to claim very much from three examples, particularly since of Micheaux's nearly forty feature films, as many as twenty-two can be considered silent. It is perhaps because he *was* so prolific that we have the three films from this period to study at all: *Within Our Gates* (1920), *The Symbol of the Unconquered* (1920, also titled *Wilderness Trail*), and *Body and Soul* (1925).[1]

It is almost too easy to claim that Micheaux's films from the 1920s are so radically unlike his later ones because they belong to a separate aesthetic tradition—that of silent film melodrama. Given the gaps in the director's oeuvre, it is somewhat more difficult to fully support my second contention—that at least some of Micheaux's silent films are engaged, although obliquely, with an earlier American literary tradition, a tradition that at least one contemporary critic has called "race melodrama."[2] Including such works as Mark Twain's *Pudd'nhead Wilson* and Dion Boucicault's *The Octoroon* as well as the important earliest African-American novels, William Wells Brown's *Clotel: or, The President's Daughter* and Frances E. W. Harper's *Iola Leroy,* this tradition takes the question of the visibility or invisibility of blood as part of its narrative investigation.[3]

In Micheaux's silent work, the race melodrama of the nineteenth century appears to have been crossed with new, post-Reconstruction concerns having to do with education, respectability, community, and opportunity. *Within Our Gates,* his one surviving silent film that bears traces of the old race melodrama, is a significantly reconceived narrative that exorcises the blood scenario at the same time that it advances what I call the opportunity scenario. I have argued before that Micheaux's narratives often conceive of Negro opportunity as maliciously thwarted, and one of the main currents in his work has to do with the criticism of those who stand in the way of race progress.[4] What I want to propose here is that while the

Advertisement for *Within Our Gates* (1920), *Chicago Defender*, 17 January 1920, 7.

old black-blood scenario appears to have been superceded by the newer opportunity (or respectability) narrative, at least one concern is carried through: the production of *melos* through the sense of having been *wronged by one's own. Melos,* meaning music in Greek, tells us something as a term about the aspirations of melodrama as a generic form, a form that speaks to the senses as a melody would.[5]

It is also clear, in Micheaux's silent work as well as in the surviving work of other race movie producers in the same period, that the concern with respectability is gradually displacing the appeal to sentiment that marked an earlier race melodrama tradition. But since banishing the blood scenario means that the particular pathos it produced is also missing, we are probably talking about the opportunity narrative as moving quickly beyond the nineteenth-century race melodrama. Here I would also like to venture the hypothesis that the wholesale rejection of *The Birth of a Nation* by race movie pioneers is more than a renunciation of its politics. It is also a rejection of D. W. Griffith's Victorian theatrical sensibility—the sensibility that translates everything into feeling's terms, that uses innocence and victimization to advance its political points, and that is willing to sacrifice the poor and helpless in order to illustrate its moral lesson. And if these race pioneers are rejecting the sentimentality of Griffith's film, they are simultaneously speaking out against the emotionality of Harriet Beecher Stowe's *Uncle Tom's Cabin.* Although it may look like I am setting up an old paradigm— culture produced by African Americans as opposed to that produced by European Americans— in fact, I want to bridge this divide. Here, I want to resist the tendency to separate the (bad) white melodramas from the (good) African-American ones, and this will mean seeing the legacy of the slave narrative—the origin of American race melodrama—as it works its way through to D. W. Griffith.

The Birth of a Nation: The Orchestration of Affect

Even with all of the critical work on the collaboration between author Thomas Dixon and director D. W. Griffith since the release of *The Birth of a Nation* in 1915, it seems to me that none of this work has come close to giving us an adequate explanation of the film's tremendous social impact. More recent criticism by scholars in film studies has, however, brought us closer to the fuller analysis that we need. Manthia Diawara has directed us to rethink spectator positioning in relation to the black audience; Mary Ann Doane has reread the film in terms of feminist film theory, Frantz Fanon, and psychoanalysis. Janet Staiger has revisited a fuller range of reception to the film than ever before made available; Clyde Taylor has reminded us that to talk about aesthetics in the film is often to *not* talk about its politics. Yet with all of the work done on early film melodrama, there has been no attempt to explain the overwhelming impact of this film by the fact that it was the *first* feature film melodrama to be mounted as a spectacular attraction on such a scale.[6]

To suggest something of the hyperbole the film inspired in the year of its release, let me quote C. F. Zittel, reviewer for the Hearst paper *The Evening Journal:*

> "The Birth of a Nation" will thrill you, startle you, make you hold onto your seats. It will make you cry. It will make you angry. It will make you glad. It will make you hate. It will make you love. It is not only worth riding miles to see, but it is worth walking miles to see.[7]

Clearly Zittel is describing sensations produced in audience members that they had never before experienced in a darkened theatre. These are the very feelings that theatrical stage melodrama has been said to elicit—at this pitch and with such fervor. The form that presents the whole world in terms of matters of the heart, that translates the political into the sensual and the intimate, that delivers its moral by means of preposterous exaggeration—this is the form taken over by the motion picture pioneers, among whom Griffith is a leading figure. Early motion picture technology was able to enlarge the already expansive gesture and elongated delivery of popular theatrical melodrama. Scholarship on early film explains how cutting, camera movement, lighting, and photographic detail provided not just punctuation but constituted a rhetoric in and of itself.[8] Perhaps it is because critics have focused so intently on rebutting the film's historical discrepancies that they have never really explained the power of the film but rather assumed it, for to study the potency of this film might seem like studying the obvious. The discourses of historical fact in *The Birth of a Nation* are no match for the rhetoric of melodrama, which carries what James Baldwin called the "Niagara force of an obsession."[9] Melodrama *is* an obsessive form—depending upon overstatement, repetition, and return and upon a stubbornly dualistic version of the world.[10] Furthermore, film melodrama has behind its obsessive force an actual machine that is able to deliver its repetitions all the more insistently.

In addition, especially in the early exhibitions of the film, every screening had behind it the full force of a live orchestra performing the Carl Joseph Briel score—again, a first—the first orchestral performance of this magnitude ever planned for a motion picture opening or organized for a major city tour. In recent criticism, Martin Marks has analyzed this important example of the early composite musical score, that is, a score produced by combining existing music rather than composing original music.[11] However, there are almost no references to the musical accompaniment in the critical outpouring against the film in the period contemporary with its release. A single reference to Thomas Dixon's initial reaction to the film contains a clue to the function of the performed musical score. The author of *The Clansman*, the notorious literary source for *The Birth of a Nation*, recalls this experience: "The last light dimmed, a weird cry came from the abyss below—the first note of the orchestra, a low cry of the anguished South being put to torture."[12] That Dixon hears in the orchestral scoring a human cry seems typical from what we know about his hypersensitivity as well as his personal investment in the plight of the American South.[13] But here I want to use Dixon's anecdote as a key to the psyche in general. That he hears a human cry suggests something about the way such musical tonality reaches the psyche—it has a more direct route than other kinds of signs in combination. It would be at this level of feeling something but not knowing how or why, of being made to feel *for* and *with* a cause, that the silent melodrama epic was experienced. It would be this achieved "orchestration of affect" that was so difficult for the NAACP and other liberal groups to combat in their long opposition to *The Birth of a Nation.*

Of all of the critical responses to *The Birth of a Nation,* Micheaux's is the only one that answers affect with affect. It has been noted that W. E. B. Du Bois, among other black leaders, called upon the African-American community to produce their own films in reply to the Dixon-Griffith epic, and it is not an exaggeration to say that a number of the first black "race movie" producers were acting in part out of a desire to correct the film's misrepresentations.[14] Micheaux, however, seems to have been the only one to have created a tumultuous fiction, a narrative with a mission, *and* a thrilling spectacle. *Within Our Gates* contains a fiery lynching scene that shows what Griffith failed to tell us about the sadism of the white mob. Micheaux's spectacular staging of the night ride of the Ku Klux Klan in *The Symbol of the Unconquered* rivals the infamous equivalent in *The Birth of a Nation* even without the famous orchestral accompaniment of Wagner's "Ride of the Valkyries." Both of Micheaux's scenes out-Griffith Griffith as visual attraction, as spectacular burst and crescendo, particularly in the use of cross-cutting, silhouette, and night-for-night shooting.[15]

I have been arguing that in "race movies," the concern with respectability was displacing sentiment, and this is clear in the type of narrative Micheaux chooses to produce. *Within Our Gates* makes no attempt to answer Griffith point for point, and it is interesting to note that like the much-touted *The Birth of a Race* (1919), Micheaux's film counters Griffith and Dixon's slander with a black middle-class demonstration of learning and deference to the value of hard work.[16] But unlike The Birth of a Race Photoplay Corporation's catalogue of Negro achievements, a kind of encyclopedia of great moments in history, Micheaux's answer is compelling entertainment. Much of the new work on race cinema has dealt with the way these films replaced the pejorative types circulated by *The Birth of a Nation* and the early motion picture versions of *Uncle Tom's Cabin.* Micheaux's work, however, is not only important because it counters negative types, it also offers alternative narratives. What kinds of stories should the new black entertainment tell? How could these stories demonstrate respectability *and* work as gripping narratives *at the same time*? Like Pauline Hopkins and other early African-American narrative writers, Micheaux acknowledged a debt to Harriet Beecher Stowe's novel, even making reference to it in his publicity campaign for *Within Our Gates.* Certainly the debt had to do with the political benefits that had accrued to African Americans from that notorious novel, but for Micheaux, the reference to *Uncle Tom's Cabin* would also have to do with a desire to associate his own story with a great cataclysmic narrative. If we speculate that any wish to emulate Stowe had to do with the promoter's respect for the book's tremendous holding power, then we must also acknowledge that Micheaux the filmmaker was also drawing on the potency of the American race melodrama. In this, Micheaux and Griffith were both dipping into the same well.

AMERICAN RACE MELODRAMA

To explain how it is possible to see continuity rather than a break between Micheaux and Griffith, I want to turn back to the legacy of American melodrama upon which they both drew, a legacy that begins with the slave narrative as it found its first outlet in novel form. It has often been noted that the American race melodrama is centered on the problem of reuniting ruptured families, a response to the way slavery tore Negro families apart and doomed them to a life of endless searching for loved ones. This structure of rupture and reunion has a corollary concern, I would argue, in the revelation that it may be family members and not strangers who are the most heartless; another way of putting this is to say that one has been doubly wronged if one has been *wronged by one's own*. This corollary is distinctly American and exceedingly productive in the way it can be made to fuel feelings of outrage (one of the goals of melodrama) against those who would withhold freedom from others in the "land of the free."

William Wells Brown's *Clotel,* a virtual catalogue of crimes against the mulatto, begins with the literal "selling of one's own," the auctioning of Thomas Jefferson's daughter on the slave block. The paradigm works its way through Frances E. W. Harper's *Iola Leroy,* in which the relatives of a plantation owner sell his entire family after his death, and takes a different turn in *Uncle Tom's Cabin.* Here the race melodrama narrative returns to its major premise— the premise that slavery produces the division of families (and refuses as well to recognize the sacred Christian institution of marriage). Although missing the scandal of "selling one's own," Stowe's narrative substitutes (for its predominantly white female readers), the scandal of treating "one like us" as a hunted criminal—for it is well known that this fiction made its political appeal to whites through the use of the fair mulatta who was white in every other way. And it is here that I want to dwell on the significance of the light-skinned Eliza's escape to freedom on the ice-covered river, bloodhounds and slave-catchers at her heels.

The enslaved heroine's ordeal at the edge of the American river—Clotel on the bridge over the Potomac, Eliza at the banks of the Ohio—has become a staple in late nineteenth and early twentieth-century American theatrical melodrama. Taking over the situation in the popular film version of *Way Down East* (1920), D. W. Griffith elaborated the mise-en-scène of the icy river, making much of the violence of the storm because his white heroine no longer has a compelling reason to flee onto the ice. Driven out into the storm by the heartless New England patriarch, Anna Moore (Lillian Gish) is doomed to a frozen death by an icy cold white society, a society as treacherous as the turbulent river beneath the ice flow, itself a metaphor for the sharp-edgedness of cinematic cutting. Although she herself is as white as the ice, Anna Moore is like Clotel and Eliza in one important way—she is not pure. But Anna's impurity stems not from racial mixture; rather, she is impure because she bore an illegitimate child.

Somewhere in the consciousness of white culture, black blood and illegitimate pregnancy have been conflated and confused, partly because of the unsanctioned union that they have in common; but beyond this, the mysteries of sexual intercourse and the consequent issue from women's bodies are hopelessly mixed up and lost in a swirl. What prevails is the mythology of uncleanness. In 1915, Griffith intervenes to save Lillian Gish from a forced marriage to a mulatto and in 1920 he defends her innocence after a false marriage that leaves her pregnant. What can the two predicaments have in common? Griffith is working with some of melodrama's favorite material—the irrevocable deed and the permanent stain. Melodramatic tension is wound around a temporal imperative and the threat of irreversability, for in melodrama the heroine so often confronts an irrevocable loss or an unbending law. It was inevitable that the historical dilemma produced in the United States by the absurdities of slave law would find its expression in melodrama, the literary form that so relishes, in Robert Heilman's words, the completely "insoluble situation."[17]

Race melodrama written by African Americans has never returned to Clotel's plight and tragic suicide at the edge of the Potomac. (And why would they need to when countless theatrical companies performed, and at least three film companies shot, versions of *Uncle Tom's Cabin*?)[18] Literary melodrama written by African Americans since the turn of the century turned to another paradigm of irrevocability, a threat of loss having less to do with the heroine's virtue than with the hero's talent. Pervading Charles Chesnutt's *The Marrow of Tradition* is the sorrow that two sisters can never be reconciled because one is black and the other white.[19] But a parallel lament is developed alongside the narrative about a family divided by race. White society cannot recognize the black doctor's talents as a professional—until circumstances force the white sister to seek his help for her sick child. Mingled with melodrama's traditional lament for a dead child (the son of the doctor and the black sister) is a new lament about the talented black professional still unreconciled with his culture, his rightful family.

Chesnutt's narrative plays a crucial role in the transition from the hidden secret of the black-blood story to the respectability narrative, the direct progenitor of the kind of uplift story Micheaux would write. It would also come from T. S. Stribling, whose novel *Birthright* (1922) Micheaux would adapt for film in 1924 and again in 1938.[20] For in Chesnutt's classically efficient narrative construction, the subplot about the secret sister joins up with the subplot about the doctor's fight to be accepted as a competent professional. Perhaps this later branch of race melodrama, the respectability narrative, also draws inspiration from Booker T. Washington's *Up from Slavery* (1901). Although one does not necessarily think of Washington's autobiography as an example of the melodrama genre, one could say that the pattern of setbacks and triumphs that structure the narrative of his life is an "opportunity" for melodrama.[21] Washington's secretary Emmett J. Scott, just before Washington's death, was negotiating with white film producers who were interested in a dramatization of *Up from Slavery* on the basis that it might provide the needed counter to *The Birth of a Nation*.[22] What Micheaux takes from the Washington biography and works into his novels as well as his film productions is this chasm between what the talented Negro has achieved and what white society believes he is capable of achieving. Perhaps this is where the professional and entrepreneurial point of view eclipses the earlier hidden-blood scenario, where the drama of professional loss replaces that of familial loss. And most important of all, these melodramas are no longer addressed to the sympathetic white lady. Their appeal is to the African-American aspiring classes.

FLASHBACK AND INTERTITLE

From what we know of race movies in the silent era, they are busy moving away from the sentimentality of the nineteenth-century novels exemplified by *Clotel* and *Iola Leroy*. Here, *The Marrow of Tradition* appears as the transitional work, looking backward to heart-wrenching sentiment and forward to opportunity through achievement. The rejection of *The Birth of a Nation* by the race movie pioneers is not only a rejection of its politics but a refusal of Griffith's Victorian sensibility, that same sensibility responsible for *Uncle Tom's Cabin* (but also for the nineteenth-century African-American classics to which I have referred). Paramount in the production of the sentimental effect is the encouragement of pity in the viewer or reader, pity produced by the enactment of situations of helplessness and victimization, often in Victorian social melodrama a plea to the viewer or reader (in a more powerful position) to do something to help, to "reach out" or to "give." The spectator thus importuned is positioned as having the resources to give or as having a social position of some kind. One indication of the shift from the white audiences of nineteenth-century fiction to the primarily black audiences of race movies is the total absence of those pitiable figures whose presence signifies the need to "give." When there is a victim in the race movie (Louise in *The Scar of Shame* [1929] and Joe Morgan's young daughter in *Ten Nights in a Barroom* [1926]), the lesson of the victim has to do with the need for community unity or for personal reformation.

Micheaux, perhaps more than any other early race movie filmmaker, had ways of averting or modifying the victimization syndrome, the most important of which was the use of the flashback as a distancing device, the very device that Griffith often used to sentimentalize by bracketing the reverie or the recollection of a lost past. In *Within Our Gates,* the heroine Sylvia's lowest moments (the lynching of her foster parents and her near rape) occur in a protected flashback. *Body and Soul,* discussed in more detail by Charles Musser in this volume, contains Micheaux's most innovative flashback. All of the traumatic events in Martha Jane's life (the theft of her life's savings, the disappearance of her daughter, and the daughter's pitiful death when the mother discovers her in Atlanta), are safely portrayed in a "dream" flashback. Cordoned off from the film's present, which ends with the daughter's return from her honeymoon to the middle-class home provided by her prosperous inventor husband, the flashback separates the worst fears of the black community from their dream life—the comfortable suburban living room.[23]

Sylvia Landry (Evelyn Preer) is befriended by Mrs. Elena Warwick (Mrs. Evelyn), a wealthy Boston matron.

Somewhat similarly, Richard D. Maurice's *Eleven P.M.* uses the flashback device, here motivated by a young reporter's dream, to present and simultaneously deny a story of crime and betrayal. Maurice's Sundaisy and his wife, robbed by the ungrateful boy he raised who has turned into a criminal, are reduced to destitution. The criminal steals their light-skinned daughter, forcing her into a life of sexual slavery as a nightclub performer; the light-skinned wife finally dies; and Sundaisy is killed when he tries to rescue his daughter. But the pathos is cancelled when the Sundaisy character is reincarnated as a dog. In a scene that suggests that he is not really dead (the dog image superimposed over his body), Sundaisy is made to come alive, although as another creature. Since the daughter is played by the same actress as the mother, we also have the sense that the mother has come alive again, and perhaps it is this double reincarnation that gives this film its surreal quality.

As a strategy, sentimentality was gradually being replaced by respectability as the old race melodrama gave way to stories featuring characters with professions—teachers, doctors, and even aviators, as in *The Flying Ace* (1926), discussed elsewhere in this volume by Phyllis Klotman. And this concern about respectability may hold the key to one of the questions asked most frequently by contemporary viewers of *Within Our Gates.* The question pertains to the status of the relationship between the heroine's real parents, and it arises at one crucial point in the flashback that explains the mystery of her past. To summarize this "elevation of the race" narrative, it is the story of Sylvia Landry (Evelyn Preer), a young schoolteacher who travels back and forth between the North and the South in an attempt to raise money for the Negro school where she teaches. Sylvia first travels to Boston to find the money that can help to keep the school from closing. In the city, she is rescued by two people who change the course of her life. First, she is rescued by Dr. Vivian, to whom she later becomes engaged, when her purse is stolen by a street thief. Second, she is hit by a car after saving a young boy in its path, but is rescued and befriended by Mrs. Warwick, the wealthy Boston matron who is a passenger. Although the Boston suffragette is nearly dissuaded from helping Sylvia's cause by Mrs. Stratton, a southerner who thinks that blacks should not be educated, Mrs. Warwick finally decides to give the school $50,000.[24] Sylvia's return to the South with money for the school doesn't bring the film to an end, because another obstacle stands in the way of her happiness. To save her reputation, she is forced to leave the school and return to Boston, where she again meets Dr. Vivian. It is the early part of Sylvia's life that appears in flashback at the end of the film, and immediately after the flashback the film concludes with an epilogue that suggests that Sylvia and Dr. Vivian are to be married.

We learn from the flashback that Sylvia lives with her brother and foster parents, who are sharecroppers. When she helps Jasper Landry, her foster father, with his accounts and he

Jasper Landry (William Starks), Sylvia's foster father, tries to settle his accounts with tyrannical landowner Philip Girdlestone (Ralph Johnson).

tries to settle with the tyrannical landowner Philip Girdlestone, an argument ensues. In the middle of the argument, an angry white man, also cheated by the landowner, shoots him through the window. Because Girdlestone's servant Ephrem, spying on them from another window, sees the Girdlestone shot but doesn't see the real killer, Landry is blamed. To return to the crucial point in the flashback, at the climactic moment, Sylvia is accosted by an older white-haired man who we later learn is her own father. Armand Girdlestone is searching for those who he believes are responsible for killing his brother, Philip, and as a member of the Landry family, Sylvia herself is suspect. The film cuts from the lynchers starting a fire to Sylvia, who is returning to the family's home for provisions, unaware that her foster parents have been caught.

I have already discussed the cutting pattern in the scene that alternates between Armand's attempt to corner Sylvia and the hanging of her foster parents. It is as she is gathering supplies for her family that she is discovered and accosted. In the act of ripping Sylvia's dress, Girdlestone discovers a telling birthmark on her breast. The close-up shot of the scar and the reverse-angle shot of Girdlestone's shocked reaction to seeing it tell us that it has deep significance for him: the mark is proof that he is assaulting his own daughter. In the English-language translation of the Spanish-language text of the next intertitle (itself a translation of an earlier English original), the awkward phraseology calls attention to the question of Sylvia's parentage: "A scar that she had on her chest saved her dishonor because on discovering it Girdlestone knew that Sylvia was his daughter which he had in legitimate marriage with a woman of her race and later adopted by the Landrys."

The assault scene, crosscut as it is with the lynching scene, calls up associations with the whole tumultuous history of sexual relations between blacks and whites in the American South—from the imagined crimes of black men against white women of the Reconstruction era to the real and originary sexual attacks of the plantation masters on slave women. I have already argued that the scene cries out against the master's sexual encounters with his own slave women, even representing the incestuousness of every one of those acts. It is as though Micheaux was recapitulating this history in the scene and foregrounding the sexual secrets left out in *The Birth of a Nation*. For never once does that film intimate that the very mulatto class it wants to discredit is the product of the indiscretion of the men of the planter class. I have also argued elsewhere that Micheaux has it both ways in this scene, since interracial rape is "enacted as well as averted."[25] The close-up that shows Girdlestone's hand on Sylvia's breast, emphasized as it is by the technical function of the shot as an insert, stands out as a shocking testimony of guilt. The frame, discovered in the film and re-emphasized here as a frame enlargement, presents irrefutable evidence that Sylvia is sexually assaulted. As a pair, the shots suggest the temporal sequence of events, so that we see his hand on her breast in one shot and going to his head in a gesture of amazement in the following shot, a shot order that tells us that he was horrified to find that the woman who he *had* molested is actually his daughter. But there is also evidence here that the father stops short—the scene cuts to the film's present just after Girdlestone rips Sylvia's bodice. This reading of the scene that suggests that rape is averted has the advantage of emphasizing Sylvia's purity, but politically it would be as important to represent Sylvia as *having been raped* as it would be to represent her as innocent and *not raped,* especially in the light of new black feminist arguments that since African-American women were historically characterized as sexually willing it was difficult to argue that they had ever been raped or sexually assaulted.[26] Conveniently, it was impossible to rape a black woman. This new black feminist work thus urges us to consider black women's respectability, a consideration that inevitably leads us to the question of Silvia's mother and the nature of the interracial relationship between her mother and father.

An angry white man who was also cheated by Philip Girdlestone shoots him through the window.

Another narrative of Sylvia's origins is offered in the evidence of contemporary reviews. The *Chicago Defender,* reviewing *Within Our Gates* just after its Chicago premiere in January 1920, describes a film dramatically different from the one that has survived. The reviewer relates: "You see the white man who claims the black child laid at his doorstep by the mother, because it is his own and he later gives the mother some money."[27] Contradicting the "legitimate marriage" story of the intertitles, this version confirms the "concubinage" to which Micheaux refers in his promotion for the film and in addition produces Sylvia not as legitimate but as illegitimate. It is tempting to look to this review as providing the "real" story, especially since the story of a white male taking sexual advantage of a poor black woman is confirmed a thousand times over in the historical record. But there is no "real" story, no final version, particularly with Micheaux, who was so adept at writing the same story a multitude of ways, beginning with the story of his own life, as Jayna Brown tells us in her study of his autobiographical novels. The existing film insists that we *interpret* what we see on the screen, and contemporary viewers want to make sense of these images in relation to the curious intertitle: "The scar that she had on her chest saved her dishonor because on discovering it Girdlestone knew that Sylvia was his daughter which he had in legitimate marriage with a woman of her race and later adopted by the Landrys." Compared with the narrative fragment provided by the reviewer for the *Defender,* the existing film raises a far more interesting question of interpretation since we are faced with the evidence of the image on screen as opposed to the evidence of the intertitles. Let us consider, then, quite strictly, only the film before us. In that film, the one set of signs (the iconic) tells us that there are a wealth of interconnected relationships, and the other (the linguistic) tells us more narrowly that there is a father and a daughter and that there was at one time a "legitimate marriage." The relatively dense semiosis of the image of the white-skinned, white-haired man chasing the light-brown-skinned, black-haired young woman is portrayed in extreme contrast to the thin meaning of the linguistic signs of the intertitle that tell a story of a respectable father who married the mother of his child, a story that would seem to completely contradict this image of irresponsible lust that we see on the screen. Would the man who would so brutally ravish a helpless black woman take the trouble to marry another? It is the image that finally calls up the historical legacies and reenacts so many scenarios simultaneously, and it is the image that *can* and *does* carry the weight, the extra freight, of signification.

In contrast, the linguistic signs, ghostly white letters stenciled through blackness, seem fragile. Although they have relatively less semiotic density, they nevertheless assert themselves with an irrefutable finality. Half book page and half theatrical title card, they give themselves

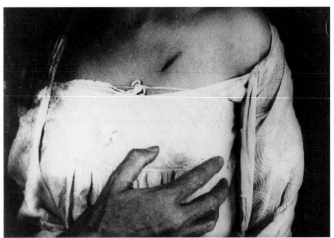

Sylvia is assaulted by Girdlestone's brother, Armand (Grant Gorman). Close-up shot: "The scar on her chest."

to the viewer as print to be read—they ask to be attended to as literary fragments. In addition to the Barthesian limitation of meaning performed by the linguistic sign in proximity to the iconic, motion picture intertitles have a special function.[28] In order to limit the meaning of the action, they must also interrupt the action, creating stoppage at timed intervals. The intertitle is also a hearkening back to the magic light-show origins of the motion picture, a momentary lapse into its prehistory, figured by the projection lamp that shines through the lettering and the absolute stillness of the title cards. Some critics over the years have argued that the speechlessness of the silent film should not be seen as a deficit.[29] At times, this argument sounds like an elitist nostalgia for aesthetic purity, at other times, a cranky suspicion of a newly arrived technology (in this case, sound on film). But perhaps the most important development to come out of these arguments is the conviction that silent film should not be seen as missing something. Rather than seeing silence as a deficit, this point of view understands the ingenious compensations of the silent film. Consider, for instance, the question of sound supplementation. If the audio is not on the track, where is it? Film theorists find it in a range of different places. All of the important work on musical scoring for the silent film locates the sound in the orchestra pit or finds it coming from the honky-tonk piano. In addition, however, the silent film image itself is full of sound substitutes. Mary Ann Doane, for instance, has theorized the way missing speech is "spread over the entire body," assigning to the gestural continuum the burden of the conveyance of meaning.[30] The eloquence missing in the spoken word is thus given to the body in silent cinema. Perhaps in the shimmering quality of silent cinema, then, we are seeing the image that exudes speech—all of which is to say once again that the silent image was never truly silent and that it never seems exactly mute.

For all of the eloquence of the silent image, however, we are still perplexed with its titles, which not only come from a mysterious non-diegetic nether-space (*not* belonging to the fiction within which we are immersed), but which also carry an authority that has the power to overrule the image, to take its apparent meaning in another direction. Flat and impassive, the intertitle interjects its lines of prose right at the point of ambiguity. We wait for the intertitle like we wait for a stop sign. We wait, just an instant, before agreeing to its meaning in the seconds between image frames, and then we go ahead to the next frame. It is, then, a kind of tyranny of the intertitle that makes spectators into reader-viewers who are concerned about taking it "at its word." And it is this tyranny that makes it necessary to deal with the phrase "legitimate

Reaction shot—Armand.

A scar on her chest saved her because, once it was revealed, Gridlestone knew that Sylvia was his daughter—his legitimate daughter from marriage to a woman of her race— who was later adopted by the Landrys.

The concluding intertitle of the flashback. A translation of the Spanish-language intertitle, from the Library of Congress restoration of *Within Our Gates*.

marriage with a woman of her race." Less interesting are the considerations that lead us to speculation about the way the Spanish titles might have been rewritten from the English or even about the way Micheaux wrote them to get around white censorship boards. More compelling is the approach that sees the reference to "legitimate marriage" as part of a development in African-American history and as a convention in nineteenth-century African-American fiction.

It is well known that part of the motivation for writing these novels in the tradition of sentimental women's fiction was to make the case that slave laws did not recognize marriage, the sacred foundation of Christian society. Perhaps it is significant that the first African-American novel, *Clotel: or, The President's Daughter,* takes the impossibility of marriage between the exquisite mulatta and the sons of the white master class as its central problematic. Its structure examines every facet of and variation on the consequences of the predicaments produced by a culture that espoused one thing and practiced another, showing up the contradictions between wife and slave and the absurdity of legally owning one's wife. The 1853 novel begins with the premise that the refined mulatta is white in every way but in the view of the law. It follows from this premise that the inability of the society to protect the sacred union will have its consequences in a string of tragedies.

What I want to advance is not a theory of influence but rather a theory of oppositionality, an approach that will find the exception to the absurd law and the prevailing code in either the imagination or in historical actuality. Reading Catterall's *Judicial Cases* from these years, one is struck by those cases that offer up historical counters to the rule that masters generally disowned their slave mistresses as well as the children they fathered.[31] The case-law record provides examples that echo the narrative of *Iola Leroy,* in which it is the family of Iola's planter father who sells her along with her mother and brother when the planter dies. Consider the analogous case of Elijah Willis. When Willis died and left property to his slaves, his will was contested by his family. Yet another man willed money to his slave, or "adopted wife." Records indicate that another slave owner, a Louisianian, took his female slave as well as their children first to Ohio and afterward to Texas and that they lived as man and wife.[32] History records even more dramatic enactments of opposition to the taboo against interracial unions, such as the story of the white daughter of a North Carolina slave owner who ran away with her father's black coachman. When apprehended and tried, she reportedly drank her lover's blood so that she could claim that she was of "mixed blood."[33]

Any mix of history, literature, and legend could and did supply these counter-examples to the African-American community, perhaps even through the Reconstruction period, when the sociological data shows interracial unions on the decline.[34] So Micheaux's fiction (contained in a single title card), a fiction about the marriage of a plantation owner's son to a woman of African descent that ostensibly took place around the turn of the century or before, just after Reconstruction, is important in the way it offers an alternative story. And as an alternative, it achieves some important political ground. First, the story of a perhaps-secret marriage is the antithesis of the prevailing mythology about illicit interracial sexuality, and as an added bonus, the marriage makes Sylvia legitimate. Second, if the marriage story is a way around censorship boards intent upon legislating morality, the assertion that Sylvia's parents were married contains an interesting irony in that as morality is upheld, interracial marriage is sanctioned.

Of course, scholars will continue to speculate about the origin of and the intent behind the curious intertitle: "The scar that she had on her chest saved her dishonor because on discovering it Girdlestone knew that Sylvia was his daughter which he had in legitimate marriage with a woman of her race and later adopted by the Landrys." Does it matter that few, if any, historical situations can be found to constitute a basis for this fiction? Since when has imaginative fiction ever required any kind of basis in historical circumstances, even when dressed up in a realist mode and when purporting to retell events from an historical past?

WRONGED BY ONE'S OWN

Micheaux pitches his stories halfway between a lament about professional loss and a complaint about those who hinder their own people. Never does he lay the blame directly at the feet of white society. Instead, Micheaux critiques the larger society indirectly; the criticism of white society is reflected off the blacks who emulate and play up to whites, as seen in the characterizations of Ephrem and Old Ned in *Within Our Gates* and Driscoll in Micheaux's *The Symbol of the Unconquered* (1920). White society is criticized, albeit in a muted way, through the scoundrels and crooks it has produced, and by the fact that Micheaux's heroes and heroines are wronged by their own people. The characters in Micheaux are "hell-bent" on causing trouble for one another, but not because they are inherently evil. Often, the troublemakers are strangely under the influence of white people. (Driscoll in *The Symbol of the Unconquered* rides with the Ku Klux Klan; Old Ned in *Within Our Gates* schemes with whites against blacks, and the adopted Naomi in Micheaux's 1938 film, *God's Step Children,* appears to have been bedeviled by her white half.)

Perhaps the turn-of-the-century African-American novel that epitomizes the way white society works through members of the black society in such a way that they betray their own is Charles Chesnutt's *The House Behind the Cedars.* Here, Chesnutt's lament has to do not with the waste of talent but about the wrong done to one's own in the climb to the top. A young black professional passing for white introduces his sister to a wealthy young white man from a promising family. When her white suitor discovers her heritage and rebukes her, she is fatally destroyed. In the narrative rewritten by Micheaux in his 1924 film by the same name, both the brother and the mother press the marriage on the light-skinned sister, who prefers a man "of her own race." What is particularly Micheauxesque about this is the turnabout: the Negro couple rebukes the conniving relatives who would marry the mulatta to a white man rather than a black one.

In one form or another, a number of examples of the surviving race cinema from the silent era contain this betrayal structure, a variation on one of the most deeply embedded patterns in the melodrama form: familial strife. Those who should be the nearest and dearest are those from whom we have the most to fear and who harm us the most. The "haven in the heartless world" is the most dangerous place on earth. Newly married, the light-skinned Louise in *The Scar of Shame* (1929) is kidnapped by her own father and an accomplice, who force her into high-class prostitution in their nightclub. Scarred for life in the gun battle that ensues during the attempt to kidnap her, the wronged and slighted heroine sends her own husband to prison—a waste of his talent as a pianist.[35] Remarkably, the family melodrama is extrapolated to the African-American community, the film openly blaming that community for the class strife that produced Louise's tragedy. The black community is a torn and riven family when it should be whole. In *Ten Nights in a Barroom* (1926), another film featuring the Colored Players Film Corporation, the Charles Gilpin character holds his former partner, the proprietor of the local tavern, responsible for his dissipation and consequent ruin. One might ask why this particular film, a version of a popular play performed primarily with a white cast to a white audience, should seem to speak to the particular attitude of the black community toward the backsliders among them who would "drag down the race." In this particular case, much of the undercurrent of criticism for what the black race has "done to itself" is produced by Gilpin's performance.

This criticism is in the elongation of Gilpin's character's suffering and the prolongation of the actor's expressivity, produced by a much more intricately inflected set of gestures that contrasts with the broad, typed gestures used by the character actors who play the crooks and barflies. Gilpin is fluid where the backdrop of hinderers are tightly constrained by their function. To some degree, this is nothing more than the use of "flat" characters to set off a fully realized, "round" protagonist, in traditional literary terminology. And here it may be important to mention the old attack on stereotypes in black cinema, exemplified by Donald Bogle's popular *Toms, Coons, Mulattoes, Mammies, and Bucks,* as critiqued in this volume by Michele Wallace.[36] Here is another place where we can move on from what Wallace identifies as a critical dead end. Typification, she says, can be both necessary and complex. In the case of the horde of cheats, scoundrels, pimps, crooks, murderers, card sharks, corrupt officials, and sluts that appear in the silent "race" cinema we are considering here, all have a significant function. And often that function is to hold back the upright character who is in danger of yielding to temptation, a character upon whom the hopes of others depend. Like the one-function characters E. M. Forster described in Dickens, their importance lies in their very reliability, predictability, and familiarity.[37] They are given but one thing to do: the crook steals, the shark cheats, and the slut lies, and the success of the good character actor in silent cinema was often the relish with which such a one-note part was played for every one of its familiar traits, often emphasized in single shots or cutaways. The character Gilpin plays, in contrast, is unfamiliar in its unpredictable multi-functionality. We really do not know if this character (who seems the epitome of physical and psychic instability, swaying and reeling at the bar), can be rehabilitated. It is as though the future of the entire race is hanging upon his fragile constitution and weak will.

Micheaux's contribution to this thematic of the hero misunderstood and wronged by his people is significant. Rewritten several times as his biography, as Jayna Brown tells us in her article, it is the story of a man who sees how to better himself as well as his race and, pulling himself up as others are dragging him down, creates what might be called an especially Micheauxesque tension. Again and again, Micheaux tells the story of how he slaved alone on the South Dakota plains, working tirelessly to stake out his claim, only to be robbed of it by his father-in-law, whose vision for his people was too narrow. Perhaps the closest silent screen exemplification of the lone black pioneer figure is Van Allen in *The Symbol of the Unconquered,* against whom Driscoll (Lawrence Chenault), one treacherous black passing for white, schemes and aids the whites who attempt to frighten Van Allen off from his valuable land. Sylvia Landry in *Within Our Gates* is similarly held back by the jealousy of her cousin Alma and Alma's brother Larry, who finally attempts to blackmail Sylvia, forcing her to leave her teaching position at the Piney Woods School. Driscoll physically abuses his own darker-skinned mother when she interrupts his courting of a white woman in *The Symbol of the Unconquered.* Reverend Jenkins in *Body and Soul* not only steals from his own collection plate but robs the hardworking mother of her savings and rapes her daughter. In Micheaux's world, the crimes committed against one's own people explain the failure of those people to rise higher and go further. It is, however, often the case that it is the educated, motivated, entrepreneurial types that climb. And yet here "climb" is the wrong word, for it has historically referred to class ascent. The black uplift characters are more accurately asserting that they belong *where they are.* That is, they are justifiably entitled to the positions within which they are shown. In this, the black uplift melodrama stands in marked contrast to the white backstage musicals or the gangster genre, where the characters are constantly trying to move up and out of their class by golddigging or bootlegging, through organized crime or sexual scheming.

One reason it makes sense to see these uplift narratives as structural melodramas is that they are so righteously persistent, particularly in Micheaux's hands. Again and again, the idealized race hero or heroine is wronged and the deep injustice threatens some vital principle of democracy as well as the existence of the black community. Something in the personal injustice is structurally similar to the deep injustice of the social crimes committed against the American Negro—historically deprived of the right to vote, the right to marry, and the right to own property. Micheaux dramatizes the consistency and the severity of the injustice, making it visible. Melodrama is the ideal form for the exposure of systematic unfairness, relishing the repetitions of the wrong, elongating the revelation of the injustice, and triumphantly rectifying matters in favor of the wronged. Motion picture melodrama perfects the reiterative mode by means of a technological enhancement of the repeat and return action of the narrative. Melodrama in African-American fiction, then, was not abandoned—only divorced from the sentimental strain with which it had come to be so closely associated for so long. One can only imagine Micheaux's delight at discovering the capabilities of the machine that intensified the moral illustrations so fundamental to the opportunity narrative.

The four pictures given the public up to date and within a period of
two years—*The Homesteader,* a stirring story of pioneer life in the
great West country; *Within Our Gates,* the action of which centers
about the Southland; *The Brute,* a dramatization of the best and the
worst in Negro life; and *The Symbol of the Unconquered,* the action
of which deals rather with condition than locale—are all powerful sermons visualizing the struggle of Dark America for a place in the sun.
—Georgia Huston Jones, unidentified magazine (Spring 1921)

7.

Oscar Micheaux's The Symbol of the Unconquered: *Text and Context*

Moving pictures have become one of the greatest vitalizing forces in
race adjustment, and we are just beginning.
—Oscar Micheaux, *The Competitor*, January–February 1921

PEARL BOWSER

AND

LOUISE SPENCE

Within two and a half years after founding the Micheaux Film Corporation, Oscar
Micheaux had produced four features, films which critic Georgia Huston Jones called "pow-
erful sermons visualizing the struggle of Dark America for a place in the sun."[1] *The Homesteader* (released in 1919), *Within Our Gates* (1920), *The Brute* (1920), and *The Symbol of the
Unconquered* (1920), according to Jones, showed "the tragedy of the Negro being enacted on
American soil and voiced the heart cry of millions in a world where the common heritage
of trials and obstacles and disappointments are intensified by the evil shadow of prejudice."
In a career that spanned thirty years, Micheaux made close to forty films, with approximately
half of his total output produced in the first decade (1918–1929). These silent films were tools
to express his personal view of the African-American experience. By addressing such contemporary social issues as concubinage, rape, lynching, peonage, and miscegenation in his
pictures, he created a textured and layered response to the social crises that circumscribed
African-American life. Oscar Micheaux's silent films and early novels were acts of recollection and imagination, creations and re-creations shaped by his personal experience and the
desire to construct an image of himself for his audience. Suspended between autobiography
and commerce, memory and dreams, his stories, though often personal, were not unique;
they were woven with threads of commonalty and communality. He spoke from his living
history and from the specific realities of his time; he referred to what lay beneath or beyond
the particular.

At the core of each of these early works is Micheaux's call for Race solidarity and self-
reliance. *The Homesteader* depicted the romance between a pioneering Negro farmer and his
white neighbor, one left unfulfilled due to the homesteader's own sense of racial solidarity.
Within Our Gates centered around fund-raising for a Black school.[2] The film also portrayed
a white man's attempt to rape a young Black woman and stripped away the anonymity of a

KU KLUX KLAN REACH PHILADELPHIA

See the inner workings of the "INVISIBLE EMPIRE," the mid-night dash of the "WHITE RIDERS" and their annihilation in the Greatest Negro Photoplay ever produced

DUNBAR ✦ THEATRE

BROAD AND LOMBARD

One Week Only Commencing Monday, Jan. 3

SPECIAL---This Picture will not be shown at the ROYAL THEATRE as previous Micheaux Productions have been

3 Shows Daily, 2:30 p. m. 7 and 9 p. m.

E. C. BROWN, . . President and General Manager

The Man who wrote, directed and produced "The Homesteader," "Within Our Gates" and "The Brute,"

OSCAR MICHEAUX

Presents

"THE SYMBOL OF THE UNCONQUERED"

A Story of The Ku Klux Klan

with Lawrence Chenault, Iris Hall, E. G. Tatum, Walker Thompson, Lee Whipper, Jim Burris and many others

Eight Tremendous Reels, Filled with Gripping action, love, intrigue and suspense. See the MURDEROUS NIGHT RIDE of the INSIDIOUS KU KLUX KLAN in the effort to drive a Black Boy off of Valuable Oil Lands and the wonderful heroism of a brave girl to save him!

One of the most thrilling and sensational Photo Plays ever Produced. A Micheaux Picture.

Exclusive Philadelphia Showing : : : : : **High Class Vaudeville Acts**

PRICES: : :

MATINEE . 40c., Box Seats 75c.
NIGHT 30c., 40c., 60c., Box Seats $1.00

Advertisement for *The Symbol of the Unconquered* (1920), *Philadelphia Tribune,* 1 January 1921, 4.

lynch mob, exposing its members as ordinary townsfolk: men, women, and even children who participate in hunting down and hanging a Black family. *The Brute* condemned racketeering and the abuse of women. And in *The Symbol of the Unconquered,* Micheaux not only exposed the economic underpinnings of the hooded night riders, the Ku Klux Klan on the frontier, but he also addressed important discourses on racial identity and preference from within the Black community. The color line was both the subtext and the context of this recently recovered film.[3]

 The Symbol of the Unconquered dramatized what W. E. B. Du Bois labeled "life within the veil," the shadowy yet substantial line that separated whites from people of African descent.[4] The film called attention to issues of color and racial identity. In race-conscious America, a person of mixed race defiled the racial classifications that organized racial relations. Elaborate segregationist sanctions and the legal and social classification of persons with known Black ancestry attempted to control race as well as define the social and political boundaries of African Americans. One cornerstone of white supremacist ideology was a fear of rampant Black sexuality. The image of the Black man as a savage brute, along with the equally fallible myth of the sanctity of white womanhood, were powerful weapons used by white men to try to reassert control over Black labor in the post-slavery era. Consensual relations between Black men and white women, inadmissible and unspeakable, were perceived as rape. Black women, viewed as wanton seductresses, were unprotected by the law from white men's aggressions. Marriage between the races was illegal in many states. Lynching upheld this repressive regime, often punishing Black men who attempted to defend Black women. The story of *The Symbol of the Unconquered* alludes to the complex politics of interracial sex and the moral dilemma it imposed on individuals of both races. It is the experiences of the children of these unions and the risk that they might act out their self-hate by attacking other Blacks that are of special concern in Micheaux's tale of romance and adventure.

As *The Symbol of the Unconquered* premiered in December 1920, *The Competitor* magazine remarked that Oscar Micheaux's film made a significant thrust at the "more than 500,000 people" in America who were "passing for white."[5] The larger context of race in America is what propels the film's narrative and complicates an otherwise simple and ordinary melodrama situated on the developing frontier of the Great Northwest, where the filmmaker spent nine years as a homesteader. Likewise, Micheaux's first novel, *The Conquest: The Story of a Negro Pioneer,* written "by the Pioneer" (1913), based on the author's own frontier experiences in Gregory County, South Dakota, cites incidences of miscegenation and hidden racial identity. The book also explores certain personal decisions concerning his own possible love relationship with a white woman (an unnamed Scottish neighbor).[6] In his other novels, Micheaux also addresses either interracial relationships or the offspring of mixed-race couples.[7] The subject of intermarriage raised in his work was not simply the union of two people of different races but also engendered questions of Race loyalty, morality, and responsibility. We miss the point of the African-American experience from slavery through much of contemporary history if Micheaux's theme of "one drop of Black blood" is read simply as his preoccupation with color. For Micheaux, miscegenation and passing were a betrayal if they produced an abandonment of the Race.

In *The Symbol of the Unconquered,* "the folly of color," as *The Competitor* put it, is the driving force of the narrative, spinning a web of deceit and hatred that threatens the well-being of two lives and destroys another. Jefferson Driscoll, at first a hotelier and then a land speculator, is a light-skinned man passing for white. Hugh Van Allen, the hero of the story, also sees Eve Mason—a lady he encounters on the road in need of assistance—as white.[8] He offers to take her to the homestead she has inherited from her grandfather, which happens to border on his own land. In this way Micheaux establishes the distinction between the two mixed-race characters: the villain who would be white and the heroine who is mistaken for white through no conscious effort on her part. Woven into the theme of "shall the races intermarry" are reflections on both the turbulence and triumphs that marked the frontier experience of the African-American pioneer.

Oscar Micheaux, son of former slaves, was the product of a generation of African-American migrants who left the land in search of "the freedom of life and limb, the freedom to work and think, the freedom to love and aspire."[9] In his semi-autobiographical novels *The Conquest* and *The Homesteader* (1917), he tells of venturing forth from his home in southern Illinois in 1901, at the age of seventeen, in search of a career. Heading north to Chicago, he supported himself at odd jobs, shining shoes, bailing water in a coal mine, laboring in a factory, toiling in the stockyards, and working as a Pullman porter. While employed as a porter, Micheaux was able to save enough money to set up an agrarian enterprise, a homestead on the Rosebud Reservation in Gregory, South Dakota.[10] His novels suggest that, like many of his white immigrant neighbors who made land purchases based on the prospects of the westward extension of the railroad, he hoped to turn a profit on the value of his holdings. However, in order to "prove-up" on the land, it was necessary to build a house on it and till the soil. In *The Conquest,* he wrote that as a boy he preferred selling the family crop to working

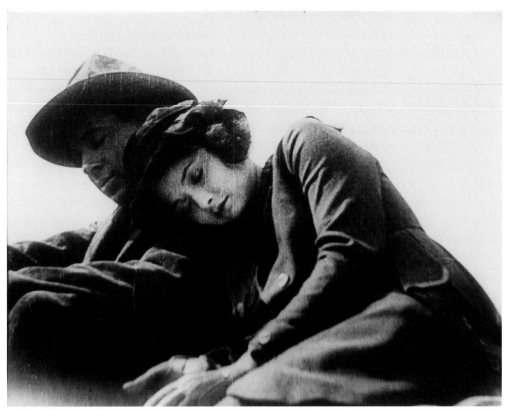

Hugh van Allen (Walker Thompson) befriends Eve Mason (Iris Hall) and drives her to her new homestead.

in the fields and that he knew little about farming.[11] Undeterred by lack of experience and armed with government pamphlets, almanacs, and the challenge of conquering the untamed land and reaping the rewards of that first harvest, he taught himself the rudiments of Great Plains farming, a process he described in painful detail, including purchasing mules, getting the right equipment to break the prairie, and turning the sod over day after day.[12] He also reflected on the need, as the only "colored man" engaged in agriculture on the Rosebud Reservation, to demonstrate to his neighbors that he was an honest, hardworking Negro determined to succeed.[13] Bent on disproving the widely held belief that "the negro," when faced with hardships of homesteading, would opt for the "ease and comfort" of the city, Micheaux bragged about having broken out three times as many acres as his neighbors.[14]

By working hard for several years, he amassed more than 500 acres by the time he was twenty-five. He approached homesteading with the same philosophy he was later to apply to his book and movie businesses: independence, persistence, and a willingness to take risks when a small investment had potentially large returns. One chapter of *The Conquest* digresses to report the history of two towns, detailing the townsfolk's speculation on the routes of the railroad's expansion. Although the "objective reporting" of the details and key players obviously attempts to distance the author from those speculators, it is given such prominence in an otherwise personal saga that one cannot help but wonder what role he had in the scheme. Indeed, the image of Micheaux as land speculator is far more in keeping with Micheaux's entrepreneurial spirit than the image of Micheaux as yeoman farmer. In his own words, he "was possessed with a business turn of mind."[15] In *The Homesteader*, for example, he boasts that after hand-writing "his life story" in a tablet and having a publisher reject it, he financed its publication (i.e., *The Conquest*) himself. With borrowed money for a suit and a trip to Nebraska, he struck a deal with a printer there and then raised money for the first payment through advance sales to his neighbors in South Dakota.[16]

Although Micheaux acquired a large holding and claimed to have been successful at wheat and flax farming,[17] he lost his land to foreclosures in 1912, 1913, and 1914.[18] He tells of liens on the homesteads and struggling to pay interest and taxes so he would not lose his land. Many homesteaders who had settled with great optimism were forced to abandon their claims. In his second novel, *The Forged Note* (1915), he refers nostalgically to the Rosebud Reservation and returning to the land.[19] By 1916, Micheaux had moved to Sioux City, Iowa, where he published a third novel, *The Homesteader,* and sold this and his earlier works through his own firm, the Western Book Supply Company.

Micheaux went on to produce an eight-reel filmed version of *The Homesteader,* the longest African-American moving picture at that time, nearly three hours. He advertised it as "Oscar Micheaux's Mammoth Photoplay," premiered it in Chicago's Eighth Regiment Armory, and declared that it was "destined to mark a new epoch in the achievements of the Darker Races."[20]

In his desire to have his life be an example for others, Micheaux fostered certain aspects of his personal vision, made artistic use of his personal history, and dramatized particular motifs. He created a legendary biography composed of selected real and imaginary events that continues to exist and exert influence today, even though many of his films are lost and forgotten. The silent features now extant (*Within Our Gates* [1920], *The Symbol of the Unconquered* [1920], and *Body and Soul* [1925]), along with his novels, promotional materials, and personal papers, illuminate the degree to which Micheaux used his "biographical legend" (his self-constructed social identity, political point of view, and status as African-American entrepreneur)[21] to create, promote, and shape the reception of his works. During that first decade of his career, he developed the public persona of an aggressive and successful businessman and a controversial and confident maverick producer—an image that was to sustain him for the next twenty years, although little of the work after his first sound picture, *The Exile* (1931), would seem to justify it.[22]

His correspondence and promotional material tell us a bit about the persona with which he confronted the world. He was able to win the confidence of noted author Charles W. Chesnutt, for instance, who granted him the right to film his novel *The House Behind the Cedars,* as well as Robert S. Abbott, publisher and editor of the *Chicago Defender,* who printed two of this unknown writer's first articles on the front page of his newspaper.[23] In one of these pieces, Micheaux was identified as a "government crop expert," and both articles urged readers to take advantage of the opportunities in the unsettled territories of the Northwest. Perhaps Abbott was persuaded because, somewhat of a visionary himself, he shared some of the aspirations of this self-propelled young man writing from South Dakota. Certainly when Micheaux made the decision to write his first novel and talked his neighbors into purchasing advance copies, he had to be convincing. Perhaps he made them feel it was about their dreams and ambitions as well as his own! And at the beginning of his career, full of energy, enthusiasm, and optimism, but no film experience, he was able to convince many small investors in Iowa and Nebraska to buy shares in his newly incorporated company to produce a Negro feature photoplay.[24] Once involved in an agrarian enterprise in which he failed, he was now marketing that romantic past. The idea of the West as an essential proving ground, which he had himself adventurously pursued, was now being adventurously reenacted as commercial entertainment for the same people whom he had been unable to attract to South Dakota land openings in the early *Defender* articles.[25]

The Symbol of the Unconquered, advertised as "A Stirring Tale of Love and Adventure in the Great Northwest," is, like *The Homesteader,* a wilderness story. Press releases for the film alluded to the characteristic elements of the popular Westerns, both serials and features, playing in theaters across the county: hard riding and red-blooded scrapping. The frontier, for Micheaux, was the mythic space of moral drama and the site of golden opportunities, seemingly free of the social arrangements and racial antagonisms of the rural South and the urban metropolis, where the characteristic model of economic expansion was entrepreneurship. *The Conquest* celebrated enterprising individuals: homesteaders, merchants, bankers, and real estate dealers.

The hero of *The Symbol of the Unconquered,* Hugh Van Allen, a man of the frontier, self-willed and self-motivated, is another articulation of Oscar Micheaux's biographical legend. Accumulating wealth through hard work and self-denial, he is almost a metaphor for the spirit of individualism. The West spoke strongly to many Americans as both a symbolic and actual place that offered an unspoiled environment in "the hollow of God's hand"[26] for individuals to fill with their own virtue: a place where social conventions and distinctions proved less important than natural ability, inner goodness, and individual achievement. Real estate promoters, railroad advertisements, news stories, dime novels, traveling shows, and movies mythologized the frontier as the site of freedom, abundance, and independence, capturing the imagination of a multitude of African Americans determined to put the residues of slavery and racial barriers behind them.

In his 1910 *Chicago Defender* article, Micheaux quoted Horace Greeley's "Go west young man and grow up with the country." Although he wrote about openings for doctors, lawyers, laborers, and mechanics, this bodacious newcomer posited the future of the West with agricultural possibilities, calling farmlands "the bosses of wealth." For Micheaux, the land openings along the frontier provided the opportune moment for the Negro to "do something for himself." Detailing the participation of the Race in agriculture, he wrote of fewer than "300 Negro farmers in the ten states of the Northwest [and] more opportunities than young men to grasp them."[27] Although such an image made him seem exceptional, enlarging his legend as a "Negro pioneer," Micheaux was, in fact, one of many thousands of African Americans who, since emancipation, saw the frontier as the place where one could realize one's own destiny.[28]

In *The Symbol of the Unconquered,* Hugh Van Allen, a gentlemanly frontiersman riding in a buckboard, embodied the Western hero, self-sufficient and calmly rugged. Race theaters, not unlike white movie houses, featured Westerns as an important part of the programming in the late teens and twenties. Edward Henry, an African-American projectionist throughout the 1920s in a neighborhood theater in Jackson, Mississippi, recalled, "When you go back, William S. Hart was one of the big men. . . . All you had to do was just put his name out there; [you] didn't have to put any pictures or anything, just William S. Hart, Wednesday, and they'd be coming. . . . William S. Hart, Tom Mix. . . . As I say, just open the door and stand back. The crowds'll come in."[29]

The great antagonist in *The Symbol of the Unconquered,* however, was not hostile elements, menacing outlaws, or "savage" Indians, as in most white Westerns, but the Ku Klux Klan. And Micheaux capitalized on that. Despite a climate of racial violence and intimidation, he advertised the film's premiere in Detroit with "SEE THE KU KLUX KLAN IN ACTION AND THEIR ANNIHILATION!"[30] When it played in Baltimore, *The Afro-American* advertisement exhorted, "SEE THE MURDEROUS RIDE OF THE INSIDEOUS KU KLUX KLAN in their effort to drive a BLACK BOY off of valuable Oil Lands—and the wonderful heroism of a traveler to save him!"[31] Another reference to the KKK (apparently quoting from Micheaux's press release) appears in the *Chicago Whip:* "Night riders rode down upon [the hero] like ghosts with fiery torches intent upon revenge."[32] And the *New York Age* review, headlined "KKK Put to Rout in PhotoPlay to be Shown at the Lafayette [Theatre]," called attention to "the viciousness and un-Americanism of the Ku-Klux-Klan which . . . is beginning to manifest itself again in certain parts of the United States. . . . [The film] is regarded as quite timely in view of the present attempt to organize night riders in this country for the express purpose of holding back the advancement of the Negro."[33] *The Competitor* magazine singled out the same part and saw a similar significance: "One of the most thrilling and realistic scenes is that of the Ku-Klux Klanners, who ride forth 'on the stroke of twelve' to pursue their orgy of destruction and terror. Coming at this time

The Ku Klux Klan in action.

when there is an attempt to revive this post-Civil War force of ignominy and barbarism denounced by the leading people of both races, in speech and editorials, North and South, the effect of disgust and determination are heightened."[34]

Many of Micheaux's silent films dealing with the social interaction between the races and miscegenation generated heated debate and were subject to censoring from official censor boards, community groups, and individuals. Passing is the central theme of *The House Behind the Cedars* (1925), and in *Birthright* (1924), a young woman is victimized by her white employer in a small southern town. When Micheaux presented *Birthright* to the Maryland State Board of Motion Picture Censors, the board demanded twenty-three eliminations. Even though the film was based on a popular novel by T. S. Stribling, a white southerner,[35] they found objectionable scenes and intertitles in all but two of the ten reels. They were particularly offended by suggestions of miscegenation, the questioning of white authority, and the depiction of racist attitudes in the everyday interactions between the races. When Micheaux showed the film in Baltimore without making all the cuts, the print was confiscated.[36] In Virginia, he deliberately ignored the jurisdiction of the State Board of Censors and affixed a bogus seal from another picture on a print of *Birthright.* It was shown in at least three theaters before the Censor Board found out.[37] This set off a flurry of activity around the state; the Board corresponded with mayors, chiefs of police, and theater owners, as well as a network of informants, to prevent future screenings.[38] Although the Board had not examined the film, they sent letters saying that *Birthright* was "a photoplay released by a negro concern which touches most offensively on the relations existing between whites and blacks."[39] In the 1925 report on *The House Behind the Cedars,* the same censor board rejected the full version of the photoplay for "presenting the grievances of the negro in very unpleasant terms and even touching on dangerous ground, inter-marriage between the races."[40] They seemed particularly concerned with the representation of the white suitor's lust for the young woman who had been passing for white: "Even after the woman has severed her relations with the man he is pictured as still seeking her society; nor does his quest end until she has become the wife of a dark-skinned suitor." *Within Our Gates,* which has a scene of an attempted interracial rape, a depiction of a lynching and burning, and may have addressed interracial concubinage, was also heavily censored.[41] In the months following the bloody Summer of 1919, the Chicago censors feared the showing of the picture could invoke further mob violence.[42] A police captain in New Orleans ordered a Race theater to discontinue showing the same film, because in his opinion it might incite a riot.[43]

Although the sole extant print of *The Symbol of the Unconquered* is only 3,852 feet, a little more than half of the seven reels advertised in 1920, several scenes hint at the complex and controversial nature of many of the representations.[44] Yet, released less than a year after *Within Our Gates, The Symbol of the Unconquered* encountered little trouble with state censor boards. Perhaps the volatile issue of the color line turned inward seemed less threatening to whites, who viewed their lives as unaffected when it was an intraracial issue. And it is a multiracial KKK which tries to run a Black man off his oil-rich land. This may have been received differently than *Within Our Gates*, where the white mob's motivation was to force Negroes into submission to white domination. *The Symbol of the Unconquered* also had a serviceable hero who embodied Booker T. Washington's philosophy that hard work and industry could catapult the Race to success. He is the type of hero that appears in many of Micheaux's early works. The film's title embraces both Van Allen's optimism—his determination to overcome the forces of evil from within (Driscoll's greed and avarice)—and his courage to challenge the symbol of hatred—the Ku Klux Klan.

Promotional materials for *The Symbol of the Unconquered* addressed the Black spectator and underscored the protest nature of the film. However, to think of the Klan as the singular antagonist is to reduce the complexity of Micheaux's representation. Homesteader Van Allen (played by Walker Thompson) is echoed by Driscoll (Lawrence Chenault), the villain who is also out to improve his lot. Both men are speculators who have migrated to the Northwest in pursuit of bigger and better opportunities. Although Driscoll is motivated by the same drives as the hero (indeed, as Micheaux himself), he acts in unscrupulous ways. He advances his standing, not by hard work and self-denial, but through coercion and deception. Through Driscoll and his cohorts, Micheaux exposes the economic origins of white-capping: Driscoll is the leader of a gang of greedy misfits plotting to intimidate Van Allen and drive him off his valuable land. It is Driscoll's participation in the Klan, his use of the same forces of intimidation that he would experience if his true racial identity were known, that disturbs the equilibrium of any clear-cut binary opposition.

Why does Micheaux superimpose the image of the KKK on an interracial band of thieves, swindlers, and connivers (including a former clergyman)? Is Driscoll the resurrected Eph from *Within Our Gates*, a betrayer (albeit in a more complex form)? Driscoll's racial ambiguity enables him to pass, but the darker-complexioned Eph must rely on a charade of obsequious behavior to gain white acceptance. Micheaux appropriated the stereotype to comment on the aspirations and social behavior of those who kowtow to whites.[45] Eph's wearing of the servile mask and his loyalty to his master represents his way of negotiating racism; however, as the mob turns on him, it is clear that his shield is precarious. In the end, he is just another "nigger." Driscoll, on the other hand, not only wants to be white, but, in order to achieve whiteness, he assumes the posture of the oppressor; in order to ward off the terror of the other, Driscoll himself becomes a terrorist. He counters racism with hatred and turns that hatred on the Race and, by extension, on himself. Both Eph and Driscoll deny their solidarity with the group. Eph, in trying to secure his own "privileged" position among the whites in the Big House, separates himself and betrays a fellow Negro.[46] Driscoll, by internalizing negative perceptions of blackness, isolates himself and betrays the Race.[47] Micheaux condemns the social behavior of both characters, and both get their just deserts.

Van Allen's triumph over hatred is even sweeter because he has overcome Driscoll's "self-hate" as well as the night riders, the symbol of racial oppression and intimidation. The unmasking of hatred is as much a part of the film as the violence perpetrated in the name of that hatred. In the character of Van Allen, Micheaux was dreaming and re-dreaming his own ambitions and desires. In the epilogue, Van Allen's good deeds are rewarded: He becomes prosperous from the oil on his land and discovers that neighboring homesteader Eve Mason (played by Iris Hall) is, despite her fair skin, really a Black woman, and thus a suitable wife. In *The Conquest,* Micheaux writes of his experiences of homesteading and falling in love with his neighbor's

Indian Fakir Tugi Boj (Leigh Whipper) on the left and Jefferson Driscoll (Lawrence Chenault) on the right, two dissemblers sitting on either side of a defrocked minister, plotting strategy for the Ku Klux Klan.

daughter, an unnamed young Scottish woman of strong character who is "anxious to improve her mind," attributes he clearly admired.[48] One of the least verifiable facts of the author's life, this interracial romance is a recurring theme and rhetorical trope in his films and novels. Micheaux replays this love, or the possibility of it, in many of his works. In *The Conquest,* although he never acts on his feelings (self-control and self-denial were guiding principles of conduct in Micheaux's biographical legend), he conveys a sense of anxiety about even considering it: To pursue an interracial relationship would call into question his loyalty to the Race. His idealism comes into conflict with erotic longing.

This type of titillation—and concession to popular mores—is more developed in his novel *The Homesteader.* The main character, the Negro pioneer Jean Baptiste, decides not to marry the woman he loves (whom he believes to be Caucasian), citing "*The Custom Of The Country, and its law.*" He goes on to note that such a marriage "would be the most unpopular thing he could do. . . . He would be condemned, he would be despised by the race that was his."[49] However, in this book (and in his later films and novels) Micheaux provided a happier ending: the hero discovers that his love is not white after all, and marriage becomes possible. Georgia Hurston Jones wrote of the "compensations" in his first four films: "Mr. Micheaux has not overlooked the sheer joy of 'living and loving,' and though some ugly conditions are set forth (to the end that they might be improved), yet his pictures leave one with the comfortable feeling that 'all's well that ends well.'"[50]

Clues to the true racial identity of the woman who seems to be an inappropriate love interest for the hero emerge in different ways in these works. In *The Exile* (1931), for example, the heroine is described as a white woman by another character early in the film. The audience gets essential narrative information at the same time as the heroine does: we share her curiosity when she examines her physical appearance before a mirror, but we do not know for certain until the heroine does, in a final scene. On the other hand, the audience knows more than the characters do in *The Betrayal* (1948), the film version of Micheaux's 1943 novel, *The Wind from Nowhere* (another reworking of his biographical legend). The script for the film opens with a scene of an elderly Black man explaining his granddaughter's lineage to a visitor; however, the heroine is not present in that scene and does not know that the gentleman is her grandfather.[51] By carefully tracing the character's origins, Micheaux informs the audience that the heroine herself is unaware of her true racial identity and therefore is neither deceitful nor disloyal. In *The Symbol of the Unconquered,* a fragment of a scene at the opening of the film shows Eve at the deathbed of her grandfather, a dark-skinned man with a large white mustache. Both the heroine and the audience, from the very beginning of the narrative, are aware of her racial identity, despite her fair skin. Consistently in all these works, it is the Micheaux-like male hero who struggles for much of the story with the political and moral dilemmas of such a marriage.[52] His is the noble fight. In *Thirty Years Later* (1928), it is the man who is unaware of his ancestry; however, he also fights the noble fight, and when he learns about his origins, the hero becomes proud of the Race and marries his love.[53]

Micheaux's treatment of miscegenation in such films as *The Homesteader, Within Our Gates, The Symbol of the Unconquered, A Son of Satan, The House Behind the Cedars, Thirty Years Later, Birthright, The Exile, Veiled Aristocrats, God's Step Children,* and *The Betrayal* and in all seven of his novels are ambitious reworkings of the conventions of melodrama from a point of view within the Black community—a resourceful reconfiguration of the genre. The story, his story, was an adaptation of the sensational tropes already prevalent in the melodramas that dominated popular theater and pulp literature, indeed, Micheaux's own novels: villainy, virtue, valor, scenes of assault and abduction, intercepted letters, false accusations, coincidences, and sudden reversals. By centering on the African-American experience, he offered a bold critique of American society. To understand the scope and complexity of this critique, we must see it, as Jane Tompkins wrote of the sentimental novel, as a political enterprise that both codified the values of the time and attempted to mold them.[54]

Although mistaken identity was a common convention of nineteenth- and early twentieth-century melodrama—the ill-suited lover who turns out not to be ill-suited after all (that is, not a sibling, a pauper, a moral indigent, etc.)—the reversals in Micheaux's stories more often involve the potential transgression of the social taboos and legal prohibitions against miscegenation. Because of confusions over lines of race difference and the subsequent fear of not being able to distinguish who is Black and who is white, legislators in some states imposed legal definitions of race. The fetishization of "black blood," as Toni Morrison puts it, "is especially useful in evoking erotic fears or desires and establishing fixed and major difference where difference does not exist or is minimal. . . . Fetishization is a strategy often used to assert the categorical absolutism of civilization and savagery."[55]

Micheaux's use of mistaken identity and the potential for miscegenation that ensues opens up the question of the problematic ambiguity of those boundaries. Such racial mixing threatens definitions of race, challenging the idea that racial identity might be "knowable." By blurring the dichotomy on which whiteness depends, miscegenation throws into disarray the basis of white supremacy, Black "inferiority." Morrison points out that it is by imagining blackness that whiteness "knows itself as not enslaved, but free, not repulsive, but desirable, not helpless, but licensed and powerful."[56]

Rather than suggesting a radical new way of seeing or attempting to create a new narrative space for representation, in *The Symbol of the Unconquered* (as in much of his other early work), Micheaux worked within the hardened conventions and presuppositions of "the Negro problem text," melding the plots and conventions of the sentimental melodrama with western settings and characters. He was "crafting a voice out of tight places," as Houston Baker wrote of Booker T. Washington's use of minstrelsy.[57] Often invoking the novel *Uncle Tom's Cabin* in his promotional material (print ads and trailers), Micheaux seems to have admired not only the enormous social impact (and commercial success) of Harriet Beecher Stowe's work, but also its evangelical piety and moral commitment.[58]

Van Allen, like many other of Micheaux's characters, represents sociological and moral forces rather than a psychologically individuated person and functions as a model to illustrate what could be accomplished through hard work and industry. Micheaux, at the beginning of his career, striking out on his own and settling on the land, was influenced by Booker T. Washington's philosophy, "not of destruction, but of construction; not of defense, but of aggression; . . . not of hostility or surrender, but of friendship and advance"; where self-reliance and "usefulness in the community" were the "surest and most potent protection."[59] *The Conquest,* a success and adventure story about a Black pioneer in the West, was dedicated to the Honorable Booker T. Washington, and many of his other books and movies aimed to galvanize the spirit of success through examples of individual triumph. In *The Symbol of the Unconquered,* a portrait of Washington appears on the wall of Eve's grandfather's frontier cabin. In his 1910 *Chicago Defender* article, Micheaux wrote that he was "not trying to offer a solution to the Negro problem, for I don't feel that there is any problem further than the future of anything, whether it be a town, state or race. . . . It depends first on individual achievement, and I am at a loss to see a brilliant future for the young colored man unless he first does something for himself." Stressing his belief that the American Negro must take advantage of opportunities, Micheaux called for individual behavior and agency that could and would eventually overcome hostile institutions and structural discrimination. This idealization of the individual was compatible not only with Washington's political philosophy but also with Micheaux's use of melodrama. That is, his melodramas gave structure to the aspirations of the individual. The genre's moral tableaux and moral certainties reiterated the ideals of the Protestant ethic: a faith in work, duty, and the redemption of the just and virtuous.

In a telling note to Charles W. Chesnutt, Micheaux suggested that the screenplay for his adaptation of *The House Behind the Cedars* should make Frank more striving—in order to make Rena's affection for him more believable! "I would make the man Frank more intelligent at least towards the end of the story permitting him to study and improve himself, for using the language as he does in the story, he would not in anyway be obvious as a lover or that the girl could have more than passing respect for him."[60]

Frank's self-improvement and industry elevate him from a minor role in the novel to a more exemplary status in the film and render him a model hero, amazingly like Micheaux's own biographical legend. Rather than claiming to represent the political and social aspirations of the Negro, by necessity speaking for the majority, as many of the Black intelligentsia did, Micheaux felt that the majority needed models, heroes, to mold public opinion and for the elevation of public sentiment. Explaining why Jean Baptiste forswore marriage with his white neighbor in *The Homesteader,* Micheaux wrote, "He had set himself in this new land to succeed; he had worked and slaved to that end. He liked his people; he wanted to help them. Examples they needed and such he was glad to have become; but if he married now the one he loved, the example was lost."[61] Mildred Latham, the love interest of the homesteader, author, and itinerant book peddler in *The Forged Note,* admires the hero as "a Negro pioneer . . . [who] blaze[d] the way for others."[62] In *The Conquest,* Micheaux stated that one of his greatest tasks in life was "to convince a certain class of my racial acquaintances that a colored man can be anything."[63]

This racial uplift, which was so important to counter accusations of "inferiority," challenged white definitions of the Race without changing the terms. Others in this period—Sterling Brown, Langston Hughes, and Zora Neale Hurston, for example—questioned those terms, demanding new definitions of Race from within Black America. Hurston's work recodified both language and story by bringing out the richness of the African-American vernacular, oral culture, and folk tales. Hughes wrote of his own use of Black culture, "Jazz to me is one of the inherent expressions of Negro life in America: the eternal tom-tom beating

Driscoll looks into Eve's eyes and "sees" her true identity.

in the Negro soul—the tom-tom of revolt against weariness in a white world, a world of subway trains and work, work, work; the tom-tom of joy and laughter, and pain swallowed in a smile."[64] Hurston and Hughes, and other New Negroes, saw themselves as reclaiming images of blackness, an attempt, as Alain Locke put it, to build Americanism on Race values.[65]

Like Brown, Hurston, and Hughes, Micheaux spoke as a Negro; the "blackness" of the author is a strong presence. He shared their optimism, in spite of failed promises. However, because of his sense of personal responsibility and uplift, he strove to provide direction and envisioned himself as an empowering interpreter of Black life for the community.

Within *The Symbol of the Unconquered,* the character of Van Allen as well as the film's very title express Oscar Micheaux's optimism for the Race. Like Micheaux's biographical legend, Van Allen is the adventurous entrepreneur, an achiever, loyal to the Race, persistent and brave in the face of adversities.

Today, however, Van Allen is one of the least provocative characters! Driscoll, on the other hand, is so overdrawn that he borders on the horrific—he is almost uncanny. "Uncanny" because he is at once so evil and so familiar. Although passing is neither uncommon nor automatically condemned by the Black community, it is Driscoll's attitude of superiority, seeing Blacks as subhuman and taking pleasure in their misfortune, that is wicked—both a betrayal and a surrender.

Driscoll refuses Abraham, a Black traveling salesman (played by E. G. Tatum, who lends a comic irony to the melodrama), a room in his hotel and leads him to the barn. When Eve arrives at the hotel later, hungry and exhausted from a long journey, Driscoll at first thinks that she is white; but, as she is about to register, he looks into her eyes and "sees" her true identity. His initially genial behavior turns to hatred; he denies her a bed in his hotel, sending her to the hayloft. During the night, Eve is awakened by a storm and is frightened upon discovering that there is someone else in the barn. She falls from the loft and runs out into a driving rain. Driscoll, watching from his bedroom window as she struggles in the storm, takes sinister joy in her suffering. Surrounded by an aura of shimmering whiteness (in white nightshirt and sheets, lit as if he were aglow), he thrashes his arms in triumph.

What is so disturbing about Driscoll is his assumption of the posture of the oppressor and his terror of discovery. He sees in Eve's pale face both his true identity and the possibility of being unmasked. In *The Conquest,* invoking a story from his experiences as a homesteader in South Dakota, Micheaux wrote about the children of a wealthy mixed-race family passing for white and living in fear of other members of the Race, dreading "that moment of racial recognition."[66] Driscoll's own racial identity is exposed early in the film by his mother, a darker-skinned lady, as he is proposing to a white woman. In this scene, the terror of racial recognition and the odiousness of racial terror come together as Driscoll attacks his own mother because she is Black.

Later, in a barroom scene, there is a fistfight between Van Allen and Driscoll, supposedly over a horse deal turned sour. The fight scene is introduced by a close shot of both Driscoll and Van Allen framed in a mirror. Driscoll looks up and recognizes Van Allen. Does he see Van Allen as the horse-trade victim he has been mocking? Or is this that moment of racial recognition? Perhaps Driscoll sees his despised self, his own blackness, in Van Allen. Driscoll pulls a gun and threatens Van Allen, but Van Allen wrestles the gun away from him and they "duke it out." After being beaten by Van Allen and declaring, "I'll get my revenge!," Driscoll is thrown out of the bar with a swift kick in the butt by the same traveling salesman whom he had refused to serve in his hotel. Is this intraracial censure or is it a matter of a Black man getting the better of a "white" man?[67] To the spectators in the bar who are unaware of his racial identity, this incident appears to be a "reversal" of the standard prank: it is a "white" man, not the dark-skinned Black, who is the butt of the joke and object of ridicule.

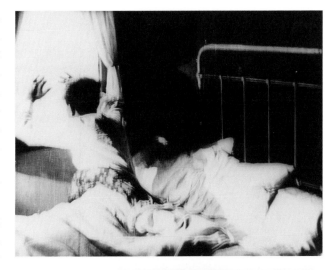

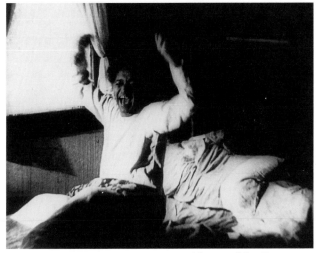

After watching Eve struggle in the storm, Driscoll raises his arms in triumph.

Lawrence Chenault's performance style throughout the film—his chalky make-up; his outlined eyes and arched eyebrows; his tense, often flailing, arms and hunched shoulders; the rigidity of his body; and the vehemence of his gestures—expresses a man driven by fear. Driscoll's self-loathing and terror of discovery provoke his attack on Van Allen; having failed, he uses the Klan as a personal instrument of revenge. It is because his identity is so tenuous that he is so vicious. Reflecting on the South Dakota mixed-race family, Micheaux wrote, "What worried me most, however, even frightened me, was that after marriage and when their children had grown to manhood and womanhood, they . . . had a terror of their race."[68] They looked upon other Blacks with a dread of discovery. Such a discovery would expose not only their racial identity but also a life of deception, threatening social and psychological upheaval. For Driscoll, race is the unspeakable, the stranger entering the gate, menacing his whiteness. Identity, to borrow from James Baldwin, "would seem to be the garment with which [he] covers the nakedness of the self."[69]

In 1909, the *Daily Ohio State Journal* noted that thousands of people were passing in Washington, D.C, alone:

> Those who just occasionally pass for white, simply to secure just recognition, and the privileges the laws vouchsafe an American citizen, should not be censured harshly. An unjust discrimination, a forced and ungodly segregation drives them to practice deception. . . . But it is an awful experience to pass for white. At all times fear—the fear of detection—haunts one. . . . Those who turn their backs upon their own color, own race and own relatives to live a life of fear, of dread, and almost isolation just to pass for white seven days in the week, while regarded with utter contempt by their colored race, really ought to be pitied, when it is known how heavy is the burden they carry, and how much they suffer in silence.[70]

Micheaux exploited these concerns in the script for *God's Step Children* (1938). Andrew, the white husband of the young woman who is passing, upon discovering his wife's "streak" says,

His own racial identity exposed, Driscoll attacks his mother because she is Black.

"You aren't the first to try this, Naomi. No, it has been tried since the days of slavery and even before that; but they can't get away with it, so you see you can't get away with it, for sooner or later, somewhere, some time after a life of fear and exemption you will be found out, and when you are they'll turn on you, loathe you, despise you, even spit in your face and call you by your right name—Naomi, Negress."[71]

The Black press often covered well-known interracial marriages and court cases of people attempting to prove that they were Negro in order to counter charges of miscegenation.[72] Stories of whites not being able to discern what is obvious to a Black person were part of the popular discourses of the time. It was thought quite funny that for whites race was not so much a matter of color and appearance as of mannerisms and deportment. Helen M. Chesnutt, in her biography of her father, tells of the family entering a restaurant while traveling and, after being seated, seeing the manager "bearing down" upon their table; they immediately began speaking French . . . and the man retreated.[73]

In an article entitled "When Is a Negro a Negro to a Caucasian?" Lester A. Walton, an amusement columnist for the *New York Age,* asked, "By what standard do they differentiate as to when is a Negro a Negro?" and laughed about vaudevillian John Hodges ("Any colored person can tell what John Hodges is") trying to eat at a restaurant and telling the waiter that he was not a Negro, but an English Jew, and getting served.[74] In another article, Walton tells the story of the white manager and cashier at the Fifty-ninth Street Theatre in New York who were discharged because "they mistook a young lady of color to be of the white race and proceeded to speak disrespectfully of their ebony-hued employer [William Mack Felton]." Walton mused, "One of the amusing features of the so-called Negro problem is the inability of the white people to recognize hundreds and hundreds of colored people who have gone on the other side of the color line. To us there is nothing so ludicrous as to observe one known as a violent Negro hater walking arm-in-arm or sitting at a table eating with a person of color, the radical Caucasian indulging in an erratic outburst of abuse on the Negro to the unconcealed delight of the colored person."[75]

In 1925, the trial of wealthy white New York socialite Leonard "Kip" Rhinelander and his wife made the front pages of the Black weeklies. Rhinelander had taken his new wife, Alice Jones Rhinelander, to court to dissolve their marriage because he said that he had just found out that she had "Negro ancestry and that she had concealed the fact from him during their courtship."[76] Mrs. Rhinelander denied any deception, insisting that anyone could tell she was a Negro. Micheaux used the notoriety of the Rhinelander case to promote *The House Behind the Cedars.*[77] But even without mentioning it in his ads, such popular discourses on crossing the "color line" certainly would have influenced the way audiences understood Micheaux's films. Press coverage, folk sayings, blues songs, and verbal exchanges are all part of the spectator's experience. As Tony Bennett and Janet Woollacott put it, "A text . . . is never 'there' except in forms in which it is also and always other than 'just itself,' always-already humming with reading possibilities which derive from outside its covers."[78] However, in what appears to be a contradiction in many of Micheaux's works, the Black romantic lead, in order to meet the demands of melodrama, must be blind to the race of his beloved until the moment of utopian revelation. In its review of *The Symbol of the Unconquered,* the *New York Age* commented: "As in nine cases out of ten Negroes instinctively recognize one of their own, some are apt to wonder why [Van Allen] did not learn the truth sooner. However, the raising of such a point does not in any way detract from the general excellence of the picture."[79]

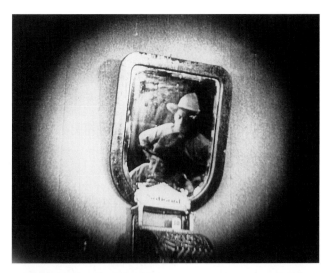

Because Driscoll's true racial identity is established early in the film, audiences watch his vileness, knowing he is Black. In his mask, he so vehemently rejects blackness that, turning his anger on the Race, he also assaults the audience. The defeat of the vengeful character at the end of the film must have given the spectator a moment of relief and joy—a blow against the oppressor. Likewise, the scene in the bar where he is kicked in the butt by the traveling salesman (one of the gestures that clustered around the "Tom" character in minstrelsy) allows the spectator to take vicarious pleasure in his humiliation.[80] Driscoll's downfall and the apocalyptic renewal of the ending is a victory not only for Van Allen but for the spectator as well, putting to rest notions of Black "inferiority." What visions of their own radical anger and omnipotence might the audience have experienced as they watched their hero!

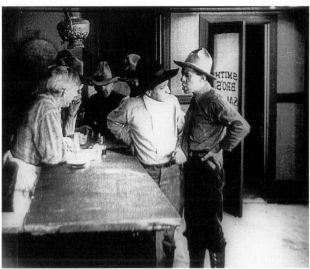

Driscoll recognizes Hugh in a mirror over the bar, then turns to confront him.

The character Driscoll is both a vehicle for exploring interracial relations and, as a person of mixed blood (the product of historical miscegenation), an expression of those relations. The question of color is of recurring interest for Micheaux. However, his is not a simple "infatuation with color," nor is it simply a narrative contrivance—that is, the melodramatic trope of someone being other than what he or she seems. It is far more complex. Although he was sometimes accused of casting by color,[81] Micheaux criticized the color-caste system within the community as destructive social behavior. And although he created a star system of fair-skinned performers (Iris Hall, Shingzie Howard, Evelyn Preer, Lawrence Chenault, Andrew Bishop, Carmen Newsome, Lorenzo Tucker, etc.), chosen for their "look" and potential appeal to audiences, he didn't necessarily associate these "looks" with certain qualities, such as "goodness." In *Body and Soul,* Paul Robeson plays both the hero and the villain with no difference in make-up, and the scoundrel, "Yellow Curley," is played by Lawrence Chenault (who also plays villains in other films where skin color is not part of the story).[82] In *The Symbol of the Unconquered,* Walker Thompson, playing the rugged outdoorsman hero, acquires his swarthy complexion with dark make-up. Carl Mahon, who did not think of himself as an actor, felt that Micheaux cast him in romantic leads because of his "exotic looks," the combination of dark skin and straight hair.[83] In several of his films—including *The House Behind the Cedars, God's Step Children,* and *The Symbol of the Unconquered*—we would argue that Micheaux was not reproducing "color prejudice" but rebuking it.

For Micheaux, the problem of miscegenation is not the mixing of the races (that was a fact of life) but the denial of racial identity and disloyalty that comes from trying to hide one's race. In *The Betrayal,* Martin Eden[84] tells the story of a mixed-race family in South Dakota with many children who would pass their father off as an "old colored servant who helped to raise them" when visitors came to call. One of the brothers was dark. Drafted into the army and assigned to a colored unit, unhappy with being unable to serve in a white regiment, "he stood before a mirror in his tent one night, took a German Luger that he had acquired—and blew his brains out."[85]

In *Within Our Gates,* Sylvia, the offspring of the plantation owner's brother, is adopted by Black sharecroppers and raised as one of their own. She sees herself as a Black woman. As a person of mixed blood, Sylvia is not automatically an outsider, someone different, a point of division. In a medium long shot of her family around a table, there are a variety of skin tones.[86] The story line is not "about" skin color per se; it is "about" the rape of Black women by white men. Although much of Eve's backstory seems to be missing from the surviving print of *The Symbol of the Unconquered,* Eve, like Sylvia, is comfortable with who she is and is not trying to pass. In an interview he gave around the time of the film's release, Micheaux said, "There is one thing aside from [making] the story interesting, that . . . I strive to demonstrate in all my pictures and that is, it makes no difference what may be a person's color, or from where a person comes, if the heart is right, that's what counts, and success is sure."[87] Eve is not only a Black woman but a Race woman. It is through a letter commending her for her service to the Race that Van Allen discovers her true identity.

The working title of *The Symbol of the Unconquered* was *The Wilderness Trail.*[88] The name change is simultaneously affirming and challenging, a call to collective consciousness and solidarity. The film sets up an oppositional imperative between individual attitudes and behavior (the villain's denial of racial identity in order to assert personal power and privilege) and the well-being of the group. Driscoll is the moral instrument through which Micheaux offers direction on social aspirations. Van Allen, our hero, is a figure of—and an inspiration toward—racial uplift. He is both a stand-in for Oscar Micheaux and a means through which Micheaux builds his biographical legend, his legend of success. In the epilogue, not only is Van Allen prosperous but so is the traveling salesman. Micheaux seems to be reading his own success as both a benefit and a catalyst for the entire community.

The white American, figuratively [forces] the Negro down into the deeper level of his consciousness, into the inner world, where reason and madness mingle with hope and memory and endlessly give birth to nightmare and to dream; down into the province of the psychiatrist, and the artist, from whence spring the lunatic's fancy and the work of art.

—Ralph Ellison

8.

To Redream the Dreams of White Playwrights: Reappropriation and Resistance in Oscar Micheaux's Body and Soul

He wanted to see a movie; his senses hungered for it. In a movie he could dream without effort; all he had to do was lean back in a seat and keep his eyes open.

—Richard Wright

CHARLES MUSSER

Scholars have found Oscar Micheaux's *Body and Soul* (filmed in late 1924, released in late 1925) to be a puzzling work which is remarkably resistant to sustained readings. Difficult to situate, it has been convenient to ignore. Although the picture was filmed in New York, was Paul Robeson's screen debut, and profoundly engaged the cultural output of the Harlem Renaissance, histories of that important movement in African-American life barely mention Micheaux or his extraordinary achievement.[1] Likewise, American film histories have either ignored the picture completely or nodded briefly in its direction.[2] Even histories of African-American cinema are remarkably cursory.[3] This is all the more intriguing because the picture's radical structure and technique make it a compelling object for analysis. Nevertheless, scholars have found it difficult to explain the ways in which these representational methods interact with the story line and subject matter to create meaning. They have ended up describing the picture as "disjointed and raggedy" with a "somewhat confusing plot."[4]

THE PROBLEM OF MICHEAUX'S STYLISTICS

The critical problems posed by *Body and Soul* (or any other Micheaux film) are highlighted by a consideration of the filmmaker's use of narrative, by the very story that he seems to be telling. In *Film Art: An Introduction,* David Bordwell and Kristin Thompson "consider a narrative to be a chain of events in cause-effect relationship occurring in time and space. . . . Typically a narrative begins with one situation; a series of changes occurs according to a pattern of cause and effect; finally a new situation arises that bring about the end of the narrative."[5]

Paul Robeson as Rev. Isiaah T. Jenkins in *Body and Soul* (1925).

In *Body and Soul* there are numerous problems with the "chain of events in cause-effect relationship occurring in time and space." To offer a blatant example, Paul Robeson plays twin brothers who live in the same small town and are involved with the same woman—one an escaped convict who is posing as a preacher, the other an aspiring inventor. Under these circumstances, the sociopathic criminal would be known to his family and the community, making problematic the story's premise as a believable tale. The film's general disregard for standard narrative logic may be one reason *Body and Soul* goes unmentioned in *Film Art*. In *Film History,* their companion text to *Film Art,* Bordwell and Thompson do mention Micheaux, positioning him as a super low-budget filmmaker whose rapid output helps to explain his disjunctive style. The peculiar narrativity of *Body and Soul* is thus explained by difficult production circumstances and limited funding. Micheaux is lauded primarily for his ability to present black concerns on the screen.[6]

Forced to account for gaps in the narrative coherence of *Body and Soul,* other scholars, such as Thomas Cripps and Donald Bogle, have suggested that surviving copies were marred by censorship problems and by the likelihood that the prints were recut and reworked as they circulated from venue to venue. What survives is a fragment, a faint suggestion of the original.[7] Analysis of the film is thus difficult and must be speculative. Certainly there is evidence for this perspective. The George Eastman House (GEH) version is 7,700 feet in length—for a film originally advertised as 9 reels (each reel able to contain 1,000 feet of film). And there appears to be missing footage. The two female leads are not introduced in a manner consistent with other characters in the story (i.e., with title cards providing the names of the actresses). Such absences suggest that certain shots and intertitles, if not actual scenes, are missing from this version. Likewise, the scene in which Rev. Isiaah Jenkins (Robeson) kills the son of Martha Jane, his most devoted parishioner, has a few jump cuts that suggest this section of the film, at least, was re-edited in response to censors eager to reduce the depiction of graphic violence. Overall, however, the GEH version seems to have its integrity intact. The print does not suffer unduly from damage due to extensive projection, suggesting that the print had not been bicycled from town to town in a way that might have undermined its textual integrity. Just because the picture was contained on nine 1,000-foot reels does not mean that 1,300 feet of film are missing. *Body and Soul* could have averaged 900 feet of film per reel—8,100 feet—or even less. (Pictures were rarely circulated on full reels because the film was more susceptible to damage. Moreover, pictures were not made to fill up reels, particularly when the number of reels was a selling point.) Given the survival of only one print, textual variation must, of course, remain a concern. Nonetheless, the GEH version of *Body and Soul* seems reasonably complete and coherent.[8]

A new analysis of *Body and Soul* has been greatly facilitated by the discovery and restoration of Micheaux's *Within Our Gates* (1920) and *The Symbol of the Unconquered* (1920).[9] What is background "noise" (i.e., print corruption) and what is the filmmaker's "voice"—his radical stylistics—is much easier to discern with the survival of two more of Micheaux's silent films. Indeed, all three share a repertoire of techniques that includes parallel editing and point-of-view structures (primarily involving eyeline matches) as well as dream and flashback constructions. The latter two techniques are particularly noteworthy for purposes of this essay. Near the end of *Within Our Gates,* it becomes evident that the film's story cannot achieve proper closure (that is, romantic union of the two main characters) because the heroine (Sylvia Landry) has a horrific past that has remained unacknowledged. Through a flashback structure, the heroine's cousin Alma tells Sylvia's frustrated suitor about her prior life: the lynching of Sylvia's adopted family and her near-rape by her white, biological father. Subsequent scenes within the flashback depict three different versions of the same event—the killing of Girdlestone—evoking the "thrice-told tale" of John Walters in Albion W. Tourgée's novel *A Fool's Errand* (1879).[10] Most notably, after depicting the events leading up to the lynchings, the cause of the race riot is retold twice—culminating with a representation of the provocative and highly distorted account appearing in a white newspaper. This rewriting of events is used to "justify" or "explain" the race riot and thus to "excuse" the resulting lynching. Indeed, as Jane Gaines has pointed out, conflicting versions of incidents leading up to these events are depicted in different modalities.[11] The truth value of dominant discourse is challenged within the framework of a racist white society that disseminates self-interested fabrications of actual events. Much earlier in the film, *Within Our Gates* contains an unusual dream sequence in which Sylvia dreams of a murder (involving a card game) as it actually takes place. Dream and reality merge in ways that are disorienting and disturbing. When she wakes from her nightmare, we find that her dream was also reality.

In *Body and Soul,* Micheaux intertwines flashbacks with dreams far more extensively, destabilizing the status of the represented event for somewhat different purposes. In this case, the film viewer comes to want the dreamer (Martha Jane) to stop dreaming, to see clearly and to face reality. To face reality, Martha Jane must be able to hear and believe her daughter Isabelle as she tells the story of her rape by Rev. Jenkins (Martha Jane's pastor, the villain posing as a man of God). Isabelle's recounting of repressed events enables Martha Jane to understand—if only for a moment—and indeed she finally seems to wake up from a nightmare. But for Micheaux, dreams are something more than manifestations of our anxieties. African Americans live life as a waking nightmare—the consequence of racism. Dream and reality often have similar structures—one which does not conform to a coherent, "logical" pattern of cause and effect. Likewise, the black characters in these films act in self-destructive ways because they are seeking to avoid and suppress certain all-too-painful events. To confront them means to confront the facade of normality and gentility. Sylvia avoids her lover rather than tell him of her past (so the cousin intervenes). Isabelle flees to Atlanta and starves to death because she knows her mother, who is tremendously invested in a proper, genteel view of the world—will refuse to listen to, and to believe, the story of her rape. Nightmare and the unspoken haunt African-American life for Micheaux. Through cinematic constructions of dream and flashback, the filmmaker found powerful ways to articulate them.

Recent scholarship has been increasingly adept at situating Micheaux's films in their historical context, both socially and culturally. Pearl Bowser and Louise Spence have done an excellent job of showing how both *Within Our Gates* and *Body and Soul* engaged contemporary events of crucial concern to the black community—subjects also treated extensively by the black press.[12] *Within Our Gates* resonated with the race riots occurring in Chicago and across the United States in 1919. *Body and Soul* addressed the problem of corruption within the black church. Jane Gaines, Cory Creekmur, and Ron Green have likewise situated *Within Our Gates* in an intertextual framework, detailing the ways Micheaux refigured the work of D. W. Griffith on one hand and Charles W. Chesnutt on the other. This essay pursues a similar mission for *Body and Soul.*

Body and Soul was simultaneously a profound reworking and a critique of three plays ostensibly about Negro life and the Negro soul. These were Nan Bagby Stephens's *Roseanne* and Eugene O'Neill's two race plays *The Emperor Jones* and *All God's Chillun' Got Wings.* All were written by white playwrights and then performed by black actors. Today Stephens and her play are virtually forgotten, but *Roseanne* had a significant reputation in 1924. Theophilus Lewis, African-American drama critic for the left-oriented *The Messenger,* believed that "'Roseanne,' excepting two plays by Eugene O'Neil[l], is the most significant dramatic work dealing with the life and psyche of the Negro yet revealed to the public."[13] In point of fact, Paul Robeson had starred in all the plays of this makeshift trilogy in the months immediately prior to the production of Micheaux's masterful picture. Talking to the press primarily about *All God's Chillun'* shortly before negotiating with Micheaux to appear in *Body and Soul,* Robeson remarked, "Jim [Harris of *All God's Chillun'*] was the third part I have played this year. I was in Ros[e]anne. I played the Emperor Jones, and now this part."[14]

To grasp how this remarkable film and its strategies of reappropriation were possible, it is useful to situate the film generically. *Body and Soul* appeared at a time when the relationship between film and theater was extensive and frequently profound. The man many considered the greatest American actor of his day, John Barrymore, worked alternately in theater and film.[15] Likewise, many of the race films of the 1920s were populated by black actors who had performed or continued to perform with the Lafayette Players Dramatic Stock Company, including Lawrence Chenault and Evelyn Preer. Film was the younger art, and cinematic adaptations and pirated reworkings of theatrical hits were common. Indeed, Thomas H. Ince had already turned Eugene O'Neill's *Anna Christie* into a film that starred Blanche Sweet and was directed by John Griffith Wray. Released in late 1923, it was praised by O'Neill as "remarkably well acted and directed, and in spirit an absolutely faithful transcript."[16] The *New York Times* hailed it as a breakthrough in the history of cinema: "Here is a picture with wonderful characterization that tells a moving and compelling story—a film that is intensely dramatic, and one that will win new audiences for the screen."[17] When the film played race movie houses in the winter of 1924, advertisements focused attention on the play and promoted the Ince production as "a picture with all the strength, the pathos and sheer beauty of the original."[18]

Not all filmic engagements with theatrical works in the 1920s were faithful or friendly adaptations. In 1925, for example, Ernst Lubitsch directed an audacious reworking of Oscar Wilde's *Lady Windermere's Fan,* which completely avoided Wilde's dialogue. In this artistic duel, Lubitsch challenged Wilde's aphorisms and verbal wit with his own visual dexterity— what critical discourse was coming to recognize as the "Lubitsch touch." Lubitsch, moreover, was not above revising the narrative construction of scenes when he felt that Wilde had handled them awkwardly. For some critics, this provided one basis for the film's success. Robert E. Sherwood praised the picture, noting that "Lubitsch filtered Wilde's manuscript through his own exceptionally sensitive mind, and then formed the resultant precipitation into the continuity for his picture."[19] For *New York Times* critic Mordaunt Hall, however, this relationship created a kind of creative interference that made it difficult for him to enjoy the film.[20] Micheaux, this essay argues, intended at least some members of his audience to appreciate *Body and Soul* within a somewhat similar intertextual framework. Micheaux did not require these viewers to have an intimate familiarity with Stephens's and O'Neill's plays, though this clearly would have been helpful: spectators who had a decent familiarity with theatrical news in the black press could have appreciated much of what Micheaux was seeking to achieve.

If this interpretation of the film's textual antecedents might at first glance seem far-fetched, it certainly suggests that Micheaux's employment of Robeson for this 1924–1925 picture was much more than the astute promotional scheme of a showman who hired a rising star cheap:

Mercedes Gilbert was a veteran of stage and screen. She had already appeared in *The Call of His People* (Reol Productions, 1921). She would later play the lead in Langston Hughes's play *Mulatto* during much of its Broadway run in 1936.

Robeson's appearance in *Body and Soul* helped to forge a crucial intertextual connection between the film and the much publicized and discussed plays. As the common denominator in this tour de force, he was the glue that bound the two sets of work together. Certainly the collective appropriation of three plays makes *Body and Soul* an audacious undertaking. One might turn to Griffith films such as *A Corner in Wheat* (1909) or *The Avenging Conscience* (1914), Jean Epstein's *Fall of the House of Usher* (1928), or Orson Welles's *Chimes at Midnight* (1966) in a search for cinematic counterparts.[21] In these instances, the author's oeuvre provides the unifying factor. Here the shift is twofold. On one hand, Micheaux equates and conflates the plays, for they share the same racial perspective, irrespective of authors. On the other, Robeson is assigned the role customarily played by the author—a not altogether complimentary assignment given Micheaux's critical assessment of the plays. Indeed, the filmmaker used an array of textual operations to constantly engage these stage works: weaving them together, playing them off each other, eliding, condensing, inverting, displacing, and finally elaborating different elements in each. In the process, he refigures the plays' most basic narratives and thematics, challenging their ideological presuppositions. He takes three plays about Negro life, written by white playwrights, and reappropriates them. That is, he reasserts not a greater black reality as such but a black critique of white racial ideology—of white stereotypes and narrative tropes.

Nan Bagby Stephens's *Roseanne* and Eugene O'Neill's *The Emperor Jones*

Roseanne was a key source for *Body and Soul,* as Hazel Carby has pointed out.[22] Although the playscript was never published and manuscript copies do not survive in major archives, it is a play that should be rescued. The *New York Tribune* provided a detailed description of its story line:

> Roseanne was one of those fine types of negro still to be found in the South, industrious, intelligent and with a religious faith that approaches the fanatical. Her loves were an adopted child, Leola, and Preacher Cicero Brown. When the play opens Roseanne has succeeded in saving a sufficient sum of money to pay for her home, Leola's home, and where it is Roseanne's greatest happiness to receive her beloved Preacher Brown. The scene shows the preacher on one of these occasional visits, surrounded by Roseanne and other adoring neighbors, worshipping literally at his feet.
>
> With various excuses he sends the women away; that is, all except the half-grown girl, Leola. It is when they are alone that the preacher shows his true colors. Seizing the girl by the throat and threatening to disclose their past relations, he forces her to give him Roseanne's savings. To make sure of the safety of his own future, he frightens Leola into writing a note to Roseanne saying that it is she who has stolen the money and then to run away to Atlanta, where he promises to join her and make good for his past sins by a legal marriage.
>
> The second act finds Leola in a bare and cheerless bedroom in an Atlanta hovel. The preacher has failed to keep his promise and the girl, half-starved and broken by remorse, is near unto death. Here Roseanne, with only love in her heart, finds her adopted child. When Roseanne asks Leola why she took the money the girl at first makes some futile excuse, and then breaks down and declares that it was the preacher who forced her to steal for him. With an hysterical outburst of rage and indignation Roseanne accuses Leola of lying, but at last, heeding the girl's supplications, she looks into her eyes and sees the truth. With a few broken sobs Leola begs Roseanne's forgiveness for her sins and then the frail body crumples and falls back on the couch lifeless.
>
> In these few brief moments everything worth while has been swept out of the life of Roseanne. She has lost Leola, whom she loved with the passionate love of a mother, and she has lost her faith in the black-faced preacher whom she loved as a man and as a symbol of her God. Nothing is now in her heart but mad desire for revenge. . . .
>
> After this it was only a question as to when and where Roseanne would again come face to face with Preacher Brown, and Miss Stephens chose the logical meeting place, which was, of course, at the Sunday service at the preacher's church, where he was surrounded by his devoted followers.
>
> There was a short sermon and the singing of many chants (for the good of the drama perhaps too many), and then, when the congregation had worked itself into a state of semi-frenzy common to negro revival meetings, Roseanne appeared and, herself half-frenzied with grief and insatiable desire for revenge, denounced the preacher. "Come down! Come down!" cries Roseanne, and the cringing, cowering preacher slinks from his pulpit, stumbles down the aisle and, with the curses of his former followers ringing in his ears, disappears into the night.
>
> The story has reached its end, but there remained the inevitable third act. Miss Stephens did her best to overcome the difficulty, but her effort was not very successful. The preacher had eluded his congregation, now bent on his destruction, by hiding in the woods. As the morning dawned he sought refuge at the cottage of Roseanne. When he met there the woman whose life he had ruined he told her that while he lay in the woods he had "seen the light"

and besought her to give him another chance. If the audience was not convinced with the sincerity of the preacher Roseanne was, assisted him to escape from his pursuers and started him on his promised reformation.[23]

This account is complemented by shorter ones in the *New York Times* and *Pittsburgh Courier:*

> Cicero Brown has been a farmhand who felt the call to exhort and save souls. The play finds him idolized by the "Ladies Aid Society" and especially by the pious and virtuous Roseanne. But power has quite turned his head. Treating the Lady's Aid with the manners of a Moro [*sic*] Sultan, he dispatches them upon trivial errands—and thus makes an opportunity to steal the money with which Roseanne is to pay off the mortgage. This deed involves Roseanne's adopted daughter, Leola, and results in her death. So we come to the great scene in which Roseanne, torn between grief for Leola and rage at the shattering of her ideal of the Reverend Cicero, breaks in upon a meeting of Mount Zion Church, denounces the pastor and incites the congregation to lynch him.
>
> This church scene has many of the elements of drama. The Reverend Cicero browbeats his "Brethren and Sisters" by name, until they "come across" to the foot of the pulpit and deposit their "voluntary offerings." Then by means of promises of heaven and threats of hell, he rouses them to an emotional hysteria which brings men and women both groveling to the floor. On the heels of this they all sing "spirituals"—an exercise that seemed especially to amuse the audience. And finally the climax which enables Crystal Herne (Roseanne) to do a particularly fine bit of rousing melodrama.[24]

> "Roseanne" is a colored washerwoman in a small Georgia town; Robeson, as the Rev. Cicero Brown, is a pastor of the Mt. Zion Church, and leader of the community. To the flock he is the "Holy Man." In his real self he has an insane desire for money.[25]

Theater critic Theophilus Lewis was fascinated by the play, though he found Cicero Brown to be a sanctimonious ass unlikely to survive as a preacher. Nonetheless, the character evoked the pastors of Lewis's youth "who entered a house, not with a text of scripture on the lips but with a joke rolling off their tongues and a twinkle in their eyes."[26] Paul Robeson, himself the son of a pastor, also found it "a very fine play."[27] And it is worth noting that his wife Eslanda began the opening chapter of a biography about her husband, *Paul Robeson, Negro* (1930), with a lengthy and highly critical description of the ways in which black communities turned their preachers into godlike figures and then spoiled them. "Preachers, being human beings, had their failings. Some remained faithful to their great responsibilities and some remained unscrupulous."[28] As W. E. B. Du Bois remarked, "The Preacher is the most unique personality developed by the Negro on American soil. A leader, a politician, an orator, a 'boss,' an intriguer, an idealist—all these he is, and ever, too, the centre of a group of men, now twenty, now a thousand in number."[29] To stage a play with a Negro pastor as a central character was to address the core of the African-American community.

As anyone who knows Micheaux's oeuvre might predict, the filmmaker was likewise drawn to Brown: the dissembling, money-hungry pastor must have conjured up similar characters from his earlier novels (the pastor and father-in-law figure of *The Homesteader*) and films (the two-faced white man's minister in *Within Our Gates*). The parallels between Rev. Isiaah Jenkins's manipulation of Martha Jane and Cicero Brown's exploitation of Roseanne are sustained (suggested by the similarities in the names of the two women). Martha Jane, like Roseanne, makes her money washing clothes, while Isiaah forces her daughter Isabelle (just as Cicero forces Roseanne's adopted daughter Leola) to give him her savings. Isabelle, like Leola, flees to Atlanta rather than stay at home and try to explain the theft to her mother. Martha Jane likewise

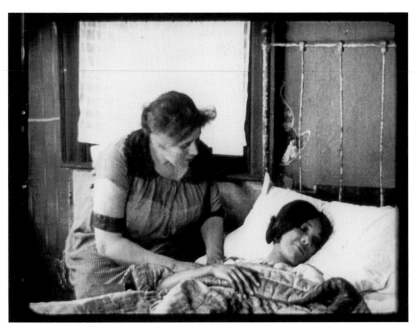

Martha Jane (Mercedes Gilbert) finds her daughter Isabelle (Julia Theresa Russell) on her deathbed and learns all.

finds Isabelle on her deathbed in a hovel and finally is told all by her dying child. Martha Jane, again like Roseanne, returns to denounce the reverend in his own church. The local population rebels, and Jenkins—like Brown—flees to the swamps for safety. Again Jenkins begs Martha Jane's forgiveness, just as Brown pleads for Roseanne's. Nevertheless, as we shall see, despite these many parallels, Micheaux parted company with Stephens's conception and narrative, turning his film into a critique of the play rather than a heartfelt adaptation.

If, at first glance, the main story of *Body and Soul* appears to be a critical adaptation of *Roseanne,* it is essential to see how this strand of the film was also a reappropriation of *The Emperor Jones.* When the play opened on November 3, 1920 (with Charles Gilpin in the role of Brutus Jones), *New York Tribune* critic Heywood Broun offered this account of the plot:

> "The Emperor Jones" tells of an American negro, a Pullman porter, who, by some chance or other, comes to an island in the West Indies, "not yet self-determined by white marines." In two years Jones has made himself emperor. Luck has played a part, but he has been quick to take advantage of it. Once a native tried to shoot him at point blank range, but the gun missed fire, whereupon Jones announced that he was protected by a charm and that only silver bullets could harm him. When the play begins he has been emperor long enough to amass a fortune by imposing heavy taxes on the islanders and carrying on all sorts of large-scale graft. Rebellion is brewing. When Emperor Jones rings the bell which should summon his servants no one appears. The palace is deserted, but from deep in the jungle there comes the sound of the steady beat of a big drum. The islanders are whipping up their courage to the fighting point by calling on the local gods and demons of the forest.
>
> Jones, realizing that his reign is over, starts to make his escape to the coast where a French gunboat is anchored. First it is necessary for him to travel through the jungle and as time presses he must go through at night. Back in the states he was a good Baptist and he begins the journey through the dark places unafraid. But under the dim moonlight he cannot recognize any familiar landmarks and, hard as he runs, the continuous drumbeat never grows any less in his ears. Then demons and apparitions begin to torment him. First it is the figure of a negro he killed back in the states. He fires and the dim thing vanishes, but immediately he reproaches himself, for in his revolver now he has only five shots left. Four are lead bullets and the fifth is a silver one which he has reserved for himself, if by any chance capture seems imminent.
>
> Other little "armless fears" creep in upon him. As his panic increases the fears become not things in his own life, but old race fears. He sees himself being sold in a slave market and then, most horrible of all, a Congo witch doctor tries to lure him to death in a river where a crocodile god is waiting. It is at this point that he fires his last bullet, the silver one.
>
> During the night he has discarded his big patent leather boots and most of his clothes in order to run faster from the drum beat. But it is louder now than ever and in the last scene we find the natives sitting about in a circle weaving spells and moulding bullets. And it is to this spot that the defenseless and exhausted emperor crawls, having made a complete circle in the jungle as his panic whipped him on.[30]

Consider, then, the basic, shared narrative of *The Emperor Jones* and *Body and Soul*: in both works Paul Robeson plays an escaped convict, an outsider, who comes to dominate a black community by concealing his past and by creating a new supernatural or religious identity. In O'Neill's play, Brutus Jones has the local populace convinced that he has divine powers and can only be killed by a silver bullet. In Micheaux's film, Rev. Isiaah T. Jenkins assumes the identity of a minister whom the women of his congregation treat as a Christ-like figure: Martha Jane and other members of the Ladies Aid grovel before Jenkins the way the islanders bow before Jones. Each has a light-skinned sidekick—a figure who

Martha Jane confronts Rev. Jenkins in his church and denounces him.

knows his past all too well and now stands by and takes what he can: Curly Hinds in *Body and Soul*, Smithers in *The Emperor Jones*.[31] Ultimately, however, each of the Robeson characters is overthrown by his subjects or supporters, whom he has cynically exploited in the course of his stay in those communities. Each then escapes into the woodlands or jungle, where he is tracked down by the angry populace. Even the surname of the Robeson character in Micheaux's film, Jenkins, shares the first and last letters with the last name of O'Neill's character, Jones.

Micheaux synthesized *Roseanne* and *The Emperor Jones* into one coherent narrative. On a superficial level, they are complementary works. The chase through the woods is not shown in *Roseanne,* but it makes up all but one of the scenes in *The Emperor Jones.* At other moments, the two plays are strikingly parallel. Cicero Brown bears significant similarities to Brutus Jones in name, position, and deed. Both are money-hungry. Brown exploits the rural southern black population in ways that evoke the methods of Jones on his Caribbean island. Only the endings are different, in that Cicero begs Roseanne's forgiveness and ostensibly reforms, while Brutus is shot down by a group of rebellious black men. Perhaps this is related to musical differences: instead of the incessant drumming of the tom-tom, Stephens's play offered Negro spirituals (the film's musical accompaniment could draw from either or ignore both). In ways that must have struck Micheaux—as it should strike us—these two plays were two versions of the same story or two sides of the same coin, and the base currency was white America's racial ideology.

Micheaux's reappropriation of *The Emperor Jones* modifies the *Roseanne*

Jenkins comes to Martha Jane's home and begs her forgiveness.

story line; and although the filmmaker's use of the O'Neill play may be somewhat less direct, it is more profound in its implications. In the mid 1920s, Eugene O'Neill's play remained highly visible and, particularly within the black community, highly controversial. In 1921, a critic for the *Negro World* called *The Emperor Jones* "a travesty of the African race."[32] At the same time, certain (presumably white) American critics were calling *The Emperor Jones* "the greatest play of modern times."[33] When it came to white dramatists depicting African Americans on the stage, *The Emperor Jones* was a touchstone—initiating a whole cycle of plays for which it was source, inspiration, and/or commercial catalyst.[34] *Roseanne* was an exemplary piece in this pattern. Superficially, *Body and Soul* was an extension of this cycle into film, but on a deeper level, it was a rejection and critique of what Micheaux consider a disturbing trend. That is, the film reappropriates these elements for African-American culture—for "the race"—and offers up a film that resists a phenomena that had strong advocates in the black community.

CHARLES GILPIN AND PAUL ROBESON

To fully appreciate the process of reappropriation and resistance that dynamizes Micheaux's *Body and Soul,* we should briefly consider the history of *Roseanne* and *The Emperor Jones* on the stage and also examine the ways in which similar processes of reappropriation and resistance occurred in the arena of performance. This means focusing on actor Charles Gilpin, and his real-life doppelganger in this period—Robeson. For it was Robeson who seemed to haunt Gilpin's every step after the elder, more established actor gave the young law student some pointers for his professional stage debut in Mary Hoyt Wiborg's *Taboo* (1922).[35] It was Gilpin who played the role of Cicero in the initial black-cast version of *Roseanne* and Robeson who replaced him. The former football star would do so again, only a month or two later, with *The Emperor Jones.*

Roseanne opened on Broadway at the very end of 1923 with a cast of respected white actors in blackface. For Chrystal Herne as Roseanne, "it was an evening of many fine moments."[36] Nonetheless, the play enjoyed only a short run. The play's producer, perhaps recognizing the credibility problems of these casting choices, reopened the play with an all-black cast in late February 1924—including Gilpin as Cicero Brown. (Such a casting choice would have emphasized the similarities, if not the actual indebtedness, of *Roseanne* to *Emperor Jones.*) It ran for two weeks at the Shubert's Pitt Theatre (Pittsburgh), and enjoyed positive reviews in the black press.[37] Now it was Gilpin as Cicero (rather than the actress in the title role) who was hailed: "His fine art is shown in the last scene when he becomes a remorseful and penitent sinner after his villainy and duplicity as a leader of the people."[38]

When the company moved to New York City, opening at the Shubert's Riviera Theatre (97th St. and Broadway) on March 10th, notices in the black press continued to be positive. Lester A. Walton enthused about Gilpin's performance in the *New York Age*:

> Charles S. Gilpin, the most distinguished and best known member of the cast, is a marked improvement over the white actor who played the part. In the Mt. Zion Church scene he is a "singing preacher" par excellence. It is agreeably noticeable that he pays strict attention to detail, such as preaching from a large Bible and wearing dust-covered clothing after spending a night in the swamp eluding his former admirers. He knows Negro life and faithfully depicts it.[39]

Gilpin, it seems, managed to smuggle in a certain degree of "black reality" that had previously been absent. But Walton may also have touched on an aspect of his performance that generated some unhappiness from Stephens and her backers: "There is a question as to whether Gilpin's interpretation is that of the author in the last act when *Cicero Brown* pleads to 'Roseanne' to save him from the mob. Is he as repentant a creature as Nan Bagby Stephens would have him to be?"[40] Perhaps these artistic (and inevitably political/ideological) choices were related to the criticisms of the *New York Times* reviewer:

> His performance turned out to be, in the main, a disappointing one. Gone is most of the authentic quality that made his performance in "The Emperor Jones" so memorable; the Gilpin who acted last night was an actor. The part of Cicero Jones is one that he should play well, but in most of the first two acts he was merely obvious. In the revival scene of act two he struck a genuine note for a few minutes.[41]

Gilpin's history of independent, even contrary performances was apparent in *Roseanne*.

When the play was "booked over the colored circuit and [would] not return to Broadway as originally planned," Gilpin quit the show.[42] Still waiting to perform the lead in Eugene O'Neill's *All God's Chillun' Got Wings*, Robeson was given the opportunity to take over the role of Cicero Brown. *Roseanne*, which featured the singing of Negro spirituals as part of its attraction, may have benefited from Robeson's voice. After a week of rehearsals, a revised cast opened for a one-week run at the Lafayette Theatre in Harlem on March 24th.[43] According to the *New York Age*, Robeson "had everything for the part of Rev. Cicero Brown but maturity."[44] The following week, he and his fellow actors performed at the Dunbar Theatre in Philadelphia.[45] Within another five weeks, he was appearing in the revival of *The Emperor Jones.*

It is fashionable, and perhaps too easy, for today's critics to lambaste *The Emperor Jones*. Although a controversial work from the outset, and one that members of the African-American community found particularly problematic, *The Emperor Jones* did possess significant progressive attributes, if not as an isolated text, then as a piece performed in 1920s America.[46] Brutus Jones can be seen as a complex, tragic figure in the tradition of Shakespeare's *Macbeth*, and playing such a role was then a rare opportunity for black performers. In fact, the play provided both Charles Gilpin and Paul Robeson, the two great African-American dramatic actors of the 1920s, with a vehicle to national recognition. Moreover, it altered the racial politics of New York's mainstream theater, where prominent black roles were routinely performed by white actors in blackface. This practice disintegrated in the wake of O'Neill's work.[47] (The production history of *Roseanne* is an effective demonstration of this shift.) Finally, the play not only has one principal character, it is particularly open to creative remolding by the actor who plays that role, and Eugene O'Neill did insist on a black actor.

Today we associate *The Emperor Jones* primarily with Robeson, due to the 1933 film adaptation in which he starred. In the 1920s, however, the O'Neill play was linked first and foremost to Gilpin, who originated the role when the play debuted at the Provincetown Playhouse in Greenwich Village on November 3, 1920.[48] Robeson's performance in the revival of *The Emperor Jones*, which opened on May 6, 1924, was thus judged against Gilpin's; and it was generally recognized that the two offered very different interpretations of the part. Robeson's size and charismatic presence made him fit naturally into the role of a larger-than-life dictator. As critic Will Anthony Madden remarked, "To begin with, Robeson has the physical build that makes him look the part of just what the character portrays and with that powerful rich voice and the ease with which he acts, I must say the theatre has gained a great deal by the addition of this sterling and promising actor to its ranks."[49] Gilpin, with his slighter build, older appearance (he was in his mid-forties by 1920), and apparent lack of sex appeal had found it effective to construct a character who achieved his aim through cunning, deceit, and guile. In the film *Ten Nights in a Barroom* (Colored Players Film Corporation, 1926), Gilpin played Joe Morgan, a character on a steady downhill slide—a trajectory similar to the one he executed

Paul Robeson as Emperor Jones in the London production of Eugene O'Neill's *The Emperor Jones* (circa September 1925).

in *Emperor Jones.* To this role he brought a sense of inner struggle and torment that was intense yet calibrated and controlled. It is this complexity that O'Neill undoubtedly found compelling in his performance, and it explains why he preferred Gilpin to Robeson—despite his praise for the latter's work in that role. O'Neill's "preference" is surprising because the actors "collaborated" or interacted with the O'Neill playscript in quite different ways.

Gilpin had established himself as an important figure in black theater before appearing in *Emperor Jones.* He had worked on the stage since the 1890s, and Sister Francesca Thompson informs us that he was the first of the Lafayette Players to be given star billing. Retaining a strong sense of independence, he quit that group when he felt his salary was insufficient.[50] Gilpin was never a mannequin who did the producer's, director's, or play-

Charles Gilpin as Emperor Jones in the New York production of Eugene O'Neill's *The Emperor Jones* (1920).

wright's bidding.[51] According to Thomas Cripps, he lost a job in a major Hollywood production of *Uncle Tom's Cabin* because he played the part of Uncle Tom with too much aggression.[52] His relationship to O'Neill was predictably stormy; that their collaboration spanned so many years is testament not only to their interdependence but to mutual, somewhat grudging, respect.

Eugene O'Neill systematically avoided characters (white or black) that might be seen as providing positive images. This refusal, not only with *The Emperor Jones* but also *All God's Chillun' Got Wings,* made many black critics and audiences unhappy. As *All God's Chillun'* went into rehearsals early in 1924, W. E. B. Du Bois publicly supported O'Neill for this avoidance, providing an endorsement that was printed in the Provincetown Players playbill:

Charles Gilpin as Joe Morgan in *Ten Nights in a Barroom* (1926). On a steady downward slide.

The Negro today fears any attempt of the artist to paint Negroes. He is not satisfied unless everything is perfect and proper and beautiful and joyful and hopeful. He is afraid to be painted as he is, lest his human foibles and shortcomings be seized by his enemies for the purposes of the ancient and hateful propaganda.

Happy is the artist that breaks through any of these shells, for his is the kingdom of eternal beauty. He will come through scarred, and perhaps a little embittered—certainly astonished at the almost universal misinterpretation of his motives and aims. Eugene O'Neill is bursting through. He has my sympathy, for his soul must be lame with the blows rained upon him. But it is work that must be done.[53]

Certainly it would be wrong to dismiss O'Neill's creations as simple, degrading stereotypes. Nevertheless, Gilpin and many black commentators of the time recognized that the problems of the plays went well beyond the question of positive or negative images. There were deeper, less easily articulated issues of racial representation, as well as the more obvious one of language.

One potentially offensive aspect of *The Emperor Jones* (and *All God's Chillun'*) was O'Neill's free use of the word "nigger," which he most often put in the mouths of his black characters. Brutus Jones constantly employs the term—referring to "bush niggers" and "common niggers." And when talking to himself, he routinely uses this term of address. Once established in the role, if not from the very outset, Gilpin avoided it. According to O'Neill's biographer Louis Shaeffer, Gilpin balked at the word "nigger" and changed it to "Negro" or "colored man." He began taking other liberties with the script as well. O'Neill eventually threatened to have him fired—or to punch him out.[54] After 204 performances in New York, *The Emperor Jones* went on the road for two years, during which time Gilpin was free from such close supervision and presumably adjusted the language to his own taste.

The Emperor Jones, as Gilpin performed it, was the product of a struggle between writer and actor. O'Neill himself was not always sure who had won, claiming that Gilpin "played Emperor with author, play and everyone concerned."[55] Certainly Gilpin felt that he had "created the role of Emperor. . . . [O'Neill] just wrote the play."[56] The play was thus Gilpin's to appropriate and reshape—at least in theory. In practice, the actor's ability to transform the play remained limited. Certainly he could not alter the basic narrative and the assumptions that underlay it. For Gilpin, alcohol became one refuge. And when he reprised his performance in 1926, at least one critic noticed that Gilpin seemed to "lend the impression of a slight loss of enthusiasm in the role."[57] His acting suggested a certain distance between actor and character, at least to those looking for such signs in his rendering of the part. Certainly this working against the grain was consistent with his aborted rendition of the Uncle Tom role in the Hollywood movie of Harriet Beecher Stowe's novel and his treatment of Cicero Brown in *Roseanne*. James Baldwin's oft-quoted remarks seem apropos:

> It is scarcely possible to think of a black American actor who has not been misused. . . . What the black actor has managed to give are moments, created, miraculously, beyond the confines of the script: hints of reality, smuggled like contraband into a maudlin tale, and with enough force, if unleashed, to shatter the tale to fragments."[58]

In his performance, Gilpin resisted, implicitly criticized, and—where possible—transformed elements of the O'Neill play which he found offensive. In this respect, Micheaux's and Gilpin's response to the play were quite similar, though the filmmaker operated with much greater freedom.

Between Gilpin's and Robeson's performances in *The Emperor Jones*, there was, according to theater reviewer Gene Fowler, "a bridge of difference."[59] In contrast to Gilpin, Robeson wholeheartedly embraced the *Emperor Jones* playscript, perhaps because of the pleasures he experienced during its rehearsal and production. Here the actor found a seemingly utopian space in which he could explore his artistic aspirations. In her 1930 biography of Paul, Eslanda (Essie) Robeson gushed about the Provincetown Players, who "wrote and produced plays entirely for intellectual and artistic self-expression and experiment."[60] She described the nature of her husband's evolving relationship with these new colleagues: "At Jimmy's [James Light], Fitzy's [Eleanor Fitzgerald], or Gig's [Harold McGhee] he had long talks with O'Neill about *Jones* and *Chillun*, about the meaning of the plays, about the purpose of the theatre. As he knew them better the talk drifted to the theatre in general, to life in general."[61] After having worked with inexperienced and second-rate playwrights, Robeson was enamored with O'Neill and his circle (a feeling that unquestionably went both ways). There were leisurely, fascinating conversations—the very type of interaction that the actor enjoyed so much. "Paul began to sense vaguely how great plays were written," Essie observed.

> When a sensitive, gifted artist like Gene went into a community, or witnessed a human experience, or felt the powerful influences of nature, he reacted emotionally to them; because of his great gift he could go back to the theatre, and, with characters, conversation, scenes and acts recreate that community, or person . . . so successfully that he could make the people who saw his play know and understand and sympathise with that community or person . . . as he did; and perhaps feel, according to their sensitivity, at least some of the emotional reactions he felt. This knowledge gave Paul an entirely new conception of the theatre. As a spectator and as an actor it meant infinitely more to him. He could now get more from a play and give more to a play.[62]

In this process, Robeson came to have a new understanding about art, about life and about himself. The Provincetown Players, concluded Essie, "were really responsible for Paul's choice of the stage as a career."[63]

Because he was working with director James Light, the twenty-six-year-old Robeson felt he was given considerable latitude to make the parts of Brutus Jones and Jim Harris his own. As Essie remarked:

> They tore the lines to pieces and Paul built them up again for himself, working out his own natural movements and gestures with Jimmy's watchful help. "I can't tell you what to do," said Jimmy, "but I can help you find what's best for you." Paul was able to bring to both *Chillun* and *Jones* not only a thorough understanding of the script itself, but a further racial understanding of the characters.[64]

This sense of a true and honest collaboration has all the earmarks of a Stanislavskian approach in which the actor absorbs himself into the role, working from his own personal experience and sense of inner truth. As Constantin Stanislavsky wrote in *My Life in Art*, published (in English) the same year Robeson appeared in O'Neill's two plays:

> I speak of the truth of emotions, of the truth of inner creative urges which strain forward to find expression, of the truth of the memories of bodily and physical perceptions. I am not interested in a truth that is without myself, but the truth of my relation to this or that event on stage, to the properties, the scenery, the other actors who play parts in the drama with me, to their thoughts and emotions.[65]

Stanislavsky's "creative if" enables the actor to take a playscript, which is "a coarse scenic lie" and transform it into something fundamentally new—something in which the actor can and must totally believe: "the most delicate truth of his relation to the life imagined."[66] This working method helps to account for Robeson's sense of artistic integrity that sustained his devotion to O'Neill and associates. Indeed, given the freedom to interpret and present the role of Brutus Jones, he was quite content to retain the script's problematic language.

As O'Neill wrote to Robeson in an inscription to a published volume of his plays:

> In gratitude to Paul Robeson in whose interpretation of "Brutus Jones" I have found the most complete satisfaction an author can get—that of seeing his creation born into flesh and blood!
> Again with gratitude and friendship.
>
> (signed) Eugene O'Neill
>
> And in whose creation of "Jim Harris" in my "All God's Chillun Got Wings" I found not only complete fidelity to my intent under trying circumstances but, beyond that, true understanding and [rarest?] integrity.[67]

Robeson's approach to acting not only was radically different than that of the actor he replaced—and, in the process, disciplined; it was also more compliant. It is hardly surprising that Gilpin, after seeing Robeson's debut performance, quarreled with O'Neill in the theater dressing room after the play.[68] If Robeson was more accommodating, it is important to recognize that Robeson's persona, as it was then emerging, nonetheless worked off and problemetized these characters to a remarkable degree. The street-smart power-hungry Brutus Jones, whose atavistic unraveling dominated the play, differed markedly from the erudite, Phi Beta Kappa graduate who was soon exploring his African-American heritage through the singing of Negro spirituals. Although Robeson played Jim Harris, who could not pass the bar exam in *All God's Chillun'*, the actor was widely known as a successful graduate of Columbia Law School (albeit one who had found his opportunities in the profession blocked by racism within the legal establishment). Less foreseeable, less public, and perhaps more controversial, the desexualized relationship between the Jim Harris character and the white woman who becomes his wife was not sustained in the backstage world that Robeson actually inhabited.[69] Of course, Robeson was supposed to find aspect of these characters inside himself; nonetheless, this gap between character and performer foregrounded the play as a construction and emphasized Robeson's talents as an actor. So did the different requirements of his performances in the two quite contrasting roles of Jim Harris and Brutus Jones.

The Emperor Jones was thus a site for struggle from the outset. Both Robeson and Gilpin found ways to engage the text in an effort to make it their own. Clearly both actors saw their performances of this play as something more than literal renderings of the O'Neill script. For both, acting was a creative process in which they brought their own considerable talents to bear, but each used his talents in opposite ways. In his exploration of African-American culture during the early decades of the twentieth century, Houston A. Baker, Jr., sees two creative tendencies at work: "the mastery of form" and "the deformation of mastery." In this respect, Robeson mastered the emergent form of Stanislavskian acting in an effort to enhance the play, giving it greater realism—greater immediacy, credibility, and artistic truth. This approach stood in opposition to the mask of minstrelsy—even as it unconsciously revitalized significant elements of it. (In fact, as I have suggested above, it sought to open up a gap between character and actor of a different order.) Robeson embraced the mastery of form. Gilpin, in contrast, engaged the text critically and, through this confrontation with O'Neill's play, achieved a performance with a high degree of intensity. His approach was certainly the deformation of mastery. Baker points to two aspects of the dynamics of deformation: "First, the indigenous comprehend the territory within their own vale/veil more fully than any intruder. . . . Second, the indigenous sound appears monstrous and deformed only to the intruder."[70] In Baker's framework, deformation is a method of reappropriation and resistance. Thus, "the Afro-American spokesperson who would perform a deformation of mastery . . . must transform an obscene situation . . . into a signal of self/cultural expression."[71] Gilpin's on-and-off battle with O'Neill is a case in point. When engaging plays about Negro life by white playwrights (or at least these plays by these white playwrights), Micheaux—like Gilpin and many commentators—did not find the mastery of form to be an appropriate way to engage these texts. Deformation seemed the only viable response to plays which Will Anthony Madden, among others, considered obscene—that is "the most damaging and insulting piece of propaganda against the Negro race that could possibly be written."[72]

MICHEAUX'S DEFORMATION OF *THE EMPEROR JONES* AND *ROSEANNE*

Because Paul Robeson is the artist that the three theatrical sources for *Body and Soul* have in common, the film's barbs are directed not only at the plays but at the actor who played the lead in all three works. That is, Micheaux plays the role of trickster as he teases and puts down his film's own star. Through the art of Signifying or naming, the filmmaker redirects the spectators' attention away from the superficial meaning to a latent one.[73] This decoding of the figure depends on the audience dismissing the apparent meaning and using the knowledge shared by storyteller and audience to reinterpret the text. Consider the first two shots following the main title of *Body and Soul*—added just as the film was being readied for release.[74] The first is an intertitle:

> The Rt. Reverend Isiaah [*sic* ?] T. Jenkins, alias, "Jeremiah, The Deliverer"—still posing as a man of God.
>
> —Paul Robeson[75]

At first glance this is a fairly typical way to introduce a character played by a movie star whom we expect to carry the picture. Openly acknowledging the actor's importance to the film from the perspective of showmanship, this introductory title prepares us for the following shot to be of Robeson in the role of Jenkins. This expectation is disappointed. Instead, there is a newspaper insert with the following information:

EX-CONVICT MAKES ESCAPE

"Black Carl" noted Negro detective, reports the escape of a prisoner whom he had arrested in Tatesville, Ga. and was bringing North for extradition to England where he was wanted on several charges. When arrested, the ex-convict and a man of many aliases, was posing as a preacher under the title of "The Rt. Reverend Isiaah T. Jenkins."

This news item undermines the previous intertitle, seemingly "by mistake," in that it makes clear that Jenkins is also an alias. We are never given the character's real name—just his aliases. This omission means that Micheaux provides us with only one "real" name—that of Robeson. The news item generates other disruptions to the narrative as well. We can only make sense of this news item, it seems to me, as a kind of alternative closure to the main narrative of the film, which the audience might otherwise come to dismiss as "just a dream." That is, if arranged chronologically, this announcement should conclude the film rather than begin it. This noirish revelation of the end at the film's beginning establishes the disjunctive quality of *Body and Soul* from the very outset.[76]

This news item must give us pause. Who is Black Carl, and why would he be bringing his prisoner north for extradition to England? This seems to be a bizarre non sequitur until one realizes that just as the film was opening in the United States, Robeson was in London enjoying a much-celebrated appearance in *The Emperor Jones*. The Urban League's *Opportunity Magazine* had just excerpted his best British reviews in a two-page spread.[77] Ads and promotional copy for *Body and Soul* also made much of Robeson's English success, noting that the film starred "Paul Robeson who electrified London audiences with his masterly acting."[78] Even before they entered the theater, audiences were thus prepared to recognize that the apparently awkward failure to provide the Robeson's character's real name is actually a purposeful joke.[79] This "joke" is a dense and dark one, for "Black Carl" was the stage name for actor Ed Johnson, "known to many for his great work on the stage years ago."[80] Johnson had been an assistant to Herman the Magician and was "the most widely acquainted colored man on the stage and was honored by all who knew him." He had been the stage manager for *Shuffle Along*, in which Robeson made a brief appearance, but in recent years had served as head carriage man at the Metropolitan Opera House—a sinecure for aging actors. That Micheaux has the Robeson character arrested by this great man of the black theater—its conscience and pioneer—was surely a clever and vicious indictment of his star. It also reinforces the intertextual engagement with the theatre.

What then were the "crimes" of which Robeson was being accused? The full implication of the film's refusal to provide Jenkins's real name now becomes evident, for these cards suggest that Jenkins is just one of *Robeson's* many aliases. Brutus Jones and Cicero Brown would be two others. Thus, undermining Gilpin and his resistant performances was perhaps one of the performer's offenses.[81] Simply acting in the O'Neill plays, which some critics found deeply disturbing ("genius productions . . . of the most insidious and damaging kind," according to one critic)[82] was another. Robeson's desire to appear in the plays are certainly understandable,[83] but these ideological and ethical issues were exacerbated by the actor's enthusiastic endorsement of the works in question. As *The Emperor Jones* had its London debut, roughly a month or so before the premiere of *Body and Soul*, Robeson mobilized his Stanislavsky-like outlook to affirm the play in the strongest and most disturbing terms. "O'Neill has got what no other playwright has—that is, the true, authentic Negro psychology. He has read the Negro soul, and has felt the Negro's racial tragedy," the actor remarked. Describing the process of playing a modern Negro who is gradually reduced to primeval man, Robeson added:

> One does not need a very long racial memory to lose oneself in such a part. . . . As I act civilization falls away from me. My plight becomes real, the horrors terrible facts. I feel the terror of the slave mart, the degradation of man bought and sold into slavery. Well I am the son of an emancipated slave and the stories of old father are vivid on the tablets of my memory.[84]

In this article, which appeared in Reynolds' *Illustrated News* (London) and was reprinted in the *Pittsburgh Courier,* Robeson comes across as egotistic, somewhat simple-minded, and an Uncle Tom. In contrast to Gilpin, whose engagement with the playscript precluded "a child-like naïveté and trustfulness,"[85] Robeson wholeheartedly embraced it. If *The Emperor Jones* was insidious, as Micheaux and many African-American critics believed, then Robeson's statements were compounding the offense. The actor was also grandstanding, and Micheaux—whose ads puffed the actor still further—opened the film with two title cards that cut him down to size. They suggest that Robeson was not an actor playing evil roles but was himself a dissembler very much like the character he was playing. Or, put another way, Robeson confused the (white) stage with real (black) life.[86] Robeson and his friends were not simple-minded. They must have realized that *Body and Soul* was a not-so-private joke made at his expense. No wonder the performer never mentioned the picture.

This approach—superficial admiration hiding serious critique—was the strategy Micheaux used to engage Stephens's and O'Neill's depictions of Negro life as well. How then did Micheaux rework these plays to create this extraordinary film, *Body and Soul*? The reworking of *Roseanne* is straightforward, at least in the beginning. This retelling is so faithful to its source that the picture seems

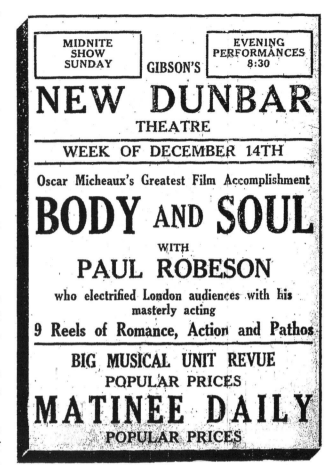

Advertisements for *Body and Soul* pointed to Robeson's London achievements. From *Pittsburgh Courier*, 12 December 1925, 11.

to be imitative, derivative—even plagiarizing. Yet this repetition is crucial to his critique of Stephens's play, which is directed at its ending. The movie reenacts Roseanne's blind faith in her pastor with Martha Jane. Martha Jane's (Roseanne's) daughter is dead, her money gone. She discovers that her beloved Rev. Jenkins (i.e., Cicero Brown) is the responsible party and denounces him in church. Pursued by the angry townspeople, he flees into the woods and returns to Martha Jane's (Roseanne's) home, where he begs her forgiveness. Arguing that she spoiled him and was responsible for his transgressions, he promises to reform. Martha Jane/Roseanne forgives him. This is how the play ends—with the playwright wanting us to believe that Rev. Brown will indeed straighten out. Micheaux—like Gilpin—found this preposterous—insulting and racist—that is, white nonsense or white minstrelsy of the worst kind. What would you do—what would *anyone* do—if someone stole your life's saving, raped your daughter, and left her to die in a garret? Well, Martha Jane realizes that it is her fault and lets Rev. Jenkins go. She turns the other cheek. And what happens? Needless to say, the fake preacher does not reform. Indeed, he quickly slaps his benefactress on the other cheek and kills her son (the helpless black youth dies calling for his mama). At this moment Martha Jane finally wakes up—as black audiences watching the film had doubtlessly been telling her to do for some time in the process of verbal engagement with the screen that characterized black movie-going.[87] This white playwright's story turns out to be "only a dream." As Henry Louis Gates, Jr., remarks in a similar context: "To dream the fantastic is to dream the dream of the Other."[88] And this is what Martha Jane has done—she has dreamed Stephens's dream of black life, which Micheaux has taken to its nightmarish but logical conclusion.

Micheaux's recounting is "repetition, with a signal difference."[89] His dogged pursuit of

Having caused Isabelle's death, Jenkins now slaps Martha Jane on the other cheek and kills her son.

Roseanne's narrative logic shows that its ending—indeed, the entire play—has been a lie. And, as the *New York Herald* review of this play makes clear, this fact needed to be stated in the most forceful terms. For Charles Belmont Davis began his column in this manner:

Had Miss Nan Bagby Stephens chosen poor white folks as the characters in her play "Roseanne," produced Saturday night at the Greenwich Village Theater, the piece would have been regarded, and rightly, as sordid melodrama. But the puppets of the authoress were all members of the negro colony of a small Southern town, and thus her excellent effort developed into a somber study of the primitive customs and almost barbaric instincts to which the black is supposed to be heir.[90]

In seeing this play—and perhaps in reading this review—must not Micheaux have felt that "sense of always looking at oneself through the eyes of others, of measuring one's soul by the tape of a world that looks on in amused contempt and pity"—in short, that peculiar sensation which Du Bois called "double consciousness."[91] *Body and Soul* was his response. Instead of Stephens's vision of Negro life in the South, we have Micheaux's biting commentary on the work of a white playwright—a reversal of power relations.

The process of deformation and engagement with *The Emperor Jones* was more complex—less repetition and more reversal—at times even using aspects of the Stephens play to further its critique. Micheaux began by taking what one Paris reviewer astutely called "an American fantasy,"[92] which Micheaux clearly believed was a white fantasy, and resituating it back in black reality. Like Du Bois and other African Americans, he saw the clergy as the center of power—the real emperors—in many black communities and eagerly explored how such power could be abused by an unprincipled con artist or impostor. In this he was transposing *Emperor Jones* and *Roseanne* via Charlie Chaplin's *The Pilgrim* (1923), in which Charlie is an escaped convict forced to play the role of village parson or face exposure and arrest. In contrast to Chaplin's picture, however, Micheaux subsumed comedy under the conventions of drama and melodrama.[93]

In *The Emperor Jones*, O'Neill underscores the theme of economic exploitation, making it clear that Jones is merely doing what he learned from watching powerful (white) heads of corporations and government, who stole bigtime. Even though O'Neill's Marxist sympathies are evident, in the end the playwright is not interested in the particulars of exploitation so much as in the psychological unravelings of an individual.[94] Brutus Jones talks about how he took the islanders' money, but the process is never shown. Micheaux, in contrast, devoted most of his film to detailing the many ways in which Rev. Jenkins exploits the black community. In this respect, to be sure, he owed something to *Roseanne.* The impostor builds his power base by endearing himself to his congregation, particularly the older women who fantasize a sexual relationship with him. Martha Jane just represents an extreme case as she seeks to have her unrequited desires played out through her daughter, Isabelle. But Jenkins is hardly a naive peasant farmer like Cicero Brown who proves to be ill-equipped to assume positions of responsibility and authority. Embedded in *Roseanne* and the character of Cicero Brown is the assumption that blacks as a race lack certain moral and ethical qualities that justify their subordinate status. Isiaah Jenkins is much more worldly and more devious. He is an escaped (or ex-) convict, a man of the underworld who has learned his tricks in prison. The film begins with Jenkins helping himself to a saloonkeeper's hard liquor and then demanding a "donation," threatening the hooch seller with an anti-liquor campaign if he protests. That is, Micheaux shows us some of the mechanisms whereby the community "leaders" pull the levers of power. These are not based on the imitation of white capitalists—as O'Neill would have it—but are embedded in the specific structures of African-American communities. Micheaux's opening up of the narrative might be compared to the 1933 film adaptation of the play itself. In that film, the filmmakers expanded on the narrative by tracing out the personal life story of Brutus Jones. His arrival at the island is touched upon, but notably absent are scenes that credibly depict the process of exploitation or make substantial the conditions of the oppressed.

This does not mean that Micheaux was uninterested in psychological issues. The portrait he created of Martha Jane is a remarkably sophisticated study of this woman's pathology: her willful blindness and girlish naiveté in the face of a difficult life of toil. As the dreamer, she is the film's psychological center; she is also the character who changes, who awakens. In contrast, Micheaux rejects the psychological devolution of the Jones/Jenkins character—the stripping away of civilization and his reduction to the primeval state of the jungle—that is the focus of the O'Neill play. Jenkins is evil: a dissembler from start to finish. His unraveling à la Jones is simple playacting as he exploits (albeit somewhat desperately) Martha Jane's known weaknesses to win her over again. But Jones's groveling on the stage was also, in the end, just playacting—by Robeson, who perhaps did it to win the support of his white benefactors (the Provincetown Players). If *Body and Soul* traces a downward spiral comparable to *The Emperor Jones*, it is not with respect to Jenkins's psychological unraveling but in the brutality with which he steals and the severity of his crimes.

Micheaux ultimately rejected O'Neill's interior psychological drama and reasserted the melodramatic tradition by reintroducing a series of clear oppositions: good and evil, victim and victimizer, innocence and corruption, and even women and men. Isabelle is an archetypal innocent, one of the long-suffering victims of villainy who, as Peter Brooks suggests, are unable to speak.[95] In her case, she cannot speak because she will not be believed by her own mother. Jenkins is clearly on the side of villainy, in ways that Brutus Jones is not. As Robeson rightly argued, Brutus is a tragic figure, caught up in a world, burdened with a fate that is beyond his control.[96] Cicero Brown is likewise too childlike, too undercivilized to be evil. Jeremiah "the deliverer" (Jenkins) possesses no such extenuating qualities.

Consider again the transpositions Micheaux introduced when the Robeson character moves through the forest. As Jones flees through the jungle, going in circles, he becomes the

Rev. Jenkins helps himself to a donation from the local saloon owner—some moonshine.

victim of his own terror, of his own return to an African primitivism. He wants to go in a straight line to safety but in circling back ensures his own demise. As Jenkins and Isabelle go in circles through the woods during a rainstorm, the circling would appear calculated on Jenkins's part. Isolated and cut off, the protection that society offers Isabelle is lost and he is free to rape her. Likewise, when he circles the table to grab Isabelle and force her to hand him her mother's money, Jenkins is reduced to an uncivilized brutality even as he remains self-conscious of his own actions (stepping back and finding a sadistic pleasure in Isabelle's pain and greeting her emotional pleadings with clever word games). And when he later flees from his congregation, he may be desperate but he does not lose his head. Rather than being killed, he turns and kills his pursuer (Martha Jane's son). This stands O'Neill on his head. For O'Neill, the mechanisms of oppression are the universal ones of white capitalism, but barbarism is tied to the African-American unconscious. Micheaux reveals that the mechanisms of exploitation are in some sense specific to small black communities deprived of other forms of leadership (elected officials, legitimate businessmen, and so on). Nonetheless, Jenkins represents a different and unracialized form of barbarism. Jeremiah/Jenkins is a sociopath not unlike Hannibal Lecter in *The Silence of the Lambs* (1991).

Micheaux's rewriting of O'Neill's play occurs along other trajectories. In *The Emperor Jones,* "the people" are savages effectively outside of civilization and its ethical distinctions. These social decencies are restored in Micheaux's film, in keeping with *Roseanne.* Micheaux reminds us how Martha Jane earned the money she saved: picking cotton, ironing other people's clothes, and so forth. Their homes and communal spaces—the domestic interiors in which they live—are shown (excepting the opening scene in the palace, O'Neill limits himself to psychological interiority). Likewise, in both *Emperor Jones* and *All God's Chillun',* it is obvious that O'Neill has an uncomfortable time dealing with black sexuality and avoids it at all costs (so, to a lesser extent, did Stephens). In *All God's Chillun',* Jim and Ella live like brother and sister. There is only one female character in *Emperor Jones,* and she is older and clearly of no sexual/romantic interest for Brutus or the audience. Brutus may be a dictator who appreciates high living, but he appears remarkably chaste. Like Cicero Brown, his principal preoccupation seems to have been the accumulating of money. This may have been credible when Gilpin played the roles, but when Robeson took over, with his charisma that exuded an intense sexuality, this absence became painfully clear. Micheaux would have none of this. It is Jenkins's attractiveness that binds and blinds the older women, making them his chief supporters. Rape and seduction are Jenkins's métier: prerogatives that come with the office.[97]

French reviewers commented that *The Emperor Jones* seemed too underdeveloped to be a truly satisfying theatrical experience. Where O'Neill was silent or retreated from a fully developed story, Micheaux was ready to confront and elaborate. He also was ready to engage issues of language, something that Gilpin had found disturbing in O'Neill's work. Through his intertitles, he did this in two ways. First, at judicious moments the film counters the associations of white with good, dark with evil—which O'Neill mobilized but leaves intact and unquestioned in *All God's Chillun'*. Isabelle at one point calls Jenkins "a white-livered, lying hypocritical beast."[98] Such constructions are carefully selected to make audiences sensitive to this use of language and aware of its arbitrariness and potential reversibility. Charlene Regester has also pointed out that Isabelle chastises her mother for using the term "nigga'," which she calls vulgar. Although the word appears in *Body and Soul* rarely, perhaps we might say judiciously, it is significant that the word is always written in dialect and is never literally spelled out. Moreover, her pronunciation of the word rhymes with that of "pastah."[99]

Jenkins (Paul Robeson) and Isabelle (Julia Theresa Russell) circle through the woods before he rapes her.

Finally, any extended engagement of *Body and Soul* must consider the Robeson doppelganger and Micheaux's use of dream, both of which have been much discussed but perhaps little understood. Suggestions that these can be explained as responses to censorship demands miss the point.[100] The playing of double roles at this time was a popular cinematic convention—Marion Davies played a double role in *Lights of Old Broadway* (1924), and dozens of other examples in American cinema of the 1910s and 1920s could be offered. It gave an actor the opportunity to display the full range of his or her acting talents. Again this can be understood, in part, as a response to *The Emperor Jones*, which was hailed as a unique opportunity for black actors. Certainly Robeson's performance in *Body and Soul* is, to my mind at least, far more inventive and impressive than his work in the film version of *The Emperor Jones*. It may well be his best screen performance.

The doppelganger is more than an artistic trope. These two brothers are linked to the Robeson characters in O'Neill's two race plays. If Jenkins is Jones's alter ego, then Sylvester is the non-neurotic, healthy counterpart to the tortured Jim Harris of *All God's Chillun'*. Heywood Broun reviewed the play for the *New York Herald*, though with little attention to the story line.

Jenkins chases Isabelle around a table—and makes her give him her mother's money.

> The play deals with the marriage of a white woman to a Negro. The first act sets forth the events leading up to the marriage. One expects that the latter half of the play will deal with the difficulties of [the] marriage in the American community.
>
> As a matter of fact, it does nothing of the sort. When next we see the white woman, she is well on the road to insanity. Before the play ends, she is stark, raving mad. No, instead of the problem of white and black, we have the problem of sane and insane. . . .

Jim Harris (Paul Robeson), on his knees, about to have his hand kissed by Ella Downey (Mary Blair) in Eugene O'Neill's *All God's Chillun' Got Wings* (1924). It was the play's most controversial moment.

> Ella Downey cannot endure the thought that Jim Harris, her husband, should pass his examination for the bar. I don't quite know why. I assume that she felt that this would make him more nearly her equal and that this she should not endure. Still, it is not clear.[101]

There are many ways in which Micheaux draws parallels between characters in his film and those in O'Neill play—often as a way to underscore differences—to create reversals or inversions. For example, Sylvester is dressed in a suit that appears to be identical to the one worn by Jim Harris.[102] Like Jim, who married Ella Downey, Sylvester is ready to marry and embrace a woman who has been seduced/raped/ corrupted by someone else. But here the parallels end. "Sylvester" as a name differs from "Jim" in every way (no letters in common, multi-syllabic, distinctive, and so forth). While Jim Harris fails to become a lawyer, Sylvester becomes a successful inventor. Jim Harris's efforts are undermined by the machinations of his white wife, Ella, while Sylvester's efforts are fostered by the devotion of his black fiancée Isabelle. "Isabelle" as a name contains all the letters of "Ella" (and shares all its letters with Leola's name); certainly she is a belle in ways that Ella is not. In *Body and Soul*, as in other Micheaux films, love and marriage become acts of racial solidarity that function as a necessary defense against societal exploitation.

As already noted, Robeson's double role in *Body and Soul* wreaks havoc with any notion of a logical plot. If Sylvester lives in the same town as his brother, then Jenkins's concealment of his past and his posturing as a minister become impossible. The full integration and logical coherence of these two narrative strands never occur on the level of story but can only be achieved by a metacritical engagement with these three plays and by a recognition of the hallucinatory state of the film's overall representational system. Martha Jane's dream state plays a crucial role in the film but provides the spectator with only a superficial and ultimately unsatisfactory solution to this problem of overall coherence. Where dream (or nightmare) ends and "reality" begins is difficult or, more accurately, impossible to

A production still for *Body and Soul* (1925) mirrors the moment of the kiss in *All God's Chillun'*. Is Robeson getting a fist or a prayer from Mercedes Gilbert? Certainly not a kiss!

establish. It means privileging certain moments, certain signs while ignoring others—which contradict them. The spectator or critic can try to read this film as a realist text, but that means s/he must be content with its manifest or superficial meaning. There are many indications that Micheaux was indeed Signifying, urging audiences to look for the latent meaning. If Jenkins is just a nightmare, a figment of Martha Jane's imagination, how does one account for the repeated intrusion of Sylvester inside that story line? How does one account for the opening title cards? The stories interpenetrate in ways that preclude this simple opposition of dream versus reality. In truth, as Micheaux's reappropriation of the plays make clear, the two narrative strands are both re-presentations of representations. They are all textual engagements. Neither is easily subordinated to the other. Rather, Micheaux shows us how two worlds—that of nightmare (Jenkins) and that of dream fantasy (Sylvester)—interrelate. Happy endings have no privileged status, in this film at least. To insist that they do (which means to treat the film as a realist text) ignores the textual operation of reversal that is the dominant trope of this film. To evoke Gates

Sylvester (Paul Robeson) and Isabelle (Julia Theresa Russell) are equals; sitting together on the ground, they look eye to eye—in contrast to Jim/Robeson on bended knee to Ella/Blair.

again, *Body and Soul* is about the fantastic ("to dream the fantastic is to dream the dream of the other"), not the real. Once these plays are understood as white fantasies—white dreams of Negro life—then we can understand how Micheaux redreamed them, reimagined them as a form of creative criticism and liberation.

Isabelle and Sylvester return from their honeymoon to find a perfect middle-class household, complete with a piano that Isabelle miraculously knows how to play. A happy ending, but how real?

BODY AND SOUL: ITS CRITICAL RECEPTION

Even as the filming of *Body and Soul* was completed, Micheaux's film *Birthright* was coming under serious criticism from the black press, particularly in Philadelphia. In a letter he sent out to African-American newspapers—published first in the *Pittsburgh Courier* of December 12, 1924—he pleaded for encouragement and assistance.

The colored producer has dared to step into a world which has hitherto remained closed to him. His entrance into this unexplored field is for him trebly difficult. He is the new born babe who must be fondled until he can stand on his own feet. If the race has any pride in presenting its own achievements in this field it behooves it to interest itself and morally encourage such efforts. I don't wish anyone to construe this as a request to suppress criticism. The producer who has confidence in his ideals solicits constructive criticism but he also asks fairness, and fairness in criticism demands a familiarity with the aims of the producer, and a knowledge of the circumstances under which his efforts were materialized.[103]

Micheaux doubtlessly recognized that *Body and Soul* would need active, supportive criticism if the film was to have a chance to succeed, and his letter must be read against the anticipated distribution of this film as much as against the travails of *Birthright.* Indeed, Micheaux may have delayed the release of *Body and Soul* in the hopes that the attitude of the press might change and that critics would come to treat his work with greater understanding and respect. At the same time, the film had an obvious potential for exploitation. Robeson's presence in the cast was a surefire selling point, for the actor's reputation had only continued to grow within the African-American community. Perhaps the film would revive those halcyon days when the *New York Age* lauded *The Symbol of the Unconquered,* asserting that it "compares favorably with screen successes put out by leading producers."[104] In that earlier film, Micheaux's attack on the resurgent Ku Klux Klan not only upended Griffith's "masterpiece," it reflected the concerns and attitudes of the nation's black weeklies, which devoted extensive news coverage to the Klan's activities. Four years later, a similar combination seemed to be at work. O'Neill's race plays had had a troubled reception in the black press: at least one writer had equated them with Thomas Dixon's *The Clansman.*[105] Once again Micheaux was reversing and reimagining racist narratives even as he was incorporating front-page news stories. The black clergy and their moral transgressions, including their compromising ties to rumrunners in the age of prohibition, were headline stories. African-American newspapers editorialized against their corruption. Was not Micheaux merely doing the same?

The film encountered resistance even before it opened. The New York Board of Censors rejected the film outright on November 7, 1925. After some radical changes, the film was approved, provided all remaining scenes of drunkenness and gambling were removed. The nine-reel picture was chopped down to five.[106] As Pearl Bowser and Louise Spence have speculated, whether the censored version was actually shown or Micheaux smuggled in the original print after receiving the necessary certificate is unclear. Descriptions of the film were sufficiently vague to cover either eventuality. Expectations certainly remained high. In New York City, *Body and Soul* opened for three days, from Sunday, November 15th through Tuesday, November 17th, at two Harlem theaters—the New Douglas Theatre, with 2,000 seats, and the Roosevelt Theatre, with more than 1,000. In an advance announcement, the *Amsterdam News* suggested that those who had seen the film were deeply moved and impressed:

> Many of our people who have deplored either the weaknesses of the story or the acting in the majority of the pictures that have been produced with an all-colored cast, will be more than agreeably surprised and proud of this sensational film
>
> The very presence of that superb super-actor, Paul Robeson, lifts a tremendously powerful story to the very heights of filmdom. . . .
>
> "Body and Soul," an appropriate title, is the signal for one of the greatest pictures ever produced with a negro cast. In nine great reels, here is a melodrama to the nth degree—a story guaranteed to hold one breathless to the very end, beautifully photographed, extraordinarily original, and acted by a cast of some of our greatest artists."[107]

After *Body and Soul* opened, there was virtual silence in the New York press. No reviews followed. The film returned several weeks later for a second three-day run (December 9–11) at the Franklin Theatre, a small (500-seat) and unprestigious movie house in Central Harlem. Located on 132nd Street and Amsterdam Avenue, the Franklin often played B-Westerns, such as *Loaded Dice* with Bill Patton and *Galloping Jinx* with Buddy Roosevelt, as well as race films, such as the Norman Film Company's *Green-Eyed Monster* (then four years old).[108] The *New York Amsterdam News,* which claimed the "Best Amusement Page in New York City," gave *Body and Soul* a peremptory two-paragraph notice: much less attention than it gave to *Don Q* with Douglas Fairbanks, then playing at the Lincoln Theatre on 135th Street and Lenox roughly five months after its New York opening, or *Lights of Old Broadway* with Marion Davies, playing at the New Douglas Theatre on 142nd and Lenox a month after its local premiere.[109]

The *New York Age,* which ran no ads for the Franklin Theatre, failed to mention the film in its columns, at least by name. Instead, the newspaper attacked the Franklin's management for decorating the theater with sensational posters and banners:

> Numerous complaints have been sent into The Age office recently, as to the character of pictures displayed each Sunday in front of the Franklin Theatre, a movie house, at 132nd Street and Lenox avenue. It is said that lurid and sensational canvases are stretched each Sunday, in front of the theatre, showing scenes from prisons, depicting the electric chair, escaping prisoners, shooting of guns, and other pictures calculated to excite and stir onlookers. In addition, it is reported that a facsimile of the electric chair used at Sing Sing prison is placed out front, with an electric buzzer whirring constantly to attract the attention of passersby.
> It is set forth that even though these displays are not illegal, they are in questionable taste, and calculated to disturb the serenity and calm which belongs to the Sabbath day.[110]

Body and Soul did play the Franklin on Sunday, and specifically the Sunday before this article appeared. Scenes of escaping convicts were consistent with the story line of the film. Perhaps Micheaux was using his talents as a showman both to attract an audience seeking sensationalism and to annoy the clergy still further.

The *Amsterdam News* publicly distanced itself from the filmmaker even as it began to "misspell" Micheaux's name: "Mischeaux," as in mischievous.[111] At least aware that Micheaux was Signifying on many levels, it reciprocated in kind:

> White theatre managers in Harlem have from time to time played the Oscar Mischeaux pictures, more from a mistaken idea of a sentiment which they feel they should exhibit in a colored community than because of the worth of the pictures. With an opportunity of viewing the best things along picture lines, it is hard to expect colored people to accept these Mischeaux pictures here in Greater New York and Northern New Jersey, and they don't. Manager Raymond Synder at the Lincoln Theatre, having been here for quite some time and with a good grasp on what should be offered at his theatre, has passed up the Mischeaux pictures because they are so far beneath what he has to offer from studios fully equipped and with high paid writers furnishing the scenarios.
> In those sections where the opportunity for witnessing the best along theatrical lines does not exist, these Mischeaux pictures would no doubt be considered the real ziz, but when it comes to competing with what our people are accustomed to see here, they are passe. Mischeaux is in the same boat in which a Marcus Garvey found himself when he tried to bring out a daily paper to compete with the O'Fays. Some years ago we bought a book written by Mischeaux. We did this on sentiment, and after the first few paragraphs we were cured. Mischeaux's pictures are along the same lines as the book which he wrote and published himself.[112]

This reworking of Micheaux's name was more than just an intentional and "clever" characterization of the man and his films. It almost certainly engaged a statement appearing in the Baltimore *Afro-American* one week earlier, one that characterized Hollywood films as "mischievous propaganda."

PLEASE GET THIS. The movies are a great institution for intellectual improvement and entertainment, and also a means of furthering schemes of MISCHIEVOUS PROPAGANDA. Your boy and girl and yourself need to know how to discriminate between the good and the bad, the true and the false. Select those pictures that offer the greatest promise of improvement material.

Learn to discriminate yourself, and teach the youngsters that they should not swallow whole all of the bunk in the films that teach the WHITE IS RIGHT. If you don't how can you expect them to grow up with the knowledge that we have a history rich with traditions of Negro soldiers, sailors, and others who have written their names on the pages of history? See all of the best of the WHITE productions, digest them and THINK. Then demand that you see more pictures with Negro casts on the screen. SAY IT WITH MONEY, that's a language all of the proprietors and managers understand.[113]

The *Amsterdam News* was challenging Micheaux and the black militancy of the *Afro-American.* It was Micheaux's films, not Hollywood's output, that was mischievous propaganda so far as the New York papers were concerned.

The *Afro-American*'s campaign for more black films culminated ten days later with the release of *Body and Soul,* which it hailed as a "magnificent combination of Negro brains and art." Indeed, if my analysis of *Body and Soul* is correct, Micheaux was using his brain to think very much along the lines of the critical reader envisioned by the *Afro-American.* In contrast to New York, Baltimore provided the film with considerable critical support and numerous theatrical play dates—the picture worked its way through almost all the movie theaters that advertised in the newspaper (see filmography in appendix). As *Afro-American* columnist Maybelle Chew remarked:

Of course, the picture is the "thing" at the Royal. Oh, boy! If some of the Reverends could see how Micheaux pictures the harm done by that Jack-leg Preacher, but, of course, they wouldn't go near that den of iniquity, a theater. And, of course, in Baltimore, the women don't buy the Reverend[s] suits, feed them on chicken dinners, hang on their slightest word and force their daughters on their attentions. Oh! No. So it wouldn't worry them. "Body and Soul" is a picture of great emotional appeal, indeed.[114]

In Baltimore, the film may have been appreciated less as a commentary on, or engagement with, the O'Neill-Stephens plays and more as a scathing, if witty, critique of the clergy and their congregations of adoring sycophants. Perhaps this is a reminder that Micheaux, like most filmmakers, wanted to make sure that his films, even though they frequently reworked literary or theatrical texts, could also be appreciated independently, free of such intertextual engagements. In Baltimore, at least, he apparently succeeded, though without such a context, its narrative coherence was always at issue.[115]

Why was *Body and Soul* rejected by New York critics and, though this is harder to definitively establish, by its audiences? Perhaps because of its very audacity, the film mocked too many groups at the same time. There was no one left to embrace the picture, to undertake the challenging critical interpretation that might have given the film its proper recognition. The intensity of Micheaux's attack on the black church and the lack of any positive images, so far as the clergy were concerned, put his film in a different category than the news exposés by African-American newspapers concerning the same problems. Of course, critics might have pointed out that Jenkins was a con artist and not a preacher, but they were silent, and Micheaux already had a track record on this point. As Charlene Regester has suggested, in attacking the clergy so relentlessly he had broken an unwritten law in the African-American community.[116] But in attacking these plays in a global fashion, the filmmaker alienated yet another group, one whose support he perhaps needed most—those cultural figures seeking to build a cultural movement that became known as the Harlem Renaissance. Putting down Robeson was also a serious miscalculation. Whatever Robeson's transgressions at home or abroad, he remained an immensely popular figure in the African-American community. Critics such as Madden might have attacked O'Neill's plays, but they had nonetheless lauded Robeson. Micheaux appeared to reject such distinctions—though he did generate an outstanding performance from the actor.

In truth, *Body and Soul* was too sophisticated and obscure for many moviegoers. Few people in the African-American community had seen all three plays. Their runs were much too limited in terms of geography and time. The presupposition that the black community shared this knowledge or frame of reference was suspect, and the critics who were knowledgeable had been alienated or were silenced.[117] Reviewers in the black press never articulated the intertextual basis for recognizing the film's achievement—in contrast to, for example, mainstream critics writing about Lubitsch's *Lady Windermere's Fan,* released at roughly the same time. Micheaux had alienated the intelligentsia, the middle class, *and* the plebeian moviegoer. It was a brilliant, courageous, and often disastrous effort—one in which the filmmaker tried to lead his audience too far and too fast.

Of course, other extraordinary films from this period were encountering similar difficulties—Buster Keaton's *Sherlock Jr.* (1924) and Sergei Eisenstein's *Potemkin* (1925), to name but two. *Potemkin* was rescued by its enthusiastic critical reception outside the Soviet Union, which forced a reevaluation at home. Keaton, like Micheaux, would lose much of his economic and artistic independence. Henry Sampson suggests that Oscar Micheaux's brother and business manager had spent the Micheaux Film Company's monies on high living and so was forced to resign on March 1, 1927. The company itself went into bankruptcy on February 28, 1928.[118] Whatever the many contributing factors (including the arrival of sound and the rural depression that preceded the stock market crash), the disastrous reception and box office for *Body and Soul* must have contributed substantially.

FINAL REFLECTIONS

Too often today's scholars have tried to analyze *Body and Soul* within the same realist framework that critics applied to the film in the 1920s. Micheaux, indeed, was somewhat guilty of fostering this misguided approach. In his letter to the black press, he maintained,

> I have always tried to make my photoplays present the truth, to lay down before the race a cross section of its own life, to view the colored heart from close range. . . . It is only by presenting those portions of the race portrayed in my pictures, in the light and background of their true state, that we can raise our people to greater heights.[119]

Of course, these plays and Robeson's performances were a significant aspect of black reality, but this statement seems to focus on the choice of stereotypic characters and plot, further obscuring Micheaux's efforts at textual engagement and reversal.[120] For if *Body and Soul* is analyzed as a simple depiction of Negro life, the picture seems to be a lunatic's fancy rather than a work of art—to mobilize Ralph Ellison's statement at the beginning of this essay.[121] Of course, scholars of cinema and/or African-American culture have not wanted to say this. White censorship or terrible production circumstances provide the necessary excuses. But in the end, such excuses cannot avoid degrading the film's value as a work of art and Micheaux's achievement as an artist. Dan Leab summed up the implications of this mapping:

> Oscar Micheaux's silent motion picture works cannot be considered outstanding. He is significant, however, because he was one of the first independent producers making popular

and for a time profitable movies with black actors and actresses for ghetto audiences. Despite his public utterances, Micheaux's films were not designed to uplift or enlighten. They were meant to entertain, to appeal to his concept of black popular taste, and to make money.[122]

The rediscovery of *Within Our Gates* and *The Symbol of the Unconquered* (as well as the greater willingness of contemporary critics to take popular film more seriously) have modified this conclusion, but only slightly. Mark Reid, for example, finds his films more impressive, if still limited:

> Micheaux's action films were forerunners of [black-oriented] 1970s film types, and for much the same reason: Micheaux's choice of controversial subjects and selection of black-oriented themes are evidence of an entrepreneur whose first goal is to make a profit and then, if popular tastes would allow, to present positive images of African-American life.[123]

Both assessments place the showman, the entrepreneur battling the Hollywood system at the forefront. The showman comes at the expense of the artist or cultural worker, and the films are seen as a means to an end (profits). This essay's analysis of *Body and Soul* points toward quite different conclusions. For an independent filmmaker such as Micheaux to survive, he must be an entrepreneur and a showman. These are the givens—the preconditions for filmmaking of any kind. But rather than be timid and stay within a narrow band of proven subject matter (the case with 1970s blaxploitation films), *Body and Soul* reveals a filmmaker who was far more daring, who was willing to risk financial loss and to offend popular taste to address issues that he felt were important.

Prior misreadings of Micheaux's work have other consequences. Because Micheaux was treated as an eccentric filmmaker focused on commerce, his place in the larger context of African-American culture was considered of little import. While this is a topic beyond the scope of my essay, a few remarks seem in order. Oscar Micheaux—former Pullman porter and homesteader in South Dakota—had been pursuing an active and increasingly successful filmmaking career in Chicago in the years after World War I, with extensive travels that included New York City as an important destination. The vitality of Harlem's cultural scene must have attracted the director who had seemingly relocated there by 1923 (though also based in Roanoke, Virginia, and frequently traveling).[124] There Micheaux found himself at odds with the literati who were forging what Huston Baker has referred to as "Harlem Renaissance, Inc."—the group of literary artists who are the subject of historian David Levering Lewis's book, *When Harlem Was in Vogue.*

Body and Soul was made at a significant moment, its origins perhaps traceable to Paul Robeson's rehearsals of *Roseanne* during the week of March 17th through 23rd in 1924. Lewis points to a soiree at the Civic Club on March 21, 1924 as an important event—the dress rehearsal for the Harlem Renaissance—that brought together young black writers and prominent cultural figures (white and black). One hundred ten people came to that dinner, though Micheaux was not among them—he apparently was not invited.[125] In the various reports of parties, meetings, and literary events, the filmmaker's name was never mentioned. This has left the impression that Micheaux was somehow on the fringes of the Harlem Renaissance, an outsider from Chicago who was operating in an entirely different cultural sphere. This may be true, but it misses the point. In background, outlook, and artistic results, Micheaux was at odds with the shapers of this emerging movement. David Levering Lewis suggests that Charles Johnson wanted "to redeem, through art, the standing of his people."[126] James Weldon Johnson and Alain Locke "both wanted the same art for the same purpose—highly polished stuff, preferably about polished people, but certainly untainted by racial stereotypes or embarrassing vulgarity. Too much blackness, too much streetgeist and folklore—nitty-gritty music, prose, and verse—were not welcome."[127] Neither was Micheaux. He was too plebeian, too crude, and even too propagandistic. The Harlem Renaissance celebrated its Phi Beta Kappa scholars from prestigious schools. Micheaux was an autodidact. His working methods and the audiences he addressed differed as well. The Harlem Renaissance Inc. was based on black-white collaboration. Micheaux's approach as a producer-director-writer ensured that he would be in full control behind the camera while the actors in the film were almost exclusively black.[128] His sympathies in this respect were with the politics of Booker T. Washington rather than the NAACP and Urban League integrationists.[129] W. E. B. Du Bois supported Eugene O'Neill; Micheaux attacked him.

"The mainspring of the Harlem Renaissance," the cutting edge of interracial collaboration in New York, did not occur in literature—that was just beginning in 1924—but, as Ann Douglas argues, in theater.[130] In 1917, Emily Hapgood produced three plays by white playwright Ridgely Torrence with black casts (*The Ride of Dreams, Simon of Cyrenian,* and *Granny Maumee*). As we have seen, Eugene O'Neill, Nan Bagby Stephens, Charles Gilpin, and Paul Robeson were, each in different ways, part of this movement. The growing popularity of plays about Negroes written by white playwrights and then enacted by blacks was a mixed advance. On one hand, this provided acting opportunities to African-American actors and encouraged the breakdown of racial barriers. Black actors might also rework and transform these works in some measure by bringing their knowledge and sensitivities to bear on the script. But it often meant that African Americans were legitimizing highly problematic texts by their appearance in the plays. Considered as isolated texts, it is certainly possible to defend *The Emperor Jones* or *All God's Chillun'.* However, taken as a group, these three plays depict African Americans as superficially civilized, amoral, conniving, dishonest, childlike failures. Jenkins may be evil, but he is not a failure. Unlike Jones, he eludes his pursuers in the end. Sylvester gets rich as an inventor, although he is never shown inventing anything. Such excessive success contrasts with the excessive failure of Jim Harris at law.

Micheaux's film engaged an important cultural nexus in the theater at the very moment that the Harlem Renaissance was moving into full swing. In this respect, the delay between the production of *Body and Soul* and its release proved costly. David Levering Lewis characterizes 1925 as year one of the Harlem Renaissance—the *Opportunity* prizes for art and literature were awarded in May of that year and Alain Locke's anthology, *The New Negro,* was published at year's end. Harlemites felt a palpable sense of possibility, and black cultural production had entered a different phase in which black writers achieved new prominence. By the time *Body and Soul* was released, Micheaux was criticizing "Harlem Renaissance, Inc." at the moment that its principles of interracial collaboration were bearing fruit. Appearing at an inopportune moment, the film's critique seemed to be ungracious, out of step, and perhaps even reactionary.

Consider again the "artistic statement" of so many Micheaux's films. As the romantic hero concludes at the end of *Within Our Gates* (1920), "It is the duty of each member of our race to help destroy ignorance and superstition." It is the message of *Body and Soul* as well. It is Martha Jane's persistent, even absurd, dream state that encourages African-American audiences to scream at her to "Wake up!" as the film unspools. Martha Jane does finally respond to the audience's cries. She does wake up. And she does do the right thing. In this non-realist text, Micheaux thus delivered a message echoed seventy years later in several films by Spike Lee, notably *School Daze* (1988) and *Do the Right Thing* (1989). For Micheaux, it was the duty of these films to awaken their audiences and to force them to reflect on their predicament. In this respect, the spectators are like Martha Jane. The film on the screen is a dream text—half nightmare, half fantasy. Reality is outside the theater. On a superficial level, the film ends and people walk out onto the street, where this trilogy of plays by white playwrights cannot be so quickly dismissed. Their impact on the realm of culture and thought is profound. Indeed, this was a message that *Body and Soul* addressed not only to audiences in Harlem and other black urban communities of the 1920s but to Robeson himself.[131] It was a message that Robeson was not then ready to hear. It would be another ten or fifteen years, after a series of unhappy experiences in the British and American film industries, before the performer's viewpoint would begin to change. Perhaps more important, it was a message that Harlemites were also not ready to hear. They were happy to savor this moment of dreamlike possibilities that was Harlem of the mid-1920s.[132] And so the movie and Micheaux were dismissed.

Martha Jane's son seeks his revenge on Rev. Isiaah Jenkins.

POSTSCRIPT

Micheaux draws our attention to endings as something that cultural producers and audiences alike must consciously problemetize; certainly such questioning is applicable to this tale of Micheaux, Robeson, and Harlem's cultural arbiters. The above ending is only one possible stopping place, but there are others, for relationships between directors and critics, between filmmakers and different sectors of their public, fluctuate. In the cultural and economic prosperity that was Harlem of the late 1920s, Micheaux was granted renewed respect by his critics. He was recognized as "the only colored motion picture producer in this country. Struggling against great odds, he has managed to produce the finest pictures in which colored players have appeared."[133] That is, the hostility that came in the aftermath of *Body and Soul* gradually abated. In 1925–1926, the *Amsterdam News* had simply edited out virtually all references to Micheaux and his films. With films such as *The Millionaire* (1927), *The Broken Violin* (1928), and *Thirty Years Later* (1928), the newspaper's staff again ran highly complimentary promotional blurbs, albeit edited as they saw fit. Indeed, the *Amsterdam News* was again spelling his name correctly—Micheaux.[134]

Here analysis gives way to speculation, but why not? It allows us to appreciate the Signifying that was once more occurring in the pages of the *New York Amsterdam News*.[135] And it lets us link it once again to Robeson and *Body and Soul*. First, Micheaux opened *When Men Betray* in New York City at the end of September 1929. It had a plot very similar to *Body and*

Soul: Two brothers seek the same girl, according to one source.[136] The woman is "cold to the love of a good and ambitious young lad" and instead believes "the rosy promises of a smooth-tongued stranger." She then runs away and follows him to the city, where unhappiness and disaster follow.[137] Meanwhile, since the release of *Body and Soul,* Robeson had grown in stature, though not without escaping controversy. He had been in London, appearing in *Show Boat.* For some dissident black critics, Robeson was once again a too-willing vehicle for expressing the Negro soul as imagined by white playwrights and lyricists—singing "Old Man River." But then, in September 1929, it was announced that he would appear in another white man's work about the Negro soul, and this was of a different order—Shakespeare's *Othello.*[138] Before this historic performance was to occur, however, Robeson embarked on an American concert tour. "The Return of Robeson" was hailed by the editor of the *New York Amsterdam News:*

> Versatile athlete, versatile actor, blessed with the qualities of that gentility which stamps the man and artist, Paul is returning to us next month. . . . Shall those of us who love this man be constrained to gaze upon him from afar and be denied the right to shout: *Well done, Paul.* We will not! Harlem will rise in her might and proclaim: *He is one of us and one of whom we are very proud.*[139]

It was at this moment that the *New York Amsterdam News* once again began to refer to the mischievous Micheaux as "Mischeaux." Perhaps *When Men Betrayed* rekindled memories of the once-despised *Body and Soul* or the newspaper's editorial staff realized that another film about two brothers—*The Wages of Sin* (also released in 1929)—was ridiculing Oscar's own brother, Swan Micheaux (in a manner reminiscent of *Body and Soul*'s critique of Robeson). But with his films appearing in Harlem's top movie houses with unprecedented frequency, this Signifying was now done in a playful, teasing way.

> The Odeon Theatre should be the Mecca for those with a desire to enjoy a real good picture created and produced by a man of color, no less than Oscar Mischeaux, who, in the face of many disappointments in those early days when he started to make pictures of and by colored people, has continued to the fore and remains the outstanding man of the race in the business.[140]

Micheaux's renegade style was appreciated even if ribbed. His old attack on Robeson, its (apparently) off-target message perhaps softened with distance and shared well-being, was recalled. Had not *The Emperor Jones,* which some had likened to an American modernist *Macbeth,* led the way for Robeson to stage Shakespeare? Stage Shakespeare on the London stage! In listing Robeson's many achievements, the editor of the *Amsterdam News* omitted any direct reference to his film work.

If Robeson was the great actor, Micheaux was still recognized as the race's great filmmaker. Now in the glow of critical respect, Micheaux could respond in kind. If the *Amsterdam News* would add a letter on one side of the "ch," he would subtract one from the other: he wrote it "Michaux" in the Odeon advertisement for *Thirty Years Later.*[141] Finally, some two weeks later, Micheaux himself added the "s" to his name. *Wages of Sin* was advertised as "Produced by OSCAR MISCHEAUX," matching the leader for the corresponding promotional blurb: "Mischeaux's Latest at The Odeon Theatre."[142] These were not casual misspellings. It was not that the *Amsterdam News* copy editors were producing text to be corrected silently or given a "*sic*" by erudite scholars. (The misspellings are not unlike some of the "mistakes" that some critics have found in Micheaux's films.) The game of naming, which not so coincidentally recognized the force of Micheaux's authorial voice, unfolded on the pages of the paper. It ended in raucous laughter over imaginary drinks at some hypothetical bar in one of the 500 speakeasies that populated Harlem at this moment.[143]

POST POSTSCRIPT

Another ending. Micheaux's part-talkie *A Daughter of the Congo* opened at Harlem's Renaissance Theatre for a week on April 5, 1930. Two days after its run ended (replaced by *The Virginian,* starring Gary Cooper), the projection booth collapsed and a patron was killed. Dramatic critic Theophilus Lewis also devoted a full column to Micheaux's film work. Lewis spelled his name correctly and began his article with amazingly laudatory comments on Micheaux's past films: "They always impressed me as being the work of a man of remarkable personal ability, handicapped only by a lack of financial resources." *A Daughter of the Congo,* however, "is thoroughly bad from every point of analysis, from continuity which is unintelligible to the caption writing, which is a crime."[144] Moreover, Lewis found Micheaux's depiction of Africans to be naive and deeply offensive: the film "makes native Africans act like half-wits."[145] Indeed, this is a criticism that would be leveled at Paul Robeson and several of his films just a few years later: *Sanders of the River* (1935), *Song of Freedom* (1937), and others. Robeson and Micheaux took two different paths, but in the minds of their critics they had more than one intersection.

Let me end this essay (for the last time) by imagining a photograph not unlike the photograph of Malcolm X and Martin Luther King that ends Spike Lee's *Do the Right Thing.* It is a now lost, always unknown photograph that may never have existed, which I have begun to see clearly in my dreams. Micheaux and Robeson are on the set of *Body and Soul,* Robeson on the right dressed in his parson's outfit, Micheaux on the left in a coat and tie. They are laughing—one warmly and heartily, the other, well, I guess somewhat Mischievously.

9.

Black Patriarch on the Prairie: National Identity and Black Manhood in the Early Novels of Oscar Micheaux

JAYNA BROWN

Oscar Micheaux's career as a writer and filmmaker spanned four crucial decades in the history of American popular culture. Tenaciously and obsessively prolific, Micheaux wrote seven novels in addition to directing and producing some forty films. From his first novel, *The Conquest,* written in 1913, to his last film, *The Betrayal,* produced in 1948, Micheaux's works reflect, as well as take part in the production of, this nation's cultural biography.

Questions abound regarding just how to evaluate the aesthetic principles of Oscar Micheaux's work. However conflicting aesthetic evaluation of his works may be, it is clear that his texts are of great social and historical importance. An exploration of the social and historical implications of his work will allow us to understand more fully how, and in what ways, Micheaux made the specific aesthetic and stylistic choices that he did. Attempting to read the interrelation between these choices and their social and historical contexts opens up new ways for us to understand the crucial work—and play—undertaken in American popular culture.

Micheaux's career as a novelist preceded his work in film. He wrote his fictionalized autobiography, *The Conquest: The Story of a Negro Pioneer,* while homesteading on the plains of South Dakota. Micheaux funded this enterprise by selling the book door-to-door to his neighbors, European immigrants farming near him on the plains. In 1915, Micheaux wrote a sequel, *The Forged Note: A Romance of the Darker Races.* Founding the Western Book Supply Company, Micheaux began publishing his books himself. In 1917, Micheaux wrote his third novel, *The Homesteader,* which he then adapted into his first film. After a twenty-three-year break, during which Micheaux focused on making films, he wrote four more novels. Micheaux's books are a strange combination of popular fiction—melodrama, romance, crime novel—and moral guidebook, espousing a Booker T. Washington–inspired code of behavior for black American success. Like his films, his novels are often roughly hewn and repeti-

Sylvia Landry (Evelyn Preer), the heroine of *Within Our Gates* (1920), reads constantly. Books provide her with an understanding of the world and with implicit moral guidance. Here she reads in the opening shot of the film.

tious. Again and again, Micheaux used his own story as material for his works. His first four novels and many of his films are revisions of *The Conquest,* while all of his works contain elements of his basic bildungsroman. Because so much of his later work was built upon themes established in his early works, they will be the focus of this study.

When I first began my investigation into the works of Oscar Micheaux, I asked myself what this devoutly conservative, aspiring businessman was *doing* writing novels and producing films. Intellectual pursuit, literature, and high art forms are part of a liberal philosophy consistently criticized in the polemic of Micheaux's works. As an ardent defender of the economic philosophies of Booker T. Washington, what kind of "art" was it that Micheaux was producing? The key to understanding Micheaux's apparently paradoxical role as a cultural producer lies in the fact that Micheaux was, first and foremost, a businessman. For him economic pragmatism, not artistic virtuosity, was the key to racial uplift. Micheaux recognized popular fiction and film as valuable cultural commodities, as profitable vehicles of self-definition and self-representation. He was interested in creating, as well as reaching, a black audience for his works, but he regarded this audience primarily as a body of consumers.

MICHEAUX'S NOVELS

Micheaux's first novel, *The Conquest,* is the story of a brave black homesteader, Oscar Devereaux, whose dream is to tame 1,000 acres of land and establish himself as an example of success for his wayward people. While on the plains, he encounters many difficulties: drought, loneliness, and a frustrated romance with a Scottish woman, Agnes Stewart, the daughter of a neighboring white settler. His homesteading endeavor therefore ends in fail-

A homesteader tills his field. Photograph from Oscar Micheaux's *The Conquest: The Story of a Negro Pioneer* (Lincoln, Neb.: Woodruff Press, 1913).

ure, compounded by an early marriage fraught with domestic conflict. His wife's father, Rev. McCraline, is Devereaux's nemesis and the prototype for the evil preachers found in Micheaux's next two novels as well as in his early silent films. *The Conquest* ends with Devereaux's decision to quit the homestead and take up writing as a career. It is in *The Conquest* that Micheaux establishes the primary themes and conflicts that his later novels and films revolve around and revise.[1]

Micheaux published his second novel, *The Forged Note: A Romance of the Darker Races,* in 1915, the year of Booker T. Washington's death. Although a sequel to *The Conquest,* in this second book the pioneer protagonist is named Sydney Wyeth. Due to a massive drought and a failed marriage, Wyeth has decided to take up writing as a career and writes his autobiography. Wyeth moves from the Rosebud Reservation in South Dakota to the southern city of Attalia (read Atlanta) to peddle his book. Having failed at his agricultural endeavor, it is now time for him to stake his claim in the city. Micheaux's protagonist is a self-promoting race man, eager to carry forth a Booker T. Washington–inspired polemic to the emerging middle and working classes. Book in hand, he prepares to "spread intelligence among people who greatly needed it."[2] *The Forged Note* reads as a guide to urban black middle-class ethics. As in Micheaux's first novel, hard work and self-sacrifice are the keys to success.

Through his protagonists, Micheaux persisted in defending Washington's platform, even as the black middle class continued in increasing numbers to reject Washington's accommodationist philosophy. Micheaux's heroes and heroines are aspiring entrepreneurs with a pragmatic vision for black economic self-sufficiency. Oscar Devereaux and Sidney Wyeth continually rail against members of an urban black professional class. Devereaux, for instance, considers the members of the growing middle-class community in suburban Chicago to be "overeducated Negroes" whose "sole object in life was obviously nothing, but who dressed up and aped the white people" (*CN*, 195). Such scathing remarks are common in the early works of Micheaux and are often transparently aimed at the young thinker W. E. B. Du Bois, who, early in his career, was known for his criticism of Washington's ideas. Du Bois first voiced criticism of Booker T. Washington in his collection of essays *The Souls of Black Folk,* published in 1903. Du Bois continued to oppose Washington's apologist and increasingly defensive posture into the 1920s, publishing editorial essays in *The Crisis,* the NAACP journal of which he was the editor. Du Bois led a growing number of members of the emerging black middle class in challenging Washington's Tuskegee platform. One of Du Bois's early ideas was his call for the development of a leading elite, composed of a highly educated ten percent of the black population. The Du Boisian talented tenth—urbane, sophisticated, and well-heeled— continue to come under fire throughout Micheaux's works.

By dedicating *The Conquest* to "The Honorable Booker T. Washington," Micheaux aligned himself with the great leader, whose own life story was published in 1901.[3] Key elements from Washington's autobiography appear in the plot of *The Symbol of the Unconquered,* and his ghostly presence presides over all of Micheaux's work. He is frequently referred to with praise in Micheaux's novels, and his photograph appears on the walls of houses and cabins in Micheaux's films. But Washington himself was never cast as a character; instead he remains a ubiquitous shadow.

Micheaux cast himself as next of kin to Washington, hanging over his own texts in a similar omniscient and ghostly relation to his central protagonists. In authoring fiction instead of straightforward autobiography, Micheaux removed himself from the line of direct criticism yet positioned himself as an example to black people.

Micheaux's third and fourth novels, *The Homesteader* and *The Wind from Nowhere,* are also autobiographical works of fiction, but the central protagonist of *The Homesteader* has been renamed Jean Baptiste. Micheaux ended this novel with a tidy resolution, compensating for the somewhat melancholy ending of *The Conquest.* Unlike Oscar Devereaux, Jean Baptiste emerges victorious over his trying circumstances. Through an unlikely chain of events, the minister, renamed McCarthy, and his daughter Orlean both die, and *The Homesteader* ends with Baptiste's marriage to Agnes Stewart. Miraculously, Baptiste discovers that Agnes's mother was mulatto, making Agnes herself black and therefore free to marry Baptiste without violating what he calls "the custom of the country and its law"[4] or threatening his status as a race man and leader of his people.

Micheaux made *The Homesteader,* published in 1917, into his first feature film, which unfortunately remains lost. How Micheaux revised his story in the third novel is revealing, in terms of how it articulates the black man's production of a new self, a process left unfinished in *The Conquest.* After completing this survey of Oscar Micheaux's novels, I will examine these two novels for what they reveal about the specific functions of Micheaux's art; how, through Micheaux's cultural production, a black man dons his "new raiments of self."[5]

Jean Baptiste and his Scottish love Agnes Stewart. Painting by W. M. Farrow from Oscar Micheaux's *The Homesteader* (Sioux City, Iowa: Western Book and Supply Company, 1917).

Detective Walter Le Baron and Dorothy Stansfield. Frontispiece to Oscar Micheaux, *The Story of Dorothy Stansfield* (New York: Book Supply Company, 1946).

In 1944, Micheaux published his fourth novel, *The Wind from Nowhere.* In this narrative, the novel's hero, Martin Eden, starts out as a prosperous landowner. Micheaux used this character to elaborate on his earlier experience writing *The Conquest,* and it is clear that his initial inspiration was partly influenced by Jack London's semi-autobiographical work *Martin Eden.* After *The Wind from Nowhere,* Micheaux tried his hand at the mystery/crime novel. In 1945, he wrote *The Case of Mrs. Wingate,* a murder mystery, and in 1946 he authored *The Story of Dorothy Stanfield,* a murder mystery/romance novel. With his detective mysteries, Micheaux sought to insert his work into the mainstream popular culture of the 1940s, but his narratives are a contrivance of crime novel and stuffy, conservative black polemic. His tenacious belief in an increasingly obsolete Washingtonian pragmatism marks his works as atavistic, and his later novels and films did not do so well with the public.

Sidney Wyeth of *The Forged Note* reappears in both of Micheaux's murder mysteries as a Micheaux persona, lauded by the other characters of the mysteries as the only black writer who truly represents the beliefs of his people. His artistic integrity is contrasted with two other black novelists, thinly veiled representations of Richard Wright (Frank Knight) and W. E. B. Du Bois (Kermit Early). In the texts, Knight and Early are accused of treasonous radicalism, the result of their overeducation. Micheaux presents their radicalism as the ultimate evil and the source of unnatural acts such as race mixing. In both mysteries, Frank Knight is accused of "getting mixed up with Communists" and marrying a Jewish woman, met through his participation in the Communist party.[6] The detective hero of *The Story of Dorothy Stanfield,* Walter Le Baron, and his bride-to-be, Dorothy Stanfield, discuss Frank Knight in scathing detail. They express shock and disdain at his choice to marry a white woman, which they interpret as a betrayal of his responsibility to the race. "Knight is *never* seen in Harlem" (*DS,* 85), according to Le Baron; implying that Knight "preaches one kind of philosophy and practices another" (*DS,* 74). In the texts' estimation, the model black male citizen is a stalwart Republican, like Wyeth (*DS,* 83).

As in many of Micheaux's later sound films, such as *The Girl from Chicago* (1932), the central male protagonists in *The Case of Mrs. Wingate* and *The Story of Dorothy Stanfield* are brave black detectives. They are not producers per se, as are the agriculturists, writers, and stage directors in his other works. But they serve a purpose within Micheaux's conservative worldview, policing the politics, bad business practices, and sexual ethics of the other characters.

Through his depiction of Kermit Early in *The Case of Mrs. Wingate,* Micheaux adopts a politically reactionary point of view. The heroine of this tale is Bertha Wingate, a wealthy white woman turned Nazi sympathizer. She and her brother Heinrich become involved in World War II as Nazi agents. Kermit Early (W. E. B. Du Bois) has an affair with Mrs. Wingate while she is married to a rich white man. Bertha supports Early through school, and as a result, Early becomes "very much over-educated." As he "[could] find nothing that he liked to do . . . [he] turned radical," Micheaux writes (*DS*, 203). According to Micheaux's reactionary and erroneous logic, Early's radicalism leads him into the Nazi party. Micheaux is alluding to Du Bois's intellectually formative years spent in Germany, insinuating that Du Bois leaned toward fascism because of them. In *The Case of Mrs. Wingate* and *The Story of Dorothy Stanfield*, socialist leanings and fascism are linked as equally un-American, both representing the potential downfall of black people. Bertha Wingate is saved only by convincing words of wisdom from Sidney Wyeth.

As we have seen, reuse and revision of material were Micheaux's trademark survival strategies. His last attempt to gain public notoriety was with *The Masquerade: A Historical Novel* in 1947. This novel was a thinly disguised rewrite of Charles Chesnutt's novel *A House Behind the Cedars*, which Micheaux had already revised into his 1932 film *Veiled Aristocrats*. Micheaux's thrift is significant for what he most often reused and revised, namely, representations of himself. Through various narrative permutations, Micheaux wrote and rewrote himself, self-consciously constructing black maleness(es) according to his own stylized projected image. Because what he wrote was popular fiction, it would prove fruitless to try to divine the real Micheaux from his works, but we can productively explore possible functions of such re-representations.

THE CONQUEST

Micheaux's first novel, *The Conquest*, and its first revision, *The Homesteader*, provide much of the material for later works. In *The Conquest* and *The Homesteader*, the achievement of black manhood and the construction of a national identity are linked. Both Oscar Devereaux of *The Conquest* and Jean Baptiste of *The Homesteader* embody Micheaux's particular formulation of the myth of the American frontier, modeling qualities of thrift, honesty, and self-sacrifice, in contrast with many of the European immigrant men homesteading the plains who are depicted as lazy, shiftless, and lacking in moral fiber. The chief rival of the protagonists is the archetypal lazy and corrupt black preacher of the urban South, and the work of the narratives is to establish the young man (Devereaux/Baptiste) as the new secular example for the black working class. Within these novels, the de-crowning of the old patriarch, the preacher-father figure, and the crowning of the son, the new, enterprising capitalist, is the fundamental process of a black man's transformation.

Despite the autobiographical nature of Micheaux's novels, we learn surprisingly little about the protagonists' families. At the beginning of *The Conquest*, Devereaux carefully controls what little information he relates regarding his early childhood in Arkansas, though his tone is one of nostalgia for an earlier generation of ex-slaves who had settled there after the Civil War. Hard-working and dedicated, this earlier generation is contrasted with members of a dissolute younger generation who move to the cities and towns in search of "society and good times," and, as Devereaux explains, "leaving the farms to care for themselves until the inevitable German immigrant came along and brought them up at his own price . . . and grew prosperous" (*CN*, 12). As a child, Devereaux is sent to market to sell the goods from the family farm. It is here that he gets his first taste of business: "I could always do better business for myself than for anyone else," the budding entrepreneur explains (*CN*, 14).

Once he has grown into a young man, Devereaux leaves home in search of work, as many young black men were forced to do. He describes his travels across the country in search of employment. He takes up a variety of back-breaking jobs, working for a car manufacturer,

Portrait of Jean Baptiste, Negro homesteader. Painting by W. M. Farrow from Oscar Micheaux's *The Homesteader* (Sioux City, Iowa: Western Book and Supply Company, 1917).

then bailing water at a coal mine. He then works at a steel mill in Joliet, Illinois. The pay he receives for his toil is scant, but Devereaux develops an iron-willed, ascetic discipline: "Economy, modesty, and frugality had become fixed habits of my life" (*CN,* 42). In addition to being industrious, he is an ambitious individualist, refraining from group leisure activities. "I didn't shoot craps or drink," he writes, "neither did I belong to a church" (*CN,* 21). After forking hay on a farm in Illinois, he finds work as a Pullman porter. The pay is much higher, and in his new job he gets to see the country. These jobs are his rite of passage, giving him the training and discipline essential for a young black man to grow into manhood.

In Devereaux's travels as a porter, he stops off in Chicago to see his brother. This event proves to be a crucial moment in his self-development. Oscar is disappointed by his brother's lifestyle, his spendthrift ways and love of luxury, and is disillusioned by what he sees as overweening materialism on the part of the urban black middle class. Having learned in his travels that land was opening up in South Dakota, Devereaux decides to migrate to the Midwest. He recites:

I turned my face westward with the spirit of Horace Greeley . . . and his words "go west, young man," ringing in my ears. So westward I journeyed, to the land of real beginning, and where I was soon to learn more than a mere observer ever could by living in the realm of a big city. (*CN,* 47)

Devereaux seeks to establish a model for black manhood through the acquisition and cultivation of untamed land. To grow into manhood, he asserts, the black man "must go where the land is new or raw and undeveloped. He must begin with the beginning and develop with the development of the country" (*CN,* 53). Devereaux depicts the raw land, "the land of real beginning," as a new Eden in which he can regain an innocence through intimacy with his native soil. At the same time, the terms of acquiring manhood within the text are those of metaphorical virility, based on Devereaux's ability to till the land and seed it, to make it produce—his ability to generate crops from raw land.

Devereaux is the only black man among the many settlers on the Rosebud Reservation. Leading businessmen and bankers compete for power in establishing towns and businesses on the frontier. As the territorial battles ensue, Devereaux maintains a distance from the goings-on, though he remains a keen observer and an admired citizen through his shrewd land purchases and hard work. In repeated comparisons with white male settlers, Devereaux is seen as an ideal man, hard-working and capable of great self-sacrifice. Here Micheaux has done a curious thing, simultaneously deracinating the new American man while painting him in black.

In his study of Micheaux's novels, Joseph Young accuses Micheaux of adopting the value systems and philosophy of "the oppressor," that is, white Anglo-Saxon America. "To adopt

Western Settlers. Photograph from Oscar Micheaux, *The Conquest: The Story of a Negro Pioneer* (Lincoln, Neb.: Woodruff Press, 1913).

the world view of the oppressor," Young writes, "requires Micheaux to reject his blackness, that is, to reject both his racial kinsmen and himself."[7] This "world view," according to Young, is that of "both the proslavery imperialist and the imperialist of industrial expansion."[8] Young's reading of Micheaux's novels is painfully reductive. His central argument, that Micheaux wanted to be white, is fundamentally flawed, because it is based on a series of conflations.[9] It obscures the central thrust obvious in all of Micheaux's texts, the creation and valorization of the black capitalist entrepreneur. Micheaux was staking a claim to the right for blacks to join the European settlers in the project of capitalist expansion, the central project upon which America was founded. But this does not imply that Micheaux adopted "proslavery ideals," nor that he harbored a desire to pass for white. On the contrary, Micheaux's texts are heavily invested in the concept of retaining black racial identity. The narrative trajectories, as we shall see, actually rely on the concept of race loyalty.

Micheaux's articulation of the black man's right to an American national identity and citizenship, however, is fundamentally conservative. The central urge within Micheaux's works is class aspiration. The rights and privileges of national identity must be earned by honest hard work, and a constant vigilance must be kept against an African-American propensity toward laziness and pleasure-seeking. What Micheaux's texts try to do is to claim the same rights that European immigrants enjoyed, the right to "shed their repulsive pasts" and enter through "the gates of class and caste." The repulsive past, for Micheaux, is a history of poverty, while the hopeful future is one of economic success, should blacks harness the limitless opportunity offered by the fertile open plains.

THE HOMESTEADER

Micheaux's novel *The Homesteader* elaborates on the themes presented in his first novel. Jean Baptiste, the principal protagonist of *The Homesteader*, is the quintessential frontiersman, "vigorous, strong, healthy and courageous" (*HS*, 24). Like Oscar Devereaux, Baptiste sees the frontier as a crucial site for the acquisition of manhood:

> [Baptiste] felt the West was the place for young manhood. Here was the unbroken prairie all about him, with its virgin soil and undeveloped resources. . . . Here a young man could work out his destiny. (*HS*, 24)

Devereaux does describe women settling the plains, among them the legendary Rattlesnake Jack, known for her fierce and fearless nature. But the central work done on the plains is the making of men.

Far from wanting to pass for white, Baptiste is a race man who casts himself as a leader selflessly dedicated to uplifting his race. Baptiste feels that his destiny also implies the destiny of his people. He dreams of taming 1,000 acres of land and explains the impetus for his dream:

> "It is not that I care so much for the fruits of my labor; but if I could actually succeed, it would mean so much to the credit of a multitude of others.—Others who need the example. . . ."
> . . . His race needed examples; they need instances of successes to overcome the effect of ignorance and animal viciousness that was prevalent among them. (*HS*, 109)

Micheaux often refers to other black people in such less-than-complimentary terms. Later in his career, he would be heavily criticized—the movie houses where his films were being shown were even picketed—for what his critics perceived were libelous depictions of African Americans. Yet in these early novels the aim of Micheaux's contentious claims was not to divorce himself from the African-American masses, it was to cast himself as a powerful example of right conduct.

In *The Homesteader,* Baptiste relates the story of another black male settler, strengthening his own position as a committed race man. This anonymous man's story, told in epic and biblical tones, operates as an object lesson for all black men. While settling his homestead in a remote region of South Dakota, the man marries a white woman and decides to pass—not as white, for his skin was too dark, but as Mexican. The man fools no one but himself; Baptiste warns that "even to merely claim being something else was a sort of compromise" (*HS*, 146). It takes uncompromising commitment and conviction, essential qualities of manhood itself, to maintain race loyalty.

Baptiste contrasts this man's compromise with his own steadfastness, for Baptiste also has an attraction to a woman of the white race. Fate draws him to Agnes Stewart, and he feels sure in his heart that she is his soul mate. Yet, exhibiting a manly restraint, he refrains from consummating their love. Baptiste's act of resisting his attraction to Agnes Stewart is key to positioning himself as a race leader, for it is out of race loyalty that he sacrifices marriage to the woman he loves. His noble sacrifice to the race is the sublimation of his passion. In so doing, Baptiste proves his manliness. Baptiste's act of self-denial establishes the particular criteria by which a black man affirms his masculinity.

Even as he writes himself as black, Baptiste's specific origins remain mysterious:

> He had no heritage, had Jean Baptiste. His father had given him only the French name that was his, for his father had been poor. . . . His heritage, then, was his indefatigable will; his firm determination to make his way; his desire to make good. (*HS*, 24)

Baptiste's lack of ethnic heritage, as well as his will and determination, contrasts with the plethora of heritages represented by the European immigrants settled near him on the plains. Baptiste describes these European immigrants as an "unusual conglomeration of kinds," making a point to draw attention to their ethnic identities. He describes his place within the community of European immigrants:

> Here in this land had come . . . the great army of discontented persons that have been the forerunners of the new world. Mingled in the crowd, Jean Baptiste regarded the unusual conglomeration of kinds. There were Germans from Germany, and there were Swedes from Sweden, Danes from Denmark, Norwegians from Norway. Here were Poles and Finns and Lithuanians and Russians; but of his race he was the only one. (*HS,* 64)

As a black man, Baptiste simultaneously sets himself apart from and aligns himself with the European immigrants settling South Dakota in the first decade or so of the century. In his description of his fellow settlers, he emphasizes their countries of origin, and by doing so, calls attention to his own status as native born. In contrast with the immigrants, coming to America burdened with ethnic histories, Baptiste is a son of American soil, born and raised in the so-called new world. His lack of "heritage" implies that he has a natural right to invent himself with the new land.

Baptiste admires the white founding fathers of Megory and Calias. They are leading businessmen who wrangle over territorial claims to prime sites along the railroad lines. These men are presented indirectly as models for the kind of leader Baptiste could be as the founder of a black town, if other blacks would join him on the frontier.

More direct comparisons are made within the text between Baptiste and the male relatives of his would-be lover, Agnes Stewart. Agnes's father, Jack Stewart, is a widower; though hard-working and honest, he lacks the financial power and fearless resolve of Baptiste. Both of Agnes's brothers, Bill and George, are disabled mentally and physically. Baptiste saves Jack from financial ruin by anonymously cosigning a loan, and to help out Agnes and her family financially, Baptiste also hires Agnes's half-witted brother Bill as a field hand. Jack and his two sons are symbolically emasculated, unable to effectively tame and seed the wilderness on their own. They are positioned in dependent, childlike relationships to Baptiste, while Baptiste consistently demonstrates a mental and physical superiority.

Baptiste's moral superiority is established in comparison with a third man, Bill Prescott, a lecherous and boorish suitor who comes begging for Agnes's hand. He is lazy, crude, and sexually lascivious, everything Baptiste is not. In the middle of a workday, when Jack is at work in the field, Prescott rudely presents himself with his intentions for Agnes. He swaggers up to Jack, chewing tobacco, and proceeds to "suck his soft mouth clean of amber and spit it tricklingly at Jack's feet" (*HS,* 126). Jack exclaims, "Don't you observe what's around you enough to see girls want some sedateness; they admire in some measure cleverness, clothes, and—well, manhood!" (*HS,* 127). Baptiste, whom Jack openly admires, demonstrates such sedateness in his relationship with Agnes.

Baptiste's moral fortitude is part of a larger principle of asceticism upon which his professional success is based. Maintaining a rigorous work ethic and level of self-denial are necessary for Baptiste to cultivate his vast crop lands, because working the land for as much as it can produce takes all of Baptiste's time, effort, and commitment. Baptiste has much at stake in ensuring the maximum amount of production from his land, because his claim to a national sense of belonging rests on his ability to productively participate in the national project of capitalist expansion.

Baptiste is successful because he can control his passions, the fulfillment of which would distract him from his work. Thus Baptiste's sublimation of his sexual desires signifies his class advancement. Consistently throughout Micheaux's works, the black man's sexual restraint is a requirement for the right to claim class status. A black man's lack of such a sexual and work

African-American homesteaders in the early 1900s on the Great Plains of Kansas, where some of Micheaux's family lived.

ethic deems him unworthy of class advancement. Accompanying a middle-class standing is the responsibility to lead the rest of the race out of poverty. He must stand as a model for other African Americans who would participate in their nation's dream of capitalist enterprise, and he must embody for them the moral fortitude needed to accumulate wealth.

Baptiste lives on the plains as the single black man among a multitude of European immigrants. In proving himself worthy among them, in the West, he is actually facing eastward and southward, toward his own people, attempting to lead them away from the cities into the new land of freedom. He sees black people as prone to urban vice and laziness. In their weakened state they are easily dominated by corrupt leaders, primarily preachers who care more for the satiation of their decadent appetites than for the welfare of their congregations. In *The Homesteader,* Rev. McCarthy is the embodiment of such an unworthy leader. Corrupt in his business practices as well as his sexual behavior, he wrongfully holds claim to the position of leader, enjoying support from various congregations across the country as well as from his own flock at home in Chicago.

Baptiste's conflict with the reverend occupies the center of the novel. Like Oscar Deveraux in *The Conquest,* Baptiste sets out to obtain a black wife after his frustrated romance with Agnes Stewart. He is heartbroken; now finding a wife is purely a business proposition, because he needs help in expanding his homestead. To this end Baptiste sends out letters to several old acquaintances, and despite reservations, he marries his third choice, Orlean McCraline of Chicago. The experience proves disastrous, as she will not stand up to her father, the corrupt and philandering reverend. *The Conquest* ends with an uneasy separation between Devereaux and Orlean. In *The Homesteader,* however, Micheaux dramatizes the conflict further and provides resolution to the tale.

Rev. McCarthy is an unrepentant adulterer. He spends most of his time on the road, traveling from congregation to congregation, exploiting the loyalty of his female congregants both financially and sexually. As a minister, he is meant to embody the moral teachings of God, but he violates his sacred trust in pursuit of sensual pleasure. His sexual sins are part of his larger lack of restraint and sense of duty. Baptiste sees him as a parasite, living off the labor of women. The reverend produces nothing, thereby violating the central requirement for manhood. He cannot model either moral or business ethics for his people and therefore wrongfully occupies his privileged place in their midst.

The tension between the old patriarch and the new man revolves around the body and soul of Orlean, her loyalty and physical dedication. The tension resides in her "subservience to her father, who insisted upon it, and obedience and loyalty to her husband, who had a right and naturally expected it" (*HS,* 242). In this fatal triad, it is through the ritual exchange of the woman that the man is born, but it is also through the woman's willing transfer of loyalty that she herself can be transformed. Again and again in Micheaux's early works the black woman is confronted with this dynamic, the necessity of resituating her loyalties from her father to the young black entrepreneur. Because Orleans will not submit to this split with her past and her familial loyalties, her life ends in tragedy.

From the beginning Orlean lacks the qualities Baptiste defines as essential to black womanhood. She is "extremely childish" and cannot seem to let go of her loyalty to her father (*HS*, 227). In her marriage, she continues to allow the reverend to influence her behavior and choices. She lacks "the strength of her convictions" and is therefore incapable of the hard work demanded of a woman homesteader (*HS*, 227). While living with Baptiste on the plains, Orlean gives birth to a stillborn baby, symbolizing her inability to produce a future generation, freed of its "repulsive past."

The final confrontation between Baptiste, Orlean, and her father takes place in Chapter Fifteen. After Orlean and Baptiste's baby is stillborn, Orlean's father travels to South Dakota to collect Orlean and return with her to Chicago. While in South Dakota, he coerces Orlean into forging a blank check Baptiste has left her. Baptiste follows them back to Chicago, but Orlean's family will not let him see her. He manages to organize a clandestine meeting, but the reverend tracks them down. Orlean falters, succumbing to her father's urgings. She lashes out at Baptiste, beating him savagely. As he falls to the ground in a faint, she kicks him viciously. Her father enters, and Orlean and the reverend embrace as they "whisper words of love" to each other over the fallen body of Baptiste (*HS*, 384). The physical ritual of

Rev. McCarthy attempts to sway the affections of his daughter Orlean away from her husband. Painting by W. M. Farrow from Oscar Micheaux's *The Homesteader* (Sioux City, Iowa: Western Book and Supply Company, 1917).

beating implies Baptiste's infantilization, echoing an earlier beating he received from his mother. It is a symbolic castration, the denial of his sexual right as husband. The text continually implies that the reverend's relationship with his daughter is sexual, further supporting the characterization of the reverend's evil nature as morally as well as economically corrupt.

As Orlean lacks the strength to willingly transfer her loyalties from father to husband, she can only act out her desire to do so in a destructive manner. In a dreamlike swoon, Orlean performs the ultimate act of retribution, as if acting out Baptiste's most heartfelt desire. In a highly eroticized act of violence, she stabs her father to death while he lies asleep in his bed. Waking to the terrible sight, she then stabs herself. Baptiste is then free to marry his true love, Agnes, and return to the Rosebud country.

* * *

During the forty years or so that Micheaux was working, a profound transformation was occurring in the United States around the meaning of art and the means of its production. In his unfinished study, *American Civilization*, C. L. R. James explains that during the 1930s and 1940s (and earlier, I would argue), the mainstream American populace registered its desires "not with votes, but with the tickets it bought and the money it spent." James writes:

> The men who seek to supply this imperative social need . . . do not consider themselves artists. They are businessmen. They find their performers where they can get them. They are care-

ful to observe in matter and manner the limitations of the economic and financial powers upon whom their business depends.[10]

Though James does not specifically address the production values and practices of African-American cultural producers, his insights into the national psyche offer a valuable perspective from which to understand Micheaux's works.

As early as the 1910s and 1920s, forms of popular culture were taking on a new importance as more and more diverse bodies of people immigrated to the United States. Vaudeville, music, and motion pictures were crucial forms through which the newly immigrated populace registered its anxieties and sought their resolution. Large numbers of African Americans, newly migrated from the rural South to southern and northern cities, were also using these forms as the ground on which to negotiate their national, and urban, identities. Micheaux's work must be located within the context of an emerging mass popular culture, as he was a product of this national phenomena as well as a participant in its production.

From the turn of the century on, the central work undertaken in popular cultural forms was the negotiation of national identity. Terms for what it meant to be an American, and who had rights to citizenship, were being heavily contested. The concept of "whiteness" deepened and intensified as a white identity became more than ever the way power—access to privileges associated with national identity—was articulated and denied.[11] From the turn of the century into the 1920s, European immigrants sought ways to claim this whiteness; not without a certain amount of ambivalence, they sought ways to release themselves from the burden of ethnic identity. Such was the promise of America: once free of rigid caste and class stigma, imbricated through racial identity on the continent, they would be welcomed into the land of boundless opportunity.

Popular cultural forms were central locations within which immigrants made their claims to racial whiteness. In early forms of popular culture, such as blackface minstrelsy and coon songs, the terms by which European settlers established their class and race identities were actively negotiated,[12] and after the turn of the century, claims to full citizenship were contested on the vaudeville circuit, on vinyl, and on screen. As immigrants donned blackface and danced to jazz music, claims to whiteness were made possible by defining themselves against, and through, a black "Other."[13] The tensions between old loyalties and new hopes were projected onto the silver screen.[14] Al Jolson's 1927 film *The Jazz Singer* illuminates the task that blackface, in the medium of film, was performing in defining a new sense of national belonging for recent Jewish immigrants. With his pulp fiction and with his films, Micheaux sought to stake a claim within this terrain of negotiation, though his was not a claim to racial whiteness. Instead, he sought to assert the same right of access, for black people, to American citizenship and class advancement.

By participating in settling the plains, Micheaux positioned himself in relation to these later European immigrants as the sole black homesteader among many European settlers. By 1905, the year Micheaux purchased his relinquishment in South Dakota, most African Americans had abandoned westward migration and were moving to the city, but Micheaux insisted that the West remained the land of opportunity for African Americans. Despite his adamant belief in an agrarian model for success, Micheaux later shifted careers, leaving his life as a western frontiersman to become an author of popular fiction and, later, a film producer. This shift in careers is not as paradoxical as it seems, for what was at stake remained the same. Through his work Micheaux sought to claim national identity, for himself and for other black people.

The power of the American dream, as Toni Morrison writes, was to not only be born again but be born again in new clothes, as it were. The new setting would provide new raiments of self. . . . Power—control of one's destiny—would replace the powerlessness felt before the gates of class, caste, and cunning persecution. . . . One could be released from a useless, binding, repulsive past into a kind of historylessness, a blank page waiting to be inscribed.[15]

Micheaux wanted to claim for black people the right to status as the new Adams and Eves of the virgin soil, the right enjoyed by European immigrants to "shed their repulsive pasts." For African Americans, the repulsive past was the experience of slavery and post-emancipation poverty. Once the past was shed, the "gates of class and caste" would be thrown open, and blacks could be reborn to the same historical innocence extended to the other settlers—the Norwegians, Swedes, Danes, and Germans—homesteading on the plains. For the latter, this innocence is written into earned identities as white citizens. In Micheaux's recast terms, this innocence, wrested from the raw soil, is divorced from ideological claims to whiteness. But it is imbued with the certainty of native-born inheritance.

In Micheaux's texts, the claiming of citizenship was made legitimate in terms which borrowed from both a European immigrant paradigm and from nativist ideologies. Micheaux borrows from a European immigrant paradigm its central conflict—the struggle to assimilate traditional ways of the old country while adopting new ways of life in America—and recasts this conflict between the old and the new. Throughout Micheaux's early works looms the presence of the lecherous and parasitic black preacher, invariably philandering, dishonest, and lazy. The preacher represents the old, or traditional, African-American way of life, while the rugged, individualistic, hard-working young black man symbolizes the possibilities for a prosperous future. Throughout Micheaux's early works, the conflicts between the two types of male leadership take on epic proportions. The de-crowning of the father and the mantling of the son are key elements in the construction of Micheaux's self-made American man.

This process mirrors the struggle of second-generation European Americans to separate themselves from old loyalties associated with the homeland and is gendered as the struggle between patriarchal leaders. What distinguishes Micheaux's narrative vision from a European paradigm is a nativist arrogance. "We were never immigrants," Dr. Vivian assures Sylvia Landry in *Within Our Gates*,[16] and in Dr. Vivian's estimation, what the black soldiers did under Roosevelt in Cuba during the Spanish-American War was to claim an Americanness over the second-wave immigrants, an Americanness legitimized by prior enlistment in imperialist conquest.

To an ex-slave population, emancipation meant many things. Above all, it meant not being owned. In Micheaux's vision, the ability to transform oneself from "property" to "propertied" was the ultimate articulation of attained freedom. It was a black man's success at economic enterprise that ultimately decided his national status. As he tamed and sowed the virgin soil of the West, a black man claimed his place in the American territory.

As Toni Morrison asserts, immigration held a transformative power for Europeans,[17] and as Micheaux's texts reveal, internal migration was a key means of self-transformation for African Americans. Migration out of the South was a means to regain innocence, a process by which they shed their "repulsive pasts," and Micheaux's texts are important in that they document earlier routes of African-American migration to the West, Midwest, and southern cities, as well as the great migration North. Before Micheaux had written his first novel *The Conquest*, movement to southern cities and to the North had taken precedence over westward migration. But within Micheaux's autobiographical fiction, migration to the West is the main migratory trope, and the structuring movement of a black man's self-definition. For Micheaux, participation in America's westward expansionism embodies a black man's claim to national belonging. By moving to the West and struggling to tame its soil, the black man proves his mettle. In doing so, he asserts his right to be considered a founding father of the frontier. Micheaux continued to privilege earlier westward migration in his films and novels, even as migratory trends shifted. His tenacious belief in an obsolete rural, agrarian model of black progress is a mark of his conservatism.

In his early texts, the process of gaining national legitimacy is gendered as male, based on a man's ability to tame wild soil and make it produce. Class advancement is written as the ability of the black man to control the means of his own production, and Micheaux was obsessed with this process of self-controlled production and the quest to be a "self-made" man. The central protagonists of his earlier novels and films are aspiring and/or prosperous agriculturists, while the heroes of his later works are writers and stage directors. Micheaux's central male protagonists are all linked in their reiteration of one goal, which was neither aesthetic nor technical virtuosity, but the act of production itself.

Examination of Micheaux's contributions is crucial in the reclaiming of lost and obscured histories. But what are the terms of that remembrance? How do we allow the texts to breathe, as we eagerly search faded and fragmented copies of his films for an African-American tradition? Micheaux's works, both novels and films, invite conflicting evaluation. He was at once reactionary and potentially progressive, as he tenaciously produced works by, about, and for black people. As hungry as we are for "positive" early representations of ourselves from outside of the mainstream American canon, we should not allow this to blind us to the political contradictions inherent to Micheaux's work. However, whatever evaluative criteria we attempt, a perspective which allows the contradictions to remain will most effectively reveal the complexity of what it has meant historically to be black in America.

Dr. Price did not like to lie, even to a negro. . . . As a gentleman, he would not care to have another gentleman, even a colored man, catch him in a lie.

This story was preposterous; it could not be true, and yet there must be something in it.

—Charles W. Chesnutt (1901)[1]

10.

Telling White Lies: Oscar Micheaux and Charles W. Chesnutt

I have always tried to make my photoplays present the truth, to lay before the race a cross section of its own life, to view the colored heart from close range. My results might have been narrow at times, due perhaps to certain limited situations, which I endeavored to portray, but in those limited situations, the truth was the predominant characteristic.

—Oscar Micheaux (1925)[2]

COREY K. CREEKMUR

*I*n a prefatory "acknowledgment" to *The Masquerade* (1947), the last of the seven novels he published before and "after" his filmmaking career, the African-American author and filmmaker Oscar Micheaux claims that the four books he has written since "retiring from the production of Motion Pictures in 1940" were all derived from scenarios that he had previously adapted into films. (Micheaux came out of "retirement" to make his final film, *The Betrayal*, in 1948.) *The Masquerade*, in fact, is identified as a novel based upon an old film scenario itself adapted "from a novel by Chas. W. Chesnutt, published almost fifty years ago" that Micheaux had "filmed . . . twice. First, as a silent picture in the early twenties, and as a talking picture early in the thirties."[3] Although apparently attempting to clarify this confusing sequence of adaptation—from novel to silent film to talkie and back to novel—Micheaux curiously avoids identifying either Chesnutt's novel or his own two films by their titles. Micheaux even suggests that *The Masquerade* is an improvement upon, or a "rounding out" of Chesnutt's unnamed novel, which neglected to include many of the historical events and personages it might have originally incorporated. After claiming "the privilege of having known Mr. Chas. W. Chesnutt, who died in 1932," Micheaux then begins his story, which by its third chapter reveals its acknowledged but unnamed source within a bit of dialogue: "'They live out of town aways, on the old Wilmington Road in a nice little cottage setting back quite aways from the road. They call it The House Behind the Cedars.'"[4]

In the only full-length study of Micheaux's fiction, Joseph A. Young's *Black Novelist as White Racist: The Myth of Black Inferiority in the Novels of Oscar Micheaux* (whose title bluntly

Charles Chesnutt. *A Pictorial View of Idlewild*. Chicago Daily News Film Service (1927).

summarizes a thesis which deserves to be questioned), Young refuses to discuss Micheaux's last novel at all, as this footnote declares: "An analysis of Oscar Micheaux's *The Masquerade: An Historical Novel . . .* is not included in this study because its plot is largely derived from Charles Chesnutt's *House Behind the Cedars* and does not reflect Micheaux's usual myth; hence it lies outside the scope of my thesis."[5] In other words, Micheaux's final novel is simultaneously too derivative and too "unique," too unlike his other novels and too much like another's novel, to intersect with Young's generalizing argument. Though Chesnutt, as Micheaux clarifies, died more than a decade before *The Masquerade* appeared, there is evidence that he too might have approved of Young's blunt omission. In a November 1926 response to a symposium published in the NAACP journal *The Crisis* on "The Negro in Art: How Shall He Be Portrayed," Chesnutt complained that "the propagandist, of whatever integumentary pigment, will, of purpose or unconsciously, distort the facts. My most popular novel was distorted and mangled by a colored moving picture producer, to make it appeal to Negro race prejudice."[6]

I want to introduce and perhaps productively complicate the relationship between these particular texts and artists because I think the tangled relations they demonstrate may accurately indicate how the process and sequence of adaptation frequently operates, in Micheaux's distinctive career, at least, if not more broadly throughout literary and cinematic history. The twists and (re)turns evident in simply providing the basic facts linking Chesnutt's novel and Micheaux's two films (and last novel) surely undermine the misleadingly straightforward claim that, for instance, Oscar Micheaux's now "lost" silent film *The House Behind the Cedars* (1924/1925), as well as his rediscovered sound film *Veiled Aristocrats* (1932), are adaptations of Chesnutt's 1900 novel.[7] But the comfortable identification of one text as an "original" and another, or others, as "derived" adaptations frequently oversimplifies the actual multimedia and multidirectional circulation of texts in a zigzag process that at moments might be better

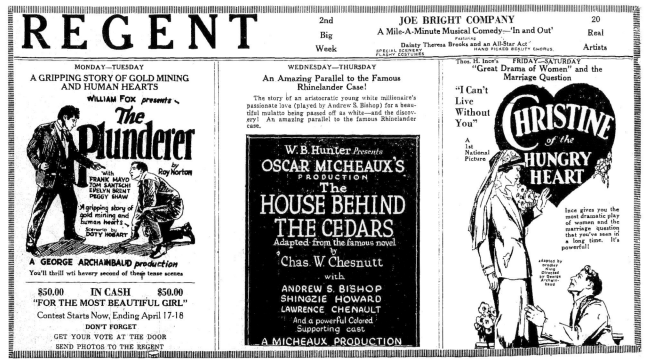

Advertisement for *The House Behind the Cedars* (1924/1925). Baltimore *Afro-American,* 14 March 1925, 5.

described as translation, allusion, deformation, parody, homage, copyright infringement, "Signifying," or (as Micheaux's title more subtly suggests) masquerade.

Given the considerable evidence that Micheaux often rewrote, remade, retitled, recut, and re-released his books and films (not to mention the basic facts of his own life), it now seems necessary to set aside the simplistic and fetishizing claims of "originality" which have often been used to generously but uncritically praise Micheaux's achievements. Let it now be said, without necessarily negative connotations, that Oscar Micheaux was often highly *unoriginal.* Indeed, his incessant refashioning of his own and others' "source" materials should be recognized as *radically* unoriginal; Micheaux's career often seems based upon an implicit rejection of the notion of "intellectual property" insofar as that literally self-ish legal concept insists upon withholding powerful narratives from those nevertheless determined to tell—indeed, to re-present—those necessary stories, legal provenance be damned. If it seems unconvincing or strained to suggest that Micheaux's "radical unoriginality" aligns him with such modernist masters of appropriation as Marcel Duchamp or Joseph Cornell, or their postmodernist heirs Andy Warhol or Jeff Koons, then perhaps we can insist upon Micheaux's unacknowledged role within an African-American aesthetic tradition that most recently has centered on the practice of "sampling." Of course, as an African American, whose predecessors could not own property because they were in fact legally owned property themselves, Micheaux may have felt righteous justification in playing fast and loose with the "laws" of "copyright," even if his works often argue passionately for the importance of African-American landownership.

When considering the texts which might be "properly" attached to Oscar Micheaux's name, it is also worth emphasizing that it remains impossible, despite important rediscoveries and ongoing critical interest, to establish Micheaux's filmography with any degree of certainty. Collating the various published lists of Micheaux's films (as I originally did for this volume), for instance, only illustrates how contradictory and incomplete our basic information about this important and fascinating filmmaker remains. Given the many gaps in the simple record of facts, it may simply seem premature to proceed with speculations and claims about Micheaux's works as adaptations—a misleading term which again must refer at least to his transformation of written material into films as well as to his own "remakes" and "novelizations" of his earlier films, themselves apparently commonly derived from prior sources. (Although rarely remarked upon, it appears as if Micheaux's actual activity as a writer and as a filmmaker did not overlap: in the two periods when he was publishing novels [1913–1917 and 1944–1947] he was apparently not making films, and vice versa, a back-and-forth shift between media which makes the otherwise dense links between his literary and cinematic productions across his entire career additionally intriguing.)

Among the limited information about Micheaux that one would wish to obtain might be some evidence of the texts that this literate African American—a category that can't be taken for granted, given Micheaux's birth in 1884—might have read. Publishing his first books almost a decade before the Harlem Renaissance, and coming to maturity in isolated South Dakota, Micheaux's access to literature generally and to turn-of-the-century African-American texts especially was probably limited until he eventually settled in Chicago and New York. The fact that his first novel, *The Conquest* (1913), is dedicated to "the Honorable Booker T. Washington" indicates Micheaux's relatively unsurprising familiarity with *Up from Slavery* (1901), Washington's extremely influential autobiography, and a much more likely source of support for Micheaux's black bourgeois perspective than W. E. B. Du Bois's *The Souls of Black Folk* (1903), despite the contemporary desire on the part of many of Micheaux's most enthusiastic critics that the case might be otherwise.[8] (Micheaux's valorization of Booker T. Washington frequently extends into the films, which often feature portraits of Washington, such as on the Mason cabin wall in *The Symbol of the Unconquered* [1920].) In either case, Washington's and Du Bois's best-known nonfiction books would not have provided Micheaux with obvious *narrative* models for his own creative work. Providing additional clues regarding Micheaux's reading, the title cards and posters for Micheaux's films often clearly identify them as adaptations, though the exact identity of these "original" sources often remains vague at the next level. For example, Micheaux's musical *Swing!* (1938) is identified as an adaptation of "Mandy" but so far as I know, no one has actually determined what "Mandy" is—is it a short story, or novel, or perhaps a play? And whatever it is, who wrote it and was it in fact published? (It seems altogether impossible that "Mandy" could refer to *Mandy Oxendine*, Charles W. Chesnutt's first, but only recently published, novel, which appeared in print approximately a century after its composition.)

Surviving promotional posters or actual title cards from Micheaux's films in fact demonstrate his ongoing but critically unexamined activity of adaptation: while a film such as *The Exile* (1931) is clearly identified as an adaptation of Micheaux's first novel *The Conquest* (1913), or *Birthright* (1924 and 1938) is advertised as an adaptation of (white author) T. S. Stribling's once well-known 1922 novel of the same title, other links remain unclear. *God's Step Children* (circa 1938) is presented as an adaptation of the story "Naomi, Negress"; *The Girl from Chicago* (circa 1932) is from the story "Jeff Ballinger's Woman"; and *Ten Minutes to Live* (circa 1932), which credits Micheaux onscreen for "Adaptation, Dialogue, Direction," is identified as derived from *three* short stories, presumably from a collection entitled "Harlem After Midnight," although an apparently original "Producer's Note" immediately following the film's main titles claims that "This photoplay is adapted from the following short stories of Negro night life in Harlem: Story No. 1 "The Faker," Story No. 2 "The Killer." *Underworld* (1937) is identified as an adaptation of "Chicago After Midnight," by Edna Mae Baker, but whether or not "Harlem After Midnight" and "Chicago After Midnight" share any relation other than similar titles remains unclear. None of these titles of Micheaux's self-identified sources appear in standard and now quite extensive research guides to African-American fiction.[9] Equally confusing is exactly how the source material for *Lem Hawkins' Confession* (circa 1935) (retitled *Murder in Harlem* in surviving prints), which posters identify as the "Stanfield Murder Case," is then related to Micheaux's novel *The Story of Dorothy Stanfield* (1946), published a decade later. Is the novel based directly upon the film or upon the film's more elusive source? (The female victim in Micheaux's film, to tangle threads further, is clearly named *Myrtle* Stanfield.) A somewhat less mysterious but no less dizzying example is provided by the poster for Micheaux's last (and apparently lost) film, *The Betrayal* (1948): the film is advertised as "The unforgettable story of Martin Eden, young Negro man of Conquest," and is explicitly identified as "Based on the immortal novel *The Wind from Nowhere*." If, as Micheaux scholars now recognize, Micheaux essentially rewrote his 1913 novel *The Conquest* as 1917's *The Homesteader*, and revised *The Homesteader* as "the immortal" *The Wind from Nowhere* (1944), does it then make any sense to speak of *The Betrayal* as a "remake" of *The Exile* (again, "clearly" an adaptation of *The Conquest*), or are the intertextual links of these two films to at least three novels better understood as "adaptations"? Once again, the common suspicion that Micheaux himself remade, re-edited, retitled, and re-released his films, though already troublesome for later research, perhaps only touches upon the full complexity of Micheaux's intricate and career-long reworking of related material. If the sequence just outlined is plausible, Micheaux's first and last creative works in different media, and a number of works in between, are all versions of the same basic story—which is, moreover, Micheaux's own fictionalized autobiography.

Despite the many gaps in our knowledge of Micheaux's sources, we can at least securely rely on straightforward evidence that Micheaux had read the novels of Charles W. Chesnutt, whose importance within African-American literature has long been acknowledged, but who has recently been the subject, like Micheaux, of renewed critical interest, perhaps exemplified by major reexaminations in Eric J. Sundquist's *To Wake the Nations: Race in the Making of American Literature* (1993) and J. Lee Greene's *Blacks in Eden: The African-American Novel's First Century* (1996), in addition to the recent publication of volumes of Chesnutt's journals (1993), letters (1997), and his first novel (1997).[10] Micheaux, however, has played almost no part in earlier or even recent Chesnutt scholarship; the collections of Chesnutt's journals (1874–1882) and letters (1889–1905) end before Micheaux could be expected to make an appearance, but Micheaux also escapes notice in the first biography of Chesnutt, a selection of journals, and letters and connecting material assembled by the writer's daughter Helen in 1952, while a 1978 biography by Frances Richardson Keller refers only to Micheaux purchasing the rights to *The House Behind the Cedars* with the intention of changing the novel's ending.[11] The first major literary study of Chesnutt, by William L. Andrews, mentions Micheaux only twice, but provided some information that had not appeared previously in Chesnutt criticism: "Micheaux Productions and Reol Productions paid $500 apiece for the film rights to *The House Behind the Cedars* and *The Marrow of Tradition*. Nothing ever came of Reol's plans for *The Marrow of Tradition*, but Oscar Micheaux produced *The House Behind the Cedars* in altered form (notably with a happy ending) and distributed it in December, 1923."[12] In fact, the film had its first-known preview a year later, in December 1924. Given this release date, one might suspect that Micheaux might have become aware of *The House Behind the Cedars* through its serialization in the *Chicago Defender* beginning in late 1921, over twenty years after its initial publication and first serialization in Cleveland's *Self-Culture* magazine in 1900 and 1901, though Charlene Regester has demonstrated that a (typically) more complicated process was at work.[13] Despite the novel's resurrection in 1922 and as a film thereafter, the publishers Houghton

Mifflin wrote Chesnutt in 1924 of their intention to destroy the plates for both *The Wife of His Youth and Other Stories of the Color Line* (1899) and *The House Behind the Cedars* unless Chesnutt wished to purchase them for $100. Chesnutt's last significant work of fiction, the short story "Baxter's Procrustes," had been published in the *Atlantic Monthly* in 1904, and when he was awarded the NAACP's Spingarn Medal in 1928 for "pioneer work as a literary artist depicting the life and struggles of Americans of Negro descent," all his works were out of print. Besides the more direct links discussed in this essay, Chesnutt and Micheaux also share careers marked by periods of relative obscurity and limited celebrity, a contrast that notably defines other African-American public careers as well: the critical retrieval and republication of Nella Larsen and Zora Neale Hurston in recent years after decades of obscurity provide now-familiar examples.

Tracing many of these scraps of information is eventually frustrated by the blunt fact that no copy of Micheaux's first version of *The House Behind the Cedars* appears to have survived; we can speculate on the still-curious fact of this adaptation but not on the more interesting process of cinematic adaptation itself. An even more elusive case related to the figures in question involves a Micheaux film that survives as little more than a rarely recorded title: some time in the 1920s Micheaux seems to have made a film called *The Conjure Woman*, presumably (relying on the evidence of the title alone) from Chesnutt's first collection of linked short stories. Until recently, very little evidence seemed to support the existence of this film. However, a publicity still of Percy Verwayen and Evelyn Preer in "Oscar Mischeaux's [*sic*] Picture Called 'The Conjure Woman'" appeared in the *New York Amsterdam News* on July 14, 1926; ads for the film's run at the Lafayette Theatre appeared the following week. Until I became aware of these confirmations, the strongest evidence I'd previously found for the actual existence of this film was its inclusion in an advertisement printed on Micheaux Film Corporation stationery used in 1926 (which also lists as the film's stars Micheaux regulars Preer and Lawrence Chenault), though it should be noted that this advertisement *also* provides two titles that appear on no other Micheaux filmographies, *Deadline at Eleven* and *Vanity*. The latter example is as tantalizing and as fully emblematic of the research difficulties still surrounding Micheaux as any other detail: this title is actually credited as "Zora Neale Hurston's 'VANITY,'" but as Hurston's many contemporary readers will know, no such title now appears among her published novels or short stories.[14]

It would certainly be fruitful to take advantage of the unanticipated possibility of examining Chesnutt's "passing" novel in relation to Micheaux's recently rediscovered sound "remake" of *The House Behind the Cedars, Veiled Aristocrats;* in its treatment of related material, Micheaux's *God's Step Children* might also be considered a relevant intertext.[15] I might even argue that Micheaux's controversial fascination, evident from many of his films and novels, with light-skinned blacks and the possibility of their passing for white, derives directly from Micheaux's creative engagement with Chesnutt, whose own obsession with the topic was a consequence of his own status as a mixed-race "bright mulatto" and the temptation to pass for white that this offered him (a temptation which he refused, perhaps to his professional detriment in his other profession as a lawyer).[16] The dark-skinned Micheaux's continued interest in passing as a narrative trope has often confused and offended his later audiences, but I suspect his interest in the topic was, unlike Chesnutt's, generated more by its rich literary and dramatic possibilities—also explored by Chesnutt's literary precursors and contemporaries such as Frances E. W. Harper (*Iola Leroy; or, Shadows Uplifted* [1892]) and Sutton E. Griggs (*The Hindered Hand* [1905]), or younger Harlem Renaissance writers such as James Weldon Johnson (*The Autobiography of an Ex-Coloured Man* [1912]), Walter White (*Flight* [1926]), Jessie Fauset (*Plum Bun* [1928]), and Nella Larsen (*Passing* [1929])—than by its central role in Micheaux's own experience.[17] Like many of Micheaux's sound films, *Veiled Aristocrats* also becomes a melodramatic musical in which questions of genre intersect with adaptation concerns: although the film's "happy ending" seems like the kind of revision of downbeat material stereotypically associated with Hollywood adaptations—despite Micheaux's enormous economic and cultural distance from the mainstream industry—its role in a narrative that has been musicalized "faithfully" matches generic expectations even as the film's ending seems "unfaithful" to its literary source.

However, instead of providing a detailed examination of these (somewhat) clearly linked works, I'd like to advance a series of broader claims and more implicit comparisons in order to argue—in the tradition of Sergei M. Eisenstein's famous identification of Charles Dickens as D. W. Griffith's narrative model for a bourgeois moral sensibility perfectly aligned with the cinematic device of crosscutting—that Chesnutt provides Micheaux with some of the narrative strategies that have often appeared odd, awkward, or unprecedented in Micheaux's films, but which, for both Chesnutt and Micheaux, provide expressive devices ideally tailored to their "stories of the color line."[18] I'd like to therefore illustrate formal or structural connections between two works that *do not* in any direct way occupy the more comfortable roles of source and version: Chesnutt's masterpiece, *The Marrow of Tradition* (1901), which Sundquist has justifiably identified as "up to that time perhaps the best political novel in American literature," and Micheaux's rediscovered and restored *Within Our Gates* (1920), arguably the most powerful act of black protest in the American cinema before *Sweet Sweetback's Baadasssss Song* (1971).[19] My emphasis will be on linking devices in the narration of each work which suggest an understanding of adaptation more fully attentive to plotting and rhetorical structure than to the formal translation of explicit story content such as setting, dialogue, character, and action from one medium to another. (In this regard, we can thus claim that Griffith's *The Birth of a Nation* constitutes an adaptation of Dickens, as Eisenstein emphasizes, or Sir Walter Scott, as James Chandler has convincingly demonstrated, in structural and stylistic ways that might support but may also diverge from the film's explicit dramatization of the narrative content of Thomas Dixon's novel *The Clansman,* Griffith's ostensible source; such a claim might be especially relevant to the first half of Griffith's film, which is not directly derived from material in Dixon's book.)[20]

There are, nonetheless, specific points of contact between the content of *The Marrow of Tradition* and *Within Our Gates,* despite their considerable story differences; both works are what film scholars have come to re-recognize and more fully appreciate as melodramas, intertwining historical and political material with domestic and personal tragedies, and both are blatant in their reliance on coincidence or fate to link characters and plot lines.[21] To take a single set of related examples, both works include semi-parodic, servile black men whose unctuous devotion to white "masters" is eventually undercut when the color line is strictly drawn. Chesnutt's character Jerry, a servant to the white-supremacist newspaper editor Carteret, who describes Jerry as "a very good negro" who "knows his place" and is "respectful, humble, obedient, and content with the face and place assigned to him by nature" is nevertheless revealed to be a comic snoop who listens at the door while his racist "master" and his cohorts organize to reverse the gains made by blacks in Reconstruction North Carolina.[22] (Jerry mishears the cry "No nigger domination!" as "No nigger damnation," and wonders why white men should demand that all blacks enter heaven since "W'en a passel er w'ite folks gits ter talkin' bout de niggers lack dem in yander, it's mo' lackly dey're gwine ter ketch somethin' e'se dan heaven!" [*MT*, 39]) Micheaux's Efrem in *Within Our Gates* is in type and effect the same character, a debased servant of the landowner Philip Girdlestone who (like Chesnutt's Jerry) steals sips of the white man's liquor and peeks in his master's windows. Both

In *Within Our Gates* (1920), Efrem, or "Eph" (E.G. Tatum), steals sips of Girdlestone's liquor and peeks in his master's window.

characters help whites apprehend innocent blacks, who might then be lynched, and then they gloat: "He had distinguished himself in the public view, for to Jerry, as to the white people themselves, the white people were the public" (*MT,* 184). And both characters come to understand that, despite their status as "good negroes," their black bodies ultimately damn them when white mobs seek "an example" to lynch.[23] Chesnutt represents the reductive, leveling logic of racism through his most violent white supremacist, McBane: "We seem to have the right nigger, but whether we have or not, burn *a* nigger. It is an assault upon the white race . . . committed by the black race, in the person of some nigger. It would justify the white people in burning *any* nigger. The example would be all the more powerful if we got the wrong one. It would serve notice on the niggers that we shall hold the whole race responsible for the misdeeds of each individual" (*MT,* 182). In Micheaux's film, the comparable moment supplies the extraordinary visualization of Efrem's own realization of his undifferentiated blackness to white eyes. Surrounded by an angry white mob that grows less and less appreciative of his services and servility, Efrem's comic "glory" dissolves into a nightmare image or projection of his own lynched body, his extended tongue a grotesque parody of the laughing face of the comic darky of the minstrel tradition.[24] Another, even more specific, link between Chesnutt's novel and Micheaux's film might at least be noted: both texts summarize a man's desperate exchange of his dignity for survival by recourse to the biblical figure of Esau, tricked by his brother Jacob into selling his birthright for a mess of pottage (Genesis 25:27–34).[25] In an extraordinary moment in Micheaux's film, to which I will return, the debased preacher Old Ned, after allowing himself to be kicked in the behind for the amusement of whites in power, declares to himself, but in effect in direct address to the film audience, "Again I've sold my birthright. All for a miserable 'mess of pottage.' Negroes and whites—all are equal. As for me, miserable sinner, Hell is my destiny."

I have compared these characters and events in order to suggest some basic thematic and descriptive correspondences between Chesnutt's novel and Micheaux's film, despite what remains their indirect relation to one another. In distinct media, each presents similar content in means appropriate to their form: Chesnutt expresses the racist logic for indiscriminate lynching through fanatical dialog, while Micheaux presents that logic's outcome through a distinctively cinematic figure, the dissolve to a fantasized and striking "vision." The next scenes in Micheaux's film, however, suggest an even more intriguing inheritance from Chesnutt's formal techniques in *The Marrow of Tradition*. Following Efrem's vision, the white mob chases him, clearly to realize his own grisly projection of their racist desires. Efrem's murder then occurs offscreen, although we have, in effect, already seen his corpse even before the murder takes place in Micheaux's proleptic narration. In a sequence of intertitles announced as "What

Like Jerry in *Marrow of Tradition*, Efrem is "a very good negro" who is lynched.

the newspapers said" we read that "Efrem, Girdlestone's faithful servant—and himself the recent victim of accidental death at unknown hands—had described the event [the earlier murder of Girdlestone] as follows . . . ." Micheaux's narrative construction of this sequence thus splits the narrative first from diegetic reality into fantasy (the image of Efrem lynched) and back to reality (the beginning of the lynching), and then offers the rewriting of that reality as a lie in the "official" form of the white-authorized written news report. The verbal report is then intercut with the visual dramatization of its lies—the drunken rampage of Landry killing Girdlestone—which we necessarily compare and counter with the more complex "actual" events depicted earlier, which demonstrated the black man's innocence, the murderer in fact a poor white unseen by Efrem, Girdlestone, or Landry. In terms which have been more often employed to discuss African-American literature, Micheaux's repeated version of events "signifies" in the sense defined by Henry Louis Gates, Jr.: in Signifying, "a second statement or figure repeats, or tropes, or reverses the first." Like Gates's Signifying Monkey, the African-American "trope for repetition and revision," Micheaux repeats and reverses "simultaneously . . . in one deft discursive act."[26] Fantasy and reality, which literally may dissolve together in the sequence of cinematic images, are carefully distinguished by the intrusion of white language which clearly lies, and which then motivates the visualization of the official misrepresentation of the truth.

The Marrow of Tradition is a novel that explicitly presents and exposes similar lies at multiple narrative levels and with various consequences, from the little "white lies" that prevent the white Dr. Price from offending his black colleague Dr. Miller when the latter is restricted from attending an operation, to the fully elaborated, vicious "White Lies" engineered by the publisher Carteret through his newspaper, the *Morning Chronicle*, calculated misrepresentations which lead to the novel's climactic riot that reestablishes white rule. (In a brilliant and chilling dialect pun, one of Chesnutt's characters refers to the publications that list runaway slave reports as "noospapers.") Besides their function as a central motif in the novel, Chesnutt also narrativizes lies and misrepresentations by describing the same events through multiple perspectives; instead of always crosscutting between narrative spaces in order to suggest simultaneity (the model Eisenstein claims Dickens provided for Griffith and which Jane Gaines has effectively interpreted in the parallel rape and lynching sequence of *Within Our Gates*), both Chesnutt and Micheaux construct portions of their narratives to repeat (and thus subtly revise) key story events in alternate versions—inevitably *racialized* as black and white. For instance, in Chesnutt's novel, another black servant, Sandy, is walking along one evening when he "saw himself hurrying along in front of himself toward [a] house" (*MT,* 167). Sandy sees a man "who wore his best clothes and looked exactly like him," "his double" whom he takes to be his "own ha'nt." The following chapter re-narrates this same event from the previously unannounced position of Lee Ellis, a sympathetic white newspaper editor who, as a Mormon, will eventually oppose his own newspaper's pro-lynching stance. Ellis clearly identifies Sandy and notes that the two figures "were as much alike as twin brothers" (*MT,* 173). But Ellis is also "vaguely conscious that he had seen the other negro somewhere" (*MT,* 173), a dim perception that will later emerge as his recognition that the second figure is the actual thief and murderer, the degenerate white aristocrat Tom Delamere, who periodically disguises himself in blackface and performs minstrelized cakewalks to amuse the white community. In other words, Chesnutt's narrative form is closely tailored to his story's content: his narration doubles itself in order to represent Delamere's act of doubling. But here, and elsewhere in less extended passages, Chesnutt illustrates a dual perspective motivated by racial difference, a view split along the color line that in formal strategy anticipates the modernist shifts in perspective common in later decades. (The segment of Jean Toomer's *Cane* [1923] entitled "Blood-Burning Moon" provides a classic African-American example, with three different perspectives distinguished by gender as well as race).[27] Within pre–Harlem Renaissance African-American literature, such narrative shifts do not suggest the modernist recognition of the radical subjectivity provided by any alternative perspective or the essential relativity of any claim to truth (the notion famously embodied by Akira Kurosawa's modernist film *Rashomon* [1950]), but demonstrate a much more direct opposition in which race (or racism, materialized through Jim Crow segregation) isolates the "official" story from actual events. W. E. B. Du Bois, of course, powerfully articulated a general version of this unequal difference in *The Souls of Black Folk* as the African American's double-consciousness or "two-ness," and this compelling characterization of the African-American's internal division has served as a model for understanding Micheaux, among many others (motivating, for example, Henry Louis Gates, Jr.'s influential discussion of African-American literary texts as "double-voiced").[28] Since Du Bois's notion is intended as an explanation of the African-American psyche, the model is certainly appropriate to a consideration of Micheaux, but it is worth recalling that many of the narrative examples preceding Du Bois which I am offering as possible models for Micheaux's style insist upon the division marked by the color line as fundamentally *external* and *material* in its strict maintenance and concrete effects. In other words, slavery and Jim Crow laws explicitly reinforced the regular construction of alternative *public narratives,* demanding at least two versions of every story (undoubtedly enforcing Du Bois's psychological divisions) in tandem with segregation's strict regulation of separate and unequal public spaces. As Craig Hansen Werner has suggested broadly (though with specific reference to Chesnutt), "Afro-Americans, individually and communally, learned quickly to exploit the gap between signifier and signified. Constructing elaborate verbal 'masks' in everyday discourse as well as in the spirituals and animal tales, 'slaves' . . . continually . . . subverted the oppositional racist association of *white* with such privileged terms as 'good,' 'God,' 'mature,' and 'civilized,' and *black* with such excluded terms as 'evil,' 'devil,' 'child-like,' and 'savage.'"[29] An exemplary dramatization of the production of alternative narratives as the result of racial difference appears in the first chapter of Frances E. W. Harper's *Iola Leroy* (1892), the best-selling novel by an African American in the nineteenth century, and thus a text Micheaux and Chesnutt might have known. After two slaves meet on the road during the Civil War and exuberantly discuss the butter, fish, and eggs on sale at the market, Harper's narrator intrudes:

> There seemed to be an unusual interest manifested by these men in the state of the produce market, and a unanimous report of its good condition. Surely there was nothing in the primeness of the butter or the freshness of the eggs to change careless looking faces into such expressions of gratification, or to light dull eyes with such gladness. What did it mean?
>
> During the dark days of the Rebellion, when the bondman was turning his eyes to the American flag, and learning to hail it as an ensign of deliverance, some of the shrewder slaves, coming in contact with their masters and overhearing their conversations, invented a phraseology to convey in the most unsuspected manner news to each other from the battlefield.[30]

Like Chesnutt and Micheaux after her, Harper suggests that the racially segregated world necessarily generates alternate narratives and narrative techniques, two ways of telling even though the maintenance of racial difference denies both versions equal validity. White versions of events, in these narratives, stand as officially recorded and validated lies, whereas black versions of the same events are consistently represented as informally circulated truths or even as the immediate oral and eyewitness testimony obscured by written and retrospective history. Given their melodramatic contexts, however, the truth from below is ultimately privileged over the lie from above, even if Chesnutt, Micheaux, and Harper demonstrate the painful price that the speaking of "unofficial" truth can exact. In one of the most curious moments in *Within Our Gates,* for example, the subservient black preacher, Old Ned, who bows and scrapes to his white "superiors," even allowing them to kick his backside, shuts the door on the space of his humiliation and degradation and instantly changes his laughter to a frown, suddenly declaring his own recognition of his self-damnation, cursing his selling of his "birthright for a mess of pottage." Like many of the major sequences of *Within Our Gates* (including virtually its entire second half, constructed as a flashback), this action is in fact represented as a full visualization of a verbal narration, an embedded tale dramatized through images rather than fully quoted description; remarkably, however, this moment is supposedly narrated by the wealthy white racist Mrs. Stratton, who is identifying Old Ned as the proper kind of Negro—servile, yet influential within his controlled domain—worthy of white patronage. But Old Ned's moment of self-recognition and confession, offered directly to the film's audience, cannot reasonably be assumed to be part of Mrs. Stratton's narration, of her impossible, shared recognition of his own self-recognition. Though this moment might appear like one of Micheaux's many examples of the loose narrative control forced by low budgets, it nevertheless serves the pattern found throughout the film of knowledge being divided along racial lines: even the ostensibly white version of a black character's life splits apart when the black character's consciousness finally must speak through another's "authoritative" narration. Another form of such doubling is perhaps evident in Micheaux's film: though I have not been able to confirm this, it appears that the same actor (E. G. Tatum) may be playing both Old Ned and Efrem, with only slight changes in make-up, though with remarkably different physical and facial gestures.[31] Since *Within Our Gates* also includes an apparently uncommon cameo appearance by Micheaux—ironically the only black character in the film to use the word "nigger" in an intertitle—such complex play in casting should not be overlooked.[32]

In later films, Micheaux will play variations on the theme and structure of alternate versions, though the fundamental racial distinction between "official lies" and "unofficial truth" will not always be so emphatically drawn as in *Within Our Gates*. For instance, in *Underworld* (1937), Paul Bronson is wrongfully accused of shooting Sam Brown until a Chinese man, Ching Li, appears with the information that he witnessed the killing from a previously unrevealed position; through a flashback, an entirely different view of the murder is re-presented to secure the truth. A more complex narration appears in *Lem Hawkins' Confession* (re-released as *Murder in Harlem*) (1935). The story of the murder of white Myrtle Stanfield, for which the innocent black watchman Arthur Vance stands accused, is partially narrated through the testimony of black Lem Hawkins, who reveals (in recreated flashback) that his white boss, Mr. Brisbane, is guilty of raping and beating Myrtle. However, the full story only emerges when the surrogate mother of Myrtle's white lover, George Epps, narrates (again through flashback) the missing segment of the complete story, in which the jealous Epps strangles Myrtle's unconscious body. The complete solution to the film's enigma, in other words, requires the accumulation and coordination of black and white narratives, assembled, appropriately enough, by the black lawyer and novelist Henry Glory. Glory's initial appearance in the film selling his own "race" novels door-to-door certainly suggests that he is a surrogate for this director, not only because of their shared profession and means of distribution (Micheaux sold his novels himself), but because Glory, like Micheaux, constructs and revises his narrative by negotiating the truths and misleading evasions of opposed, racialized versions of the same story events.[33]

While there is clear evidence that Oscar Micheaux frequently adapted the work of Charles W. Chesnutt throughout his career as a filmmaker and novelist, I have attempted to demonstrate that Micheaux's most significant inheritance from Chesnutt may be in form rather than content; more precisely, Chesnutt provides a formal means for narrating—and exposing—the "white lies" that otherwise declare themselves as truth. While I still believe it will be valuable, as the critical examination of Micheaux continues, to trace and consider Micheaux's work of adaptation in the conventional sense—work that has barely begun—I would suggest that ongoing research also recognize from the start that in Micheaux's hands the process of adaptation might always involve more transgression than translation. There is little real value in continuing to uncritically praise Micheaux's often spurious "originality" when the forms his "unoriginality" so often takes are far more adventurous and revealing.

III

MICHEAUX'S
CONTEMPORARIES

11.

Planes, Trains, and Automobiles: The Flying Ace, *the Norman Company, and the Micheaux Connection*

PHYLLIS R. KLOTMAN

THE NORMAN STUDIOS PRESENT:
The Greatest Airplane Thriller Ever Filmed.
Six Smashing Reels of Action!
Love! Laughs! Mystery!

So exults the multihued *Flying Ace* publicity poster, with flaming plane, parachuting villain, primping heroine (in seductive heart inset), and stalwart hero in the uniform of his country—the "flying ace" himself. All this *and* an "all colored cast" in the six-reel film which Richard Norman completed in 1926.

The Flying Ace (1926; sometimes referred to as *The Fighting Ace* or *The Black Ace*) is about Captain William Stokes, World War I flyer-hero and former railroad detective, who is called upon by his former boss to solve the mystery of a disappearing paymaster and the $25,000 payroll he was carrying. With his partner (and one-legged sidekick), Stokes unravels the clues to the crime, apprehends the villain, clears the stationmaster (who was falsely accused), and woos the stationmaster's daughter. But the real star of the film is the plane—prop though it was—at least according to the publicity. It is the symbol of Captain Stokes's heroism, his past triumphs, and his ability to use the new technology to good purpose. Melodrama abounds, but the audience is primed for aerial exploits.

BACKGROUND

The origins of *The Flying Ace* can be traced to a number of factors: the beginning of the film medium itself; nineteenth-century melodrama, which fed the new medium with standard plots; stock characters and easily understood conventions; the development and phenome-

Poster for *The Flying Ace* (1926).

nal success of the serial (from the teens to the fifties); the fascination with aviation and avia-tors, especially after World War I, as reflected in popular pulp fiction; and Richard Norman's interest in targeting the Negro audience for his all-black-cast film productions.

From the beginning of cinema, audiences were excited by seeing images moving on screen, any image—*Workers Leaving a Factory* (the Lumière Brothers, 1895) or street scenes such as *Herald Square* (Edison, 1896). "From 1895 until about 1900 movies continued to seek their material directly from life. Nothing was too slight to photograph as long as it moved: people strolling in the streets, trees swaying in the wind, trains speeding."[1]

Although the plane never gets off the ground in *The Flying Ace,* the film acknowledges the great interest of the public in technology by focusing on the excitement generated by the movement of planes, trains, and automobiles (a car also figures in the solution of the mys-tery), an excitement already exploited by the popular film serial. "The thrills of flying were incorporated into virtually all serials whose setting did not predate the invention of the air-plane."[2] *The Flying Ace* has a number of the characteristics of the most popular serials of the teens and twenties. For example, *The Hazards of Helen,* a forty-eight-chapter series produced first by Kalem, then Universal, starred Helen Holmes as a telegraph operator who "keeps the railroad running regardless of the obstacles placed in her path."[3] Unlike the continued-next-week convention that brought audiences back to the theater again and again, *The Flying Ace* follows the format of one *Hazards of Helen* episode, "Escape on the Fast Freight" (1914), in which the conflict is resolved at the end: Helen battles the payroll thieves on a moving train and, like Captain Stokes, rounds them up at the end of the episode. A later episode even has Helen escaping from a train by climbing the kind of rope ladder on which Ruth, the station-

The airplane rivaled the actors for attention when it came to publicizing *The Flying Ace*. Here villain Finley Tucker (Harold Platts) is about to strike Captain William Stokes (J. Lawrence Criner) while Ruth Sawtelle (Kathryn Boyd) lies unconscious in the cockpit.

master's daughter, escapes from the burning plane in *The Flying Ace*. In addition, using intertitles, Norman divided his film into four parts which could have been, but apparently never were, shown separately.

The Flying Ace was the fifth all-black-cast film made by the Norman Film Manufacturing Company. Shot at the Eagle Studios in Arlington (Jacksonville), Florida,[4] it was screened in segregated theaters from Alabama to Texas, many of them managed and some owned by African Americans, as well as in churches and schools in the black community.

According to the Norman Studios' records (contracts and box-office receipts), during its near-decade distribution life, *The Flying Ace* grossed approximately $20,000. And, although Norman seems to have exhausted its distribution possibilities in the United States by 1935, in October of that year he received an inquiry from S. Raymond Horace, Managing Director of "Wer" Motion Picture Company in Monrovia, Liberia, expressing special interest in *The Flying Ace:* "A picture that would seem most thrilling, judging from the correspondence and Posters, is 'The Flying Ace.' Is this picture still available?" Horace wanted to know. Norman's reply indicated that not only were *The Flying Ace, Black Gold,* and *Crimson Skull* available, but he could also furnish used prints for the bargain price of $75 each, or two for $125. "It would pay you to snap them up" he wrote Horace two months later. What we don't know from the records is whether or not the deal with "Wer" was ever consummated. Nor do we know exactly what *The Flying Ace* cost to make. However, in a letter to D. Ireland Thomas, owner-manager of the Lincoln Theatre in Charleston, South Carolina and columnist for the *Chicago Defender,* regarding Thomas's suggestion that Norman use Bessie Coleman, the "Only Colored Girl Aviator in the World, in a production with a story built around her and her plane,"

Norman estimated that it would cost between four and five thousand dollars "to make the proper kind of picture for her, and one which will bring the biggest returns."[5] Norman was acutely aware of the cost of a five- to six-reel feature of the sort that Coleman wanted to produce jointly with him because, as he wrote Thomas, "I am just starting a new picture called 'The Flying Ace,' in which there are many thrilling airplane stunts, therefore am equipped to supply all props Miss Coleman would require for a picture."[6] Although Norman was not completely candid in this correspondence—there are no "thrilling airplane stunts" (there are simulated stunts, creative special effects), we can still conjecture that he cleared $13,000 to $14,000 after deducting the cost of production, marketing, and distribution. What we cannot know for sure is if he intended to shoot real stunt footage of a flyer with his or her own plane, to use footage he hoped to acquire as he had with the train-wreck footage for *The Green-Eyed Monster,*[7] or if he expected to resort to special effects using the prop that sat on the ground at Eagle Studios.[8]

AFRICAN AMERICANS AND AVIATION

"I *could* fly a plane if I had a chance," Bigger said.
  "If you wasn't black and if you had some money and if they'd let you go to that aviation school, you *could* fly a plane," Gus said.

—Richard Wright, *Native Son*

More than twenty years before Richard Wright put these words in the mouth of Bigger Thomas and his friend Gus, African Americans had taken to the skies, but their air flight was not legitimated by state or federal licensing agencies *or* the United States Air Force. The history of African Americans in the United States armed services, and especially in the air force, flies in the face of the storied "reality" of *The Flying Ace,* even assuming the conventional latitude of the movie serial. There is no way that the handsome hero could have flown missions in France for the U.S. Air Force during World War I. Not until October 1940 did the War Department announce that "Negroes were in training as pilots, mechanics, and technical specialists, and that Negro Aviation units would be organized as soon as the necessary personnel were trained."[9] William Miles's fine documentary, *Men of Bronze,* depicts the experiences of African-American soldiers during the war that was to save the world for democracy, World War I. The assignments of the 369th Infantry Regiment (the New York 15th), for example, before the transfer of the unit to the Fourth French Army, where they fought heroically and were awarded the Croix de Guerre, were much more grounded and circumscribed: digging trenches and latrines and loading and unloading supplies—the work of stevedores. Given that racist reality, writer-director Norman seems to have reached beyond the headlines and produced a hero his intended audience hungered to see and identify with.

Eugene Bullard

The model for the "Flying Ace" could have been Eugene Bullard, whose unique story as a volunteer in the French Foreign Legion and then in the French army was first known to readers (perhaps including Richard Norman) in this country through an article in a popular magazine, the *Saturday Evening Post,* by Will Irwin, who wrote a series of weekly feature articles entitled "Flashes from the War Zone." On July 15, 1916, he wrote an article on Bullard, to whom he'd been introduced by the United States consul while Bullard was recovering in a hospital in Lyons from wounds he suffered at the battle of Verdun. Irwin ended the article with a typical southerner's elicited response from Bullard: "You wouldn't a' believed it, boss, if you'd seen it in a cinema show!"[10] Yet Bullard's journal, which is ingeniously woven into the biography, has no trace of dialect. Bullard was so badly wounded that he had no hope of getting back into the fray, but miraculously he was able to convince one of his French supporters, Captain Ferrolino, that he should go into French aviation. He was transferred to the French Air Service on October 6, 1916, to train as a gunner, then fifteen days later to the aviation school for pilots at Tours, where he learned to fly *cages au poules* (chicken coops), as the French called their training planes. On November 5, 1917, he received his pilot's license. However, discrimination dogged his steps even in France, where he had lived as an expatriate since he was nineteen. Although Bullard flew missions against the Germans and comported himself well, he was constantly thwarted by unseen forces, usually his own countrymen once they had arrived in France. Learning that "Uncle Sam would accept all pilots serving France and, additionally would advance them in rank," Bullard took and passed the physical and waited, and waited, while all the other pilots were transferred. Finally it dawned on him that they were all white. "Later, I learned that in World War I, Negroes were not accepted as flyers by the United States Army."[11]

Hubert Fauntleroy Julian

Hubert Fauntleroy Julian is another possible model for Captain William Stokes—a picture of Julian labeled "Flying Ace" appears in a 1993 publication of the

Stunts were simulated on sets in the Norman Studio, Arlington, Florida. Trapped in an airplane with the villain, Ruth Sawtelle (Kathryn Boyd) is rescued by Captain Stokes (J. Lawrence Criner), the flying ace, via a ladder suspended from his plane.

Smithsonian Institution.[12] This handsome young Trinidadian, partially educated in London, sailed off to Canada in 1914 to attend a Jesuit high school in Montreal, but his great ambition was to fly. His chance came when he attracted the attention of flight instructor William A. Bishop, who had distinguished himself in the Royal Canadian Flying Corps during World War I. Bishop was impressed with the boy's daily vigil at Montreal's aerodrome and taught him to fly. Julian's biographer, John Peer Nugent, reports: "On a chilly November Sunday

Hubert Julian climbed down from a ten-minute solo flight in 'Billy' Bishop's Sopwith Camel. He had just become the first Negro aviator in history."[13] However, the year was 1919, and Eugene Bullard had already flown missions against the Germans in France.

Bessie Coleman

Bessie Coleman, the young aviatrix from Texas, who had to go to France in order to fulfill her ambition to fly, also saw herself as the "first Negro flier." In her letter to Norman of February 3, 1926, Coleman states unequivocally that she is the "world's first col[ored] Flyer, man or woman." Firsts are always difficult to confirm, and Julian became such a flamboyant figure in Harlem during the twenties that he made the pages of, among others, the *Chicago Defender,* the *New York Times,* and the *New York World Telegram* with his daring exploits in the air, in Harlem and around the world. He may well have launched his career as a daredevil on September 3, 1922, by parachuting from the wing of Coleman's plane when she made her first exhibition flight in the United States at Curtiss Airfield in Garden City, Long Island.[14] Both of them participated in the excitement of barnstorming and both of them made the black as well as the white press.[15] Captain E. C. McVey, who is the most likely model for Captain Billy Stokes in *The Flying Ace,* escorted Coleman to her plane that memorable day and was a passenger in the plane for the first part of her performance.

Captain Edison C. McVey

Norman corresponded with both Coleman and McVey, especially with the latter (from May 20 to October 25, 1924), whom he had evidently met in San Antonio. The first letter from Norman indicates that the filmmaker knew about McVey's stunt flying and wanted to use him in a film. In fact, if McVey did well, Norman would consider a proposition to finance the flyer in a picture in which he would be starred. However, Norman wanted to make sure that McVey was in a position to come to Jacksonville the summer of 1924, or in the near future, and urged McVey to give up the "scheme" he was "framing" in order to join him where he would earn *real* money. Any offer was contingent upon whether McVey had already filmed his own picture and intended to show it, because Norman believed that it would hurt McVey's reputation to appear in anything that wasn't "strictly professional."

What is illuminating about this correspondence with McVey is that he not only describes the kind of daredevil stunts he can and has already performed ("changing from plane to plane, from top of train to plane, catching an aeroplane on the ground from a flying start . . . there is [sic] no possible feats that I am afraid to undertake on Land Sea or in the Air"), enclosing a sample of the 1800–2000 feet of negative he had already shot, but he also enclosed a brochure of his company, the Afro-American Film Producers, Galveston, Texas, with his picture superimposed on an ace of spades.[16] McVey is the flying black ace, down to the uniform we see on Captain Billy Stokes. His enthusiasm for Norman's proposition is reflected in all of his letters from Galveston and Flatonia, Texas: he offered to travel across the country by plane; to send his own story, "Coming from the Clouds," some of which he'd already shot; and to adjust his schedule to suit Norman's. Yet McVey, who could perform all of the stunts Norman advertised in his publicity for *The Flying Ace,* which seem to out-hazard Helen, never appeared in this or any other Norman film. The only inference we can draw from the exchange of letters is that the two men were unable to come to terms on the schedule. McVey expected to start working on October 15th, but since Norman was in Norfolk and didn't receive McVey's letter of confirmation until the first week in October, he assumed that McVey wouldn't be able to make it and changed the starting date to November 1st. For his part, McVey felt that Norman had put him at a great disadvantage because he had turned down other film and lecture propositions: he wanted a more rigorous agreement and would wait for two weeks before attempting anything else. Norman replied by the deadline, this time from Washington, D.C., and, while he apologized for any embarrassment his change of plans may have caused McVey, would not be pinned down since he was on the road looking after "percentage dates" for *Regeneration*. Norman indicated that he could still use McVey's services, but he wouldn't stand in McVey's way: "I will substitute Clarence Brooks of California who has quite a bit of picture experience."[17] As it turned out, Brooks was not available and he "substituted" J. Lawrence Criner.

McVey's value, apparently, was in his reputation as a flyer and the possibility of using some of the footage he had already shot. It was not in his ability to perform the stunts required by a script, because although there were planes available in Jacksonville, Norman wrote him, "no pilot will let a stranger fly his machine, unless we put up the full price . . . in case of damage. This is a thing we don't want to do because [of] the element of risk, therefore it will be necessary in case we use you, to double your part in any actual flights—using the original pilot with his plane."

There is no question that an eager audience existed for films that showed African Americans in roles that they should have had but were in reality denied. Norman had proved that with his first all-black-cast film, *The Green-Eyed Monster,* a remake of the all-white version, which he advertised as spectacular and stupendous: the thrilling scenes were "even more interesting than the usual 'thrillers' because of the fact that the characters are colored people, splendidly assuming the different roles of Railroad President, Financial Backer, Traffic Manager, Directors, Superintendent, Railroad Contractor . . . representing the cream of the colored race."[18] *The Flying Ace,* like *The Green-Eyed Monster,* required the audience's suspension of disbelief. Yet the leap from intrepid flying performer to heroic flying ace was less a challenge to the spectator than buying the American screen dream of rising to the pinnacle—president of the railroad or president of the country.

RICHARD NORMAN AND THE NORMAN FILM MANUFACTURING COMPANY

Richard Edward Norman was born in Middleburg, Florida, on July 13, 1891; he died on November 7, 1960. He had two brothers: Earl, who volunteered and served with the Royal Canadian Forces during World War I, and Kenneth Bruce, who became his partner in the film production business. Richard attended Massey Business College in Jacksonville. An inventor and entrepreneur (he concocted a drink called Pasi-Kola and designed a sound device for film projectors which he called a Camera Phone or resynchronizer), he started his film production career around 1912, traveling through the Midwest and contracting to film local events using residents and businesses. He sold tickets to screenings in schools, churches, and at the local theater, splitting with them 60–40 percent. In Marinette, Wisconsin, he met (and later married) a young woman whom he featured in two films, *The Wrecker* and *Marinette Adopts a Baby*. Their son, Richard Norman, Jr., told an interviewer with the *Jacksonville Times-Union and Journal:*

> Father traveled all through the Midwest writing scenarios and filming as he went along. Approaching the mayor and the commissioners of each town, he would ask them to allow him to use their sons and daughters in his productions—usually as stars. The movies were love stories, and the same type of situation was used over and over, but adapted to suit each city's surroundings. They would always end happily with a church wedding.[19]

Richard E. Norman
in 1925, age 34.

One of his most inventive early films was *Sleepy Sam the Sleuth,* a short comedy enhanced by interesting cinematic techniques, that he shot in Des Moines, Iowa, with local residents. In the film, Sam dreams he is hired by farmer Brown to catch a couple of chicken thieves, but he ends up being chased all over the countryside by an ever-growing bomb hurled at him by bearded anarchists. Norman touted it as a "Home Talent Moving Picture: A Local Photoplay Comedy Made in this City. 1000 laughs in 1000 feet. Acted by your Friends. Directed by a Master Comedy Director [himself]." Although he shot the film several times in different locations with different local casts, only one version survives.

Norman returned to Florida, making his home in Jacksonville, and began producing feature-length films for national distribution. In 1916, he made *The Green-Eyed Monster* with an all-white cast, a melodrama of romance and treachery involving competition in the railroad industry and in love. It capitalizes on the audience's interest in men, machines, and movement. In 1919, he remade the film with an all-black cast, adding a stereotypical comic sequence, which he later removed and marketed separately as *The Love Bug.* There are no clues in the correspondence to help us understand the catalyst for his decision to make films targeting the black audience, no contracts for the original *Green-Eyed Monster* to indicate its success or failure. Norman was certainly an astute observer of the market. Perhaps he knew of Lincoln's and Micheaux's successes, particularly on the west and the east coasts. Certainly Norman's painstaking research, represented by the file he developed of theaters catering to black audiences, and his records of the "colored" population in Florida and the other southern states where those theaters were located, are an indication of a decision not lightly taken. Reception of the shorter, five-reel version of *The Green-Eyed Monster,* released in 1920, encouraged Norman to produce more films for this newfound audience.

In 1921, Norman went to the all-black town of Boley, Oklahoma, to make a film about black cowboy Bill Pickett, a hand on the Miller Bros. 101 Ranch. Pickett had become a star of the 101's rodeo by virtue of his "bull-dogging" specialty—pinning a steer to the ground with his teeth. Norman's original plan was to put all of the Oklahoma footage that he shot into a film on Pickett to be entitled *A Rodeo Star [A Round-up Star].* Although wiry, muscular, and physically powerful, Pickett was in his fifties and had lost most of his upper front teeth. Disappointed that Pickett was older and less prepossessing than he expected, Norman decided to assign him a lesser role and foreground a drama set in the west starring Anita Bush, the "Mother of Negro drama" and founder of the Anita Bush Players, and Lawrence Chenault,[20] a member of her company, later leading man of the Lafayette Players and a Micheaux star. Norman shot enough footage of Pickett at the 101 and at a round-up in Wellington, Kansas, to make two films, *The Bull-Dogger* and *The Crimson Skull* (he even had in mind a third film, *The Fairytale,* which apparently was never made), both capitalizing on essentially the same cast. The latter was the tale of a peaceful town on the prairie beset by outlaws. According to the *Cleveland Gazette* of February 12, 1923, "No expense was spared to make it a typical picture of the old swash-buckling west, with the added attraction of a cast composed of our ac-

Advertising material for *The Love Bug* (1920).

tors and actresses who could ride and shoot in true western style."[21] Bush played Anita, the cattleman's daughter, and Chenault had a challenging triple role. Also featured was Steve "Peg" Reynolds, the versatile one-legged actor who not only appeared from then on in every Norman black-cast film, but also made personal appearances at screenings to enhance the box office. Norman released both films the same year, but *The Crimson Skull* was shown only in Oklahoma in 1921. Its eight reels were cut to six before it was released in other states the following year. Both were enthusiastically received by black filmgoers who had never seen black cowboys on or off the screen.

Norman's next feature film was *Regeneration* (1923), a melodrama about buried treasure,

Press book material for *The Bull-Dogger* (1920), featuring cowboy star Bill Pickett.

violence, and lovers stranded on an island in the South Pacific. The scenario of shipwrecked lovers on a desert island they call "Regeneration" echoed Vitagraph's 1915 film, *Island of Regeneration,* which was re-released in 1920. Norman's added touches were a search for treasure, a villainous cutthroat, and some nude scenes:

> I am endeavoring to work in several nude and artistic scenes on the desert island that will not offend and can be nicely removed . . . one of them showing this bathing scene with villain peering lustfully through bushes at the terrified girl—it will draw like mustard poultice.[22]

However, there is no record that the film was shown with the nude scenes. Stella Mayo played the heroine Violet Daniels, M. C. Maxwell one of the leads, Alfred Norcom one of the heavies. Norman offered J. Albert English, stage actor and manager of the Pekin Theatre in Montgomery, Alabama, the part of the villainous "Knife" Hurley, but English never appears in the publicity.[23]

ZIRCON, OR THE FIGHTING FOOL

M. C. Maxwell was both a performer and a businessman. His career as a magician spanned more than twenty years; his business activities were mainly confined to the "selling end of the film game," according to J. A. Jackson.[24] Maxwell tried to help Norman get his fifteen-reel serial *Zircon* into production by suggesting possibilities for the female lead. Mystery still surrounds this serial, which Norman wanted very much to make. It is advertised, along with the company's other productions, on the Norman Film Manufacturing Company letterhead, dated February 8, 1924:

> Coming!   "Zircon."
> A Colored Serial Supreme.
> 15 Smashing 2-reel Episodes,
> featuring "The Fighting Fool."
> Big Fights!   Suspense!
> Thrills!

Letters to theater managers that year indicate that Norman tried to guarantee distribution of the serial before he undertook the project. To the manager of the Grand in West Palm Beach, he wrote: "Every Colored Exhibitor catering to colored audiences must book this serial or we can't afford the venture."[25] He even offered a "profit sharing rental franchise" and indicated to other managers that the

Steve "Peg" Reynolds was regularly featured in Richard Norman's films from the 1920s. In *The Flying Ace*, he played Captain Stokes's mechanic and all-round associate. His crutch, like Charlie Chaplin's cane, served many purposes. In *The Flying Ace*, he uses it as a gun in one scene and a mock guitar in another.

serial had to be "booked solid" to be released. Apparently it was not, because as late as June 21, 1927, he replied to a query from Guy Shriner, manager of the Gem Theatre in Kansas City, Missouri, that he was "hampered by lack of proper financing to take care of it, tho I have every facility to make such a serial." What's more, there are no validated contracts or box-office receipts for the serial, although *The Fighting Fool,* which may be an alternate title, is included on occasion as a companion piece to another film. In fact, the *Regeneration* press kit includes a section on "Coming Attractions" in which *The Fighting Fool* is touted as "15 Two-Reel Episodes Teeming with Big Fights, Thrilling Situations, Suspense Mystery, Adventure, Love," with an "ALL COLORED CAST"; yet there are no posters, lobby cards, or stills to verify the production or the cast. Nonetheless, all the episodes are titled, hero, heroine and villain named, and dramatic conflict limned. Each suspense-filled episode is designed to captivate the audience, for example "The Wheel of Death" (#2), "The Poison Cloud" (#3), "The Living Tomb" (#5), "The Sky Demon" (#8), "Sands of Death" (#13), and "The Vanishing Prisoner" (#14). Norman had a cast in mind: Clarence Brooks in the role of the hero John Manning, a young chemist and mining engineer who discovers a new substance he names "Zircon"; Anita Thompson as Helen, Manning's sweetheart; J. Albert English as "Spider," the villain, who promised to "try and make Lon Chaney take notice"; and Steve Reynolds as "Peg," Manning's friend. But there are no contracts in the correspondence and no firm date set for shooting. In spite of the strong cast, Norman may not have gotten the exhibitor commitments he needed to fund the project, but one of the episodes, "The Sky Demon" (#8), was about a "Colored Aviator" who rescues Manning from the "Crocodile's Jaws" (#7)[26] It was a "colored aviator" who became the hero of Norman's next film, *The Flying Ace,* the only complete Norman feature film that survives.

Black Gold, set in Oklahoma and touted as a story of "oil, greed, love and heroism," was the last of Norman's black-cast films. He began shooting in July of 1927 with Criner and Boyd, his two stars of *The Flying Ace,* and released it the same year. It seems reasonable to conjecture that his decision to stop producing race films was taken with the same seriousness as his decision to undertake that new enterprise.

MICHEAUX'S CIRCLE

The correspondence between Richard Norman and Oscar Micheaux in the Norman Collection at the Black Film Center/Archive (Afro-American Studies Department, Indiana University) establishes the connection between the two men, who were both filmmakers and potential rivals wooing the same audience. Yet the language of the letters reflects a genuinely warm and friendly relationship. While Micheaux was turning out a quartet of films and struggling to exhibit almost a dozen more, he paused to write Richard Norman, whom he had apparently seen on a previous Norman visit to New York. Micheaux's letter may well be a response to a query from Norman after the latter's production of *Regeneration.* Micheaux addresses him warmly as "Friend Norman":

> The Franklin Theatre here, would like to play your "REGENERATION." So if you will get in touch with them, the Franklin Theatre Lenox Avenue at 132nd Street, you will be able to consummate a deal with them if your rental is not too high. Understand that you have produced a new feature and should like to hear from you.[27]

That new feature was probably *The Flying Ace.* From the warm respectful tone of his letter, it is obvious that Micheaux relates to Norman as a fellow filmmaker in the struggle. He certainly does not relate in the same way to "the Jews" who produced *A Prince of His Race* and *Ten Nights in a Barroom* (the Colored Players Film Corporation, headed by David Starkman), who "seem to think they know it all, and regard all of us who have endured through the years gone by as dubbs [who] know nothing . . . about production or distribution."

Norman's reply two days later is in kind—warm, with the same friendly salutation—and thanking Micheaux for "a tip" about the Lenox Theatre, which apparently had not lived up to its contract with Norman. He also commiserates with Micheaux about the Philadelphia company "which has brought out more pictures to hinder the progress of the colored picture." Norman had a solution to the distribution problem that plagued them both, and he was not averse to using blandishments to get Micheaux's attention: "You are a genius in producing pictures," he writes, "but your genius has led you astray by producing pictures that you haven't been able to intensively distribute, and you have had to rely on help that has taken advantage of you." Norman believed that the only solution was to "organize the exhibitor, let him pay for the picture when it is released, and play it when he wants to." He tried to do that with his proposed serial *Zircon*, in which he hoped to feature Evelyn Preer, the star of Micheaux's first film, *The Homesteader*, as well as *Within Our Gates*—Norman recognized the need for box-office stars with drawing power. His proposition to Micheaux: "By controlling the distribution, or solving it, we could take on any independent production of merit and show them where they would make more money by letting us distribute for them." And they could divide the country—Micheaux in the North, Norman in the South.

Norman was certainly right about trying to counteract the exhibitors' pernicious practice of playing the filmmakers against each other and told Micheaux that "when the exhibitor gleefully pits us both against each other, he is only taking advantage of our foolishness, and slowly killing the goose that has laid the golden egg for him."

Although Norman later distributed some Micheaux films—the sound version of *The Spider's Web* (1926), *The Millionaire* (1927), *The Exile* (1931), and *The Girl from Chicago* (1932)—as late as 1938, the two were in fact competitors in a highly competitive business, and exhibitors did take advantage. For example, one of Norman's front men wrote to him from Beaumont, Texas, that the exhibitor had given them a "dirty deal" in Orange and Beaumont on Norman's *Regeneration* in favor of Micheaux's *The Spider's Web*.[28] Other producers of "colored" films also felt the pressure of competition. George P. Johnson, Noble's brother and general booking manager of the Lincoln Motion Picture Company, understood the pressures of the "race film" business that so many fly-by-night companies had entered for quick profit. In fact, Johnson wrote Norman explaining the financial problems of independent producers such as Micheaux—and Norman—as he saw them, offering advice on distribution and production and a proposition:

> If you have not obligated yourself on present release of your pictures and are in a position to shelve same for a few months, why not consider holding back your present release until fall and in the meantime get in touch with us and lets see if we cannot work out some combination, some co-operation that will be beneficial to both of us in the better times that are coming.[29]

Johnson also suggested that Norman incorporate and combine with Lincoln on a stock flotation. But Norman demurred. In fact, he obliquely criticized both Lincoln and Micheaux for their unnecessarily cumbersome organizations:

> That is the reason we never could see how a $75,000 Corporation of your size could realize a good profit on the investment, or a firm like Michaux [*sic*] Producing Corporation could satisfy their stockholders. We are not a corporation and have a very limited number in our company, therefore we are in a better financial condition than most producers catering to Colored Theatres. We owe this fact to our careful management and our abstainance [*sic*] from entangling alliances.[30]

Apparently Johnson never pursued the matter after this exchange. The only partner Richard Norman ever had in his business was his brother Bruce, and they eventually parted company.[31]

Box office statement for *The Flying Ace* at the Maceo Theater in Tampa, Florida. Norman split the receipts with the theater, taking home about $100 per night.

THE ACTING ENSEMBLE: THE MICHEAUX, LINCOLN, AND NORMAN COMPANIES

Operating without a studio system, independent filmmakers were never able to develop their own "stable," as Hollywood moguls later referred to their actors under contract. Yet Micheaux developed a kind of acting ensemble, in part by mining the talent from the black theater, especially the Lafayette Players. Norman was able to tap into Micheaux's and Johnson's resources because he had made a place for himself in the circle, as the above correspondence with both men demonstrates. He also developed contacts with black reviewers and theater owner-managers, such as D. Ireland Thomas and J. A. Jackson, who knew what was selling at the box office. Although he advertised for actors in the black press and received a number of responses, for the most part he employed professionals who had experience on the boards or before the camera, as long as they agreed to the salaries he set.

Lawrence Chenault apparently came to Norman's attention through Anita Bush; however, Chenault had already played opposite Evelyn Preer in Micheaux's *The Brute* (1920). In 1921, he also starred with Edna Morton in Reol's *The Burden of Race*. From 1920 to 1932, he appeared in twenty-two black films, more than any other "race movie" actor of the period.[32] Norman cast him in both *The Bull-Dogger* and *The Crimson Skull*, but when Shingzie Howard suggested Chenault later for the role of the villain in *The Flying Ace*, Norman declined to use him again because he wouldn't "keep sober on the job," thereby costing Norman time and money.[33]

J. Lawrence Criner, a featured actor with the Lafayette Players, appeared in Micheaux's *The Millionaire* (1927). He signed an agreement with Norman on June 24, 1926, for "his services, his wife's, Samuel Jordan and Lyons Daniels for the making of a motion picture for a period of two weeks for a total salary for the four people of $550.00." The agreement letter provides for an additional $175 for three extra days if necessary, but it does not indicate the film in which he was to appear. We know that Criner and Kathryn Boyd appeared in *The Flying Ace* and in *Black Gold,* both shot in 1926. It may be that Norman made the second film with Boyd/Criner without negotiating another contract. This modus operandi seems to follow the Anita Bush/Lawrence Chenault pattern of two for one with *The Bull-Dogger* and *The Crimson Skull.*

Shingzie Howard, who had made *The Dungeon* and *The Virgin of Seminole* (both in 1922) and then *A Son of Satan* and *The House Behind the Cedars* (both in 1924) with Micheaux, corresponded with Norman about the role of Ruth Sawtelle in *The Flying Ace.* She recommended Harry Henderson for one of the leads, but he was under contract with the Colored Players Film Corporation, the Philadelphia-based company headed by David Starkman, whom Micheaux had savaged to Norman. Henderson appeared in four films by the Colored Players, the company that historian Thomas Cripps considers to be Micheaux's only real rival. In 1926, when Norman wanted him for *The Flying Ace,* Henderson and the Colored Players were involved in three back-to-back productions. Perhaps the Boyd-Criner deal made the issue moot.

Edna Morton, who played in Micheaux's *A Son of Satan* (1924), negotiated in 1923 with Norman for a role in *Regeneration,* but they were never able to agree on terms. He planned to start to work on *Regeneration* around the 14th of August in Jacksonville, and his letter urged her to quote a reasonable figure for which she would work, emphasizing that the market had fallen off 50% "due to poor business and a crowding of the field with pictures that have not had drawing power." He also claimed that "present conditions in the Colored picture field will not warrant high salaries." Several letters and telegrams later, she agreed to lower her salary to $100 a week plus transportation,[34] but Norman was able to get Stella Mayo for $50.

Evelyn Preer, leading actress with the Lafayette Players and a Micheaux star, never made a picture for Norman; however, contact with her was apparently initiated by Edward G. Tatum, who appeared in seven of Micheaux's films from 1920 to 1927. Tatum's July 24, 1923, letter indicates Norman's interest in acquiring Preer's services for *Zircon,* the serial Norman planned to make.

Popular stars Anita Thompson ("known as the Mary Pickford of negro [sic] films" according to Y. Andrew Roberson's *New York Tribune* article) and Clarence Brooks ("who gets more 'fan letters' than any other colored star"[35]) were both in Lincoln Motion Picture productions. (Brooks was also secretary of the company and the person most likely to assume ownership.) They appeared together in Lincoln's *By Right of Birth* (1921). Norman contracted with them to star in his much-touted serial, *Zircon.* Brooks suggested to Norman that he use them as the stars in *Regeneration* and to promote the feature film and the serial simultaneously, but Norman had apparently already cast the leads in *Regeneration* (Stella Mayo and M. C. Maxwell). However, he proposed a permanent position for Brooks as a producer and distributor, offering him a salary, commission on bookings and pictures he produced, and stock in the corporation. In a lengthy letter to Brooks assessing the "colored picture situation" as chaotic, with too many companies in the market undercutting prices, Norman aligned himself with Lincoln and Micheaux, who was doing what he could to hold up prices and pro-

J. Lawrence Criner as Captain Stokes, with his wife Kathryn Boyd as Ruth Sawtelle.

duction but was forced to make more pictures than he would have in order to offset Reol: "As long as Lincoln, Michaux [*sic*] and Norman were the only ones in the field, they were doing their utmost to hold up prices, by personal exploitation and a minimum of productions." Norman's idea was to forge a permanent connection with Brooks, who combined both star power and business acumen, demonstrated by his track record with Lincoln and his detailed analysis of the general conditions of "colored" picture production and distribution which he prepared for the officers and directors of the Lincoln Motion Picture Company in February 1922, and which he later shared with Norman, who admonished him: "Think this letter over carefully, and decide for yourself if you are willing to come to Jacksonville and put your 'shoulder to the wheel' and guide 'Clarence Brook's [*sic*] Productions' to financial success."[36] But Brooks was involved in real estate as well as in film production, and he and his wife were very happy in California. Although his reply to Norman wasn't completely negative, from the tone of the letter—and without evidence to the contrary—it is safe to assume that the connection, like the serial, was never made.

Ida Anderson, another Micheaux actress (*A Son of Satan* [1924]), was negative in her reply to Norman:

> Your letter received and carefully read. My salery [*sic*] is $200.00 Two hundred dollars per week including concessions. I am an experienced artist and am not giving my services for try-out to any one. Lasky and Selznick pay me $40.00 forty dollars per day. However, should you really wish to talk business I am at your service.[37]

Her response made it eminently clear that she had no intention of working for the $50 a week Norman offered in his letter of June 17, 1923, or the $75 that Norman's reply indicates he could negotiate with several other actresses. He also tried to convince Anderson that she was laboring under a delusion:

> White pictures have a possible distribution of over 15000 theatres, including all colored theatres. Colored Pictures have a distribution of a bare 100 theatres. The greatest colored picture ever produced played in only 105 theatres in boom times. . . . Revenues have decreased 50% in the last 2 years. Colored Pictures have ceased to be a novelty and have lost their original drawing power.[38]

While Norman complained to M. C. Maxwell that Ida Anderson and Edna Morton's demands were absolutely unreasonable—the salaries were all right for New York, but he didn't care to invest all his profit in a New York cast—he did recognize that they were "finished artists and much in demand on account of their talent."[39]

The challenge was the same for all the producers of race films—how to stay solvent. Maxwell agreed with Norman about limiting salaries because there were so many inferior films being made for limited distribution. "There is an audience for *good* films," he wrote Norman. "Micheaux filmed one recently at Roanoke, Va. [*A Son of Satan*], but there is no telling when it will be released" and therefore he urged Norman to release *Regeneration* immediately.[40]

Norman continued to make race films for four more years and to distribute them for at least another decade. Neither he nor Lincoln survived the transition to talkies, as Micheaux did. Lincoln discontinued operations in 1923, a few weeks after announcing that the company's next production would be *The Heart of a Negro*.[41] Norman's last race film was released four years later. However, he continued to operate Eagle Studios, to distribute black-and-white films, to manage a theater in Winterpark, Florida, and in later years to make industrial training films. And he has left a remarkable record that expands our knowledge of Micheaux's circle and of the racial practices in this country that produced a separate cinema.

12.

Colored Players Film Corporation

An Alternative to Micheaux

CHARLES MUSSER

Colored Players Film Corporation, a Philadelphia-based production company, was a leading maker of race films in the late 1920s, releasing four feature films between mid-1926 and early 1929: *A Prince of His Race* (June 1926), *Ten Nights in a Barroom* (November 1926), *Children of Fate* (April 1927), and *The Scar of Shame* (April 1929).[1] Enjoying remarkable initial success with its first two pictures, the company increased its budgets.[2] Despite the critics' praise for its films, the company encountered difficulties in finding desirable bookings and, by the time of its third release, had become financially overextended.[3] Reorganized in mid-1927, the company was ultimately doomed by the rapidly growing popularity of sound films. By the time its last film was completed, many of the leading theaters catering to black audiences in Chicago, New York, Los Angeles, and Philadelphia were wired for sound.[4] The company always faced limited opportunities to recoup its investment, but these difficulties became insurmountable as the 1920s came to a close, however excellent the qualities of its silent films.

Colored Players Film Corporation (CPFC) was launched by European-American Jews: producers David Starkman and Louis Groner and Roy Calnek, who directed the first three films and was also part owner.[5] Nonetheless, admittedly fragmentary evidence indicates that this company was the site of substantive interracial collaboration. After visiting the set of *Children of Fate,* a reporter noted that the crew included "a number of race artists, electricians and cameramen."[6] Pearl Bowser also reports, based on her interview with Starkman's daughter, that Starkman was a close personal friend of Sherman H. Dudley, a prominent African-American impresario, who invested in shows and owned a theater in Washington, D.C. When CPFC faced economic difficulties after the completion of its first three films, Dudley became a public advocate for its pictures and assumed the role of company president in the summer of 1927 (perhaps contributing a badly needed infusion of capital as well).[7] This eventually led

A Prince of his Race

In "A PRINCE OF HIS RACE," the Colored Players Film Corporation present what is universally regarded as the last word in photoplay production, and when one realizes that each and every one of the players have been carefully directed with this one picture in view for a period covering over six months time, a small idea of its tremendous cost can be obtained.

The story is one that teaches that we must be in complete control of our passions and no matter what the provacation let them not get the best of us. It also tells a story with heart interest—filled with occasional thrills and moments of suspense.

Tom Bueford a member of a good family has fallen into disgrace through unscrupulous associates and is found in jail serving the last six months of a five year sentence for manslaughter.

His sweetheart's appeal to the Governor results in a twenty-four hour respite so that he can solace his dying mother in her last moments on Earth. A nerve racking, death defying ride in a dashing plunging auto over the State highways at break neck speed all night, brings him to her bedside in time for him to see her breathe her last. The auto in one of its stops is seen by James Stillman whose false testimony sent Tom to jail and as he gazes at Tom in prison garb, a mental picture recalls to Jim's guilty mind the scenes of the night that resulted in Tom's conviction, and shows the actions and events that led up to the actual crime. After Tom's release from custody he is thwarted in his attempt to see his sweetheart who has remained loyal and true through it all, by Jim who not only advises he leave town and intercepts his mail to her, but also tries his hand at love making. He succeeds in gaining the consent of her hand in marriage through her father and the wedding is about to be solemnized when Tom, who has by this time reached wealth and affluence, reads of it in the newspapers. All is in readiness; the Minister stands ready to tie the knot; the groom has the ring; the bridesmaids are in the aisle; the organ is pealing the wedding march, but at the very last moment there is an unexpected—but it is all shown in "A PRINCE OF HIS RACE," SO BE SURE AND SEE IT.

"A PRINCE OF HIS RACE"

IT BEGINS WITH A THRILL—FOLLOWED BY A SOB
ATTENDED WITH A GASP—AIDED BY A DANCE
ACCOMPANIED WITH SHAKES, SHUDDERS AND SHOUTS AND
FINISHES WITH A SURPRISE THAT YOU HOPE FOR,
BUT DON'T EXPECT.

DOUGLAS THEATRE

355 BROADWAY, MACON, GEORGIA

TUESDAY AND WEDNESDAY,
MARCH 29TH AND 30TH

DAVID STARKMAN and LOUIS GRONER
present

The Supreme Spectacular Success

A Prince of his Race

WITH A CAST OF ALL-STAR
COLORED PLAYERS

INCLUDING

Harry Henderson,

Shingzie Howard,

William A. Clayton, Jr.,

Lawrence Chenault,

Arline Mickey,

Ethel Smith

AND THE STRONGEST SUPPORTING
CAST POSSIBLE TO
ASSEMBLE.

Written and Directed by ROY CALNEK

The Treat of a Lifetime!

POSITIVELY THE GREATEST ACTORS OF THE RACE.
PRESENTING THE GREATEST PLAY OF THE AGE.
ACCLAIMED BY PRESS AND PUBLIC.
FEATURE WITHOUT A PEER—A PICTURE THAT WILL LIVE FOREVER.

THE SURPRISE CREATION
OF THE CENTURY

"A PLAY WITH A PURPOSE"

THE MOST ELABORATE ALL-COLORED PRODUCTION
EVER CONCEIVED

FULL OF THRILLS—PUNCH—ACTION—LAVISH SCENES
GORGEOUS GOWNS

SIX MONTHS IN THE MAKING AND AT
A TREMENDOUS COST

A Prince of his Race

PRODUCED BY

COLORED PLAYERS FILM CORPORATION
1322 VINE STREET
Philadelphia, Pa.

A herald for *A Prince of His Race* (1926), the first release of Colored Players Film Corporation.

to the production of a fourth film, *The Scar of Shame,* with director Frank Perugini and cameraman Al Liguori, both Italian. Colored Players Film Corporation is noteworthy, therefore, not only for interracial but also for interethnic collaborations.

Philadelphia, the CPFC's home base, was a center for insurgent filmmaking throughout the silent period. This had been true at least since Siegmund Lubin went into production in 1897, challenging Thomas A. Edison and New York capital. Lubin remained the dominant force in Philadelphia filmmaking until his business closed in 1916.[8] The movie mogul's failure left a reservoir of trained personnel and a tradition of independent—even guerrilla—filmmaking, enabling Philadelphia subsequently to become a center for the production of Yiddish as well as race films.[9] David Starkman had made his living working in and around this enterprising industry. He owned the Standard Film Exchange as well as a local theater on Ridge Avenue, which catered to a largely African-American clientele. Keeping the film exchange, he sold the theater to raise capital for his new venture.[10] Roy Calnek was an experienced filmmaker by the time he became involved with Colored Players. He directed at least three race films made by Superior Art Motion Pictures, Inc., also based in Philadelphia: the features *Hearts of the Woods* (1921) and *Smiling Hate* (1924), as well as the two-reel comedy *Steppin' High.*[11] Calnek then wrote and produced *Abie's Imported Bride* (1925), a Jewish comedy for the Temple Theater Amusement Company.[12] Harry Henderson, Howard Augusta, and possibly Ethel Smith had their motion picture debuts in *Smiling Hate,* then subsequently worked with Calnek at Colored Players. Henderson was the company's leading man, appearing in all four of its pictures.

Colored Players had a strong Philadelphia identity and repeatedly emphasized its close relations to the city's African-American community. Advertisements for *A Prince of His Race* in the *Philadelphia Tribune* promoted "an Excellent Supporting Cast of Local Talent."[13] While living in Philadelphia, William A. Clayton, Jr. was selected to play the villain in *A Prince of His Race* and then appeared in the company's next two pictures. On Monday, December 27, 1926, during the making of *Children of Fate,* the actors of the Colored Players Film Corporation hosted "The First Annual Movie-Artists Camera Dance and Frolic" for the studio staff, the local colored press, and the larger black community, with tickets ranging from 25¢ to $1.[14] Alonzo Jackson, who appeared in *Children of Fate,* subsequently provided acting lessons to local residents through the company.[15]

The Scar of Shame, according to one article, featured over 200 Philadelphians, including several of the film's stars. Lucia Moses, the female lead, a former city resident, was the daughter of Rev. William H. Moses, pastor of the Zion Baptist Church on North Broad Street. Cousins and family visited her on the set and in some cases appeared as extras, probably in the party scenes near the end of the film.[16] Norman Johnstone, who played the villain Eddie Blake, was a Philadelphia native who was enjoying some success with the Lafayette Players. William E. Pettus, manager of the local Strand Ballroom, proved tremendously successful in the role of the weak-willed alcoholic stepfather.[17]

Colored Players combined local talent with seasoned professionals. Lawrence Chenault, who appeared in all four productions, was a veteran who was often billed as the race's foremost motion picture actor. A new director and a new cameraman, who probably collaborated on the film's overall production, were used for the company's fourth and final picture.[18] Although *The Scar of Shame* is Frank Perugini's only known credit as a director, he was a cameraman on two small, independent productions: *The Devil's Confession* (directed by John S. Lopez, 1921) and *The Valley of Lost Souls* (directed by Carlyl S. Fleming, 1925).[19] The film's cinematographer, Alphonso Liguori, had a more impressive background, having shot three feature films for Famous Players in 1916: *The Innocent Lie, The Smugglers,* and *The Daughter of*

MacGregor—all for veteran director Sidney Olcott. He worked throughout the late 1910s and 1920s, remaining one of Olcott's favorite cameramen. He shot Olcott's *Salomé of the Tenements* (1925). None of these production personnel (Calnek, Perugini, Liguori) would continue with feature filmmaking in the sound era, at least if the credits in the *American Film Institute Catalog: Feature Films, 1931–1940* are any indication. In this, they were not unlike Philadelphia's motion picture production companies.

All the evidence, fragmentary though it may be, suggests that Colored Players was David Starkman's particular passion. As a showman with an African-American clientele, he believed in the importance of films that were free from negative black stereotypes. This was his vision. He not only sold his theater business to pursue it, he borrowed heavily from friends and, when the company failed, became impoverished. Starkman contributed in many different ways, providing the story for *The Scar of Shame* and using the furnishings from his own home to dress the sets for his pictures.[20] The impresario also assumed chief responsibilities for getting the film into the theaters, perhaps through his company the Standard Film Exchange. In short, he was involved in many aspects of finance, pre-production, production, and distribution.

Micheaux and Colored Players

Colored Players Film Corporation was, in many respects, the mirror image of the Micheaux Film Company. CPFC was initially financed by European Jews with Calnek as writer-director and Starkman as the driving force, while Micheaux's company was black financed, with African-American Micheaux as producer, writer, director, and the mastermind of distribution. When Starkman and Groner faced a financial crisis, they turned to Sherman H. Dudley. When faced with a similar situation one year later, Micheaux was aided, in turn, by Jewish theatrical entrepreneur Frank Schiffman, who controlled most of the race theaters in Harlem.[21] Moreover, despite Micheaux's overt cultural nationalism, his productions were, to some degree, interracial: Micheaux's cameramen are generally thought to be white, and some of his actors in more minor roles were also white. In contrast, Colored Players used black actors exclusively, conforming to general theatrical practices of the period and working within a paradigm of racial segregation. It was a paradigm Micheaux was seemingly ready to challenge. Nevertheless, both Colored Players and the Micheaux Film Company stood in marked contrast to the mainstream American film industry, where blacks were kept in subordinate positions on the set and were generally assigned demeaning, stereotypical roles. Hollywood, moreover, gave virtually no consideration to the interests, desires, and fantasies of race audiences. Colored Players and Micheaux may have disagreed about the nature of those needs, but they both catered to and addressed them.

A none-too-friendly rivalry existed between Oscar Micheaux and the Colored Players Film Company. In a letter to Richard Norman, Micheaux denigrated the quality of Colored Players' first two films and then complained,

> Some Jews have produced a couple of features, the first of which appears to draw very well although mighty badly acted and poorly photographed due to the use of some Cooper-Hewitt banks alternating current which flicker alternatingly through all the interiors and refuse to permite [*sic*] a fade-out with any degree of smoothness at all. The first is called "A Prince of His Race" which, while having drawn very well at the Royal in Philadelphia, and I understand at the Royal in Baltimore, if they screen the same, have serious difficulties in getting a booking with critical houses . . . .

Shingzie Howard was discovered by Micheaux, then found work at Colored Players Film Corporation in *A Prince of His Race* (1926) and *Children of Fate* (1927). By the fall of 1928, she was studying to be a school-teacher. Baltimore *Afro-American*, 27 October 1928, 8.

We could help them a great deal, but since they seem to think they know it all, and regard all of us who have endured through the years gone by as dubbs[who] know nothing, I am letting them find out for themselves the things we have learned from experience. Their second picture is "Ten Nights in a Bar Room" which I am advised is not as good as the first. Since they expect to make between one hundred seventy-five and two hundred thousand dollars, you can appreciate the disappointment in store for them.[22]

These complaints are only symptomatic of other tensions. Certainly Micheaux and Starkman "stole" each other's actors. Lawrence Chenault, who had appeared in half a dozen Micheaux films, including *Symbol of the Unconquered* and *Body and Soul,* was the chief prize. His last silent film for Micheaux was *The Conjure Woman* (1926), and he then appeared in all four Colored Players pictures. Shingzie Howard, who had been in several Micheaux films in the early 1920s—the last being *A Son of Satan* (1924), appeared in *A Prince of His Race* and *Children of Fate.*[23] Micheaux subsequently lured away William A. Clayton, Jr. during Colored Players' protracted hiatus in production. Clayton appeared in Micheaux's *The Broken Violin,* (1928), *The Wages of Sin* (1929), and *When Men Betray* (1929)—but not in *The Scar of Shame.*[24] If Micheaux was able to star Paul Robeson in *Body and Soul* (1925), Colored Players boasted Charles S. Gilpin for *Ten Nights in a Barroom* (1926). Advertisements for each film claimed to be featuring "the world's greatest Negro actor." Indeed, Gilpin's intense rivalry with Robeson helps to explain his commitment to this project.

The Micheaux–Colored Players rivalry also played out in the field of exhibition. In Chicago, Micheaux and Colored Players competed for attention throughout 1927, and their films were often booked in rival theaters on alternate weeks. With Micheaux playing *The Spider's Web* in the week following *Ten Nights in a Barroom,* promotional announcements for his picture were adjacent to Tony Langston's enthusiastic review of *Ten Nights*—and were more prominently displayed.[25] In New York City, while *Ten Nights in a Barroom* was playing an unprecedented four weeks at the Grant Theatre, Micheaux opened *The Spider's Web,* starring Evelyn Preer, at both the M & S Douglas Theatre and the M & S Roosevelt Theatre for four days.[26] When *The Scar of Shame* had its Philadelphia debut at Gibson's Theatre, Micheaux booked *The Broken Violin* at the Royal Theatre for the same week: it starred former Colored Players actor William Clayton, Jr. (assigned the first credit, lest anyone miss the point).[27] After *Children of Fate* opened in April 1927 (if not before), Starkman also went on the road to book his films into smaller cities and towns in the South and West. Here, as in many other respects, he followed a pattern that Micheaux had developed to a high art. At a time when both organizations faced financial bankruptcy, the rivalry in some locations was doubtless filled with tension.

The rivalry between these two concerns was not only commercial, it was ideological. Nor did it take place in a vacuum. Micheaux was coming off several films—notably *Birthright* (1924) and *Body and Soul* (1925)—which had been widely condemned in the black press. Micheaux, or Mischeaux as he was sometimes dubbed, was out of favor. Colored Players seemed calculated to fill the void with a desirable alternative. Sherman H. Dudley's position in this debate is particularly interesting. He became a vocal advocate for race films in 1927, particularly those made by Colored Players. In his *Chicago Defender* column he wrote:

Race pictures is my subject this week. We need them. I don't believe any manager lost a dime on a Race picture regardless of how rotten the picture was. If that be the case why can't they make money with good pictures with good Race scenarios written carefully around Race atmosphere. I think we should write around ourselves and stop trying to ape the white man.

An advertisement for *Children of Fate* (1926). Baltimore *Afro-American*, 16 April 1927, 12.

I do believe that if the Lafayette Players when first organized and made such a wonderful success in New York and other eastern cities, Chicago also, if these wonderful actors had had special plays, I mean Race plays instead of playing the same shows that the white actors have played they would not have suffered comparison and would have made an everlasting success.[28]

The irony is that Micheaux's pictures conformed much more fully to the type of films that Dudley seemed to be advocating.

By dealing with lynching, the KKK, the black clergy, language, black-white relationships, passing, and even racial self-hatred, Micheaux was addressing issues that pervaded African-American life.[29] In contrast, the scenarios chosen by Colored Players Film Corporation could have easily been enacted by white actors. They were both about race and not about race: these two positions were active simultaneously and in tension with each other. This is most obvious with *Ten Nights in a Barroom,* which fits the Lafayette Players paradigm of adapting a traditional European-American play to the black stage. The issue of race, as opposed to the issue of alcoholism and a moral life, is never directly addressed in that film. The white world has no overt impact on this all-black community; indeed, for purposes of the film, it does not exist. African-American audiences might have brought to bear their awareness of the predicament faced by a black community existing in the larger white society or nation. Alcohol could be seen as this community's self-destructive solace from racism. (As Thomas Cripps has pointed out, the theme may have been particularly relevant to the black community during prohibition.)[30] However, these are creative, contextual readings that are not

Ten Nights in a Barroom (1926) featured two of the greatest actors (and the two most famous drunks) of the African-American stage: Charles S. Gilpin as Joe Morgan and Lawrence Chenault as Simon Slade.

dictated by the film. Audiences might have as easily been complicit in its apparent silence. For example, they may have seen this tale of alcohol's ravages as a play with personal relevance for its performers, for it was enacted by the two most famous drunks on the African-American stage—Gilpin and Chenault. This relationship between actors and their roles brought an emotional intensity and inward connection that could have had a powerful impact on audiences. Such a film could thus serve as a refuge from the ordeal of everyday racial dynamics. Above all else, *Ten Nights in a Barroom* was a classic American play, and its production by a black cast was an assertion of American identity and full citizenship. The film worked within the sophisticated framework and established conventions of adaptation from theater to film. In this context, it was seen as a superior version to a somewhat earlier film adaptation made with an all-white cast in 1921.[31] It was thus a film in the spirit of the Harlem or Negro Renaissance.

The tension between race consciousness on one hand and a lack of engagement with race and racism on the other is also evident with *A Prince of His Race,* a fairly conventional melodrama that European Americans could easily have performed. The term "race" in the title could as readily apply to a self-contained Italian or Jewish community. This applies to *The Scar of Shame* as well. Compare the scar (both literal and metaphorical) in *The Scar of Shame* to the scar in Micheaux's *Within Our Gates.* In the Colored Players' film, the scar is a scar of upbringing and environment. Louise Howard, like her stepfather, is weak-willed and cannot escape the curse of her inheritance. The fact that Spike Howard is not her biological father emphasizes the influence of upbringing over that of blood or genetics, in the tradition of Emile Zola's *L'Assomoir* and Frank Norris's *McTeague* (the basis for Eric von Stroheim's *Greed* [1925]). The physical manifestation of this metaphorical scar comes when she is wounded in the process of leaving her noble husband for the evil Eddie Blake. It signifies her weakness and thus the shortcomings embedded in the black community. The answer is "uplift." Hillyard's noble effort to lift her up are thwarted by corrupt elements within the lower strata of the black community as well as by misplaced elitism among its upper reaches. In *Within Our Gates,* the scar on Sylvia Landry's breast is a sign of her mixed-race past. It saves her from being raped by her white father by revealing her parentage. It is what is hidden yet must be revealed if she is to be reunited and reconciled with her white father and honestly embraced by her true love Dr. Vivian (Charles D. Lucas).[32] Louise Howard's scar is not a fact of birth but is inflicted by society. And it is adorned, fetishized by an elegant scarf until she is confronted by her heroic ex-husband who has miraculously escaped and resumed his life as a musician. His efforts to become a great composer are likewise thwarted by unsavory elements in black society; these forces of darkness are only defeated with Louise's suicide and confession. The issue of race, of African Americans living in a hostile white society, lurks at the edges of Colored Players films, but it is never addressed overtly.

For many African Americans embracing cultural refinement, Micheaux's films were an embarrassment: they lacked taste.[33] The acting was often uneven, the sets rough, the narrative structures demanding to the point of superficial incoherence. Micheaux often attacked the black church (or at least its leaders) and included the word "niggah" in his intertitles (to be sure, for purposes of linguistic engagement). Cultural arbiters in the black community were looking for pictures that would conform more closely to their agenda of uplift—films that would showcase the race. In this respect, Colored Players had unequaled success. All agreed that *A Prince of His Race* represented "a decided step forward in the

Mediated by alcohol, the relationship between actor and role brought an unusual intensity to Gilpin's performance as Joe Morgan. Morgan holds his dying daughter.

field of cinema art as it pertains to the Negro."[34] It was "a commendable picturization of the better element of Negro life" and "teaches [that] we must be in complete control of our passions and no matter what the provocation let them not get the best of us."[35] Its high production values and consistently outstanding, uniform acting foregrounded African-American achievement. According to the *California Eagle*, "Critics are convinced, after having seen *A Prince of His Race*, that race artists are entitled to a prominent place in the art of Motion Pictures."[36]

The critical acclaim for Colored Players was only extended with *Ten Nights in a Barroom*, for which Gilpin delivered an outstanding performance that was effectively supported by the entire cast. White Hollywood did, in fact, take notice. Gilpin was given the opportunity to appear in at least three Hollywood features. He began to play the role of Uncle Tom in Universal's *Uncle Tom's Cabin* (1927), only to quit after two days of filming.[37] He was also scheduled to appear in *Hearts in Dixie* (1929).[38] In the end, Colored Players' ability to work with Gilpin, when Hollywood could not, is testimony to the fundamental differences between the two forms of production. Nonetheless, they shared a similar commitment to production values. The barroom of *Ten Nights in a Barroom* need only be compared to similar locales in Micheaux films to see the fundamental difference. The Colored Players' barroom *is* a barroom: a substantial, carefully constructed simulacrum—large, roomy, and detailed. The social club in *Body and Soul* is at best a makeshift back room, with Micheaux using a handful of decorative elements to signify the nature of the space. This commitment on the part of Colored Players continued with *The Scar of Shame* which, according to one report, set "a new standard of excellence for picture features with colored talent."[39]

In terms of acting virtuosity and mise-en-scène, Colored Players movies were understood as heroic achievements—demonstrations of high levels of cultural attainment. As such, these elements functioned in tandem with the black heroes played by Harry Henderson in *A Prince of His Race* and *The Scar of Shame*. In the company's first film, he defies death to reach the bedside of his dying mother, makes a fortune, and takes action to rescue his girlfriend

In *Within Our Gates* (1920), Sylvia Landry's scar is revealed as she resists being raped by Armand Girdlestone (white), revealing that her would-be rapist is, in fact, also her biological father. In *The Scar of Shame* (1929), Louise Howard's scar is fetishized: concealed and adorned by an elegant scarf.

from a disastrous marriage. We can see these same elements in *The Scar of Shame:* Alvin Hillyard rescues Louise Howard (Lucia Moses) from her drunken stepfather and later climbs a fire escape and crashes through a window to protect his wife. His character sees the world through high-angle, point-of-view shots—able to discern the terrain clearly and so take effective action. Micheaux's men often misrecognize the situation (in *The Symbol of the Unconquered,* hero Hugh Van Allen does not realize that Evon Mason is a person of color) or are extraordinarily passive (the inventor Sylvester played by Paul Robeson in *Body and Soul,* for example). Colored Players offered heroes who put African-American men in a more active, positive light. They are daring, self-confident, and debonair.

The pictures made by Colored Players Film Corporation often appear to be in conscious dialogue with Micheaux's films: this is particularly true for *Ten Nights in a Barroom* as a response to *Body and Soul.* Gilpin's performance as Joe Morgan sketches a downward spiral, a complex losing battle with alcohol until—with his daughter's death—he finds redemption. It is a clear moral tale—a Christian tale, one might add. As such it comments critically on *Body and Soul.* Rev. Isiaah T. Jenkins does not struggle with his behavior. He is a sociopath who is not redeemed by Isabelle's death or Martha Jane's forgiveness. This difference is also active in the realm of cinematic form. *Ten Nights in a Barroom* is told through flashbacks, but in a clear and easily understood structure that is fundamentally different from the use of dream and flashbacks in the Micheaux film. Finally, both films engage works by white playwrights but in ways that are very different. *Ten Nights in a Barroom* masters the classical mode of adaptation. These black actors take a white playtext and make it their own. *Body and Soul,* as a reworking and critique of three plays by white playwrights about the "Negro soul," exemplifies what Huston Baker calls "the deformation of mastery."[40]

Colored Players Film Corporation produced two surviving race films that are important

The saloon in *Ten Nights in a Barroom* is rendered with elaborate detail.

achievements in their own right. They display outstanding production values and consistently strong performances by black stars and nonprofessionals alike. Joe Morgan (Charles Gilpin) and Alvin Hillyard (Harry Henderson) are two quite different kinds of heroes. Yet both are courageous and take action—men who make costly mistakes but then persevere in the face of terrible adversity. Lucia Moses as Louise Howard is filmed with soft-focus cinematography and attentive lighting that makes her the most glamorous of black actresses on the silent screen. Understood in relation to the work of the filmmakers' contemporaries, we can see that these pictures participated in a complex and productive dialogue about the methods, means, values, and purposes of race films.

Lost, Then Found: The Wedding Scene from *The Scar of Shame* (1929)

PEARL BOWSER

The "wedding scene" was not in the 35mm print that the American Film Institute acquired on or before 1970 (the year I first saw *The Scar of Shame*). Indeed, I did not realize the scene was missing until the mid-1970s when I acquired what proved to be a more complete 16mm print, which included the wedding, for African Diaspora Images. According to Ken Weissman of the Library of Congress, this was made from a circa-1975 dupe negative that, in turn, came from a 1930 16mm positive stock print. This dating suggests a very early move into the non-theatrical market, perhaps in a desperate effort to exploit whatever limited commercial value *The Scar of Shame* might still have had. Although I have lectured about the importance of this missing scene over the last two decades, this 16mm version may have been more widely seen than the version at the American Film Institute. Video changed this, and it is the American Film Institute material that was used for the video released by the Library of Congress and Smithsonian Video in 1993. The Library of Congress is now adding a blowup from the African Diaspora Images print to its 35mm materials, and this addition will be seen in the 35mm print in our touring program. Unfortunately, the Library of Congress has no immediate plans to change the video, due to cost considerations. Each of the following frame enlargements represent a shot from the "rediscovered" scene.

In this "rediscovered" scene, Louise and Alvin Hillard's marriage takes place in the boardinghouse where the bride found refuge from her abusive stepfather and his cohorts. The witnesses present for the ceremonies are the owner of the house, Mrs. Green, and the staff. This is the turning point in Louise's life—away from all the negative influences of those who would exploit her beauty. The wedding establishes the seemingly peaceful domestic scene that follows of the couple "at home." The scene opens with Alvin seated at the piano and Louise in the background, playing with what at first appears to be a baby. A close-up shot reveals a hand puppet of a black doll. In the absence of the wedding scene, the Library of Congress print poses a "joke" not easily lost on the audience—suggesting the possibility that six months after Alvin proposed, Louise gave birth to a child. Rather than a setup for the joke, the doll scene introduces the subplot of the drama—a complex issue of class and caste. In a later scene the black doll is crushed beneath the foot of the hero as he races off to see his mother, whom he believes is seriously ill, leaving his wife behind. Alone, the despondent wife first tries to put the pieces of the broken puppet back together, then tosses it across the room, destroys a photo of her mother-in-law, tears up her marriage certificate, and packs a bag to leave.

The missing 18-shot wedding scene from *The Scar of Shame* (1929).

OWL—Two days of vaudeville, Vanishing Dagger, Girl in the Web, Mirlous Mrs. Lysle and Hairpins, Sun-Kings and Little Cafe. Sunday, The Adorable Savage.

PICKFORD—Daughters of Men, two days each of Prince Chap and Notorious Mrs. Lysle and Hairpins. Sunday, Elsie Ferguson in Lady Rose's Daughter.

ATLAS—Dancing Fool, Beckoning Road, Beggar Prince, World and Its Women, Double-Dyed Deceiver and The Gauntlet. Sunday, Norma Talmadge in Yes or No.

ELBA—Six Best Cellars, The Heart of Twenty, Hearts in Exile, His House in Order, Whims of Society and The Dark Lantern. Sunday, Seccue Hayakama in Li Ting-Ling. Monday and Tuesday, 27th and 28th, The Brute.

DOPING 'EM

The following arrived from Jack Williams of New York: "Jim Burris' company opened at the Putnam theater, Brooklyn, and Jim Burris and Lawrence Chenault did their parts fine. Lena Landford Roberts and Lottie Gee were the feature attractions. Miss Wilson needs to study the business a little more, then she may be able to do a leading part."—Jack Williams.

LIZZIE HART DORSEY

Lizzie Hart-Dorsey, who has been very ill for several months, and who successfully withstood a serious operation a short time ago, is fast regaining her health. Mail will reach her if addressed to 4619 Prairie avenue, Chicago, Ill.

Billy E. Jones, the popular balladist, is featuring songs for the Watterson & Snyder music house.

mysterious yacht offshore to seek a safer harbor. The girl swims to it to escape from the natives and learns the two passengers aboard are seeking a man named Milton Craig. Templeton had confessed to her that his name was Milton Craig and that he had fled from America after killing a man. The storm breaks as the yacht drifts off Marama's home and she plunges overboard and is washed ashore half drowned.

She finds her father wandering insane in the storm and both are struck down by a falling tree. The next morning Templeton finds them there, and the two men fight. The American is victorious, but the natives come up and the couple escape in a canoe through the surf. They are borne toward the yacht and Marama suddenly remembers why the craft is there. But Templeton recognizes the two passengers as his uncle and his best friend. They tell him the man he thought he had killed did not die after all. Then Marama and Templeton realize that their love dreams can come true in the civilized surroundings to which both their natures are suited.

COLUMBUS HOUSE

Columbus, Ohio, Sept. 17.—The only place for the Race's performers to show in Columbus, Ohio, is Dreamland, situated at 4th and Long streets, and under the management of Billy Smith, one of the most progressive showmen in the business. He gives but one show a night and none on Sunday. Billy would like to hear from acts and entertainers who have open time. His fall and winter season opens soon. Get in line.

Advertisements in the *Chicago Defender*, 18 September 1920, 4. Announcements for *Nobody's Children* (1920) appeared months before the film's completion and release. Here they compete for attention with ads for Oscar Micheaux's *The Brute* (1920).

13.

Richard D. Maurice and the Maurice Film Company

PEARL BOWSER AND CHARLES MUSSER

*T*he Maurice Film Company released two feature-length films almost ten years apart: *Nobody's Children* (1920) and *Eleven P.M.* (circa 1929). Company founder Richard Maurice produced, directed, wrote, and starred in both films. The production company was formed in July 1920 and "consists of a dozen clean cut young men, whose present place of abode is Detroit, Mich."[1] It was located at 184 E. High Street, Detroit, and later moved to the Northcross Bank Building, 2302 St. Antoine St., Detroit. Officers of the corporation included Richard Maurice as president, G. Walter Davis as vice-president, M. A. Cary as secretary and treasurer, and James T. Diggs as managing director.[2]

According to James Wheeler, a local historian and collector, Maurice's office and most likely his home were located in the black neighborhood known as Paradise Island—a thriving community with its own theaters, banks, insurance companies, and other businesses owned and operated by African Americans. Urban removal has destroyed all trace of the community. Even the street names are gone. The Maurice family (he included his wife, daughter, and other family members in his pictures) seems to have disappeared without a trace, except for materials related to the company's few films (it made at least one short—*Home Brew*—in 1920).[3] Toni Cade Bambara, in viewing Maurice's only surviving film—*Eleven P.M.*—injected the possibility that the family may have "passed for white" after leaving Detroit.[4] Wheeler is currently trying to unearth some of the history of the former Detroit middle-class community and its institutions, including race theaters that showed the films of Maurice, Micheaux, and others in the 1920s.[5]

The Maurice Film Company illustrates some of the problems historians encounter when trying to piece together the history of many peoples and companies making race movies. The company's initial production, announced in July 1920, had the working title of *Our Christianity and Nobody's Children*.[6] Week by week, the company used small advertisements to whet the public's appetite, including two different production stills and a brief description of the

A Scene From "Our Christianity and Nobody's Children"
A MAURICE PRODUCTION
MAURICE FILM CO.
184 E. HIGH STREET   DETROIT, MICH.

Advertisement for
Nobody's Children (1920)
under the working title
of "Our Christianity
and Nobody's Children."
Chicago Defender, 14
August 1920, 5.

plot: "A rousing story of two illegitimate children and their dying mother. The desperate fight of the brother against heavy odds to save his sister from the evil grip of his unnatural father."[7] People were told, "If You Do Not or Do Believe in Christianity, See This Play. If You Have or Have Not a Sister, See This Play."[8]

By September the Maurice Film Company had shortened the film's title to *Nobody's Children* and advertised it as "PRODUCED BY RACE PEOPLE" with an all-star colored cast.[9] The cast included Richard Maurice, Jacque Farmer, Alex Griffin, Joe Green, Max Johnson, Vivian Maurice, Howard Nelson, and others.[10] The story was later described as follows:

It tells of the death of the mother of two illegitimate children, a boy and a girl. A deathbed promise is made by the former that he will look after and protect his sister. The stepfather is a no-account type whose time is spent in the resorts of the underworld. It is during the search in a resort for him by the boy that a murder is committed and of which the lad is falsely accused, tried, convicted and sentenced to hang. The step-parent abducts the girl and takes her to one of the resorts where he is known. The actual slayer is a dope fiend. He discovers the girl's presence in the resort and decides to aid the brother to escape from the jail so that he might rescue his sister. The consummation of this escape and the hand-to-hand fight which takes place in the room in which the stepfather had placed the girl, and in which the boy kills the unnatural parent, furnishes one of the most gripping climaxes ever seen on the screen.[11]

Nobody's Children premiered at E. B. Dudley's Vaudette Theatre, 224 Gratiot Avenue in Detroit for one week, commencing Monday, September 27th.[12] (Two months later, the same theater would premiere Micheaux's *The Symbol of the Unconquered*.)[13] Maurice originally released *Nobody's Children* as a 6,000-foot feature, playing the Vaudette in Detroit and Engineer's Auditorium in Cleveland (October 14–16) at this length.[14] It was possibly tightened to 5,500 feet and eventually promoted as a 5-reeler by the time it unspooled in Chicago at States Theatre (December 22–25), Owl Theatre (December 27–29), and Lincoln Theatre (December 30–31) during the final two weeks of 1920.[15]

Promotional materials indicated that Maurice was an experienced director and that in the process of filmmaking "every modern idea was used."[16] The picture began with a "handsome novelty initial title," suggesting that Maurice was already interested in special effects and innovative filmic techniques that he would further develop in *Eleven P.M.*[17] It was also praised for its "wonderful acting by a group of performers, all of whom are capable and who have been selected with great discrimination."[18] It was considered "one of the best pictures turned out by colored people" and played widely in the eastern United States, showing at Philadelphia's Olympia Theatre for three days in late December and Norfolk's Attucks Theatre for three days in mid-February 1921.[19] In Norfolk, it drew large crowds, packing the theater on Thursday and Friday nights; an even bigger crowd was expected the following day.[20] When *Nobody's Children* played the New Frolic Theatre in Jacksonville, Florida, for three days in the spring of 1921, the Maurice Company was receiving $25 per day, or $75 for that run.[21]

The film remained in circulation, playing Pittsburgh's New Lincoln Theatre for three days in March 1925 and, "by popular request," two days at Harlem's Franklin Theatre in August 1926.[22]

The early 1920s saw a burst of film production that used black casts and catered to African-American audiences. *Nobody's Children,* as well as the short *Home Brew,* both made in 1920, were part of this trend. It was at this time that Robert Levy's Reol Pictures and other smaller firms such as the Royal Gardens Film Company moved into production.[23] Indeed, by late 1921, African-American critic J. A. Jackson could list seventeen "Colored Film Producing Companies" in his amusement columns.[24] The economics of race filmmaking proved daunting, however, and few of these companies

Louis (Frank?) Perry (Sammie Fields) at the typewriter, trying to finish a story. *Eleven P.M.* (circa 1929).

continued. According to one notice, Richard Maurice had "abandoned the plan for a big corporation and is single handedly making one and two reel comedies for release to exhibitors catering to either colored or white audiences."[25] He refrained from making another feature until the decade's close.

If significant newspaper documentation exists for Maurice's lost feature, that is not the case for *Eleven P.M.* When it was made and where it was shown are questions that remain to be answered. An avant-garde or experimental film, *Eleven P.M.* did not find its way into prominent race movie houses in major cities such as New York, Chicago, or Baltimore. Although it is generally dated 1928, it possesses a cinematic style and internal evocations of other race films that suggest a date of 1929 or possibly even 1930. Certainly its use of dream and flashbacks and many of its narrative tropes strongly evoke Micheaux's earlier work.[26]

Eleven P.M. opens with Louis Perry (Frank Perry in the head credits, played by Sammie Fields), a young black writer, trying to finish a story. He gives an incomplete manuscript to the editor of the journal *Search Light,* and the final chapter is due at 11 P.M. that night. Ultimately he falls asleep and dreams the story's conclusion, which is the remainder of the film, excepting a brief conclusion when he awakes and begins to write. The film has a mystical theme in which the main character, Sundaisy (Richard Maurice), a street musician and violinist, dies but comes back as a dog and attacks the man who has shattered his family, killing him with a vicious bite to the throat. While the film is not in any way derivative, Micheaux hovers over it: The con artist posing as a preacher is straight out of *Body and Soul* (1925), while the fact that Sundaisy plays the violin perhaps

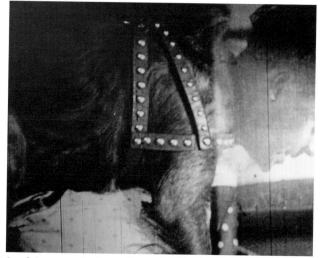

Sundaisy comes back as a dog and seeks revenge. Maurice uses a split-screen technique to depict this aspect of his story.

Extreme camera angles and other unusual techniques mark *Eleven P.M.* as a remarkably avant-garde achievement.

evokes *The Broken Violin* (1928). It riffs with many of the narrative tropes established in earlier films of the Oscar Micheaux and His Circle retrospective—including *The Scar of Shame,* which it seems to appropriate and invert in strategic ways. For instance, although Sundaisy's marriage to June Blackwell turns out to be fake, he remains fiercely loyal to it and her. Alvin Hillyard marries Louise Howard for the same reasons but, in contrast, quickly abandons her despite the marriage's legitimacy. Maurice's innovative use of cinematography—location filming, unusual angles, and tracking shots as well as special, almost surrealist effects—distinguish the film from its surviving counterparts of race cinema.

14.

Cinematic Foremothers: Zora Neale Hurston and Eloyce King Patrick Gist

GLORIA J. GIBSON

*B*lack women understood the power of the motion picture camera from the very beginning. During the early decades of the twentieth century, they envisioned themselves in front of and behind the camera and were cognizant of the camera's potential to capture African-American talent as well as to document day-to-day experiences. Black women, however, were also aware of one other aspect, the inaccessibility of this new technology, primarily because of financial constraints. The result is a paucity of films produced by African-American women during the early part of the century.

A few exceptions exist, though by and large academic research has not assisted in the search for these lost pieces of history. Since references are few and footage scant, queries sometime arise such as Can these women be considered "filmmakers?" or How important are film fragments? These are serious questions with dire consequences for film studies scholarship, especially as it pertains to filmmakers of color.

Even today, many women of color find funds too limited to produce works on a regular basis. Film projects can take years, even a decade (as did Julie Dash's *Daughters of the Dust*), to come to fruition. After such grueling struggles, some still question how a person who has only produced one or two films can be called a filmmaker. Perhaps this debate may have some legitimacy with regard to current makers, but in terms of unearthing the early history of black women's contributions to cinema, each and every frame of footage qualifies the person as a filmmaker because each frame qualifies as a historical and cultural artifact. The designation of filmmaker comes not in the number of frames, but in the women's realization and utilization of the power of the camera.

Early male filmmakers, such as Oscar Micheaux and the Johnson Brothers, have been recognized and celebrated; but because of the makers' gender and their limited number, the early frames of black women remain invisible and neglected. My objective is to begin to ex-

Jessie Fauset, Langston Hughes, and Zora Neale Hurston (1927) traveling through the South, shortly before Hurston went to Florida to do her fieldwork.

cavate the early history of black women's achievements and to argue simply that numbers must not be held as the primary factor in determining one's contribution to film studies. As archeologists unearth bones, they do not discard them because they don't add up to a complete, intact skeleton. Every fragment, no matter how small, helps reconstruct evolutionary history. And every frame of film, no matter how fragile and incomplete, helps scholars to understand the history of our relationship to culture and ultimately to ourselves.

Zora Neale Hurston and Eloyce King Patrick Gist each left her mark with a camera. It is only now, many decades later, that their frames are being exposed, viewed, studied, and—we would hope—celebrated.

GENESIS: A CULTURAL EYE, CRUDE CAMERA, AND INSPIRATIONAL LIGHT

Zora Neale Hurston and Eloyce King Patrick Gist were in some respects as different as night and day. In other respects, their lives mirrored each others in extraordinary ways. There is no evidence to suggest Zora Neale Hurston and Eloyce Gist ever met, knew each other, or even viewed each other's work. But it is indisputable that they were both creative women who truly lived before their time. They were both risk-takers who expressed great concern about their people, and although the manifestations differed, both realized the power of the camera as a way to capture, preserve, and critique African-American culture. Additionally, Gist strove to ultimately expose elements of black society she felt were detrimental to, in Micheaux's words, "racial uplift." And for each of them, their communities—Hurston's Florida and Gist's Washington, D.C.—functioned as the nucleus for their creative expressions.

Eloyce King Patrick Gist.

The ways in which Hurston and Gist differed are no less compelling. Their educational backgrounds and social affiliations contributed to different lifestyles and class status. Gist attended Howard, while Hurston received a bachelor's degree from Barnard and continued her graduate studies at Columbia University. Their circles of friends were quite different. While Hurston interacted with the intelligentsia of the Harlem Renaissance, Gist's life, during the time she produced film, revolved around her partner/husband, her daughter, and the church.

The two women's approaches to filming African-American life also reflected their differences. Hurston's footage is an outgrowth of her work as an anthropologist. Consequently, her footage is ethnographic, similar to the research methodology of Margaret Mead and Franz Boas. Gist's work is religious, based on her teachings as a Baha'i and her husband's influence as a Christian.[1] Though on the surface these seem to be disparate influential forces, there is a vital link: both women recognized the importance of folk culture.

Hurston appreciated folk culture, using it as her filmic focus and subsequently integrating aspects of it into her creative and scholarly writings. The Gists structured their films by incorporating beliefs and behaviors from African-American folk culture. For example, both Hurston and Gist incorporate music and dance (even though the films are silent). In several scenes, one of a child on the playground and another of a woman, Hurston highlights improvisational performance. Gist also integrated dance and music in her work in a dynamic way, but in her films, they are aligned with sinful living. In both instances, their audiences could identify with and relate to the imagery, and consequently it served as a foundation for self-reflection or self-affirmation.

Finally, Hurston and Gist both waged a war with time. The consequences of time emerge as a common denominator for each, but in different ways. As an anthropologist, Hurston realized that time brought about change, so it was important to preserve behavior and beliefs as cultural artifacts. As religious individuals, the Gists believed that time would also effect change—but perhaps for the worse. Their work promotes a return to values and behaviors that preserve a lifestyle of morality. In a way, time served and betrayed both filmmakers. Contemporary folklorists and anthropologists study continuity and change. African-American religious practice remains one of the primary elements which represents black culture even as it constantly wages moral struggles with the behavior of members of that culture. In the final analysis, contemporary audiences have much to learn as they view the Hurston and Gist film footage almost seventy years later. Scholars and film enthusiasts are able to assess their documentary style and creative ingenuity as artifacts of African-American culture and film history.

Folklore and Folklife

In a recent article, film scholar Clyde Taylor argues that the new black cinema can be identified by core features or aesthetic principles, namely, "its realness dimension, its relation to Afro-American oral tradition, and its connections with black music."[2] Likewise, scholar Vattel Rose also argues for the importance of oral tradition in the development of black literary and cinematic aesthetics. Whereas both scholars acknowledge the contribution of oral tradition, their discussion is limited to its applicability to new black cinema. In point of fact, various aspects of folklore (oral tradition, music performance) and folklife (the realness dimension) have always been essential ingredients which inform black independent cinema.

According to scholar Barre Toelkin, folklore, like culture, is all encompassing because "it represents a tremendous spectrum of human expression that can be studied in a number of ways and for a number of reasons."[3] Folklorists ascertain how groups communicate the essence of who they are, including their fears, beliefs, values, cultural practices, and performances. By investigating "the folk," Hurston and Gist demonstrated their appreciation of and concern for capturing the richness of African-American life.

Because folklore practice must be studied within a specific cultural framework, when examined contextually, African-American folklore reveals "the history of black people in this country and their psychological reactions to their experience."[4] H. Nigel Thomas elaborates:

> To study folklore of black Americans is to examine their dreams, their aspirations, the mental curtains they designed to shut out the brutality of slave and postslave reality, the psychic wings on which they bore themselves temporarily away from oppressive pain, as well as the aesthetic objects—the blues, spirituals, folktales, toasts, etc. they fashion from their pain. Therefore, the study of black American folklore is essentially a study of the survival of black people in America.[5]

To study the folkloric elements in the Hurston and Gist footage is to begin to understand the genesis and development of specific cultural traditions and behaviors.

During the 1920s and 1930s, Hurston's research, as well as that of other folklorists and anthropologists during that period, embraced the notion of "disappearing" cultural artifacts. Scholars felt that cultural performance and beliefs must be expeditiously collected and documented because they would soon be gone forever. This fear is articulated in Hurston's first line of *Mules and Men,* when she states, "I was glad when somebody told me, 'You may go and collect Negro folk-lore.'"[6] This validation suggests that in her mind the stories, games, rhymes, and so forth she heard growing up were now academically legitimized. They need not be considered only "old wives' tales" that reflected the mindset of uneducated people lacking sophistication.

Hurston was introduced to the importance of oral tradition by Franz Boas, one of the world's most celebrated anthropologists. In her studies with Boas she gained not only general knowledge and social science methodology but also a profound appreciation of African-American culture. *Mules and Men* is the first book of African-American folklore collected by an African American (woman or man) and published by a major company. While the fact that she collected and published folklore in itself is remarkable, her vision to use the camera is almost bewildering.

While Hurston sought to capture folklife as it was, Gist's footage was more concerned with depicting life as it should be. It examines black folk experience and pitfalls that must be avoided. Although there is no written documentation to support their filmic objective, it seems to be advancing social uplift and religious morality. Because the Gists combine religious folk drama with the "realness dimension," their work embraces social realism. According to Gladstone Yearwood, social realism represents

Zora Neale Hurston conducting fieldwork in Florida.

one of the primary developments in the African-American artistic tradition. Moreover, "its orientation was social in nature; it presented models of character traits considered to be most desirable for black Americans. Among these values were a strong belief in the redemptive powers of Christianity."[7] Unmistakably, Gist's work is saturated with religious symbolism mediated by social realism.

The film footage of Hurston and Gist functions as documented expressions of African-American cultural experience, not unlike collected and published folk tales, personal narratives, or music. Additionally, their films evoke culture-specific images; they establish a unique synthesis of folk elements derived from the everyday experiences and cinematic practice of African Americans in the late twenties and early thirties.

Eloyce Gist's name fades in and out of the history of African-American cinema.[8] Although the complete story of her work may never be known, the importance of her contributions have recently come more into focus. Eloyce Gist's story represents significant frames from the history of black cinema. Unfortunately, these frames are figuratively and literally difficult to reconstruct. Eloyce Gist worked with her husband James. Exactly where her contributions started and his left off may forever remain unclear.

Eloyce King Patrick Gist was born on October 21, 1892 in Hitchcock, Texas, to Walter and Josephine King.[9] The family relocated to Washington, D.C. during the early part of this century. Gist attended Howard University, where she studied music. Later she studied beauty culture and established the Patrick School of Beauty Culture and Personal Improvements. Like entrepreneur Madam C. J. Walker, Gist felt strongly that African-American women should not only be well-groomed, but, more important, they should have a means to support themselves financially.

The course of Gist's life changed abruptly when she met and married her second husband James Gist sometime in the late twenties or early thirties. James was a self-made Christian evangelist, and Eloyce embraced the Baha'i faith because she felt it promoted racial harmony. Despite the difference in denominations, the Gists agreed upon basic Christian principles, which became deeply entrenched in their productions.

Their goal as filmmakers was more than entertainment; their mission was one of moral and spiritual education for men and women. Like Micheaux, they sought ways to encourage racial uplift and deter the destructive behavior of their people. During the mid-thirties the couple toured with their two films *Hell Bound Train* and *Verdict Not Guilty* in and around Washington, D.C. Both films advocate Christian behavior and the importance of family, and because of the films' high moral standards, their popularity spread.

While the programming records of the Gist films remain undiscovered, a few surviving documents suggest the films encountered a broader venue. Correspondence dated May through June 1933 documents the interest of the NAACP in screening the Gist films. The NAACP endorsement and co-sponsorship meant that its branches would cover the cost of advertisement. The Gists would provide the films, music, and projection equipment. As NAACP field secretary Irving S. Hammer wrote to Roy Wilkins:

> Mr. Gist is a producer of religious motion pictures which have an entire Negro cast and for the past four days we at the Harlem branch have done business with him and have found him a Negro of high caliber, also his picture "VERDICT NOT GUILTY" represents an ambitious effort and one worth while seeing.[10]

Clearly the NAACP respected the Gists' work and felt that a collaboration between the two could prove fruitful for both parties. In a follow-up letter, Wilkins acknowledged "our branches could solicit patronage directly from the churches in their communities,"[11] and Wilkins viewed the films as a potential means by which to increase membership in the NAACP. It is not known how many screenings materialized in conjunction with the NAACP.

According to Gist's daughter, Homoiselle Patrick Harrison, the usual format of the service was for Eloyce to play the piano and lead the congregation in hymns. The film would then be shown, followed by a sermonette by James Gist. Tickets were sold prior to the screening or a collection was taken at the close of the service; either way, the monies were split between the Gists and the church.

I've focused the following analysis on *Hell Bound Train* because it is the longer film and, more important, the one to which Eloyce Gist contributed more substantially. Gist's daughter makes this assertion, and it is reinforced by Amy Petrine's research. Petrine states, "Eloyce's first contribution was to rewrite a complete script. . . . James' original script was revamped and improved."[12] In all probability, Eloyce Gist not only rewrote the script but also aided in reshooting certain segments.

Historically, the black church has exercised enormous power as a religious and cultural entity. Additionally, religious doctrine and folk drama have a long-established relationship. Stories of faith, whether personal or biblical, remain central to African-American church fellowships. These narratives supply strength, courage, and comfort. Moreover, the narrative text of these dramas—whether *Hell Bound Train, Old Ship of Zion,* or *Heaven Bound*—is not only religious but one which reflects the African-American worldview. Worldview functions as "a general way of referring to the manner in which a culture sees and expresses its relation to the world around it."[13] Within Christian doctrine "the world" is believed to be basically a wicked place, replete with temptation and sin. Christian doctrine and an African-American worldview establish a religious and moral blueprint of how believers should govern their lives and a rationale for conversion for those who don't believe.

In African-American culture, as in many cultures, religion is a communal, collective structure. While there may be some room for interpretation, religious principles are usually based on an unwavering doctrine—for example, the Christian Bible—and individuals are granted free will to conform to or to reject religious principles. Accordingly, within many folk dramas, scenarios of choice are presented as personal accounts or narratives. In such dramas the characters' behavior is fluid and dynamic, responding to social circumstances and individual issues. Through the personal journey, religion—or the lack thereof—shapes the quality of their lives. The bottom line is that religious maturity and conformity serve as the keys to a better life.

Deborah Bowman Richards outlines the specific characteristics of the black religious drama as being "episodic performances which: (a) employ a variety of techniques to focus attention; (b) exist as public action of a small, community-level group sharing a system of understood motives and symbols; (c) have a foreknown resolution; and (d) are related to a game, play, and ritual."[14] Whether live or filmed, these folk dramas serve as vehicles to deliver dramatic performance and instill religious power. Like some games, there are clearly defined winners and losers. Unlike games, in many instances the outcome is known beforehand, based on the character's religious conviction.

Hell Bound Train is an intense examination of the tension between religious doctrine and individual free will. Utilizing a primarily black cast, the film is structured as a journey, much like Spencer Williams's *The Blood of Jesus* (1941).[15] The scenarios are personal accounts of struggles between right and wrong, good and evil. Quite simply, those who stray from God are punished. The goal is for the audience to "connect," to identify with the narratives, and, if they are engaging in similar unrighteous practices, to repent. The film is not strictly entertainment, but it encourages the audience to be active participants rather than spectators or voyeurs.

The Devil's objective is clearly stated in the opening frames: "Free admission to all—just give your life and soul. No round trip tickets—one way only." The message is signed by "Satan, Lucifer." Several people are lined up to receive tickets. After the opening sequence, the film surveys various types of sin. The Devil, who is the engineer running the train, serves as

The devil as engineer . . .   . . . on the Hell-bound train.

"The Devil loves a man who lets another woman get his money, while his wife suffers."   *"I knew I'd catch you sooner or later."*

Scenes from *Hell Bound Train.*

a recurring icon. Sinners are continuously enticed and placed on the train to begin their journey to Hades. Each car on the train is reserved for specific groups of sinners. For example, the first coach is designated for dancers, while the second coach is reserved for those who partake of alcohol.[16]

Hell Bound Train also utilizes many traditional symbols and images found in other African-American films from the early period. First and foremost, the train has historically served as an important symbol in African-American history and culture. It functioned to transport one's body, mind, or spirit to another location. Hymns such as "I'm Going Home on the Evening Train" express the joy of salvation and a spiritual home in heaven. During slavery, the "underground railroad" was a possible means to freedom. The train, however, could hold potential danger, especially as it transported one to places unknown such as "up North" or "to the city." An interesting parallel can be drawn between the truck which transports sinners to Hades in the climactic scene of *The Blood of Jesus* and the train in *Hell Bound Train.* Each vehicle helps facilitate the delivery of the unrighteous to their final spiritual resting place—Hell.

The Devil in *Hell Bound Train* continuously tempts his victims, but he, too, is reminiscent of a character type in Williams's film. He is not solely villainous and occasionally supplies comic relief as he dances around his victims, oils the wheels of the train, and sells one-way tickets to Hell. The role of the Devil is a significant one in most religious folk dramas, and as William Wiggins suggests, his performance is deeply rooted in pantomime. Analyzing the actors playing the Devil in the religious pageant *Heaven Bound,* Wiggins explains that the core of each of their "artistry has laid in mime. For example, as each pilgrim makes his or her heavenly march, he or she is taunted, tempted, and teased, with the hope of being diverted from Heaven to Hell."[17] While the Devil's role is significant, he in no way assumes the persona of a horror or science-fiction character. The audience must perceive him as evil, cunning, and real.

Other familiar symbols of good and evil mediate between the spiritual and physical world in *Hell Bound Train,* including portraits of Jesus, the cross, and the Bible. Issues of drinking, gambling, fornication, and murder are among those placed under scrutiny. Interestingly, sin is committed by male and female, old and young, righteous and unrighteous. In so doing, the film demonstrates that no one is above reproach.

One of the coaches, number three, is earmarked for those who listen to secular music, especially music associated with cabaret life. Several cards read, "Then as enjoyment to sporting women. It may bring happiness to you through life—But at the point of death. Mary, Emma, Come quick, stop those blues, Bring Hymn Book. Too late then." The woman who only minutes before had been listening to the phonograph player turns to the hymn "Rock of Ages" and then suddenly dies.

A similar warning of the inherent dangers of cabaret life is found in *The Scar of Shame* (1929) and *The Blood of Jesus* (1941). The conflict between sacred and secular music genres reflect conflicts between urban and rural lifestyles. Danger lurks in the city, where temptations are greatly enhanced by alcohol and the music is more than ornamental backdrop. It serves to dramatically inform the visual and narrative action, evoking individual and communal spirituality or individual and communal sin.[18]

The next car is reserved for "thieves, crooks, and grafters." Various scenarios are presented depicting theft among friends and among those unacquainted with each other. Murders and gamblers are located in the next coach. Here one episode chronicles an unfortunate man who loses everything, even his suit. The next coach is "immorality, women and men with no care and respect." Coach number seven is overcrowded with liars, and the last coach is reserved for "backsliders, hypocrites, and Used to be Church Members." A title card appears which tells sinners to "Get Off This Train By Repenting, believing, and being baptized, before it is too late." Interestingly, no one is ever shown leaving the train. Instead, the passengers continue to engage in their sinful activities.

While most of the scenarios attack and dramatize commonplace sin, two episodes deviate slightly. The first attacks those who are backsliders, ministers in particular. The card reads, "False preachers will get with the officers and steal the church's money." The identification of corrupt ministers was also a theme in Micheaux's controversial *Body and Soul* (1925). Corrupt ministers are dramatized here in similar fashion, lusting after and stealing the church's money.

One other episode seems to hint at either birth control or abortion. As a woman lies in bed, a doctor unsuccessfully tries to save her. The card reads, "She has taken medicine to avoid becoming a mother. SHE'D better get right with GOD, for it's murder in COLD BLOOD." It is not clear whether the woman took medicine to prevent pregnancy or to aid in aborting the child. Either way, to broach such a sensitive issue in film during this time is extremely rare.

Throughout the film, biblical scriptures are presented on the title cards, including "The wages of sin is death, Romans 6:23" and "The wicked shall be turned into hell; and all nations that forgot God" [Psalms 9:17]. The scriptural quotes reinforce the stark imagery for the Gists, who are basing their narrative on religious principles. One can serve only one master—God or the Devil. Because actual scriptures are integrated into the film text, *Hell Bound Train* appears as an authentic dramatization of the black community's religious faith.

The dramatic cinematic climax captures a train moving faster and faster toward Hell. Death is depicted as a flagman holding a sign that says "Entrance to Hell." The train bursts Hell wide open (it enters a tunnel), crashing and exploding into flames. The Devil circles the train to further torment the victims. Even though it is obviously a miniature train set afire, the mise-en-scène so strongly suggests Hades that the audience momentarily suspends disbelief.[19] In the final scene a man, perhaps James Gist, states, "Thus I've demonstrated to you this picture which I painted as a vision from hearing a sermon in a revival meeting." Behind him is a large poster or flowchart of the hell-bound train's journey. This scene may have functioned as a segue to Gist's sermonette after the film.

For the most part, the camera shots are quite straightforward; however, some scenes showed technical and aesthetic ingenuity. Most fascinating are the tracking shots as the train moves down the railroad tracks. Here the cameraperson is either on another train or in a car, holding the camera parallel to the moving train. Another scene begins and ends with a fade in and out as the dying sinner reads from a hymn book and promptly expires. In addition, there are a few pan shots and reaction shots; but by and large, the camera is stationary and unobtrusive. Most of the footage is shot on the same interior set, though there are several location shots, including a bus stop, a church, a factory, and an ice house.

According to Harrison, her mother continued to travel with the films, a projector, and an assistant to screen the films after James Gist's death in 1940. She soon realized, however, that she couldn't shoulder the diverse responsibilities alone. Additionally, amid the glamour and spectacle of the growing sound film industry after 1927, the appeal of the silent film diminished. From the forties to her death, Gist continued to live in Washington, D.C., where she wrote a novel, occasionally published newspaper articles, and enjoyed her family. She died suddenly while on vacation in 1974. The bits and pieces of the Gist films were deposited in the Library of Congress in the seventies after her death.

The Gists' overall message is clear. While one's lifestyle may be considered personal, it can also become the object of collective observation and evaluation. In their films, the folk drama functions as a religious narrative encouraging spiritual and social uplift. *Hell Bound Train* captures the essence and dynamics of African-American culture during the early decades of the twentieth century. It surveys the lives of African Americans within a communal context that depicted the good and the not so good.

ZORA NEALE HURSTON: FIELDWORK AND FOOTAGE

In the social sciences as well as some disciplines of the humanities, fieldwork, whether recorded with audio or visual technology, is an instrumental component of most research projects. According to Robert Emerson, "The initial and in some senses foundational task of fieldwork is to provide rich, empirically based *descriptions* of the distinctive social life and activities of those studied.[20] When scholars conduct fieldwork they produce an ethnography of a cultural group or environment that functions as a characterization of a way of life, or culture; it also "identifies the behaviors and the beliefs, understandings, attitudes, and values they imply found in that social world."[21] The scholar's goal, then, is to depict not only the person or object but also the social and environmental context of that person and object. Hurston recognized the power of the camera to capture not only activities but also a way of life.

Ethnographic film utilizes one of the basic components of social science, fieldwork, but incorporates a camera. Plainly stated, "in ethnographic film, film is the tool and ethnography the goal."[22] In his introduction to the book *Ethnographic Film*, Karl Heider elaborates: "When we are talking about 'ethnographic film,' ethnography must take precedence over cinematography. If ethnographic demands conflict with cinemagraphic demands, ethnography must prevail."[23] In other words, the content of footage, especially in light of the historical period, must not take a back seat to the cinematic creativity used to capture the footage. Moreover, the ethnographic content should emerge from an understanding of the people and the culture. Since Hurston was considered an insider to the culture she was documenting, she probably had easier access to study its people and traditions. As Hurston makes clear in *Mules and Men,* she actively participated in the lives of the people she studied.

One of Hurston's early mentors was Franz Boas, who is recognized as the father of American anthropology. He helped shape her intellectual development as well as influence her research direction and focus. Boas was also an enigma. His relationship to African Americans was fraught with personal and social controversy. Historian Vernon J. Williams, Jr. explains:

> Since the 1950s, historians and historically minded social scientists have celebrated the monumental role that Franz Uri Boas played in eviscerating the racist world view that prevailed in the American social sciences during the years before 1930. Nevertheless, between 1894 and 1938, when Boas addressed the issue of the capabilities of African Americas, his writing exhibited contradictions between his commitment to science and his commitment to the values of his liberal ideology.[24]

During the latter part of the nineteenth century and into the twentieth century, social scientists sought to answer questions pertaining to racial difference based on Darwinism. Initially, Boas and his contemporaries felt answers lay in measuring skulls, testing blood samples, and other "scientific" experimentation. Boas later abandoned this racist approach.

Hurston met Boas when she was a student majoring in anthropology at Barnard College. In 1927, he was instrumental in obtaining a fellowship for her to collect folklore, though according to a letter between Boas and Hurston dated May 3, 1927, he was not particularly impressed with the results. As he told her, "I find that what you obtained is very largely repetition of the kind of material that has been collected so much."[25] This led to another fieldwork trip later that year funded by a patron, Charlotte van der Veer Quick, or, as she was affectionately called, "Godmother" or "Mrs. Mason."

In Robert Hemenway's extensive biography of Hurston, he explains that "the soul Zora Hurston sought to define needed very little spiritual help from Mrs. Mason. The need was quite material, and Hurston knew it, whether she admitted it to herself or not. To 'do something,' however, one needed money, and Mrs. Mason personified wealth."[26] During Hurston's subsequent trip, Mason "agreed to pay Zora $200 per month for a year, and promised to provide a motion picture camera and an automobile to facilitate the collecting."[27] What remains unclear is why Hurston decided to use the camera to document her fieldwork. More than likely she was influenced by Boas or Margaret Mead. According to Heider, Mead "did play a major role in the development of ethnographic film in the late 1930s."[28]

Hurston's footage, however, was made a decade earlier. Perhaps the camera was another tool Boas used as he sought to find answers to racial issues, or perhaps its use resulted from

Film frames from footage shot by Zora Neale Hurston in Florida. Logging (April 1928), Baptism (April 1929), Kossula, last of the Takkoi slaves (February 1928), and Children's Games (April 1928).

Hurston's own ingenuity. Maybe she or Boas had been introduced to documentary filmmaker Robert Flaherty's "exotic" research locations of the late 1920s. Also unclear is whether the footage was to be used as an ethnographic film or as strictly research footage. Would the films of children at play, for example, accompany published game songs or did she mean for the footage to stand alone for analysis? Even though there are no game songs in *Mules and Men*, the first black-and-white drawing in the book is of children playing a ring game.

According to *The African-American Mosaic: A Library of Congress Resource Guide for the Study of Black History and Culture*, Hurston "shot ten rolls of motion pictures in the southern United States in 1927–1929 to document logging, children's games and dances, a baptism, a baseball crowd, a barbecue, and Kossula, last of the Takkoi slaves."[29] This footage may well represent the earliest film footage shot by an African-American woman. Without a doubt, it is the earliest ethnographic footage by an African-American folklorist. The footage, like her writing, is celebratory, showcasing the diverse talents, rituals, and creativity of African-American people. The following discussion focuses on footage of several children's games and dances, since they represent the largest portion of the fragments we have. The footage exemplifies the merger of early ethnographic filmmaking conventions and the knowledge and appreciation of the people Hurston sought to capture with her camera. As the footage is viewed it is important to remember that "the way in which a film project is conceptualized, shot, and edited is inseparable from the interactions of our gendered selves . . . [as] much as it is inseparable from anthropological discourses of the time."[30]

The Games

The footage seems to indicate that Hurston assumed directorial authority. Seemingly, her intent was to spend a great deal of time filming children's play and game songs. We may never know exactly why—perhaps because they are performance. She was dealing with crude silent camera equipment, and the familiar motions within the games help to suggest sound and to convey meaning. Clearly, she was using the camera as a notation device knowing that the intricate kinesic performance would be more precisely documented with a camera than with a pen.

As usual, Hurston selected a familiar location and immersed herself within the culture. This footage was taken in the South, probably in Florida, and she was well aware of the richness of local folklore and folk performance. Intensive immersion was a well-established approach in ethnographic research and certainly characterized the work of the "father of ethnographic film," Robert Flaherty. His approach involved conducting lengthy fieldwork with the people and observing and learning their traditions *before* he began shooting.

When viewing Hurston's footage, it is significant to observe what she shot in the foreground and the background. In most instances she uses long takes with no editing. She primarily uses long shots with a few close-ups, allowing the audience to evaluate kinesic and proxemic behavior. In some instances she keeps the camera on after the game is finished, so that even if the game play itself has been "staged," the behavior captured afterward appears spontaneous. Because of her insider relationship, Hurston's presence probably changed the actual event in only a small way.

Before some of the games commence, the children hold up (illegible) cards that probably give their names. Since many of the same children are in several games, this acknowledgement serves as a recognition of each child's importance. The children perform freely and uninhibitedly, primarily against an open field or on the school playground. Some are dressed to perform; others are dressed in everyday clothes. By concentrating on the background, the audience may surmise information regarding the socioeconomic levels of the members of this rural community. The children's bodies and faces make it clear that they evaluate each others' performances. Hurston's visual composition communicates the ingenuity, talent, and cultural aesthetics of the children (intricate rhythmic movements, hand-clapping, improvisational style, and call and response).

There is no record of Hurston's training to use a motion picture camera; however, the image is well framed, and, for the most part, the footage remains in focus. Where scenes are technically flawed—usually from loss of focus—the effectiveness of the sequence is not hindered.

The children in the footage play ring, line, performance, and "it" games, a reflection of their carefree life. Several studies of children's games suggest that the importance of such games lies in their ability to socialize and enculturate the game-players. In other words, the games are more than games for the sake of play. Children learn physical skills, but, perhaps more important, they also develop and sharpen social skills such as taking turns, winning and losing, negotiation, and compromise. Additionally, in these games the point is not only *what* you do but *how* you do it. Hurston's decision to record children's game songs on film reflects her understanding of the importance of play to children and to the total sociocultural development of the child.

One of the games Hurston's footage captures appears to be "Sissy in the Barn." Here the children form a large circle with two small children in the center. Hurston uses a medium shot which, although it does not capture all the children within the frame, does reveal the entire bodies of those filmed. The children then break into pairs and shake index fingers in each other's faces, finally grabbing a partner and performing a social dance. Hurston keeps the camera stationary throughout the majority of the shots.

Various versions of this game are documented by folklorist Brian Sutton-Smith (*The Folkgames of Children*), collectors Bessie Jones and Bess Lomax Hawes (*Step It Down: Games, Plays, Songs, and Stories from the Afro-American Heritage*), and scholar Grace Fox, whose study specifically investigates games in Florida during the early 1950s.[31] The following, taken from Fox's dissertation, is probably a variant of the filmed game and could be understood as the words "missing" from Hurston's silent footage.

> Sissy in the barn, join the wedding,
>
> Prettiest little couple I ever did see, [*action:* child in center chooses another to come into the circle with him]
>
> Oh bye and bye, [*action:* both clap hands sharply]
>
> Throw your arms around me, Say, little Sissy, won't you marry me? [*action:* take social dance position and walk around each other]
>
> Now step back gal, [*action:* shake forefinger at each other]
>
> Don't you come around me.
>
> All those sassy words you say. [*action:* turn away from each other]
>
> Oh, bye, and bye. [*action:* both clap hands once sharply]
>
> Throw your arms all around me, Say, little Sissy, won't you marry me? [*action:* take social dance position and turn around each other. As this couple moves out of the center of the circle they indicate another couple to take their place.][32]

Another identifiable game is "Little Sally Walker/Water." Here Hurston begins with a medium shot of the children as they circle. There are two children in the center, one of them approximately two to three years old. The older child is either babysitting or teaching the younger one. They both stoop in the center, then rise as the older one wipes her eyes. She then picks the one "she loves the best." Hurston pans the camera slightly to capture the hip movement as they obviously sing "shake it to the east, shake it to the west." The children perform this game as described in *Step It Down* (version two, page 108).

The games Hurston filmed conform to two of the four categories outlined by folklorist Brian Sutton-Smith: games of physical skill and games of chance. While in some games, "winning" or "losing" is an important concept, it is clearly not the only concern. Performance style—how the dance is executed and the intricacy of the rhythm—remains an important evaluative consideration. Even in "Little Sally Water" there is a focus on performance, and Hurston's camera focuses on feet, hips, and hands to underscore its importance. One game even seems to be exclusively performance orientated: a young boy dances intricate steps while the other children who circle him clap their hands and cheer him on.[33]

Hurston's footage is extremely important to folklorists, anthropologists, and cultural critics. Even though it is silent, it concisely demonstrates (1) ethnographic filming technique and anthropological practice during that time; and (2) various performance styles within a communal context.

Synthesis

There are many questions yet to answer regarding the footage of Gist and Hurston. How did Hurston intend to use the footage? Who or what was her inspiration to use the camera? How did the Gists finance their films? What exactly was Eloyce's role? How successful were they? Much more research needs to be conducted before these and other questions can be answered.

In both cases, however, the footage does provide us with certain very important insights. We learn what an African-American female anthropologist thought was important enough to record visually. We learn what religious filmmakers thought were destructive modes of behavior for African Americans and the measures needed to correct that behavior. The footage of Hurston and Gist in many ways mirror the aesthetics and social themes found in Micheaux's work.

Understanding folklore and folklife within a historical context is crucial to understanding this historic footage and its legacy. In both the games and the dramas there are clear winners and losers, although in the children's games, the consequences of losing are not as great as in the religious folk dramas. There, one can potentially lose everything, including, as the Devil warns, "your very soul." Games also teach socialization. Thus, Hurston's footage represents microcosms of life, instilling skills of how to play and how to lose. Just as some games have strategic modes of behavior, so too does religion. As some games rely on physical skill and strategy, navigating through life requires both. According to the Gists, life should not be lived by chance, but by design. While many questions remain, one fact is indisputable: Zora Neale Hurston and Eloyce Gist appreciated "the(ir) folk" and used the motion picture camera to examine and preserve the African-American way of life.

APPENDIX A

The Reemergence of Oscar Micheaux: A Timeline and Bibliographic Essay

J. RONALD GREEN

THE 1960S

The current groundswell of interest in Oscar Micheaux began with the 1969 publication in *Negro Digest* of an article by Thomas Cripps that characterizes Micheaux as "by far the most famous, and best, of the black silent filmmakers."[1] Cripps's early appreciative position regarding the value of Micheaux's silent films was courageous, since it was diametrically opposed to a prevailing disdain for Micheaux expressed by a number of Cripps's respected colleagues at Morgan State University.[2]

Micheaux's first and third novels were reprinted;[3] so was Peter Noble's *The Negro in Films,* an obscure book on black cinema that was first published in 1948.[4]

THE 1970S

The legend of Oscar Micheaux, which had persisted in parts of the black community since Micheaux's time, began to emerge into wider streams of American culture in 1970. Between March 24 and May 14 of that year, the Jewish Museum in Manhattan screened a program of films by black producers, curated by black cinema activists Pearl Bowser, Charles Hobson, and others. This was repeated a few months later at the Brooklyn Academy of Music; Penelope Gilliatt published, in *The New Yorker,* a two-column notice of the Jewish Museum's press screening of Micheaux's film *God's Step Children;*[5] and Thomas Cripps published a scholarly article that included discussion of Paul Robeson's role in Micheaux's film *Body and Soul.* Bowser's film programs and her continuing activism also signify the presence of an unbroken current of interest in black-produced cinema in the African-American community, a current that began virtually with the advent of movies and erupted into history with the black response to the release of *The Birth of a Nation* in 1915.

A flyer for Oscar Micheaux's *Veiled Aristocrats* (1932).

Cripps's article on Robeson[6] and Peter Noble's reissued book point backward across a hiatus in interest in Micheaux since before his death in 1951. The forward glance of Noble's book in 1948 seems to project across the era of the House Un-American Activities Committee and Eisenhower conservatism to the Civil Rights movement of the 1950s and 1960s, even to the time when Noble's own book would be re-issued in 1969 and (again) in 1970; it also seems to anticipate Cripps's early research and publications in the 1960s leading to his articles on race movies.

A small surge of Micheaux literature occurred in 1973. James P. Murray's book on black cinema treats Micheaux's successful entrepreneurial strategies as worthy of emulation and interprets his films as anti-stereotypic and as black-centered.[7] Donald Bogle's *Toms, Coons, Mulattoes, Mammies, and Bucks,* which has become a classic, features Micheaux prominently, recognizing the importance of Micheaux's entrepreneurship and calling him "fiendishly aggressive."[8] Bogle points to the criticism Micheaux received for selecting "light-bright" actors for prominent roles, for selecting genres of film that seemed to imitate Hollywood, and for the technical inferiority of Micheaux's films compared to Hollywood films. Bogle, however, mentions two films as outright racial achievement films, one of them, *God's Step Children,* "capturing the entire racial philosophy of the black middle classes in the 1930s and 1940s."[9] Bogle points out that though Micheaux's bourgeois values are held against him, the reflection in his films of the interests of the black middle class is his greatest contribution—"[Micheaux] was moving as far as possible away from Hollywood's jesters and servants."[10] Bogle was probably the first critic to defend the artistry and rhetoric of Micheaux's films in an extended and reasoned manner, although his treatment of black stereotypes has been recently challenged by Michele Wallace in her essay included in this book.

Janis Hebert worked out the historical names of the fictionalized towns and people of Micheaux's early autobiographical novels about South Dakota, providing quotations from interviews with Micheaux's neighbors about Micheaux's ambitions in land speculation and in his early novels. Ernest Jackson—a locally famous entrepreneur who, as the character Ernest Nicholson, is treated sympathetically in Micheaux's fiction—is reported by Hebert to have seen Micheaux later in life in Chicago and found him prosperous, having "grown to 300 pounds" and having acquired a chauffeur-driven car.[11]

212 | APPENDIX A

Jim Pines's book on black American cinema, *Blacks in Films* (1974), addresses some of the issues of racial identity in Micheaux's work, introducing them with a quotation from Ken Jacobs: "[Micheaux's films reveal] 'a series of shocking, inadvertent disclosures, *a terrifying portrait of Black self-devouring rage*. . . . their 'stories' are the products of minds which live in a racist nightmare.'"[12] Pines says that Jacobs is "referring to the role colour caste and class play in the films, and the almost pathological obsession with race-identity versus social recognition the films seem to project."[13] He also argues that Micheaux could not finally transcend or demystify the caste and class problems he portrayed, but that he could not be expected to, considering his own history and the working-class and rural nature of his audience. Pines's concluding questions revolve around the dynamics of ethnically oriented self images:

> How effective was Micheaux as a black myth-maker? Did his films help to reinforce, or did they help to break down ethnic caste and class barriers? Or were such possibilities obscured by melodrama and the general novelty of the ethnic-orientated medium? How effective really were race movies in forming a sense of cohesion and identity within the black communities in the United States at the time? And finally, what was the political and ideological substance of various attacks made by civil rights organizations against the "naiveté and latent Tomism" in Micheaux's films?[14]

Because we are only in the early stages of scholarship on black film, Pines's questions are still unanswered.

Variety carried a short report of the opening of the "first Hall of Fame for black filmmakers," sponsored by the Oakland Museum; since the awards given by the hall of fame are named after Oscar Micheaux, *Variety* provides some biographical information.[15] The Black Filmmakers' Hall of Fame continues to conduct the Oscar Micheaux Awards.

The avant-garde–oriented Collective for Living Cinema in New York mounted a program of early black cinema, curated by Pearl Bowser partly through the initiative of filmmaker Ken Jacobs. J. Hoberman wrote an appreciative article in the *Village Voice*, which included detailed descriptions and criticisms of the films screened.[16] Hoberman's enthusiasm for the films, based on his eclectic taste in art, suggested avenues for appreciation that had not been considered before. Penelope Gilliatt's early excitement about Micheaux was based on the historical significance of the work, and Bogle's was based on Micheaux's themes, but Hoberman was the first publicly to express excitement about the *style* and artistry of early black cinema. Hoberman's schooling in the de-trained ways of seeing the work of underground filmmakers Ken Jacobs, Stan Brakhage, and Jack Smith helped him to be open to what Micheaux has to offer.

Daniel Leab's groundbreaking book on black cinema, *From Sambo to Superspade* (1975), treats Micheaux at some length, but Leab's judgments about Micheaux lack analytic foundation. Leab states that Micheaux's silent films "cannot be considered outstanding," but, although Leab discusses several of the silent films, he could only have seen one of them (*Body and Soul*), since the others were not then extant. Further, Leab's quotations from the black press are hard to evaluate since they cannot easily be traced to their sources, and his assessment that "despite his public utterances, Micheaux's films were not designed to uplift or to enlighten" is mistaken.[17]

Gary Null's discussion of Micheaux in his book *Black Hollywood* (1975) is marked by errors in fact and judgment and unfair criticisms.[18] To criticize Micheaux for failing to use blacks in technical positions in the filmmaking process is to ignore the power and the racism of the unions.

Clinton Cox's article on early black cinema includes new information about Micheaux derived from interviews with black film actors.[19] Actor Lorenzo Tucker, for example, answered the criticism that Micheaux was imitating whites: "'We all tried to make pictures that would elevate,' the 68-year-old Tucker replied. 'We weren't imitating whitey. . . . I didn't and never will play an Uncle Tom, even if I never eat.'" Cox also sheds light, through these interviews, on Micheaux's business practices, such as Micheaux's attempt to get blacks to buy movie theaters, and his desire, after spending time in a wheelchair because of arthritis, to quit traveling with his films and to be able to sit in his office and just ship films, like the "boys on the coast."

In *The New Yorker*, Penelope Gilliatt—again responding to a public screening curated by Pearl Bowser, this time at the Whitney Museum—recognized a cogency in Micheaux's films that transcended their peculiar style of delivery, or, as she put it, "[Micheaux's] approach to his life still comes to us as a clear voice through air chattering with accents less blithe."[20]

Arlene Elder's reading of the autobiographical novels that are based in South Dakota finds the following set of contradictions: Micheaux wanted to inspire African Americans while defining himself in contrast to them; he treated Chicago as a mecca, on the one hand, and as a constraint to black progress, on the other; Micheaux combined individualism and utopian socialism as solutions for uplift. Elder's eye for contradiction opens interesting issues for future scholarship.[21]

1977 was a watershed year because of the publication of two books on black cinema, each of which remains indispensable. Thomas Cripps's *Slow Fade to Black,* a thickly documented history of African-American cinema, cogently demonstrates the effort made by blacks to produce a cinema of their own in competition with a hostile Hollywood.[22] Cripps's treatment of Micheaux is extensive and basically sympathetic to his entrepreneurial accomplishment; however, Cripps's negative conclusions about Micheaux's artistic quality are plagued by faulty film analysis, as discussed at length elsewhere.[23]

Henry Sampson's *Blacks in Black and White,* a sourcebook on black cinema, contains one of the best summaries of Micheaux's career.[24] Sampson made extensive use of the black press, and thus his facts are testable. Sampson's sources make it possible to correct some of the Spanish titles found in the rediscovered film, *Within Our Gates;* the heroine is *not* the product of a marriage between a southern white male aristocrat and a female slave-descendant, which would be an anomaly; she is—as one of Sampson's sources has described—illegitimate, clearly the result of white-on-black rape or concubinage, commonplaces in the antebellum South. Sampson concludes his discussion of Micheaux by reprinting the full text of the famous open letter to the black press in which Micheaux answered his critics and stated his artistic intentions.[25]

On the west coast the Black Filmmakers Hall of Fame mounted its fifth annual production of its Oscar Micheaux Awards Ceremony, which occasioned a catalog statement on Micheaux. Though barely three columns long, the text is characterized by accuracy and seems to be founded on original interviews with actors who worked with Micheaux, making the case that "Micheaux . . . was not unconcerned about how his films appeared . . . [since he] secured the best Black actors of the period[, he] employed the best available technicians, Black and White, that . . . budgets would allow[, and he] was intolerant of phlegmatic actors." The article states that "for all the [t]echnical know-how and directorial skill commanded by Hollywood, the filmic statements about Black people were dehumanizing and destructive," a state of affairs that entirely justified Micheaux's determination to affirm his own humanity by any technical means that were available to him, no matter how modest.[26]

In *Black Film as Genre* (1979), Thomas Cripps finds that "Micheaux's production style gave texture to black genre films even if his work was not noted for its excellence of cinematic technique" and that Micheaux's production companies, "by sharing poverty, late paychecks, and shabby working conditions, somehow managed to give a generic texture to their films."[27] Cripps pays tribute to Micheaux's courage by comparing him to Orson Welles, who also "had the gall to be opinionated in the presence of more experienced filmmakers," and who also worked from "a vantage point outside the system."[28] What Joseph Young and other critics would later call Micheaux's racial self-hatred, Cripps describes as Micheaux's "power to say . . . the unnameable, arcane, disturbing things that set black against black," which Cripps characterizes (sympathetically) as irony rather than self-hatred.[29] By focusing on Micheaux's work as *specifically* black in genre, Cripps raises *Body and Soul*—one of the films that he had excoriated in his previous book for failings of coherency and artistry—as a central example of the willingness of black genre films to assault problems within the black community. In his critique of Donald Bogle's book, Cripps calls for more attention to black genre movies: "Bogle was clearly happiest at the enjoyable task of puncturing the pink bubbles sent aloft by Hollywood studios. There seemed to be no room for a methodic analysis of aberrant film . . . or for the outlaw tradition of race movies."[30] Cripps answers his own call for analysis with an extended discussion of Micheaux and six case studies of difficult, non-mainstream films by other filmmakers.

Phyllis Klotman published an extensive and thoroughly indexed filmography of black cinema, *Frame by Frame* (1979), in which Micheaux figures prominently; unfortunately, its recent reissue does not include updated information about recent discoveries of three Micheaux films.[31]

Bernard Peterson's descriptive article on Micheaux includes an extensive annotated filmography. As Peterson himself points out, no filmography of Micheaux's can yet be considered definitive, and, in fact, Peterson's own revision in 1992 remained out of date.[32]

THE 1980S

Madubuko Diakité's dissertation on black cinema uses Micheaux's work extensively to refute the two claims that black film is incompetent and that it addresses itself to the bourgeoisie.[33] Diakité discusses style as a reflection of society; for example, in complex societies undergoing rapid evolution one might expect dynamism, motion, and "informalism" of style, and in rural or semiurban societies, styles might lean toward simplicity, "naturalism," and middle-class values. A number of critics have criticized Micheaux's films because they are too middle class; Communists even picketed some of Micheaux's films in the 1930s for similar reasons. Diakité gives further insight into Micheaux's relation to radical politics through the writings of Communist critic V. J. Jerome, pointing to a seeming contradiction in black politics of the 1930s—the role of the black middle class in black militancy. Diakité has shown that even the communist Jerome recognized that the continuing struggles of the "Negro liberation movement" included "a section of Negro midd[le]-class intellectuals [who were] advanced in thinking and fired with zeal for the freedom of their people." Diakité credits Micheaux's "defiance of Holl[y]wood's overwhelming influence [as] radical and perhaps militant."[34] Objecting to Thomas Cripps's statement that Micheaux succumbed to Hollywood because Micheaux developed no aesthetics of his own, Diakité implies that the attraction of technology itself may have blinded critics and audiences to the aesthetic qualities of race movies.

J. Hoberman suggests a refreshingly perverse approach to adverse criticisms. Of the hostile contemporary reception of Micheaux's last film, *The Betrayal* (1948), including the *Her-*

A publicity still for Oscar Micheaux's *Temptation* (1936).

ald-Tribune reviewer's remark that "the fact that Micheaux expects one to watch this [trash] for more than three hours is a monstrous piece of miscalculation," Hoberman responds: "Were the above reviews to greet a film opening tomorrow, one might rush to see it on the assumption that only a powerful originality could goad the jaded reviewers of the daily press to such fury. Edward Wood may be the Worst, but Oscar Micheaux . . . is the Baddest—with all that implies." Hoberman locates the most sensitive point in Micheaux's reception in the "painful ambivalence" of his racial attitudes, noting that Micheaux is on one hand offered as a role model for black directors and on the other hand is depicted by some black critics as producing "a fantasy world where blacks were just as affluent, just as educated, just as 'cultured,' just as well-mannered—in short, just as white—as white America."[35] Much of the controversy over Micheaux's films over the years has had to do with questions of racial identity—self hatred, skin-color caste, black-on-black criticism—and with the contradictions of black class mobility. Hoberman argues that the fact that Micheaux may have internalized some white American values is inevitable, and that Micheaux's unwillingness or inability "to directly confront America's racism," caused him to "displace his rage on his own people," and that his "internalization of America's racial attitudes" caused "his horrified fascination with miscegenation and 'passing,' his heedless blaming of the victim, his cruel baiting of fellow blacks." While accepting the general direction of Hoberman's rebuttal, I would like to note that Micheaux, in fact, *did* confront racism directly—a fact made clear by two films rediscovered after the publication of Hoberman's article—and that Micheaux's "rage" toward his own people was calculated, principled, and intended as progressive; Micheaux's "fascination with miscegenation and 'passing'" was not "horrified," but practical, considered, and racially loyal.

Hoberman, finally, is correct in his more positive judgment that *God's Step Children,* which epitomizes "Micheaux's complex, contradictory mixture of self-hatred and remorse forms an essential triptych with *The Birth of a Nation* and *The Searchers*," and he is justified in calling this triptych "the three richest, most harrowing delineations of American social psychology to be found on celluloid."[36] Hoberman's concluding paragraph expresses in daredevilish language intimations of genius in Micheaux's work:

> Three more things: 1) In *The Exile,* Micheaux uses titan of industry Charles Schwab's Riverside Drive mansion to represent the exterior of a Chicago whorehouse; 2) It's been said that Micheaux deliberately left mistakes in his finished films "to give the audience a laugh"; 3) The longer Micheaux made films, the badder they got. I'm haunted by these facts because they suggest that Micheaux knew what he was doing. And if Oscar Micheaux was a fully conscious artist, he was the greatest genius the cinema ever produced.[37]

Carol Munday Lawrence produced the first film about Micheaux. *Oscar Micheaux, Film Pioneer* features interviews with veteran actors of Micheaux's movies Bea Freeman and Lorenzo Tucker and is illustrated by fictional re-creations of events from Micheaux's life, with Danny Glover playing Micheaux.[38] The interviews with Micheaux's contemporaries are invaluable, though their memories are understandably questionable after sixty years. Tucker, for instance, places Paul Robeson incorrectly in Micheaux's first film, *The Homesteader,* instead of in *Body and Soul* six years later. Nevertheless, the eyewitness accounts of Micheaux's personality and working methods are based on personal experience. Bea Freeman says that Micheaux always knew exactly what he wanted from an actor and that he would not let anybody tell him what to do. She calls his stories "corny," but says the excitement lay in seeing a "clean, decent, uplifting" colored cast that was not picking cotton; Freeman describes the exhilaration of watching Micheaux's black actors who "were really dressed up and talking like people talk." Freeman's first meetings with Micheaux surprised her because he did not make a pass; non-harassment was so unusual as to make her wonder if she should be insulted. She was pleased, nonetheless, with his "all-business" attitude, which continued throughout her career with him. Freeman also reports on Micheaux's method of financing each film from proceeds of the previous film; but she adds the fact, which if true could eventually lead to a gold mine of rediscovered films, that *most* of Micheaux's sales returns came from South America, where his films were tremendous hits.

Lorenzo Tucker's description of Micheaux's knowledge of the business of race movies conveys a sense of Micheaux's utter competence; Tucker says he knew "to the penny" how much he could spend—and thus he knew how far off his white competition was in their own expenditures. He knew his public intimately from coast to coast, a fact that is also deducible from his novels, as well as from the legend of Micheaux's constant travels and inquisitiveness. Tucker also confirms that Micheaux "was trying to contradict D. W. Griffith," adding evidence that Micheaux's artistic intentions included rebuttal of Griffith and Hollywood, a point Michele Wallace expands on in her essay included in this book.

Finally, Tucker confirms what any scholar knows who has spent time with Micheaux's extant letters, novels, and films—that Micheaux was very kind, a humane, thoughtful, loving, and responsible person. He and his wife treated Tucker like a son, lending money whenever he needed it, feeding him, entertaining him in their home on Sundays. Whenever Micheaux was in Philadelphia, he would drop by Tucker's mother's house just to tell her Lorenzo was alright and that the Micheauxs were looking after him (and no doubt to report on her well-being to Tucker as well). Such stories, and a wealth of other evidence, run counter to the occasional scholarly generalization that Micheaux was a ruthless, self-promoting exploiter of all around him. While it is no doubt true that many small investors lost money in

Micheaux's companies, and that many actors were paid little or nothing, it is also true that Micheaux himself often faced bankruptcy, and that his actors knew precisely what their payment was going to be[39]—often when the payment was nothing, it was understood that they would "do it for exposure." Micheaux was pragmatic, and frankly so, rather than ruthless; and his pragmatism was fueled not only by ambition but also by larger goals that uplifted all who worked with him (and almost certainly will have done so in the eyes of history), as Tucker and Freeman imply unequivocally throughout their interviews.

David Levering Lewis's book on the Harlem Renaissance, *When Harlem Was in Vogue* (1981), brings to light a rare reference to Micheaux's connection (or, rather, his lack of a connection) with the cultural life of Harlem:

> Nan Bagby Stephens's unmemorable *Glory,* a melodramatic story about evil Reverend Cicero Brown ravishing a credulous parishioner's daughter, James Weldon Johnson considered remarkably good, musing how strange it was that "in most cases the Southern white writers can dig so deep down into Negro life, often a good deal deeper than the Negro writers themselves." Johnson was obviously unaware that *Glory* owed characters and plot to a brilliant 1924 silent film, *Body and Soul,* starring Paul Robeson and written, produced, and directed by Oscar Micheaux.[40]

Chester Fontenot's essay on Micheaux's life in South Dakota provides readings of three of Micheaux's novels set in the homesteading region (unaccountably, the other such novel, *The Wind from Nowhere* [1941] is not discussed, though it is more midwestern in focus than *The Forged Note* [1915], which Fontenot does include).[41] In analyzing his films, Fontenot casts Micheaux's positive portrayals of middle-class values as a reaction to Hollywood stereotyping, as a reaction to a tendency for black urban intellectuals to "glorify the black lower class" and "stigmatize . . . black middle-class people as plastic replicas of white society incapable of sustaining African and Afro-American cultural traditions," and "as a symbol of . . . race pride" seen from the point of view of goal orientation and black achievement.[42]

Fontenot's claim that Micheaux's attitude toward pioneering in "the great northwest" was virtually a Rousseauesque vision of utopian significance for ambitious black Americans and that cities were a trap of dystopian proportions ignores evidence that Micheaux was also drawn to the life of the city (see Jayna Brown's essay in this book)—its plays, movies, nightlife—and was interested in improving that life through the building of black YMCAs and businesses. Micheaux, after all, worked the greater part of his life in Chicago and New York, and his portrayals of life in those cities were in many ways positive.

Black Cinema Aesthetics,[43] a collection of essays on black cinema edited by Gladstone Yearwood, features Micheaux prominently throughout, beginning with the forceful call by film historian Thomas Cripps for a critical effort to follow up his own historical research. Pearl Bowser highlights Micheaux's female characters in perhaps the first serious critical treatment of *Body and Soul.* Bowser redirects critical attention from the preacher to the mother, whose "unconscious sexual fantasies about her minister are revealed in her nightmare, a long segment [that] constitutes three-qua[r]ters of the film. Micheaux shook his audiences with this strong, complex and emotional woman; and the story is as much about her as it is the expos[ur]e of the venal jackleg preacher."[44] Bowser adds further examples of Micheaux's serious treatment of black women on the screen, suggesting a line of analysis that remains relatively unexplored.

Gladstone Yearwood's own essay in his volume lays foundations for a theory of a black film aesthetic. Yearwood faults the prevailing critical assessment of black cinema for its failure to found its criteria outside the hegemony of Hollywood, and he uses Micheaux as an implicit example of a strong figure who has been denigrated by the application of inappropriate Hollywood-oriented criticism. Yearwood insists that black film criticism must be oppositional to the Hollywood institution of representation and that it must be founded on a material understanding of the films and their processes of production as opposed to a founding of black aesthetics on merely iconic references (e.g., counting black faces on the screen) or merely indexical references (e.g., whether the filmmaker was black) or intentional references (e.g., whether the filmmaker seemed to propose something African American).[45]

Pearl Bowser was guest curator for screenings of seven of Micheaux's films at the Whitney Museum of American Art on the occasion of the filmmaker's 100th birthday. Bowser's continuing commitment to a deeper and broader understanding of Micheaux is reflected in the authority of the program note, which includes interpretive insight and some new information. Bowser suggests, for example, that the deafness and muteness of one of the characters in *Ten Minutes to Live* was in part a cost-saving measure during the transition from silent to sound movies.[46]

J. Hoberman reviewed virtually every film of the Whitney series in three consecutive issues of the *Village Voice*. Hoberman's response to the dual role—one bad character, one good—played by Paul Robeson in *Body and Soul* (discussed by Charles Musser in this volume) was not unduly swayed by the unconventionality of the narrative: "Of course, however bizarre this [split role] seems on the narrative level, Robeson's schizoid figure makes perfect allegorical sense: he represents what Micheaux saw as the two alternatives open to black men, namely the hustler-trickster Stagger Lee or the bourgeois disciple of Booker T. Washington."[47] Hoberman's writings on Micheaux again demonstrate the efficacy of an avant-garde point of view and the inefficacy of an over-reliance on conventional aesthetics. Sympathy with the idea of the avant-garde and experience outside the canons of mainstream culture loosen the preconceptions of what constitutes successful art, and that loosening can work to the benefit of ethnic diversity.

Richard Dyer discusses *Body and Soul* in the context of a lengthy consideration of the significance of Paul Robeson's acting career. Just before discussing the Micheaux film, Dyer identifies four aspects of Robeson's star presence that were potentially disturbing to ethnically white America and Europe—"his physique, his moral character, his level of achievement, [and] his association with ideas of freedom."[48] Dyer then focuses on Robeson's widely recognized sexual attractiveness, presumably an aspect of the disturbing quality of "physique" (though not limited to physique). *Body and Soul,* the only Robeson film directed by an African American, might be expected to avoid some of the problems white filmmakers had with black male sex appeal. White films, according to Dyer, tended to "deactivate" Robeson's disturbing qualities, including his sex appeal. Micheaux's film, while presenting Robeson's attractiveness in all its power, also demonstrates some problems with what it is presenting: "There is a central dilemma in most black thought of the period. . . . Is celebrating black sensuality insisting on an alternative to white culture or, on the contrary, playing into the hands of white culture, where such sensuality could be labelled as a sign of irrational inferiority and more grossly read as genital eroticism, as 'sexuality'?"[49] Micheaux deals with those problems by splitting the Robeson character in two. The viewer is allowed to experience Robeson's sexual powers undiluted but then is invited to reject him as "bad" and to accept a more middle-class, respectable character, who is also played by Robeson; though one aspect of Robeson replaces the other, both aspects get into the film. Dyer recognizes the special contribution Micheaux makes in registering, within the filmic discourse, the problem of "handling" a black star of Robeson's magnitude.

Black Film Review carried a report by contributing editor (and Hollywood actress) Saundra Sharp on the special award given to Oscar Micheaux by the Directors Guild of America.[50] A new high point, of sorts, in the reemergence of Micheaux must be recognized, ironically symbolized by President Ronald Reagan's telegram to the Guild, which said, "'Oscar Micheaux stands tall in the history of the cinema. . . . Nothing daunted him and his work remains a testament to courage and artistic excellence.'" Part of the irony of Reagan's telegram is the fact that Micheaux's *artistic* excellence had seldom been granted. In the course of her report, Sharp includes her own version of the reemergence of Micheaux, emphasizing the work of the Directors Guild of America's first black member, Wendell James Franklin; the strong support of film director William Crain; the cooperation of Academy Award–winning director Robert Wise; the film on Micheaux made by Carol Munday Lawrence; the festival mounted by Mayme Clayton, founder of the Western States Black Research Center; the scholarly documentation of Henry Sampson; and the television productions of Gail Choice and Tony Brown. Sharp notes that the Black Filmmaker Hall of Fame confers its Oscar Micheaux Award on new inductees each year in Oakland, California.

In the subsequent issue of *Black Film Review,* a poster of Micheaux's film *Underworld* is featured on the cover to illustrate the subject of another article by Saundra Sharp, this time about black cinema collectors, featuring Micheaux more prominently than any other filmmaker.[51] Sharp's article, which might easily be overlooked in a bibliography on Micheaux, is one of the few instances in which full credit is given to private collectors such as James Wheeler in Detroit, Pearl Bowser in Brooklyn, and Henry Sampson and Mayme Clayton in Los Angeles, without whose work the reemergence of Micheaux into the public sphere would be difficult to imagine.

A short article in the *Chicago Defender* reported the ceremony for the erection of a headstone over Micheaux's grave in Great Bend, Kansas, also mentioning that a star for Micheaux had been placed on Hollywood Boulevard and tributes had been paid him by the Screen Actors Guild (probably this is a mistaken reference to the Directors Guild) and the Black Filmmakers Hall of Fame.[52]

In an article in *The Independent,* black South African filmmaker Ntongela Masilela credits Micheaux with dealing with race but faults him once again for not taking "this question beyond the class boundaries of the black bourgeoisie."[53] Masilela also credits Micheaux with themes that were "far-reaching, ranging from the problems of interracial romance to the traumas of collapsing black marriages to the corruption of the church." Although he approves of such themes, Masilela compares Micheaux unfavorably with filmmakers from the Soviet golden age: "Unlike Eisenstein, [Micheaux's] contemporary, whose films revolve around a central thematic object—the glorification and celebration of the past—or Vertov, who attempted to explain and clarify the struggle of the present moment, Micheaux's work lacks a conceptual center or philosophical object that would have established [its] coherence and rigor." This latter point is incorrect, however; and comparing Micheaux to "his contemporaries" in the Soviet avant-garde makes no sense because the political cultures do not bear comparison.

Of the African-American critics of the 1980s, Donald Bogle continued to be among the most sympathetic toward Micheaux while avoiding uncritical enthusiasm. His encyclopedia *Blacks in American Films and Television* features Micheaux repeatedly as the most important, and among the most fascinating, founders of independent black cinema.[54] Every time Bogle notes negative qualities of some of Micheaux's work, he also mentions compensating qualities. Bogle characterized *God's Step Children* as "absurd," "trite," and "knuckle headed," but also as "deliriously enjoyable," as "funny and often appealing," as being "without major studio guile or glamour," characterized instead by "directness" and a sense of gritty reality.[55]

Like Pearl Bowser, Bogle also notes Micheaux's foregrounding of women characters, "[Micheaux's] independent, strong-willed heroines often [overshadow] the rather pallid males." Bogle characterizes *God's Step Children* (1938) as "part women's film, part race-theme movie, its haughty heroine Naomi punished with death perhaps precisely because of her free-wheeling independence."[56] Bogle is partly right about Naomi's punishment, but Naomi can also be seen as more representative of whiteness in the black community than she is of female independence; there are other Micheaux films that do not punish independent, intelligent women. Micheaux's film work is, as Bogle has suggested, saturated with a kind of protofeminist sensibility in spite of Micheaux's overriding "bourgeois" ideal.

Returning again to Micheaux's apparent espousal of bourgeois ideals, "viewed by some contemporary black audiences as his severest shortcoming," Bogle defends Micheaux: "Though his films rarely centered on the ghetto, few race movies did. . . . Micheaux in his later films concentrated on the problems facing black 'professional people.'"[57] Bogle places Micheaux's middle-class aspirations in historical context.

Of the three books in 1988 that most reflect the rising interest in Micheaux, Richard Grupenhoff's book on Lorenzo Tucker, the black actor who Micheaux built into a race movie star, clearly is the most extensive and original contribution to historical scholarship.[58] Given the paucity of factual knowledge about Micheaux's life and career, the detailed information gathered from interviews with people who knew Micheaux is invaluable. For example, Grupenhoff demonstrates that the characters in *Wages of Sin* (not extant) represent Micheaux and his brother Swan, and that the drama plays out Swan's ostensible mismanagement of the finances of Oscar's film company. Thus, the contemporary descriptions of the plot of the film can be read as factual, with appropriate caution.[59]

Grupenhoff also provides the most historically grounded discussion of Micheaux's alleged color-caste fetishism. Introducing damning quotations from the black press concerning Micheaux's seeming preference for light-skinned heroines, Grupenhoff finds that the perception of fetishism does not fit the facts. Tucker himself clearly states that Micheaux's goal was "to depict the black race in its natural settings, facing everyday problems. . . . He gave all different kinds of roles to different shades. He used different-looking people, not stereotypes. I played bad guys, too, and I was light-skinned. He wrote his stories to use all the shades of the black race, because that's the way we are."[60]

Though Grupenhoff argues that Micheaux's "directing technique was primarily pragmatic" rather than artistic,[61] and thus the book does not explicitly probe the possibilities of an art of an unconventional sort, Grupenhoff nevertheless points the way to just such an unconventional approach, providing an example of Micheaux's pragmatics that also conjures modernist theories of stage acting: "In *The Girl from Chicago* . . . one can hear Micheaux's off-camera voice cueing the actors as they gesture on camera for him to be quiet. . . . Micheaux's films are replete with these strange, revealing moments in which we are able to see both the character and the actor behind the character in self-conscious behavior."[62]

In the same year, Grupenhoff also published another version of his interviews with Lorenzo Tucker[63] and an article that uses much of the material on Micheaux from Grupenhoff's book on Tucker, subtracting the discussion of Micheaux's color-caste controversies but adding the full text of a letter written by Micheaux's wife, Alice B. Russell, that describes Micheaux's physical condition and spirit toward the end of his life. One statement by Grupenhoff in this latter article, to the effect that "there were no negative stereotypes held up to ridicule,"[64] occasioned a rebuttal by J. Ronald Green and Horace Neal, Jr., published in the same journal later that year.[65]

Though references to Micheaux proliferate in an issue of the French journal *CinémAc-*

tion devoted entirely to black American film, it contains no original contribution to Micheaux scholarship. Pearl Bowser's article focuses on Micheaux, but it is a translation into French of her note for the Whitney Museum discussed above.[66]

The second of Mark Reid's articles appeared in *Black Film Review,* emphasizing the historical fact that after the advent of sound, race movie producers raised most of their capital from white sources. Reid concludes that, although it is not historically accurate to call Micheaux's post-1931 films "Black independent cinema," Micheaux nonetheless left an important legacy for today's black filmmakers.[67]

Joseph Young's *Black Novelist as White Racist* is the first book devoted to Micheaux. It focuses on Micheaux's fiction, adds nothing original about his films, and is relentlessly negative in its judgment of Micheaux's accomplishment.[68] The value of Young's book is in its interpretation of many of the factual double meanings of Micheaux's romans à clef.[69]

THE 1990S

The most significant events of the 1990s have been the rediscovery and public exhibition of two of Micheaux's silent films and one of his early sound films. The first to emerge, *Within Our Gates* (1920), was actually discovered in the mid-1970s, though it was not exhibited in this country until the 1990s. Not surprisingly, the rediscovery involved the perspicacity of Lawrence Karr (an archivist at the American Film Institute), the cooperation of two dedicated archivists at the Spanish national film archives (La Filmoteca Española), Florentino Sopria and Catherine Gauthier, and the knowledge of scholar Thomas Cripps.

An early sound film, *Veiled Aristocrats* (1932), was rediscovered in 1992, again as the result of the perspicacity of a film collector and distributor, Jack Hard, of Grapevine Video in Phoenix, Arizona, who discovered the film in a garage in Tennessee. Hardy contacted Richard Grupenhoff, who confirmed the identity and value of the find and brought the film to the attention of Jan-Christopher Horak, archivist at the George Eastman House in Rochester, New York. Horak reconstructed the film, using the print discovered in Tennessee plus some additional footage owned by the Library of Congress.

Sometime in 1992 or shortly before, a print of Micheaux's early silent film *The Symbol of the Unconquered* was acquired from the Belgian film archive by the Museum of Modern Art. The film, screened with French and Flemish subtitles but with an English-language translation, was the centerpiece of a monthly meeting of the University Seminar on Cinema and Interdisciplinary Interpretation, held at the Museum and co-chaired by Charles Musser; the presentation by Pearl Bowser and Louise Spence was one of several talks on Micheaux that the seminar sponsored in this period.

A panel presentation on Oscar Micheaux at the Society for Cinema Studies annual conference in Los Angeles was accompanied by a screening of the newly discovered *Within Our Gates.* That year also marks the first meeting at the conference of scholars interested in Micheaux. The meeting gave rise to a loosely knit ongoing organization that would later be called the Oscar Micheaux Society, which now publishes a newsletter of the same name.[70]

Micheaux loomed large in a book about the discovery of a cache of early African-American films in a Texas warehouse, *Black Cinema Treasures,* by G. William Jones.[71] The author, the late director of the Southwest Film/Video Archives at Southern Methodist University, helped to discover the films eight years earlier and raised the money to have them preserved at his archive. The book is more celebratory than critical. Jones's section on Micheaux includes no original scholarly or critical information, except the fascinating observation that

A publicity still for Oscar Micheaux's 1938 sound version of *Birthright*.

the role of one of the detectives in the film *Murder in Harlem,* a minor speaking part, is played by Micheaux.

Perhaps the most appealing contribution of Jones's book is a transcribed conversation among film artists and professionals—Herman Abrams, Barbara Bryant, Ossie Davis, William Greaves, and Harrel Gordon Tillman—who provide many points of guidance about the importance of race movies, about the conditions of race movie production, and the reception of race movies by black audiences. Harrel Tillman (a 1940s race movie actor), for example, notes: "I don't care how black you were or how fair you were—you could see someone in those films that looked like you."[72]

American Film published a feature article and a sidebar by Richard Gehr on Micheaux's career, novels, films, and critical reception.[73] Details and judgments are plentiful and sometimes original, but unfortunately they are largely undocumented.

Three events in the 1990s constitute a breakthrough with regard to specifically African-American scholarly and critical reassessment of Micheaux. First, an article by bell hooks characterizes Micheaux as a pioneer who challenged racist representations of blackness, mastered codes of "signifying" and indirection, employed melodrama to undermine accepted forms of language, and explored sexual politics within a context of color caste.[74] hooks claims that Micheaux's mixing of the color codes of whiteness and blackness constitutes not only an interrogation of the color caste system but also a challenge to the mainstream audience's need for a "bad guy" and the black audience's need for a totally positive image of blackness. hooks shows how even so-called bad guys are constructed by Micheaux to be sexually appealing to female spectators, complicating the notion of "badness." The so-called badness of the seductive villain in *Ten Minutes to Live* (1932) is qualified by the facts that the villain respects his mother, who advises him constantly by mail, and that he has been on a chain gang. hooks suggests that Micheaux's inclusion of such historical references "(that would have been immediately understood by his audience) situate representations of black male 'criminality' in a social and political context, contesting notions of inherent biological propensity toward evil perpetuated in racist ideology—and in white cinema."[75] In that single observation, one of many such in her article, hooks has refuted the argument that Micheaux exploited melodrama merely to pander to his audience to make a profit. She shows how Micheaux reclaims his character from melodramatic villainy by inserting him into an African-American history shared by his audience. More on the way Micheaux productively used the genre of melodrama can be found in the essay by Jane Gaines in this collection.

hooks has interpreted Micheaux's treatment of sexual looking not as exploitative of women's availability but as aesthetically, psychologically, and sociologically healthy: "The body movements [of Micheaux's skimpily dressed black female dancers] resemble those of Josephine Baker, calling attention to their breasts, legs, and asses. Yet this display does not evoke pornographic gazes from folks in the nightclub; it is presented not as exposure of taboo sexuality but as comfortable expression of bodily delight."[76]

hooks suggests that Micheaux, far from advocating a white value system, gave an important place to the connection of the world of his films with Africa and with the values of African ancestors.[77] Africanisms extend to the privileged importance of the mother, and of women in general, in Micheaux's stories. hooks points out that it is the advice of the mother that saves the villain, the hero, and the heroine in *Ten Minutes to Live* and also causes the demise of the immoral vamp. The "men in the film lack insight. They can only apprehend the world fully, grasp the true nature of reality, by learning from women."[78]

The second breakthrough was the publication of Mark Reid's *Redefining Black Film*, which includes a section titled "Oscar Micheaux and Black Action Films."[79] Like bell hooks, Reid emphasizes Micheaux's appeal to sophisticated African Americans rather than to any white values that may be a part of such sophistication. According to Reid, "Micheaux's action films . . . were imaginative reflections of a proud, aggressive New Negro whose new morality condoned retaliatory action against white racist aggressions. New cultural 'objects' such as black action films were created for this new group of urbanized, race-conscious blacks who were learning to lessen their need for approval by white America."[80]

One of Reid's most important historical insights is that Micheaux anticipated by fifty years the commercial black-oriented films of the 1970s, suggesting that "[Micheaux's] 'colored man with bricks'[the hero in *The Symbol of the Unconquered*] who defeats the Klan is a superhero, an ancestor of such heroes of the 1970s as Sweetback, who appears in Melvin Van Peebles's *Sweet Sweetback's Baadasssss Song*" (1971).[81]

Reid gives Micheaux a prominent and respected place in the history of early cinema, but Reid downplays Micheaux's films after the silent era, owing to the fact that Micheaux needed white financing in order to make sound films. As a consequence, Reid does not discuss Micheaux's more difficult sound films with anything like the attention he gives to the silent films. As it happens, it may be those sound films—because of the stylistic problems caused by the special difficulties of working in sound—that have kept some scholars from wanting to embrace Micheaux as a major artist.

The third breakthrough was Manthia Diawara's *Black American Cinema*, an anthology published by Routledge that includes articles on Micheaux by Jane Gaines, J. Ronald Green, and Thomas Cripps.[82] Gaines's essay is the first extended textual and thematic analysis of a Micheaux film, *Within Our Gates*. Green argues for a reassessment of Thomas Cripps's criticisms of Micheaux's artistic accomplishment; and Cripps responds to Green and reviews the context of Micheaux scholarship.

The next major event of Micheaux scholarship by African Americans in the 1990s was the publication of a special issue of *Black Film Review,* edited by Pearl Bowser and Jane Gaines, in which most of the contributions are by African-American writers.[83] Deserving particular mention is Clyde Taylor's article on "the crisis of 1937–1939," when independent black cinema was successfully choked off by Hollywood, not to reemerge until the 1960s.[84] Since that crisis was precisely the period in which Micheaux made his last films and, because of Hollywood competition, had to return to writing novels, Taylor's thesis has relevance to a critical reevaluation of Micheaux. Taylor says that the sense of what constituted high quality in black cinema was changing because of increased urbanization and sophistication in the black community and the growing call for an integrated society. One of the consequences of this exposure of Micheaux to those audiences was a shift in the criteria of film quality. Integrated audiences seemed to call for higher production values than race movies could provide; the resulting crossover films resulted in gangster melodramas or "goo-goo success stories, using Negro actors,"[85] which distorted African-American reality in a way true race movies did not. An important contribution is Taylor's identification of the historical shift in values that helped to bury Micheaux until the current reemergence.

In the same issue, Pearl Bowser's interview with writer Toni Cade Bambara and documentary filmmaker Louis Massiah is one of the fresher discussions of Micheaux. Bambara points out that "the backstory is the real meat of [*Within Our Gates*]. We get the backstory of [the sharecropper's] daughter, which consists of . . . her education, and that allows Micheaux to talk about issues of the day and urgency of saving the Black land grant colleges."[86] Massiah makes a similar point: "There's an extraordinary amount of exposition in [*Symbol of the Unconquered*] . . . by our standards now of what drama is, there's so much filling in the past. . . . In drama classes or in filmmaking classes they say it's too much exposition, but it is interesting."[87]

Bambara also explains how Western cinema has tended to shut down cinematic space, after a certain number of establishing shots, to a very confined referencing of psychological space, where solutions to problems always relate to the individual rather than the social or the systemic. She finds Micheaux's films more like *Daughters of the Dust,* where there is a collective point of view and the focus "is on the group and social space. It's shared space and it's democratic space, as opposed to idealized space and hierarchical space dominated by one hero. The way [African Americans] handle space allows us to make that connection, and ask the spectator to make that connection, between this story and contiguous reality."[88] Both Massiah and Bambara notice that Micheaux always has a consciously economic argument. Massiah says that Micheaux shows the Klan's "terrorism is not even vaguely racial; it's really about economic subjugation."

All of these points, and several others in Bowser's interview, suggest ways that Micheaux is vitally relevant to scholars, critics, and filmmakers today, ways that open windows on unconventional strategies of filmmaking. They show that people in other times and other places, when engaged fiercely with problems resistant to change, can produce strategies, such as an expositional writing style or a spatially democratic shooting style, that may look odd to audiences used to conventional fare but may be appropriate to conditions of struggle or be just plain pragmatic. The realization that a once commercially successful but later declining filmmaker such as Micheaux was also artistically sophisticated justifies interest in Micheaux, since such history lends encouragement to those who are working today who may find themselves marginalized. Insight into Micheaux's methods might help in bringing some independently minded artists of today into a broader current, nourishing them and enriching the fields of their endeavor downstream. That is one reason the reemergence of Micheaux is so important.

Another reason is the effect of this reemergence on film studies and possibly on African-American studies. One of the issues accompanying the reemergence of Micheaux centers around a question posed by bell hooks in her book *Yearning*: "Isn't it time to look closely at how and why work by white scholars about nonwhite people receives more attention and acclaim than similar work produced by nonwhite scholars?"[89] During the reemergence of Micheaux that began in the 1960s, academic interest has included both black and white writers and a steadily growing number of black academics, but white interest has certainly been a key factor. Of the four persons in those first panels at the Society for Cinema Studies, only one, Charlene Regester, was African American, and she had not been a member of the Society until that time. Pearl Bowser had been approached to give papers at the Society's annual conference but was initially unable to do so. The three articles on Micheaux that appear in Diawara's book on black American cinema were all by white scholars—Cripps, Gaines, and Green—but the rest of the book is comprised primarily of essays by black scholars. It is not surprising that three of the nineteen essays are focused on Micheaux, but it is interesting that all three are by white scholars. Whatever the reason for this somewhat characteristic past phenomenon of Micheaux scholarship of the reemergence, recent activity shows that black and white scholars in film studies are being drawn together in a new conversation.

The flurry of Micheaux events below attests to the vitality of that conversation: (1) Thomas Cripps's *Making Movies Black* discusses Micheaux's last films;[90] (2) Brian Taves discusses Micheaux in a book on the Library of Congress holdings of African-American documents;[91] (3) *In Touch with the Spirit: Black Religious and Musical Expression in American Cinema*, the proceedings from a conference convened by Phyllis R. Klotman and Gloria J. Gibson in Indianapolis, includes articles on Micheaux by J. Ronald Green and Charlene Regester;[92] (4) a conference, "Oscar Micheaux: Film Pioneer," organized by David Schwartz and featuring an array of speakers thoroughly representative of the reemergence, is held at the Museum of the Moving Image in New York;[93] (5) filmmaker Arthur Jafa (cinematographer for *Daughters of the Dust*) discusses Micheaux's film style in *Black Film Bulletin*;[94] (6) Jane Gaines and Richard Dyer hold a dialogue about *The Birth of a Nation* and *Within Our Gates* at a conference titled Contemporary Perspectives on U.S. Southern Culture at the University of Warwick, U.K.; (7) an article by Jane Gaines on the release of an English-language version of Micheaux's *Within Our Gates* by the Smithsonian; an article by J. Ronald Green on Micheaux filmographies; and a film review by Arthur Knight of *Midnight Ramble: Oscar Micheaux and the Story of Race Movies* appear in volume three of the *Oscar Micheaux Society Newsletter*; (8) the long-awaited broadcast of *Midnight Ramble: Oscar Micheaux and the Story of Race Movies*—Pamela Thomas, producer, Bestor Cram and Pearl Bowser, directors, Clyde Taylor, writer—takes place; (9) Micheaux's first and third novels, *The Conquest* (1913) and *The Homesteader* (1917) are republished in facsimile by the University of Nebraska Press; (10) the posthumous publication of James Snead's *White Screens/Black Images*[95] includes discussion of Micheaux; (11) Mark Reid conducts panels on *Within Our Gates* at the annual conferences of the Modern Language Association and the Society for Cinema Studies; (12) Charlene Regester's article, "Lynched, Assaulted, Intimidated: Oscar Micheaux's Most Controversial Films," appears in *Popular Culture Review*;[96] (13) the conference Oscar Micheaux and His Circle, organized by Pearl Bowser, Jane Gaines, Charles Musser, and Hazel Carby, is held at Yale University; (14) the Yale conference is covered in a feature article by the *Chronicle of Higher Education*;[97] (15) Charlene Regester publishes a thorough review of the literature on Micheaux;[98] (16) Richard Dyer's article on whiteness in *The Birth of a Nation* and Jane Gaines's comparison of *The Birth of a Nation* and *Within Our Gates* in the light of the culture of the American South are included in *Dixie Debates: Perspectives in Southern Culture*;[99] (17) several papers are presented on Micheaux on various panels at the Society for Cinema Studies conference; (18) two of Micheaux's films plus the documentary about Micheaux, *Midnight Ramble,* are featured in a major series called "Cinéma noir" at the Cinémathèque Française; (19) the first article—a study of the Micheaux legend in relation to *The Symbol of the Unconquered*—from the important project on Micheaux by Pearl Bowser and Louise Spence appears in *The Birth of Whiteness: Race and the Emergence of United States Cinema;*[100] (20) Richard Papousek, Francie Johnson, and other members of the community of Gregory, South Dakota, where Micheaux homesteaded at the turn of the century, create an annual Oscar Micheaux festival that includes screenings; a gathering of historians, film scholars, and South Dakotans who knew Micheaux; and a sunrise ceremony at Micheaux's old homestead site, which has been reconstructed meticulously (this magnificent small festival in its second year won the National Endowment for the Humanities' prize for best state humanities council project for 1997); (21) Charlene Regester's well-researched account of Oscar Micheaux's battles with censorship in New York, Virginia, and Chicago appears in *Movie Censorship and American Culture;*[101] (22) the Pordenone Silent Film Festival shows *Within Our Gates* and publishes J. Ronald Green's "Micheaux v. Griffith" in its journal, *Griffithiana;* Green's Micheaux article, "America in bianco et nero," appears in the Sunday supplement to the Italian daily paper *L'Unità;*[102] (23) Charlene Regester's detailed study of the financial negotiations between Micheaux and Charles Chesnutt, the author of *The House Behind the Cedars,* appears in the *Journal of Film and Video;*[103] and (24) numerous Micheaux sites emerge on the Internet.

The rapidly expanding activity on Micheaux indicates that in the late 1990s his reemergence can no longer be reviewed adequately in a single article. The list above is no doubt incomplete, and most of the events listed deserve extensive discussion that is beyond the scope of this essay; from this point any continuing review of the literature will need to be more selective, as is the case with most established research subjects. Publications such as the *Oscar Micheaux Society Newsletter*—with its subject headings on conferences, screenings, bibliography, audio/visual resources, Web sites, and other categories—will become ever-more-essential tools. Because of the importance of Micheaux's life and work to the state of filmmaking and of film studies, such an overflowing cup is a welcome problem and an appropriate image with which to conclude an overview of Micheaux's reemergence.

There now can be no doubt that there was a formidable champion in the field, a Great Black Hope, in early cinema. That champion was fiercely and successfully independent, as well as socially and politically engaged, over a thirty-year career. He wrote, published, and distributed seven novels; he wrote, produced, directed, distributed, and promoted about forty films that were race conscious, class conscious, gender conscious, and aesthetically innovative in ways that philosophically and politically challenged the contemporary standards. He anticipated concerns that may mature only in the twenty-first century, when class issues could overtake race issues in the consciousness of Micheaux's society. The historical and biographical information, interpretive reassessments, and theoretical speculation that scholars and critics have produced, and the public forums of his work provided by exhibitors and festival organizers, are making a difference in the picture we have of this champion. But there is need for much more. All the important issues—aesthetics, race, class, gender, and just facts—are very much in contention; much work and many points of view are still needed. What is no longer seriously in contention is that Oscar Micheaux's achievement is worthy of such an effort.

APPENDIX B

An Oscar Micheaux Filmography: From the Silents through His Transition to Sound, 1919–1931

COMPILED BY CHARLES MUSSER, COREY K. CREEKMUR, PEARL BOWSER,
J. RONALD GREEN, CHARLENE REGESTER, AND LOUISE SPENCE

*T*his Oscar Micheaux filmography is a collective effort that took its current form as the catalog neared completion. Corey Creekmur initiated this undertaking by assembling information on the producer's films by collating the published efforts from a wide range of sources up to 1992. While illuminating, the result proved highly problematic, for it produced many contradictions and unresolved questions. Creekmur's filmography only underscored the need for a more definitive reference work. In response, Charles Musser began a more or less systematic search of the *New York Amsterdam News,* the *Chicago Defender* (City Edition), the *Pittsburgh Courier,* and the *Philadelphia Tribune.* Creekmur's manuscript was then reworked based on this new information. Once this process was well underway, a revised filmography was sent out to Pearl Bowser, Charlene Regester, Ron Green, and Louise Spence. They each provided information from the George P. Johnson Negro Film Collection, Special Collections, Young Library, UCLA, which included descriptions of films, cast information, and selected articles as well as additional references gathered from various newspapers (including overlooked citations from newspapers that Musser had consulted). Regester also provided a wealth of information from censorship records in Chicago, New York, and Virginia; the Charles Chesnutt correspondence; additional screening dates; and cast information. Musser double-checked and refined these references, pursued further references in the Baltimore *Afro-American, Norfolk Journal and Guide,* and the otherwise untapped *Washington Tribune* and organized the information in its present form. Bowser and Spence reviewed the filmography, provided editorial judgment based on their immense knowledge, and provided a wide range of additional information, ensuring that we avoided numerous errors and enriching the overall results immeasurably.

The fiction films that follow were all "written, directed, and produced" by Micheaux. (He produced only one news film, a short subject shown before his first feature, *The Homesteader* [1919].) Since the names of his cameramen are unknown, we have not listed production personnel (as opposed to cast members). Although this filmography has its genesis in

Oscar Micheaux's *The Wages of Sin* (1929). A production still featuring William A. Clayton, Jr.

secondary sources, it is now firmly based on primary research. We have either omitted information or given source information in brackets when we could not independently verify material.

We have tried to create a preliminary, admittedly circumscribed, sense of where and when films were shown, promoted, and discussed. The degree of incompleteness cannot be overemphasized. Micheaux's films were shown widely in the South and also overseas, but little of these activities is documented in this filmography. Although we relied heavily on newspaper research, there are significant gaps in available microfilm editions for all the black newspapers we consulted. In many cases, these involve isolated missing issues, but often there are months or even years of missing documentation. This shortfall is only one dimension of the larger problem: in 1929, the *Amsterdam News* estimated that there were twenty movie theaters in Harlem. Perhaps six or seven of these venues were then advertising in the *Amsterdam News,* and even fewer advertised in the *New York Age.* There were also surely more black theaters in Harlem in the early 1920s than advertised. Nor has our own survey of even these newspapers been exhaustive. It is absolutely certain that Micheaux's films were screened much more extensively, even in the cities on which we have focused.

Past filmographies of Micheaux's work have enjoyed or suffered from a certain level of mystery and mystification. What follows, while still tentative in some areas, is an effort at delimitation. A number of Micheaux pictures were said to be in production or even completed but apparently never found their ways into theaters. Some of these have proved to be working titles. *The Ghost of Tolston's Manor* (often dated 1923), for example, has proved to be the working title for *A Son of Satan* (1924). Other films might themselves be called "ghosts" and are listed at the end of the filmography proper. These include *Jasper Landry's Will* (1923) and *A Fool's Errand* (1923), which might have been working titles for subsequent releases. Or they may be never-completed films or minor efforts which received very limited distribution (in which case they should be "moved up" to the filmography proper).

Our filmography is arranged chronologically in order of release. Additional information on Micheaux-related activities, primarily in the form of short news articles, is interspersed within the overall time line. From his first film, *The Homesteader* (1919), to his last, *The Betrayal* (1948), the present filmography attributes thirty-eight films to Micheaux. We have focused on the first twenty-five of these—twenty-three features and two shorts. That is, we effectively conclude our filmography once Micheaux's transition to sound has been completed—with *The Exile* (1931) and *Darktown Revue* (1931). *A Daughter of the Congo* (1930) was a "part talkie" that included one or more synchronous sound sequences. However, Micheaux's next film, *Easy Street* (1930), was seemingly still a "silent" (though there is contradictory evidence on this score). This complex transition, while little addressed in the present catalog, is of considerable potential interest.

Films have been dated by their earliest documented public exhibition. In only one established instance—*The House Behind the Cedars* (1924/1925), did Micheaux give a public preview at the end of one year and premiere the film in the next. Micheaux routinely showed footage to exhibitors before a premiere, but we cannot assume that such films were actually in a finished state at that time. Censorship records suggest that Micheaux refined his pictures until very shortly before their exhibition and may have changed them many times in the course of their exhibition history. We provide the length of each picture in forms that were advertised or noted in censorship reports—often in 1,000-foot units or reels, with each reel containing as much as 1,000 feet of film, which would translate into approximately fifteen minutes of screen time. In many cases, a given film varied substantially in length and meaning as the result of censorship directives or anticipated problems. Micheaux sometimes submitted the same film to different censorship boards in different lengths. Thus, New York censors saw a 10,000-foot version of *Birthright,* while two months later those in Chicago saw one that was only 8,000 feet in length. These varying lengths are noted, whether footage, reels or both. Nonetheless, Micheaux did not always show what had been approved. More than any other commercial producer perhaps, Micheaux recognized that censorship was an ideological issue.

Unless a film is extant, we are dependent on newspaper accounts for cast lists. There one finds a person's name given in various forms, often with multiple spellings. And names sometimes changed over time. A. B. DeComathiere eventually went by the name of A. B. Comathiere, though his names had many variant spellings (De Comathiere, DeComatheirs, Comatheire, and so on). In a few cases we depend on secondary sources (primarily Henry T. Sampson's *Blacks in Black and White*) and indicate this with the author's name in brackets. Under the headings "production dates" and "locations," we indicate the time and place—when and where a film was shot. Micheaux did not necessarily release films in the order they were shot. Moreover, some of his films, made in the early 1920s, were probably shot in Roanoke, Virginia, over a period of time. With a very substantial gap between the initial production of a film and its release (one year or even more in some cases), the processes of production and post-production were protracted and complicated. When Micheaux adapted (or claimed to adapt) a film from another source, we provide this antecedent under the "source" heading. This includes novels Micheaux said he had written himself but were apparently never published (or perhaps never even realized). Other sources noted in advertisements or publicity have yet to be identified and may have never existed. On the other hand, Micheaux often appropriated and engaged material without formal acknowledgment. The use of Nan Bagby Stephens's play *Roseanne* (1923) in *Body and Soul* (1925) is one example, though whether it is an adaptation or something else can be debated.

Descriptions of each Micheaux film come from various primary source documents of the period. Rather than try to synthesize them into a seamless narrative, we simply quote from multiple sources and leave it to the reader to construct a more or less coherent, more or less complete story from them. When a film is extant, we provide its archival sources. When not, the archive spot is left open, hoping our collective scholarship will generate more work in the area and new "finds." For each picture in the filmography, we list as many venues and dates for exhibition as we can. In many cases, this establishes a useful pattern that allows us to judge a production's commercial history. In one area we ask the reader's forbearance: to provide an accurate and/or consistent name for a theater is often impossible. Names for theaters were unstable and varied. "The New Dunbar" and "the Dunbar" were monikers that coexisted for the same Baltimore theater; whether it was the Vendome Theat*er* or the Vendome Theat*re* in Chicago is a pointless speculation, since commentary and advertisements oscillated between the two. A general shift in spelling from "Theater" to "Theatre" can be traced in the pages of the *Chicago Defender* over the course of 1920, but the standard then reverts to "Theater" by late 1922.

African-American newspapers are the single most important source for information on Micheaux's films, so the citations under the "press" heading provide the basis for the information we have incorporated into each entry. Finally, the note sections offer a variety of information relevant to each film, including information on censorship and illustrations of Micheaux's silent films in pre-1997 publications. The results, we believe, are a significantly clearer overview of Micheaux's film activities between 1919 and 1931.

1) *The Homesteader* (1919)

©No reg. **Length:** 8,000 ft. (8 reels).
Cast: Charles D. Lucas (Jean Baptiste, the homesteader), Iris Hall (Agnes Stewart), Charles S. Moore (Jack Stewart, Agnes's father), Evelyn Preer (Orlean, Baptiste's wife), Inez Smith (Ethel), Vernon S. Duncan (N. Justine McCarthy), Trevy Wood (Glavis, Ethel's husband), William George (Bill Prescott, Agnes's white lover).
Production dates: Fall 1918.
Locations: Tripp County & Gregory County, South Dakota; Ebony Studio, Chicago.
Source: Oscar Micheaux's novel *The Homesteader* (1917).
Description: "The Homesteader" involves six principal characters the leading one being Jean Baptiste, the Homesteader far off in the Dakotas, living where he alone was black. In him we have the embodiment of strength, courage and conviction. To this wilderness came in time Jack Stewart, a Scotchman, with his motherless daughter Agnes. In Agnes, Baptiste meets the girl of his dreams, only to make a discovery in the same instance upon which the story has its first climax.

But Agnes didn't know that she was not white. Peculiar fate threw her in the company of the Homesteader, and their love, forbidden by the custom of the country, is the most appealing and idealistic ever created. Of how Baptiste sacrificed the love of this girl of his dreams, went back to his own people, marrying the daughter of a preacher, and the circumstances that came of it, marks the second epoch in the development of the story.

In the case of N. Justine McCarthy the author has done a work that is typical of our life today, and the whole public in any way acquainted with the present race minister must appreciate it—narrow, spiteful, envious. McCarthy is the very embodiment of vanity, deceit and hypocrisy. He really admired the marriage his daughter had made—was proud of it. He spoke of the "rich" young man she had married, eulogized him to the highest—but Baptiste did not understand that McCarthy, to be satisfied, was in the habit of having people praise him. This Baptiste forgot in the first to do; in the second, he was not of the temperament to do it, and upon this failure grew the tragedy of a marriage and the happiness of McCarthy's daughter, Orlean, a sweet girl, kind and good, but, like her mother, without the strength of her convictions.

Of how then Baptiste was sacrificed to the altar of McCarthy's hatred and vanity; of how Orlean failed him at those crucial moments; of how Ethel, her sister, like her father, possessed with all the evil a woman is capable of, forces her weak-kneed husband, Glavis, to assist her and her father in their persecution of Baptiste; and then, of how in the end Orlean, made insane by the evil she had been the innocent cause of, rights a wrong, bringing Baptiste back to his land. He comes back to the girl he has discovered the truth about and the story has a beautiful ending after a life of storm and misery ("The Homesteader," *Chicago Defender,* 22 February 1919, 14).

Archive:

Screenings: 20–23 February 1919, 8th Regiment Armory, Chicago (premiere); 3–5 March 1919, Hammond & Sons Vendome Theater, Chicago; 6 March 1919, Dooley's Atlas Theater, Chicago; 7–8 March 1919, Pickford Theater, Chicago; 2–8 March 1919, New Centre Theater, Kansas City, Mo.; 12–15 March, Crawford Theater, Wichita, Kan.; 16 March 1919, Convention Hall, Kansas City, Mo.; 18–19 March 1919, Lyceum Theater, St. Joseph, Mo.; 24–29 March 1919, The Grand, Topeka, Kan.; 30 March–2 April 1919, Brandeis Theater, Omaha, Neb.; 11 April 1919, States Theater, Chicago; 9 May 1919, Star Theater, Florence, Ala.; 27–28 May, Bijou Theater, Nashville, Tenn.; 30 May 1919, Fields Theater, Sheffield, Ala.; 31 May–2 June 1919, Sykes Theater, Decatur, Ala.; 3–4 June 1919, Grand, Chattanooga, Tenn.; 2–4 June 1919, Metro Theater, Memphis, Tenn.; 5–7 June 1919, Champion Theater, Birmingham, Ala.; 9 June 1919, Dixie Theater, Bessemer, Ala.; 14–15 June 1919, Pike Theater, Mobile, Ala.; 17–18 June 1919, Pekin Theater, Montgomery, Ala.; 20–21 June 1919, Shreveport, La.; 22–29 June 1919, Pythias Temple Theater, New Orleans; 26 June 1919, Alexandria, La.; 27 June 1919, Monroe, La.; 28 June 1919, Baton Rouge, La.; 5–7 July 1919, Atlas Theater, Spartenberg, S.C.; 8–9 July 1919, New Lincoln Theater, Columbia, S.C.; 12 July 1919, Gem Theater, Reidsville, N.C.; 10–12 July 1919, Auditorium Theater, Atlanta, Ga.; 20 September 1921, The Carey, Baltimore; 27 September 1921, Dunbar Theatre, Baltimore.

Press: Advertisement and "The Homesteader," *Chicago Defender,* 22 February 1919, 14; Advertisements and "The Homesteader," *Chicago Defender,* 1 March 1919, 11, 12, and 13; "Last Chance," *Chicago Defender,* 5 April 1919, 8; Advertisement, *Chicago Defender,* 5 April 1919, 9; Advertisement, *Chicago Defender,* 31 May 1919, 9; Advertisement, Baltimore *Afro-American,* 16 September 1921, 4; Advertisement, Baltimore *Afro-American,* 23 September 1921, 4; Evelyn Preer, "Evelyn Preer Nearly Drowned in Realistic Movie Scene," *Pittsburgh Courier,* 11 June 1927, 1B.

Note: The premiere of *The Homesteader* in the 8th Regiment Armory came as that regiment, known as the "Black Devils," returned to Chicago from Europe. Music was played by Byron Bros.' Celebrated Symphony Orchestra, while "the Race's Greatest Tenor," George R. Garner, Jr., sang at each performance. David B. Peyton provided "original music settings." Chicago Censors viewed the film on 20 February 1919 and rejected it for "a tendency to disturb the public peace." Reviewed again on the following day, they ordered substantial cuts, including the complete elimination of the characters Orlean and Ethel. It was subsequently advertised as "Passed by the Censor Board Despite the Protests of Three Chicago Ministers Who Claimed That It Was Based Upon the Supposed Hypocritical Actions of a Prominent Colored Preacher of This City" (Advertisement, *Chicago Defender*, 1 March 1919, 11). The film was advertised as 7 reels (7 acts) when shown in Baltimore in September 1921. The film received a New York State license on 30 September 1922. An advertisement and publicity still are in Sampson, *Blacks in Black and White*, 150 and 253; still in Cripps, *Slow Fade to Black*, 185.

2) [8TH REGIMENT IN CHICAGO] (1919)

© No reg.   *Length:* 1 reel.
Cast: 8th Regiment, 370th Infantry.
Production dates: Between 17 and 19 February 1919.
Locations: Chicago.
Source:
Description: SEE THEM IN THEIR OWN ARMORY. Motion pictures of the return of the "victorious" Eighth, the "Black Devils" who sent the Kaiser into oblivion.

   Note.—The day was dark and dreary and snow was falling the day this Great Regiment returned. To secure clear, bright and recognizable Motion Pictures requires sunlight. The pictures you may have seen, and which were made the day the regiment returned, are dark and obscure. WE SENT OUT CAMERA MAN AND DIRECTOR TO GRANT, where bright, clear pictures of each company and their officers were taken, so YOU CAN SEE AND RECOGNIZE THEM. See, therefore the REAL pictures of your heroes, which are shown only in their own armory this week (Advertisement, *Chicago Defender*, 22 February 1919, 14).
Archive:
Screenings: 20–23 February 1919, 8th Regiment Armory, Chicago.
Press: Advertisement and "The Homesteader," *Chicago Defender*, 22 February 1919, 14.
Note: Micheaux's authorship is uncertain; possibly the 8th Regiment Armory took the footage.

3) WITHIN OUR GATES (1920)

©No reg.   *Length:* 8,000 ft. (8 reels)/7 reels.
Cast: Evelyn Preer (Sylvia Landry), William Starks (Jasper Landry), Mattie Edwards (Jasper Landry's wife), Grant Edwards (Emil Landry), E. G. Tatum (Eph or Efrem, Girdlestone's faithful servant), Jack Chenault (Larry Prichard), S. T. Jacks (Reverend Wilson Jacobs), Grant Gorman (Armand Girdlestone), Flo Clements (Alma Prichard), Jimmie Cook, Charles D. Lucas (Dr. V. Vivian), Ralph Johnson (Philip Girdlestone), James D. Ruffin (Conrad Drebert), Bernice Ladd (Mrs. Geraldine Stratton), Mrs. Evelyn (Mrs. Elena Warwick), William Smith (Philip Gentry, detective), LaFont Harris (Emil as a young adult).
Production dates: 1919.
Locations: Capitol City Studios, Chicago; Chicago area.
Source:

Description: This is the picture that it required two solid months to get by the Censor Board, and it is the claim of the author and producer that while it is a bit radical, it is withal the biggest protest against Race prejudice, lynching and "concubinage" that was ever written or filmed and that there are more thrills and gripping, holding moments than was ever seen in any individual production.

The scenes of this story are laid in the South, where the outrages are most predominant, and the author has not minced words in presenting the facts as they really exist. To give you a slight idea of what the story is like, we publish the following paragraph, taken from the middle part of the scenario:

"It was in late September in Mississippi: the cotton had been picked, ginned, baled and delivered. There was to be a picnic and night festival, and on the preceding afternoon, Jasper Landry, with a statement of account, prepared by his daughter Sylvia, who was 'going away to school,' went to the plantation offices of Philip Girdlestone, white, to make a settlement. Now there was a worthless, unlikable fellow named Eph. He was known as a spreader of 'news,' who had told Girdlestone something that had fanned the flame of hatred in his breast against Landry. Eph, secreted to peep upon the controversy which he had planned, turned away to giggle when a shot rent the air. He whirled—and saw Girdlestone falling to the floor, mortally wounded, with Landry standing over him holding a smoking revolver. So away went Eph with a greater tale than ever to tell."

People interested in the welfare of the Race cannot afford to miss seeing this great production and remember, it TELLS IT ALL ("Within Our Gates," *Chicago Defender*, 17 January 1920, 6).

The scenes of this story are laid in the South amongst our people.

It was in late September, the cotton had been picked, ginned, baled and delivered and Jasper Landry, a cropper, had prospered, clearing a nice balance according to statement of account prepared by his adopted daughter, Sylvia, who had "been off to school."

In the same community dwelt "Eph" the "tattle-tale," making no effort toward his own betterment, but who made it his business to "spread news." Going to Girdlestone, wealthy planter, aristocrat and owner of everything for miles around, "Eph" told him that Landry was "buying land," "owned a mule," and was "edicatin'" their children and was therefore "gittin' sma't." "Now day," said he, "am keepin' books, and when he comes to settle, ain' gwine to take yo' figgers, but will bring a bill."

Landry came, "bringin' his bill." Eph secreted to "peep" upon the mischief he had made, watched. There arose a dispute. Eph turned his head away to giggle; when suddenly a shot rang out. Eph whirled and saw Girdlestone, falling to the floor mortally wounded—and Landry standing over him holding a smoking revolver.

What Happened is told in seven reels ("'Within Our Gates' at Putnam, B'klyn," *New York Age*, 17 July 1920, 6).

Archive: Library of Congress, United States; La Filmoteca Española, Spain.

Screenings: 12–17 January 1920, Hammond's Vendome Theater, Chicago; 18–22 January 1920, Pendleton Theater, St. Louis, Mo.; 19 January 1920, Pekin Theater, Montgomery, Ala.; 20 January 1920, Pike Theater, Mobile, Ala.; 21 January 1920, Pekin Theater, Springfield, Ill.; 21–22 January 1920, Auditorium Theater, Atlanta, Ga.; 26 January–1 February 1920, E. B. Dudley's Vaudette Theater, Detroit; 29–31 January 1920, Hammond's Pickford Theater, Chicago; 1–4 February 1920, Temple Theater, New Orleans; 2–5 February 1920, Atlas Theater, Chicago (restored version); 24 February 1920, States Theater, Chicago; 11–13

March 1920, New Rainbow Theatre, Baltimore; 23–24 March 1920, Dunbar Theatre, Baltimore; 20 January 1920, Rex Theatre, Durham, N.C.; 21 January 1921, Reidsville, N.C.; 21–22 January 1920, Atlas Theatre, Spartensburg, S.C.; 23–24 January 1920, Community Center, Charlotte, N.C.; 27–28 January 1920 Star Theatre, Asheville, N.C.; 29 January 1920, Dixie Theatre, Greenwood, S.C.; 30–31 January 1920, Lincoln Theatre, Columbia, S.C.; 3 February 1920, Palmetto Theatre, Orangeburg, S.C.; 4 February 1920, Globe Theatre, Wilson, N.C.; 6 February 1920, Rex Theatre, Goldsboro, N.C.; 9 February 1920, Globe Theatre, New Bern, N.C.; 10 February 1920, Victoria Theatre, Washington, N.C.; 11 February 1920, Palace Theatre, Kingston, N.C.; 17–18 February 1920, Pekin Theatre, Brunswick, Ga.; 20 February 1920, Crystal Theatre, Dublin, Ga.; 23–24 February 1920, Dixie Theatre, Sandersville, Ga.; 26 February 1920, Lennox Theatre, Augusta, Ga.; 28 February 1920, 81 Theatre, Atlanta, Ga.; 1 March 1920, Morton Star Theatre, Athens, Ga.; 2 March 1920, Douglas Theatre #2, Macon, Ga.; 14 March 1920, Dream Theatre, Columbus, Ga.; 15 March 1920, Gem Theatre, Fort Valley, Ga.; 16 March 1920, Elite Theatre, Cordele, Ga.; 17 March 1920, Opera House, Americus, Ga.; 19–20 March 1920, Star Theatre, Waycross, Ga.; 12–13 April 1920, Schenley Theater, Pittsburgh; 13–16 May 1920, Lincoln Theatre, New York City; 19–25 July 1920, Putnam Theatre, Brooklyn; 12–13 May 1922, Dunbar Theater, Savannah, Ga.

Press: Advertisement and "Within Our Gates," *Chicago Defender,* 10 January 1920, 6; Advertisement, "Within Our Gates," and "Great Lesson," *Chicago Defender,* 17 January 1920, 6; Advertisements, *Chicago Defender,* 17 January 1920, 6 and 7; Advertisement, "Within Our Gates," and "The Vaudette," *Chicago Defender,* 24 January 1920, 7; Advertisements and "Within Our Gates," *Chicago Defender,* 31 January 1920, 8; "Within Our Gates," *Chicago Defender,* 21 February 1920, 6; Advertisement, Baltimore *Afro-American,* 5 March 1920, 8; Advertisement, Baltimore *Afro-American,* 12 March 1920, 2; Advertisements, Baltimore *Afro-American,* 19 March 1920, 6; Advertisement, *Chicago Defender,* 10 April 1920, 8; Advertisement, *New York Age,* 15 May 1920, 6; "'Within Our Gates' at Putnam, B'klyn," *New York Age,* 17 July 1920, 6; "Motion Picture News," *Chicago Defender,* 20 May 1922, 7; Evelyn Preer, "My Thrills in the Movies," *Pittsburgh Courier,* 18 June 1927, 2B.

Note: Sometimes given the full title of *Within Our Gates: A Story of the Negro* (Advertisement, Baltimore *Afro-American,* 19 March 1920, 6). According to Evelyn Preer, "the entire picture was filmed in Chicago" ("My Thrills in the Movies," *Pittsburgh Courier,* 18 June 1927, 2B). When *Within Our Gates* was first screened in Chicago, censors forced the removal of 1,200 feet of film. They were subsequently restored at the end of January (Advertisement, *Chicago Defender,* 31 January 1920, 8). At the Vendome premiere, the price was 30¢ for adults, 15¢ for children; and Tates Symphony Orchestra provided the musical accompaniment. Landry's first name tended to change in publicity material. It was given as Joseph in "Within Our Gates," *Chicago Defender,* 17 January 1920, 6. A subplot involving Sylvia Landry and Emil as a young adult (played by LaFont Harris), not in the extant version of the film, was featured in advertisements appearing in the Baltimore *Afro-American* (12 March 1920, 2). The name Girdlestone comes from newspaper publicity; it is spelled Gridlestone in the 35mm print and video circulated by the Library of Congress. Screening dates (January–March) for the film in North Carolina, South Carolina, and Georgia are from a Micheaux Ledger page, African Diaspora Images; the year is presumed to be 1920. Publicity still in Sampson, *Blacks in Black and White,* 278; advertising leaflet in Cripps, *Slow Fade to Black,* 187; publicity still in Cripps, *Black Film as Genre,* 28.

GOING ABROAD

Noted Motion Picture Producer Soon Sails for Europe

Oscar Micheaux, author and producer of "The Homesteader" and "Within Our Gates," will be in Europe 30 days from now. He is going abroad to arrange world distribution of his "Within Our Gates" and a series of new Racial features which he will produce upon his return. The first of these will be "The Brand of Cain," which he has just completed in book form, and which will be published simultaneously with the release of the picture. Mr. Micheaux states that plans are all complete for the financing of these productions, which will be the greatest achievement ever made by the Race.

"The appreciation my people have shown my maiden efforts convinces me that they want Racial photoplays, depicting Racial life, and to that task I have consecrated my mind and efforts" (*Chicago Defender,* 31 January 1920, 8).

PRODUCER RETURNS

BUSY MAKING NEW PRODUCTIONS WHICH WILL APPEAR SOON

Oscar Micheaux, the prominent moving picture producer, who recently returned to the city after extensive travelling, during which he has written a series of features as well as comedies, has already started the production of a new picture.

During his absence Mr. Micheaux contracted with some of the most prominent and widely known actors and actresses of the Race; their names and photos will appear from time to time in these columns. He reports great activity in the building of new picture theaters by and for the Race in the East and South and the subsequent demand for more and better photoplays acted by Racial casts from stories concerning the lives of our people. The first new production will be ready about July 1 (*Chicago Defender,* 29 May 1920, 7).

4) *The Brute* (1920)

© No reg.   *Length:* 8,000 ft. (8 reels)/7,000 ft.

Cast: Evelyn Preer (Mildred, the mistreated wife), A. B. DeComathiere ("Bull" Magee, the brute), Susie Sutton (Aunt Clara), Lawrence Chenault (Herbert Lanyon, the lover), Alice Gorgas (the vamp), Sam Langford and Marty Cutler (prizefighters), E. G. Tatum, [Laura Bowman, Mattie Edwards, Virgil Williams, Flo Clements, Louis Schooler, Henry Plater, Al Gaines—Sampson, *Blacks in Black and White,* 241].

Production dates: June–July 1920.

Locations: Chicago.

Source:

Description: The Story of a Beautiful and Tender Girl in the Toils of a Shrewd Gambler and Boss of the Underworld, Bull McGee, Whose Creed is 'TO MAKE A WOMAN LOVE YOU, KNOCK HER DOWN' (Advertisement, *Chicago Defender,* 14 August 1920, 4).

They were engaged when he went across the seas in search of gold—and then the papers reported his ship wrecked and all on board lost. After that, through sordid influences, she had fallen into the web of "Bull" McGee, the power in the underworld; and then Herbert Lanyon returned, but she was lost to him forever(?) (Advertisement, *Chicago Defender,* 14 August 1920, 4).

Mr. Micheaux has written something that carries much more than an ordinary moral lesson.

It tells of the entering, through his money, of an underworld character into the life of an innocent girl; it shows the manner in which he gains his point by playing upon the cupidity of the girl's aunt and guardian, whose ambition to see the girl do well in the matrimonial field blinds her to all else until it is too late. What the girl suffers and the manner in which the man's brutal treatment of her is avenged by the aunt forms the most interesting part of the tale, although there is a great prize fight, introducing Sam Langford and Marty Cutler, and a world of comedy and a screaming character ("Great Picture," *Chicago Defender,* 28 August 1920, 4).

So far as the story which "The Brute" unfolds, it is neither original nor any too pleasing to those of us who desire to see the better side of a Negro life portrayed. A dive where colored men and women congregate to gamble, the susceptibility of a devoted aunt who takes money from a dive keeper seeking the hand of a niece, a detailed exhibition of a crap game in which a woman is the central figure, are included in some of the important scenes. As I looked at the picture I was reminded of the attitude of the daily press, which magnifies our vices and minimizes our virtues . . . .

There is much to commend in Oscar Micheaux's latest photoplay. It is a very creditable endeavor in many respects. There is one feature that is bound to make the picture a success—the prize fight in which Sam Langford defeats Marty Cutler. This is the one big scene and it is a genuine thriller. When Langford floors Cutler with a knockout wallop with his mighty right, my such noise from the audience! Men, women and children get excited as if at a real fight and cheer. Mr. Micheaux showed rare judgment in putting on this scene (Lester A. Walton, "Sam Langford's Wallop Makes 'The Brute' A Screen Success," *New York Age,* 18 September 1920, 6).

The story of a gambler posing as a gentleman and winning over the girl he desires by giving money to her aunt who believes him true. He later proves a brute. See how brutes are to be handled. See the great gambling den where a fight is framed for the championship of the world. Does Sam Langford fake the fight? Come and see.

This picture broke all records in New York, Philadelphia and Chicago (Advertisement, Baltimore *Afro-American,* 1 October 1920, 4).

Archive:

Screenings: 16–20 August 1920, Hammond's Vendome Theatre, Chicago; 16–20 August 1920, E. B. Dudley's Vaudette Theatre, Detroit; 29–30 August 1920, Western Theater, Chicago; 7–9 September 1920, Dooley's Atlas Theatre, Chicago; 13–19 September 1920, Lafayette Theatre, New York City; 17–18 September 1920, Hammond's Phoenix Theatre, Chicago; 21–22 September 1920, Dooley's Atlas Theatre, Chicago; 27–28 September 1920, Elba Theatre, Chicago; 5–9 October 1920, New Rainbow Theatre, Baltimore; 12–13 October 1920, Dunbar Theatre, Baltimore; November 1920, Omaha; 3 April 1921, Gilmor Theatre, Baltimore; 30 September–1 October 1921, American Theatre, Baltimore; 10–11 October 1921, The Carey, Baltimore; 18 October 1921, Dunbar Theatre, Baltimore; 15 January 1922, The Rialto, Johnson, Tenn.; 3 January 1925, Dunbar Theatre, Baltimore; 7 January 1925, The Carey, Baltimore.

Press: Advertisement, *Chicago Defender,* 10 July 1920, 7; Advertisement, "Big Feature" and "The Brute," *Chicago Defender,* 14 August 1920, 4; Advertisement, *Chicago Defender,* 14 August 1920, 5; Advertisement and "The Vendome," *Chicago Whip,* 21 August 1920, 3; "Great Picture," *Chicago Defender,* 28 August 1920, 4; "The Brute," *Chicago Defender,* 28 August 1920, 5; Advertisement and "The Brute," *Chicago Defender,* 4 September 1920, 4; Advertisement and "'The Brute,' Photoplay, at Lafayette," *New York Age*, 11 September 1920, 6; Lester A. Walton, "Sam Langford's Wallop Makes 'The Brute' A Screen Success," *New York Age*, 18 September 1920, 6; Advertisements, *Chicago Defender*, 18 September 1920, 4; "The Brute," *Chicago Defender*, 25 September 1920, 4; Advertisement, Baltimore *Afro-American*, 1 October 1920, 4; Advertisement and "Coming to Rainbow Theatre," Baltimore *Afro-American*, 1 October 1920, 5; Advertisement, Baltimore *Afro-American*, 8 October 1920, 5; Advertisement, Baltimore *Afro-American*, 1 April 1921, 5; "American," Baltimore *Afro-American*, 23 September 1921, 4; Advertisement, Baltimore *Afro-American*, 7 October 1921, 5; Advertisement, Baltimore *Afro-American*, 14 October 1921, 4; "Here and There," Baltimore *Afro-American*, 3 February 1922, 11; D. Ireland Thomas, "Motion Picture News," *Chicago Defender*, 22 March 1924, 7A; Advertisement, Baltimore *Afro-American*, 27 December 1924, 6; "Are Race Pictures a Failure," *Chicago Defender*, 27 December 1924, 8A; Advertisement, Baltimore *Afro-American*, 3 January 1925, 7; Evelyn Preer, "My Thrills in the Movies," *Pittsburgh Courier*, 18 June 1927, 8.

Note: Sometimes given the title *The Brute: The Story of a Gambler* (Advertisement, Baltimore *Afro-American*, 8 October 1920, 5). The fight between Sam Langford and Marty Cutler was staged at the Royal Gardens, 459 East 31st Street in Chicago on Thursday evening, July 8th. Readers of the *Chicago Defender* were encouraged to be movie extras: "See Yourself in the Movies by Being a Spectator at the Ringside During This Mighty Battle" (Advertisement, *Chicago Defender*, 10 July 1920, 7). Sam Langford fought Sam McVey in East Chicago on 15 August 1920, drawing 10,000 fans ("Langford and McVey Draw Big House," *Chicago Defender*, 21 August 1920, 6). The fight was uneventful, but the *Chicago Defender* awarded the fight to Langford. The next day, *The Brute* had its joint premiere at Hammond's Vendome Theatre in Chicago and E. B. Dudley's Vaudette Theatre in Detroit. Promotional information for this film in the *New York Age* announced that Evelyn Preer was about to join the Lafayette Players (11 September 1920, 6). A play of the same title by Frederick Arnold Kummer had its Broadway premiere 8 October 1912 (*New York Times*, 9 October 1912, 13). A film adaptation of Kummer's *The Brute* was released by Famous Players Film Company in 1914. The play, which was performed by the Lafayette Players in New York and Chicago around the time that Micheaux's film was released, had a different story line ("The Brute," *Chicago Defender*, 3 January 1920, 6). According to Henry T. Sampson, Micheaux's *The Brute* was shown in Sweden as *Mr. Bull Magee* (*Blacks in Black and White*, 241). Chicago Censors reviewed a 7,000-foot print of *The Brute* on 9 August 1920 and demanded selected edits. Advertisement and still in Sampson, *Blacks in Black and White*, 153 and 242; still in Cripps, *Slow Fade to Black*, 190.

GONE EAST

Iris Hall, of the Perrin-Henderson Co., left this week for New York, where she will be starred in the forthcoming film production, "Wilderness Trail." Miss Hall played a prominent part in "The Homesteader," which had such a successful career. Mail will reach her if addressed to 143 West 140th Street, New York, N.Y. (*Chicago Defender*, 18 September 1920, 4).

5) THE SYMBOL OF THE UNCONQUERED (1920)

© No reg.   **Length:** 8,000 ft. (8 reels)/7,000 ft. (7 reels).

Cast: Iris Hall (Evon Mason), Walker Thompson (Hugh Van Allen), Lawrence Chenault

(Jefferson Driscoll), George Catlin (Dick Mason), Edward E. King (Tom Cutschawl), Jim Burris, Mattie V. Wilkes (Driscoll's mother), E. G. Tatum (Abraham), Leigh "Lee" Whipper (Tugi Boj, Indian Fakir), James Burroughs, [Edward Fraction (Peter Kaden), Lena L. Loach (Christina)—Sampson, *Blacks in Black and White*, 271].

Production dates: Fall 1920.

Locations: New York.

Source: Elements of the story can be found in Oscar Micheaux's novel *The Homesteader* (1917).

Description: Hugh Van Allen, a young Race man, goes into the great Northwest, where fences were unpopular, to seek his fortune. There he meets Evon Mason, a young lady of his own Race, from Selma, Ala. The beautiful girl is very light complected and is naturally mistaken for a white person by Van Allen. In the same neighborhood dwelt Tom Cutschawl, formerly of the South, and prejudiced to a degree. There also [is] Jefferson Driscoll, "passing" for white, who had vowed to make it hard for all Race people with whom he came in contact, owning to a love affair in his youthful days and to conceal his real nationality. These two conspire, along with others, to drive Van Allen and the girl from the country.

The manner in which they go about it and the romance between the objects of their machinations makes it one of the most interesting and thrilling pictures released this season ("The Vaudette," *Chicago Defender*, 27 November 1920, 5).

Dick Mason, an aged Negro who had taken a homestead in the wilds of the great Northwest, returns to his former home in the South where he dies, leaving the claim to his granddaughter and the last of his kin, Evon Mason, a beautiful quadroon, who later goes therewith to make proof on the same. Arriving in Oristown, she proceeds to the little hotel wherein one Jefferson Driscoll, night clerk and a Negro but masquerading as white, refuses her accommodations. Hungry, tired, and discouraged, she wanders into the forest; a storm comes up, she becomes lost and is picked up in a miserable condition the next morning by Hugh Van Allen, colored, and a prospector, whom she had met on the street the afternoon before, but who, because he had and was still, unknown to her, mistaking her for white, is merely courteous, while with her—she had fallen in love with him at first sight. . . . When later Van Allen discovered how Driscoll had treated her, he goes and beats that one up—result, to get even, Driscoll schemes and succeeds in selling Van Allen what he, Driscoll, thought to be a tract of the most worthless land in the country. When he discovered later that those selfsame lands were underlaid with a sea of oil and valuable beyond description, and he was unable to persuade Van Allen to sell them back to him, in league with a Negro hating Squawman, he launches a plot to drive Van Allen off the lands and out of the country by recourse to the insidious———. At the hour of midnight, robed in white, like ghosts, and with fiery torches, they ride down on Van Allen. In the meantime, Evon, who had gotten word of the plot, dashes into the village and gets the settlers, who ride with her to Van Allen's rescue. In due time oil is discovered on Van Allen's land, he becomes a millionaire—and then of how Evon came back into his life and he discovered at last that she was of his own blood, makes up one of the most stirring, yet sweetest love stories ever screened ("Synopsis 'The Symbol of the Unconquered'," *Philadelphia Tribune*, 1 January 1921, 6).

Archive: Museum of Modern Art, United States; Cinémathèque Royale, Belgium.

Screenings: 29 November–5 December 1920, E. B. Dudley's Vaudette Theater, Detroit (premiere); 27 December 1920–2 January 1921, Lafayette Theatre, New York City; [29] December 1920–1 January 1921, Attucks Theatre, Norfolk, Va.; 3–8 January 1921, Dunbar Theatre, Philadelphia; 3–8 January 1921, Rainbow Theatre, Baltimore; 10–15 January 1921,

Putnam Theater, Brooklyn; 10–15 January 1921, Hammond's Vendome Theatre, Chicago; 17–22 January 1921, Palace Theatre, Memphis; 25–27 January 1921, Olympia Theatre, Philadelphia; 27–29 January 1921, Pickford Theater, Chicago; 9 February 1921, Gem Theatre, Knoxville, Tenn.; 5–7 March 1921, New Dixie Theater, Bessemer, Ala.; 7–12 March 1921, Lincoln Theater, Cincinnati; 14–16 March 1921, New Lincoln Theater, Louisville, Ky.; 17–19 March 1921, Lyric Theater, New Orleans; 28 March 1921, Liberty Theater, Berkley, Va.; 29–31 March 1921, Pike Theater, Mobile, Ala.; 31 March–1 April 1921, Lincoln Theater, Alexandria, Va.; 19–20 April 1921, Frolic Theater, Birmingham, Ala.; 20–21 April 1921, Pekin Theater, Montgomery, Ala.; ca. 22 May 1921 (one day), States Theatre, Chicago; ca. 24 May 1921 (one day), Owl Theatre, Chicago; May 1921 (three days), Frolic Theatre, Jacksonville, Fla.; 12–14 September 1921, American Theatre, Baltimore; 19–20 September 1921, Dunbar Theatre, Baltimore; 31 October 1921, The Carey, Baltimore; 22 May 1924, Argonne Theatre, Baltimore; 4–5 April 1926, Franklin Theatre, New York City.

Press: Advertisement and "The Vaudette," *Chicago Defender,* 20 November 1920, 6; "The Vaudette," *Chicago Defender,* 27 November 1920, 5; Advertisement and "Ku Klux Klan Put to Rout in Photoplay To Be Shown at Lafayette," *New York Age,* 25 December 1920, 6; Advertisement, Baltimore *Afro-American,* 31 December 1920, 4; "'The Symbol of the Unconquered' and Musical Program Unique Lafayette Bill," *New York Age,* 1 January 1921, 6; "Attucks to Present Many Features Next Week," *Norfolk Journal and Guide,* 1 January 1921, 8; Advertisement, *Chicago Defender,* 1 January 1921, 5; Advertisement, *Philadelphia Tribune,* 1 January 1921, 4; "Synopsis 'The Symbol of the Unconquered,'" *Philadelphia Tribune,* 1 January 1921, 6; "The Dunbar Theatre," *Philadelphia Tribune,* 8 January 1921, 10; "Micheaux Film," *Chicago Defender,* 8 January 1921, 4; Advertisement, *Chicago Defender,* 8 January 1921, 5; "Another Oscar Micheaux Picture," *Chicago Whip,* 8 January 1921, 3; Advertisement and "Vaudeville and Movie Reviews," *Chicago Whip,* 15 January 1921, 3; Advertisement, *Chicago Defender,* 15 January 1921, 5; Advertisement, *Chicago Defender,* 22 January 1921, 4; Advertisement, *Philadelphia Tribune,* 22 January 1921, 4; Advertisement, *Chicago Defender,* 5 February 1921, 4; "The Week's Movies," *Chicago Defender,* 28 May 1921, 6; *The Competitor* (Pittsburgh), January/February 1921, 61 (clipping, Micheaux file, Black Film Center/Archive at Indiana University); Advertisement, Baltimore *Afro-American,* 9 September 1921, 4; Advertisement, Baltimore *Afro-American,* 16 September 1921, 4; Advertisement, Baltimore *Afro-American,* 28 October 1921, 4; Advertisement, Baltimore *Afro-American,* 16 May 1924, 4; Advertisement, *New York Amsterdam News,* 31 March 1926, 5.

Note: Some advertisements and reference works shorten the title to *Symbol of the Unconquered.* The film's working title was *The Wilderness Trail,* according to Micheaux's letters in the George P. Johnson Collection. The character of Evon Mason was listed as Eva and Driscoll as Drescola in one advertisement (Baltimore *Afro-American,* 28 October 1921, 4). Leigh Whipper's name appeared in various forms in advertisements, often as Lee Whipper and at least once as Lee Whipple (Baltimore *African American,* 31 December 1921, 4). James Burroughs as a cast member, according to *Chicago Whip,* 15 January 1921, 3. Walker Thompson died on 19 September 1922 at the age of 34 ("Actor Dead," *Chicago Defender,* 23 September 1922, 7). James Burris died 3 June 1923 at the age of 49 ("'Jim' Burris Died at Dudley's Country Home," *New York Age,* 16 June 1923, 6). Mattie V. Wilkes died on 6 July 1927 ("Theatrical Stars Mourn Mattie V. Wilkes' Demise," *New York Amsterdam News,* 13 July 1927, 1–2). The film was sometimes said to be only 7 reels ("The Vaudette," *Chicago Defender,* 27 November 1920, 5; Advertisement, Baltimore *Afro-American,* 28 October 1921, 4). On 18 November 1920, Chicago Censors reviewed a 7,000-foot version of the film and demanded selected cuts, particularly scenes related to interracial romance or lust. The extent to which the extant version of this film is incomplete is underscored by the following comments by Chicago Film Censors, who ruled:

Cut Outs—Reel II Subtitle—ending: "That they had often lynched his kind for a smaller offense . . . talking to a white girl on street." Cut all views of colored man holding white girl's hand in [love] scenes. Reel III Subtitle relating to sign of Britain married to young lady of color—"No visitors—no visiting." All scenes of Britain killing & talking to his colored wife. Reel 4 All scenes of Englishman looking at colored girl after subtitle "strongly desirous." "Why should you worry, he is nothing but a Negro." Change subtitle "Old Darkeys" to "Old Negro's [sic]."

6) *THE GUNSAULUS MYSTERY* (1921)

© No reg.   *Length:* 7,000 ft. (7 reels).

Cast: Evelyn Preer (Ida May Gilpin), Lawrence Chenault (Anthony Brisbane), Mattie V. Wilkes, Ed "Dick" Abrams (Sidney Wyeth), Louis DeBulger (Lem Hopkins), Bessye Bearden, Ethel Williams, Edward "Eddie" Brown, Ethel Watts, E. G. Tatum, and Miss Harris, [Mabel Young, Hattie Christian, W. D. Sindle, George Russell, Alex Kroll—Sampson, *Blacks in Black and White,* 331].

Production dates: [early 1921.]

Locations: New York studios.

Source: The Leo Frank lynching case and elements of Oscar Micheaux's novel *The Forged Note: A Romance of the Darker Races* (1915).

Description: The piece is an interesting story built around a West Indian young man, who comes to America with his literary abilities, writes a book and starts out to sell them from door to door. In his travels many adventures he encounters, and finally he looms up as the prosecutor of the man who commits a murder and convicts him ("The Gunsualus [sic] Mystery," *Chicago Whip,* 7 May 7, 1921, 6).

"The Gunsaulus Mystery" deals with Myrtle Gunsaulus, a young girl who is found mysteriously murdered in the basement of a factory by Alfred Gilpin, the Negro night watchman, who is arrested and charged with the crime. Sidney Wyeth, a young Negro lawyer, who had once been in love with his sister, but who, through an error, had got the impression that she was immoral, is engaged by the girl to defend her brother. The incidents surrounding the tragedy, the motive of the crime, and the strange manner in which the girl came to her death, makes one of the most complicated cases the courts had ever been confronted with. Strange murder notes found upon the floor, covered with white substance, strands of her hair scattered here and there, all add to the mystery.

Out of it all, there was one fact that was self-evident—the girl was the victim of assault—but not in the usual way. Lem Hawkins, Negro janitor, falls under suspicion and is arrested; but the police are unable to get much out of him before suspicion is directed to Anthony Brisbane, the superintendent and general manager of the factory.

A great trial follows, Wyeth succeeds in proving Ida May's brother innocent, at the same time wringing a confession from Lem Hawkins in which he told the story of Anthony Brisbane's double life; of how he, Brisbane, a sexual pervert, had committed the unspeakable crime and killed the girl to try to hide it.

After his success in placing the crime where it belonged, Wyeth writes another book, in which he reveals a secret. Ida May reads the same, sees where he was laboring under the wrong impression and in answer to a letter she sends him, the whole thing is cleared up, and the old, old story ("Latest Race Photo Play and Vaudeville Features at Lafayette," *New York Age,* 23 April 1921, 6).

This is a story based on the Leo Frank case. It is one of the most mysterious murder cases on record. The evidence shows that Leo Frank committed the crime and got a COLORED MAN to help him dispose of the body. And then tried to blame the crime on the COLORED MAN.

Lawrence Chenault plays the part of Leo Frank (Advertisement, Baltimore *Afro-American,* 6 April 1923, 4).

Archive:

Screenings: 18–24 April 1921, Lafayette Theatre, New York City (premiere); 2–7 May 1921, Hammond's Vendome Theatre, Chicago; 24–26 May 1921, Dooley's Atlas Theatre, Chicago; 5–7 June 1921, Dunbar Theatre, Washington; 13–14 June 1921, Foraker Theatre, Washington; 15–16 June 1921, Hiawatha Theatre, Washington; 23–25 June 1921, Regent Theatre, Baltimore; 27–28 June 1921, Star Theatre, Baltimore; 1–2 July 1921, American Theatre, Baltimore; 8–10 December 1921, Attucks Theatre, Norfolk, Va.; 28–29 November 1922, Owl Theater, Chicago; 11–13 February 1923, Broadway Theatre, Washington; 27 March 1923, Dunbar Theatre, Baltimore; 9 April 1923, The Carey, Baltimore; 26 May 1924, Argonne Theatre, Baltimore; 25–27 October 1925, Franklin Theatre, New York City; 4–5 April 1927, Lafayette Theatre, Baltimore.

Press: Advertisement (advance announcement), *Chicago Defender,* 26 March 1921, 5; and "Latest Race Picture To Be Seen on Screen for First Time at Lafayette," *New York Age,* 16 April 1921, 6; "Latest Race Photo Play and Vaudeville Features at Lafayette," *New York Age,* 23 April 1921, 6; "Gunsaulus Mystery," *Chicago Defender,* 30 April 1921, 6; Advertisement and "The Gunsualus [*sic*] Mystery," *Chicago Whip,* 7 May 1921, 6; Advertisement and "Gunsaulus Mystery," *Chicago Defender,* 21 May 1921, 8; Advertisement, *Washington Tribune,* 4 June 1921, 4; Advertisements, *Washington Tribune,* 11 June 1921, 4; Advertisement, Baltimore *Afro-American,* 17 June 1921, 4; Advertisement, Baltimore *Afro-American,* 24 June 1921, 4; Advertisement, *Norfolk Journal and Guide,* 3 December 1921, 8; "Gunsaulus Mystery," *Chicago Defender,* 25 November 1922, 7; Advertisement, *Washington Tribune,* 10 February 1923, 5; Advertisement, Baltimore *Afro-American,* 23 March 1923, 5; Advertisement and "Carey," Baltimore *Afro-American,* 6 April 1923, 4; Advertisement, Baltimore *Afro-American,* 23 May 1924, 4; "Franklin Theatre," *New York Amsterdam News,* 21 October 1925, 7; Advertisement, Baltimore *Afro-American,* 2 April 1927, 9.

Note: Oscar Micheaux included a film entitled *Circumstantial Evidence* (1919) in a prospectus for *The Homesteader* (1919). It is described as a story based on the Leo M. Frank case, for which Micheaux states he was in the courtroom during the famous trial in Georgia. This suggests that Micheaux wrote the script for *The Gunsaulus Mystery* two years before its 1921 production and release. In a promotional announcement for the film, giving a release date of 20 April 1921, the murdered girl was described as "Little Mary," while the actual name of the girl murdered in the Leo Frank case was Mary Fagan (George P. Johnson Negro Film Collection). The change in title from *Circumstantial Evidence* bore the girl's fictitious last name. Mary Gunsaulus then came to be Myrtle Gunsaulus when the film was finally released. Chicago Film Censors viewed a 7,000-foot print of *The Gunsaulus Mystery* on 27 April 1921 and asked for a few minor cuts. It was advertised as *The Gonzales Mystery* in *New York Amsterdam News,* 21 October 1925, 7 and *The Gonzalas Mystery* in *Norfolk Journal and Guide,* 3 December 1921, 8. According to one source, Ethel Waters appeared in this film, perhaps under the name of "Ethel Watts" ("Ethel Waters

Grand Daughter of Douglas," Baltimore *Afro-American,* 19 December 1925, 4). Lobby card reprinted in Sampson, *Blacks in Black and White,* 155.

MICHEAUX IN FLORIDA

Oscar Micheaux, President and producing director of the Micheaux Film Corporation, is in Florida selecting locations for two new pictures that require tropical atmosphere and surroundings. He announces that he is now casting and that they will be ready for release within three months (Baltimore *Afro-American,* 27 January 1922, 11).

I am glad to note that Micheaux will start producing again (*Chicago Defender,* 18 March 1922, 8).

The Micheaux Film Company has removed its offices from downtown to 3457 [South] State street, third floor. Back amongst the old folks once gain ("Micheaux Moves," *Chicago Defender,* 1 April 1922, 7).

7) *The Dungeon* (1922)

© No reg.   *Length:* 7,000 ft. (7 reels).

Cast: William E. Fountaine (Stephen Cameron), Shingzie Howard, Blanche Thompson, W. B. F. Crowell ("Gyp" Lassiter), Earle Brown "Carl" Cooke, J. Kenneth Goodman.

Production dates: ca. March 1922.

Locations: Roanoke, Va.

Source:

Description: Stephen Cameron, a fine, manly and courageous youth, and Myrtle Downing, a beautiful girl of exceptional character, are engaged to marry. At 2 o'clock on the morning set for the marriage she calls him on the phone and relates a terrible dream, which she has just experienced. A few hours later she is shown the morning paper in which is the announcement of her marriage to "Gyp" Lassiter, a notorious crook. This ceremony is said in the article to have occurred the night before. The girl has no recollection whatever of such a thing having happened. What had occurred? Was the report true? The denouement and preceding action will certainly hold you spellbound. There are thrills galore in the seven great reels required in the telling of the story ("The Dungeon," *Chicago Defender,* 31 March 1923, 7).

Myrtle Downing, a beautiful young lady, is engaged to Stephen Cameron, a young lawyer. One night Myrtle comes to his office and they decide to marry the following day. The next morning he reads that she has just been married the night before to "Gyp" Lassiter, his bitterest enemy and whom she herself despises. Discouraged, Cameron goes to Alaska and settles on a claim, while Myrtle is carried to a strange and lonely house. She is carried below the surface of the earth to a dungeon where her husband after showing and acquainting her with many gruesome details concerning the house, tells her the story of Hector, a bigamist, a man of many wives, all of whom he murdered when they exposed him or tried to escape. She realizes that her husband is Hector himself and that any attempt at exposure on her part she would be the next to meet the fate of the terrible dungeon. In the meantime in Alaska Cameron has struck it rich on his claim, when one afternoon he is set upon by claim-jumpers and is saved by the timely arrival of "Chick" Barton, a pugilist, who after fighting off the bandits informs him that through redistribution of the congressional district in Cartersville, from whence Cameron came, it has been made possible for a Negro to be elected to Congress and that "Gyp" Lassiter is groomed for the office. Cameron is amazed at the audacity of the man and decides to try and save his Race from such a calamity as the election of Lassiter, returns with Barton to Cartersville to oppose Lassiter in the approaching election. Myrtle overhears a plot between her husband and certain real estate interests, whereby in consideration for a seat in congress and a large sum of money Lassiter agrees to secretly permit residential segregation, which deal would compel Colored people to move out of the best section of the city. But before she can escape and warn the Race of their danger, she is discovered and locked in a room by her husband; from which she escapes before the election and publishes the exposure in a Negro newspaper. Upon reading it and realizing that it was his wife who exposed him, Lassiter, enraged, sets out to murder, and coming upon her before she is able to escape, carries her fighting to the dungeon, where he proceeds to kill her by slow torture. Of how, then, Cameron hears of her danger and rushes to her rescue, and how it was Lassiter himself who suffered the last fate of his own dungeon (D. Ireland Thomas, "Motion Picture News," *Chicago Defender*, 8 July 1922, 6).

Archive:

Screenings: 22 May 1922, New York City [Peterson]; 5–7 June 1922, Regent Theatre, Baltimore; 5–6 July 1922, Auditorium Theater, Atlanta; 4–10 March 1923, Royal Theatre, Philadelphia; 4–7 March 1923, Lincoln Theatre, Washington; 20 March 1923, The Carey, Baltimore; 2–3 April 1923, Goldfield Theatre, Baltimore; 5–6 April 1923, Owl Theater, Chicago (Chicago premiere); 9–10 April 1923, Dunbar Theatre, Baltimore; 23–24 October 1923, Lincoln Theater, Charleston, S.C; 2–4 December 1923, Broadway Theatre, Washington; 12 May 1924, Argonne Theatre, Baltimore.

Press: Advertisement (advance announcement), *Chicago Defender,* 8 April 1922, 6; Advertisement, Baltimore *Afro-American,* 2 June 1922, 4; "The Dungeon," Baltimore *Afro-American,* 9 June 1922, 4; D. Ireland Thomas, "Motion Picture News," *Chicago Defender,* 8 July 1922, 6; D. Ireland Thomas, "Motion Picture News," *Chicago Defender,* 15 July 1922, 6; Advertisement, *Washington Tribune,* 24 February 1923, 4; Advertisement, Baltimore *Afro-American,* 16 March 1923, 4; "Dunbar," Baltimore *Afro-American,* 6 April 1923, 4; D. Ireland Thomas, "Motion Picture News," *Chicago Defender,* 17 March 1923, 7; "The Dungeon," *Chicago Defender,* 31 March 1923, 7; "Race Screen Star Becomes Popular New York Favorite," *New York Age,* 31 March 1923, 6; Advertisement, Baltimore *Afro-American,* 30 March 1923, 5; D. Ireland Thomas, "Motion Picture News," *Chicago Defender,* 3 November 1923, 7; Advertisement, *Washington Tribune,* 1 December 1923, 4; Advertisement, Baltimore *Afro-American,* 9 May 1924, 5.

Note: The advance announcement in the *Chicago Defender* (8 April 1922, 6) failed to identify the picture as a race film. Noting that "The characters are very bright, in fact, almost white," D. Ireland Thomas remarked, "'The All-Star Colored Cast' that is so noticeable with nearly every Race production, is omitted on the cards and lithographs. Possibly Mr. Micheaux is relying on his name alone to tell the public that it is a Race production, or maybe he is after booking it in white theaters ("Motion Picture News," *Chicago Defender,* 8 July 1922, 6). Thomas later remarked, "The *Dungeon* is very much like *The Brute,* only *The Brute* is the best production for many reasons, the main reason being that there were better actors in the cast" (*Chicago Defender,* 5 August 1922, 6). A critic for the Baltimore *Afro-American* found the acting to be good but the story was "a rambling maze of incidents that have a tendency to confuse the spectator" ("The Dungeon," Baltimore *Afro-American,* 9 June 1922, 4). Major W. B. F. Crowell, a businessman in Roanoke, Virginia, was the auditor of the Hampton Theater, Inc., and district manager of the North Carolina Mutual Life Insurance Company, the largest Negro insurance company in the world

("Salem Sez," *Chicago Defender*, 21 July 1923, 6). He not only acted in several Micheaux films, playing the villain in *The Dungeon*, but shared responsibility for the distribution of Micheaux's films in the Eastern District with Tiffany Tolliver (aka C. Tifany Toliver), president of the company that owned the Hampton Theater. In this dual capacity of actor and distributor, Crowell appeared in person at a number of theaters in the South, where he was billed as "The Meanest Man in the World" (D. Ireland Thomas, "Motion Picture News," *Chicago Defender*, 8 July 1922, 6). Crowell, a leader of the Knights of Pythias and other fraternal organizations, died 1 August 1929 ("W. B. F. Crowell, Va. Fraternal Figure, Is Dead," *Norfolk Journal and Guide*, 3 August 1929, 1, 13). For more on William E. Fountaine's acting career see "William Fountaine," *Chicago Defender*, 15 December 1928, 11A. Censors reviewed a 7,000-foot print of *The Dungeon* and demanded moderate cuts involving scenes of "girl shimmying" and other sexually suggestive movements as well as scenes related to the committing of various crimes.

8) *The Virgin of Seminole* (1922)

© No reg.   *Length:* 7,000 ft. (7 reels)/6,000 ft./5 reels.

Cast: William E. Fountaine, Shingzie Howard.

Production dates: May–August 1922.

Locations: Studio, Bronx, N.Y. (May 1922); Roanoke, Va. (July–August 1922).

Source:

Description: This production is a splendid one from every point of view, and the story is one of gripping interest and thrilling episodes from beginning to end. It is laid in the Northwest and Southeast and tells of the adventures of a young man who goes into the Canadian wilds and through his manly character is made a member of the famous Canadian mounted police. Through his clever work as an officer and by the fame he gains through a gun fight with a desperado he wins a large financial reward. He buys a ranch and becomes a successful ranchero. A love story of a most enthralling sort is carried throughout the feature and the many vicissitudes and adventures through which himself and the girl are led forms one of the best parts of this remarkable picture ("Virgin of Seminole," *Chicago Defender*, 2 December 1922, 6).

Archive:

Screenings: 5–8 December 1922, Owl Theater, Chicago; 5–9 December 1922, States Theater, Chicago; 19–22 December 1922, Joseph's Lincoln Theater, Chicago; ca. 25–27 March 1923, New Douglas Theatre, New York City (all three days with personal appearance of Shingzie Howard); 27–29 September 1923, Dunbar Theater, Washington; 3–4 October 1923, Roosevelt Theatre, Baltimore; 26 November 1923, The Carey, Baltimore; 20 February 1924, Colonial Theatre, Portsmouth, Va.; 3 December 1925, Lafayette Theatre, Baltimore; 9–11 May 1926, Royal Theatre, Philadelphia.

Press: J. A. Jackson, "Here and There," Baltimore *Afro-American*, 19 May 1922, 13; J. A. Jackson, "Here and There," Baltimore *Afro-American*, 4 August 1922, 11; D. Ireland Thomas, "Motion Picture News," *Chicago Defender*, 26 August 1922, 6; "Racial Feature," *Chicago Defender*, 25 November 1922, 6; "Virgin of Seminole," *Chicago Defender*, 2 December 1922, 6; Advertisement, *Chicago Defender*, 2 December 1922, 7; J. A. Jackson, "Micheaux Pictures," *Billboard*, 27 January 1923, 50; Advertisement and "Colored Film at New Douglas Theatre," *New York Age*, 24 March 1923, 6; "Race Screen Star Becomes Popular New York Favorite," *New York Age*, 31 March 1923, 6; Advertisements, *Washington Tribune*, 22 September 1923, 5 and 6; Advertisement, Baltimore *Afro-American,* 28 September 1923, 4; "Carey," Baltimore *Afro-American,* 23 November 1923, 2; Advertisement, Baltimore *Afro-American,* 23 November 1923, 5; Advertisement, *Norfolk Journal and Guide,* 16 February 1924, 4; Advertisement, Baltimore *Afro-American,* 28 November 1925, 5; Advertisement and "Royal Theatre," *Philadelphia Tribune,* 8 May 1926, 3.

Note: There was standing room only all day Sunday, 25 March 1923, for the film (and Shingzie Howard's guest appearance) at the 2,200-seat Douglas Theatre in New York City. Chicago Film Censors viewed a 6,000-foot version of the film on 29 November 1922 and demanded minor cuts. The version shown in Baltimore on 26 November 1923 was 5 reels. The film was advertised as "C. Tifany Toliver presents" for its October 1923 playdates (Advertisement, Baltimore *Afro-American,* 28 September 1923, 4).

MICHEAUX PICTURES

Among the recent callers at the Billboard office in New York, was Oscar Micheaux, head of the picture concern that bears his name. For the past half year, he has spent most of his time in and about Roanoke, Va., and in the coal districts of West Virginia, where practically all of the [caller's] activities have been centered . . . .

The Chicago Office has general charge of distribution with Swan Micheaux in Charge and G. A. O'Neill as General Agent. Tiffany Tolliver and W. B. Crowell have the eastern district with offices in Roanoke, while the releases in the southwest are being handled by A. N. Odams of the Verdun Theater, Beaumont, Texas (Baltimore *Afro-American,* 26 January 1923, 13).

9) *DECEIT* (1923)

© No reg.   *Length:* 6,000 ft. (6 reels).

Cast: Evelyn Preer (Doris Rutledge, Evelyn Bently), Norman Johnstone (Alfred DuBois, Gregory Wainwright), A. B. DeComathiere (Rev. Christian P. Bently), Cleo Desmond (Charlotte Chesboro), Louis De-Bulger (Charlotte Chesboro's husband), Mabel Young (Mrs. Levine), Cornelius Watkins (Wainwright as a boy), Mrs. Irvin Miller (Mrs. Wainwright), Ira O. McGowan (Mr. Wainwright); Lewis Schooler (an actor, a waiter), Jerry Brown (an actress), James Carey (a crooked banker), Viola Miles, Mary Watkins, and N. Brown (teachers), J. Coldwell, F. Sandifier, Jessie R. Billings, and Allen D. Dixon (preachers), Leonard Galezio, William Patterson, Sadie Carey (censors—all white); William Patterson and Melton Henry (rescue party—all white) [Source: George P. Johnson Negro Film Collection.]

Production dates: 1921.

Locations:

Source:

Description: "DECEIT" is the story of a motion picture. Alfred DuBois, played by Norman Johnstone, organizes a film corporation, and with the assistance of his secretary, played by Evelyn Preer, produce their first picture, advertised to be released under the title of "THE HYPOCRITE." On reaching the Censor Board for its approval, [DuBois] is surprised to find, waiting there to see it, a delegation of preachers, headed by one Christian P. Bently, in whom he recognizes . . . an arch enemy of his youth. After viewing the picture along with the Censors, Bently registers a violent complaint and succeeds in having the censor reject the picture. Persistent, DuBois finally succeeds in having the case appealed and an audience selected without bias is permitted to view the picture to judge whether the portions objected to by the ministers justifies the rejection of the picture.

The committee take seats and for an hour and a half look upon the events to which the ministry raised such violent objections to; and the events which are unfolded are what you will see by going to the REGENT THEATRE, Monday, Tuesday and Wednesday, October 22, 23, 24th. Don't miss it, DECEIT A MICHEAUX PRODUCTION, starring EVELYN PREER, the race's most popular star ("Deceit," Baltimore *Afro-American,* 19 October 1923, 5).

Should a girl marry to satisfy her wish for love, or should she marry to satisfy her sister and parents? This girl married the man of her heart, and said she would fight the world if necessary to keep him. Her parents tried to separate them, and then she starts to fight, and Oh, Mama, come see the hair fly (Advertisement, Baltimore *Afro-American,* 11 April 1924, 5).

Archive:

Screenings: 22–24 October 1923, Regent Theatre, Baltimore; 18–21 November 1923, Broadway Theatre, Washington; 15 April 1924, The Carey, Baltimore; 29–30 April 1924, Dunbar Theatre, Baltimore; 16–17 June 1924, Elmore Theatre, Pittsburgh, Pa.; 26 November 1925, Lafayette Theatre, Baltimore; 20–26 June 1927, Indiana Theater, Chicago.

Press: Advertisement, Baltimore *Afro-American,* 19 October 1923, 4; "Deceit," Baltimore *Afro-American,* 19 October 1923, 5; Advertisement, *Washington Tribune,* 17 November 1923, 4; Advertisement, Baltimore *Afro-American,* 11 April 1924, 5; Advertisement, Baltimore *Afro-American,* 25 April 1924, 5; Advertisement and "Uncrowned Blues Queen at Lincoln; Evelyn Preer Plays Star Role in Deceit," *Pittsburgh Courier,* 14 June 1924, 10; Advertisement, Baltimore *Afro-American,* 21 November 1925, 5; Advertisement, *Chicago Defender,* 18 June 1927, 9A; Evelyn Preer, "My Thrills in the Movies," *Pittsburgh Courier,* 25 June 1927, 2B.

Note: The film was billed as the latest Micheaux production but was not yet released, according to D. Ireland Thomas, "Motion Picture News," *Chicago Defender,* 21 January 1922, 7. *The Hypocrite* was probably a working title for this film. A film of this title was mentioned as a future production in D. Ireland Thomas, "Motion Picture News," *Chicago Defender,* 4 November 1922, 7; and as a completed film in J. A. Jackson, "Micheaux Pictures," *Billboard,* 27 January 1923, 50. Micheaux booked the film for D. Ireland Thomas's Lincoln Theater in Charleston, South Carolina for 19–20 November 1923, but the film proved unavailable ("Motion Picture News," *Chicago Defender,* 1 December 1923, 6A). This was one of many "miss outs" reported by Thomas (D. Ireland Thomas, "Motion Picture News," *Chicago Defender,* 29 December 1923, 8A). The Motion Picture Commission of the State of New York State viewed a 6,000-foot print on 21 February 1923 (which was to be released 1 March 1923); it was said to be a film manufactured in 1921. A few scenes of violence were eliminated because they are "inhuman" and would "tend to incite crime." Advertised at one point as "A Sister Show to the 'Brute'" (Advertisement, Baltimore *Afro-American,* 25 April 1924, 5).

10) *BIRTHRIGHT* (1924)

© No reg.   *Length:* 10 reels/8,000 ft.

Cast: Evelyn Preer (Cissie Deldine), Salem Tutt Whitney (Tump Pack), J. Homer Tutt (Peter Siner), Lawrence Chenault (Henry Hooker, Captain Renfrew), Callie Mines (Aunt

Caroline), E. G. Tatum (The Persimmon), Ed Elkins (Dawson Bobbs), Alma Sewall (Old Rose), W. B. F. Crowell. [Source: Promotional materials provided by Virginia Film Censor Board Records.]

Production dates: July 1923.

Locations: Roanoke, Va.

Source: Thomas S. Stribling's novel *Birthright* (1922).

Description: Peter Siner, Colored, a graduate of Harvard university, on reaching Cairo on his way South with plans to establish a school for Colored youth, is told to get out of the Pullman and go forward to the Jim Crow car for the rest of his journey. On the platform he meets "Tump Pack," a burley and loud spoken Negro, wearing a distinguished service badge, who is just returning from overseas. On arriving at their home up the Tennessee river, Tump is accorded a great welcome, in the midst of which he is arrested by a constable, Dawson Bobbs, and thrown in jail on a four-year old charge of shooting craps. A few days later Bobbs raids the village, where Siner is living with his mother, in search of a Turkey Roaster. The Siner cabin is ransacked and a few minutes after the constable leaves the house the roaster shows up mysteriously, causing Siner serious embarrassment. He meets Cissie Dildine (Evelyn Preer) with whom he falls in love, to learn that she is Tump Pack's girl. A local lodge raises $100, which Siner uses to purchase ground for his school—discovering after he had signed the papers, that the deed contained a clause prohibiting all Colored people from occupying the land. His Race comes down on him and discounts his education, all but Cissie. Tump Pack, furiously jealous, meets him on the street with her and administers a severe beating which adds to his disgrace. On his way to shoot Peter later, Tump Pack is arrested and sent to the chain gang. Cissie and Peter become engaged. Peter's mother dies and he is visited by a strange old white man, Captain Renfew, with whom he goes to live. The night before he is married Cissie confesses that she is immoral and unfit to be his wife. Mysterious events come thick and fast, and then on the night before the day of great tragedy, Peter is visited in his room by Cissie. Dawson Bobbs, tipped off by "The Persimmon," a "white folks man" waits outside. Cissie comes out and events from there on until the end of the story become dynamic with excitement (D. Ireland Thomas, "Motion Picture News," *Chicago Defender,* 15 March 1924, 6A).

In adapting the story for the screen, Mr. Micheaux followed the book very closely, even using in the headlines the identical language contained therein. So if you read "Birthright" and liked it you will probably like the picture. It is a descriptive story of a small southern town—a sort of colored "Main Street." All of the ignorance, prejudice and many of the crimes of both races in this town is graphically depicted.

Although it is two hours long and drags at times, it is the best colored moving picture that has so far been produced. With few exceptions the cast is well selected and the acting good. Salem Tutt Whitney as Tump Pack (the colored bully of the town who was decorated for heroism during the World War), has the best part ever seen him in. Evelyn Preer was also exceptionally good as Cissie Deldine. In the book Peter Siner did not appear as a real character to the writer. Few colored Harvard graduates go South nowadays with the intention of reforming that section of the country and none of them have been as ignorant of conditions there as Peter appears to be. J. Homer Tutt succeeds in bringing some life to this character, but even he cannot make it the outstanding part in the picture. Next to Miss Preer the southern sheriff had the most convincing part ("At the Lafayette Theatre," *New York Age,* 19 January 1924, 6).

Archive:

Screenings: 14–20 January 1924, Lafayette Theatre, New York City (premiere); 21–26 January 1924, Douglass Theatre, Baltimore (announced but either postponed one week or cancelled); 28–29 January 1924, Attucks Theatre, Norfolk, Va.; February 1924, Renaissance Theater, New York City; 2–4 April 1924, Dunbar Theatre, Baltimore; 24–25 April 1924, Roosevelt Theatre, Baltimore; 9 June 1924, The Carey, Baltimore; summer 1924, Lyric Theater, New Orleans; summer 1924, Paramount Theater, Atlanta; summer 1924, Douglass Theater, Macon, Ga.; mid-September 1924, Lincoln Theater, Charleston, S.C.; 19–22 November 1924, Royal Theatre, Philadelphia; 17 December 1925, Lafayette Theatre, Baltimore; 21–25 March 1927, 20th Century Theater, Chicago; late November 1927, 18th Street Theater, Kansas City.

Press: Advertisement and "At the Lafayette Theatre," *New York Age,* 12 January 1924, 6; Advertisement, Baltimore *Afro-American,* 18 January 1924, 2; "Douglass," Baltimore *Afro-American,* 18 January 1924, 5; "At the Lafayette Theatre," *New York Age,* 19 January 1924, 6; J. A. Jackson, "'Birthright,' in New York," *Billboard,* 19 January 1924, 54; J. A. Jackson, "Birthright," Baltimore *Afro-American,* 25 January 1924, 10; J. A. Jackson, "Birthright," *Billboard,* 26 January 1924, 52; Advertisement and "In the Theatres," *Norfolk Journal and Guide,* 26 January 1924, 4; D. Ireland Thomas, "Motion Picture News," *Chicago Defender,* 1 March 1924, 6A; D. Ireland Thomas, "Motion Picture News," *Chicago Defender,* 15 March 1924, 6A; Advertisement, Baltimore *Afro-American,* 28 March 1924, 2; "'Birthright' at the Dunbar," Baltimore *Afro-American,* 28 March 1924, 10; Advertisement, Baltimore *Afro-American,* 18 April 1924, 4, 10; Advertisement and "Evelyn Preer at the Carey," Baltimore *Afro-American,* 6 June 1924, 4; D. Ireland Thomas, "Motion Picture News," *Chicago Defender,* 5 July 1924, 6A; D. Ireland Thomas, "Motion Picture News," *Chicago Defender,* 16 August 1924, 7A; D. Ireland Thomas, "Motion Picture News," *Chicago Defender,* 27 September 1924, 6A; D. Ireland Thomas, "Motion Picture News," *Chicago Defender,* 4 October 1924, 9A; "Motion Picture News," *Chicago Defender,* 25 October 1924, 6A; Advertisement and "The Royal Theatre," *Philadelphia Tribune,* 15 November 1924, 3; "'Birthright' at Royal Theatre Draws Praise," *Philadelphia Tribune,* 22 November 1924, 3; Advertisement, *Baltimore Afro-American,* 12 December 1925, 5; Advertisement, *Chicago Defender,* 19 March 1927, 8A; Evelyn Preer, "Evelyn Preer Nearly Drowned in Realistic Movie Scene," *Pittsburgh Courier,* 11 June 1927, 1B; "In Old Kaysee," *Chicago Defender,* 26 November 1927, 9A.

Note: Sometimes advertised as *Birthright: A Story of the Negro and the South* (Advertisement, *New York Age,* 12 January 1924, 6). Charles Waddell Chesnutt wrote Oscar Micheaux, "I had the pleasure of seeing your picture of *The Birthright* about a week ago. It was very well done, and was certainly extremely realistic. Neither the author nor the picture flattered the negro one article, and they both showed up the southern white in his least amiable characteristics, which seem always to come to the front in his dealings with the negro" (Charles Waddell Chesnutt to Oscar Micheaux, 29 January 1924, Charles Waddell Chesnutt Papers, Western Reserve Historical Society, Cleveland, Ohio). Evelyn Preer had been engaged to play the lead in *Birthright* by early July 1923 (J. A. Jackson, "Motion Picture News" *Billboard,* 14 July 1923, 50). Salem Tutt Whitney had a regular column, "Salem Sez," in the *Chicago Defender* during the 1920s. He reported from Roanoke, Virginia, while making the film (14 July 1923, 7). Whitney and J. Homer Tutt formed the duo "Whitney and Tutt" and billed themselves as "The Race's Great Comedy Kings." In 1924, they were touring with the song-and-dance stage show *Come Along, Mandy* (Advertisement, *Chicago Defender,* 3 May 1924). The working title for the film was *Hooker's Bend* ("Motion Picture News," *Chicago Defender,* 28 July 1923, 9A). It is the film Micheaux said would be finished after *The House Behind the Cedars* in J. A. Jackson, "Micheaux Film Ready," *Billboard*, 5 May 1923, 50. It was just being released at the end of 1923, according to D. Ireland Thomas, along with *Jasper Landry's Will, Ghost of Tolston's Manor,* and the much-announced *House Behind the Cedars* ("Motion Picture News," *Chicago Defender,* 15 December 1923, 7A). The Motion Picture Commission of the State of New York reviewed a 10-reel print of *Birthright* on 17 January 1924 and approved the film for exhibition with substantial eliminations. The film was scheduled for a week-long run at Baltimore's prestigious Douglass Theatre, starting 21 January 1924, but at the last moment the film proved unavailable, probably due to censorship problems and maybe even to opposition within the black community itself. J. A. Jackson remarked, "Micheaux has made a really great picture. It is a modern "Uncle Tom's Cabin," and may not be popular in some quarters, a fact that will but confirm its value" ("Birthright," Baltimore *Afro-American,* 18 January 1924, 10). The film was rescheduled for the following week, though the absence of any advertising or publicity makes it unlikely that this run actually took place ("Douglass," Baltimore *Afro-American,* 18 January 1924, 5). Moreover, Maryland Film censors reviewed *Birthright* and ordered substantial eliminations on 26 January 1924. Chicago Film Censors reviewed an 8,000-foot print of the film on 2 March 1927 and ordered substantial cuts. Micheaux attempted to exhibit *Birthright* in several Virginia theaters without obtaining a license and encountered difficulty with Virginia film censors.

OSCAR MICHEAUX MOVES FAST.

Not long since we reported his presence in Texas, under date of June 20, we get a letter that advises us that he is in the vicinity of Birmingham. By the time this gets into print, the fast moving movie man will perhaps be far from there. Anyhow, he leaves every town with contracts for his films. His latest is booked into the Famous Theater, Birmingham for mid-July dates (Baltimore *Afro-American,* 4 July 1924, 4).

Oscar Micheaux of the Micheaux Film Corporation is in Roanoke, Va., making preparations for more business (D. Ireland Thomas, "Motion Picture News," *Chicago Defender,* 12 July 1924, 6A).

The great and only Oscar Micheaux advises that he is now releasing "A Son of Satan," to be followed by "The House Behind the Cedars" next month (Ireland Thomas, "Motion Picture News," *Chicago Defender,* 26 July 1924, 6A).

Oscar Micheaux writes that his latest feature, "Birthright," broke all records at the Lyric theater, New Orleans; Paramount theater, Atlanta, and Douglass theater, Macon, Ga., and that he expects to continue breaking records at [the] "81" theater, Atlanta; Strand theater, Jacksonville; Lincoln theater, Miami; and at Nassau. He informs me that the great Leon is traveling with the print (D. Ireland Thomas, "Motion Picture News," *Chicago Defender,* 16 August 1924, 7A).

11) *A Son of Satan* (1924)

© No reg.   *Length:* 8 reels/6,000 ft. (6 reels).

Cast: Andrew S. Bishop (the sea captain), Lawrence Chenault, Edna Morton, Shingzie Howard, Ida Anderson, Monte Hawley, Emmett Anthony (comic role), Evelyn Ellis, Marie Dove, Margaret Brown, Walter Robinson (the father), Dink Stewart, Olivia Sewall, E. G. Tatum, Mildred Smallwood (dancer), Miller and Lyles, and the chorus from the original Shuffle Along Company.

Production dates: March–April 1923.

Locations: Clason's Point, N.Y.; Bronx Studio, N.Y.; Roanoke, Va.

Source: Oscar Micheaux's original story "The Ghost of Tolston's Manor."

Description: Some may not like the production because it shows up some of our Race in their true colors. They might also protest against the language used. I would not endorse this particular part of the film myself, but I must admit that it is true to nature, yes, I guess, too true. We have got to hand it to Oscar Micheaux when it comes to giving us the real stuff. This is all the criticism that I could find and I am a hard critic when it comes to Race pictures, and like Sylvester Russell, I do not want to see my Race in saloons or at crap tables. But it is not what we want, that gets the money, it is what the public clamors for that makes the coin jingle (D. Ireland Thomas, "Motion Picture News," *Chicago Defender,* 31 January 1925, 6A).

Archive:

Screenings: 27–29 October 1924, Attucks Theater, Norfolk, Va. (blocked by state); 25–27 December 1924, Attucks Theater, Norfolk, Va.; early January 1925, Dunbar Theater, Savannah, Ga.; late January 1925, Lincoln Theater, Charleston, S.C.; 13–15 April 1925, Franklin Theatre, New York City; 14–16 February 1926, Royal Theatre, Philadelphia; 23–26 June 1926, Royal Theatre, Baltimore; 18–19 October 1926, New Dunbar, Baltimore.

Press: J. A. Jackson, "Micheaux Shooting a Picture," *Billboard,* 7 April 1923, 48; "Micheaux Shooting Thrilling 8-Reeler," *Pittsburgh Courier,* 7 April 1923, 12; J. A. Jackson, "Micheaux Film Ready," *Billboard,* 5 May 1923, 50; "Micheaux Releases Film," Baltimore *Afro-American,* 31 October 1924, 7; Advertisement, *Norfolk Journal and Guide,* 25 October 1924, 4; Advertisement and "Andrew Bishop and Lafayette Players at Attucks," *Norfolk Journal and Guide,* 25 October 1924, 5; "Oscar Micheaux Releases Film," Baltimore *Afro-American,* 31 October 1924, 7; "'A Son of Satan' Barred By the Va. Censors," *Norfolk Journal and Guide,* 1 November 1924, 4; *Billboard,* 8 November 1924, 49; Advertisement and "'Son of Satan' Passes Board of Censors," *Norfolk Journal and Guide,* 20 December 1924, 4; "Son of Satan Played," *Baltimore Afro-American,* 24 January 1925, 4; D. Ireland Thomas, "Motion Picture News," *Chicago Defender,* 31 January 1925, 6A; Advertisement, *New York Amsterdam News,* 8 April 1925, 6; Advertisement, *Philadelphia Tribune,* 13 February 1926, 6; Advertisement, Baltimore *Afro-American,* 29 May 1926, 4; Advertisement, Baltimore *Afro-American,* 19 June 1926, 4; Advertisement, *Baltimore Afro-American,* 16 October 1926, 14.

Note: Sometimes advertised as *A Son of Satan: The Story of a Haunted House* (Advertisement, *Norfolk Journal and Guide,* 20 December 1924, 4). Also *The Son of Satan* (Baltimore *Afro-American,* 29 May 1926, 4). Prior to its release, the film was referred to as *The Ghost of Tolston's Manor.* A cast list for the film under that title is given by J. A. Jackson, "Micheaux Film Ready," *Billboard,* 5 May 1923, 50. *Billboard,* 7 April 1923, 48, mentions a somewhat different cast that includes Andrew Bishop, Dink Stewart, W. B. F. Crowell, and Olivia Sewall. D. Ireland Thomas indicated the film was newly finished with Andrew S. Bishop in "Motion Picture News," *Chicago Defender,* 23 December 1923, 7A—again under the title *Ghost of Tolston's Manor.* This pre-release title was mentioned so frequently that it has generally been considered a different film. However, we have been unable to identify a single screening of the film under such a title. Moreover, an advertisement for *A Son of Satan* in the Baltimore *Afro-American* indicates it was "adapted from the story of 'The Ghost of Tolston Manor.' A hair-raising story of adventure in a haunted house, where rattling chains and walking ghosts are as common as parrots and puppies" (19 June 1926, 4). A flyer for the film in the Virginia Censorship files echoes this connection and also mentions that the film was presented by W. B. Hunter. Edna Morton had appeared in fourteen race films made by either Oscar Micheaux or Reol Productions by the summer of 1923, when she was hired by Famous Players-Lasky to appear in supporting roles for such films as *The Ne'er Do Well* (1923) with Thomas Meighan (J. A. Jackson, "Edna Norton [*sic*] Signed by Famous Players," Baltimore *Afro-American*, 3 August 1923, 5).

The Motion Picture Commission of the State of New York reviewed a 6,000-foot, 6-reel print of *Son of Satan* on 22 July 1924 and rejected the picture. In a letter to Micheaux, the censors stated:

> The picture is filled with scenes of drinking, carousing and shows masked men becoming intoxicated. It shows the playing of crap for money, a man killing his wife by choking her, the killing of the leader of the hooded organization and the killing of a cat by throwing a stone at it. There are many scenes of crime. The film is of such character that in the opinion of the commission, it is "inhuman" and would "tend to incite to crime" (Motion Picture Commission of the State of New York to Oscar Micheaux, 20 September 1924).

After Micheaux eliminated offending passages, the New York censors reviewed the film again in September and October 1924, finally approving the film for exhibition.

The Virginia State Board of Censors reviewed *A Son of Satan* [exact date unknown] and rejected the film in toto. Film censors stated:

> The film entitled A Son of Satan was released by a colored concern engaged in the distribution of motion pictures and has an all-negro cast. The central figure in the plot is a mulatto whose villainies justify the significant title of the photoplay. By implication at least the audience is led to believe that the criminal tendencies of the man are inherited from his white forefathers.
>
> A Son of Satan, at best, is unwholesome as it touches unpleasantly on miscegenation. Furthermore, many of its scenes and sub-titles will prove irritating if not hurtful alike to quadroons, octoroons, half-breeds and those of pure African descent. In some of the scenes—notably at the "fashionable" dance where a white orchestra furnishes music for blacks—there is an intermingling of the two races which would prove offensive to Southern ideas. The most serious feature of the picture, however, is the series of race riots incited by the Son of Satan, who uses a white man as his tool. While it might be argued that these riots, in reality, are attributable to the villainous negro, it should not be forgotten that a white man is his partner in crime.
>
> Riot scenes of any sort are calculated to arouse the passions, and even the mildest presentation of race conflict is inflammatory material of the most dangerous sort for treatment on the screen. The scenes in A Son of Satan smack far too much of realism and race hatred to be classified as mild, and in the opinion of this Board, might lead to serious results. In this connection it should be remembered that the picture, in all probability, will be offered only to negro theatres where a large proportion of the audiences will doubtless be illiterate, or so ignorant as to misinterpret even what is good in the films.
>
> A Son of Satan is rejected on the ground that it might tend to corrupt morals or incite to crime.

The film was advertised as 8 reels when shown at the Royal Theatre, Baltimore, in early June 1926 (Baltimore *Afro-American*, 29 May 1926, 4).

MICHEAUX CALLS

Oscar Micheaux, the well-known producer of the famous Micheaux Race photoplays was a caller at the Desk on Friday of last week [November 28], looking the picture of health and prosperity. He was very anxious to see and have a chat with the Old Roll Top Desk Man [Tony Langston], but his honor was at that time in the East where he had just attended the Lincoln-Howard "grid" set-to. However, our honored visitor was shown every courtesy at the command of the staff. Mr. Micheaux is contemplating a trip to South America, intending to start about January 10. He left for the East, where he has some important matters to look after in that territory (*Chicago Defender*, 6 December 1924, 6A).

W. B. Hauser [*sic*, Hunter], vice president and fiscal agent of the Micheaux Film corporation, passed through Charleston, S.C. en route to the North on important business. While there he booked "Birthright" for Nashville, Tenn." (D. Ireland Thomas, "Motion Picture News," *Chicago Defender*, 14 February 1925, 6A).

12) THE HOUSE BEHIND THE CEDARS (1924/25)

© No reg.   *Length:* 9,000 ft. (9 reels).

Cast: Andrew Bishop (wealthy young white aristocrat), Lawrence Chenault, Shingzie Howard (mulatto passing for white).

Production dates: October–November 1922.

Locations: Roanoke, Va.

Source: Charles W. Chesnutt's novel *The House Behind the Cedars* (1900).

Description: The story of an aristocratic young white multi-millionaire's passionate love (played by Andrew S. Bishop) for a beautiful mulatto being passed off as white—and the discovery. An amazing parallel to the famous Rhinelander case (Advertisement, Baltimore *Afro-American*, 28 March 1925, 6).

Archive:

Screenings: 7 December 1924, Royal Theatre, Philadelphia (preview); 7–10 January 1925, Royal Theatre, Philadelphia (local premiere); 28–29 January 1925, Regent Theatre, Baltimore (scheduled, then cancelled due to late arrival of advertising paper), 15–18 March 1925, Franklin Theatre, New York City; 16–18 March 1925, Attucks Theatre, Norfolk, Va.; 18–19 March 1925, Colonial Theater, Portsmouth, Va.; 18–19 March 1925, Regent Theatre, Baltimore; 31 March–1 April 1925, Dunbar Theatre, Baltimore; 10 November 1925, Lafayette Theatre, Baltimore; 16–18 September 1926, Royal Theatre, Baltimore.

Press: D. Ireland Thomas, "Motion Picture News," *Chicago Defender*, 14 October 1922, 6; D. Ireland Thomas, "Motion Picture News," *Chicago Defender*, 4 November 1922, 7; "The House Behind the Cedars' Shown at Royal Sunday," *Philadelphia Tribune*, 13 December 1924, 1, 3; "Micheaux Answers His Philly Critics," Baltimore *Afro-American*, 27 December 1924, 7; Advertisement and "The Royal Theatre," *Philadelphia Tribune*, 3 January 1925, 3; "Newest Film Like Rhinelander Case," Baltimore *Afro-American*, 24 January 1925, 5; "Film Cancelled," Baltimore *Afro-American*, 31 January 1925, 5; Advertisement and "Chesnut's [*sic*] Famous Story at the Franklin Theatre," *New York Amsterdam News*, 11 March 1925, 6; Advertisements and "New Micheaux Picture Tops Attucks Bill," *Norfolk Journal and Guide*, 14 March 1925, 4; Advertisement and "'House Behind The Cedars' Regent," Baltimore *Afro-American*, 14 March 1925, 5; "Rhinelander Case at Regent," Baltimore *Afro-American*, 21 March 1925, 5; Advertisement, Baltimore *Afro-American*, 28 March 1925, 6; Advertisement, Baltimore *Afro-American*, 7 November 1925, 9; "Producers Clean Up on Rhinelander Film," Baltimore *Afro-American*, 12 December 1925, 4; Sylvester Russell, "In the Theatrical World," *Pittsburgh Courier*, 19 December 1925, 9; Advertisement, Baltimore *Afro-American,* 11 September 1926, 4; Advertisement, Baltimore *Afro-American,* 18 September 1926, 4; "House Behind the Cedars," Baltimore *Afro-American,* 18 September 1926, 5.

Note: For clarification over the dating of this film, see Charlene Regester, "Oscar Micheaux the Entrepreneur: Financing *The House Behind the Cedars," Journal of Film and Video* 49, nos. 1–2 (Spring–Summer 1997): 17–27. The Virginia State Board of Censors reviewed *The House Behind the Cedars* on 9 March 1925 and again on 10 March 1925. The board rejected the film in toto, offering the following explanation:

> The House Behind the Cedars, aside from presenting the grievances of the negro in somewhat infelicitous sub-titles, touches even more dangerous ground—the intermarriage of the two races. Its plot is based on a love affair between a white man (described in the film as the scion of an aristocratic North Carolina family) and a colored woman who masquerades as a white. Even after the woman has severed her relations with the men he is pictured as still seeking her society, nor does his quest end until she has become the wife of a dark-skinned suitor.
>
> The photodrama, at best, is hardly the medium for handling of so delicate a theme, and The House Behind the Cedars assuredly proves inadequate for such a purpose. In the opinion of the Va. Board of Censors this film, whatever its good points, should not be displayed in this State—especially in negro houses for which it is intended—since many of its scenes, as well as sub-titles, are liable to cause friction between the races and might therefore incite to crime. Furthermore, the picture, either purposely or through the maladroitness of the producers, at least indirectly contravenes the spirit of the recently enacted anti-miscegenation law which has put Virginia in the forefront as a pioneer in legislation aimed to preserve the integrity of the white race (Virginia State Board of Censors to Oscar Micheaux, 10 March 1925).

Micheaux then tried to rework the film to the censors' satisfaction, including the elimination of reel two (Micheaux to Virginia State Board of Censors, 13 March 1925). Chicago Film Censors reviewed a 9,000-foot, 9-reel print of *The House Behind the Cedars* on 1 December 1925 and approved the picture for exhibition with minor cuts (all involving intertitles).

"THE HOUSE BEHIND THE CEDARS" SHOWN AT ROYAL SUNDAY
Producer, On Hand, Makes Statement Explaining His Aims; Invited Guests Impressed

----

Something new in the line of catering to the patrons of a motion picture theatre was attempted by the owners and management of the Royal Theatre on Sunday, December 6th [*sic*], [with] a private screening of Charles Chestnut's [*sic*] famous novel, "The House Behind the Cedars" produced for the screen by Mr. Oscar Micheaux, the greatest Negro producer of motion pictures. In fact Mr. Micheaux is the pioneer of the Negro Film, and is deserving of the greatest support that colored people can give him for the great strides he has made in giving them a place in the Motion Picture field.

This picture was witnessed at the Royal Theatre by at least two hundred specially invited guests of the owners and management. It was an opportunity offered to those persons of the city who may have heard of the producer but had never met him or heard him discuss his work and the great [strides] it means for the advancement of the race in this particular line of art and education. As to the picture it was a very faithful adaptation of the novel modernized in such a manner as not to destroy the story and at the same time making it a little more appealing. The photography was splendid and the direction in the picture is proven by the smoothness and well placed and not exaggerated in any manner. It may be accorded by many critics as being the greatest work of this producer and for one who has carefully followed the marvelous developments of this producer from the beginning through the various stages of hardships due to failure to secure the necessary financial backing, he may well be placed on a par with any of the greatest producers of photoplays who have at their fingertips the necessary finance to make their productions as they would have them. The lobby criticisms were loud in the praise of this work and it is safe to reason that it will be well supported by the public. The Owners and management of the Royal Theatre are to be congratulated upon the manner in which they have interested themselves in this producer and bringing his efforts before the Philadelphia public. Assisting on the program were Mr. Lord, a baritone soloist and organist, and Mr. Andrew Bishop who starred in the picture, read a brief, but educational statement by the producer.

Mr. Micheaux's statement follows:

"Unless one has some connection with the actual production of photoplays, it is impossible fully to recognize the tremendous scope which the motion picture embraces. The completed picture is a miniature replica of life and all the varied forces which help to make life so complex. The intricate studies and problems of human nature all enter into the physical make-up of the most lowly photoplay. The mastery, therefore, of the art of production, for indeed it is an art, is no small attainment and success can only be assured when assisted by the most active encouragement and financial backing. The colored producer has dared to step into a world which has hitherto remained closed to him. His entrance into this unexplored field is for him trebly difficult. He is limited in his theme, in obtaining casts that present genuine ability and in his financial resources. He requires encouragement and assistance. He is the new born babe who must be fondled until he can stand on his own feet. If the race has any pride in presenting its own achievements in this field it behooves it to interest itself and morally encourage such efforts. I don't wish anyone to construe this as a request to suppress criticism. The producer who has confidence in his ideals solicits constructive criticism but he also asks fairness, and fairness in criticism demands a familiarity with the aims of the producer, and a knowledge of the circumstances under which his efforts were materialized. I have been informed that my last production "Birthright" has occasioned much adverse criticism in Philadelphia. Certain newspaper men have denounced me as a colored Judas merely because they were either unaware of my aims or were not in sympathy with them. What then are my aims to which such critics have taken exception? I have always tried to make my photoplays present the truth[,] to lay before the race a cross section if its own life—to view the colored heart from close range. My results might have been narrow at times due perhaps to certain limited situations which I endeavor to portray. But in these limited situations Truth was the predominate characteristic. It is only by presenting those portions of the race portrayed in my pictures in the light and background of their true state that we can raise our people to greater heights. I am too much imbued with the spirit of Booker T. Washington to engraft false virtues upon ourselves to make ourselves that which we are not. Nothing could be a greater blow to our own progress. The recognition of our true situations will react in itself as a stimulus for self advancement. It is these ideals that I have enjected into my pictures and which are now being criticised. Possibly my aims have been misunderstood but criticisms arising from such misunderstanding only double the already overburdened labors of the colored producer. If I have been retarded by unjust criticism from my own race it has amply been made up by the aid of the Royal Theatre, which from the very beginning has encouraged the production of colored photoplays, and in the face of burning criticism has continued to foster my aims and helped place my organization on a strong footing. It is only by constructive criticism arising from an intelligent understanding of the real problem however, that the colored producer can succeed in his efforts and produce photoplays that will not only be a credit to the race but be on a par with those of the white producer (*Philadelphia Tribune,* 13 December 1924, 3).

PAUL ROBESON, MISS RUSSELL STAR IN MICHEAUX'S LATEST MOVIE FILM, "BODY AND SOUL"

WASHINGTON, D.C., Feb. 9—Oscar Micheaux, president of the Micheaux Film Corporation, was in the city last week in connection with a private showing of his latest picture, "The House Behind the Cedars," from the novel by Charles W. Chestnut [*sic*]. This picture will be shown soon at one of the local theaters.

Mr. Micheaux says he is going abroad in April. He plans to visit London and all of the larger cities on the continent, probably Cairo, and several Russian cities. The purpose of this trip, he says, is to obtain world distribution of Micheaux films (*Pittsburgh Courier,* 14 February 1925, 3).

13) *The Devil's Disciple* (1925)

© No reg.   *Length:* 6 reels/5,000 ft. (5 reels).
Cast: Evelyn Preer, Edward Thompson, Lawrence Chenault, Percy Verwayen.
Production dates:
Locations: New York City.
Source:
Description: The picture is really the first story of Negro night life in Harlem ever brought to the screen. Every scene is taken in this locality and every one will recognize the hundred and one landmarks that are so familiar to us.

The story centers about a beautiful but vain girl who falls in love with a degenerate. She determines to reform him, but fails miserably, and is in turn dragged down and down.

Besides being intensely gripping and dramatic, the picture contains a good moral lesson for our stage struck sisters ("The Douglas Theatre," *New York Amsterdam News,* 14 October 1925, 7).

The story is of a man, disciple of Satan himself, a character of the underworld, who employs women of the streets to earn money for him. He seduces innocent girls from their homes with promises of wealth and happiness to offer them only disillusionment and degradation. A young man hateful of women comes in contact with one of these girls and puts her to the acid test. What ensues makes a story of such nerve-tingling suspense and dramatic situations that you are gripped in an ecstasy of entertainment from which you are not released until the end is flashed before your eyes ("Devil's Disciple, Mighty Race Drama At Royal Next Week," *Pittsburgh Courier,* 11 February 1928, 10A).
Archive:
Screenings: 12–15 October 1925, Owl Theater, Chicago; 18–20 October 1925, New Douglas Theatre and Roosevelt Theatre, New York City; 4–6 November 1925, Lincoln Theater, Chicago; 5–10 November 1925, Franklin Theatre, New York City; 23–25 November 1925, Attucks Theatre, Norfolk, Va.; 13–15 May 1926, Royal Theatre, Baltimore (local premiere);

19–20 May 1926, Dunbar Theatre, Baltimore; 31 May 1926, The Carey, Baltimore; 27–29 June 1926, Broadway Theatre, Washington (local premiere); 7 July 1926, Roosevelt Theater, Baltimore; early October 1927, 18th Street Theater, Kansas City; 31 March–2 April 1927, Royal Theatre, Philadelphia (local premiere); 16–18 February 1928, Royal Theatre, Philadelphia.

Press: "At the Movies," *Chicago Defender,* 10 October 1925, 6A; Advertisement, *Chicago Defender,* 10 October 1925, 8A; Advertisement and "The Douglas Theatre," *New York Amsterdam News,* 14 October 1925, 7; Advertisement, *New York Age,* 17 October 1925, 6; Advertisement and "Evelyn Preer at The New Douglass," *New York Age,* 24 October 1925, 6; publicity still, *Chicago Defender,* 24 October 1925, 8A; publicity still, *Chicago Defender,* 31 October 1925, 6A; "The Lincoln," *Chicago Defender,* 31 October 1925, 7A; Advertisement, *New York Amsterdam News,* 4 November 1925, 7; Advertisement and "'Devil's Disciple' at Attucks Theatre 3 Days Next Week," *Norfolk Journal and Guide,* 21 November 1925, 4; Sylvester Russell, "In the Theatrical World," *Pittsburgh Courier,* 19 December 1925, 9; Advertisement, Baltimore *Afro-American,* 8 May 1926, 4; Advertisement and "'Devil's Disciple,' With Colored Cast At Royal Three Days This Week," Baltimore *Afro-American,* 15 May 1926, 6; Advertisement, Baltimore *Afro-American,* 29 May 1926, 6; Advertisement and "All Colored Cast in Devil's Disciple," *Washington Tribune,* 25 June 1926, 7; Advertisement, Baltimore *Afro-American,* 3 July 1926, 6; Advertisement and "Theatres," *Philadelphia Tribune,* 26 March 1927, 3; "In Old Kaysee," *Chicago Defender,* 15 October 1927, 9A; Advertisement and "Royal Theatre," *Philadelphia Tribune,* 9 February 1928, 6; Advertisement and "Devil's Disciple, Mighty Race Drama At Royal Next Week," *Pittsburgh Courier,* 11 February 1928, 10.

Note: Evelyn Preer (assisted by her husband Edward Thompson) made a personal appearance with this film at its Chicago debut. Preer was on her way to New York, where she was to star in David Belasco's play, *Lulu Belle* (Advertisement, *Chicago Defender,* 10 October 1925, 8A). Race films had not been advertised as playing in Chicago theaters for some time and the *Chicago Defender* remarked, "It goes without saying that it is quite an innovation for this house [the Owl Theater] to book a Race film" ("At the Movies," *Chicago Defender,* 10 October 1925, 6A). When *The Devil's Disciple* played in Philadelphia in February 1928, Percy Verwayen (also Verwayn) was starring in the stage play *Porgy.* The film was presented by A. F. Brooks. Chicago Film Censors reviewed a 5,000-foot, 5-reel print of *The Devil's Disciple* on 9 October 1925 and ordered moderate cuts.

MICHEAUX PRODUCTIONS

Cincinattus Major, long identified with the publicity field in this city and a "live one," is now travelling for the Micheaux film company, as Eastern representative. He reports that a growing demand from the public for Negro films is indicated by the successful trip that he has just completed. Another straw that shows the blowing of the wind is the removal of the general offices from Roanoke, Virginia, to New York City.

Recently the "Devil's Disciple," the firm's latest release, played the Owl Theatre, Chicago, and the Douglass and Roosevelt, New York simultaneously. The "Son of Satan," is also showing profits. A complete reorganization of the sales force, and other up-to-date innovations are now in progress by the firm.

"Body and Soul" with the distinguished Paul Robeson starring will be the next production (Baltimore *Afro-American,* 31 October 1925, 5).

TWO NEW COLORED FEATURES

It would not be amiss to see the "Devil's Disciple" and "The Son of Satan" on local programs before they become commercial. Both of these films have had "first runs" in all the large cities, and from the accounts of the reviewers, have pleased the patrons mightily. They are Micheaux productions, which means an all colored cast, producer and distributor. WHY NOT REQUEST YOUR MANAGER FOR THEM ON HIS BILLS? (Baltimore *Afro-American*, 7 November 1925, 4).

14) *Body and Soul* (1925)

© No reg.   *Length:* 9,000 ft. (9 reels)/7,000 ft.

Cast: Paul Robeson (Rgt. Rev. Isiaah T. Jenkins, Sylvester), Mercedes Gilbert (Martha Jane), Lawrence Chenault (Yellow Curly Hinds), Julia Theresa Russell (Isabelle), Marshall Rodgers (saloon owner), Chester A. Alexander (Deacon Simpkins), Walter Cornick (Brother Amos), Madame Robinson (Sister Lucy), Lillian Johnson (Sister Ca'line), and Tom Fletcher.

Production dates: late 1924.

Locations: New York studios; New Jersey; Atlanta, Georgia.

Source: Uncredited appropriation of Nan Bagby Stephens's play *Roseanne* (1923) with elements of Eugene O'Neill's *The Emperor Jones* (1920) and O'Neill's *All God's Chillun' Got Wings* (1924) as well as Charles Chaplin's *The Pilgrim* (1923).

Description: Mr. Robeson plays a dual role, that of Rev. Jenkins, a rascal masquerading as a minister of the gospel, and that of his twin brother, a hard-working, conscientious lad. During the course of the story complications arise out of which develops one of the most tragic, yet sympathetic stories ever filmed ("Robeson Making His Bow as Movie Star Next Week," *New York Amsterdam News*, 11 November 1925, 5).

Not since "Over the Hill to the Poor House" has there been filmed a story that touches the heart strings with as great a force as "Body and Soul," the new Micheaux photo-production. The story is of a good but helpless girl in the toils of a hypocritical beast. The story is jammed with action, love and suspense, it is one of those pictures of the simple life and of the lowly, but faithful Negro which the world has heard much, but is in no position to know much about. The settings are in the Great American Black Belt of which a story is evolved around that has held audiences spell bound ("Paul Robeson Tops Big Bill at Attucks," *Norfolk Journal and Guide*, 19 June 1926, 5).

Not since "Over the Hill" has there been a story that touches the heart with greater force than this story of a good but helpless girl in the toils of a hypocritical beast, who ruins her very "Body and Soul" for his greed for lust (Advertisement, Baltimore *African American*, 25 September 1926, 6).

Archive: George Eastman House.

Screenings: 15–17 November 1925, New Douglas and Roosevelt theaters, New York City; 6–8 December 1925, Franklin Theatre, New York City; 14–20 December 1925, Gibson's New Dunbar Theatre, Philadelphia; 31 December 1925–2 January 1926, Royal Theatre, Baltimore; 21–23 June 1926, Attucks Theater, Norfolk, Va.; 30 August–5 September 1926, Royal Theatre, Baltimore; 20–21 September 1926, New Dunbar, Baltimore; 27 September 1926, The Carey, Baltimore; 30 September 1926, Lafayette Theatre, Baltimore; 26–29 January 1927, Broadway Theatre, Washington; 21–27 February 1927, 20th Century Theater, Chicago; 13 May 1927 (Friday), Dunbar Theatre, Washington; 24–25 November 1927,

Metropolitan Theater, Chicago; 25 December 1927 (midnight show), Royal Theatre, Philadelphia.

Press: "Beautiful Colored Film Player," *Variety,* 26 November 1924, 1; "Paul Robeson, Miss Russell Star in Micheaux's Latest Movie Film, 'Body and Soul,'" *Pittsburgh Courier,* 14 February 1925, 3; "New Micheaux Film Stars Robeson," *Baltimore Afro-American,* 14 February 1925, 5; Advertisement and "At the New Douglas Theatre," *New York Age,* 7 November 1925, 6; "Robeson Making His Bow as Movie Star Next Week," *New York Amsterdam News,* 11 November 1925, 5; Advertisement, *New York Amsterdam News,* 11 November 1925, 7; Advertisement and "Paul Robeson's Next Play Will Tell The Story of a Negro Prizefighter," *New York Age,* 14 November 1925, 6; "Robeson and Chenault in 'Body and Soul,'" *New York Amsterdam News,* 2 December 1925, 5; Advertisement, *New York Amsterdam News,* 2 December 1925, 7; "Body and Soul at the Dunbar All Next Week," *Pittsburgh Courier,* 12 December 1925, 10; Advertisement, *Pittsburgh Courier,* 12 December 1925, 11; "Paul Robeson and All-Colored Cast at Royal," Baltimore *Afro-American,* 26 December 1925, 4; Advertisement, Baltimore *Afro-American,* 26 December 1925, 15; "Paul Robeson Tops Big Bill at Attucks," *Norfolk Journal and Guide,* 19 June 1926, 5; Advertisement, Baltimore *Afro-American,* 28 August 1926, 4; Advertisement, Baltimore *Afro-American,* 4 September 1926, 3; Maybelle Chew "Along the White Way," Baltimore *Afro-American,* 11 September 1926, 5; Advertisement, Baltimore *Afro-American,* 18 September 1926, 6; Advertisements, Baltimore *Afro-American,* 25 September 1926, 6; Advertisement and "Paul Robeson, Premier Actor at Broadway Theatre," *Washington Tribune,* 21 January 1927, 7; "Correcting Oscar Micheaux," *Chicago Defender,* 22 January 1927, 2B; Advertisement, *Chicago Defender,* 12 February 1927, 8A; "Body and Soul Race Film at 20th Century Theater," *Chicago Defender,* 12 February 1927, 9A; Sylvester Russell, "Sylvester Russell's Review," *Pittsburgh Courier,* 5 March 1927, 2B; Advertisement, *Washington Tribune,* 6 May 1927, 9; Advertisement, *Chicago Defender,* 19 November 1927, 10A; Advertisement, *Philadelphia Tribune,* 22 December 1927, 6.

Note: The Motion Picture Commission of the State of New York reviewed a 9,000-foot, 9-reel print of *Body and Soul* on 5 November 1925 (the date of the application license) and rejected the film in toto. Reviewers stated, "Body and Soul is the story of a man, minister of the gospel, whose habits and manner of life are anything but the life of a good man. He associates with the proprietor of a notorious gambling house, extorts money from him, betrays a girl of his parish, forces her to steal from the bible her mothers savings, forces the girl to leave home, and finally kills the girl's brother when he comes to the sister's protection. . . . The film is of such a character that in the opinion of the Commission it is 'sacrilegious,' 'immoral' and would 'tend to incite to crime.'" Micheaux discovered that the print was missing "some titles and a photograph," added them, and resubmitted the film on 9 November 1925. They made clear that Jenkins was "a man of many aliases and in the development of the plot was only masquerading as a minister." The commission rejected his appeal on 10 November 1925. On 11 November 1925, Micheaux radically edited the film, reducing it to 5 reels—"changing the theme and transferring the villainy from the minister to another character." This version was passed on 12 November 1925, with the understanding that all scenes of drinking and gambling would be eliminated. Chicago Film Censors reviewed a 7,000-foot print of *Body and Soul* on 18 February 1927 and rejected the film for exhibition, noting that "this picture is rejected because it is immoral and exposes to contempt and obloquy a minister of the Protestant Church." *Body and Soul* was re-inspected on 21 February 1927 and the Chicago censors approved this bowdlerized version. Micheaux's promotional material compared *Body and Soul* to *Over the Hill,* performed as a play at New York's Lafayette Theatre in mid-April 1922, a few months after the film version had been shown in Harlem ("At the Lafayette Theatre," *New York Age,* 15 April 1922, 6).

MICHEAUX TO SAIL

Oscar Micheaux, the film producer, dropped into the office last week and told of a planned trip that will include a tour of the West Indies, and South America. The objective of the journey is to place the Micheaux product in those places. A publicity campaign will also be launched to acquaint the citizens with colored productions.

The producer is greatly encouraged over the outlook in this country and the ultimate results of the foreign invasion. "Body and Soul," the "Devil's Disciple," and the "House Behind the Cedars" are all swimming along nicely. There are four more pictures in the course of preparation that will have an early release. Cincinnatus Major, of Baltimore, is now sole Eastern representative (Baltimore *Afro-American,* 12 December 1925, 4).

Swan Micheaux has left his real estate employment in Chicago and gone to New York to open the New Oscar Micheaux Film Exchange in Gotham, it is intimated from a private source (Sylvester Russell, "In the Theatrical World," *Pittsburgh Courier,* 19 December 1925, 9).

MICHEAUX WEDS

Oscar Micheaux, the film magnate, has joined hands in matrimony with Miss Alice Burton. The ceremony took place at Montclair, N.J., the home of the bride, Saturday, March 20.

It was quite a social event and was attended by hundreds. Mr. Micheaux is the producer of the well-known race films, "The Homesteader," "The House Behind the Cedars," and many other educational screen successes. The writer extends to them many congratulations (*Chicago Defender* [National Edition], 3 April 1926, 6A).

15) *The Conjure Woman* (1926)

© No reg.   *Length:*
Cast: Evelyn Preer, Lawrence Chenault, Percy Verwayen, Alma Sewell, Mattie V. Wilkes, Sidney Easton.
Production dates:
Locations:
Source: Charles W. Chesnutt's short story from *The Conjure Woman* (1899).
Description:
Archive:
Screenings: 19–25 July 1926, Lafayette Theatre, New York City; 23–24 September 1926, Republic Theatre, Washington; 24–26 March 1927, Royal Theatre, Baltimore; 26–28 April 1927, Broadway Theatre, Washington; late November 1927, 18th Street Theater, Kansas City.
Press: Publicity still, *New York Amsterdam News,* 14 July 1926, 10; "'Liza' to Follow Connie's Revue Next Week," *New York Amsterdam News,* 21 July 1926, 11; Advertisement and "Evelyn Preer at the Republic," *Washington Tribune,* 17 September 1926, 7; Advertisement, Baltimore *Afro-American,* 19 March 1927, 10; Advertisement, *Washington Tribune,* 22 April 1927, 9; "In Old Kaysee," *Chicago Defender,* 26 November 1927, 9A.
Note: In a letter to Charles Chesnutt, Micheaux wrote, "I think you could develop a good synopsis from the first story of *The Conjure Woman.* Write the case of the man and woman

into a good love story, let there, if possible, be a haunted house, the haunts being intriguers to be found out near the end, the heroine to have ran off there and in hiding — anything that will thrill or suspend, but have a delightful ending and give opportunity for a strong male and female lead" (Oscar Micheaux to Charles Waddell Chesnutt, 30 October 1921, Charles Waddell Chesnutt Papers, Western Reserve Historical Society, Cleveland, Ohio). When this film opened at New York's Lafayette Theatre, Evelyn Preer was then appearing in David Belasco's production of *Lulu Belle* on Broadway. The comparatively few screening dates and general dearth of publicity for *The Conjure Woman* remain to be explained. It is tempting to relate these gaps to a statement made by the Royal Theatre management one week after it screened the film, apologizing for recent shortcomings in the programming and announcing that its future policy would be "to give the public amusement that will be high class in every respect. Pictures will be the best obtainable in keeping with the high standard set by the stage attraction" ("Royal Management Makes Statement," Baltimore *Afro-American*, 21 March 1927, 10). This may not have been a very successful film.

16) THE SPIDER'S WEB (1926)

© No reg.   *Length:* 7,000 ft. (7 reels).

Cast: Evelyn Preer (Norma Shepard, the niece), Lorenzo McLane (Elmer Harris, detective for the Department of Justice), Edward "Eddie" Thompson (Martinez, a Cuban numbers banker), Zodie Jackson, Grace Smythe (Madame Boley), Henrietta Loveless (Mary Austin, a widow), Marshall Rodgers, Billy Gulport, Cy Williams, Josiah Diggs, Cincinnatus Major (the lawyer), Edna Barr (Creole belle), Palestine Delores Williams.

Production dates: late summer and fall 1926.

Locations: New York City; Baltimore.

Source: Oscar Micheaux's story "The Policy Players" (date of publication, if any, unknown).

Description: Mary Austin, a widow, dwelling in a small Southern delta town, is the recipient of a visit from her niece, Norma Shepard (Evelyn Preer) of New York, who informs her on arrival that on the way from the depot, the man who directed her, and a stranger, advised that he would call on her late that night. Her aunt recognizes the man as Ballinger, a planter's son, and tells her niece that he is notorious and must sweetheart with any colored girl that comes to town, otherwise she must flee. She is terribly upset and frightened.

Meanwhile, to the village from Chicago, has come Elmer Harris, a detective, connected with the Department of Justice, United States Secret Service, looking for a man accused of practicing peonage. When he calls that night, Harris recognizes Ballinger as the man he wants and places him under arrest. Ballinger's associates gather later, however, and Norma is compelled to flee, so returns to New York, taking her aunt, Mary Austin, with her.

In strained circumstances later, her aunt begins to play "the numbers" (policy) and soon loses all self-control, playing every penny she gets hold of in a desperate but vain effort to win. Continuing to plunge, she takes the rent money one day and places it all on a single number to come up—and it does. Knowing that she will be rich after collecting her winnings, she rushes excitedly to the "banker's" office. A few minutes later, carrying a large package of money, she is seen by a passer-by stealing out of the office mysteriously. Upon investigation, the passer-by discovers the banker dead upon the floor, his safe rifled. Mary is arrested, tried and sent to prison.

Certain people, including Harris, do not believe she committed the crime, how-ever,—but WHO did? Harris sets out to unravel the mystery and how he came in time to succeed, free Mary Austin and place the crime where it belonged, makes up as good a story as you can hope to see. A great picture! ("Royal," Baltimore *Afro-American,* 22 January 1927, 10).

Deals with the well-known evil of "number" gambling in the black belt of New York. A Cuban number banker, played by Eddie Thompson, is reported refusing to pay off af-ter being hit hard for a winning by the players and is found mysteriously murdered a few minutes later. Suspicion points to Mary Austin, who is subsequently arrested and sent to prison for the crime. How the guilty parties are at last discovered and brought to jus-tice makes up as interesting a story of Negro life as one can wish to see (*Chicago De-fender,* 15 January 1927, 8A).

Charlotte a young negro girl graduate with no purpose or plans for the future de-cides to visit an aunt in a small southern village. Ballanger, a white man, is shown ac-costing her upon her arrival in village. Mary Austin, aunt of Charlotte, is distressed and appeals to Doc. Harris a young negro sent to the village by the attorney General to in-vestigate conditions peonage, etc. Ballanger who threatens Mary Austin, saying he will be there "Thursday night" and "no monkey business" is later seen casting off a creole girl and upon arrival at Mary Austin's home to force his attentions on Charlotte is ar-rested by "Doc. Harris." Scene shifts to Harlem—Mary Austin is shown playing the "num-bers" hoping to make enough to send for her crippled daughter and have her operated on. Real Estate Office is shown where negroes combine forces to cheat the unfortunate players of these "Numbers" (detailed system of which is fully given in subtitles) and car-rying out their plans. Mary Austin after losing everything finally picks the winning num-ber, goes to get her money from the "number Banker" Martinez, finding him dead, steals the amount of her winnings. She is accused of Martinez murder and imprisoned. A ne-gro woman, Madame Boley from Oklahoma, with great wealth, is shown entertaining lavishly. She takes a fancy to Doc. Harris, who is secretly working to free Mary Austin and visits Madame Boley's home, who invites him upstairs (subtitles very bad) and in a drunken condition confesses to the murder of Martinez and stealing his money, because of his unfaithfulness. Mary Austin is thereby exonerated. Action bad and subtitles very suggestive (Motion Picture Commission of the State of New York, 3 January 1927).

Archive:

Screenings: 1 November 1926, Royal Theatre, Baltimore (preview); 27–30 December 1926, Royal Theatre, Philadelphia (local premiere); 8–11 January 1927, M.&S. Douglas Theatre and M.&S. Roosevelt Theatre, New York City (local premiere); 10–12 January 1927, Attucks Theatre, Norfolk, Va.; 17–23 January 1927, 20th Century Theater, Chicago; 24–29 Janu-ary 1927, New Royal Theatre, Baltimore; 31 January–1 February 1927, New Dunbar The-atre, Baltimore; 23–26 February 1927, Broadway Theatre, Washington.

Press: "The 'Spider's Web' New Micheaux Film," Baltimore *Afro-American,* 6 November 1926, 14; Advertisement and "Royal Theatre," *Philadelphia Tribune,* 25 December 1926, 3; "'The Spider's Web' at Roosevelt and Douglas," *New York Amsterdam News,* 5 January 1927, 10; Advertisement, *New York Amsterdam News,* 5 January 1927, 11; "Latest Colored Pic-ture at the Roosevelt and New Douglass Theatres," *New York Age,* 8 January 1927, 6; Ad-vertisement and "'Spider's Web' with a Colored Cast, Attucks," *Norfolk Journal and Guide* 8 January 1927, 4; Advertisement and "Does Lead Role in 'The Spider's Web,'" *Chicago Defender,* 15 January 1927, 8A; "Twentieth Century," *Chicago Defender,* 22 January 1927,

6A; Advertisement and "Royal," Baltimore *Afro-American,* 22 January 1927, 10; "Along the White Way," "Local Folks in Micheaux Film," and "Royal," Baltimore *Afro-American,* 29 January 1927, 7; Advertisement, Baltimore *Afro-American,* 29 January 1927, 8; "Evelyn Preer Ranks First As Stage and Movie Star," *Pittsburgh Courier,* 16 April 1927, 1A; Advertisement and "'The Spider's Web' with All Colored Stars at The Broadway," *Washington Tribune,* 18 February 1927, 7.

Note: Palestine Dolores Williams was the runner-up for the beauty contest staged by the Royal Theatre in Baltimore on Saturday, 11 September 1926 (Advertisement, Baltimore *Afro-American,* 11 September 1926, 4; "The 'Spider's Web' New Micheaux Film," Baltimore *Afro-American,* 6 November 1926, 14). Several actors from this film were appearing in David Belasco's play *Lulu Belle,* which opened at the Belasco Theatre on Broadway on 12 February 1926 and was still running when the film had its New York premiere. Grace Smythe was a recently adopted stage name for Grace Smith. Attendance was heavy at the 20th Century Theater in Chicago: "You have to get in line if you go there after 7 P.M. The picture is accompanied by pipe organ music played by Celesta Morris" ("Twentieth Century," *Chicago Defender,* 22 January 1927, 6A). The film's title was part of a fad: *The Spider Web Revue* was performed at the Lafayette Theatre, New York City, in December 1926 (*New York Amsterdam News,* 15 December 1926, 12). Chicago Film Censors reviewed *The Spider's Web* (7,000 feet, 7 reels) on 6 January 1927 and approved the film for exhibition with no cuts ordered. The Motion Picture Commission of the State of New York, however, reviewed *The Spider's Web* (7 reels) on 31 December 1926 and rejected the film. As the Commission ruled on 3 January 1927, "the picture clearly violates the statues in that much of it is 'immoral,' and 'incite[s] to crime.'" Micheaux apparently appealed their decision, because on 11 January 1927, a letter submitted to the Commission from J. A. Koerpel, who was associated with Agfa Raw Film Corporation, stated: "I have . . . instructed Mr. Micheaux to make up a list of all the eliminations we made on the *Spider's Web.* I hope to have them the first thing in the morning . . . for your files" (New York State Censorship Records).

OSCAR MICHEAUX IN

The czar of Race filmdom, Oscar Micheaux, was a visitor at the Scribe's office in the plant of the Chicago Defender this week. The motion picture magnate was somewhat gleeful over the outlook for the coming season with his master photoplays. He arrived in Chicago from a seven-thousand mile trip by auto through the South, where he lined up the bookings of his films for the coming season. "The Millionaire" is his latest release and had its premier showing to the trade agents in Chicago several months ago. All pronounced it a wonderful picture from every angle. He attended to some business in Chicago for a few days and expects to leave for New York the last of the week. Mail will reach him at the New York office, 200 West 125th Street. Grace Smith, William Edmons [*sic*], J. Lawrence Criner, Lyonal Monagas are the stars in the film, "The Millionaire" (*Chicago Defender,* 24 September 1927, 9A).

17) *The Millionaire* (1927)

© 15 February 1928, Oscar Micheaux; LU24983   *Length:* 9,000 ft. (9 reels).
Cast: Grace Smythe (Celia Wellington), Lionel Monagas (Trevy Dureau, the Lizard), J.

Lawrence Criner (Pelham Guitry), Cleo Desmond, William Edmondson, Vera Bracken, S. T. Jacks, E. G. Tatum, Robert S. Abbott (editor and publisher of the *Chicago Defender*), and Mrs. Robert Abbott.

Production dates: [Spring–Summer 1927.]

Locations: New York City, Chicago.

Source:

Description: The Millionaire deals with the adventures of Pelham Guitry, a soldier of fortune, a man who, as a youth, possessing great initiative and a definite objective, hies himself far from the haunts of his race—thousands of miles away to South America. There, upon the wild, billowy plains of the Argentine, he becomes a sort of "Wild Bull of the Pampas." Fifteen years fly by, and, having amassed a huge fortune, he returns to America, his heart anxious and hungry for that most infinite of all things—woman. In New York he meets Celia Wellington, the siren—a woman with an inferiority complex—a beautiful, dazzling talented—but unworthy creature; the concubine of the Lizard, a most notorious underworld character in New York, who, in league with Brock, king of the underworld, seek to inveigle him into marriage with the vampire ("Editor Abbott and Wife Star in Movies," *Chicago Defender*, 19 November 1927, 10A).

. . . In New York he meets Celia Wellington, cabaret dancer and love maid. This soldier of fortune, Pelham Guitry, allows himself to become infatuated while the check[s] he hands to his intended go to the "Lizard," a notorious Harlem crook.

How he comes to his senses and how the words of his old school teacher come to him in times of need, form a tale that is not often portrayed in race productions ("'The Millionaire,' Drama of Soldier of Fortune, With Race Cast, On Dunbar Screen," Baltimore *Afro-American*, 21 January 1928, 7).

Archive:

Screenings: 21–24 November 1927, Metropolitan Theater, Chicago; 28 November–1 December 1927, Royal Theatre, Philadelphia; 5–11 December 1927, Lafayette Theatre, New York City; 26–27 December 1927, Regent Theatre, Baltimore; 30 January–4 February 1928, Elmore Theatre, Pittsburgh; 6–7 February 1928, Dunbar Theatre, Baltimore; 7–9 December 1929, Odeon Theater, New York City.

Press: "Micheaux's Latest Picture Coming To Lafayette Theatre," *New York Age*, 19 November 1927, 6; Still, *Chicago Defender*, 19 November 1927, 9A; Advertisement and "Editor Abbott and Wife Star in Movies," *Chicago Defender*, 19 November 1927, 10A; Advertisement and "Royal Theatre," *Philadelphia Tribune*, 24 November 1927, 6; Advertisement, *New York Amsterdam News*, 30 November 1927, 13; Advertisement, *New York Age*, 3 December 1927, 6; "Stage and Screen Hits at Lafayette," *New York Amsterdam News*, 7 December 1927, 13; Advertisement, *New York Age*, 10 December 1927, 6; "'The Millionaire,' Featuring Local Girl, at Regent Two Days," Baltimore *Afro-American*, 24 December 1927, 7; Advertisement, Baltimore *Afro-American*, 24 December 1927, 8; "'The Millionaire,' Drama of Soldier of Fortune, With Race Cast, On Dunbar Screen," Baltimore *Afro-American*, 21 January 1928, 7; Advertisement and "Dunbar To Play 'Millionaire,' With Race Cast," Baltimore *Afro-American*, 4 February 1928, 7; Advertisement, *Pittsburgh Courier*, 28 January 1928, 12A; "At the Elmore," *Pittsburgh Courier*, 4 February 1928, 3B; "At the Odeon," *New York Amsterdam News*, 4 December 1929, 8.

Note: The film was largely shot in Chicago: "The Dreamland cabaret, South parkway and many other familiar places have been used as locations." It thus gave black Chicagoans "many opportunities of seeing yourself and friends on the screen" ("Editor Abbott and Wife Star in Movies," *Chicago Defender*, 19 November 1927, 10A). On opening night at the

Chicago screening, "long lines awaited entry to the second show, which was packed, and the third show was also a sold out house" ("The Metropolitan," *Chicago Defender,* 26 November 1927, 8A). Chicago Film Censors reviewed a 9,000-foot, 9-reel print of *The Millionaire* on 21 October 1927 and approved the film for exhibition with moderate cuts. The State of New York Motion Picture Division reviewed *The Millionaire* (9 reels) 3 January 1928 (even though date was incorrectly written on the document; the stamped date is 1928) and approved the film for exhibition with extensive eliminations. Poster in Cripps, *Slow Fade to Black,* 201.

18) *Thirty Years Later* (1928)

© 15 February 1928, Oscar Micheaux: LU245007   *Length:* 6,000 ft. (6 reels)

Cast: William Edmundson (George Eldridge Van Paul), A. B. DeComathiere (Habisham Strutt), Adelle Dabney (Clara Booker), Harington Garter, Gertrude Snelson (Mrs. Van Paul), Mme. Robinson, Arthur Ray, Ruth Williams, Mabel Kelly (Hester Morgan). [Roles of individual actors from Sampson, *Blacks in Black and White,* 344.]

Production dates:

Locations:

Source: Henry Francis Downing's play *The Racial Tangle* (aka *The Tangle*).

Description: The theme of the picture deals with a question of the day, "should a colored girl marry a white man?" and the method in which Mr. Micheaux deals with the issue is unfolded to a surprising and interesting manner. Several of the more outstanding colored performers are included in the cast of "Thirty Years Later" ("All Colored Cast Appear On Bill at Pearl," *Philadelphia Tribune,* 16 February 1928, 6).

This production is a tribute to the Colored race and is crammed full of many interesting, exciting and pathetic moments, the climax of which is the love of a mother for her son ("The Met Next Week," *Chicago Defender,* 19 May 1928, 10A).

The gripping plot hinges about the mixing of the races. George Eldridge Van Paul, wealthy clubman, falls in love with a race girl and poses as a man of color to be near her. Later he finds that he is the son of his housekeeper, upon whom he had looked with scorn because of her color.

The play is redolent with action, with all the jealousy and envy capable of being created by racial differences and wealth ("Royal," Baltimore *Afro-American,* 14 April 1928, 7).

Archive:

Screenings: 20–25 February 1928, Pearl Street Theatre, Philadelphia; 17–23 March 1928, Renaissance Theatre, New York City; 16–22 April 1928, Lincoln Theater, Kansas City; 19–21 April 1928, Lincoln Theatre, Washington; 23–26 April 1928, Royal Theatre, Baltimore; 21–22 May 1928, Dunbar Theatre, Baltimore; 22–25 May 1928, Metropolitan Theater, Chicago; 28–31 May 1928, Broadway Theatre, Washington; 4 June 1928, The Carey, Baltimore; 26–28 October 1929, Odeon Theatre, New York.

Press: Advertisement, *Philadelphia Tribune,* 16 February 1928, 3; Advertisement, *Washington Tribune,* 13 April 1928, 10; Advertisement, *New York Amsterdam News,* 14 March 1928, 8; "In Movies," *Pittsburgh Courier,* 14 April 1928, 3; "Royal," Baltimore *Afro-American,* 14 April 1928, 7; Advertisement, Baltimore *Afro-American,* 21 April 1928, 9; Obie McCollum, "Things Theatrical: Mr. Micheaux Pioneers," Baltimore *Afro-American,* 5 May 1928, 8; Clipping, 6 May 1928, George P. Johnson Negro Film Collection; Advertisement, Baltimore *Afro-American,* 19 May 1928, 9; Advertisement and "The Met Next Week,"

Chicago Defender, 19 May 1928, 10A; Advertisement, *Washington Tribune,* 25 May 1928, 8; "The Metropolitan," *Chicago Defender,* 26 May 1928, 10A; "Chicago Theatrical News," *Chicago Defender,* 26 May 1928, 11A; Advertisement, Baltimore *Afro-American,* 2 June 1928, 8; Advertisement and "Colored Company at Odeon," *New York Amsterdam News,* 23 October 1929, 8.

Note: Henry Francis Downing (1851–1928) was hailed as an African-American dramatist "deserving of serious consideration" in 1920 when his play *The Racial Tangle* was slated for production by the Lafayette Players ("Race Playwright," *Chicago Defender,* 17 July 1920, 6). Micheaux's *Daughter of the Congo* (1930) was also adapted from a literary work by Downing. Downing may have enjoyed some renewed attention with the publication of *Liberia and Her People* (New York: 1925), which had an introduction by Heywood Broun. He died shortly after *Thirty Years Later* had its premiere ("Royal," Baltimore *Afro-American,* 14 April 1928, 7). Mabel [Mable] Kelly was Miss Lincoln of the 1927 Howard-Lincoln football classic and went on to star in Swan Micheaux's film *The Mid-Night Ace* (1928) with A. B. "Abe" DeComathiere ("Scenes from 'The Midnight Ace,'" *Pittsburgh Courier,* 24 March 1928, 3B). Abe's last name was publicized as both Decomathiere ("Royal," Baltimore *Afro-American,* 14 April 1928, 7) and Comathiere ("Colored Company at Odeon," *New York Amsterdam News,* 23 October 1929, 8) in conjunction with *Thirty Years Later.* The film was advertised as a story "patterned after Alice Rhinelander's famous case" ("In Movies," *Pittsburgh Courier,* 14 April 1928, 3). Chicago Film Censors reviewed a 6,000-foot, 6-reel print of *Thirty Years Later* on 18 May 1928 and approved the film for exhibition with very minor cuts.

MICHEAUX FILM CO. BANKRUPT

NEW YORK, N.Y., Mar 1.—The Micheaux Film Corporation with offices at 200 West 135th street, and for the past 10 years one of the best known firms producing race films, has filed a voluntary bankruptcy in the U.S. 7th District Court through its attorney, Morris Kohn, 103 152nd street.

The petition states the assets as $1,400 and the liabilities as $7,837 (*Pittsburgh Courier,* 3 March 1928, 2B).

Oscar Micheaux's "Thirty Years Later" has been given the biggest reception received by any of his photoplays. The picture played to the biggest business in the history of the Pearl Theatre, Philadelphia, during a week's run there. The production was adapted from the play "The Tangle," by Henry F. Downing, celebrated playwright who died only a few weeks ago ("Coming Photoplays, Royal," Baltimore *Afro-American,* 14 April 1928, 7).

19) *The Broken Violin* (1928)

© No reg.   *Length:* 7,000 ft. (7 reels).

Cast: William A. Clayton, Jr., Ethel Smith, Homer Tutt Whitney, J. Homer Tutt, Ardelle Dabney, Alice B. Russell, Ike Paul, Daisy Foster, Gertrude Snelson, "Boots" Hope, and W. "Pickaninny" Hill.

Production dates:

Locations:

Source: Oscar Micheaux's story "House of Mystery" (date of publication, if any, unknown).

Description: A synopsis of the story points out that Lelia Cooper, young, intelligent and beautiful daughter of a lowly washwoman, is possessed with a gift for music and plays the violin with much feeling. One eventful day her father, a drunkard, loses his week's pay in a game, and, returning home intoxicated and disgruntled, demands money from her mother. Upon being refused, he secures the violin, after a desperate struggle, and smashes it over her mother's head. Her young brother coming up, rushes to his mother's rescue—but is severely beaten by the father, who seeks then to take the boy's pay by force. A struggle and a prolonged chase—a huge auto truck passing—the father rushes blindly across its path and—is run down and killed!

Seven sensational reels—Don't miss it! ("Daisy Theater Will Present Broken Violin," clipping, George P. Johnson Negro Film Collection).

Archive:

Screenings: 22–27 October 1928, Elmore Theatre, Pittsburgh; 15–17 April 1929, Royal Theatre, Philadelphia; 10–11 May 1929, Douglas Theatre, Philadelphia; 13–15 June 1929, Lincoln Theatre, Baltimore; 19 August 1929, The Carey, Baltimore; mid-August 1929, Broadway Theatre, Washington; 1–4 October [1929], Daisy Theater, [unknown locale]; 19 November 1929, Lafayette Theatre, Baltimore.

Press: "New Movie to Be Out Soon," *Pittsburgh Courier,* 25 August 1928, 2B; "Micheaux' Broken Violin," *Pittsburgh Courier,* 15 September 1928, 2B; Advertisement, *Pittsburgh Courier,* 20 October 1928, 9A; "'The Broken Violin' on Elmore Bill," *Pittsburgh Courier,* 27 October 1928, 3B; Advertisement, *Philadelphia Tribune,* 11 April 1929, 6; Advertisement and "Great Colored Picture at Douglas Next Week," *Philadelphia Tribune,* 2 May 1929, 6; Advertisement, *Washington Tribune,* 16 August 1929, 6; Advertisement, Baltimore *Afro-American,* 17 August 1929, 8; Advertisement, Baltimore *Afro-American,* 8 June 1929, 8; "Daisy Theater Will Present Broken Violin," clipping, George P. Johnson Negro Film Collection; Advertisement, Baltimore *Afro-American,* 16 November 1929, 9.

Note: Chicago Film Censors reviewed a 7,000-foot, 7-reel print of *The Broken Violin* on 31 May 1929 and approved the film for exhibition. They remarked that "some cut[s] have been made in the first two reels."

> "The Midnight Ace," a Swan Micheaux picture, was seen at the Vendome last week. While it was only fair it is a slight improvement on his brother, Oscar ("Sylvester Russell's Review," *Pittsburgh Courier,* 20 October 1928, 3B).

ALONG RIALTO
MICHEAUX PICTURES DRAW.

> Saw Mr. Oscar Micheaux in Tob's restaurant a couple of nights ago and after a talk on his profession I was a much wiser man of colored pictures. The pioneer of Negro films says that his pictures receive great patronage from our people, and that in every city where they are shown crowded houses greet them. From the "House Behind the Cedars," one of the first screened, to "The Broken Violin," one of his latest, everywhere they are shown to packed houses. Mr. Micheaux scouts the country for the best talent obtainable for every picture. For his newest picture, now being made in his New York studio, he has chosen the best actors and some of the prettiest and brainiest of our feminine kind (Chappy Gardner, "Along the Rialto," *Pittsburgh Courier,* 5 January 1929, 1C).

20) *THE WAGES OF SIN* (1929)

© No reg.   *Length:* 7,000 ft. (7 reels).

Cast: Lorenzo Tucker (Winston Le Jaune), Katherine Noisette, William A. Clayton, Jr. (Jefferson Le Jaune aka Jefferson Lee), Rudolph Hind, Ardelle Dabney, [Bessie Gibbens, Sylvia

Birdsong, Alice B. Russell, William Baker, Gertrude Snelson—Sampson, *Blacks in Black and White,* 345].

Production dates: late 1928–early 1929.

Locations: New York studio.

Source: Oscar Micheaux's unpublished story "Alias Jefferson Lee."

Description: Oscar Micheaux's latest contribution to the screen, "The Wages of Sin," an adaptation from the story 'Alias Jefferson Lee,' with an all-star cast, tells the story of two brothers who meet shortly after the opening of the story, when the elder, Winston Le Jaune, goes home to bury his mother. His elder sister when they are alone delivers the mother's dying message, which was for him to bear with the younger brother. J. Lee, who has already been shown while they were soldiering together in France to be a coward.

Accordingly, after returning to his office in the city he sends for his brother and gives him a job. Winston is a motion picture producer and shortly after J. Lee arrives he begins to steal the company's money which he spends on women in cabarets and on wild parties. Soon Winston finds his company in financial needs and is compelled to go away repeatedly to raise funds to carry on. On one of these trips he meets a girl with whom he falls in love. About to marry, she suddenly disappears. Unable to find her, Le Jaune later in Chicago meets his brother, whom he had finally discharged.

In a weak moment he reinstates him. In the beginning J. Lee had only crippled the firm by his thefts, but once reinstated he sets out to wreck it, and succeeds, betraying his brother in the meanwhile. At this point the story takes an unexpected turn, a new and unusual character enters the picture, and the activities that follow adds thrills and the heroism is of an unusual nature, bringing [the] story to a logical and happy climax that should please everybody who chances to see it. "The Wages of Sin" is an improvement over the usual photoplay of this character and a long step forward in the production of racial photoplays ("Micheaux's Picture," *Chicago Defender,* 8 December 1928, 11).

Has to do with the life of two brothers, one of whom goes straight while the other goes wrong, led on by wild life. Thrills and heroism make this an unusual production ("At the Renaissance," *New York Amsterdam News,* 30 January 1929, 8).

Archive:

Screenings: 2–6 February 1929, Renaissance Theatre, New York City; 4–6 February 1929, Royal Theatre, Philadelphia; 18–21 March 1929, Royal Theatre, Baltimore; 25–29 March 1929, Apollo Theater, Chicago; 1–5 April 1929, Elmore Theater, Pittsburgh; 1–3 April 1929, Attucks Theatre, Norfolk, Va.; 1–2 May 1929, Lafayette Theatre, Baltimore; 6 May 1929, The Carey, Baltimore; 9–13 November 1929, Odeon Theatre, New York City.

Press: "Micheaux's Picture," *Chicago Defender,* 8 December 1928, 11; Advertisement and "At the Renaissance," *New York Amsterdam News,* 30 January 1929, 8; Advertisement and "Royal Theatre," *Philadelphia Tribune,* 31 January 1929, 6; Advertisement and "'The Wages of Sin,' With Colored Cast, To Be At The Renaissance Theatre," *New York Age,* 2 February 1929, 6; Advertisement and "Royal," Baltimore *Afro-American,* 16 March 1929, 7; Advertisement, *Chicago Defender,* 23 March 1929, 10A; "Coming to Apollo" and publicity still, *Chicago Defender,* 23 March 1929, 11A; Advertisement, *Pittsburgh Courier,* 30 March 1929, 8A; Advertisement, *Norfolk Journal and Guide,* 30 March 1929, 3; "Fine Photoplay and Classy Stage Show on Elmore Bill," *Pittsburgh Courier,* 6 April 1929, 8A; Advertisement, Baltimore *Afro-American,* 27 April 1929, 10; Advertisement, Baltimore *Afro-American,* 4 May 1929, 12; "Harlem's Sheik," *Chicago Defender,* 8 June 1929, 8; Advertisement and "Micheaux's Latest at The Odeon Theatre," *New York Amsterdam*

News, 6 November 1929, 8; "She Likes Being a Movie Actress," *Norfolk Journal and Guide*, 19 April 1930, 10; "The Villain of The Wages of Sin Now Wants to be a Priest," Baltimore *Afro-American*, 18 January 1936, 10.

Note: Wages of Sin was the title of a novel by Victor Vallon that was serialized in the black press around 1927 (see *Philadelphia Tribune*, August–September 1927); a popular stage melodrama of that name was also being performed in urban black theaters (e.g., at the Pearl Theatre, Philadelphia for the week beginning 22 October 1928). Henry T. Sampson has argued convincingly that Micheaux's story has strong autobiographical elements and is based on difficulties he encountered with his brother Swan Micheaux, who had run the business until fired in 1927 (*Blacks in Black and White*, 160). Chicago Film Censors reviewed a 7,000-foot, 7-reel print of *The Wages of Sin* on 23 March 1929 and approved the film for exhibition with minor cuts. Publicity still in Cripps, *Slow Fade to Black*, 194.

21) WHEN MEN BETRAY (1929)

© No reg. **Length:** 6,000 ft. (6 reels).

Cast: Katherine Noisette, William A. Clayton, Jr., Bessie Gibbens, Gertrude Snelson, Lorenzo "Alonzo" Tucker, Ethel Smith, Alice B. Russell.

Production dates:

Locations: New York City.

Source:

Description: Two brothers in love with the same girl, see these brothers love, thrilling, love drama. Oh boy! (Advertisement, Baltimore *Afro-American*, 16 November 1929, 8).

An exceptionally strong melodrama of night life in Chicago and New York, with an all-colored cast.

Briefly, it is the story of a beautiful girl who was cold to the love of a good and ambitious young lad. Believing the rosy promises of a smooth-tongued stranger, she runs away and follows him to the city. The unhappiness and disaster which follow can easily be imagined. Deserted on her wedding night, alone, penniless, in a foreign city, left to the none too tender mercy of strangers ("At the New Douglas," *New York Amsterdam News*, 25 September 1929, 9).

Archive:

Screenings: 7–13 August 1929, Royal Theatre, Baltimore; 2–4 September 1929, Royal Theatre, Philadelphia; 28–30 September 1929, New Douglas Theatre, New York City; 5–7 October 1929, Odeon Theatre, New York City; 16–19 October 1929, Royal Theatre, Philadel-

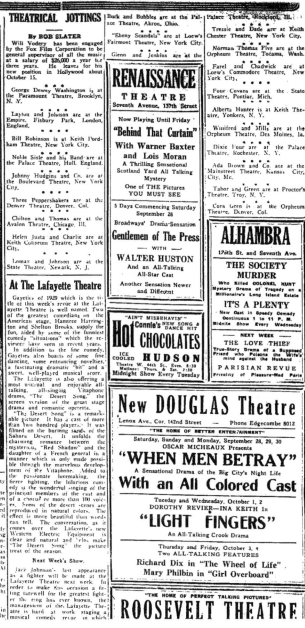

Advertisement for *When Men Betray* (1929). *New York Age*, 28 September 1929, 6.

phia; 22–27 October 1929, Alhambra Theatre, New York City; 9–13 November 1929, Odeon Theatre, New York City; 18 November 1929, Dunbar Theater, Baltimore.

Press: Advertisement, Baltimore *Afro-American,* 3 August 1929, 10; Advertisement and "Season's Greatest Colored Picture at The Royal Theatre," *Philadelphia Tribune,* 29 August 1929, 6; Advertisement, *New York Amsterdam News,* 25 September 1929, 9; Advertisement, *New York Age,* 28 September 1929, 6; "At the Odeon," *New York Amsterdam News,* 2 October 1929, 8; Advertisement, *Philadelphia Tribune,* 10 October 1929, 6; Advertisement and "Artie Cain Back at the Alhambra," *New York Amsterdam News,* 23 October 1929, 8; Advertisement and "Mischeaux's Latest at The Odeon Theatre," *New York Amsterdam News,* 6 November 1929, 8; Advertisement, *Philadelphia Tribune,* 10 October 1929, 6; Advertisement, Baltimore *Afro-American,* 16 November 1929, 8; "Coming Films," Baltimore *Afro-American,* 16 November 1929, 9.

Note: Chicago Film Censors reviewed a 6,000-foot, 6-reel print of *When Men Betray* on 31 October 1929 and rejected the film, stating: "This picture is rejected because it tells of the betrayal of a girl, repeated scenes of women who are evidently prostitutes, a man giving money to one of the women for an immoral purpose. Deliberate murder for revenge, which is justified by the subtitles and by a jury (in a newspaper article)." Censorship records are incomplete, but *When Men Betray* was reinspected by the Chicago film censors on 16 November 1929 and approved for exhibition with moderate cuts.

22) *A Daughter of the Congo* (1930)

© No reg.   *Length:* 7 reels.

Cast: Katherine Noisette (Lupelta), Salem Tutt Whitney (Kojo, the rumhound president), Daisy Harding (singer), Lorenzo Tucker (Capt. Paul Dale), Roland C. Irving (Lieut. Brown), [Joe Byrd (Wheraboe), Wilhelmina Williams (Ressha), Clarence Redd (Lodango), Alice B. Russell (Miss Pattie), Charles Moore (John Calvert), Gertrude Snelson (Calvert's sister), Percy Verwayen (Pidgy Muffy), Mme. Robinson (Lobue), Willor Lee Guilford (Hulda), "Speedy" Wilson (Mwamba), Rudolph Dawson (tap dancer)—Sampson, *Blacks in Black and White,* 296].

Production dates:

Locations:

Source: Henry Francis Downing's novel *The American Cavalryman: A Liberian Romance* (New York: Neale Publishing, 1917).

Description: The story of Lupelta, a beautiful mulatto girl, who has been stolen as a baby and brought up among the savages of the Jungle.

    The plot opens with Lupelta, on her way to the kraals of Lodango, powerful Chief of the Imbundas, to become his bride. She has paused to bathe in a brook, when she and her maid are surrounded, captured and made prisoners by slave hunters. In the meantime, Captain Paul Dale, colored, United States Army, assisted by his First Lieutenant, Ronald Brown, who have been sent to the little black republic by their Government, to organize a constabulary, are on a reconnoiter. They encounter the Arabs, who have taken Lupelta prisoner, promptly seize the slave hunters, making them prisoners and rescuing Lupelta (Advertisement, Baltimore *Afro-American,* 20 September 1930, 9).

Archive:

Screenings: 5–11 April 1930, Renaissance Theatre, New York City; 27–28 August 1930, Regent Theatre, Baltimore; 8–9 September 1930, Dunbar, Baltimore; 22–23 September 1930,

Lafayette Theatre and The Carey, Baltimore; 13–15 October 1930, Royal Theatre, Philadelphia.

Press: Advertisement and "At the Renaissance Theatre," *New York Amsterdam News,* 2 April 1930, 9; Advertisement and "Renaissance Theatre," *New York Age,* 5 April 1930, 6; "N.Y. Youths Write Theme Song of Film," *Chicago Defender,* 5 April 1930, 11; Advertisement and "At the Renaissance," *New York Amsterdam News,* 9 April 1930, 9; Advertisement and "Renaissance Theatre," *New York Age,* 12 April 1930, 6; Geraldyn Dismond, "Micheaux Produces Another," *Pittsburgh Courier,* 12 April 1930, 7B; Theophilus Lewis, "The Harlem Sketch Book," *New York Amsterdam News,* 16 April 1930, 10; Geraldyn Dismond, "*A Daughter of the Congo* Features Roland C. Irving," *Negro World,* 19 April 1930, 5; "'Daughter of the Congo' on Regent Screen," Baltimore *Afro-American,* 23 August 1930, 8; Advertisement, Baltimore *Afro-American,* 23 August 1930, 9; Advertisement and "Coming Films," Baltimore *Afro-American,* 6 September 1930, 8; Advertisement and "Coming Films," Baltimore *Afro-American,* 20 September 1930, 9; Advertisement, *Philadelphia Tribune,* 9 October 1930, 6.

Note: Roland C. Irving, who plays Lieut. Brown in the film, and Earl B. Westfield composed the theme music for the film, entitled "That Gets It" ("Micheaux Produces Another," *Pittsburgh Courier,* 12 April 1930, 7B). Although the picture had sound elements, including a female character singing "Kiss Me Again," Micheaux was still working within the silent film tradition. The singing of Daisy Harding was praised in the *New York Age* as "really superb and honestly worthwhile" (12 April 1930, 6), but it was criticized in the *New York Amsterdam News* (16 April 1930, 10) and elsewhere. Film still in Bogle, *Toms, Coons, Mulattoes, Mammies, and Bucks,* 113.

23) *Easy Street* (1930)

© No reg.   *Length:* 5 reels.

Cast: Richard B. Harrison, William A. Clayton, Jr., Alice B. Russell, Willor Lee Guilford, Lorenzo Tucker.

Production dates:

Locations:

Source: Original story "Caspar Olden's Will" (author and publication unknown).

Description: The plot deals around a sensational story of love, finance and gang life. It shows the "inside actions" of city slickers in their attempt to swindle an old man of honestly earned money. It's a plot sensational with surprise, action, love, suspense and intrigue ("Easy Street, Great All-Colored Talkie at Lando Next Week," *Pittsburgh Courier,* 11 October 1930, 9B).

Archive:

Screenings: 26–28 July 1930, Roosevelt Theatre, New York City; 16–18 October 1930, Lando Theatre, Pittsburgh; 27–28 October 1930, Dunbar Theatre, Baltimore.

Press: Advertisement and "Harrison in Micheaux's Picture," *New York Amsterdam News,* 23 July 1930, 8; Advertisement, *New York Age,* 26 July 1930, 6; Advertisement, *Pittsburgh Courier,* 11 October 1930, 8B; "'Easy Street,' Great All-Colored Talkie at Lando Next Week," *Pittsburgh Courier,* 11 October 1930, 9B; Baltimore *Afro-American,* 25 October 1930, 8.

Note: The State of New York Motion Picture Division reviewed a 5-reel print of *Easy Street* on 22 July 1930 and approved the film for exhibition with moderate cuts (many involving intertitles). Publicity still in Cripps, *Slow Fade to Black,* 194.

NEW YORK. Jan. 8—The Micheaux Film Corporation, founded in 1918 by Oscar Micheaux, and which has specialized in the production and distribution of Negro feature photoplays ever since, has been reorganized with new capital. It will continue the production and distribution of photoplays of Negro life, except that from now on the product will be all-talking pictures and will be produced on a larger and more expensive scale.

The company, which operated as a Delaware corporation until a few years ago, when the Delaware charter was allowed to expire, is being incorporated as a new company, under the laws of the state of New York, with the capital all paid up and no stock for sale. It will be officered as follows: Oscar Micheaux, president; Frank Schiffman, vice president and secretary; Leo Bracher, treasurer.

The company has leased the Metropolitan Studios at Fort Lee, N.J., the largest and most fully equipped studios in the East for independent production, and will commence making the first feature, "The Exile," under the direction of Oscar Micheaux, Jan 15.

The cast, which has been in rehearsal for some time, includes, among others, Charles Moore, Eunice Brooks, George Randol, Lorenzo Tucker, Nora Newsome, Stanley Morrell, Inex Persaud, A. B. DeComatheire, Katherine Noisette, Norman Reeves, Lou Vernon, Carl Mahon and a number of singers and dancers from "Black Birds," "Brown Buddies," Connie's Inn and the Cotton Club, who will appear in cabaret scenes in the picture.

The production when completed will make a tryout on Broadway. Although Oscar Micheaux has produced 25 silent pictures since he commenced directing 12 years ago, all subjects of present-day Negro life, this will be his first offering of a picture of modern Negro life to the general public. The two Negro talking features to precede this, "Hearts in Dixie" and "Hallelujah," both had their settings in the South and dealt with the Negro in his native state. Micheaux contends that since there are more than 4,000,000 Negroes in the North, he feels that a public is in position to possibly appreciate a theme dealing and laying somewhere among these 4,000,000.

The company is contemplating making a couple of short subjects to be used as "fillers" for the Broadway showing, in conjunction with the feature, and should the general public's appreciation warrant it, as may be evidenced by the Broadway exhibition, the company will seek a special road show engagement in a large number of key cities before the picture is released for general distribution.

The production is expected to make its Broadway appearance some time during February (*Pittsburgh Courier,* 10 January 1931, 8B).

24) *THE EXILE* (1931)

© 16 May 1931, Oscar Micheaux: LP2489   *Length:* 9 reels (93 minutes)/7 reels.
Cast: Eunice Brooks (Edith Duval), Stanley Morrell (Jean Baptiste), Nora Newsome (Agnes Stewart), Katherine Noisette (Madge), George Randol (Bill Prescott) A. B. DeComathiere (an outlaw), Charles Moore (Jack Stewart, Agnes's father), Carl Mahon ("Jango," an Abyssinian student), Lou Vernon ([Asst.] District Attorney). Celeste Cole (a singer), Louise "Jota" Cook (dancer), Roland Holder (tap dancer), George Cooper, Sr., Donald Heywood's Band, Leonard Harper's Connie Inn Chorus, members of Donald Heywood's chorus (extras on the dance floor).

Production dates: 15 January–early March 1931.

Locations: Metropolitan Studios, Fort Lee, N.J.; New York City.

Source: Oscar Micheaux's novels *The Conquest* (1913) and *The Homesteader* (1917).

Description: The story is laid in Chicago and tells of Edith Duval, a sensuous and beautiful woman, who has turned a beautiful mansion into a gambling den. Several men come under her spell. One of them madly infatuated with her is stung by the kind of life she is living and goes West to forget. There he encounters unlooked for obstacles on account of his Race. He falls in love with a girl but realizes that the barriers of race prejudice can never be overcome.

He encounters cattle thieves and other outlaws. Finally when life becomes most bitter he returns to his old haunts and to Edith Duval. But the hand of the avenger is already stretched to punish her! Intrigue follows, a murder, and an innocent man is brought within the shadow of the electric chair ("Chicago Film, 'The Exile,' Brings Race Cast to Regal for Week," *Chicago Defender,* 18 July 1931, 6).

[Carl Mahon] takes the part of the student from Abyssinia who has become ensnared in the clutches of the vamp—played by Miss Brooks—and when she tries to throw him over for an old sweetheart, he kills her ("'The Exile' At Lafayette Theatre," *New York Age,* 23 May 1931, 6).

Archive: Library of Congress (16mm only).

Screenings: 16–22 May 1931, Lafayette Theatre, New York City (world premiere); 30 May–2 June 1931, Douglas Theatre, New York City; 6–8 June 1931, Odeon Theatre, New York City; 18–24 July 1931, Regal Theater, Chicago; 5–8 August 1931, Michigan Theater, Chicago; 16–20 November 1931, Broadway Theatre, Baltimore.

Press: "Micheaux's 'Exile' Being Prepared: All-Talking Picture of Modern Negro Life Now in the Cutting Room," *New York Amsterdam News,* 18 February 1931, Tuskegee Institute Files, Fisk University; "Sidelights on New Picture, 'The Exile,'" *New York Age,* 7 March 1931, 6; Publicity still, *New York Age,* 7 March 1931, 7; "'The Exile' Best of Micheaux's Productions," Baltimore *Afro-American,* 14 March 1931, 8; Advertisement and "Lafayette Theatre," *New York Age,* 16 May 1931, 6; "'The Exile' at Lafayette Theatre," *New York Age,* 23 May 1931, 6; Advertisement, *New York Age,* 30 May 1931, 6; Advertisement, *New York Age,* 6 June 1931, 6; "Chicago Film, 'The Exile,' Brings Race Cast to Regal for Week," *Chicago Defender,* 18 July 1931, 6; Advertisement and "Two-Picture Policy Stays at Michigan," *Chicago Defender,* 25 July 1931, 5; Advertisement and "Michigan to Show 4 Films During Week," *Chicago Defender,* 1 August 1931, 5; Advertisement and "'The Exile' to be Broadway Feature," Baltimore *Afro-American,* 14 November 1931, 2.

Note: Actors for *The Exile* were recruited from *The Green Pastures,* a highly successful and long-running all-black-cast Broadway musical, and from Harlem's leading nightclubs ("Lafayette Theatre," *New York Age,* 16 May 1931, 6). Photographed by Lester Lang and Walter Strenge. Dances and ensembles staged by Leonard Harper. Musical score and synchronization by Donald Heywood. Presented by Frank Schiffman. Rushes were shown (still in need of final editorial touches) and a preview presentation also occurred in the form of a midnight show at the Ogden Theatre in early March ("Sidelights on New Picture, 'The Exile'," *New York Age,* 7 March 1931, 6; "'The Exile' Best of Micheaux's Productions," Baltimore *Afro-American,* 14 March 1931, 8). Whether these were the same or different screenings is unclear. It is evident from the Baltimore *Afro-American* that *Darktown Revue* (1931) was already shot and was being shown as a prologue to *The Exile.* The genesis and casts of these two productions were intertwined. This prologue was probably separated from *The Exile* after copyrighting, reducing the original running time from

93 to 75 minutes—the length of the surviving print. If so, scenes with A. B. DeComathiere as the outlaw did not make their way into the release version. According to one advertisement, the film was distributed by the Fayette Pictures Corp., New York City (*New York Age*, 16 May 1931, 6). Posters and credits for the film refer to Micheaux's *The Conquest* as its literary source, even though it more closely follows *The Homesteader* (1917). The hero is named Oscar Devereaux in *The Conquest* but Jean Baptiste in *The Homesteader*. The latter novel also ends with the marriage of Baptiste and Agnes Stewart along the lines of the marriage that took place in *The Exile*.

25) *The Darktown Revue* (1931)

© No reg.   *Length:* 2 reels.

Cast: Andrew Tribble, Tim Moore, Amon Davis, Celeste Cole, Donald Heywood's Choir.

Production dates: 15 January–early March 1931.

Locations: Metropolitan Studios, Fort Lee, N.J.

Source:

Description: Another treat that is in store for Regal patrons along with "The Exile" is a cabaret revue called "Darktown Follies," that has in its cast Celeste Cole, whom all Chicagoans know ("Chicago Film, 'The Exile,' Brings Race Cast to Regal for Week," *Chicago Defender*, 18 July 1931, 6).

Archive: Library of Congress.

Screenings: 18–24 July 1931, Regal Theater, Chicago; 16–20 November 1931, Broadway Theatre, Baltimore.

Press: "Chicago Film, 'The Exile,' Brings Race Cast to Regal for Week," *Chicago Defender*, 18 July 1931, 6; Advertisement and "Lincoln Has Stars on Stage and Screen," Baltimore *Afro-American*, 14 November 1931, 2.

Note: Produced in conjunction with *The Exile* (1931) as a kind of prologue but then released separately. Sometimes advertised as *The Darktown Review* and referred to as *Darktown Follies*. (Pathé produced a short film in 1929 known as *Dark Town Follies* with Buck and Bubbles.) Andrew Tribble's last name is misspelled on the head title for the film (i.e., Trible).

Subsequent Micheaux Films

26) *Veiled Aristocrats* (1932)

27) *Ten Minutes to Live* (1932)

28) *The Girl from Chicago* (1932)

29) *Harlem After Midnight* (1934)

30) *Lem Hawkins' Confession* (1935), aka *Murder in Harlem*

31) *Temptation* (1936)

32) *Underworld* (1937)

33) *God's Step Children* (1938)

34) *Birthright* (1938)

35) *Swing!* (1938)

36) *Lying Lips* (1939)

37) *The Notorious Elinor Lee* (1940)

38) *The Betrayal* (1948)

The following titles have often been included as part of Oscar Micheaux's filmography but in fact they lack strong evidence of either their existence or Micheaux's authorship:

The Shadow (1921)

Received New York State license October 1921, according to Bernard L. Peterson, Jr., "A Filmography of Oscar Micheaux: America's Legendary Black Filmmaker," in *Celluloid Power: Social Criticism from "The Birth of a Nation" to "Judgment at Nuremberg,"* ed. David Platt (Metuchen, N.J.: Scarecrow Press, 1992), 124; Mapp, *Directory of Blacks in the Performing Arts* (Metuchen, N.J.: Scarecrow Press, 1990), 348.

Jasper Landry's Will (1923)

Length: 5 reels.

Cast: William E. Fountaine, Shingzie Howard.

Note: *Jaspar Landry's Will* mentioned as a future production in D. Ireland Thomas, "Motion Picture News," *Chicago Defender,* 4 November 1922, 7; as a completed film entitled *Joseph Lander's Will* in J. A. Jackson, "Micheaux Pictures," *Billboard,* 27 January 1923, 50; as a completed film starring Shingzie Howard in "Race Screen Star Becomes Popular New York Favorite," *New York Age,* 31 March 1923, 6; and as a new release entitled *Jasper Landry's Will* in D. Ireland Thomas, "Motion Picture News, *Chicago Defender,* 15 December 1923, 7. Peterson (126) mentions a New York City screening in 1922, though we have located no primary source evidence to this effect.

A Fool's Errand (1923)

Production dates: early 1923.

Locations: Roanoke and Norfolk, Va.

Source: Albion W. Tourgee's novel *A Fool's Errand* (1879).

Note: Mentioned as a future production in D. Ireland Thomas, "Motion Picture News," *Chicago Defender,* 4 November 1922, 7; and J. A. Jackson, "Micheaux's Pictures," *Billboard,* 27 January 1923, 50. The latter indicated it would be shot at Nassau in the Bahamas. "Being shot now at Roanoke and Norfolk, Va.," according to "Race Screen Star Becomes Popular New York Favorite," *New York Age,* 31 March 1923, 6. J. A. Jackson, "Micheaux Film Ready," *Billboard,* 5 May 1923, 50, indicates it would be the next film to finish, now that *The Ghost of Tolston's Manor* [released as *A Son of Satan*] was completed. It was to be followed by *The House Behind the Cedars.* Clearly this was a novel that Micheaux found compelling, but we have found no mention of the film's exhibition in the press. Micheaux listed it near the end of his filmography in *Who's Who in Colored America: A Biographical Dictionary of Notable Living Persons of African Descent in America,* ed. Joseph J. Boris. 2nd edition (New York: Who's Who in Colored America Corp., 1928–29), 262. This may have been the revival of an old idea, or reflected an interest in the unpublished play *The Fool's Errand* by Eulalie Spence, which was awarded one of the Samuel French prizes for best unpublished plays in the Little Theater Tournament of 1927. See James Weldon Johnson, *Black Manhattan* (1930; New York: Da Capo Press, 1991), 181.

Marcus Garland (1928)

Production dates: Summer of 1928.

Source: Marcus Garvey is the likely model for Marcus Garland.

Note: According to the *Pittsburgh Courier,* 25 August 1928, 2B, "Mr. Micheaux is now photographing another of his great stories entitled 'Marcus Garland.' It is an exciting story of love, intrigue and the gamble for the control of a continent. Salem Tutt Whitney and Amy Birdsong are featured in this production." Peterson (128) states Micheaux applied for a New York State license in 1925.

Dark Princess
Source: W. E. B. Du Bois's novel *Dark Princess: A Romance* (1928).
Note: Dark Princess is listed at the end of Micheaux's filmography in *Who's Who in Colored America: A Biographical Dictionary of Notable Living Persons of African Descent in America,* ed. Joseph J. Boris. 2nd edition (New York: Who's Who in Colored America Corp., 1928–29), 262. This entry was repeated in subsequent editions. *Dark Princess* was almost certainly a production that Micheaux contemplated but did not pursue.

Bibliography for Initial Filmography

Belda, Rita. "Race Advancement and Race Pride: The African American Middle Class Images of Oscar Micheaux and James Van Der Zee 1920–1940." Honors Thesis, American Studies, University of Iowa, 1998.

Bogle, Donald. *Blacks in American Films and Television: An Encyclopedia.* New York: Garland, 1998.

———. *Toms, Coons, Mulattoes, Mammies, and Bucks: An Interpretive History of Blacks in American Films.* 3rd ed. New York: Continuum, 1994.

Cripps, Thomas. *Slow Fade to Black: The Negro in American Film, 1900–1942.* New York: Oxford University Press, 1993.

Gevinson, Alan, ed. *The American Film Institute Catalog: Within Our Gates: Ethnicity in American Feature Films, 1911–1960.* Berkeley: University of California Press, 1997.

Kisch, John, and Edward Mapp. *A Separate Cinema: Fifty Years of Black Cast Posters.* New York: The Noonday Press, 1992.

Klotman, Phyllis Rauch. *Frame by Frame: A Black Filmography.* Bloomington: Indiana University Press, 1979.

Mapp, Edward. *Directory of Blacks in the Performing Arts.* Metuchen, N.J.: Scarecrow Press, 1990.

Peterson, Jr., Bernard L. "A Filmography of Oscar Micheaux: America's Legendary Black Filmmaker." In *Celluloid Power: Social Film Criticism from "The Birth of a Nation" to "Judgment at Nuremberg,"* ed. David Platt. Metuchen, N.J.: Scarecrow Press, 1992, 113–141.

Regester, Charlene. "The Misreading and Rereading of African American Filmmaker Oscar Micheaux: A Critical Review of Micheaux Scholarship." *Film History* 7 no. 4 (Winter 1995): 426–449.

Richards, Larry. *African American Films through 1959: A Comprehensive, Illustrated Filmography.* Jefferson, N.C.: McFarland & Company, 1998.

Sampson, Henry T. *Blacks in Black and White: A Source Book on Black Films.* 2nd ed. Metuchen, N.J.: Scarecrow Press, 1995.

N.B.: A letter from Oscar Micheaux to Richard Norman, 7 August 1926 on printed Micheaux Film Corporation stationery is in the Richard Norman Collection, Lilly Library, Indiana University. It provides the following information advertised in a box at the bottom of the page:

8 Features Starring	1 Feature Starring	2 Features Starring
EVELYN PREER	PAUL ROBESON	WM. E. FOUNTAINE
"THE HOMESTEADER"	"BODY AND SOUL"	& SHINGZIE HOWARD
"DECEIT"	2 Features Starring	"THE DUNGEON"
"WITHIN OUR GATES"	ANDREW S. BISHOP	"VIRGIN OF SEMINOLE"
Supported By	Supported By	3 ALL STAR CAST
LAWRENCE CHENAULT	LAWRENCE CHENAULT	Productions
"THE DEVIL'S DISCIPLE"	& SHINGZIE HOWARD	"THE SPIDER'S WEB"
"THE BRUTE"	"HOUSE BEHIND THE CEDARS"	Zora Neale Hurston's
"THE GUNSAULUS MYSTERY"	"A SON OF SATAN"	"VANITY"
"BIRTHRIGHT"	Starring Lawrence Chenault	Louis De Bulger's
"THE CONJURE WOMAN"	"A SYMBOL OF THE	"DEADLINE AT ELEVEN"
	UNCONQUERED"	

Vanity and *Deadline at Eleven* are not listed on any Micheaux filmographies, perhaps because these were eventually unrealized projects. Both titles remain intriguing, however. Despite the resurgence of interest in Hurston's work, the title *Vanity* does not appear among her published works. The title *Deadline at Eleven* suggests the 1929–1930 film by Richard Maurice, *Eleven P.M.,* though that film credits its story to Maurice.

APPENDIX C

A Colored Players Film Corporation Filmography

COMPILED BY CHARLES MUSSER

A Prince of His Race (1926)

© No reg.   *Length:* 8 reels.

Cast: Harry Henderson (Tom Bueford), Shingzie Howard (Tom's sweetheart), William A. Clayton, Jr. (James Stillman), Lawrence Chenault (the father), Arline Mickey (the maid), Ethel Smith.

Production credits: Written and directed by Roy Calnek; presented by David Starkman and Louis Groner.

Production dates: January–February 1926.

Locations: Studio, 58th Street and Woodlawn Avenue (5813 Woodlawn Avenue), Philadelphia.

Source:

Description: The story is one that teaches we must be in complete control of our passions and no matter what the provocation let them not get the best of us. It also tells a story with heart interest, filled with occasional thrills and moments of suspense.

Tom Bueford, a member of a good family, has fallen into disgrace through unscrupulous associates and is found in jail serving the last six months of a five-year sentence for manslaughter.

His sweetheart's appeal to the Governor results in a 24 hour respite so that he can solace his dying mother in her last moments on earth. A nerve racking death defying ride in a dashing, plunging auto over the state highways at breakneck speed all night brings him to her bedside in time for him to see her breathe her last. The auto in one of its last stops is seen by James Stillman, whose false testimony sent Tom to jail, and as he gazes at Tom in prison garb, a mental picture recalls to Jim's guilty mind the scenes of the night that resulted in Tom's conviction and shows the actions and events that led up to the actual crime. After Tom's release from custody he is thwarted in his attempt to see his sweetheart, who has remained loyal and true through it all, by Jim, who not only advises he leave town and intercepts his mail to her but also tries his hand at love making. He succeeds in gaining the consent of her hand in marriage through her father, and the wedding is about to be solemnized when Tom, who has by this time reached wealth and influence, reads of it in the newspapers. All is in readiness: the minister is ready to tie the knot; the groom has the ring; the bridesmaids are in the aisles; the organ is pealing the wedding march; but at the very last moment there is—but it is all shown in "A Prince of His Race" so be sure and see it. ("Great Race Picture Coming to the Grand October 17," *Chicago Defender,* 16 October 1926, 7A)

Screenings: 13 June 1926, Astor Theatre, Philadelphia (preview); 19–24 July 1926, Royal Theatre, Philadelphia (premiere); 2–6 August 1926, Howard Theatre, Washington; 30–31 August 1926, Lafayette Theatre, Baltimore; 6–7 September 1926, The Carey, Baltimore; 18–24 October 1926, Grand Theater, Chicago (local premiere); 28–30 October 1926, Broadway Theatre, Washington; 4–7 December 1926, M. & S. Douglas Theatre and M. & S. Roosevelt Theatre, New York City (local premiere); 17–19 January 1927, Royal Theatre, Baltimore; 24–30 January 1927, Grant Theatre, New York; 28 March–3 April 1927, Grand Theater, Chicago; 15–16 April 1927, The New Aladdin Theatre, West Baltimore; 1–6 May 1927, 20th Century Theater, Chicago; 24–30 October 1927, Grand Theater, Chicago; 7–10 October 1928, Rosebud Theatre, Los Angeles.

Press: "Colored Film Players," *Washington Tribune,* 26 February 1926, 9; "Private Showing of New Race Picture Reveals Promising Talent" and "Gilpin Enters Movie's Realm," *Philadelphia Tribune,* 19 June 1926, 3; Advertisement, publicity still, and "Stellar Colored Picture at Royal Theatre Next Week," *Philadelphia Tribune,* 17 July 1926, 3; Advertisement and "A Prince of His Race," *Washington Tribune,* 30 July 1926, 7; "A Prince of His Race," *Washington Tribune,* 6 August 1926, 7; Advertisement, Baltimore *Afro-American,* 28 August 1926, 7; Advertisement, Baltimore *Afro-American,* 4 September 1926, 5; "Great Race Picture Coming to the Grand October 17," *Chicago Defender,* 16 October 1926, 6A; Advertisement, *Chicago Defender,* 16 October 1926, 7A; "A Prince of His Race," *Pittsburgh Courier,* 16 October 1926, 8B; "Great Picture Packs Grand; 'Jazz Wild' at the Monogram," *Chicago Defender,* 23 October 1926, 6A; Advertisement, *New York Amsterdam News,* 1 December 1926, 10; Advertisements and "Colored Picture Gets 1st Showing at the Douglass and Roosevelt Theatres," *New York Age,* 4 December 1926, 6; "Royal," Baltimore *Afro-American,* 15 January 1927, 8; Advertisement, Baltimore *Afro-American,* 15 January 1927, 10; "'The Prince of His Race,' at the Grant," *New York Amsterdam News,* 19 January 1927, 12; Advertisement and "'A Prince of His Race' Returns to Grand," *Chicago Defender,* 26 March 1927, 8A; Advertisement, Baltimore *Afro-American,* 16 April 1927, 12; Advertisement and "Prince of His Race for 20th Century," *Chicago Defender,* 30 April 1927, 9A; "A Prince of His Race," *Chicago Defender,* 7 May 1927, 8A; Advertisement, *Chicago Defender,* 22 October 1927, 8A; Advertisement and "Rosebud Theater To Show All-Colored Cast Picture," *California Eagle,* 5 October 1928, 7; "'Ten Nights in a Bar Room' to Show at the Rosebud Theatre," *California Eagle,* 19 October 1928, 7.

Note: Although the film was advertised as "Written and Directed by Roy Calnek" (e.g., *Chicago Defender,* 16 October 1926, 7A), a news article about the film after a preview screening listed it as co-directed by Calnek and Bob Martin. ("Private Showing of New Race Picture Reveals Promising Talent," *Philadelphia Tribune,* 19 June 1926, 3). According to one source, the film cost $14,000 ("'Children of Fate' Latest Production," *Pittsburgh Courier,* 27 November 1926, 3A). The description of the film's story reprinted above is very similar to one appearing in "Stellar Colored Picture at Royal Theatre Next Week," *Philadel-*

phia Tribune, 17 June 1926, 3; it was undoubtedly based on the company's own promotional material.

The Colored Players Film Corporation was formally incorporated in February 1926, with a capitalization of $100,000, only after the production of *A Prince of His Race.* David Starkman, owner of the Standard Film Exchange, was named president ("Colored Film Players," *Washington Tribune,* 26 February 1926, 9).

TEN NIGHTS IN A BARROOM (1926)

© No reg.   *Length:* 8 reels.

Cast: Charles S. Gilpin (Joe Morgan), Lawrence Chenault (Simon Slade), Harry Henderson (Willie Hammond, the Judge's son), Arline Mickey (Mehitable Cartwright), Myra Burwell (Jannie Morgan, Joe's wife), William A. Clayton, Jr. (Harvey Green), William R. Johnson (Judge Hammond), Edward Moore (Sample Swichel), William F. Milton (Alfred Romaine), Reginald Hoffer (William Carr), Ethel Smith, Sam Sadler, Boxana Mickelby.

Production credits: Written and directed by Roy Calnek; presented by David Starkman and Louis Groner.

Production dates: June 1926.

Locations: Studio, 58th Street and Woodlawn Avenue, Philadelphia.

Source: William W. Pratt's play *Ten Nights in the Bar Room* (1858).

Description: The story shows, in brief, how Joe Morgan, part proprietor of the lumber mill, loses his interest in the property by his drinking habits and accidently his daughter is killed. After several dramatic situations—there is rough house stuff at times: any number of fights; a scene on the rapids of a river, which thrill you by its exciting movement, he reforms and there is promise of peace if not happiness between him and his wife ("Carey," Baltimore *Afro-American,* 22 January 1927, 10).

Screenings: 17 November 1926, Gladstone Theatre, Philadelphia (preview); 19 December 1926–16 January 1927 (4 weeks), Grant Theatre, New York City; 3–8 January 1927, Royal Theatre, Baltimore; 10–16 January 1927, Grand Theater, Chicago; 24–25 January 1927, The Carey, Baltimore; 31 January–2 February 1927, Attucks Theatre, Norfolk, Va.; 2–3 May 1927, The Aladdin, West Baltimore; 24 May 1927, Dunbar Theatre, Baltimore; 7–11 August 1927, Broadway Theatre, Washington; 5–6 October 1927, Broadway Theatre, Washington; 1–3 December 1927, Gem Theatre, New York City; 28 October–1 November 1928, Rosebud Theatre, Los Angeles.

Press: "Gilpin Enters Movie's Realm," *Philadelphia Tribune,* 19 June 1926, 3; Daniel W. Chase (for Associated Negro Press), "Gilpin Enters Movie's Realm," *California Eagle,* 25 June 1926, 7; "Is Charles Gilpin Through?" *Pittsburgh Courier,* 16 October 1926, 8B; "'Ten Nights in a Bar Room' Gets Showing," *Philadelphia Tribune,* 20 November 1926, 3; Advertisement and production still, *New York Amsterdam News,* 29 December 1926, 13; Advertisement, Baltimore *Afro-American,* 1 January 1927, 10; Production still and "Royal," Baltimore *Afro-American,* 8 January 1927, 11; Advertisement, *New York Amsterdam News,* 5 January 1927, 11; Advertisement, publicity still, and "Star of New Race Picture at Grand," *Chicago Defender,* 8 January 1927, 6A; Advertisement, *New York Amsterdam News,* 12 January 1927, 11; Tony Langston, "Race Picture Packs Grand; Dad James Gives a Fine Show," *Chicago Defender,* 15 January 1927, 6A; Advertisement, Baltimore *Afro-American,* 22 January 1927, 9; "Carey," Baltimore *Afro-American,* 22 January 1927, 10; Advertisement and "'Ten Nights in A Bar Room' at Attucks," *Norfolk Journal and Guide* 29 January 1927, 4; Advertisement, Baltimore *Afro-American*, 30 April 1927, 10; Advertisement, Baltimore *Afro-American*, 21 May 1927, 8; Advertisement and "Charles S. Gilpin at the Broadway," *Washington Tribune*, 5 August 1927, 6; Advertisement, *New York Amsterdam News*, 30 November 1927, 13; "Ten Nights in a Bar Room to Show at the Rosebud Theatre," *California Eagle*, 19 October 1928, 7; Advertisement and "Charles S. Gilpin, Famous Race Actor, at the Rosebud Theatre," *California Eagle*, 26 October 1928, 8.

Note: Additional credits for cast are taken from "Race Picture Packs Grand; Dad James Gives a Fine Show," *Chicago Defender*, 15 January 1927, 8A. William W. Pratt's play *Ten Nights in a Bar-Room* had its New York premiere on 9 August 1858 at the National Theatre (George C. D. Odell, *Annals of the New York Stage.* Vol. VII: 1857–1865 [1931; reprint, New York: AMS Press, 1970], 52). It was based in turn on a novel by T. S. Arthur: *Ten Nights in a Bar Room* (1854). David Starkman had difficulties finding a prominent Philadelphia venue for this film ("'Ten Nights in a Bar Room' Gets Showing," *Philadelphia Tribune*, 20 November 1926, 3).

> The actors of the Colored Players Film Corporation sponsor "The First Annual Movie-Artists Camera Dance and Frolic" on 27 December 1926, at the Strand Ballroom, Philadelphia (Handbill, African Diaspora Images Collection).

CHILDREN OF FATE (1927)

© No reg.   *Length:* 8 reels.
Cast: Harry Henderson, Lawrence Chenault, Shingzie Howard, Arline Mickey, Howard Augusta, Alonzo Jackson, and William A Clayton, Jr.
Production credits: Directed by Roy Calnek.
Production dates: November 1926–[March 1927].
Locations: Studio, 58th Street and Woodlawn Avenue, Philadelphia.
Source:
Description: The story is one that teaches a great lesson, warning us that he who lives for self alone finds not the gems of contentment.

> "While the wheel of life spins on
>   Weaving friendship, love and hate,
> Life, the Jester, takes a hand
>   And guides the destiny of Fate."

And when Life, that unrelenting Jester, guides the destiny of Ross Hampton's fate, it takes him from "The Nest," a famous gambling palace, wherein society's night life mingles with the professional gamester, transplanting him, through the medium of a train wreck, amid the scenes of his boyhood, where he meets Virginia Lee, a sweetheart of childhood days.

The white plague has fastened its talons upon the lungs of the great gambler and the doctors have given him but a year to live.

For the first time, the desire to live and love enters his life. It is then that fate deals the cards again and Ross Hampton is separated from the girl of his choice.

For long months she waits, bravely bearing silent days, until at last, from out of the long silence, sad news of Ross Hampton's death arrives—but you must wait and see for yourself, this, the greatest of pictures, wherein the Providence that guides the lives of we poor mortals here on earth guards the destiny of Virginia Lee.

A laugh—a sob—a tear—a smile—a thrill—a fear—and then the sun breaks through the dark clouds, bathing the world in its radiant glow ("At the Elmore," *Pittsburgh Courier,* 13 August 1927, 10A).

Screenings: 18–24 April 1927, Royal Theatre, Philadelphia; 18–23 April 1927, Royal Theatre, Baltimore; 9 May 1927, Dunbar Theatre, Baltimore; 23–24 May 1927, The Carey, Baltimore; 8–14 August 1927, Elmore Theatre, Pittsburgh; 6–10 September 1927, Broadway Theatre, Washington.

Press: "Colored Film Players Corporation Working Again," *Pittsburgh Courier,* 27 November 1926, 3B; Advertisement and "Royal Theatre," *Philadelphia Tribune,* 16 April 1927, 6; Advertisement, Baltimore *Afro-American,* 16 April 1927, 12; Advertisement, Baltimore *Afro-American,* 7 May 1927, 9; Advertisement, Baltimore *Afro-American,* 21 May 1927, 7; Advertisement and "At the Elmore," *Pittsburgh Courier,* 6 August 1927, 10A; Advertisement and "Colored Stars in 'Children of Fate' at the Broadway," *Washington Tribune,* 2 September 1927, 7.

Note: In the *Pittsburgh Courier* of 6 August 1927, the film was titled "Children of Hate" (in both advertisements and promotional copy). This was corrected in the subsequent issue of the newspaper.

Sherman H. Dudley, who was a popular columnist in black newspapers during the 1920s, published a series of articles generally supportive of race films and particularly those of the Colored Players Film Corporation in his column "Dud's Dope," appearing in the *Chicago Defender* (12 March 1927, 8A; 19 March 1927, 8A; 26 March 1927, 9A), *Washington Tribune* (18 March 1927, 7; 8 April 1927, 7; 22 April 1927, 8; 13 May 1927, 9; 10 June 1927, 9; 8 July 1927, 9; 16 December 1927, 9; 23 December 1927, 9) and the Baltimore *Afro-American.* In June 1927, he announced that David Starkman had offered him the presidency of Colored Players Film Corporation (*Chicago Defender,* 25 June 1927, 9A). By July he was announcing plans for the revamped company (*Chicago Defender,* 9 July 1927, 6A).

The following advertisement appeared in *Philadelphia Tribune,* 11 August 1927, 6:

BE A MOVIE ACTOR!

Students Prepared Quickly and Efficiently. Instruction Given.

STUDIO, 5813 WOODLAWN AVE.

On Mondays and Wednesdays at 8 P.M. with all Lighting and Scenic Effects. Male and Female classes. Terms Reasonable and Convenient.

Colored Players Film Corporation

S. H. Dudley President
Apply: 1227 Vine Street
Phone Rtt 2563
Alonzo Jackson, Instructor

Movie Corporation Plans Big Picture

WASHINGTON, D.C.—Directors and stockholders of the Colored Film Corporation meeting here, elected S. H. Dudley, president; J. Finley Wilson first vice-president; David Starkman, general manager; and Louis Gro[n]er secretary-treasurer.

The company is offering stock to the public. The next big picture has already been outlined and calls for 1,500 people drawing salaries from $30 to $500 weekly, and plans to star the most beautiful brown-skin women in the world (Baltimore *Afro-American*, 26 November 1927, 8).

Plan New Photoplays

PHILADELPHIA—Plans for the filming of a series of new photoplays with race casts were announced here Monday by David Starkman of Colored Film Players Corporation (Baltimore *Afro-American*, 19 May 1928).

THE SCAR OF SHAME (1929)

© No reg.   *Length:* 8,023 ft. (8 reels).

Cast: Harry Henderson (Alvin Hillyard), Lucia Lynn Moses (Louise Howard), Lawrence Chenault (Ralph Hathaway), Pearl McCormack (Alice Hathaway), Norman Johnstone (Eddie Blake), William E. Pettus (Spike Howard), Ann[ie] Kennedy (Lucretia Green).

Production credits: Directed by Frank Perugini; story: David Starkman; cinematography: Al Liguori.

Production dates: February–March 1929.

Locations: Studio, 58th Street and Woodlawn Avenue, Philadelphia.

Source:

Description: Louise Morgan, who drudges daily to the Music of the Washboard that she may satisfy the cravings for liquor of her brutal stepfather, but who instinctively has higher ideals and greater ambitions in life, can be seen daily rubbing at the washtub, but even in that miserable environment looks as beautiful as the Rose of Shannon [*sic*] with whom King Solomon fell so madly in love. While she was being attacked by her stepfather, she is rescued by our hero, Harry Henderson, who plays the part of Alvin T. Hillyard, who also has higher ideals and who is in thorough sympathy with the sufferings of the "womanhood" of the race. He makes every effort to give her an education and teach her music. Soon, however, a great dissatisfaction arises to mar their happiness. Because he is afraid to have her meet his mother, as she (his wife) does not belong to his select set, his wife becomes highly incensed and is later involved with the villain who has plotted to steal her and then comes "THE SCAR OF SHAME." From here on the story carries its way through a wonderful plot of intrigue, romance and suspense (Advertisement, Baltimore *Afro-American*, 13 April 1929, 13).

Screenings: 13–17 April 1929, M & S Douglas Theatre, New York; 15–20 April 1929, Gibson's Theatre, Philadelphia; 15–20 April 1929, Royal Theatre, Baltimore; [22–28 April 1929], Elmore Theater, Pittsburgh; 27–29 April 1929, Odeon Theatre, New York City; 13–19 May 1927, Howard Theatre, Washington; 27 May–1 June 1929, Pearl Theatre, Philadelphia; 9–15

Head title for *The Scar of Shame* (1929).

Louise Howard (Lucia Lynn Moses) tears up the wedding license.

Alvin Hillyard (Harry Henderson) in prison.

June 1929, Alhambra, New York City; 14–15 October 1929, The Carey, Baltimore; 5 November 1929, Lafayette Theatre, Baltimore; 11 November 1929, Princess Theatre, Baltimore; 25 December 1929, New Dunbar Theatre, Baltimore.

Press: "New Star of Silver Screen," *Pittsburgh Courier*, 23 February 1929, 1A; "Lucia Moses Is the Beautiful Star in 'Scar of Shame'," Baltimore *Afro-American*, 6 April 1929, 27; Advertisement, *New York Age*, 6 April 1929, 6; Advertisement and "'Scar of Shame' A Big Colored Movie at Gibson's," *Philadelphia Tribune*, 11 April 1929, 6; Advertisement, *New York Age*, 13 April 1929, 6; Advertisement, Baltimore *Afro-American*, 13 April 1929, 13; "Royal," Baltimore *Afro-American*, 13 April 1929, 15; "Race Film Is Classic," *Pittsburgh Courier*, 20 April 1929, 9A; "At the Odeon" and "Colored Players at Odeon" *New York Amsterdam News*, 24 April 1929, 12; "Race Film Is Classic," *Pittsburgh Courier*, 27 April 1929, 3B; "She's a Jewel," Baltimore *Afro-American*, 4 May 1929, 13; Advertisement and "Bob (Uke) Williams at Howard," *Washington Tribune*, 10 May 1929, 7; Advertisement, *New York Amsterdam News*, 12 June 1929, 12; Advertisement, Baltimore *Afro-American*, 12 October 1929, 9; Advertisement, Baltimore *Afro-American*, 2 November 1929, 9; Advertisement, Baltimore *Afro-American*, 9 November 1929, 8; Advertisement, Baltimore *Afro-American*, 21 December 1929, 8.

Note: In the film, Hillyard receives a telegram sent to 5813 Woodlawn Avenue, the address of the studio. The date on this missive (19 January 1927) has led historians to believe that the film was made two or three years earlier. The Library of Congress, for example, has dated the film 1926. Sampson and the American Film Institute catalog date it as 1927. A front-page announcement of the film's *forthcoming* production, appearing in the *Pittsburgh Courier* of 23 February 1929, puts this popular notion to rest. Lucia Moses had been with the *Dixie to Broadway* and *Blackbirds* companies by the time the film was released ("'Scar of Shame' A Big Colored Movie at Gibson's," *Philadelphia Tribune*, 11 April 1929, 6). *Blackbirds* No. 2 Company opened at the Garrick Theatre in Philadelphia on 29 January 1929 and ran to April 13th—its close coinciding with the opening of the film. One is tempted to place Lucia Moses in this company, since her employment there would have been highly convenient from the point of view of the producers. With Sherman Dudley, Jr.—the son of Colored Players Film

Corporation president Sherman Dudley, Sr.—also appearing in the Philadelphia cast, there were plenty of opportunities for Lucia to be "discovered." A popular account of Lucia Lynn Moses's selection for the starring role has David Starkman visiting New York and "discovering" her on the stage. Perhaps he visited the Blackbirds No. 2 company in rehearsal at Dudley's suggestion ("Blackbirds No. 2 Co. Equals New York Troupers in Class," *Pittsburgh Courier,* 9 February 1929, 1C). Nonetheless, it is her sister Ethel Moses who is listed as appearing in the cast for the musical's Philadelphia run (*Blackbirds* playbill, 18 February 1929). Furthermore, a third Moses sister, Julia, was listed as a dancer in a playbill for *Blackbirds* at the Liberty Theater, New York, on 17 September 1928 (Geraldine Duclow, head of the Theatre Collection, Free Library of Philadelphia, to Charles Musser, 23 July 1999). Finally, Lucia Moses recalled working as in the chorus of the Cotton Club and commuting between New York and her hometown. Whether her quite vague memory was improperly "refreshed" with inaccurate dating is unclear (see "*The Scar of Shame:* Why the Fuss Over This Old, Made-in-Philadelphia, Silent Black Film," Sunday Bulletin, *Philadelphia Bulletin,* 17 November 1974, 16–20). In any case, Pearl McCormack, the second female lead in *The Scar of Shame,* was featured in another musical comedy *Jazzbo Regiment,* then being whipped into shape at Philadelphia's Gibson Theatre, in a run from February 6th to March 2nd ("Jazzbo Regiment Is a Classy Show," *Philadelphia Tribune,* 14 February 1929, 6). The *Pittsburgh Courier* also fostered interest in *The Scar of Shame,* by publishing a number of elegant photographs of McCormack ("Pearl McCormick [sic]," *Pittsburgh Courier,* 30 March 1929, 3B; and "Me, Oh My," *Pittsburgh Courier,* 20 April 1929, 5A). The Philadelphia opening was billed as "the premiere showing," though the film opened two days earlier in New York City. The company's energies went into the Philadelphia opening, however, as the film was accompanied by a playlet, "Night Life in Philadelphia," featuring Lucia Moses. The film's other stars also attended the Philadelphia opening (*Philadelphia Tribune,* 11 April 1929, 6). A full-page advertisement in the Baltimore *Afro-American* claimed the film was "The First All-Colored Talking Picture!" (15 April 1929, 15). An advertisement for the film's Philadelphia premiere also indicated that it was "with sound," though this went unmentioned in the promotional announcements and reviews (Advertisement and "'Scar of Shame' A Big Colored Movie at Gibson's," *Philadelphia Tribune,* 11 April 1929, 6).

Norman Film Manufacturing Company: Production and Theatre Release Dates for All-Black-Cast Films

COMPILED BY PHYLLIS R. KLOTMAN

	PRODUCTION DATE	RELEASE DATE
The Green-Eyed Monster Original 8-reel version	1919	1920
The Love Bug 2 reels	(cut from above)	1920
The Bull-Dogger 5 reels	1921	1921
The Crimson Skull* 7 reels	1921	1921
6 reels	1921	1922
Regeneration 6 reels	1923	1923
The Flying Ace** 6 reels	1926	1926
Black Gold 6 reels	1926	1927

* Released only in Oklahoma in 1921.
** Norman usually negotiated a 50–50 split with theatre managers, and 60–40 or 70–30 with churches and schools. However, he released *The Green-Eyed Monster, The Love Bug, The Bull-Dogger, The Crimson Skull,* and *Regeneration* as straight rentals, then did a 50-percent split on second runs (or if theater operators could not afford rental prices). After a certain amount of time, the films were contracted out for straight rental, sometimes in combination with another film. *The Green-Eyed Monster* started at $100-a-day rental. He did show *The Flying Ace* mostly at 50 percent, due to "hard times for colored films." The price of the tickets ranged from 5–20 cents for children and from 25–50 cents for adults. Occasionally there was a 75-cent charge for adults.

Publicity still for *The Flying Ace* (1926). With J. Lawrence Criner (Captain William Stokes), Steve Reynolds ("Peg," Stokes's mechanic), and Kathryn Boyd (Ruth Sawtelle).

Cast Lists

The Green-Eyed Monster [sometimes advertised as Green Eyed Monster, without the article or the hyphen]
Featured: Jack Austin and Louise Dunbar, Steve Reynolds, Dr. R. L. Brown. In its original version, it also included the cast of *The Love Bug* listed below.

The Love Bug
Featured: Billy Mills and Maud Frisbie; supported by the Billy Mills Company. Additional Cast: Robert Stewart, Maud Johnson (the "425 pound marvel") and "real Colored Triplets."

The Bull-Dogger [sometimes advertised as Bull Dogger, without the article or the hyphen]
Featured: Anita Bush, Lawrence Chenault, Steve Reynolds, Bennie Turpin; supported by Bill Pickett with George Larkin, Pete Haddon, Buck Lucas.

The Crimson Skull
Featured: Anita Bush (Anita) and Lawrence Chenault (Bob Calem, et al.); supported by Bill Pickett (sheriff's deputy), Steve Reynolds (marshal) and "30 Colored Cowboys."

Regeneration
Featured: Stella Mayo (Violet Daniels), M. C. Maxwell (Jack Roper), Alfred Norcom, Charles Gaines, Dr. R. L. Brown, Clarence Rucker, Steve Reynolds.

The Flying Ace

Featured: J. Lawrence Criner (Captain William Stokes), George Colvin, (Thomas Sawtelle), Kathryn Boyd (Ruth Sawtelle), Harold Platts (Finley Tucker), Steve Reynolds ("Peg"), Boise DeLegge (Blair Kimball), Lyons Daniels (Jed Spivens), Sam Jordan (Dr. Maynard), Dr. R. L. Brown (Howard Mac Andrews).

Credits in order of appearance. (Press kits and posters feature Criner and Boyd, who are supported by the rest of the cast.)

Black Gold

Featured: J. Lawrence Criner and Kathryn Boyd, with Steve Reynolds, Alfred Norcom, R. L. Brown, Marshal L. B. Tatums and the "entire all-colored city of Tatums, Oklahoma."

For a complete list of the films in the AFI Norman Collection, preserved by the Library of Congress, some of which Norman made, most of which he distributed, write or call the Motion Picture, Broadcasting and Recorded Sound Division, Library of Congress, Madison Building, Washington, D.C. There are some 22 items available for viewing; three more remain to be preserved.

Note: A Debtor to the Law (1924) is erroneously attributed to the Norman Film Manufacturing Company in Richard A. Nelson's *Florida and the American Motion Picture Industry 1898–1980* (New York: Garland Publishing, 1983, 439) from information listed in *The American Film Institute Catalog, Feature Films, 1921–1930,* vol. 2 (New York: R. R. Bowker Company, 1971), 1286. *A Debtor to the Law* was produced by Peacock Productions, Inc., with executive offices in Tulsa, Oklahoma; it was a *white-cast* film, starring the "Last of the Great Western Outlaws," Henry Starr, who is billed in the advertising materials as "The Man Who Stole A Million." Norman did distribute the film, as he did a number of others that he did not produce—Micheaux's *The Millionaire, The Exile,* and *Girl from Chicago,* for example. If Norman ever made a black-cast version of *A Debtor to the Law,* it has not yet been found.

2. THE NOTION OF TREATMENT

1. Spencer Williams produced, wrote, and directed his first film, *Tenderfeet,* in 1928. He studied comedy with the master of the art—Bert Williams—and is best known for his role as Andy Brown in the *Amos 'n Andy* television show.

2. "Bad Movies," *Film Comment* (July 1980), reprinted in J. Hoberman, *Vulgar Modernism: Writing on Movies and Other Media* (Philadelphia: Temple University Press, 1991), 13–22.

3. See, for example, "Oscar Micheaux Writes on Growth of Race and Movie Field," *Pittsburgh Courier,* 13 December 1924, 10.

3. FROM SHADOWS 'N SHUFFLIN' TO SPOTLIGHTS AND CINEMA

1. Taped interview with Clarence Muse, 23–29 August 1969, Perris, California.

2. Henry T. Sampson, *Blacks in Black and White: A Source Book on Black Films,* 2nd ed. (1977; Metuchen, N.J.: Scarecrow Press, 1995), 212–214, 549–550.

3. Interview with Lincoln Perry (Step 'n Fetchit); Indianapolis, Indiana, 12 April 1970.

4. Interview with Clarence Muse.

5. Article from Baltimore *Afro-American,* 20 June 1936, in Anita Bush's personal scrapbook.

6. Taped interview with Anita Bush, January 1969, New York City.

7. Ibid.

8. Thomas Cripps, *Slow Fade to Black* (London: Oxford University Press, 1977), 195–196.

9. Ibid.

10. Ibid., 191.

11. Ibid., 186.

12. See Sampson, *Blacks in Black and White,* 280–347, 664; Charles Musser, "Colored Players Film Corporation Filmography," Appendix C in this volume.

13. G. William Jones, *Black Cinema Treasures: Lost and Found* (Denton, Texas: University of North Texas Press, 1991), 39–40.

14. "Thousands at Bier of Nation's Most Popular Colored Actress Whose Demise Causes Great Shock," *California Eagle,* 25 November 1932, 1.

15. Advertisement, *New York Amsterdam News,* 18 April 1923, 5.

16. Copy of Dreiser's letter in personal scrapbook of a fan of Evelyn Preer's, in author's possession (hereafter Preer Scrapbook). I should mention that, because of my personal association, I possess more material on Evelyn Preer than on any of the other members of the Lafayette. I will endeavor to be as objective as possible but hope to be forgiven any bias in regard to the accomplishments and career of my mother, Evelyn Preer.

17. "Evelyn Preer at the New Douglas," *New York Age*, 24 October 1925, 6.

18. Interview with Leigh Whipper, New York City, 1969.

19. Floyd J. Calvin, "Evelyn Preer Ranks First as Stage and Movie Star," *Pittsburgh Courier*, 16 April 1927, 1.

20. *Pittsburgh Courier*, 11, 18 and 25 June 1927, 1 and 2.

21. Brian Rust, *Discography: Jazz Records, 1897–1942* (London: Storyville Publishers, 1970). I thank James Lindsay, a private record collector from Indianapolis, Indiana, for bringing this information to my attention.

22. Ina Duncan, "Evelyn Preer Pioneered in Hollywood for Race Movie Stars, Declares Ina Duncan," clipping, ca. August 1930, Preer Scrapbook.

23. Interview with Clarence Muse.

24. Unidentified newspaper articles, Preer Scrapbook.

25. "Evelyn Preer Awaits Visit of Stork," *Pittsburgh Courier*, 19 December 1931, 8.

26. "Stage Mourns Evelyn Preer," *Chicago Defender*, 26 November 1932, 4.

27. "Death of Famous Actress a Shock to New York Friends," *New York Age*, 26 November 1932, 1.

28. "Thousands at Bier of Nation's Most Popular Colored Actress," 1.

29. "Clarence Muse Pays Perfect Tribute to the Late Evelyn Preer on Behalf of a Grateful Theatrical Profession," *Pittsburgh Courier*, 10 December 1932, 6

30. "Depression Hits Stage and Screen," *California Eagle*, 13 February 1931, 10.

31. Interview with Anita Bush.

4. THE AFRICAN-AMERICAN PRESS AND RACE MOVIES, 1909–1929

1. Martin E. Dann, ed., *The Black Press 1827–1890* (New York: Capricorn Books, 1971), 12.

2. Lester Walton, "The Degeneracy of the Moving Picture Theatre," *New York Age*, 5 August 1909, 6.

3. Ibid.

4. *New York News*, 24 September 1914, Tuskegee Newsclipping File.

5. Quoted in Daniel Leab, *From Sambo to Superspade* (Boston: Houghton Mifflin, 1975), 22.

6. "The Clansman," *Western Outlook*, 15 May 1915.

7. Rosalie M. Jonas, "What the People Say, 'The Birth of a Nation,'" *New York Age*, 25 March 1915, 5.

8. Jane Gaines, "*The Scar of Shame*: Skin Color and Caste in Black Silent Melodrama," *Cinema Journal* 26, no. 4 (Summer 1987): 6.

9. "Foster's Colored Photo Plays," Indianapolis *Freeman*, 30 August 1913, 6.

10. Henry T. Sampson, *Blacks in Black and White: A Source Book on Black Films* (Metuchen, N.J.: Scarecrow, 1977), 68.

11. Juli Jones, Jr., "Moving Pictures Offer the Greatest Opportunity to the American Negro in History of the Race from Every Point of View," *Chicago Defender*, 9 October 1915. Juli Jones is a pseudonym for William Foster.

12. James W. Johnson, "Views and Reviews," *New York Age*, 15 April 1915, 4.

13. "In Filmdom," *Chicago Defender*, 22 December 1917.

14. "*A Man's Duty*," *Chicago Defender*, 27 September 1919, 8.

15. "Great Picture," *Chicago Defender*, 11 December 1920, 6.

16. "Does Well," *Chicago Defender*, 9 July 1921, 7.

17. "Racial Film," *Chicago Defender*, 25 June 1921, 6.

18. "*The Green-Eyed Monster*," *Chicago Defender*, 9 July 1921, 6.

19. "*Call of His People*," *Chicago Defender*, 6 August 1921, 7.

20. "*Spitfire* Misses Fire," Baltimore *Afro-American*, 8 December 1922, 15.

21. "Reviewing Service: *Hearts of the Woods*," *Chicago Defender*, 4 February 1922, 8.

22. J. A. Jackson, "*His Great Chance* Is Newest Film," Baltimore *Afro-American*, 18 May 1923, 4.

23. D. Ireland Thomas, "Motion Picture News," *Chicago Defender*, 2 June 1923, 6.

24. "*His Great Chance*," Baltimore *Afro-American*, 15 June 1923, 4.

25. D. Ireland Thomas, "Motion Picture News," *Chicago Defender*, 22 July 1922, 7.

26. Ibid.

27. D. Ireland Thomas, "Motion Picture News," *Chicago Defender*, 21 October 1922, 6.

28. D. Ireland Thomas, "Motion Picture News," *Chicago Defender*, 16 January 1923, 7.

29. D. Ireland Thomas, "Motion Picture News," *Chicago Defender* (national edition), 10 January 1925, 6A.

30. D. Ireland Thomas, "Motion Picture News," *Chicago Defender*, 24 January 1925, 6.

31. "Are Race Pictures a Failure?," *Chicago Defender*, 27 December 1924, 7. The same article was reprinted in *Billboard*, 27 December 1924, 49.

32. Ibid.

33. "Picture Producing Cemetery," Baltimore *Afro-American*, 23 January 1926, 5.

34. "The Spotlight," Baltimore *Afro-American*, 31 July 1926, 5.

35. Will H. Smith, "Says Million Dollar Film Company Would Be Small," Baltimore *Afro-American*, 11 June 1927, 7.

36. W. R. Arnold, "Believes in Future of Colored Motion Pictures," Baltimore *Afro-American*, 2 July 1927, 8.

37. "Liked *Scar of Shame*," *New York Amsterdam News*, 22 May 1929, 8.

38. Thomas Cripps, *Slow Fade to Black: The Negro in American Film 1900–1942* (1977; reprint, New York: Oxford University Press, 1993), 179–180.

39. Ibid., 180.

40. J. Ronald Green, "'Twoness' in Style of Oscar Micheaux," in *Black American Cinema*, ed. Manthia Diawara (New York: Routledge, 1993), 32.

41. Ibid.

42. bell hooks, *Black Looks: Race and Representation* (Boston: South End Press, 1992), 133.

43. Ibid.

44. "*The Homesteader*," *Chicago Defender*, 22 February 1919, 14.

45. "Last Chance," *Chicago Defender*, 12 April 1919, 8.

46. "*Within Our Gates*," *Chicago Defender*, 10 January 1920, 6.

47. Advertisement, *Chicago Defender*, 10 January 1920, 6.

48. Advertisement, *Houston Informer*, 20 March 1920, 8.

49. Lester A. Walton, "Sam Langford's Wallop Makes *The Brute* Screen Success," *New York Age*, 18 September 1920, 6.

50. Ibid.

51. J. A. Jackson, "*Birthright*," Baltimore *Afro-American*, 25 January 1924, 10.

52. "Producer Can Succeed Only with Our Aid," *Pittsburgh Courier*, 13 December 1924, 10.

53. Sylvester Russell, "Sylvester Russell's Review," *Pittsburgh Courier*, 5 March 1927, 2.

54. William Henry, "Correcting Oscar Micheaux," *Chicago Defender*, 22 January 1927, 2B.

55. "Film Tips: Reader Writes Us on Film," Baltimore *Afro-American*, 11 September 1926, 6.

56. Richard Grupenhoff, *The Black Valentino: The Stage and Screen Career of Lorenzo Tucker* (Metuchen, N.J.: Scarecrow Press, 1988), 65, 74–81.

57. Obie McCollum, "Things Theatrical: Mr. Micheaux Pioneers," Baltimore *Afro-American*, 5 May 1928, 8.

58. "Magnificent Show at the Regal," *Chicago Defender*, 26 May 1928, 10.

59. "Sylvester Russell Looks 'Em Over," *Pittsburgh Courier*, 2 June 1928, 3.

60. Geraldyn Dismond, "*A Daughter of the Congo* Features Roland C. Irving," *Negro World*, 19 April 1930, 5.

61. Cripps, *Slow Fade to Black,* 198.

62. W. E. Burghardt Du Bois, *The Souls of Black Folk* (1902; reprint, Millwood, N.Y.: Kraus-Thomson Organization, 1973), 3.

63. hooks, *Blacks Looks,* 143.

64. Ibid.

5. Oscar Micheaux's *Within Our Gates:* The Possibilities for Alternative Visions

1. Sander Gilman, *Difference and Pathology: Stereotypes of Sexuality, Race, and Madness* (Ithaca, N.Y.: Cornell University Press, 1985), 27.

2. Richard Dyer, *The Matter of Images: Essays on Representations* (New York: Routledge, 1993), 16.

3. Donald Bogle, *Toms, Coons, Mulattoes, Mammies, and Bucks: An Interpretive History of Blacks in American Films* (New York: Viking Press, 1973); Thomas Cripps, *Slow Fade to Black: The Negro in American Film 1900–1942* (New York: Oxford University Press, 1977).

4. Ella Shohat and Robert Stam, *Unthinking Eurocentrism: Multiculturalism and the Media* (New York: Routledge, 1994). I have also supported this approach to stereotypes in my introduction ("Negative/Positive Images") to *Invisibility Blues: From Pop to Theory* (New York: Verso, 1990). Although I still believe that what we automatically consider "positive" should be regarded as questionable and what we see as "negative" should be scrutinized more closely for pragmatic and/or constructive value, I also think that in dealing with a particular national/historical tradition of stereotypes, it is best to be more specific rather than less. When speaking in an international or global context, positive and negative are clearly relative terms. But on the regional or national level, these terms become rigid and inflexible and cannot be diffused by rising above them.

5. Gilman, *Difference and Pathology;* Eve Sedgwick, *Epistemology of the Closet* (Berkeley: University of California Press, 1990); Richard Dyer, *Stars* (London: British Film Institute, 1979); Richard Dyer, *Now You See It: Studies on Lesbian and Gay Film* (New York: Routledge, 1990); and Dyer, *The Matter of Images.*

6. Bogle, *Toms, Coons,* 3, 10–16.

7. Ibid., 4.

8. Ibid.

9. Gilman, *Difference and Pathology,* 24.

10. Sedgwick, *Epistemology of the Closet,* 22–24. As Sedgwick says, "People are different from each other" and "It is astonishing how few respectable conceptual tools we have for dealing with this self-evident fact."

11. Nell Irvin Painter, *Standing at Armageddon: The United States, 1877–1919* (New York: W.W. Norton, 1987), 141–169, 216–230; Ronald Takaki, *Strangers from a Different Shore: A History of Asian Americans* (New York: Penguin, 1989). Concerning the resulting images, see Gary D. Keller, *Hispanics and United States Film: An Overview and Handbook* (Tempe, Ariz.: Bilingual Review Press, 1994); Peter C. Rollins and John E. O'Connor, eds., *Hollywood's Indian: The Portrayal of the Native American in Film* (Lexington: University of Kentucky Press, 1998); Matthew Bernstein and Gaylyn Studlar, eds. *Visions of the East: Orientalism in Film* (New Brunswick, N.J.: Rutgers University Press, 1997); Gina Marchetti, *Romance and the "Yellow Peril": Race, Sex, and Discursive Strategies in Hollywood Fiction* (Berkeley: University of California Press, 1993).

12. Dyer, *The Matter of Images,* 2.

13. Mel Watkins, *On the Real Side: Laughing, Lying, and Signifying—The Underground Tradition of African-American Humor that Transformed American Culture, from Slavery to Richard Pryor* (New York: Simon & Schuster, 1994); Robert Toll, *Blacking Up: The Minstrel Show in Nineteenth Cen-*

tury America (New York: Simon & Schuster, 1994); Henry T. Sampson, *The Ghost Walks: A Chronological History of Blacks in Show Business 1865–1910,* 2nd ed. (Metuchen, N.J.: Scarecrow Press, 1995); Allen Woll, *Black Musical Theatre: From Coontown to Dreamgirls* (Baton Rouge: Louisiana University Press, 1989); Albert Murray, *Stomping the Blues* (New York: Vintage, 1982); Robert Palmer, *Deep Blues: A Musical and Cultural History of the Mississippi Delta* (New York: Penguin Books, 1980); and many other books, recordings and documents.

14. Gilman, *Difference and Pathology,* 25.

15. Cripps, *Slow Fade to Black,* 45.

16. Joseph Boskin, *Sambo: The Rise & Demise of an American Jester* (New York: Oxford University Press, 1986), 3–16; Eric Ledell Smith, *Bert Williams: A Biography of the Pioneer Black Comedian* (Jefferson, N.C.: McFarland & Company, 1992).

17. This idea first came to me as I was pondering the preoccupation of racial characterization in silent films within the context of slavery and the Civil War, and the juxtaposition of this "drama," in turn, with a seemingly comedic form, that of blackface minstrelsy. Racial stereotypes often boil down to awkward juxtapositions of drama and humor. And yet, if there is an American aesthetic of literature and performance that explains the figure of the black, it is forged precisely of this counterintuitive combination. See Constance Rourke, *American Humor: A Study of the National Character* (New York: Harcourt, Brace, 1931); Albert Murray, *The Omni-Americans: Black Experience & American Culture* (New York: Da Capo Press, 1970).

18. In the many stage versions of *Uncle Tom's Cabin* that were presented from the book's first publication through the silent period, one particular songwriter and minstrel performer, Sam Lucas, emerges as the first black on record to play the title role on the stage in the 1870s. By the time he performed the role on film in 1914, he was not only elderly and thin but apparently bent over with arthritis, and yet in the light of the emerging star system, he was still the logical choice.

19. Joel Chandler Harris, *Uncle Remus: His Songs and His Sayings* (New York: Penguin Classics, 1982); Albert Murray, *South to a Very Old Place* (New York: Vintage, 1971), 41–67.

20. Conversations with Cuban-American cultural critic Coco Fusco, Puerto Rican American cultural critic Yasmin Ramirez, and Brazilian cultural critic Catherine Benamou.

21. Grace Hale and M. M. Manring, *Slave in a Box: The Strange Career of Aunt Jemima* (University Press of Virginia, 1998).

22. Joel Williamson, *New People: Miscegenation and Mulattoes in the United States* (New York: Free Press, 1980), 111–139.

23. James Baldwin, "Everybody's Protest Novel," in *Notes of a Native Son* (New York: Dial Press, 1961), 9–17.

24. Williamson, *New People,* 75–91.

25. Fredi Washington Papers, Schomburg Research Center for Black Culture, New York Public Library, New York; Gail Lumet Buckley, *The Hornes: An American Family* (New York: Knopf, 1986).

26. Henry Louis Gates, Jr., "The Face and Voice of Blackness," in *Modern Art and Society: An Anthology of Social and Multicultural Readings,* ed. Maurice Berger (New York: Harper Collins, 1994); Michele Wallace, "De-Facing History," *Art in America,* December 1990, 120–129, 184–186; Patricia Turner, *Ceramic Uncles & Celluloid Mammies* (New York: Anchor, 1994).

27. Richard Schickel, *D. W. Griffith: An American Life* (New York: Simon and Schuster, 1983), 212–302. Despite the fact that Henry Walthall, who plays Ben Cameron, the lead, was in his mid-thirties and a hopeless alcoholic, the stark white make-up they wore in those days seems to have suited his classical features. Lillian Gish as Elsie is, of course as always, a peach. Or, as Griffith would later defend the seeming violence of his politics in defending the Ku Klux Klan, "Beauty's the answer. Beauty is my fetish. I don't care what anyone says to the contrary" (290).

28. Richard Dyer gives credit to the potentially magical qualities of cinematic whiteness (as opposed to its literary articulation) in *White* (New York: Routledge Press, 1998). Art historian Kirk Savage points out how American ideals of racial whiteness in the nineteenth century drew directly

upon classical Greek sculpture in *Standing Soldiers, Kneeling Slaves: Race, War, and Monument in Nineteenth Century America* (Princeton, N.J.: Princeton University Press, 1997), 3–20. As Savage writes, "The importance of the aesthetic dimension of racial theory cannot be overemphasized, and sculpture served as the aesthetic standard" (10).

29. Patricia Morton, *Disfiguring Images: The Historical Assault on Afro-American Women* (Westport, Conn.: Greenwood Press, 1991), 21.

30. Jane Gaines, "Fire and Desire: Race, Melodrama and Oscar Micheaux," in *Black American Cinema,* ed. Manthia Diawara (New York: Routledge, 1993), 49–70.

31. Williamson, *New People.*

32. I am thinking of such recent films as *Mississippi Burning* (1988).

6. *WITHIN OUR GATES:* FROM RACE MELODRAMA TO OPPORTUNITY NARRATIVE

1. Charlene Regester, "Oscar Micheaux on the Cutting Edge: Films Rejected by the New York State Motion Picture Commission," *Studies in Popular Culture* (Spring 1995): 61–72.

2. For the development of the concept of the "race melodrama," see Susan Gilman, "The Mulatto, Tragic or Triumphant? The Nineteenth-Century American Race Melodrama," in *The Culture of Sentiment: Race, Gender, and Sentimentality in Nineteenth-Century America,* ed. Shirley Samuels (New York: Oxford University Press, 1992).

3. Mark Twain, *Pudd'nhead Wilson* (1894; reprint, New York: Bantam Books, 1959); Dion Boucicault, *The Octoroon: or, A Lover's Adventures in Louisiana* (1856; reprint, Miami: Mnemosyne Publishing Co., 1969); William Wells Brown, *Clotel: or, The President's Daughter* (1853; reprint, Secaucus, N.J.: Carol Publishing Co., 1969); Frances E. W. Harper, *Iola Leroy* (1892; reprint, Boston: Beacon Press, 1987).

4. Jane Gaines, "*The Birth of a Nation* and *Within Our Gates:* Two Tales of the American South," in *Dixie Debates: Perspectives on Southern Culture,* ed. Richard H. King and Helen Taylor (London: Pluto Press, 1995).

5. For a basic introduction to the way melodrama theory has been developed in film studies, see *Home Is Where the Heart Is,* ed. Christine Gledhill (London: British Film Institute, 1987) and *Melodrama: Stage/Picture/Screen,* ed. Christine Gledhill (London: British Film Institute, 1994).

6. Manthia Diawara, "Black Spectatorship: Problems of Identification and Resistance," *Screen* 29, no. 4 (Winter 1988): 66–76; Mary Ann Doane, "Dark Continents: Epistemologies of Racial and Sexual Difference in Psychoanalysis and Cinema," in *Femmes Fatales* (New York: Routledge, 1991), 209–248; Janet Staiger, "*The Birth of a Nation:* Reconsidering its Reception," in *The Birth of a Nation,* ed. Robert Lang (New Brunswick, N.J.: Rutgers University Press, 1994), 195–213; Clyde Taylor, "The Re-Birth of the Aesthetic Cinema," *Wide Angle* 13, no. 3–4 (July–October 1991): 12–30; Neil Lerner and Jane Gaines, "The Orchestration of Affect," in *Proceedings from the Domitor Conference on Early Sound,* ed. Rick Altman and Richard Abel (Bloomington: University of Indiana, forthcoming).

7. As quoted in Richard Schickel, *D. W. Griffith: An American Life* (New York: Simon and Schuster, 1984), 277.

8. See, for instance, Noel Burch, *Life to Those Shadows* (Berkeley: University of California Press, 1991); Tom Gunning, *D. W. Griffith and the Origins of American Film Narrative* (Urbana: University of Illinois Press, 1991); Thomas Elsaesser, ed., *Early Cinema: Space-Frame-Narrative* (London: British Film Institute, 1990).

9. James Baldwin, *The Devil Finds Work* (New York: Dell, 1976), 53.

10. See, for instance, Jane Gaines, "The Melos in Marxist Theory," in *The Hidden Foundation: Film and the Question of Class,* ed. David James and Rick Berg (Minneapolis: University of Minnesota Press, 1995).

11. Martin Marks, *Music and the Silent Film: Contexts and Case Studies, 1895–1924* (New York: Oxford University Press, 1997), Chapter 4.

12. As quoted in Schickel, *D. W. Griffith,* 267.

13. See, for instance, Raymond A. Cook, *Fire from the Flint: The Amazing Careers of Thomas Dixon* (Winston-Salem, N.C.: John F. Blair, 1968); Joel Williamson, *A Rage for Order: Black/White Relations in the American South since Emancipation* (New York: Oxford University Press, 1986), especially 98–116.

14. Thomas Cripps, *Slow Fade to Black: The Negro in American Film, 1900–1942* (New York: Oxford University Press, 1977), 69.

15. Jane Gaines, "Fire and Desire: Race, Melodrama, and Oscar Micheaux," in *Black American Cinema,* ed. Manthia Diawara (New York: Routledge/American Film Institute, 1993), 55–59.

16. Henry Sampson, *Blacks in Black and White: A Source Book on Black Films,* 2nd ed. (Metuchen, N.J.: Scarecrow Press, 1995), 208–209; Thomas Cripps, "*The Birth of a Race:* A Lost Film Rediscovered in Texas," *Texas Humanist* (March/April 1983): 10–11.

17. See Robert Heilman, *Tragedy and Melodrama: Versions of Experience* (Seattle: University of Washington Press, 1968) on the "insoluble situation."

18. See Harry Birdoff, *The World's Greatest Hit: Uncle Tom's Cabin* (New York: S. F. Vanni, 1947).

19. Charles Chesnutt, *The Marrow of Tradition* (1901; reprint, Ann Arbor: University of Michigan Press, 1969).

20. T. S. Stribling, *Birthright* (1922; reprint, Delmar, N.Y.: Scholars' Facsimiles & Reprints, 1987).

21. For an excellent analysis of Washington's biography as a work of literature, see Robert Stepto, *From Behind the Veil* (Urbana: University of Illinois Press, 1979).

22. Cripps, *Slow Fade to Black,* 61.

23. Richard Dyer argues that the dream represents the mother's fears about black male sexuality in *Heavenly Bodies: Film Stars and Society* (London: Macmillan, 1987), 109–115.

24. See J. Ronald Green, "Micheaux v. Griffith," *Griffithiana* no. 60/61 (October 1997) for the argument that Mrs. Stratton has affinities with the Lillian Gish character from *The Birth of a Nation,* particularly as Gish comes to develop southern sympathies (45).

25. Gaines, "*The Birth of a Nation* and *Within Our Gates,*" 188.

26. See Valerie Smith, "Split Affinities: The Case of Interracial Rape," in *Conflicts in Feminism,* ed. Marianne Hirsch and Evelyn Fox Keller (New York: Routledge, 1990).

27. *Chicago Defender,* 7 February 1920, quoted in Henry T. Sampson, *Blacks in Black and White: A Source Book on Black Film,* 2nd ed. (Metuchen, N.J.: Scarecrow, 1995), 279.

28. See Roland Barthes, "The Rhetoric of the Image," in *Image/Music/Text* (New York: Hill and Wang, 1977), for the theory of the way linguistic signs limit the meaning of the image. Kristin Thompson discusses the transition from expository intertitles to dialogue intertitles in David Bordwell, Janet Staiger, and Kristin Thompson, *The Classical Hollywood Cinema: Film Style and Mode of Production to 1960* (New York: Columbia University Press, 1985), 186–88. This particular title appears to have qualities of both.

29. Rudolph Arnheim, *Film as Art,* 2nd ed. (Berkeley: University of California Press, 1966) is the most extreme but eloquent example.

30. Mary Ann Doane, "The Voice in Cinema: The Articulation of Body and Space," *Yale French Studies* no. 60 (1980): 33–50. Reprinted in Philip Rosen, ed. *Narrative, Apparatus, Ideology: A Film Theory Reader* (New York: Columbia University Press, 1986), 335–348.

31. Helen T. Catterall, ed., *Judicial Cases Concerning American Slavery and the Negro* (Washington, D.C.: Carnegie Institution of Washington, 1926–1937; reprint, New York: Octagon Books, 1968).

32. John D'Emilio and Estelle Freedman, *Intimate Matters: A History of Sexuality in America* (New York: Harper and Row, 1988), 103.

33. C. Van Woodward, "History from Slave Sources," in *The Slave's Narrative,* ed. Charles T. Davis and Henry Louis Gates, Jr. (New York: Oxford University Press, 1985), 56.

34. See Joel Williamson, *New People: Miscegenation and Mulattoes in the United States* (New York: Free Press, 1980).

35. For more on this film see Thomas Cripps, "'Race Movies' as Voices of the Black Bourgeoisie: *The Scar of Shame,*" in *American History/American Film,* ed. John E. O'Connor and Martin A. Jackson (New York: Ungar, 1979); and Jane M. Gaines, "*Scar of Shame:* Skin Color and Caste in Black Silent Melodrama," in *Black Issues in Film and Visual Media,* ed. Valerie Smith (New Brunswick, N.J.: Rutgers University Press, 1997).

36. Donald Bogle, *Toms, Coons, Mulattoes, Mammies, and Bucks: An Interpretive History of Blacks in American Films* (New York: Continuum, 1989).

37. For the classic explanation of this difference, see E. M. Forster, *Aspects of the Novel* (New York: Harcourt Brace Jovanovich, 1927), Chapter 3.

7. OSCAR MICHEAUX'S *THE SYMBOL OF THE UNCONQUERED*

Much of the material in this essay is from the authors' book *Writing Himself into History: Oscar Micheaux, His Silent Films, and His Audiences* (New Brunswick, N.J.: Rutgers University Press, 2000). Some of it has also appeared in "Identity and Betrayal: *The Symbol of the Unconquered* and Oscar Micheaux's 'Biographical Legend,'" in *The Birth of Whiteness: Race and the Emergence of United States Cinema,* ed. Daniel Bernardi (New Brunswick, N.J.: Rutgers University Press, 1996). Shorter versions were presented at the Columbia Seminar on Cinema and Interdisciplinary Interpretation, January 1994, and at the conference "Oscar Micheaux and His Circle: African-American Filmmaking and Race Cinema of the Silent Era," Whitney Humanities Center, Yale University, January 1995.

1. Unidentified magazine clipping, [Spring 1921], Tuskegee Institute files.

2. We have used the terms Black and African American interchangeably in this essay. The currently outmoded term Negro is sometimes used when it seems appropriate to the historical context. We capitalize "Black" because it refers not to skin pigmentation but to a specific social identity and heritage, akin to other ethnic identities, and use the lowercase for "white" because it refers not to a specific ethnic group or ethnic identity, but to many. This is also the form of capitalization that was employed by most of the Negro press in the late teens and twenties.

3. *The Symbol of the Unconquered* was repatriated in 1992 from the Belgian national film archives (Cinémathèque Royale/Koninklijk Filmarchief) with French and Flemish titles.

4. Henry Louis Gates, Jr., and Nellie Y. McKay, eds., *Norton Anthology of African American Literature* (New York: W.W. Norton, 1997), 607.

5. *The Competitor,* January–February 1921, 61.

6. Oscar Micheaux, *The Conquest: The Story of a Negro Pioneer, by the Pioneer* (Lincoln, Neb.: Woodruff Press, 1913).

7. Oscar Micheaux, *The Forged Note* (Lincoln, Neb.: Western Book Supply Company, 1915); Oscar Micheaux, *The Homesteader* (Sioux City, Iowa: Western Book Supply Company, 1917); Oscar Micheaux, *The Wind from Nowhere* (New York: Book Supply Company, 1943); Oscar Micheaux, *The Case of Mrs. Wingate* (New York: Book Supply Company, 1945); Oscar Micheaux, *The Story of Dorothy Stanfield* (New York: Book Supply Company, 1946); Oscar Micheaux, *The Masquerade* (New York: Book Supply Company, 1947).

8. We are using the name of the character as it appears in the repatriated print of the film. In three newspaper notices (*The Chicago Defender* [27 November 1920], *The Philadelphia Tribune* [3 January 1921], and *The Chicago Whip* [15 January 1921]), however, she is referred to as "Evon."

9. W. E. B. Du Bois, *The Souls of Black Folk,* in *W. E. B. Du Bois Writings,* ed. Nathan Huggins (New York: Library of America, 1986), 370.

10. Micheaux, *The Conquest,* 47. Richard Slotkin suggests that the Homestead Act that divided Indian lands into homestead-type allotments was planned as both a safety valve for urban dis-

content and a way to integrate Native Americans into "civilized society" by making them into yeoman farmers. However, "unlike homesteading in the well-watered and forested Middle West, plains farming required considerable investment of capital and a larger scale of operations to make it profitable. . . . Indeed, the greatest beneficiaries of the Homestead legislation were railroad, banking, and landholding corporations; and thirty years after the first Homestead Act, land ownership in the Great Plains states was being steadily consolidated in fewer and fewer hands." See Richard Slotkin, *The Fatal Environment: The Myth of the Frontier in the Age of Industrialization, 1800–1890* (New York: Atheneum, 1985), 284–285. Micheaux himself seldom mentions the Native American population or the appropriation of their land. But in a short passage in *The Conquest* he does refer to the Indians as "easily flattered" who, rather than developing their allotments, sold them and spent their money as quickly as possible, "buying fine horses, buggies, whiskey, and what-not" (178). His pragmatic self-deception was consonant with the vision of degraded Indians, free land, and progress that held the popular imagination of most of the rest of the non-Native population.

11. Micheaux, *The Conquest,* 14–15.

12. Ibid., 74–85.

13. Ibid., 145.

14. Ibid., 98–99.

15. Micheaux, *The Homesteader,* 407.

16. Ibid., 401–411.

17. Oscar Micheaux, "Colored Americans Too Slow to Take Advantage of Great Land Opportunities Given Free by the Government," *Chicago Defender,* 28 October 1911, 1.

18. Gregory County Register of Deeds, Burke, South Dakota.

19. Micheaux, *The Forged Note,* 541.

20. *Chicago Defender,* 22 February 1919; "The Eighth Regiment Armory at 35th Street and Forest Avenue is a monument to the sacrifice and persistence of the military lover of the race. It was erected when Colonel [Franklin A.] Denison was in charge of the regiment. It is often used for large gatherings, as it has a seating capacity of about 8000" ("Negro Life in Chicago," *The Half-Century Magazine,* May 1919).

21. The term "biographical legend" is Boris Tomasevskij's [Tomashevsky]. "Thus the biography that is useful to the literary historian is not the author's curriculum vitae or the investigator's account of his life. What the literary historian really needs is the biographical legend created by the author himself." See Boris Tomasevskij, "Literature and Biography," in *Readings in Russian Poetics: Formalist and Structuralist Views,* ed. Ladislav Matejka and Krystyna Pomorska (Ann Arbor: University of Michigan Press, 1978), 55.

22. A previous film, *Daughter of the Congo,* 1930, was billed by Micheaux as a "talking, singing and dancing" picture; however, the sound sequence, according to one reviewer, John Mack Brown, is confined to "one short and unnecessary scene." "Oscar Micheaux Makes No Big Hit with His 'Talkie' Venture," *Norfolk Journal and Guide,* 12 April 1930, 3.

23. Oscar Micheaux, "Where the Negro Fails," *The Chicago Defender,* 19 March 1910, 1; and Oscar Micheaux, "Colored Americans Too Slow to Take Advantage." Abbott and his family later appeared in Micheaux's 1927 film *The Millionaire* (Clipping, *The Chicago Bee,* n.d.).

24. His stock prospectus stated, "Aside from the general public, who themselves, [have] never seen a picture in which the Negro race and a Negro hero is so portrayed, . . . twelve million Negro people will have their first opportunity to see their race in [a] stellar role. Their patronage, which can be expected in immense numbers, will mean in itself alone a fortune."

25. See Micheaux, *The Conquest,* 147.

26. Micheaux used this phrase in both *The Homesteader,* 25, and *The Wind from Nowhere,* 133.

27. Micheaux, "Where the Negro Fails."

28. Nell Irvin Painter, *Exodusters: Black Migration to Kansas after Reconstruction* (New York: W.W. Norton, 1992) is a study of one such group of homesteaders. Micheaux's own family had migrated West from southern Illinois to Kansas and, later, to Colorado and California (Verna Crowe

[Micheaux's niece] to Pearl Bowser, Los Angeles, California, 29 January 1991, for the film *Midnight Ramble* [Bester Cram and Pearl Bowser, 1994]).

29. Edward Henry to the authors, Jackson, Mississippi, 18 June 1993. Mr. Henry, well-respected in the Farish Street community, worked at race theaters in Jackson from 1919 to 1977 and trained several other African-American operators.

30. *Chicago Defender,* 20 November 1920, 6.

31. Baltimore *Afro-American,* 31 December 1920, 4.

32. "The Symbol of the Unconquered," *Chicago Whip,* 15 January 1921, 3.

33. *New York Age,* 25 December 1920, 6.

34. *The Competitor,* January–February 1921, 61.

35. T. S. Stribling, *Birthright* (New York: Century, 1922). The Black press noted how closely the film followed the book. According to the *New York Age,* 19 January 1924, 6, "In adapting the story for the screen, Mr. Micheaux followed the book very closely, even using in the [intertitles] the identical language contained therein." D. Ireland Thomas wrote, "Mr. Micheaux is not the author of *Birthright.* He is not responsible for the bad language used in the production. He filmed the production as the author wrote it" ("Motion Picture News," *Chicago Defender,* 25 October 1924, 6A). Micheaux made a sound version of the film in 1939.

36. Maryland State Board of Motion Picture Censors, "List of Eliminated Films," Week ending 26 January 1924; and Micheaux to Virginia State Board of Censors, 14 October 1924, both in Virginia Division of Motion Picture Censorship, Virginia State Library and Archives.

37. *Birthright* was shown with a bogus seal at the Attucks Theatre in Norfolk, the Idle Hour in Petersburg, and the Dixie in Newport News (and perhaps other venues). "Correspondence Regarding Controversial Pictures, 1924–1965," Virginia Division of Motion Picture Censorship, Virginia State Library and Archives.

38. Ibid.

39. See, for example, E. R. Chesterman, Virginia State Board of Censors, to C. C. Collmus, Jr., of Norfolk, 28 February 1924, Virginia Division of Motion Picture Censorship, Virginia State Library and Archives.

40. "List of films rejected in toto since August 1, 1922," 4 February 1930, Commonwealth of Virginia, Department of Law, Division of Motion Picture Censorship, Virginia State Library and Archives. In his 1925 review of *The House Behind the Cedars,* the board's chair, Evan Chesterman, wrote that the film "contravenes the spirit of the recently enacted anti-miscegenation law which has put Virginia in the forefront as a pioneer in legislation aimed to preserve the integrity of the white race."

41. The only known print of *Within Our Gates* was repatriated from La Filmoteca Española, the National Film Archive of Spain, in 1988 under the title, *La Negra.* It is only three-fourths of the original advertised length. While the intertitle in the film currently in distribution, which is translated from the Spanish print, describes the young woman, Sylvia, as the product of a "legitimate marriage," ads and descriptive material in the press, although they do not use the words incest or rape, do refer frequently to concubinage. Concubinage is not represented in the existing print, but even if it had not been depicted, the reference to concubinage in the promotional material and a knowledge of how endemic concubinage was within the sharecropping system would have been enough to suggest this as a likely backstory for Sylvia's mother. There may also have been a more overt representation of white paternity. According to one review, "You see the white man [presumably Armand Girdlestone] who claims the black child laid at his doorstep by the mother because it is his own and he later gives the mother some money" (quoted in Henry T. Sampson, *Blacks in Black and White: A Source Book on Black Films,* 2nd ed. [Metuchen, N.J.: Scarecrow Press, 1995], 152.) The Spanish intertitle may have been a concession to local mores, or censors, or a misinterpretation. For a different interpretation, see Jane Gaines's "*Within Our Gates:* From Race Melodrama to Opportunity Narrative," in this volume, which argues that the title card is a reference to a "legitimate marriage," is in keeping with "history, literature, and legend," and that interracial

marriage is a device Micheaux used to offer an "alternative story" to the "prevailing mythology about illicit interracial sexuality."

42. Clipping, American Negro Press, 20 January 1920, George P. Johnson Negro Film Collection, Department of Special Collections, Young Research Library, University of California, Los Angeles.

43. Police Captain Theodore A. Ray to Frank T. Monney, Superintendent of Police, 19 March 1920, George P. Johnson Collection, UCLA.

44. This print, repatriated from Brussels in 1992, is now in the archives of the Museum of Modern Art in New York. The opening of the film (including the story of Eve and her grandfather) and a good part of the Klan attack toward the end appear to be missing.

45. See the authors' paper, "'I may be crazy, but I ain't no fool': The Strategic Use of Stereotypes in Oscar Micheaux's *Within Our Gates,*" presented at the Society of Cinema Studies Conference, New York City, March 1995.

46. Eph is a peripheral character in *Within Our Gates,* living on the edges of both Black and white society. In the existing print, he is only seen in white-dominated spaces and he is never in the same space or frame with another Black person.

47. This is interesting in contrast to the mulattos in Chesnutt's works, characters who continue to have ties to the community (for example, in the title story in *The Wife of His Youth and Other Stories of the Color Line* [Boston: Houghton, Mifflin and Company, 1899]) or who have affection for and the support of their family, even though they are bitterly missed, as in *The House Behind the Cedars* (Boston: Houghton, Mifflin and Company, 1900).

48. Micheaux, *The Conquest,* 153–154.

49. Micheaux, *The Homesteader,* 147. Italics and capitalization in original.

50. Ibid.

51. Oscar Micheaux, *The Betrayal* (film script), the Motion Picture Commission of the State of New York, New York State Archives, Albany, New York. The film does not seem to be extant.

52. South Dakota did not have an anti-miscegenation law until 1909.

53. Bernard L. Peterson, Jr., *Early Black American Playwrights and Dramatic Writers: A Biographical Directory and Catalogue of Plays, Films, and Broadcasting Scripts* (Westport, Conn.: Greenwood Press, 1990), 139.

54. See Jane P. Tompkins's "Sentimental Power: Uncle Tom's Cabin and the Politics of Literary History," in *The New Feminist Criticism: Essays on Women, Literature and Theory,* ed. Elaine Showalter (New York: Pantheon, 1985), 84–85.

55. Toni Morrison, *Playing in the Dark: Whiteness and the Literary Imagination* (Cambridge, Mass.: Harvard University Press, 1992), 68. Morrison is elaborating linguistic categories from James A. Snead, *Figures of Division: William Faulkner's Major Novels* (New York: Methuen, 1986).

56. Morrison, *Playing in the Dark,* 52.

57. Houston A. Baker, Jr., *Modernism and the Harlem Renaissance* (Chicago: University of Chicago Press, 1987), 33.

58. *Within Our Gates,* for example, was advertised as "the most sensational story of the race question since *Uncle Tom's Cabin.*" Micheaux described *Birthright* as "a grim, gripping story of Negro life in the South today, more crowded with action, thrills, romance, comedy and suspense than any story on this subject since *Uncle Tom's Cabin.*" His novelization of *Veiled Aristocrats* and *The House Behind the Cedars,* entitled *The Masquerade* (New York: Book Supply Company, 1947), opens with a reference to Stowe's novel.

59. Booker T. Washington, *World's Work,* November 1910; reprinted in *A Documentary History of the Negro People in the United States, 1910–1932,* ed. Herbert Aptheker (New York: Citadel Press, 1973), 3–15.

60. Oscar Micheaux to C. W. Chesnutt, 18 January 1921, Western Reserve Historical Society, Cleveland, Ohio. The extant version of the sound remake, *Veiled Aristocrats,* suggests that Micheaux, in the sound version at least, did make these changes in the character.

61. Micheaux, *The Homesteader,* 147.

62. Micheaux, *The Forged Note*, 48.

63. Micheaux, *The Conquest*, 145.

64. Langston Hughes, "The Negro Artist and the Racial Mountain," *The Nation*, 23 June 1926, 692–694.

65. Alain Locke, ed., *The New Negro: An Interpretation* (New York: A. and C. Boni, 1925), 12.

66. Micheaux, *The Conquest*, 160–162.

67. This social taboo was so entrenched that when boxer Jack Johnson defeated his white opponent, films of his bouts were banned from interstate commerce. See Dan Streible's "A History of the Boxing Film, 1894–1915: Social Control and Social Reform in the Progressive Era," *Film History* 3, no. 3 (1989): 235–257.

68. Micheaux, *The Conquest*, 162.

69. James Baldwin, *The Devil Finds Work: An Essay* (New York: Dial Press, 1976), 77.

70. *Daily Ohio State Journal*, quoted in the *New York Age*, 16 October 1909.

71. Oscar Micheaux, *God's Stepchildren* (film script), copyrighted 1937, New York State Archives. The author's preface to the script declares that "all the characters appearing herein, regardless how bright in color they may seem, are members of the Negro Race." In a film that deals with the sensitive subject of an interracial marriage, Micheaux seems to be assuring the censors, and perhaps even his distributors and exhibitors, that the cast is all Black. There exists no record of the determination of the Motion Picture Commission of the State of New York; however, this scene does not exist in the print currently in circulation. The film is titled *God's Step Children*, the script, *God's Stepchildren;* one reason for confusion over this film's precise title.

72. See, for example, *New York Age*, 21 August 1913, 1. In one article, "Can't Tell Who's Who: Denver Authorities Think Woman Married to Coal Black Negro Is White," Mrs. Nora Harrington Frazier offers samples of her blood to prove that she is Black. The article also discusses several tests that the woman submitted to in order to convince the marriage license bureau clerk to give her a license, including looking for dark blotches at the root of her hair and pressing her fingernails. Just below that notice is a piece entitled "Gives Up All for Negro: Pretty Daughter of Wealthy White Farmer Marries Samuel De Frees Against the Wishes of Her Parents" about a Ringwood, New Jersey, couple.

73. Helen M. Chesnutt, *Charles Waddell Chesnutt: Pioneer of the Color Line* (Chapel Hill: University of North Carolina Press, 1952), 274.

74. Lester A. Walton, "When Is a Negro a Negro to a Caucasian?" *New York Age*, 22 April 1909, 6.

75. *New York Age*, 1 May 1913. The theater, near a neighborhood known as San Juan Hill, catered to the residents of the vicinity, both Black and white.

76. *Norfolk Journal and Guide*, 28 November 1925, 1. During the proceedings, Mrs. Rhinelander was asked to bare her back to the jury so that they could tell how dark her skin was.

77. See, for example, "The Parallel of the Rhinelander Case," *New York Amsterdam News*, 4 March 1925.

78. Tony Bennett and Janet Woollacott, *Bond and Beyond: The Political Career of a Popular Hero* (London: Methuen, 1987), 90–91.

79. "'The Symbol of the Unconquered' and Musical Program Unique Lafayette Bill," *New York Age*, 1 January 1921, 6.

80. In *Within Our Gates*, the preacher "Old Ned" meets with two white men to receive his weekly "contribution" and afterward turns for what seems to be a ritualized "friendly" kick in the butt before exiting.

81. See, for example: Theophilus Lewis, *New York Amsterdam News*, 16 April 1930, 10. Speaking of *Daughter of the Congo*, Lewis accused Micheaux of associating "nobility with lightness and villainy with blackness." More recently, Charlene Regester has revived this discussion in "Oscar Micheaux's Multifaceted Portrayals of the African American Male: The Good, The Bad, and The Ugly," in *Me Jane: Masculinity, Movies, and Women*, ed. Pat Kirkham and Janet Thumin (New York: St. Martin's Press, 1995). The practice of individual performers making up light was well es-

tablished on stage and may have carried over to early film, where many performers also made themselves up. As early as 1911, Sherman H. Dudley admonished the female members of the Smart Set Company's chorus not to use light "paint and powder." Lester A. Walton reprinted part of Dudley's speech in the *New York Age* and elaborated on it, condemning the practice of making up "brown-skinned girls light and the bright girls lighter" and praising Aida Overton Walker as a performer who "has never shown a disposition to be other than a 'brownie,' and it cannot be said that she has suffered any for using such good judgment" (*New York Age,* 28 September 1911, 6).

82. Richard Grupenhoff discusses Tucker playing both romantic leads and gangsters in Micheaux's later films. See Grupenhoff, *The Black Valentino: The Stage and Screen Career of Lorenzo Tucker* (Metuchen, N.J.: Scarecrow Press, 1988), 61–81.

83. Interview with Carl Mahon, Julius Lester's *Free Time* (PBS), aired 18 October 1971. Mahon was a New York City schoolteacher with good diction but little acting experience.

84. The name seems to have been borrowed from or an homage to Jack London's semi-autobiography *Martin Eden* (New York: Grosset & Dunlap, 1909). Micheaux also used the title of Gertrude Sanborn's novel, *Veiled Aristocrats* (Washington, D.C.: The Associated Publishers, 1923), as the name of his sound remake of C. W. Chesnutt's *The House Behind the Cedars.*

85. Oscar Micheaux, *The Betrayal* (film script), New York State Archives.

86. Most African Americans are familiar with a wide variety of skin colors in the community and their own families. For example, painter and illustrator Elton Fax commented, "We all knew there were light-skinned blacks who were our cousins, our brothers and sisters, so there was nothing new in that. To white people, this might have been new but it wasn't to us" (Elton Fax to Pearl Bowser, 7 January 1991, New York City, for the film *Midnight Ramble* [Bester Cram and Pearl Bowser, 1994]).

87. *The Competitor,* January–February 1921, 61. Micheaux's thoughts here seem similar to Booker T. Washington's: "Every persecuted individual and race should get much consolation out of the great human law, which is universal and eternal, that merit, no matter under what skin found, is in the long run, recognized and rewarded." See Booker T. Washington, *Up From Slavery: An Autobiography* (1901; reprint, Garden City, N.Y. Doubleday, 1963), 29.

88. Swan Micheaux to George P. Johnson, 27 October 1920, George P. Johnson Collection, UCLA. A Tom Mix film, *The Wilderness Trail,* had opened in July of 1919.

8. To Redream the Dreams of White Playwrights

1. This essay would not have been written without the generosity and support of Pearl Bowser and Jane Gaines. The Schomburg Center for Research in Black Culture, New York Public Library, has proved an invaluable resource for this undertaking, which was first given as a paper at the conference Oscar Micheaux and His Circle at Yale University in January 1995. As the centennial of Paul Robeson's birth approached, Rae Alexander-Minter invited me to participate in the Paul Robeson: Artist and Citizen project being organized by the Paul Robeson Cultural Center (Rutgers University). Elements of the paper were further developed as "Troubled Relations: Paul Robeson, Eugene O'Neill and Oscar Micheaux," in *Paul Robeson: Artist and Citizen,* ed. Jeffrey Stewart (New Brunswick, N.J.: Rutgers University Press, 1998), 81–103. What follows is a substantial reconceptualization of that work. In particular, Hazel Carby provided a crucial insight that rearranged many pieces of the historical puzzle: Micheaux's *Body and Soul* was a reworking of Nan Bagby Stephens's play *Roseanne.* See Carby's *Race Men: The Body and Soul of Race, Nation and Manhood* (Cambridge, Mass.: Harvard University Press, 1998), 69–70. Thanks also to Charlene Regester, Martin Duberman, Henry Louis Gates, Jr., Louise Spence, John MacKay, Logan Hill, and Ron Green.

Harold Cruse deals with the Harlem Renaissance at considerable length in *The Crisis of the Negro Intellectual: A Historical Analysis of the Failure of Black Leadership* (1967; reprint, New York: Quill Press, 1984). Although he seems to long for the kind of black-oriented media consciousness of an Oscar Micheaux, Cruse was apparently unaware of his existence. Nathan Irvin Huggins, *Harlem Renaissance* (New York: Oxford University Press, 1971) ignores film, Micheaux, and *Body and Soul* completely. David Levering Lewis mentions Micheaux only briefly in *When Harlem Was in Vogue* (New York: Alfred Knopf, 1981), suggesting that Nan Bagby Stephens's novel *Glory* was a rip-off of Micheaux's *Body and Soul* (264). In fact, it was a reworking of her earlier play, *Roseanne*, which Micheaux swiped for his own purposes. Micheaux goes unmentioned in Jervis Anderson, *This Was Harlem: A Cultural Portrait 1900–1950* (New York: Farrar, Straus & Giroux; 1981); and Victor A. Kramer, ed., *The Harlem Renaissance Re-examined* (New York: AMS Press, 1987). Houston A. Baker, Jr., declines to consider film in *Modernism and the Harlem Renaissance* (Chicago: University of Chicago, 1987): "The constellation I have in mind includes Afro-American literature, music, art, graphic design and intellectual history" (8). Cary D. Wintz (*Black Culture and the Harlem Renaissance* [Houston: Rice University Press, 1988]); James L. de Jongh (*Vicious Modernism: Black Harlem and the Literary Imagination* [New York: Cambridge University Press, 1990]); and George Hutchinson (*The Harlem Renaissance in Black and White* [Cambridge, Mass.: Belknap Press of Harvard University Press, 1995]) ignore Micheaux completely, while Ann Douglas, *Terrible Honesty: Mongrel Manhattan in the 1920s* (New York: Farrar, Straus & Giroux, 1995), makes only tangential reference to him. Such marginalization can be traced back to the 1920s and such important journals as *Opportunity Magazine, The Messenger,* and *The Crisis.* In Alain Locke, ed., *The New Negro* (1925; reprint, New York: Simon & Schuster, 1992), various authors make brief reference to O'Neill's plays, Gilpin, and Robeson (35, 157–158, 167), but film is completely ignored. Micheaux is cited only as the author of *The Conquest* in the volume's concluding bibliography of African-American literature (428)—even his other books go unmentioned. Micheaux was not listed in *Who's Who in Colored America* (New York: Who's Who in Colored America Corp., 1927), though he does appear in all subsequent editions. See also Arna Bontemps, ed., *The Harlem Renaissance Remembered* (New York: Dodd, Mead, 1972). Bruce Kellner, ed., *Harlem Renaissance: A Historical Dictionary for the Era* (New York: Methuen, 1987) gives a substantial and somewhat admiring capsule biography of the filmmaker, but then concludes: "None of Micheaux's films had any critical reputation, but their popularity was considerable, largely because of their maker's ability to sell himself" (242). Not only Carby's *Race Men* but also Jeffrey C. Stewart's essay "Paul Robeson and the Problem of Modernism" in *Rhapsodies in Black: Art of the Harlem Renaissance* (Berkeley: University of California Press, 1997), 90–100, have begun to change this silence about or dismissal of Micheaux and his 1925 film.

In *The Signifying Monkey: A Theory of African-American Literary Criticism* (New York: Oxford University Press, 1988), Henry Louis Gates, Jr., analyzes only one film: *Charleston* (1927), made by French filmmaker Jean Renoir. Indeed, as this essay shows, Gates's illuminating approach could be applied to Micheaux (and African-American cinema) with even greater effectivity.

2. For example, *Body and Soul* goes unmentioned in David Bordwell, Janet Staiger, and Kristin Thompson, *The Classical Hollywood Cinema: Film Style & Mode of Production to 1960* (New York: Columbia University Press, 1989); Robert Sklar, *Movie-Made America,* 2nd ed. (1975; New York: Vintage, 1994); and Garth Jowett, *Film, The Democratic Art: A Social History of American Film* (Boston: Little, Brown, 1976). The film is briefly referenced in Richard Koszarski, *An Evening's Entertainment: The Age of the Silent Feature Picture, 1915–1928* (New York: Scribners, 1990), 189.

3. *Body and Soul* goes unmentioned and Micheaux is only referred to twice in Peter Noble, *The Negro in Film* (London: Skelton & Robinson, 1948); as well as twice in Ed Guerrero, *Framing Blackness: The African-American Image in Film* (Philadelphia: Temple University Press, 1993). Dan Leab, *From Sambo to Superspade: The Black Experience in Motion Pictures* (New York: Houghton, Mifflin Co., 1975), offers no analysis of *Body and Soul* but astutely suggests that Robeson must have regretted his involvement (78–79). In *Redefining Black Film* (Berkeley: University of California Press, 1993), Mark Reid mentions the film once, as an example of how black actors such as Paul Robeson started their movie careers by appearing in race films, only to be lured away by white studios (15). In his otherwise outstanding and lengthy treatment of Oscar Micheaux and the Micheaux Film Company, Henry T. Sampson mentions *Body and Soul* only in passing, noting that it has a

"somewhat confusing plot of a minister gone corrupt" (*Blacks in Black and White: A Source Book in Black Films,* 2nd ed. [1977; Metuchen, N.J.: Scarecrow Press, 1995], 149, 287–288). Thomas Cripps deals with the film more extensively in *Slow Fade to Black: The Negro in American Film, 1900–1942* (New York: Oxford University Press, 1977), 189–193. Despite his reservations about the film, he characterizes it as Micheaux's outstanding achievement.

4. Donald Bogle, *Blacks in American Film and Television: An Encyclopedia* (New York: Garland, 1988), 32–33; Sampson, *Blacks in Black and White,* 287.

5. David Bordwell and Kristin Thompson, *Film Art: An Introduction,* 5th ed. (New York: McGraw Hill, 1997), 90.

6. David Bordwell and Kristin Thompson, nonetheless, failed to even mention *Body and Soul* in *Film History: An Introduction* (New York: McGraw Hill, 1994), 181. This position is also articulated in James Snead, *White Screens/Black Images: Hollywood from the Dark Side* (New York: Routledge, 1994), 113. It is perhaps a somewhat simplified synopsis of the position argued by Ron Green, who celebrates a "poor cinema." See Ron Green, "'Twoness' in the Style of Oscar Micheaux," in *Black American Cinema,* ed. Manthia Diawara (New York: Routledge, 1993), 26–48.

7. Thomas Cripps, *Slow Fade to Black,* 191–193; Bogle, *Blacks in American Film and Television,* 32–33.

8. Print variation and corruption are pervasive realities for any historian studying film—particularly silent film. Films by Edwin S. Porter, D. W. Griffith, Charles Chaplin, and Erich von Stroheim (his *Foolish Wives* and *Greed,* to offer two extreme examples) have suffered serious alteration; nonetheless, such problems have not prevented analysis of their work.

9. The Library of Congress restored Micheaux's *Within Our Gates* (1920), found with Spanish intertitles in Spain, in 1995; *The Symbol of the Unconquered* was restored in 1998 by the Museum of Modern Art and Turner Entertainment.

10. *Within Our Gates* functions as a reworking and evocation of both Albion Tourgee's *A Fool's Errand: A Novel of the South during Reconstruction* and—as Corey Creekmur has pointed out—Charles Chesnutt's *Marrow of Tradition* (1901) about the race riots in North Carolina during 1898. From this perspective, *Within Our Gates* can be seen as the third stage in this genealogy of race-riot epics, this one in the immediate post–World War I period.

11. Jane Gaines, "Fire and Desire: Race, Melodrama and Oscar Micheaux," in *Black American Cinema,* ed. Manthia Diawara (New York: Routledge, 1993), 49–70. One is struck, however, with how these retellings invert the thrice-told tale in *A Fool's Errand.* This chapter (Chapter 30) begins with several white newspaper accounts and ends with an account from a black servant who overheard the perpetrators discussing the crime in detail. Micheaux goes in the opposite direction, but he also focuses on the death of a white racist plantation owner rather than on a white radical.

12. Pearl Bowser and Louise Spence, *Writing Himself into History: Oscar Micheaux, His Silent Films, and His Audiences* (New Brunswick, N.J.: Rutgers University Press, 2000).

13. "Roseanne," *The Messenger,* March 1924, 73.

14. *New York Herald-Tribune,* 6 July 1924, in *Paul Robeson Speaks: Writings, Speeches, Interviews, 1918–1924,* ed. Philip S. Foner (New York: Citadel Press, 1978). Negotiations for Robeson's participation in *Body and Soul* were apparently concluded in mid-October, a few weeks before filmmaking commenced. When Robeson began talking about the project with Micheaux is unclear. See Martin Bauml Duberman, *Paul Robeson* (New York: Random House, 1989), 76, 593 n. 24.

15. Marian Keane, "The Great Profile: John Barrymore's Acting on Stage and on Film" (Ph.D. diss., New York University, 1991).

16. Louis Sheaffer, *O'Neill: Son and Artist* (Boston: Little, Brown, 1973), 104.

17. "The Screen," *New York Times,* 10 December 1923, 20.

18. Advertisement, Baltimore *Afro-American,* 29 February 1924, 2. See also, "'I Hate All Men' She Hissed," Baltimore *Afro-American,* 29 February 1924, 10.

19. "The Film of the Month," *McCall's Magazine,* April 1926, clipping, Irene Rich Collection, Academy of Motion Picture Arts and Sciences.

20. As Hall remarked about *Lady Windermere's Fan,* "Those who have seen or read the play will be disappointed in the pictorial results" (Mordaunt Hall, "The Screen," *New York Times,* 28 December 1925, 19). Hall longed for a transparent rendering of the play, one in which the filmmaker's creative input was in the opening up of the play and the rendering of its text in cinematic form. Sherwood, in contrast, appreciated the way that Lubitsch disrupted the easy correspondence of play and film. In this regard, we might think of Lubitsch's *Lady Windermere's Fan* as a resistant text.

21. See Kevin J. Hayes, *American Literature and Silent Film* (Iowa City: University of Iowa Press, forthcoming).

22. Carby, *Race Men,* 69–70.

23. Charles Belmont Davis, "'Roseanne' Somber Study of Primitive Customs of Negro," *New York Tribune,* 31 December 1923, 6. A number of reviews suggest that Leola was Roseanne's sister rather than her adopted daughter. See "The Stage," *New York Herald,* 31 December 1923; and "'Roseanne' Coming to Gibson's New Dunbar," *Pittsburgh Courier,* 29 March 1924, 10.

24. "All Negro Religious Drama," *New York Times,* 31 December 1923, 9.

25. "'Roseanne' Coming to Gibson's New Dunbar," *Pittsburgh Courier,* 29 March 1924, 10.

26. Lewis, "Roseanne," *The Messenger,* March 1924, 75.

27. *Opportunity Magazine,* November 1925, 346.

28. Eslanda Goode Robeson, *Paul Robeson, Negro* (New York: Harper & Brothers, 1930), 8–9.

29. W. E. B. Du Bois, *The Souls of Black Folk* (1903; New York: Washington Square Books, 1970), 155.

30. Heywood Broun, "'The Emperor Jones' by O'Neill Gives Chance for Cheers," *New York Tribune,* 4 November 1920, 8.

31. The parallels between Yellow Curly Hinds and Smithers deserve serious consideration. (Note, for example, that Smithers's "pasty face" is described by O'Neill as a "sickly yellow" in the playscript.) Smithers, Brutus Jones suggests, was himself once in prison. He does not know for sure, perhaps because segregation had kept them apart. Hinds and Jones, however, were in the same prison cell.

32. *The Negro World,* 26 March 1921, quoted in David Krasner, "Whose Role Is It Anyway?: Charles Gilpin and the Harlem Renaissance," *African American Review* 29, no. 3 (Fall 1995): 486. See also William Stanley Braithwaite, "The Negro in American Literature" in *The New Negro,* 36.

33. *The Outlook,* quoted in *Opportunity Magazine,* November 1925, 346. For example, Heywood Broun called it "the most interesting play which has yet come from . . . the best of American playwrights" (*New York Tribune,* 4 November 1920, 8).

34. Stephens was worried that *Roseanne* would be considered derivative of *Emperor Jones,* so much so that she took pains to claim that she wrote the play while she was still in college when she was presumably unaware of O'Neill's effort. Even if this were the case, however, it is impossible to imagine that *Roseanne* would have ever been staged without the success of *The Emperor Jones.*

35. Duberman, *Paul Robeson,* 43, 582 n. 24.

36. *New York Tribune,* 31 December 1923, 6.

37. "'Roseanne' Drama Coming to Local Theatre, Feb'y 25," *Pittsburgh Courier,* 23 February 1924, 10. It was held over for a second week.

38. "At the Pitt," *Pittsburgh Courier,* 1 March 1924, 10.

39. "'Roseanne,' With All Negro Cast, Strikes Higher Average Than When Given by White Co.," *New York Age,* 15 March 1924, 6.

40. Ibid.

41. "Negroes Play 'Roseanne,'" *New York Times,* 11 March 1924, 16.

42. "Gilpin Quits 'Roseanne,' Paul Robeson Takes His Place," *New York Age,* 22 March 1924, 1. Other members of the cast also quit at this time, including Evelyn Ellis, who had played Leola, and C. Edward Brown, who had played Rodney.

43. Advertisement, *New York Age,* 22 March 1924, 6.

44. "At the Lafayette Theatre," *New York Age,* 29 March 1924, 6.

45. "'Roseanne' Coming to Gibson's New Dunbar," *Pittsburgh Courier,* 29 March 1924, 10.

46. The progressive impact of *The Emperor Jones,* as performed by Gilpin in the early 1920s, is amply documented in the black press. According to one article, entitled "Bright Future for Study of Dramatic Art," "One sign of the race consciousness so rapidly developing among the Race is the interest its members are now manifesting in dramatic art. The remarkable achievement of Charles Gilpin in the title role of 'The Emperor Jones' doubtless has been an incentive to greater effort on the part of other Race actors" (*Chicago Defender,* 18 February 1922, 5). Gilpin and the Provincetown Players often used the play to confront and undermine the "color line" as they toured the country.

47. The demise of blackface in American theater at this time was heavily indebted to the extraordinary performance of Charles Gilpin. This was part of a larger transformation of American theater, a change that was preceded and facilitated by the establishment of a serious black theatrical repertory company, the Lafayette Players. In addition, the Lafayette Players mounted a play in Harlem using an integrated cast at virtually the same moment that *The Emperor Jones* was staged in Greenwich Village ("'Justice' to Be Presented at Lafayette with a Mixed Cast," *New York Age,* 27 November 1920, 6).

48. For an inventory of important productions of Eugene O'Neill's plays and listing of relevant reviews, see Jordan Y. Miller, *Eugene O'Neill and the American Critic: A Bibliographic Check List,* 2nd ed. (1962; Hamden, Conn.: Archon Books, 1973).

49. "Paul Robeson Rises to Supreme Heights," *Pittsburgh Courier,* 17 May 1924, 8.

50. Sister Francesca Thompson, "The Lafayette Players, 1917–1932," in *The Theater of Black Americans,* vol. 2, ed. Errol Hill (Englewood Cliffs, N.J.: Prentice Hall, 1980). See also David Krasner, "Charles S. Gilpin: The Actor before the Emperor," *Journal of American Drama and Theatre* 4, no. 3 (Fall 1992): 62–75.

51. David Krasner very effectively describes the many conflicting pressures with which Gilpin had to contend (Krasner, *African American Review,* 483–496).

52. Cripps, *Slow Fade to Black,* 159.

53. Provincetown Players, playbill no. 4, 1923–1924 season, cited in Sheaffer, *O'Neill, Son and Artist,* 138.

54. Ibid., 35.

55. Ibid., 36–37.

56. Duberman, *Paul Robeson,* 62.

57. "Gilpin Again Stars in 'The Emperor Jones,'" *Pittsburgh Courier,* 24 March 1926, 10.

58. James Baldwin, *The Devil Finds Work: An Essay* (New York: Dial Press, 1976), 100; cited in Richard Dyer, *Heavenly Bodies: Film Stars and Society* (New York: Macmillan, 1986), 71. It is a fascinating contradiction, therefore, that Gilpin's one significant and only surviving film role is in *Ten Nights in a Barroom,* a black-cast rendering of an European-American play. Yet the use of mainstream white plays in which the question of racial politics appeared to be absent or peripheral was, according to Sister Francesca Thompson, one of the hallmarks of the Lafayette Players. It certainly had advantages over the playing of black roles as conceived by white playwrights, who inevitably introduced their own racial ideology. This approach was consistent with one strand of Gilpin's work both before and after *Emperor Jones.*

59. "The Stage and Its People," *New York American,* 8 May 1924, 10.

60. Robeson, *Paul Robeson, Negro,* 77. In fact, Essie is quoting here from a 1929 Provincetown Players manifesto.

61. Ibid., 78.

62. Ibid., 79–80.

63. Ibid., 76.

64. Ibid., 81.

65. Constantin Stanislavsky, *My Life in Art,* trans. J. J. Robbins (Boston: Little, Brown, and Company, 1924), 466.

66. Ibid., 466–467.

67. Eugene O'Neill to Paul Robeson, inscription in *The Complete Works of Eugene O'Neill* (New York: Boni and Liveright, January 1925).

68. Eslanda Robeson, diary, 7 May 1924, displayed for the exhibition Paul Robeson: Bearer of Culture, New-York Historical Society, April–July 1998. See also Duberman, *Paul Robeson*, 61.

69. Martin Duberman's biography devotes substantial attention to Robeson's extramarital romances with white women (Duberman, *Paul Robeson*).

70. Baker, *Modernism and the Harlem Renaissance*, 51–52.

71. Ibid., 56.

72. Will Anthony Madden, "Why Did Eugene O'Neill Write 'All God's Chillun' Got Wings'?," *Pittsburgh Courier*, 5 April 1924, 13.

73. In his discussion of Signifying, Henry Louis Gates, Jr., explains, "In one of several ways, manifest meaning directs attention away from itself to another latent level of meaning. We might compare this relationship to that which obtains between the two parts of a metaphor, tenor (the inner meaning) and vehicle (the outer meaning)" (*The Signifying Monkey*, 86). In this process of refiguration, the "apparent meaning serves as a key which directs hearers to some shared knowledge, attitudes, and values or signals that reference must be processed metaphorically" (Claudia Mitchell-Kernan, "Signifying," in *Mother Wit from the Laughing Barrel: Readings in the Interpretation of Afro-American Folklore,* ed. Alan Dundes [Englewood Cliffs, N.J.: Prentice Hall, 1973], 325.)

74. Oscar Micheaux to Motion Picture Commission of the State of New York, 9 November 1925, courtesy of Charlene Regester.

75. We can only speculate about Micheaux's "misspelling" of Jenkins's first name—Isiaah rather than Isaiah. Many scholars have silently corrected this. Given Micheaux's sense of play with the names of his characters, this is probably a mistake. Isaiah was the great messianic prophet—something that Isiaah Jenkins certainly is not (except perhaps in a negative sense), though his congregation seems to treat him this way. The misspelling signals his fraudulence. Or could it be I si aah—"dialect" for I see her? Who? The girl who is a belle (Isabelle). Readers are invited to entertain other explanations.

76. The temporal disjunction in moving from the opening title to the news item is underscored by the intertitle that immediately follows: "while in the meantime." This expresses a temporality of dream that anticipates in some respects Luis Buñuel and Salvador Dali's *Un Chein Andalou* (1928).

77. "'The Emperor Jones' in London," *Opportunity Magazine,* November 1925, 346.

78. Advertisement, *Pittsburgh Courier,* 12 December 1925, 11.

79. This type of playful humor can be found elsewhere. An advertisement for Charlie Chaplin's *The Pilgrim* (1923) in the black press provided the following text:

CHARLES CHAPLAIN

In his latest success

REWARD! ESCAPED CONVICT

Believed to be masquerading as a parson in this neighborhood.
Calls himself, "The Pilgrim." Said to be a familiar figure hereabouts! (Baltimore *Afro-American,* 18 May 1924, 5).

Chaplin is thus said to be the escaped convict, or "The Pilgrim," while his name is misspelled with an extra "a" to become chaplain. *The Pilgrim* was an important antecedent for Micheaux's *Body and Soul.*

80. "'Black Carl' Is Stricken," *California Eagle,* 30 November 1928, 7. He was, according to Salem Tutt Whitney, "the greatest magician the Race has produced" and "for many years was a conspicuous figure upon the vaudeville stage" (Salem Tutt Whitney, "Timely Topics," *Chicago Defender,* 24 November 1928, 11A). See also "Carl a Caller," *Chicago Defender,* 16 August 1924, 8.

81. Micheaux must have known Charles Gilpin through the Lafayette Players, whom he employed on his films.

82. "Paul Robeson Rises to Supreme Heights," *Pittsburgh Courier,* 17 May 1924, 8.

83. "I needed money. The $175 a week which they offered me was a good salary . . . and I accepted" (quoted at the Paul Robeson: Bearer of Culture exhibition at the New-York Historical Society, April–July 1998).

84. "Paul Robeson, Son of Slave Parents, Reaches Pinnacle," *Pittsburgh Courier,* 7 November 1925, 10.

85. Stanislavsky, *My Life in Art,* 466.

86. Marcus Garvey would also come to criticize Paul Robeson in terms similar to the criticisms of Madden and Micheaux. For these individuals, Robeson's uncritical association with white cultural producers was highly problematic. See *Black Man,* October 1935, 10–11, 32; and "Grand Speech of Hon. Marcus Garvey at Kingsway Hall, London, Denouncing Moving Picture Propaganda to Discredit the Negro," *Black Man,* June 1939, cited in Tony Martin, *Literary Garveyism* (Dover, Mass.: Majority Press, 1983), 117–118. *Black Man* was a Garvey newspaper published in England. Jeffrey Stewart kindly brought this information to my attention. Since Brutus Jones was generally assumed to be modeled on Garvey, Robeson's appearance in the play and movie version of *The Emperor Jones,* as well as his long-standing defense of O'Neill's work, made the actor a likely target for Garvey.

87. The "call and response" which black urban audiences often mobilize to engage the screen has been frequently commented upon. When I showed *Body and Soul* to a class on "Race and Representation in American Cinema" for New Haven Public School teachers, half of whom were African Americans, they responded actively during the film. In our discussion of the film, several participants argued that the film dictated this response, though it would have been articulated somewhat differently if the audience was exclusively black. Indeed, according to the Baltimore *Afro-American,* the movie audience was "talking out loud to the picture, tearfully and wrathfully" (Maybelle Crew, "Along the White Way," Baltimore *Afro-American,* 11 September 1926, 5).

88. Gates, *Signifying Monkey,* 59.

89. Ibid., 51.

90. Davis, "'Roseanne' Somber Study," 6.

91. Du Bois, *The Souls of Black Folk,* 3.

92. "Gilpin Again Stars in 'The Emperor Jones,'" *Pittsburgh Courier,* 24 March 1926, 10.

93. Micheaux's engagement with Chaplin's *The Pilgrim* involves the same sustained parallels, reversals, and critiques as with the three plays examined in this essay. For example, Charlie meets an old cellmate, Howard Huntington, who is a man of many aliases ("Nitro Nick" and "Picking Pete"). Picking Pete sees Charlie, dressed as a parson, in a chance encounter on the street and recalls their days together in a jail cell. When "Yellow Curley" Hinds meets Jenkins preaching in the pulpit, it is Jenkins who recalls their time together in a cell. Both films mobilize these strikingly similar memory flashbacks, the only significant difference being that a stand-in played the Robeson role, so the Robeson character was seated with his face effectively covered. In *The Pilgrim,* Charlie loves Mrs. Brown's daughter and repeatedly rescues her money (meant for the church mortgage) from the quick hands of Picking Pete. (For a period, the money is in the top drawer of a chest of drawers—exactly where the mother in *Body and Soul* hides it.) Returning the money is a way for Charlie to ingratiate himself with Mrs. Brown and, more important, her daughter, whom he loves. In *Body and Soul,* the escaped convict has no such sentimental and moralistic compulsion. He rapes the girl and makes her give him her mother's money. Chaplin's sentimentality is exposed as fraudulent. Such sustained parallels with yet another work of this period underscore ways in which this film is not an "adaptation" of any single text. It has no single source but moves between sources, evoking them with certain striking similarities and sustained parallels but always engaging in a profound creative remolding. In its mobilization of multiple sources, the film involves a collision of texts, forcing the reader to consider their relationship and the underlying ideological mission of each.

94. This stripping away of the facade of civilization, which certainly was part of the experience

of World War I, was first and foremost a crisis in European life, and so we—like Micheaux—might wonder about the suitability of its projection onto a black character. See John Cooley, "In Pursuit of the Primitive: Black Portraits by Eugene O'Neill and Other Village Bohemians," in Kramer, ed., *The Harlem Renaissance Re-examined;* and Joel Pfister, *Staging Depth: Eugene O'Neill & The Politics of Psychological Discourse* (Chapel Hill: University of North Carolina Press, 1995).

95. Peter Brooks, *The Melodramatic Imagination* (New Haven, Conn.: Yale University Press, 1976), 56–80. bell hooks also emphasizes the importance of melodrama for Micheaux and makes use of Brooks's analysis in "Micheaux: Celebrating Blackness," *Black American Literature Forum* 25, no. 2 (Summer 1991): 351–360; reprinted in bell hooks, *Black Looks: Race and Representation* (Boston: South End Press, 1992).

96. Robeson wrote, "What a great part is 'Brutus Jones.' His is the exultant tragedy of the disintegration of a human soul" ("Reflections on O'Neill's Plays," *Opportunity Magazine,* December 1924, 368).

97. Indeed, Jenkins's rape of Isabelle evokes Girdlestone's near-rape of his daughter in an earlier Micheaux film, *Within Our Gates.* Girdlestone is a member of the white elite, and in this respect, at least, Jenkins's behavior is a different version of exploitation that is based on the model of white actions.

98. It is with *Symbol of the Unconquered* (1920) that Micheaux seemed to engage the language of race most extensively.

99. An African-American student once argued that "niggah" was a different if perhaps related word to "nigger." (The same point is made by a white student in James Taback's feature film *Black and White* [2000].) Although *Body and Soul* does not contradict such an argument, literature of the Harlem Renaissance, for example Claude McKay's *Banjo* (1929), certainly suggests that such subtle distinctions were often lost. In fact, the widespread use of the "N word" in Harlem Renaissance writing by blacks and whites makes it inappropriate to criticize O'Neill, MacKay, and Robeson as insensitive or indifferent. Robeson was involved in the adaptation of *Banjo* for the screen—it was the basis for the Robeson star vehicle *Big Fella* (1937). Their embrace of the word can be seen as a bohemian rejection of refined language and bourgeois propriety. Nonetheless, it is appropriate for commentators to single out both Micheaux and Gilpin for their courageous sensitivity to language and its relationship to racial politics.

100. Cripps, *Slow Fade to Black,* 191–193.

101. Heywood Broun, "The New Play," *New York Herald,* 16 May 1924, 13. Broun's realist reading of this play—consistent with Madden's—may be mistaken. *All God's Chillun'* could be seen as an allegorical, psychological depiction of the black-white marriage or embrace that has been central to American life for the last several centuries.

102. See the illustration in Robeson, *Paul Robeson, Negro,* opposite page 102.

103. "'The House Behind the Cedars' Shown at Royal Sunday," *Philadelphia Tribune,* 13 December 1924, 3. The article is reprinted in this catalog's Micheaux filmography (228–277). Another version of this statement appears in "Oscar Micheaux Writes on Growth of Race in Movie Future," *Pittsburgh Courier,* 13 December 1924, reprinted in Sampson, *Blacks in Black and White,* 54.

104. "'The Symbol of the Unconquered' and Musical Program Unique Lafayette Bill," *New York Age,* 1 January 1921, 6.

105. Madden, "Why Did Eugene O'Neill Write 'All God's Chillun' Got Wings'?," 13.

106. Charlene Regester has generously made available her research on the censorship of *Body and Soul* by the Motion Picture Commission of the State of New York. She reports that the commission received a 9,000 feet/ nine-reel print of *Body and Soul* on 5 November 1925 (date of application for license) and rejected the film in toto on 7 November 1925. Reviewers stated that "Body and Soul is the story of a man, minister of the gospel, whose habits and manner of life are anything but the life of a good man. He associates with the proprietor of a notorious gambling house,

extorts money from him, betrays a girl of his parish, forces her to steal from the bible her mothers savings, forces the girl to leave home, and finally kills the girl's brother when he comes to the sister's protection. A story against religion morals and crime. The film is of such a character that in the opinion of the Commission it is 'sacrilegious,' 'immoral' and would 'tend to incite to crime.'" Micheaux discovered the print was inadvertently missing titles and a photograph that made clear that Jenkins was an escaped convict posing as a preacher. He added these and resubmitted the film on 9 November 1925. The commission rejected his appeal on 10 November 1925. On 11 November 1925, Micheaux radically edited the film, reducing it to five reels—"changing the theme and transferring the villainy from the minister to another character." This version was passed on 12 November 1925, with the understanding that all scenes of drinking and gambling would be eliminated. See introductory comments, *Body and Soul* videotape, Kino International. (Released in April 1998, for the Robeson centennial, this tape is the first high-quality video of the film.) This re-edited version may be the one described by Thomas Cripps in *Slow Fade to Black*, 191–193.

107. "Robeson Makes His Bow as Movie Star Next Week," *New York Amsterdam News*, 11 November 1925, 5. A similar announcement appeared in the *New York Age* of 11 November 1925 (quoted in Sampson, *Blacks in Black and White*, 287).

108. Advertisement for Franklin Theatre, *New York Amsterdam News*, 30 December 1925, 5.

109. *New York Amsterdam News*, 2 December 1925, 5.

110. "Complain of Picture Shown Front of Franklin Theatre," *New York Age*, 12 December 1925, 6.

111. Ralph Ellison remarks, "The Negro community is deadly in its ability to create nicknames and to spot all that is ludicrous in an unlikely name or that which is incongruous in conduct" ("Hidden Name and Complex Fate," in *The Collected Essays of Ralph Ellison*, edited with an introduction by John F. Callahan [New York: Modern Library, 1995], 194).

112. "About Things Theatrical," *New York Amsterdam News*, 23 December 1925, 5. This article also puts down a film, *Easy Money*, starring S. H. Dudley, who was later involved with the Colored Players Film Corporation. Sections are quoted in Cripps, *Slow Fade to Black*, 180, but Micheaux's name is played straight (i.e., corrected silently). In fact, the alteration of a name by adding (or occasionally subtracting) letters has a rich history in the black press. For example, the *New York Amsterdam News* often added an "s" to the "Douglas" in Douglas Theatre to evoke the name of the great Frederick Douglass.

113. "Film Tips," Baltimore *Afro-American*, 19 December 1925, 4.

114. Maybelle Crew, "Along the White Way," Baltimore *Afro-American*, 11 September 1926, 5. Thanks to Louise Spence for bringing this to my attention. The three plays by O'Neill and Stephens were extensively discussed in the *Afro-American*, but neither *Roseanne* nor *All God's Chillun'* appeared on Baltimore stages. Micheaux's critical engagement with the plays remained in the background as overtones.

115. Of course, we should recognize—as did the surrealists in the 1920s—that many mainstream films lack narrative coherence. These are viewed and often embraced by moviegoers interested in other dimensions of the screen experience.

This was one of the rare times that the film's success with popular audiences was acknowledged. This is not entirely surprising, in that the *Afro-American* was more "movie-crazy" and embraced black popular theater far more enthusiastically than other black weeklies in this period. Nonetheless, it is worth noting that Micheaux was staying at Baltimore's Royal Hotel while the film had its week-long run at the Royal Theatre ("Around Town," Baltimore *Afro-American*, 11 September 1926, 5). His charming presence probably had something to do with columnist Maybelle Chew's laudatory comments.

116. Charlene Regester, "Oscar Micheaux's *Body and Soul*: A Film of Conflicting Themes," in *In Touch with the Spirit: Black Religious and Musical Expression in American Cinema*, ed. Phyllis Klotman and Gloria Gibson (Bloomington: Black Film Center/Archive and the Department of Afro-American Studies, Indiana University, 1994), 59–71. In point of fact, Micheaux and O'Neill both expressed strong anti-religious viewpoints in their work. This was a point of continuity between

O'Neill's plays and Micheaux's films, a way in which their work was part of a circuit of expression and not simply opposing texts.

117. The exceptions—those best-case scenarios—only underscore Micheaux's miscalculation of the theatrical knowledge the film's audiences needed to share. In Philadelphia, *Body and Soul* played the New Dunbar Theater during mid-December, where Robeson had performed *Roseanne* for one week some twenty months earlier. In the process of promoting the film, at least one newspaper mentioned Robeson's performances in both *Emperor Jones* and *All God's Chillun'* ("Body and Soul at the Dunbar All Next Week," *Pittsburgh Courier*, 12 December 1925, 10). *All God's Chillun'* had been discussed in the newspapers the previous year and was available in printed form, while Gilpin had played Philadelphia in *Emperor Jones*. Obviously, this involved a small, highly cultured audience, which Micheaux was alienating for other reasons.

118. Sampson, *Blacks in Black and White*, 160; "Micheaux Film Co. Bankrupt," *Pittsburgh Courier*, 3 March 1928, 2B.

119. *Pittsburgh Courier*, 13 December 1924, reprinted in Sampson, *Blacks in Black and White*, 54–55.

120. From this vantage point, Micheaux began to circulate a more useful promotional item for the film in mid-1926, during what may have been a second and somewhat more successful effort to release the film. "It is one of those pictures of the simple life and of the lowly, but faithful Negro [about] which the world has heard much, but is in no position to know much about," the blurb remarks ("Paul Robeson Tops Big Bill at Attucks," *Norfolk Journal and Guide*, 19 June 1926, 5). Indeed, as this later characterization at least hints, *Body and Soul* is very much about those white playwrights who had heard much but knew little about Negro life and the Negro soul. This item was also run as part of an advertisement in the Baltimore *African American*, 25 September 1926, 6. Unfortunately, the quoted portion was removed in favor of other sections.

121. Ralph Ellison, "Beating That Boy," *The New Republic*, 22 October 1945, reprinted in *The Collected Essays of Ralph Ellison*, 149.

122. Leab, *Sambo to Superspade*, 81.

123. Reid, *Redefining Black Film*, 14.

124. Several of Micheaux's films from the early 1920s were shot in the New York area, including *The Symbol of the Unconquered* (1920), *The Gunsaulus Mystery* (1921), and *A Son of Satan* (1924). *The Brute* (1920) was apparently the last Micheaux film to be shot in Chicago before he moved to New York.

125. "The Debut of the Younger School of Negro Writers," *Opportunity Magazine*, May 1924, 143–144; David Levering Lewis, *When Harlem Was in Vogue*, 89–91.

126. Lewis, *When Harlem Was in Vogue*, 90.

127. Ibid., 95.

128. Jeffrey C. Stewart has also emphasized the ways Micheaux's work differed from the interracial collaboration said to characterize the Harlem Renaissance. See Stewart, "Paul Robeson and the Problem of Modernism," 92–94.

129. As Micheaux told Lester A. Walton, "The large and increasing demand for colored motion pictures should mean much to the race from an economic standpoint. There is no reason why all photo plays of this description should not be written, played and produced by Negroes. Here is a new and fertile field offering wonderful opportunities where we should be complete masters. If we lose our stranglehold it will be because we have failed to measure up and keep pace with the times ("Colored Motion Pictures Are in Great Demand," *New York Age*, 6 March 1920, 6).

130. Douglas, *Terrible Honesty*, 100; Lewis, *When Harlem Was in Vogue*, 91.

131. In searching for a parallel to this all-too-public address to Robeson, one might think of Jean-Luc Godard's *A Letter to Jane* (1972).

132. Lewis, *When Harlem Was in Vogue*, 91. A text-centered interpretation of this ending might see this fantasy as a critique of black bourgeois values and "false consciousness." On the other hand, Micheaux's reliance on happy endings in both *Within Our Gates* and *Symbol of the Unconquered* would seem to challenge such a radical interpretation from an authorial perspective.

Doubtless there are possibilities in this ambiguity and contradiction. While such endings may be commercial concessions to popular taste, they simultaneously address the whole question of endings—which is certainly one of the subjects of *Body and Soul,* since it rewrites the endings of the plays. The excessively happy ending—the cliched ending—creates contradictions that foster discussion and reflection—as Spike Lee has demonstrated more recently with *Jungle Fever* (1991).

133. "Mischeaux's Latest at The Odeon Theatre," *New York Amsterdam News,* 6 November 1929, 8. Although Richard Maurice was making *Eleven P.M.,* his film was not mentioned in the New York press.

134. "At the Renaissance," *New York Amsterdam News,* 30 January 1929, 8.

135. The analysis that follows is based on the assumption that Micheaux controlled the advertising for his films, while the *New York Amsterdam News* received promotional copy but edited this material as it wished.

136. Advertisement, Baltimore *Afro-American,* 16 November 1929, 8.

137. "At the New Douglas," *New York Amsterdam News,* 25 September 1929, 9.

138. Duberman, *Paul Robeson,* 122, 607 n. 36.

139. "The Return of Robeson," *New York Amsterdam News,* 16 October 1929, 8.

140. "At the Odeon," *New York Amsterdam News,* 2 October 1929, 9.

141. Advertisement, *New York Amsterdam News,* 23 October 1929, 8. "Michaux" was a common misspelling of the filmmaker's name. It had appeared in New York advertisements at the beginning of the decade (see advertisement for *The Virgin of Seminole, New York Age,* 24 March 1923, 6).

142. *New York Amsterdam News,* 6 November 1929, 8.

143. "Is This Really Harlem?," *New York Amsterdam News,* 23 October 1929, 9.

144. Theophilus Lewis, "The Harlem Sketch Book," *New York Amsterdam News,* 16 April 1930, 10.

145. Ibid.

9. Black Patriarch on the Prairie

1. Oscar Micheaux, *The Conquest: The Story of a Negro Pioneer* (1913; reprint, Lincoln: University of Nebraska Press, 1994). (Hereafter, quotations from this novel will be cited as *CN* in the text.)

2. Oscar Micheaux, *The Forged Note: A Romance of the Darker Races* (Lincoln, Neb.: Western Book Supply Company, 1915), 168. (Hereafter, quotations from this novel will be cited as *FN* in the text.)

3. According to African-American historian David Levering Lewis, Washington's autobiography was actually ghostwritten by a white man, Max Bennett Thrasher, a newspaper journalist from Vermont. See Lewis, *W. E. B. Du Bois: Biography of a Race, 1865–1919* (New York: Henry Holt, 1993), 262–264.

4. Oscar Micheaux, *The Homesteader: A Novel* (1917; reprint, Lincoln: University of Nebraska Press, 1994), 138. (Hereafter, quotations from this novel will be cited as *HS* in the text.)

5. Toni Morrison, *Playing in the Dark: Whiteness and the Literary Imagination* (Cambridge, Mass.: Harvard University Press, 1992), 34.

6. Oscar Micheaux, *The Story of Dorothy Stanfield* (New York: Book Supply Company, 1946), 82. (Hereafter, quotations from this novel will be cited as *DS* in the text.)

7. Robert Young, *Black Novelist as White Racist* (New York: Greenwood Press, 1989), ix.

8. Ibid.

9. Young conflates the concepts of industrial expansion and pro-slavery imperialism, obscuring the differences into one viewpoint, that of the white oppressor. He conflates the concept of race with political perspective, a strategy that Micheaux's work itself belies.

10. C. L. R. James, *American Civilization* (London: Routledge, 1994), 37.

11. For more on the construction of whiteness, especially in relation to nineteenth-century class formation, see David Roediger, *The Wages of Whiteness: Race and the Making of the American Work-*

ing Class (New York: Verso, 1991), Chapter 5: "Class, Coons and Crowds in Antebellum America," 95–114. See also Eric Lott, *Love and Theft: Blackface Minstrelsy and the Making of the American Working Class* (New York: Oxford University Press, 1993).

12. See Lott, *Love and Theft,* Chapter 2: "Love and Theft: 'Racial' Production and the Social Unconscious of Blackface."

13. In *The Location of Culture* (New York: Routledge, 1994), Homi K. Bhabha writes eloquently about the uses of blackness as an imagined construct, particularly with regard to the development of the modern nation-state.

14. Michael Rogin, "Blackface, White Noise: The Jewish Jazz Singer Finds His Voice," *Critical Inquiry* 18, no. 7 (Spring 1992): 417–453.

15. Morrison, *Playing in the Dark,* 34–35.

16. Yet this is not a citizenship based solely on claims of prior residence. In *The Conquest,* for example, Devereaux describes Native Americans as "easily flattered spendthrifts," who sell their government land allotments to the European immigrants only to spend the money "as quickly as they get it" *(178).*

17. Morrison, *Playing in the Dark,* 35.

10. TELLING WHITE LIES

I wish to thank Jane Gaines and Charles Musser for encouragement, the Oscar Micheaux Society (especially stalwarts Jane Gaines, Charlene Regester, Ron Green, and Arthur Knight) for ongoing enthusiasm, and Micheaux-scholar-in-the-making Rita Belda for helpful leads and sources.

1. Charles W. Chesnutt, *The Marrow of Tradition* (1901; reprint, New York: Penguin, 1993), 75, 277.

2. Oscar Micheaux, *Philadelphia Afro-American,* 24 January 1925, 3. This "open letter" was also published in the *Pittsburgh Courier,* 13 December 1924, 10, and resembles a talk Micheaux delivered to a film audience on 7 December 1924, according to *Billboard,* 27 December 1924, 49. The larger quote includes a response to negative criticism of Micheaux's first version of *Birthright* (1924), which he remade in 1938. These lines are also quoted in bell hooks, "Micheaux: Celebrating Blackness," *Black American Literature Forum* 25, no. 2 (Summer 1991): 351–360; and J. Ronald Green, "Oscar Micheaux's Interrogation of Caricature as Entertainment," *Film Quarterly* 51, no. 3 (Spring 1988): 16–31.

3. Oscar Micheaux, *The Masquerade: An Historical Novel* (New York: Book Supply Co., 1947), 7.

4. Ibid., 24. Charlene Regester finds "no evidence to suggest that the two ever actually met," despite a lengthy correspondence between Chesnutt and the Micheaux Film Corporation (often represented by Swan Micheaux, Oscar's brother) regarding the purchase of Chesnutt's novel. See Charlene Regester, "Oscar Micheaux the Entrepreneur: Financing *The House Behind the Cedars," Journal of Film and Video* 49, no. 1–2 (Spring–Summer 1997): 18. My work in this essay is indebted to Regester's painstaking research of primary documents linking Micheaux and Chesnutt.

5. Joseph A. Young, *Black Novelist as White Racist: The Myth of Black Inferiority in the Novels of Oscar Micheaux* (New York: Greenwood Press, 1989), 168, n. 1. Jayna Brown's essay in this volume effectively challenges Young's extremely reductive thesis.

6. Charles W. Chesnutt, "The Negro in Art: How Shall He Be Portrayed: A Symposium," *The Crisis* 33, no. 1 (November 1926): 29.

7. Regester, "Oscar Micheaux the Entrepreneur," 18–23. As Regester demonstrates, the film was still playing in New York and Baltimore as late as March 1925, with its superficial and unanticipated associations with the sensational 1924 Rhinelander case fully exploited.

8. For instance, see J. Ronald Green, "'Twoness' in the Style of Oscar Micheaux," in *Black American Cinema,* ed. Manthia Diawara (New York: Routledge, 1993), 26–48.

9. For example, William L. Andrews, Frances Smith Foster, and Trudier Harris, eds., *The Oxford Companion to African American Fiction* (New York: Oxford University Press, 1997); or *The Black Literature Index: A Guide to Black Periodical Literature 1827–1940*, CD-ROM, ed. Henry Louis Gates, Jr. (Chadwyck-Healey, Inc., n.d.).

10. Eric J. Sundquist, *To Wake the Nations: Race in the Making of American Literature* (Cambridge, Mass.: Harvard University Press, 1993); and J. Lee Greene, *Blacks in Eden: The African-American Novel's First Century* (Charlottesville: University Press of Virginia, 1996). Other significant recent reappraisals of Chesnutt include Craig Werner Hansen, *Playing the Changes: From Afro-Modernism to the Jazz Impulse* (Urbana: University of Illinois Press, 1994); Samira Kawash, *Dislocating the Color Line: Identity, Hybridity, and Singularity in African-American Literature* (Stanford, Calif.: Stanford University Press, 1997); and Henry B. Wonham, *Charles W. Chesnutt: A Study of the Short Fiction* (New York: Twayne Publishers, 1998). Recent publications of Chesnutt material include *The Journals of Charles W. Chesnutt*, ed. Richard Brodhead (Durham, N.C.: Duke University Press 1993); *"To Be an Author": Letters of Charles W. Chesnutt 1889–1905*, ed. Joseph R. McElrath and Robert C. Leitz, III (Princeton, N.J.: Princeton University Press, 1997); and Charles W. Chesnutt, *Mandy Oxendine*, ed. Charles Hackenberry (Urbana: University of Illinois Press, 1997). Another heretofore unpublished Chesnutt novel, *Paul Marchand: F.M.C.*, appeared from the University Press of Mississippi in 1998.

11. Frances Richardson Keller, *An American Crusade: The Life of Charles Waddell Chesnutt* (Provo, Utah: Brigham Young University Press, 1978), 270. See Helen M. Chesnutt, *Charles Waddell Chesnutt: Pioneer of the Color Line* (Chapel Hill: University of North Carolina Press, 1952). Regester's essay "Oscar Micheaux the Entrepreneur" greatly clarifies the relationship between Chesnutt and Micheaux.

12. William L. Andrews, *The Literary Career of Charles W. Chesnutt* (Baton Rouge: Louisiana State University Press, 1980), 265 n. 7. As Regester demonstrates, the process of payment was in fact unusually complex and extended; see Regester, "Oscar Micheaux the Entrepreneur," 18–23. White independent Robert Levy's Reol Productions operated in New York City from 1920 to 1924 and produced over ten feature "race" films. On Reol Productions see Henry T. Sampson, *Blacks in Black and White: A Source Book on Black Films*, 2nd ed. (Metuchen, N.J.: Scarecrow Press, 1995), 214–215.

13. Although the Micheaux Film Corporation seems to have initiated the serialization of Chesnutt's story in the *Chicago Defender*, by the time of publication, only Chesnutt and the newspaper were involved. See Regester, "Oscar Micheaux the Entrepreneur," 20–21.

14. This stationery is in the Richard E. Norman Collection in the Lilly Library, Indiana University. The relevant portion of the stationery is quoted at the end of the Oscar Micheaux Filmography, included in this volume.

15. The trailer for *God's Step Children*, which now, curiously, precedes most versions of the film, explicitly identifies its debts to the Hollywood films *Imitation of Life* (1934) and *These Three* (1936, an adaptation of Lillian Hellman's controversial play *The Children's Hour*), and the ending suggests a direct reworking of the classic maternal melodrama *Stella Dallas* (1925 and 1937). Though my essay considers Micheaux's possible literary sources, it seems clear that Micheaux was also extremely attentive to mainstream cinema as a potential source of narrative material.

16. According to Eric J. Sundquist, Chesnutt's "very light skin emblematically incorporated the essence of the race crisis and dictated the perspective of much of his fiction" (*To Wake the Nations*, 275).

17. For recent perspectives on passing narratives, see Elaine K. Ginsberg, ed., *Passing and the Fictions of Identity* (Durham, N.C.: Duke University Press, 1996). The texts cited here are Frances E. W. Harper, *Iola Leroy; or, Shadows Uplifted* (Philadelphia: Garrigues Brothers, 1892); Sutton E. Griggs, *The Hindered Hand* (Nashville: Orion Publishing Co., 1905); James Weldon Johnson, *The Autobiography of an Ex-Colored Man* (New York: Sherman, French, 1912), reprinted as *The Autobiography of an Ex-Coloured Man* (New York: Knopf, 1927); Walter White, *Flight* (New York: Knopf, 1926); Jessie Redmond Fauset, *Plum Bun* (New York: Frederick A. Stokes Co., 1928); and Nella

Larsen, *Passing* (New York: Knopf, 1929). A number of these works have appeared in many other later editions. Among many "passing" short stories, one might highlight Langston Hughes's chilling "Passing" in *The Ways of White Folks* (New York: Knopf, 1934), 51–55. Hughes's story, about a light-skinned son who fears that his dark-skinned mother will reveal his racial heritage in public, uncannily suggests the early flashback in Micheaux's *The Symbol of the Unconquered* when the mulatto Jefferson Driscoll recalls his own traumatic exposure by his dark mother before his white lover.

18. See S. M. Eisenstein, "Dickens, Griffith, and the Film Today," in *Film Form,* ed. Jay Leyda (New York: Harcourt Brace Jovanovich, 1949), 195–255. Also see James Chandler, "The Historical Novel Goes to Hollywood: Scott, Griffith, and Film Epic Today," in *The Birth of a Nation,* ed. Robert Lang (New Brunswick, N.J.: Rutgers University Press, 1994), 225–249. Jane Gaines also discusses Eisenstein's essay in relation to Griffith and Micheaux in "Fire and Desire: Race, Melodrama, and Oscar Micheaux," in *Black American Cinema,* ed. Manthia Diawara (New York: Routledge, 1993), 49–70.

19. Sundquist, *To Wake the Nations,* 409.

20. See Eisenstein, "Dickens, Griffith, and the Film Today"; and Chandler, "The Historical Novel Goes to Hollywood."

21. On black silent melodrama specifically, see the illuminating work of Jane Gaines, to which this essay and my appreciation of Micheaux's *Within Our Gates* are deeply indebted. In addition to "Fire and Desire: Race, Melodrama, and Oscar Micheaux," see "*The Birth of a Nation* and *Within Our Gates:* Two Tales of the American South," in *Dixie Debates: Perspectives on Southern Cultures,* ed. Richard H. King and Helen Taylor (New York: New York University Press, 1996): 177–192; and "*The Scar of Shame:* Skin Color and Black Caste in Black Silent Melodrama," *Cinema Journal* 26, no. 4 (Summer 1987), reprinted in Valerie Smith, ed., *Representing Blackness: Issues in Film and Video* (Brunswick, N.J.: Rutgers University Press, 1997), 61–81. Eric J. Sundquist's brilliant analysis of *The Marrow of Tradition* seeks to demonstrate "careful links between the political plot of the novel—the disfranchisement of black voters and accompanying white violence—and the melodramatic plot of family romance and generational, cross-racial conflict," a summary that also suits Micheaux's film. See *To Wake the Nations,* 271. Gaines's essay in this volume also acknowledges the importance of Chesnutt's work in an African-American melodramatic tradition.

22. Chesnutt, *The Marrow of Tradition,* 87. (Hereafter cited in the text as *MT.*)

23. Jane Gaines makes a similar point in her discussion of lynching in "Fire and Desire: Race, Melodrama, and Oscar Micheaux," 54. Gaines emphasizes Micheaux's startling depiction of a lynch mob that includes "savage" white women and children.

24. In a brief shot in *The Symbol of the Unconquered,* a cowboy twirling a rope tosses it around the neck of the same actor (E. G. Tatum). This small "joke," which could be taken as an inheritance from the moment in *The Great Train Robbery* (1903) when western cowboys tease an eastern dude by firing their guns at his feet, in effect revises the Western genre from its typical basis in the opposition between East and West toward a Reconstruction-era tension between white and black. Here the famous title of Ralph Ellison's 1958 essay on the African-American trickster figure comes to mind: "Change the Joke and Slip the Yoke." See Ellison, *Shadow and Act* (New York: Random House, 1964), 45–59.

25. See Chesnutt, *The Marrow of Tradition,* 127. The importance of this allusion for African-American self-consciousness throughout the period is additionally signaled by its appearance as the final line of James Weldon Johnson's "passing" novel, *The Autobiography of an Ex-Colored Man,* published anonymously in 1912 and under Johnson's name in 1927.

26. Henry Louis Gates, Jr., *The Signifying Monkey: A Theory of African-American Literary Criticism* (New York: Oxford University Press, 1988), 44–88. Eric J. Sundquist emphasizes "the troping dimension of signifying—its capacity to revise a given text . . . by revising or subverting its cul-

tural assumptions," a definition that also seems immediately applicable to Micheaux's strategies of repetition. See *To Wake the Nations,* 280.

27. Jean Toomer, *Cane* (New York: Boni & Liveright, 1923), 28–35. The story was first published in *Prairie* (March–April 1923).

28. See W. E. B. Du Bois, *The Souls of Black Folk* (1903; reprint, New York: Vintage Books/The Library of America, 1986); and Gates, *The Signifying Monkey,* xxv–xxvi. Again, I am thinking here of the work of J. Ronald Green, who has explicitly employed Du Bois's notion of "two-ness" to examine Micheaux: see his "'Twoness' in the Style of Oscar Micheaux."

29. Werner, *Playing the Changes,* 9.

30. Harper, *Iola Leroy,* 8–9.

31. Available cast lists for *Within Our Gates* identify the actor playing Efrem as E. G. Tatum (who appears in other early Micheaux films, including *The Symbol of the Unconquered* as the comic figure Abraham). See the notes by Scott Simmons for the Smithsonian Video copy of the film, as well as the cast lists in Henry T. Sampson, *Blacks in Black and White,* 277–288; and Alan Gevinson, ed., American Film Institute Catalog: *Within Our Gates: Ethnicity in American Feature Films, 1911–1960* (Berkeley: University of California Press, 1997), 1149. None of these cast lists identifies the actor playing Old Ned, although Pearl Bowser has suggested (through personal communication) that he is played by Leigh Whipper. Whipper, who also plays Tugi in *The Symbol of the Unconquered,* indeed somewhat resembles the actor playing Old Ned, although I still find that the man playing Old Ned more fully resembles Tatum. Even if different actors actually play these two parts, their visual similarities can only emphasize their similar moments of self-awareness in otherwise unrelated sections of the film. Micheaux's most extensive use of an actor in a dual role is certainly for *Body and Soul,* starring Paul Robeson, but other films also employ this device. For example, a single actor clearly plays both Tump Pack and his brother in *Birthright* (1938). In this regard, Michael Rogin's analysis of D. W. Griffith's use of actors in multiple (and multiracial) parts within single films is suggestive: see Michael Rogin, "'The Sword Became a Flashing Vision': D. W. Griffith's *The Birth of a Nation,*" in *Ronald Reagan, the Movie and Other Episodes in Political Demonology* (Berkeley: University of California Press, 1987), 190–235.

32. Micheaux plays the man who plans to help Larry "the Leech" in his scheme to swindle black workers in Piney Woods. In the surviving films, Micheaux's only other cameo seems to be at the beginning of *Lem Hawkins' Confession* (aka *Murder in Harlem*), where he (convincingly) plays a police detective.

33. *Lem Hawkins' Confession* begins with the murder in 1935 and moves back to 1932 for a long flashback, where we meet Henry Glory as a novelist. When the film returns to 1935 he has become a successful lawyer. The novel that he writes about the events covered in the flashback is entitled *A Fool's Errand,* itself the title of a once-well-known 1879 Reconstruction novel by Albion W. Tourgee (originally published, like Glory's novel, anonymously—"By One of the Fools"). There is incomplete evidence that Micheaux made a film with this title, presumably adapted from Tourgee's book.

11. Planes, Trains, and Automobiles

The information in this essay is taken from the Norman Collection located in the Black Film Center/Archive of the Afro-American Studies Department and the Lilly Library, Indiana University. The collection was graciously donated to the university by Richard E. Norman, Jr., in 1985. We are extremely grateful to him for his gift and for his support of our work. I have also consulted Henry Sampson's *Blacks in Black and White: A Source Book on Black Films,* 2nd ed. (Metuchen, N.J.: Scarecrow Press, 1995), to reconcile dates and names of cast members when on-screen data were not available.

Special acknowledgment to Jill Moniz, Black Film Center/Archive Archival Project Assistant, who has completed the inventory of the Norman collection housed in the Black Film Center/Archive's Collections Room at Smith Research Center.

1. Lewis Jacobs, *The Documentary Tradition: From Nanook to Woodstock* (New York: Hopkinson and Blake, Publishers, 1971), 2.

2. Jim Harmon and Donald F. Glut, *The Great Movie Serials: Their Sound and Fury* (Garden City, N.Y.: Doubleday, 1972), 142.

3. The Library of Congress has a number of episodes of *The Hazards of Helen;* for example, "The Grit of the Girl Telegrapher," "The Rival Railroad Plot," and "Escape on the Fast Freight." For more information about Helen Holmes's role and on the silent serial phenomenon, see Kalton C. Lahue, *Bound and Gagged: The Story of the Silent Serials* (New York: Castle Books, 1968); and Buck Rainey, *Those Fabulous Serial Heroines, Their Lives and Films* (Metuchen, N.J.: Scarecrow Press, 1990).

4. *The Flying Ace* may have been the first black-cast film made at the Eagle Studios. In a letter dated 16 October 1924, Norman's lawyer Frank E. Jennings reported to him: "The Motion pic property [Eagle Film Manufacturing Company] was sold the first Monday in October by the Court and bought in your name for $3250." Earlier in that year, June 17th, Norman wrote to Edison McVey, who expected to be in Norman's next film—presumably *The Flying Ace,* explaining that his production plans were held up because "we have been working on our new studio and when we have moved into same, we will have the largest plant in the South-East, fully equipped to make both comedy and dramatic subjects." It may be that Norman occupied the property before purchasing and renovating it because Richard Norman, Jr., told me in a telephone conversation, 30 December 1995, that his father began making films at Eagle Studios in 1920.

5. Richard Norman to D. Ireland Thomas, 19 January 1926, Indiana University Black Film Center/Archive.

6. Norman was certainly interested in Coleman's idea of putting her life work into a film which she entitled "Yesterday, Today and Tomorrow," and he responded positively to her letter of 3 February 1926: "There is no doubt that . . . a picture of five or six reels, properly acted and full of action with you in the leading role, would be a good drawing card in the colored theatres" (8 February 1926). Unfortunately he was never able to make a film with Coleman. The irony is that she was killed in Jacksonville, Florida, on 30 April 1926, testing a plane in which she intended to perform the next day for the Negro Welfare League (Elizabeth Amelia Hadley Freydberg, *Bessie Coleman: The Brownskin Lady Bird* [New York: Garland Publishing, 1994], 94–95). *The Flying Ace* was released in August of that year.

7. Thomas Cripps calls "outright fraud" the promise of a "spectacular wreck costing $80,000" in *The Green-Eyed Monster* which turned out to be stock footage from earlier movies (Thomas Cripps, *Slow Fade to Black: The Negro in American Film, 1900–1942* [New York: Oxford University Press, 1977], 85). In fact, the press kit also boasted "$1,000,000 Worth of Railroad Equipment." (In Norman's files there is a signed agreement, dated 29 April 1920, between the Norman Film Mfg. Co. of Chicago, Ill., with offices at No. 1614 Laura Street, Jacksonville, Fla., and Florida East Coast Railway Company "for use of an engine on the Mayport Branch between its yards at South Jacksonville and Merrill-Stevens plant in connection with the taking of certain moving pictures by certain agents and employees of said Norman Film Mfg Co on May 4th, 1920." Since *The Green-Eyed Monster* was released in its original 8-reel version in 1920, that could have been the million dollars' worth of railroad equipment the press kit boasts. Norman did use the Mayport Station in the opening sequences of *The Flying Ace,* although that film was shot six years later.

8. In an attempt to impress Ruth, the heroine in *The Flying Ace,* the villainous Finley explains some rudimentary flying procedures to her before he "takes her up" in the plane. When I asked Norman's son, (Captain) Richard Norman, Jr., who is a commercial pilot, if his father had been a flyer or knew anything about flying, he said: "No, Father probably did research on elements of

flying. The plane was nothing but a prop, probably modeled on a plane Father had seen" (Telephone conversation, 29 June 1995).

9. Charles E. Francis, *The Tuskegee Airmen* (Boston: Branden Publishing Company, 1988), 12.

10. P. J. Carisella and James W. Ryan, *The Black Swallow of Death* (Boston: Marlborough House, 1972), 137.

11. Ibid., 182–183.

12. Deborah Willis-Braithewaite, *James Van Der Zee, Photographer, 1886–1983* (Washington, D.C.: Harry N. Abrans, Inc., in association with the National Portrait Gallery, Smithsonian Institution, 1993), 162. The portrait is signed by Van Der Zee and labeled "Flying Ace (Hubert Fauntleroy Julian), 1934." The accompanying note explains that Julian "enlisted with the Royal Canadian Air Corps in World War I. He later moved to Harlem, where he became an officer in the UNIA. He parachuted twice, in 1922 and 1923 into Harlem, the second time while playing a gold-plated saxophone; he missed his target each time. He became a popular hero and the *New York Telegram* dubbed him 'The Black Eagle.' In 1930, Haile Selassie chose him to head Ethiopia's Imperial Air Force."

13. John Peer Nugent, *The Black Eagle* (New York: Stein and Day, 1971), 19. Nugent does not mention Julian's appearance with Bessie Coleman at Curtiss Airfield. He does discuss Julian's first practice jump (at the end of 1922), arranged by Charles "Casey" Jones, a pilot with Curtiss Aircraft: "The chute opened . . . and after about three minutes the world's first Negro parachutist landed on a Nassau County chicken farm" (28). He also describes Julian's first paid jump for a Harlem optician and the New York distributor for a St. Louis–based hair-straightener company on 23 April 1923. Julian mistakenly landed on the roof of the post office building at 140th and Seventh Avenue; he was drawn into the arms of the waiting crowd and was handed a summons for inciting a riot (34).

14. Freydberg, *Bessie Coleman*, 87.

15. Nugent, *The Black Eagle*, 38. A number of news writers also described Julian as "the Ace of Spades" which is the way Texas stunt flyer Edison C. McVey saw himself (cf. brochure in Norman files).

16. I am grateful to Anna Peebler and Shelley Henley at the Rosenberg Public Library in Galveston for their help in trying to track down Edison C. McVey. The brochure for his company, the Afro-American Film Producers, has a 23rd and Avenue E address and a 3303 Ave. I residential address for "Capt. E. C. McVey, King of Stunts." (In one of his letters to Richard Norman, however, McVey wrote 3302 Avenue I.) On a research trip to Galveston (6 June 1995) I found a vacant lot at 23rd and E, no 3302 or 3303 Avenue I, and a twenty-year resident at 3304 who had never heard of McVey. But he is listed in the *City Directory* of 1928–1929 and may have lived in a boarding house on Avenue I earlier in the twenties. During that period, Galveston identified African Americans in the *City Directory* by a "C" but didn't keep birth or death records of "colored" people.

17. Richard Norman to Edison C. McVey, 25 October 1924, Black Film Center/Archive, Indiana University.

18. Norman Film Manufacturing Company, flyer for *The Green-Eyed Monster,* ca. 1920.

19. Richard Norman, Jr., to Lyn Lazarus, 30 November 1975, Black Film Center/Archive, Indiana University.

20. See Sister Francesca Thompson's discussion of Anita Bush, Lawrence Chenault, and the Lafayette Players in this volume.

21. *Cleveland Gazette,* 12 February 1923, quoted in Sampson, *Blacks in Black and White,* 295.

22. Richard Norman to A. Rosen, 4 September 1923, Black Film Center/Archive, Indiana University.

23. Exchange of letters between Richard Norman and Albert English, 4 May–24 July 1923, Black Film Center/Archive, Indiana University.

24. *Billboard,* November 17, 1923.

25. Richard Norman to manager of the Grand, West Palm Beach, Fla., 13 June 1924, Black Film Center/Archive, Indiana University.

26. To complicate matters even more, Norman wrote to the Amusu Theatre in Chattanooga that he had held up release of the fifteen-episode serial (*The Fighting Fool*) "because of the dwindling number of colored theatres and cost of production" (23 October 1929).

27. Oscar Micheaux to Richard Norman, 7 August 1926, Black Film Center/Archive, Indiana University.

28. David Regan to Richard Norman, 5 June 1927, Black Film Center/Archive, Indiana University.

29. George P. Johnson to Richard Norman, 1 March 1922, Black Film Center/Archive, Indiana University.

30. Richard Norman to George P. Johnson, 20 March 1922, Black Film Center/Archive, Indiana University.

31. In a letter to Norman from True Film Co. of Dallas, Texas, True Thompson wrote that he was sorry to hear that Bruce no longer worked with Richard (20 April 1925).

32. Sampson, *Blacks in Black and White,* 509.

33. Richard Norman to Shingzie Howard, 15 March 1926, Black Film Center/Archive, Indiana University.

34. Edna Morton to Richard Norman, 26 August 1923, Black Film Center/Archive, Indiana University.

35. Y. Andrew Roberson, "The Darkest Side of the Movie Business," *New York Tribune,* 22 April 1923, 7–8.

36. Richard Norman to Clarence Brooks, 17 May 1923, Black Film Center/Archive, Indiana University.

37. Ida Anderson to Richard Norman, June 1923, Black Film Center/Archive, Indiana University.

38. In his negotiations with Anita Bush several years earlier (31 August 1921), Norman contended that there were 22,000 white theaters and only 120 theaters where race films could be exhibited.

39. Richard Norman to M. C. Maxwell, 23 August 1923, Black Film Center/Archive, Indiana University.

40. M. C. Maxwell to Richard Norman, 27 August 1923, Black Film Center/Archive, Indiana University.

41. Sampson, *Blacks in Black and White,* 141.

12. An Alternative to Micheaux

I am grateful to Pearl Bowser, Larry Richards, and Cheryl Finley for their assistance in the development of this essay.

1. Little scholarly attention has been paid to the Colored Players Film Corporation. This essay is indebted to Henry T. Sampson's pioneering historiography of this company in particular and race cinema in general. See Sampson, *Blacks in Black and White: A Source Book on Black Films,* 2nd ed. (Lanham, Md.: Scarecrow Press, 1995), 218, 293–294, 328, 329–330, 340–341. There are, nonetheless, significant differences between our two accounts, both of which must be considered preliminary. See also Al Gevinson, ed., *American Film Institute Catalog: Within Our Gates: Ethnicity in American Feature Films, 1911–1960* (Berkeley: University of California Press, 1997); as well as Kenneth Munden, ed., *American Film Institute Catalog of Motion Pictures Produced in the United States: Feature Films, 1921–1930* (New York: R. R. Bowker, 1971). This essay relies heavily on information in the black press, notably the *Philadelphia Tribune.* See also Larry Richards, *African-American Films through 1959: A Comprehensive Illustrated Filmography* (Jefferson, N.C.: McFarland, 1998). Richards is a librarian at the Philadelphia Free Library.

2. "'Children of Fate' Latest Production," *Pittsburgh Courier,* 27 November 1926, 3B. One scene in the film supposedly cost $25,000. Even assuming that such claims were inflated, it is evident that costs had increased substantially since the first film.

3. "'Ten Nights in a Bar Room' Gets Showing," *Philadelphia Tribune,* 20 November 1926, 3. All producers of race films generally encountered difficulties finding venues for their work: Micheaux often had to wait a year or more after a film's initial release before opening it in a given city.

4. "Scores of Race Theaters Install Talkies," *Pittsburgh Courier,* 30 March 1929, 9A. Race theaters that were wired for sound included Chicago's Metropolitan theater in October 1928 (*Chicago Defender,* 6 October 1928, 10A); Harlem's New Lincoln Theatre in December 1928, the Lafayette in January 1929 and the Renaissance in March 1929 (*New York Amsterdam News,* 12 December 1929, 6; 9 January 1929, 8; 13 March 1929, 6); Philadelphia's Pearl Street Theatre in February 1929 (*Philadelphia Tribune,* 14 February 1929, 60); and Los Angeles's Rosebud Theatre in May 1929 (*California Eagle,* 3 May 1929, 11.) Warner Brothers launched its first synchronized recorded sound program with *Don Juan* and a program of shorts in August 1926, followed by *The Jazz Singer* in October 1927.

5. Roy Calnek's last name has appeared in a variety of forms, including Cainick (Sampson, *Blacks in Black and White,* 511). Most sources use "Roy" as his first name.

6. "'Ten Nights in a Bar Room' Gets Showing," 3.

7. S. H. Dudley, "Dud's Dope," *Chicago Defender,* 25 June 1927, 9A; Advertisement, *Philadelphia Tribune,* 11 August 1927, 6. Dudley's relationship to Colored Players has been a source of wide disagreement. Thomas Cripps, who suggests that Dudley was involved with Colored Players throughout its four-year history, describes him as a black "front" (*Slow Fade to Black,* 196). Sampson sees him as becoming involved only after the company ceased production and thus sees his involvement as peripheral and virtually irrelevant (Sampson, *Blacks in Black and White,* 218). Without idealizing this relationship, we can imagine Dudley having a significant role that was not based on exploitation, manipulation, or hot air. What both historians lack is a vision of—or faith in—the possibilities of interracial collaboration. While their skepticism has a strong historical basis, interracial collaboration was a marked feature of the Harlem Renaissance.

8. Joseph P. Eckhardt, *The King of the Movies: Film Pioneer Siegmund Lubin* (Madison, N.J.: Fairleigh Dickinson University Press, 1997), 226. Remnants of Lubin's efforts continued as the Bretzwood Film Company, headed by Lubin's son-in-law Ira Lowry into 1921 (228–236). In many respects, Philadelphia and Chicago, where Micheaux began his filmmaking career, had similar relationships to New York and, eventually, to Hollywood. They were the two leading rivals—insurgent alternatives—to New York and Los Angeles throughout the silent period.

9. J. Hoberman, *Bridge of Light: Yiddish Film between Two Worlds* (New York: Museum of Modern Art, 1991).

10. "Colored Film Players," *Washington Tribune,* 26 February 1926, 9; Ronald Goldwyn, "*The Scar of Shame:* Why the Fuss over this Old, Made-in-Philadelphia, Silent Black Film," Sunday Bulletin, *Philadelphia Bulletin,* 17 November 1974, 16.

11. Although the director of *Smiling Hate* is not given in Gevinson, ed., *American Film Institute Catalog: Within Our Gates,* Roy Calnek is listed as director in an advertisement in the *Philadelphia Tribune,* 22 November 1924, 3. The film played 24–28 November 1924 at the Premier Theater, Philadelphia, along with the two-reel comedy *Steppin' High.* These films also played the Dunbar Theatre in Baltimore for two days on 29–30 April 1925 (Advertisement, Baltimore *Afro-American,* 25 April 1925, 14). See also "The Premier Theater," *Philadelphia Tribune,* 22 November 1924, 3.

12. Sampson, *Blacks in Black and White,* 320, 336; Gevinson, ed., *American Film Institute Catalog: Within Our Gates;* Munden, ed., *American Film Institute Catalog of Motion Pictures Produced in the United States: Feature Films, 1921–1930.*

13. Advertisement, *Philadelphia Tribune,* 17 July 1926, 3.

14. Colored Players Film Corporation, handbill, 27 December 1926, African Diaspora Images Collection. Thanks to Pearl Bowser for sharing this document with me.

15. Advertisement, *Philadelphia Tribune*, 11 August 1927, 6.

16. Goldwyn, "*The Scar of Shame:* Why the Fuss," 21.

17. "'Scar of Shame' A Big Colored Movie at Gibson's," *Philadelphia Tribune*, 11 April 1929, 6. While interethnic collaboration was far more typical of mainstream American filmmaking than Neal Gabler suggests in *An Empire of Their Own* (New York: Crown Publishers, 1988), the combination of Jewish, Italian, and African-American work on *The Scar of Shame* is certainly noteworthy.

18. When interviewed about the film late in life, Lucia Moses confessed to few clear memories of the production, except that she took direction from two white men. See Thomas Cripps, *Slow Fade to Black: The Negro in American Film, 1900–1942* (New York: Oxford University Press, 1977), 198. The fact that Perugini and Liguori were experienced cameramen but had little or no experience as directors supports this supposition that they worked collaboratively. For a discussion of this approach to filmmaking, particularly its early and continued history, see Charles Musser, "Pre-Classical American Cinema: Its Changing Modes of Film Production," *Persistence of Vision* 9 (Fall 1991): 46–65; a somewhat revised version appears in Richard Abel, ed., *Silent Film* (New Brunswick, N.J.: Rutgers University Press, 1996), 85–108.

19. Munden, ed., *American Film Institute Catalog of Motion Pictures Produced in the United States: Feature Films, 1921–1930.*

20. Goldwyn, "*The Scar of Shame:* Why the Fuss," 16, 18.

21. Henry T. Sampson, *Blacks in Black and White*, 161; "Schiffman Leads Amusement World," *New York Amsterdam News*, 24 April 1929, 12. Sampson indicates that Micheaux and Schiffman soon had a falling out.

22. Oscar Micheaux to Norman Film Manufacturing Company, 7 August 1926, Black Film Center/Archive, Indiana University. I thank Phyllis Klotman and Pearl Bowser for bringing this letter to my attention.

23. Unfortunately, none of Shingzie Howard's silent films are extant.

24. The loose dating that has been assigned to these films in the past might suggest that actors such as Chenault and Clayton moved back and forth between Colored Players and Micheaux (see Sampson, *Blacks in Black and White*, 664, 665). This was not the case. Working for one after having worked for the other seems to have been viewed as a betrayal.

25. *Chicago Defender*, 15 January 1927, 8A.

26. *New York Amsterdam News*, 5 January 1927, 11.

27. *Philadelphia Tribune*, 11 April 1929, 6.

28. "Dud's Dope," *Chicago Defender*, 12 March 1927, 8A.

29. For example, Micheaux tried to undermine if not invert associations of "white" with purity and goodness and black with evil. One can find a few traces of these concerns in Colored Players films; in the description of *Children of Fate*, the hero has the "white plague"—tuberculosis (see description of *Children of Fate* in the filmography).

30. Cripps, *Slow Fade to Black*, 196. Cripps's negative assessment of this film was not shared by critics at the time of the film's release.

31. *Ten Nights in a Bar Room* (Oscar Apfel, 1921). One reel of the Apfel film survives at the Library of Congress.

32. For two discussions of *The Scar of Shame*, see Thomas Cripps, "'Race Movies' as Voices of the Black Bourgeoisie: *The Scar of Shame* (1927)," in *American History/American Film: Interpreting the Hollywood Image*, ed. John E. O'Connor and Martin A. Jackson (New York: Frederick Ungar, 1979), 39–55; and Jane Gaines, "*The Scar of Shame:* Skin Color and Cast in Black Silent Melodrama," *Cinema Journal* 26 (Summer 1987): 4, 3–21, reprinted in *Black Issues in Film and Visual Media*, ed. Valerie Smith (New Brunswick, N.J.: Rutgers University Press, 1997). Like Vincent Canby in his review of the film ("'Scar of Shame,' Pioneering Black Film," *New York Times*, 18 March 1976, 60), they somehow assume that this film is "about" skin color. I agree with Pearl Bowser that this is

not the case: skin color crosses class boundaries and ignores other characterological, ethical, and moral distinctions.

33. Both Jews such as Starkman and Calnek and Italians such as Perugini and Liguori could intimately appreciate the issue of cultural legitimization within refined mainstream culture, and indeed they were enacting that issue in making these films.

34. "Private Showing of New Race Picture Reveals Promising Talent," *Philadelphia Tribune,* 19 June 1926, 3.

35. Ibid.; "Great Race Picture Coming to the Grand October 17 [*sic*]," *Chicago Defender,* 16 October 1926, 6A.

36. "Ten Nights in a Bar Room to Show at the Rosebud Theatre," *California Eagle,* 19 October 1928, 7.

37. Gilpin was replaced by James Lowe on *Uncle Tom's Cabin* ("James Lowe To Play Uncle Tom; Gilpin Quits," *Philadelphia Tribune,* 18 September 1926, 3). Cripps suggests that Gilpin's work on *Uncle Tom's Cabin* came before that on *Ten Nights in a Barroom* (*Slow Fade to Black,* 196). The situation, in fact, was more complicated. Gilpin was cast first in the role of Uncle Tom at Universal Studios, but his start was delayed when director Harry Pollard became seriously ill while filming Eliza's escape across the ice floes in Plattsburgh, New York ("Gilpin to Start 'Uncle Tom's Cabin' Role About Aug. 1," *Pittsburgh Courier,* 26 June 1926, 9). This postponement may have provided Gilpin with the opening in his schedule to make *Ten Nights in a Barroom.* For a time it appeared that Pollard and Universal might have to start their production without him ("Actual Production of 'Uncle Tom's Cabin' Is Now On at Universal City," *Pittsburgh Courier,* 26 June 1926, 9), but Pollard's lingering illness made this potential conflict moot.

Universal must have hired Gilpin to play Uncle Tom based on *The Emperor Jones* and his overall theatrical reputation. Universal President Carl Laemmle was probably annoyed that Gilpin was appearing in a race film during the hiatus (a few years earlier Universal had told Noble Johnson that he had to stop making race films or be dropped from its roster), fostering the tensions and "creative differences" between them. (Gilpin's successful completion of *Ten Nights in a Barroom* nonetheless gave the actor some useful movie experience that Universal had to respect.) After their falling out, Gilpin's performance in *Ten Nights in a Barroom* would have encouraged other Hollywood studios to give the actor a second and even third chance.

If Gilpin had remained on *Uncle Tom's Cabin,* the Colored Players Film Corporation could have built a marketing strategy for *Ten Nights in a Barroom* that took advantage of his emerging mainstream movie celebrity. As plays, *Ten Nights in a Bar-Room* and *Uncle Tom's Cabin* were first performed in the 1850s: one was the cultural icon of abolition, the other of prohibition. Both were also based on popular novels. The two works are twins. For Gilpin to star in the Colored Players adaptation of one and then the Hollywood version of the other was a potential tour de force, which he declined, or was unable, to embrace.

38. "Charles Gilpin Is Ousted," *California Eagle,* 14 December 1928, 8. See also "Charles Gilpin Here to Make 'Lonesome Road,'" *California Eagle,* 2 November 1928, 8.

39. "At the Alhambra," *New York Amsterdam News,* 12 June 1929, 13.

40. Houston A. Baker, Jr., declines to consider film in *Modernism and the Harlem Renaissance* (Chicago: University of Chicago, 1987), 51–56.

13. RICHARD D. MAURICE AND THE MAURICE FILM COMPANY

1. "New Film Co.," *Chicago Defender,* 24 July 1920, 6.

2. Advertisement, *Chicago Defender,* 14 August 1920, 5; Henry T. Sampson, *Blacks in Black and White: A Source Book on Black Films,* 2nd ed. (Lanham, Md.: Scarecrow Press, 1995), 187.

3. Sampson, *Blacks in Black and White,* 187, 594.

4. Likewise, in an interview with Pearl Bowser in 1970, George P. Johnson, manager of Lincoln

Motion Pictures, one of the first nationally recognized African-American race movie companies, suggested that his brother Noble Johnson, founder of the company, whom he had not seen in a number of years, had severed all ties with his background in order to cross the color line.

5. The process of reconstructing the history of Detroit's black community in the 1920s is particularly difficult because Detroit's black newspapers for this period do not survive.

6. Advertisement, *Chicago Defender,* 24 July 1920, 6.

7. Advertisements, *Chicago Defender,* 24 July 1920, 6; 14 August 1920, 5; and 28 August 1920, 5.

8. Advertisement, *Chicago Defender,* 21 August 1920, 5.

9. Advertisement, *Chicago Defender,* 18 September 1920, 4.

10. Advertisement, *Chicago Defender,* 8 January 1921, 5; Advertisement, *Norfolk Journal and Guide,* 12 February 1921, 8.

11. "Nobody's Children Is Drawing Large Crowds," *Norfolk Journal and Guide,* 19 February 1921, 8.

12. Advertisement, *Chicago Defender,* 25 September 1920, 5.

13. Advertisement, *Chicago Defender,* 20 November 1920, 6.

14. Advertisement, *Chicago Defender,* 9 October 1920, 4.

15. Advertisement, *Chicago Defender,* 11 December 1920, 5.

16. "New Film Co.," *Chicago Defender,* 24 July 1920, 6.

17. "A Thriller," *Chicago Defender,* 11 December 1920, 5.

18. Ibid.

19. Advertisement, *Philadelphia Tribune,* 25 December 1920, 5; Advertisement, *Norfolk Journal and Guide,* 12 February 1921, 8. In Baltimore, *Nobody's Children* also played the Goldfield Theatre on 22–23 February 1921 and the Dunbar Theater on 7–8 March 1921 (Advertisements, Baltimore *Afro-American* 18 February 1921, 4; and 4 March 1921, 5).

20. "Nobody's Children Is Drawing Large Crowds," *Norfolk Journal and Guide,* 19 February 1921, 8.

21. Frolic Theatre to George P. Johnson, 3 June 1921, George P. Johnson Negro Film Collection, Special Collections, Young Library, UCLA.

22. Advertisement, *Pittsburgh Courier,* 21 March 1925; Advertisement, *New York Amsterdam News,* 4 August 1926, 11.

23. Royal Gardens Film Company opened *In the Depths of Our Hearts* in Chicago in early December 1920 (before *Nobody's Children* played in that city [Advertisement, *Chicago Defender,* 11 December 1920, 5]). Robert Levy announced his intentions to offer a regular monthly release in the *Chicago Defender,* 29 January 1921, 5.

24. "A List of Colored Film Producing Companies," Baltimore *Afro-American,* 9 December 1921, 10.

25. Baltimore *Afro-American,* 23 December 1921, 10.

26. Toni Cade Bambara also has suggested that *Eleven P.M.* be examined in light of contemporary literature, particularly the writings of Jean Toomer.

14. Cinematic Foremothers

1. The Baha'i religion arose in the last half of the nineteenth century in the Middle East. The first American group was established in the late 1890s. According to *Eerdman's Handbook to the World's Religions,* the Baha'i faith promotes world peace, the resolution of all social problems, and the achievement of racial equality (Grand Rapids, Mich.: W. B. Eerdmans Publishing Co., 1982, 270).

2. Clyde Taylor, "New U.S. Cinema," in *Movies and Mass Culture,* ed. John Belton (New Brunswick, N.J.: Rutgers University Press, 1996), 231.

3. Barre Toelkin, *The Dynamics of Folklore* (Boston: Houghton Mifflin Co., 1979), 28.

4. Daryl Dance, *Shuckin' and Jivin': Folklore from Contemporary Black Americans* (Bloomington: Indiana University Press, 1978), xvii.

5. Thomas H. Nigel, *From Folklore to Fiction: A Study of Folk Heroes and Rituals in the Black American Novel* (New York: Greenwood Press, 1988), 11–12.

6. Zora Neale Hurston, *Mules and Men* (Bloomington: Indiana University Press, 1978), 3.

7. Gladstone Yearwood, "Expressive Traditions in Afro-American Visual Arts," in *Expressively Black: The Cultural of Cultural Identity,* ed. Geneva Gay and Willie L. Barber (New York: Praeger, 1987), 138–139.

8. Perhaps one of the earliest references to Eloyce Gist is in Thomas Cripps, *Black Film as Genre* (Bloomington: Indiana University Press, 1979). He states, "In the 1930s . . . Eloise Gist used highly personal films depicting literal symbols of her fundamentalist faith" (87).

9. An interview with Homoiselle Patrick Harrison, Eloyce Gist's daughter, was the source for information regarding Eloyce King Patrick Gist's life. Portions of the interview are published in my article, "Recall and Recollect: Excavating the Life History of Eloyce King Patrick Gist," *Black Film Review* 8, no. 2 (1994): 20–21.

10. Irving S. Hammer to Roy Wilkins, 11 May 1933, James and Eloyce Gist file, Motion Picture, Broadcasting, and Recorded Sound Division, Library of Congress, Washington, D.C.

11. Roy Wilkins to James E. Gist, Jr., 16 May 1933, ibid.

12. Amy Kael Petrine, "Hell Bound, Heaven Bound, The Journey: Black America, 1930s Quest for Personal Advancement Using Motivational Imagery in Dramatic Productions," unpublished paper, ibid.

13. Toelkin, *The Dynamics of Folklore,* 225.

14. Deborah Bowman Richards, "A Bibliographic Essay on Afro-American Folk Drama," *Ohio Folklife: Journal of the Ohio Folklore Society* 6 (1982): 39.

15. The primary cast members in *Hell Bound Train* are African American. In several instances, a white man portrays either a store owner, a prison warden, or a boss. In the case of the latter, he is paying the worker his salary. All the police in the film are African American.

16. Consecutive numbering of the train cars served as a structuring device to help reconstruct the footage.

17. William Wiggins, "Pilgrims, Crosses, and Faith: The Folk Dimensions of Heaven Bound," *Black American Literature Forum* 25, no. 1 (Spring 1991): 96–97.

18. A number of independent and Hollywood films use music to draw clear parallels between urban and rural, righteous and unrighteous lifestyles. See the following dissertations which analyze the roles of music in African-American film: Gloria J. Gibson, "The Cultural Significance of Music to the Black Independent Filmmaker" (Ph.D. diss., Indiana University, 1987); and Adrienne Lanier Seward, "Early Black Film and Folk Tradition: An Interpretive Analysis of the Use of Folklore in Selected All-Black Feature Films" (Ph.D. diss., Indiana University, 1985).

19. I would compare this scene to the climactic scene in *The Flying Ace*. The damsel in distress climbs a rope from a burning plane to the hero's plane hovering up above her. It is obvious that the planes are not even in the air. In both cases, the film structure aids the audience in suspending disbelief.

20. Robert Emerson, *Contemporary Field Research: A Collection of Readings* (Prospect Heights, Ill.: Waveland Press, Inc., 1983), 19.

21. Ibid.

22. Karl G. Heider, *Ethnographic Film* (Austin: University of Texas Press, 1976), 4.

23. Ibid.

24. Vernon J. Williams, Jr., *Rethinking Race: Franz Boas and His Contemporaries* (Lexington: The University Press of Kentucky, 1996), 4.

25. Quoted in Robert Hemenway, *Zora Neale Hurston: A Literary Biography* (Urbana: University of Illinois Press, 1977), 91.

26. Ibid., 108.

27. Hemenway, *Zora Neale Hurston,* 109.

28. Heider, *Ethnographic Film,* 19.

29. Debra Newman Ham, ed., *The African American Mosaic: A Library of Congress Resource Guide*

for the Study of Black History and Culture (Washington, D.C.: Library of Congress, 1993), 203. Additional footage that was either shot or supervised by Hurston during the early 1940s in South Carolina is also available at the Library of Congress. The sound track is not present on the footage.

30. Linda Connor and Patsy Asch, "Subjects, Images and Voices: Representing Gender in Ethnographic Film," *Visual Anthropology Review* 11, no.1 (Spring 1995): 5.

31. Brian Sutton-Smith, *The Folkgames of Children* (Austin: University of Texas Press, 1972); Bessie Jones and Bess Lomax Hawes, *Step It Down: Games, Plays, Songs and Stories from the Afro-American Heritage* (New York: Harper & Row, 1972).

32. Grace Fox, "Ring Plays and Other Games of the Florida Negro" (Ph.D. diss., Indiana University, 1953), 105.

33. Hurston's focus on performance style is evident in her other footage. It is not just footage to capture the men splitting logs, it is their style as they swing the ax. It is not just men smoking meat, but the dynamic interchange and interaction they engage in as the meat is cooked.

Appendix A. The Reemergence of Oscar Micheaux

1. Thomas R Cripps, "Black Films and Film Makers: Movies in the Ghetto B.P. (Before Poitier)," *Negro Digest,* Feb. 1969, 25. The endnotes in this article provide sources for each event discussed; since the notes are, with some exceptions, in chronological order, they can, like the essay itself, also be used as a timetable. This survey is thorough but not definitive.

2. Telephone conversation with Thomas Cripps, 29 July 1993.

3. Oscar Micheaux, *The Conquest: The Story of a Negro Pioneer* (1913; reprint, Miami, Fla.: Mnemosyne Publishers, 1969; and College Park, Md.: McGrath, 1969); *The Homesteader* (1917; reprint, College Park, Md.: McGrath, 1969).

4. Peter Noble, *The Negro in Films* (London: S. Robinson, 1948; reprint, Port Washington, N.Y.: Kennikat Press, 1969). Noble's book was reprinted again in 1970 by Arno Press.

5. Jewish Museum, press release for The Black Film Series, 19 March 1970; Penelope Gilliatt, "Black Film," *The New Yorker,* April 18, 1970, 34–35.

6. Thomas Cripps, "Paul Robeson and Black Identity in American Movies," *The Massachusetts Review* (Summer 1970): 468–485.

7. James P. Murray, *To Find an Image: Black Films from Uncle Tom to Super Fly* (New York: Bobbs-Merrill, 1973).

8. Donald Bogle, *Toms, Coons, Mulattoes, Mammies, and Bucks: An Interpretive History of Blacks in American Films* (New York: Continuum, 1973; revised and expanded, 1989), 109.

9. Ibid., 115.

10. Ibid.

11. Janis Hebert, "Oscar Micheaux: A Black Pioneer," *South Dakota Review* (Winter 1973–1974): 62–69.

12. Jim Pines, *Blacks in Films: A Survey of Racial Themes and Images in the American Film* (London: Studio Vista, 1974), 36. Published in the United States in 1975.

13. Ibid.

14. Ibid., 38

15. "Black Pantheon for Film Talent," *Variety,* 13 February 1974, 5.

16. J. Hoberman, "A Forgotten Black Cinema Resurfaces," *The Village Voice,* 17 November 1975, back page, 85–86, 88.

17. Daniel J. Leab, *From Sambo to Superspade: The Black Experience in Motion Pictures* (Boston: Houghton Mifflin, 1975), 81.

18. Gary Null, *Black Hollywood: The Negro in Motion Pictures* (Secaucus, N.J.: Citadel, 1975).

19. Clinton Cox, "'We Were Stars in Those Days,'" New York *Sunday News* [Magazine], 9 March 1975, 15–16, 18, 26–27.

20. Penelope Gilliatt, "Retorts to *The Birth of a Nation*," *The New Yorker,* 29 March 1976, 89–91.

21. Arlene Elder, "Oscar Micheaux: The Melting Pot on the Plains," *The Old Northwest: A Journal of Regional Life and Letters* 2, no. 3 (September 1976): 299–307.

22. Cripps, *Slow Fade to Black: The Negro in American Film, 1900–1942* (New York: Oxford University Press, 1977).

23. See J. Ronald Green, "'Twoness' in the Style of Oscar Micheaux"; and see Cripps's response to Green, "Oscar Micheaux: The Story Continues," both in Manthia Diawara, ed., *Black American Cinema* (New York: Routledge, 1993), 26–48, 71–79.

24. Henry T. Sampson, *Blacks in Black and White: A Source Book on Black Films,* 2nd ed. (1977; Metuchen, N.J.: Scarecrow, 1995).

25. Sampson, *Blacks in Black and White: A Source Book on Black Films,* 1st ed. (Metuchen, N.J.: Scarecrow, 1977), 53–55.

26. "Oscar Micheaux: Some Recollections." Quotations are taken from a copy of a catalog or brochure found in the Oscar Micheaux file at the Black Film Center/Archive at Indiana University at Bloomington. A handwritten note dates the copy 1978 and attributes it to the "BK Filmmaker Hall of Fame." No author is credited.

27. Thomas Cripps, *Black Film as Genre* (Bloomington: Indiana University Press, 1979), 26.

28. Ibid., 27.

29. Ibid.

30. Ibid., 151.

31. Phyllis Rauch Klotman, *Frame by Frame: A Black Filmography* (1979; reprint Bloomington: Indiana University Press, 1997).

32. Bernard L. Peterson, Jr., "The Films of Oscar Micheaux: America's First Fabulous Black Filmmaker," *Crisis,* April 1979; revised and republished as "A Filmography of Oscar Micheaux: America's Legendary Black Filmmaker," in *Celluloid Power: Social Film Criticism from "The Birth of a Nation" to "Judgment at Nuremberg,"* ed. David Platt (Metuchen, N.J.: Scarecrow, 1992), 113–141.

33. Madubuko Diakité, *Film, Culture, and the Black Filmmaker: A Study of Functional Relationships and Parallel Developments* (New York: Arno, 1980). Since Diakité's book does not provide an index, it might be useful to note that the pages with significant references to Micheaux include 52, 53, 64–73, 93–104, 105, 115, 120–121, 127–130, 133, 148, 152, 154, 156, 157, 166–170, 181–182.

34. Ibid., 129.

35. "Bad Movies," *Film Comment,* July 1980, 7–12, reprinted in J. Hoberman, *Vulgar Modernism: Writing on Movies and Other Media* (Philadelphia: Temple University Press, 1991), 13–22.

36. Ibid., 20.

37. Ibid., 22.

38. The anecdotes by Freeman and Tucker provide an occasion to mention that many of the people from Micheaux's era who are alive today, including these two, as well as Oliver Hill, pronounce Micheaux's name either "Me-*shaw*" or "*Me*-shaw." Most scholars of Micheaux today pronounce it "Me-*show*," as if it were French or Cajun; Richard Grupenhoff, who has interviewed many of the surviving contemporaries of Micheaux, feels the latter pronunciation is, in fact, correct.

39. This fact is confirmed, with details as to typical payments, in Murray, *To Find an Image,* 10; Clinton, "We Were Stars in Those Days," 16; and Sampson, *Blacks in Black and White,* 52.

40. David Levering Lewis, *When Harlem Was in Vogue* (New York: Alfred A. Knopf, 1981), 264. Lewis also refers elsewhere to "the curious folk novels of filmmaker Oscar Micheaux" (89).

41. Chester J. Fontenot, Jr., "Oscar Micheaux, Black Novelist and Film Maker," in *Vision and Refuge: Essays on the Literature of the Great Plains,* ed. Virginia Faulkner with Frederick C. Luebke (Lincoln: University of Nebraska Press, 1982), 109–125.

42. Ibid., 121, 124.

43. Gladstone L. Yearwood, ed., *Black Cinema Aesthetics: Issues in Independent Black Filmmaking* (Athens, Ohio: Center for Afro-American Studies, Ohio University, 1982).

44. Pearl Bowser, "Sexual Imagery and the Black Woman in American Cinema," *Black Cinema*

Aesthetics: Issues in Independent Black Filmmaking, ed. Gladstone L. Yearwood (Athens, Ohio: Center for Afro-American Studies, Ohio University), 47–48.

45. Gladstone Yearwood, "Towards a Theory of a Black Cinema Aesthetic," in *Black Cinema Aesthetics,* 67–81.

46. Pearl Bowser, program notes, "Oscar Micheaux (1884–1951)," *New American Filmmakers Series,* no. 17, Whitney Museum of American Art, 22 May–10 June 1984. Films included *Body and Soul* (1925), *The Exile* (1931), *Ten Minutes to Live* (1932), *Underworld* (1937), *God's Step Children* (1938), and *Lying Lips* (1939).

47. J. Hoberman, "Blankety-Blank," *Village Voice,* 29 May 1984, 58.

48. Richard Dyer, *Heavenly Bodies: Film Stars and Society* (New York: St. Martin's Press, 1986), 109.

49. Ibid., 111.

50. Saundra Sharp, "At Long Last: Director's Guild Honors Oscar Micheaux," *Black Film Review* (Summer 1986): 33–34.

51. Saundra Sharp, "Collectors' Dreams: Tracking Down Lost Frames and Lobby Cards," *Black Film Review* (Fall 1986): 16–20.

52. Earl Calloway, "Oscar Micheaux's Headstone Ceremony Announced," *Chicago Defender,* 6 August 1988, 35.

53. Ntongela Masilela, "Interconnections: The African and Afro-American Cinemas," *The Independent,* Jan./Feb. 1988, 15.

54. Donald Bogle, *Blacks in American Films and Television: An Encyclopedia* (New York: Garland, 1988).

55. Ibid., 92.

56. Ibid., 424.

57. Ibid.

58. Richard Grupenhoff, *The Black Valentino: The Stage and Screen Career of Lorenzo Tucker* (Metuchen, N.J.: Scarecrow Press, 1988).

59. Ibid., 64–65.

60. Ibid., 70–71.

61. Ibid., 61, 74–75.

62. Ibid., 75.

63. Richard Grupenhoff, "Interview: Lorenzo Tucker: The Black Valentino," *Black Film Review* (Spring 1988): 3–5.

64. Richard Grupenhoff, "The Rediscovery of Oscar Micheaux, Black Film Pioneer," *Journal of Film and Video* (Winter 1988): 46.

65. J. Ronald Green and Horace Neal, Jr., "Oscar Micheaux and Racial Slur: A Response to 'The Rediscovery of Oscar Micheaux,'" *Journal of Film and Video* (Fall 1988): 66–71.

66. *CinémAction,* no. 46 (1988): 40–42. Bowser's article is introduced as a translation from the Museum of Modern Art catalog, which may be true, but the text follows almost exactly that of the Whitney Museum note of 1984.

67. Mark A. Reid, "Pioneer Black Filmmaker: The Achievement of Oscar Micheaux," *Black Film Review* (Spring 1988): 7.

68. Joseph A. Young, *Black Novelist as White Racist: The Myth of Black Inferiority in the Novels of Oscar Micheaux* (New York: Greenwood Press, 1989).

69. Young's book, though beyond the scope of this essay, is examined in J. Ronald Green, *Straight Lick: The Cinema of Oscar Micheaux* (Bloomington: Indiana University Press, 2000), 193–224.

70. The Oscar Micheaux Newsletter, Film and Video Program, 104 Crowell Hall, Box 90671, Duke University, Durham, NC, 27708, Editors: Charlene Regester and Jane Gaines.

71. G. William Jones, *Black Cinema Treasures: Lost and Found* (Denton: University of North Texas Press, 1991).

72. Ibid., 172.

73. Richard Gehr, "One-Man Show," and "Saving Mr. Micheaux," *American Film* (May 1991): 34–39.

74. bell hooks, "Micheaux: Celebrating Blackness," *Black American Literature Forum* 25, no. 2 (Summer 1991): 351–360; reprinted in bell hooks, *Black Looks: Race and Representation* (Boston: South End Press, 1992).

75. Ibid., 355.

76. Ibid., 358.

77. Ibid., 359.

78. Ibid., 359–360.

79. Mark A. Reid, *Redefining Black Film* (Berkeley: University of California Press, 1993).

80. Ibid., 11–12.

81. Ibid., 14.

82. Manthia Diawara, *Black American Cinema* (New York: Routledge, 1993).

83. *Black Film Review* 7, no. 4 (1993).

84. Clyde Taylor, "Crossed Over and Can't Get Black: The Crisis of 1937–1939," *Black Film Review* 7, no. 4 (1993): 22–27.

85. Ibid., 26.

86. "The Micheaux Legacy," *Black Film Review* 7, no. 4 (1993): 12–13. "Backstory" is the term used by scriptwriters for the background material that defines characters and actions but that is not actually included in the script. Backstories are sometimes actually written without the intention to use them for anything more than to help the *writer* more fully understand the background forces that will define characters and motivate actions that *are* included in the script.

87. Ibid., 13.

88. Ibid.

89. bell hooks, *Yearning: Race, Gender, and Cultural Politics* (Boston: South End Press, 1990), 55.

90. Thomas Cripps, *Making Movies Black: The Hollywood Message Movie from World War II to the Civil Rights Era* (New York: Oxford University Press, 1993).

91. Debra Newman Ham, ed., Brian Taves and David L. Parker, motion picture eds., *The African-American Mosaic: A Library of Congress Resource Guide for the Study of Black History and Culture* (Washington, D.C.: Library of Congress, 1993).

92. Phyllis R. Klotman and Gloria J. Gibson, eds., *In Touch with the Spirit: Black Religious and Musical Expression in American Cinema* (Bloomington: Indiana University, Black Film Center/Archive and the Department of Afro-American Studies, 1994); Charlene Regester, "Oscar Micheaux's *Body and Soul:* A Film of Conflicting Themes"; and J. Ronald Green, "Oscar Micheaux's *Darktown Revue:* Caricature and Class Conflict," both in Klotman and Gibson.

93. Reviewed briefly in the *Oscar Micheaux Society Newsletter* 3 (Summer 1994); speakers included Charlene Regester, Jane Gaines, Pearl Bowser, Richard Grupenhoff, Richard Foreman (the dramatist), Manthia Diawara, J. Hoberman, Ken Jacobs, Clyde Taylor, Ed Guerrero, Toni Cade Bambara, and David Schwartz. The conference was held in conjunction with a film exhibition, From Harlem to Hollywood, curated by Pearl Bowser.

94. Arthur Jafa (a.k.a. A. J. Fielder), *Black Film Bulletin* (Autumn/Winter 1993/1994); see reference in *Oscar Micheaux Society Newsletter* 3, "Bibliography Update."

95. James Snead, *White Screens/Black Images* (New York: Routledge, 1994), 112–114.

96. Charlene Regester, "Lynched, Assaulted, Intimidated: Oscar Micheaux's Most Controversial Films," *Popular Culture Review* 5, no. 1 (February 1994).

97. Scott Heller, "A Pioneering Black Filmmaker: Scholars Have Rediscovered Oscar Micheaux and Established Him as a Key Figure," *Chronicle of Higher Education,* 3 March 1995, A6–7, A12–13.

98. Charlene Regester, "The Misreading and Rereading of African American Filmmaker Oscar Micheaux: A Critical Review of Micheaux Scholarship," *Film History: An International Journal* 7, no. 4 (1995): 426–449. Regester's review provides a point of view that can be contrasted with that of this essay. She, for example, interprets J. Hoberman's writing on Micheaux as negative, whereas

I read Hoberman as a major champion of Micheaux's "problem" films. Regester's recent articles present a steady flow of new historical information.

99. Richard Dyer, "Into the Light: The Whiteness of the South in *The Birth of a Nation*"; and Jane Gaines, "*The Birth of a Nation* and *Within Our Gates:* Two Tales of the American South," in *Dixie Debates: Perspectives in Southern Cultures,* ed. Richard H. King and Helen Taylor (London: Pluto Press, 1996).

100. Pearl Bowser and Louise Spence, "Identity and Betrayal: *The Symbol of the Unconquered* and Oscar Micheaux's 'Biographical Legend,'" in *The Birth of Whiteness: Race and the Emergence of United States Cinema,* ed. Daniel Bernardi (New Brunswick, N.J.: Rutgers University Press, 1996).

101. Charlene Regester, "Black Films, White Censors: Oscar Micheaux Confronts Censorship in New York, Virginia, and Chicago," in *Movie Censorship and American Culture,* ed. Francis G. Couvares (Washington, D.C.: Smithsonian Institution Press, 1996).

102. J. Ronald Green, "Micheaux v. Griffith," *Griffithiana,* nos. 60/61 (Fall 1997): 33–49; Green, "America in bianco e nero," *Diaria della settimana,* no. 39 (8–14 October): 56–58.

103. Charlene Regester, "Oscar Micheaux the Entrepreneur: Financing *The House Behind the Cedars,*" *Journal of Film and Video,* Spring–Summer 1997, 17–27.

BIBLIOGRAPHY

Compiled by Kristen Barnes,
Jane Gaines, Fred Neumann, and Hank Okazaki

Abel, Richard, ed. *Silent Film*. New Brunswick, N.J.: Rutgers University Press, 1996.

Albright, Alex. "Micheaux, Vaudeville, and Black Cast Film." *Black Film Review* 7, no. 4 (1992): 6–9, 36.

Aptheker, Herbert. *A Documentary History of the Negro People in the United States, 1910–1932*. New York: Citadel Press, 1973.

Attille, Martina. "Still." In *Rhapsodies in Black: Art of the Harlem Renaissance,* ed. Richard J. Powell and David A. Bailey. London: Hayward Gallery, The Institute of International Visual Arts; Berkeley: University of California Press, 1997.

Baker, Houston A., Jr. *Modernism and the Harlem Renaissance*. Chicago: Chicago University Press, 1987.

Baldwin, James. *The Devil Finds Work: An Essay*. New York: Dial Press, 1976.

Balio, Tino, ed. *The American Film Industry*. Madison: University of Wisconsin Press, 1985.

Barthes, Roland. *Image/Music/Text*. Trans. Stephen Heath. New York: Hill and Wang, 1977.

Bernardi, Daniel, ed. *The Birth of Whiteness: Race and the Emergence of the United States Cinema*. New Brunswick, N.J.: Rutgers University Press, 1996.

Bernstein, Matthew, and Dana F. White, "'Scratching Around' in a 'Fit of Insanity': The Norman Film Manufacturing Company and the Race Film Business in the 1920s." *Griffithiana* 62/63 (maggio 1998): 81–128.

Bhabha, Homi K. *The Location of Culture*. New York: Routledge, 1994.

———. "The Other Question: The Stereotype and Colonial Discourse." *Screen* 24, no. 4 (November–December 1983): 18–36.

Billops, Camille, Ada Griffin, and Valerie Smith, eds. "Special Issue on Black Film." *Black American Literature Forum* 25, no. 2 (Summer 1991).

Birdoff, Harry. *The World's Greatest Hit: Uncle Tom's Cabin*. New York: S. F. Vanni, 1947.

Bobo, Jacqueline. *Black Women as Cultural Readers*. New York: Columbia University Press, 1995.

———. "'The Subject Is Money': Reconsidering the Black Film Audience as a Theoretical Paradigm." *Black American Literature Forum* 25, no. 2 (Summer 1991): 421–432.

Bogle, Donald. "'B' for Black." *Film Comment* 21, no. 5 (September–October 1985): 32.

———. *Blacks in American Films and Television: An Illustrated Encyclopedia*. New York: Garland, 1988.

———. *Dorothy Dandridge: A Biography*. New York: Boulevard Books, 1997.

———. *Toms, Coons, Mulattoes, Mammies and Bucks: An Interpretive History of Blacks in American Films*. New York: Continuum, 1973; revised and expanded, 1989.

Bone, Robert A. *The Negro Novel in America*. New Haven, Conn.: Yale University Press, 1958.

Bordwell, David, Janet Staiger, and Kristin Thompson. *The Classical Hollywood Cinema: Film Style and Mode of Production to 1960*. New York: Columbia University Press, 1985.

Boskin, Joseph. *Sambo: The Rise and Demise of an American Jester.* New York: Oxford University Press, 1986.

Bowser, Pearl. "Portrait of a Pioneering Spirit." *African Voices* (Spring 1999): 16–19.

———. "Sexual Imagery and the Black Woman in American Cinema." In *Black Cinema Aesthetics: Issues in Independent Black Filmmaking,* edited by Gladstone L. Yearwood. Athens, Ohio: Afro-American Studies at Ohio University, 1982.

Bowser, Pearl, and Jane Gaines. "New Finds/Old Films." *Black Film Review* 7, no. 4 (1992): 2–5.

Bowser, Pearl, and Louise Spence. "Identity and Betrayal: *The Symbol of the Unconquered* and Oscar Micheaux's 'Biographical Legend.'" In *The Birth of Whiteness: Race and the Emergence of the United States Cinema,* ed. Daniel Bernardi. New Brunswick, N.J.: Rutgers University Press, 1996.

———. "Oscar Micheaux's *Body and Soul* and the Burden of Representation," *Cinema Journal* 38, no. 3 (Spring 2000): 3–29.

———. *Writing Himself into History: Oscar Micheaux, His Silent Films, and His Audiences.* New Brunswick, N.J.: Rutgers University Press, 2000.

Boyd, Todd. *Am I Black Enough for You?* Bloomington: Indiana University Press, 1997.

Brown, Nick. "Griffith's Family Discourse: Griffith and Freud." *Quarterly Review of Film Studies* 6, no. 1 (Winter 1981): 67–80.

Brown, William Wells. *Clotel: or, The President's Daughter.* 1853. Reprint, Secaucus, N.J.: Carol Publishing, 1969.

Burch, Noel. *Life to Those Shadows.* New York and Berkeley: University of California Press, 1991.

Calloway, Earl. "Oscar Micheaux's Headstone Ceremony Announced." Chicago *Defender,* 6 August 1988, 35.

Campanella, Jr., Roy. "Lorenzo Tucker: 'Valentino noir.'" Trans. Francis Bordat. *CinémAction* 46 (1988): 53–55.

Carbine, Mary. "'The Finest Outside the Loop': Motion Picture Exhibition in Chicago's Black Metropolis, 1905–1928." *Camera Obscura* 23 (May 1990): 9–41. Reprinted in *Silent Film,* ed. Richard Abel (New Brunswick, N.J.: Rutgers University Press, 1996).

Carby, Hazel. *Race Men: The Body and Soul of Race, Nation and Manhood.* Cambridge, Mass.: Harvard University Press, 1998.

———. *Reconstructing Womanhood: The Emergence of the Afro-American Woman Novelist.* New York: Oxford University Press, 1987.

Carisella, P. J., and James Ryan. *The Black Swallow of Death.* Boston: Marlborough House, 1972.

Cham, Mbye B., and Claire Andrade-Watkins, eds. *Blackframes: Critical Perspectives on Black Independent Cinema.* Cambridge, Mass.: MIT Press, 1988.

Cherchi Usai, Paolo. *Burning Passions: An Introduction to the Study of Silent Cinema.* London: British Film Institute, 1994.

Chesnutt, Charles Waddell. *The Conjure Woman, and Other Conjure Tales.* Edited by Richard H. Brodhead. Durham, N.C.: Duke University Press, 1993.

———. *The House Behind the Cedars.* Boston: Houghton, Mifflin and Company, 1900. Reprint, Athens, Ga.: University of Georgia Press, 1988.

———. *The Marrow of Tradition.* 1901. Reprint, Ann Arbor: University of Michigan Press, 1969.

———. *The Wife of His Youth and Other Stories of the Color Line.* Boston: Houghton, Mifflin and Company, 1899.

Chesnutt, Helen M. *Charles Waddell Chesnutt: Pioneer of the Color Line.* Chapel Hill: University of North Carolina Press, 1952.

Cox, Clinton. "We Were Stars in Those Days." New York *Sunday News* [Magazine], 9 March 1975, 15–6, 18, 26–27.

Cox, Oliver C. *Caste, Class and Race: A Study in Social Dynamics.* New York: Doubleday, 1948.

Cripps, Thomas. "*The Birth of a Race:* A Lost Film Rediscovered in Texas." *Texas Humanist* (March–April 1983): 10–11.

———. *Black Film as Genre*. Bloomington: Indiana University Press, 1979.

———. *Hollywood's High Noon: Moviemaking and Society Before Television*. Baltimore and London: Johns Hopkins University Press, 1997.

———. "Movies in the Ghetto B. P. (Before Poitier)." *Negro Digest* (February 1969): 24–29.

———. "Oscar Micheaux: The Story Continues." In *Black American Cinema*, ed. Manthia Diawara. New York: Routledge, 1993.

———. "Paul Robeson and Black Identity in American Movies." *Massachusetts Review* 11, no. 3 (Summer 1970): 468–485.

———. "'Race Movies' as Voices of the Black Bourgeoisie: *The Scar of Shame*." In *American History/American Film*, ed. John E. O'Connor and Martin A. Jackson. New York: Ungar, 1979.

———. *Slow Fade to Black: The Negro in American Film, 1900–1942*. 1977. Reprint, New York: Oxford University Press, 1993.

Crusz, Robert. "Black Cinemas, Film Theory and Dependent Knowledge." *Screen* 26, no. 3–4 (May–August 1985): 152–156.

Dance, Daryl. *Shuckin' and Jivin': Folklore from Contemporary Black Americans*. Bloomington: Indiana University Press, 1978.

Daniels, Therese, and Jane Gerson, eds. *The Color Black*. London: BFI, 1989.

Danky, James P., and Maureen Hady, eds. *African-American Newspapers and Periodicals: A National Bibliography*. Cambridge, Mass.: Harvard University Press, 1998.

Diakité, Madubuko. *Film, Culture, and the Black Filmmaker: A Study of Functional Relationships and Parallel Developments*. New York: Arno, 1980.

Diawara, Manthia. "Black Spectatorship: Problems of Identification and Resistance." *Screen* 29, no. 4 (Autumn 1988): 66–76.

Diawara, Manthia, ed. *Black American Cinema*. New York: Routledge, 1993.

———. "Cinema Studies, the Strong Thought, and Black Film." *Wide Angle* 13, no. 3–4 (July–October 1991): 4–11.

Doane, Mary Ann. *Femmes Fatales: Feminism, Film Theory, Psychoanalysis*. New York: Routledge, 1991.

Douglas, Ann. *Terrible Honesty: Mongrel Manhattan in the 1920s*. New York: Farrar, Strauss and Giroux, 1995.

Drake, St. Clair. *Black Folk Here and There*. 2 vols. Los Angeles: UCLA Center for Afro-American Studies, 1987, 1990.

Duberman, Martin B. *Paul Robeson: A Biography*. New York: Knopf, 1989.

Du Bois, W. E. B. *The Souls of Black Folk*. 1903. Reprint, New York: Washington Square Books, 1970.

Dyer, Richard. *Heavenly Bodies: Film Stars and Society*. New York: Macmillan, 1986. See chapter on Paul Robeson.

———. "Into the Light: The Whiteness of the South in *The Birth of a Nation*." In *Dixie Debates: Perspectives in Southern Cultures*, ed. Richard H. King and Helen Taylor. London: Pluto Press, 1996.

———. *The Matter of Images: Essays on Representations*. New York: Routledge, 1993.

———. *White*. London and New York: Routledge, 1997.

Dyson, Michael. "Film Noir." *Tikkun* 4, no. 5 (1989): 75–78.

———. *Reflecting Black*. Minneapolis: University of Minnesota Press, 1993.

Eisenstein, Sergei. "Dickens, Griffith, and the Film Today." In *Film Form*, ed. Jay Leyda. 1949. Reprint, New York: Harcourt Brace, 1977.

Elder, Arlene. "Oscar Micheaux: The Melting Pot on the Plains." *The Old Northwest: A Journal of Regional Life and Letters* 2, no. 3 (September 1976): 299–307.

Ellison, Ralph. *Shadow and Act*. New York: Random House, 1964.

Elsaesser, Thomas, ed. *Early Cinema: Space/Frame/Narrative*. London: British Film Institute, 1990.

Fanon, Frantz. *Black Skin, White Masks*. New York: Grove Press, 1967.

———. *The Wretched of the Earth.* New York: Grove Press, 1966.

Fiedler, Leslie. *The Inadvertent Epic: From Uncle Tom's Cabin to Roots.* New York: Simon & Schuster, 1980.

Fontenot, Jr., Chester J. "Oscar Micheaux, Black Novelist and Film Maker." In *Vision and Refuge: Essays on the Literature of the Great Plains,* ed. Virginia Faulkner and Frederick C. Luebke, 109–125. Lincoln: University of Nebraska Press, 1982.

Fowler, Carolyn. *Black Arts and Black Aesthetics: A Bibliography.* Atlanta: Atlanta University Press, 1976.

Fox, Grace. "Ring Plays and Other Games of the Florida Negro." Ph.D. diss., Indiana University, 1953.

Francis, Charles E. *The Tuskegee Airmen.* Boston: Branden Publishing Company, 1988.

Freydberg, Elizabeth Amelia Hadley. *Bessie Coleman: The Brownskin Lady Bird.* New York: Garland Publishing, 1994.

Friedman, Lester, ed. *Unspeakable Images: Ethnicity and the American Cinema.* Carbondale: University of Illinois Press, 1991.

Gaines, Jane M. "*The Birth of a Nation* and *Within Our Gates:* Two Tales of the American South." In *Dixie Debates: Perspectives in Southern Cultures,* ed. Richard H. King and Helen Taylor. London: Pluto Press, 1996.

———. *Fire and Desire: Mixed Blood Relations in Silent Cinema.* Chicago: University of Chicago Press, 2000.

———. "Fire and Desire: Race, Melodrama and Oscar Micheaux." In *Black American Cinema,* ed. Manthia Diawara. New York: Routledge, 1993.

———. "*Scar of Shame:* Skin Color and Caste in Black Silent Melodrama." *Cinema Journal* 26, no. 4 (Summer 1987): 3–21. Reprinted in *Imitations of Life: A Reader on Film and Television Melodrama,* ed. Marcia Landy (Detroit: Wayne State University Press, 1991). Also reprinted in *Representing Blackness: Issues in Film and Video,* ed. Valerie Smith (New Brunswick, N.J.: Rutgers University Press, 1997).

Gates, Jr., Henry Louis. *Black Literature and Literary Theory.* London: Methuen, 1984.

———. "The Face and Voice of Blackness." In *Modern Art and Society: An Anthology of Social and Multicultural Readings,* ed. Maurice Berger. New York: Harper Collins, 1994.

———. *Figures in Black.* New York: Oxford University Press, 1987.

———. ed. *"Race," Writing and Difference.* Chicago: University of Chicago Press, 1986.

———. *The Signifying Monkey: A Theory of African-American Literary Criticism.* New York: Oxford University Press, 1988.

Gehr, Richard. "One-Man Show." *American Film* 16, no. 5 (May 1991): 34–39.

———. "Saving Mr. Micheaux." *American Film* 16, no. 5 (May 1991): 39.

George, Nelson. *Blackface: Reflections on African-Americans and the Movies.* New York: HarperCollins, 1994.

Gevinson, Alan, ed. *Within Our Gates: Ethnicity in American Feature Films, 1911–1960.* Berkeley and Los Angeles: University of California Press, 1997.

Gibson-Hudson, Gloria J. "The Cultural Significance of Music to the Black Independent Filmmaker." Ph.D. diss., Indiana University, 1987.

———. "The Norman Film Manufacturing Company." *Black Film Review* 7, no. 4 (1992): 16–20.

———. "Recall and Recollect: Excavating the Life History of Eloyce King Patrick Gist." *Black Film Review* 8, no. 2: 20–21.

Gilliatt, Penelope. "Black Film." *The New Yorker,* 18 April 1970, 34–35.

———. "Retorts to *The Birth of a Nation.*" *The New Yorker,* 29 March 1976, 88–91.

Gilman, Sander. *Differences and Pathology: Stereotypes of Sexuality, Race and Madness.* Ithaca, N.Y.: Cornell University Press, 1985.

Gilman, Susan. "Micheaux's Chesnutt." *PMLA* 114, no. 5 (October 1999): 1080–1088.

———. "The Mulatto, Tragic or Triumphant? The Nineteenth-Century American Race Melodrama." In *The Culture of Sentiment: Race, Gender, and Sentimentality in Nineteenth-Century America,* ed. Shirley Samuels. New York: Oxford University Press, 1992.

Gilroy, Paul. *There Ain't No Black in the Union Jack.* London: Hutchinson, 1987.

Green, J. Ronald. "The Micheaux Style." *Black Film Review* 7, no. 4 (1992): 32–34.

———. "Micheaux v. Griffith." *Griffithiana* 60/61 (October 1997): 32–49.

———. "Oscar Micheaux's *Darktown Revue:* Caricature and Class Conflict." In *In Touch with the Spirit: Black Religious and Musical Expression in American Cinema,* ed. Phyllis Klotman and Gloria-Gibson Hudson. Bloomington: Indiana University, Black Film Center/Archive and The Department of Afro-American Studies, 1994.

———. *Straight Lick: The Cinema of Oscar Micheaux.* Bloomington: Indiana University Press, 2000.

———. "'Twoness' in the Style of Oscar Micheaux." In *Black American Cinema,* ed. Manthia Diawara. New York: Routledge, 1993.

Green, J. Ronald, and Horace Neal, Jr. "Oscar Micheaux and Racial Slur: A Response to 'The Rediscovery of Oscar Micheaux.'" *Journal of Film and Video* 40, no. 4 (Fall 1988): 66–71.

Grupenhoff, Richard. *The Black Valentino: The Stage and Screen Career of Lorenzo Tucker.* Metuchen, N.J.: Scarecrow Press, 1988.

———. "Interview: Lorenzo Tucker: The Black Valentino." *Black Film Review* 4, no. 2 (Spring 1988): 3–5.

———. "The Rediscovery of Oscar Micheaux, Black Film Pioneer." *Journal of Film and Video* 40, no. 1 (Winter 1988): 40–48.

Gubar, Susan. *Race Changes: White Skin, Black Face in American Culture.* New York and Oxford: Oxford University Press, 1997.

Gunning, Tom. *D. W. Griffith and the Origins of American Narrative Film: The Early Years at Biograph.* Urbana: University of Illinois Press, 1991.

Guerrero, Ed. *Framing Blackness.* Philadelphia: Temple University Press, 1993.

Hall, Stuart. "Notes on Deconstructing 'The Popular.'" In *People's History and Socialist Theory,* ed. Rafael Samuel. Boston: Routledge and Kegan Paul, 1981.

———. "What Is This 'Black' in Black Popular Culture?" In *Black Popular Culture,* ed. Gina Dent. Seattle, Wash.: Bay Press, 1992.

———. "The Whites of Their Eyes: Racist Ideologies and the Media." In *Silver Linings,* ed. George Bridges and Rosalind Brunt. London: Lawrence and Wishart, 1981.

Harmon, Jim, Glut Harmon, and Donald F. Date. *The Great Movie Serials, Their Sound and Fury.* Garden City, N.Y.: Doubleday, 1972.

Harper, Frances E. W. *Iola Leroy.* 1892. Reprint, Boston: Beacon Press, 1987.

Hebert, Janis. "Oscar Micheaux: A Black Pioneer." *South Dakota Review* 11, no. 4 (Winter 1973–1974): 62–69.

Heider, Karl G. *Ethnographic Film.* Austin: University of Texas Press, 1976.

Hemenway, Robert. *Zora Neale Hurston: A Literary Biography.* Urbana: University of Illinois Press, 1977.

Hoberman, James. "Bad Movies." *Film Comment* 16, no. 4 (July–August 1980): 7–12.

———. "Blankety-Blank." *Village Voice,* 29 May 1984, 58.

———. "Film: American Fairy Tales." *Village Voice,* 12 June 1984.

———. "A Forgotten Black Cinema Resurfaces." *Village Voice,* 17 November 1975, 85–86, 88.

———. "Race to Race." *Village Voice,* 22 February 1994, 47.

———. *Vulgar Modernism: Writing on Movies and Other Media.* Philadelphia: Temple University Press, 1991.

hooks, bell. *Black Looks: Race and Representation.* Boston: South End Press, 1992.

———. "Micheaux: Celebrating Blackness." *Black American Literature Forum* 25, no. 2 (Summer 1991): 315–360.

Huggins, Nathan Irvin. *Harlem Renaissance.* New York: Oxford University Press, 1971.

Hughes, Langston. "The Negro Artist and the Racial Mountain." *The Nation,* 23 June 1926, 692–694.

Hurston, Zora Neale. *Mules and Men.* 1935. Reprint, Bloomington: Indiana University Press, 1978.

Jacobs, Lewis. *The Documentary Tradition: From Nanook to Woodstock.* New York: Hopkinson and Blake, 1971.

James, C. L. R. *American Civilization.* London: Routledge, 1994.

Johnson, M. K. "'Stranger in a Strange Land': An African American Response to the Frontier Tradition in Oscar Micheaux's *The Conquest: The Story of a Negro Pioneer.*" *Western American Literature* 33, no. 3 (1998).

Jones, William. *Black Cinema Treasures: Lost and Found.* Denton: University of North Texas Press, 1991.

Julien, Isaac and Kobena Mercer, eds. "The Last 'Special' Issue on Race?" *Screen* 29, no. 4 (Autumn 1988).

Kaplan, E. Ann. *Looking for the Other: Feminism, Film, and the Imperial Gaze.* New York: Routledge, 1997.

Kellner, Bruce, ed. *Harlem Renaissance: A Historical Dictionary for the Era.* New York: Methuen, 1987.

King, Richard H., and Helen Taylor, eds. *Dixie Debates: Perspectives in Southern Cultures.* London: Pluto Press, 1996.

Klotman, Phyllis Rauch. *Frame by Frame: A Black Filmography.* Bloomington: Indiana University Press, 1979.

Klotman, Phyllis Rauch, ed. *Screenplays of the African-American Experience.* Bloomington: Indiana University Press, 1991.

Klotman, Phyllis R., and Janet K. Cutler, eds. *Struggles for Representation: African American Documentary Film and Video.* Bloomington: Indiana University Press, 1999.

Klottman, Phyllis Rauch, and Gloria Gibson-Hudson, eds. *In Touch with the Spirit: Black Religious and Musical Expression in American Cinema.* Bloomington: Indiana University, Black Film Center/Archive and the Department of Afro-American Studies, 1994.

Kochman, Thomas. *Black and White Styles in Conflict.* Chicago: University of Chicago Press, 1981.

Koszarski, Richard. *An Evening's Entertainment: The Age of the Silent Feature Picture, 1915–1928.* New York: Scribners, 1990.

Krasner, David. "Charles S. Gilpin: The Actor before the Emperor." *Journal of American Drama and Theatre* 4, no. 3 (Fall 1992): 62–75.

Lahue, Kalton C. *The Story of the Silent Serials.* New York: A. S. Barnes and Company, 1968.

Landay, Eileen. *Black Film Stars.* New York: Drake Publishers, 1973.

Lang, Robert, ed. *The Birth of a Nation.* New Brunswick, N.J.: Rutgers University Press, 1994.

Leab, Daniel J. *From Sambo to Superspade: The Black Experience in Motion Pictures.* Boston: Houghton Mifflin, 1975.

———. "A Pale Black Imitation: All-Colored Films 1930–60." *Journal of Popular Film* 4, no. 1 (1975): 72.

Lewis, David Levering. *W. E. B. Du Bois: Biography of a Race, 1865–1919.* New York: Henry Holt, 1993.

———. *When Harlem Was in Vogue.* New York: Alfred A. Knopf, 1981.

Library of Congress. *The African American Mosaic: A Library of Congress Resource Guide for the Study of Black History and Culture.* Washington, D.C.: Library of Congress, 1993.

Locke, Alain, ed. *The New Negro: An Interpretation.* New York: A. and C. Boni, 1925. Reprint, New York: Simon and Schuster, 1992.

Lott, Eric. *Love and Theft: Blackface Minstrelsy and the Making of the American Working Class.* New York: Oxford University Press, 1993.

Mapp, Edward. *Directory of Blacks in the Performing Arts.* Metuchen, N.J.: Scarecrow, 1978.

Marable, Manning. *How Capitalism Underdeveloped Black America.* Boston: South End Press, 1983.

Masilela, Ntongela. " Interconnections: The African and Afro-American Cinemas." *The Independent,* January/February 1988, 15.

Memmi, Albert. *The Colonizer and the Colonized.* New York: Orion Press, 1965.

Merritt, Russell. "Rescued from a Perilous Nest: D. W. Griffith's Escape from Theatre into Film." *Cinema Journal* 21, no. 1 (Fall 1981): 21–30.

Micheaux, Oscar. *The Case of Mrs. Wingate.* New York: Book Supply Company, 1945. Reprint, New York: AMS Press, 1975.

———. *The Conquest: The Story of a Negro Pioneer.* 1913. Reprint, Lincoln: University of Nebraska Press, 1994.

———. *The Forged Note: A Romance of the Darker Races.* Lincoln, Neb.: Western Book Supply Company, 1915.

———. *The Homesteader: A Novel.* 1917. Reprint, Lincoln: University of Nebraska Press, 1994.

———. *The Masquerade: An Historical Novel.* New York: Book Supply Company, 1947. Reprint, New York: AMS Press, 1975.

———. *The Story of Dorothy Stanfield.* New York: Book Supply Company, 1946.

———. *The Wind from Nowhere.* New York: Book Supply Company, 1944.

Miller, Randall M., ed. *The Kaleidoscope Lens: How Hollywood Views Ethnic Groups.* Englewood, N.J.: Jerome Ozer, 1980.

Morrison, Toni. *Playing in the Dark: Whiteness and the Literary Imagination.* Cambridge, Mass.: Harvard University Press, 1992.

Morton, Patricia. *Disfiguring Images: The Historical Assault on Afro-American Women.* Westport, Conn.: Greenwood Press, 1991.

Murray, Albert. *Stomping the Blues.* New York: Vintage, 1982.

Murray, James P. *To Find an Image: Black Films from "Uncle Tom" to "Superfly."* New York: Bobbs-Merrill, 1973.

Muse, Clarence. *The Dilemma of the Black Actor.* Self-published, 1924.

Musser, Charles. *The Emergence of Cinema: The American Screen to 1907.* New York: Scribners, 1990.

———. "L-O-V-E and H-A-T-E: Spike Lee's *Do the Right Thing,*" *Cineaste* 17, no. 4 (1990): 37–38.

———. "Troubled Relations: Paul Robeson, Eugene O'Neill, and Oscar Micheaux." In *Paul Robeson: Artist and Citizen,* ed. Jeffrey C. Stewart, 81–103. New Brunswick, N.J.: Rutgers University Press, 1998.

Nelson, Richard Alan. *Florida and the American Motion Picture Industry, 1898–1980.* Vol. II. New York: Garland Publishing, 1983.

Nesteby, James. *Black Images in American Films, 1896–1954.* Washington D.C.: University Press of America, 1982.

Nigel, Thomas H. *From Folklore to Fiction: A Study of Folk Heroes and Rituals in the Black American Novel.* New York: Greenwood Press, 1988.

Noble, Peter. *The Negro in Films.* London: S. Robinson, 1948. Reprint, New York: Arno, 1970.

Nugent, John Peer. *The Black Eagle.* New York: Stein and Day, 1971.

Null, Gary. *Black Hollywood: The Negro in Motion Pictures.* Secaucus, N.J.: Citadel, 1975.

Painter, Nell Irvin. *Exodusters: Black Migration to Kansas after Reconstruction.* New York: W. W. Norton, 1977.

———. *Standing at Armageddon: The United States, 1877–1919.* New York: W. W. Norton, 1987.

Palmer, Robert. *Deep Blues: A Musical and Cultural History of the Mississippi Delta.* New York: Penguin Books, 1980.

Parkinson, David. *History of Film.* New York: Thames and Hudson, 1995. See reference to Micheaux on page 46.

Patterson, Lindsay, ed. *Black Films and Filmmakers.* New York: Dodd, Mead and Company, 1975.

Peterson, Jr., Bernard L. *Early Black American Playwrights and Dramatic Writers: A Biographical Directory and Catalogue of Plays, Films, and Broadcasting Scripts.* Westport, Conn.: Greenwood Press, 1990.

———. "A Filmography of Oscar Micheaux: America's Legendary Black Filmmaker." In *Celluloid Power: Social Film Criticism from "The Birth of the Nation" to "Judgment at Nuremberg,"* ed. David Platt, 113–141. Metuchen, N.J.: Scarecrow Press, 1992.

———. "The Films of Oscar Micheaux: America's First Fabulous Black Filmmaker." *The Crisis* 84, no. 4 (April 1979): 136–141.

Pieterse, Jan Nederveen. *White on Black: Images of Africa and Blacks in Western Popular Culture.* New Haven, Conn.: Yale University Press, 1992.

Pines, Jim. *Blacks in Films: A Survey of Racial Themes and Images in the American Film.* London: Studio Vista, 1975.

Pines, Jim and Paul Willemen, eds. *Questions of Third Cinema.* London: BFI, 1989.

Powell, Richard J. "Re/Birth of a Nation." In *Rhapsodies in Black: Art of the Harlem Renaissance,* ed. Richard J. Powell and David A. Bailey. London: Hayward Gallery, the Institute of International Visual Arts; Berkeley: University of California Press, 1997.

Ravage, John W. *Black Pioneers: Images of the Black Experience on the North American Frontier.* Salt Lake City: University of Utah Press, 1997.

Regester, Charlene. "African American Extras in Hollywood during the 1920s and 1930s." *Film History* 9, no. 1 (Fall 1997): 95–115.

———. "African Americans in the Early Period of Cinema: A Period of Protest and Self-Assertion." In *Cinema at the Turn of the Century: Proceedings of the Third International Conference at Domitor,* ed. Clair Dupre la Tour, Andre Gaudreault, and Roberta Pearson. New York: New York University Press, 1994. Reprint, Quebec: Nuit Blanche editeur, 1996 and Lausanne: Payot-Laussane, 1996.

———. "Black Films, White Censors: Oscar Micheaux Confronts Censorship in New York, Virginia, and Chicago." In *Movie Censorship and American Culture,* ed. Francis G. Couvares. Washington, D.C.: Smithsonian Institution Press, 1996.

———. "The Duplicity of Oscar Micheaux's Male Characters." In *Me Jane: Masculinity, Movies and Women,* ed. Pat Kirkham and Janet Thumin. New York: St. Martin's Press, 1995.

———. "Headlines to Highlights: Oscar Micheaux's Exploitation of the Rhinelander Case." *Western Journal of Black Studies* 22, no. 3 (Fall 1998).

———. "Lynched, Assaulted, and Intimidated: Oscar Micheaux's Most Controversial Films." *Popular Culture Review* 5, no. 1 (February 1994): 47–55.

———. "The Misreading and Rereading of African American Filmmaker Oscar Micheaux." *Film History* 7, no. 4 (Winter 1995): 426–449.

———. "Myth and Reality: How Many Books Did Oscar Micheaux Publish?" *Oscar Micheaux Newsletter* 2 (November 1993): 1–2.

———. "Oscar Micheaux on the Cutting Edge: Films Rejected by the New York State Motion Picture Commission." *Studies in Popular Culture* 17, no. 2 (Spring 1995): 61–72.

———. "Oscar Micheaux's *Body and Soul:* A Film of Conflicting Themes." In *In Touch with the Spirit: Black Religious and Musical Expression in American Cinema,* ed. Phyllis Klotman and Gloria Gibson-Hudson, 59–71. Bloomington: Indiana University, Black Film Center/Archive and The Department of Afro-American Studies, 1994.

———. "Oscar Micheaux's Multifaceted Portrayals of the African American Male: The Good, the Bad, and the Ugly." *Studies in Popular Culture* 17, no. 2 (April 1995): 166–183.

———. "Oscar Micheaux the Entrepreneur: Financing *The House Behind the Cedars.*" *Journal of Film and Video* 49, nos. 1–2 (Spring–Summer 1997): 17–27.

———. "The Reading of a Still: The Evocation of Death in Dorothy Dandridge's Photograph." *Art Criticism* 13, no. 1 (Spring/Summer 1998): 41–47.

———. "The Reel and Real Dorothy Dandridge: Hollywood's Construction of Their 'Dark Star.'" *Camera Obscura* (forthcoming).

———. "Stepin Fetchit, the Man, the Image and the African American Press." *Film History* 6, no. 4 (Winter 1994): 502–521.

Reid, Mark A. "Early Black Independents." *Black Film Review* 2, no. 4 (1986): 21–22.

———. "Pioneer Black Filmmaker: The Achievement of Oscar Micheaux." *Black Film Review* 4, no. 2 (Spring 1988): 7.

———. *Redefining Black Film.* Berkeley: University of California Press, 1993.

Rhines, Jesse. *Black Film/White Money.* New Brunswick, N.J.: Rutgers University Press, 1996.

Richards, Deborah Bowman. "A Bibliographic Essay on Afro-American Folk Drama." *Ohio Folklife: Journal of the Ohio Folklore Society* 6 (1979–1981): 37–55.

Robeson, Eslanda Goode. *Paul Robeson, Negro.* New York: Harper and Brothers, 1930.

Robinson, Cedric. "In the Year 1915: D. W. Griffith and the Whitening of America." *Social Identities* 3, no. 2 (1997): 161–192.

Roediger, David. *The Wages of Whiteness: Race and the Making of the American Working Class.* New York: Verso, 1991.

Rogin, Michael. "Blackface, White Noise: The Jewish Jazz Singer Finds His Voice." *Critical Inquiry* 18, no. 3 (Spring 1992): 417–453.

———. "The Great Mother Domesticated: Sexual Difference and Sexual Indifference in D. W. Griffith's *Intolerance.*" *Critical Inquiry* 15, no. 3 (Spring 1989): 510–555.

Rose, Phyllis. *Jazz Cleopatra: Josephine Baker in Her Time.* New York: Random House, 1989.

Rose, Tricia. *Black Noise.* Middletown, Conn.: Wesleyan University Press, 1994.

Rust, Brian. *Discography: Jazz Records (1897–1942).* London: Storyville Publishing, 1970.

Sampson, Henry T. *Blacks in Black and White: A Source Book on Black Films.* Metuchen, N.J.: Scarecrow Press, 1977; revised and expanded, 1989.

———. *The Ghost Walks: A Chronological History of Blacks in Show Business, 1865–1910.* 2nd ed. Metuchen, N.J.: Scarecrow Press, 1995.

———. *That's Enough, Folks: Black Images in Animated Cartoons, 1900–1960.* Lanham, Md.: Scarecrow Press, 1998.

Schickel, Richard. *D. W. Griffith: An American Life.* New York: Simon & Schuster, 1984.

Schuyler, George. *Black No More.* 1931. Reprint, Boston: Northeastern University Press, 1989.

Seward, Adrienne Lanier. "Early Black Film and Folk Tradition: An Interpretive Analysis of the Use of Folklore in Selected All-Black Feature Films." Ph.D. diss., Indiana University, 1985.

Shaeffer, Louis. *O'Neill, Son and Artist.* Boston: Little, Brown, 1973.

Sharp, Saundra. "At Long Last: Director's Guild Honors Oscar Micheaux." *Black Film Review* 2, no. 3 (Summer 1986): 33–34.

———. "Collectors' Dreams: Tracking Down Lost Frames and Lobby Cards." *Black Film Review* 2, no. 4 (Fall 1986): 16–20.

Shohat, Ella, and Robert Stam. *Unthinking Eurocentrism: Multiculturalism and the Media.* New York: Routledge, 1994.

Silva, Fred, ed. *Focus on "The Birth of a Nation."* Englewood Cliffs, N.J.: Prentice Hall, 1971.

Slotkin, Richard. *The Fatal Environment: The Myth of the Frontier in the Age of Industrialization, 1800–1890.* New York: Atheneum, 1985.

Smith, Valerie, ed. *Representing Blackness: Issues in Film and Video.* New Brunswick, N.J.: Rutgers University Press, 1997.

———. *Self-Discovery and Authority in Afro-American Narrative.* Cambridge, Mass.: Harvard University Press, 1987.

———. "Split Affinities: The Case of Interracial Rape." In *Conflicts in Feminism,* ed. Marianne Hirsch and Evelyn Fox Keller. New York: Routledge, 1990.

Snead, James. *White Screens/Black Images: Hollywood from the Dark Side.* New York: Routledge, 1994.

Snowden, Frank M. *Before Color Prejudice: An Ancient View of Blacks.* Cambridge, Mass.: Harvard University Press, 1983.

Staiger, Janet. *Interpreting Films: Studies in the Historical Reception of American Cinema.* Princeton, N.J.: Princeton University Press, 1992.

Stecopoulos, Harry and Michael Uebel, eds. *Race and the Subject of Masculinities.* Durham, N.C.: Duke University Press, 1997.

Stepto, Robert. *From behind the Veil.* Urbana and Chicago: University of Illinois Press, 1979.

Steven, Peter, ed. *Jump Cut: Hollywood, Politics, and Counter Cinema.* New York: Praeger, 1985.

Stewart, Jeffrey C. "Paul Robeson and the Problem of Modernism." In *Rhapsodies in Black: Art of the Harlem Renaissance,* ed. Richard J. Powell and David A. Bailey. London: Hayward Gallery, the Institute of International Visual Arts; Berkeley: University of California Press, 1997.

Stewart, Jeffrey C., ed. *Paul Robeson: Artist and Citizen.* New Brunswick, N.J.: Rutgers University Press, 1998.

Stowe, Harriet Beecher. *Uncle Tom's Cabin.* 1852. Reprint, New York: Penguin Books, 1981.

Streible, Dan. "A History of the Boxing Film, 1894–1915: Social Control and Social Reform in the Progressive Era." *Film History* 3, no. 3 (1989): 235–257.

Stribling, T. S. *Birthright.* 1922. Reprint, Delmar, N.Y.: Scholars' Facsimiles & Reprints, 1987.

Taylor, Clyde R. "The Birth of Black Cinema: Overview." In *Black International Cinema Berlin: 1–5 February 1989,* 115–117. West Berlin: Arsenal Cinema, 1989.

———. "Crossed Over and Can't Get Black: The Crisis of 1937–1939." *Black Film Review* 7, no. 4 (1992): 22–27.

———. *The Mask of "Art": Breaking the Aesthetic Contract—Film and Literature.* Bloomington: Indiana University Press, 1998.

———. "New U.S. Cinema." In *Movies and Mass Culture,* ed. John Belton. New Brunswick, N.J.: Rutgers University Press, 1996.

———. "The Re-birth of the Aesthetic Cinema." *Wide Angle* 13, nos. 3–4 (July–October 1991): 12–30.

Thompson, Sister Francesca. "The Lafayette Players, 1917–1932." In *The Theater of Black Americans,* vol. 2, ed. Errol Hill. Englewood Cliffs, N.J.: Prentice Hall, 1980.

Toelkin, Barre. *The Dynamics of Folklore.* Boston: Houghton Mifflin Company, 1979.

Toll, Robert. *Blacking Up: The Minstrel Show in Nineteenth-Century America.* New York: Simon & Schuster, 1994.

Tompkins, Jane P. *Sensational Designs.* Oxford and New York: Oxford University Press, 1985.

———. "Sentimental Power: *Uncle Tom's Cabin* and the Politics of Literary History." In *The New Feminist Criticism: Essays on Women, Literature and Theory,* ed. Elaine Showalter. New York: Pantheon, 1985.

Turner, Patricia. *Ceramic Uncle and Celluloid Mammies.* New York: Anchor, 1994.

Van Epps-Taylor, Betti Carol. *Oscar Micheaux: Dakota Homesteader, Author, Pioneer Film Maker— A Biography.* Sioux Falls: South Dakota Press, 1999.

Wallace, Michele. "De-facing History." *Art in America* (December 1990): 120–129.

———. *Invisibility Blues.* London and New York: Verso, 1990.

———. "Passing, Lynching, and Jim Crow: A Genealogy of Race and Gender in U.S. Visual Culture, 1895–1929." Ph.D. diss., Tisch School of the Arts, New York University, 1999.

Waller, Gregory A. *Main Street Amusements: Movies and Commercial Entertainment in a Southern City, 1896–1930.* Washington, D.C., and London: Smithsonian Institution Press, 1995. See chapter 7, "Another Audience: Black Moviegoing from 1907 to 1916."

Washington, Booker T. *Up from Slavery.* 1901. Reprint, Garden City, N.Y.: Doubleday, 1963.

Watkins, Mel. *On the Real Side: Laughing, Lying, and Signifying—The Underground Tradition of African-American Humor That Transformed American Culture, from Slavery to Richard Pryor.* New York: Simon & Schuster, 1994.

Wiggins, William. "Pilgrims, Crosses and Faith: The Folk Dimensions of *Heaven Bound.*" *Black American Literature Forum* 25, no. 1 (Spring 1991): 93–100.

Williams, Christopher, ed. *Cinema: The Beginnings and the Future.* London: University of Westminster Press, 1996.

Williams, Jr., Vernon J. *Rethinking Race: Franz Boas and His Contemporaries.* Lexington: University Press of Kentucky, 1996.

Williamson, Joel. *The Crucible of Race: Black-White Relations in the American South since Emancipation.* New York: Oxford University Press, 1984.

———. *New People: Miscegenation and Mulattoes in the United States.* New York: Free Press, 1980.

Willis-Braithwate, Deborah. *James Van Der Zee, Photographer, 1886–1993.* Washington, D.C.: Harry N. Abrams, Inc., in association with The National Portrait Gallery, Smithsonian Institution, 1993.

Woll, Allen L. *Black Musical Theatre: From Coontown to Dream Girls.* Baton Rouge: Louisiana State University, 1989.

Woll, Allen L., and Randall Miller. *Ethnic and Racial Images in American Film and Television.* New York: Garland, 1987.

Woodward, C. Van. "History from Slave Sources." In *The Slave's Narrative,* ed. Charles T. Davis and Henry Louis Gates, Jr. Oxford and New York: Oxford University Press, 1985.

Yearwood, Gladstone L., ed. *Black Cinema Aesthetics: Issues in Independent Black Filmmaking.* Athens, Ohio: Afro-American Studies at Ohio University, 1982.

———. "Expressive Traditions in Afro-American Visual Arts." In *Expressively Black: The Cultural Basis of Cultural Identity,* ed. Geneva Gay and Willie L. Barber. New York: Praeger, 1987.

Young, Joseph A. *Black Novelist as White Racist: The Myth of Black Inferiority in the Novels of Oscar Micheaux.* New York: Greenwood Press, 1989.

Young, Lola. *Fear of the Dark: "Race," Gender and Sexuality in the Cinema.* London and New York: Routledge, 1996.

Zito, Stephen. "The Black Film Experience." In *American Film Heritage: Impressions from the American Film Institute Archives,* ed. Tom Shales and Kevin Brownlow. Washington D.C.: Acropolis Books, 1972.

ABOUT THE CONTRIBUTORS

Jayna Brown was coordinator for the Oscar Micheaux and His Circle conference at Yale University (January 1995). Her master's thesis, entitled "Acts of Blackness: The Production of Race and The Labor Of Performance in the Films and Novels of Oscar Micheaux," was written in Yale's African & African-American Studies Program. She recently completed her dissertation, "Babylon Girls: African American Women Performers and the Making of the Modern," and is currently an Assistant Professor in the Ethnic Studies Program and English Department at the University of Oregon.

Pearl Bowser is founder and director of African Diaspora Images, a collection of historical and contemporary African-American and African films and memorabilia. Since 1970 she has curated film programs in Europe, Asia, Africa, and throughout the United States, including the Whitney Museum, the American Museum of the Moving Images, the Brooklyn Museum, the Pacific Film Archives (Berkeley), and the Cleveland Museum of Art as well as a tour of black colleges. Her production credits include *Mississippi Triangle* (1984), *Namibia Independence Now* (1986), and *Stories About Us* (1988). She was co-director and director of research for *Midnight Ramble: Oscar Micheaux and the Story of Race Movies* (1994). With Louise Spence, she co-authored *Writing Himself into History: Oscar Micheaux, His Silent Films, and His Audiences* (2000).

Corey K. Creekmur is an Associate Professor of English and Cinema & Comparative Literature at the University of Iowa, where he also directs the Institute for Cinema and Culture. He is the co-editor of *Out in Culture: Gay, Lesbian, and Queer Essays on Popular Culture* and the author of *Cattle Queens and Lonesome Cowboys: Gender and Sexuality in the Western.* He is currently completing a study of the film musical and co-editing a volume on popular Indian cinema.

Jane Gaines is Professor of Literature and English at Duke University, where she directs the Film and Video Program, which she founded in 1985. She has co-edited *Fabrications: Costume and the Female Body* (1990), edited *Classical Hollywood Narrative Cinema: The Paradigm Wars* (1992), and published *Contested Culture: The Image the Voice and the Law* (1991) for which she received the Katherine Singer Kovacs Award. Her recent work is in African and African-American literature and film melodrama. Her book *Fire and Desire: Mixed-Race Movies in the Silent Era* has been recently published by University of Chicago Press (2001).

GLORIA J. GIBSON is Associate Professor in the Department of Folklore & Ethnomusicology and Associate Vice Chancellor for the Office of Multicultural Affairs at Indiana University. She was previously Director of the Archives of Traditional Music and assistant director of the Black Film Center/Archives. Her essays have appeared in numerous anthologies and journals, among them *Feminism and Documentary, Point of Contact,* and *Quarterly Review of Film and Video.* She is also a recipient of a National Endowment for the Humanities award used to produce the interactive multimedia CD-ROM "Music and Culture of West Africa: The Straus Expedition," which will be published later this year by Indiana University Press. She is also working on a book-length manuscript on the history of black women's cinema throughout the African diaspora entitled *Moving Tableaux of Consciousness: The Films and Videos of Black Women.*

J. RONALD GREEN teaches film studies as an Associate Professor in the Department of History of Art at Ohio State University. He has recently published a book called *Straight Lick: The Cinema of Oscar Micheaux* (Indiana University Press, 2000) and is currently working on a second, related volume titled *Vision of Uplift: The Films of Oscar Micheaux.* He has also written on video artist Nam June Paik, collage across various media, and other topics.

ARTHUR JAFA is a visual artist who has worked extensively in film and video. As director of photography he worked on numerous projects, including Julie Dash's *Daughters of the Dust* (for which he received the cinematography award at the 1991 Sundance Film Festival), John Akomfrah's *Seven Songs for Malcolm X* (1993), Spike Lee's *Crooklyn* (1994), and Louie Massiah's *W. E. B. DuBois: A Biography in Four Voices* (1995). His published thinking on questions of Black aesthetics, diafra and trauma, and film includes "69," in Michele Wallace's *Black Popular Culture* (1992), and "Like Rashomon but Different," *Art Forum* (Summer 1993). He was selected by Kiki Smith for inclusion in a three-person exhibition at Artist Space (April 1999). His work has since been included in numerous exhibitions, including the Mirror's Edge, curated by Okwui Enwezor (BildMuseet, Umea, November 1999); Black Box (CCAC Institute, Oakland, Calif., 2000); the 2000 Biennial Exhibition (Whitney Museum of American Art, New York); media_city (Seoul, Korea, 2000); and Bitstreams, curated by Lawrence Rinder (Whitney Museum of American Art, 2001). Jafa notes that (1) jazz improvisation, classically, is first and foremost signified self-determination; (2) Pollock's "crisis" was provoked by his inability to decipher the meaning of the aesthetic modality, jazz improvisation, which he himself had appropriated; (3) because Black creativity is generally a matter of treatment more so than material, its full complexity is often underestimated; (4) "Black potention" lies at the core of Black being in America; (5) the split between Black specificity and universality must be abolished; (6) Miles Davis is the supersign of Black Consciousness.

PHYLLIS R. KLOTMAN is Professor of Afro-American Studies and Founder/Director of the Black Film Center/Archive at Indiana University. Her publications on film include *Screenplays of the African American Experience; Frame by Frame: A Black Filmography; Frame by Frame II: A Filmography of the African American Image, 1978–1994* (with Gloria Gibson); *Struggles for Representation: African American Documentary Film and Video* (coedited with Janet Cutler); and over thirty articles, essays, and book chapters on African-American film and literature.

CHARLES MUSSER is Professor of American Studies and Film Studies at Yale University, where he co-chairs the Film Studies Program. His books include *The Emergence of Cinema: The American Screen to 1907* (1990) and *Edison Motion Pictures, 1890–1900: An Annotated Filmography* (1998). He produced, directed, and co-wrote the hour-long documentary film *Before the Nickelodeon: The Early Cinema of Edwin S. Porter* (1982). With Ed Guerrero and Mark Reid, he curated Paul Robeson film retrospectives at UCLA Film & Television Archives and the Museum of Modern Art, mounted in conjunction with the touring exhibition Paul Robeson: Artist and Citizen. In 1996, he received the Prix Jean Mitry from the Giornate del Cinema Muto for his contribution to the study of silent film.

CHARLENE REGESTER is co-editor of the Oscar Micheaux Society Newsletter (published by Duke University) and Visiting Assistant Professor in the Department of African & Afro-American Studies at the University of North Carolina at Chapel Hill. She is an editorial board member for the *Journal of Film and Video*. She has articles published in *Journal of Film and Video, Film History, Art Criticism, Studies in American Culture,* and *Popular Culture Review*. She has also had articles published in the following books: *Me Jane: Masculinity Movies and Women,* edited by Pat Kirkham and Janet Thumim (1994), and *Movie Censorship and American Culture,* edited by Francis Couvares (1996).

LOUISE SPENCE is Associate Professor and Coordinator of Media Studies at Sacred Heart University in Fairfield, Connecticut. The co-author (with Pearl Bowser) of *Writing Himself into History: Oscar Micheaux, His Silent Films, and His Audiences* (Rutgers University Press, 2000), she has published extensively on film and television. Her article (co-authored with Robert Stam) "Colonialism, Racism and Representation: An Introduction" has been reprinted in several anthologies. A recipient of two National Endowment for the Humanities grants and an American Council of Learned Societies grant, Dr. Spence has also been a fellow at the McDowell Colony, the Virginia Center for the Creative Arts, and the Anderson Center for Interdisciplinary Studies.

CLYDE R. TAYLOR, film scholar and literary/cultural essayist, is Professor at the Gallatin School and in Africana Studies, New York University. His publications include *The Mask of Art; Breaking the Aesthetic Contract-Film and Literature* (1998); and *Vietnam and Black America: An Anthology of Protest and Resistance* (1973). He wrote the script for *Midnight Ramble,* a documentary about early black independent cinema, and appeared extensively as an on-screen commentator for St. Claire Bourne's documentary *Paul Robeson* (1998).

SR. FRANCESCA THOMPSON, O.S.F., is Assistant Dean, Fordham University, Rose Hill Campus, Bronx, New York. The daughter of Evelyn Preer and Edward Thompson, she wrote a ground-breaking dissertation on black theater of the 1920s: *The Lafayette Players, 1915–1932*. Conversations with her father, who died in Indianapolis in 1960, were inspirational to her project. Other important information came from personal interviews with the late Clarence Muse and Edna Thomas, both former members of the Lafayette Players, as well as Leigh Whipper. Sister Francesca made effective use of black newspapers from 1915–1932: the *Chicago Defender;* the *Indianapolis Freeman;* the *New York Age;* the *New York Amsterdam News;* the *Pittsburgh Courier;* and the *California Eagle*. A scrapbook of news articles, film stills, and pictures of Miss Preer's various performances on stage and screen remain in her possession.

Michele Wallace, who has recently completed her Ph.D. in Cinema Studies at New York University ("Passing, Lynching and Jim Crow in U.S. Visual Culture"), is Professor of English, American Studies, and Women's Studies at the City College of New York and professor of the film certificate program at the CUNY Graduate Center. She is the author of *Black Macho and the Myth of The Superwoman* (1979) and *Invisibility Blues: From Popular Culture to Theory* (1990), and was the organizer for *Black Popular Culture* (1992), edited by Gina Dent.

PHOTO CREDITS

INDEX

*Page numbers in **boldface** refer to illustrations*

213, 214, 216, 217, 224, 225; and "Africanisms," 13; articles by, 16, 122–23, 254–56; bankruptcy of, xxviii–xix, 43, 49, 126, 266; and black press, 34, 43–49; as businessman, 133, 212, 214, 217, 227, 236, 243, 250, 252–53, 257, 263; and censorship, 5–6, 44, 61–66, 86–87, 123, 230, 252, 308–309n106; cost cutting by, 46–48, 61–62, 98; and CPFC, 181–87; filmography, difficulties of, 149–51, 226, 228–31, 275–76; "legendary biography" use, 85; life of, xvii–xix, 83–86; and literary forms, xxvii–xxviii; marriage to Alice Burton Russell, 260; and Maurice, 193–94; and melodrama, 66, 67, 70–72; misreadings of, 126–28; misspelling of name, 124–25, 130–31, 182; music use by, 13–14; narrative style of, 97–102; and Norman, 172–73, 177, 181–82; novels of, xvii–xviii, 81–85, 132–49, 212, 214, 218, 222; and O'Neill, 104–18; and Preer, 28, 31–32; production values, 64–66, 214, 217, 225; recutting by, 230; recycling of material, 79–86, 136–37, 147–58; and Robeson, xxiv, 113–15; silent films of, xviii, 43–44, 81–82, 126–29, 231–71; and skin color, 62–63, 94–96, 152–53, 212, 300–301nn71,81,82,87; and stereotypes, 53–66; versus Hollywood, 125, 127, 218, 219, 225; and Washington, 90–91; and whites, 78–79
Micheaux, Swan, 48, 126, 130, 246, 260, 266, 267, 269
Micheaux Book and Film Company, xvii, 126
Micheaux Film Corporation, 266, 272
Mickelby, Boxana, 280
Mickey, Arline, 278, 280, 281
middle-class characters and values, 48, 122, 133–35, 212, 215, 218, 221. *See also* class
Midnight Ace, The (Swan Micheaux film, 1928), 266, 267
Midnight Ramble (Thomas, Cram, and Bowser documentary, 1994), 226, 227
Miles, Viola, 246
Miles, William, 164
Miller, Mrs. Irvin, 246
Miller and Lyles, 250
Millionaire, The (Micheaux film, 1927), 129, 175, 263–65, 288
Mills, Billy, 287
Milton, William F., 280
Mines, Callie, 247
ministers in film. *See* preacher figure
Minnelli, Vincente, **8**
minstrelsy, 7, 21, 26, 31, 56–66, 90–91, 113, 293n17
miscegenation, xxvii, 5–6, 58–59, 74–78
Mississippi Triangle, **13**
modernism, 15–16
Moi, Un Noir (Rouch film, 1958), 15–16
Monagas, Lionel, 263
Moore, Charles, **20**, 231, 270, 272
Moore, Ed, 280
Moore, Tim, 274

Morrell, Stanley, 272
Morrison, Toni, 90, 144–45
Morton, Edna, 174, 175, 251–52
Morton, Patricia, 60
Moses, Ethel, 285
Moses, Lucia Lynn, **xxviii**, 180, 187, 283–85, **284**, 320n18
Motion Picture Commission of the State of New York. *See* New York Motion Picture Division
Movie Censorship and American Culture (Couvares, 1996), 227
movie theaters, xxvi, 41, 123–24, 130, 177, **190**, 192, 229, 265
Mulatto (Hughes play, 1936), 101
mulatto figure, 58–61, 63, 71, 77–78, 299n47
Mules and Men (Hurston, 1978), 199, 205
Murder in Harlem (Micheaux film, 1935), 223. *See also* *Lem Hawkins' Confession* (original title of film)
Murray, James P., 212
Muse, Clarence, 21–25, **23**, 28, 32
Museum of Modern Art, xxiii–xxiv
Museum of the Moving Image, 226
music, black, and film aesthetics, 12–18
musical theatre, African-American, 30–31, 56–57
Musser, Charles, 222, 226
"My Thrills in the Movies" (Preer articles, 1927), 29, 235

NAACP, 62, 70, 128, 135, 148, 152, 200
narrative style, 97–102
Native Son (Wright novel, 1940), 61, 97
Neale, Horace, Jr., 221
negative characters, 46–49, 88–89
Negro in Film (Noble, 1948), 211
Negro Digest, 211
Negro World, 47, 48
New Negro, The (Locke, 1925), 128
New York Age, xxv, 25, 34–35, 44–45, 106, 123, 124, 127, 229, 234, 241–42, 248, **269**
New York Amsterdam News, 43, 123–25, 129–30, 228–29, 268, 269
New York Herald, 116
New York Motion Picture Division, 123, 227, 233, 247, 250, 252, 259, 262, 263, 265, 271
New York News, 35
New York Times, 101, 103, 107
New York Tribune, 102–103, 104
New Yorker, The, 214
Newsome, Carmen, 95
Newsome, Nora, 272
newsreels, xix–xx, 162, 233
"nigga"/"nigger" term, use of, 110, 119, 185
Noble, Peter, 211, 212
Nobody's Children (Maurice film, 1920), xxiii, 37–38, **190**, 191–94, **192**
Noisette, Katherine, 267, 269, 270, 272
non-theatrical venues, xxiii, 167–68, 188, 200–204
Norcom, Alfred, 170, 287–88
Norfolk Journal and Guide, 228
Norman, Bruce, 173
Norman, Earl, 167

Norman, Kenneth, 167
Norman, Richard, xx, xxix, 38–39, 161–77, **168**
Norman, Richard, Jr., 26, 167–68
Norman Film Manufacturing Company, xx, xxix, 161–77, 286–88
Notorious Elinor Lee (Micheaux film, 1940), 274
nude scenes, 170
Null, Gary, 213

Octoroon, The (Boucicault play, 1859), 67
Odams, A. N., 246
Olcott, Sidney, 181
Old Ship of Zion, 201
one drop rule, 5–6, 58–59
O'Neill, Eugene, 21, 25, 100, 104–20, 123, 126, 128, 258
Opportunity Magazine, 114
opportunity narrative, 67–72, 80
oral tradition, 199–200
Oscar Micheaux and His Circle project, xvii–xxx, 226
Oscar Micheaux Awards (Black Filmmakers Hall of Fame), 213, 214
Oscar Micheaux, Film Pioneer (Lawrence documentary, 1980), 217
Oscar Micheaux Society and newsletter, 222, 227
Othello (Shakespeare play), 130
Over the Hill to the Poor House (play, 1922), 28, 258, 260
Ozu, Yosujiro, 14

Papousek, Richard, 227
Paramount Studio, 31
Paradise Island, 191
passing narratives, 83, 87, 92–96, 152–53, 191, 216, 313–14n17
Patrick School of Beauty Culture and Personal Improvements, 200
Patterson, William, 246
Paul, Ike, 266
Paul Robeson, Negro (Eslanda Robeson biography, 1930), 103, 111–12
Peebles, Melvin van, 5
Perry, Louis, **193**
Perugini, Frank, 180, 283, 320n18
Peterson, Bernard L., Jr., 215, 275
Pettus, William E., 180, 283
Philadelphia Tribune, **82**, 228, 254–56, 265
Pickett, Bill, 168–69, **170**, 287
Pictorial View of Idlewild, A (Chicago Daily News Film Service film, 1927), xix, **xx, 148**
Pilgrim, The (Chaplin film, 1923), 116, 258, 306n79
Pines, Jim, 213
Pinky (Kazan film, 1949), 59
Pittsburgh Courier, 29, 47, 103, **115**, 122, 228, 256, 266, 267, 271, 272, 281–82
Plater, Harry, 236
Platts, Harold, **163**
playwrights, white, xxvii, 25, 97–131
Poitier, Sidney, 59
popular culture, 143–46